Fortean Studies

Fortean Studies

Volume 1

Edited by Steve Moore

Produced by Bob Rickard

JOHN BROWN PUBLISHING
London 1994

Editorial enquiries should be sent to Fortean Studies at
PO Box 2409, London NW5 4NP.
E-mail: stevem@fortstudy.win-uk.net
Submissions are invited of not less than 3000 words.
Authors are responsible for obtaining permission to reproduce copyright material.
Submissions should be typed, and (ideally) supplied on floppy disk –
please discuss acceptable format with the editor first.

This edition was prepared by Fortean Times
for publication by John Brown Publishing Ltd :
The Boathouse, Crabtree Lane, Fulham, London SW6 8NJ.
No ongoing subscriptions are currently available for Fortean Studies,
but copies can be purchased by mail order from the Frome address below.

Fortean Times is published every two months
by John Brown Publishing Ltd.
It is also available on subscription - inquiries to:
Fortean Times, 20 Paul Street, Frome, Somerset BA11 1DX, UK.
☎ 0373 451777.

British Library Cataloguing-in-Publication data available.

Fortean Studies - Volume 1.

ISBN   1 - 870870 - 557

Printed in Great Britain by
Redwood Books, Trowbridge, Wilts.

Cover illustration from Olaus Magnus, *Historia de gentibus*, 1555.

CONTENTS

Many Parts
by Charles Fort & Mr. X
- Introduction. 8
- The Manuscript 9
- Thayer's Commentary & Notes . 44
- Additional Material 47

**The Luminous Owls
of Norfolk**
by David Clarke. 50

**The New England Airship
Invasion of 1909**
by Joseph Trainor. 59

**The Devil's Hoofmarks:
Source Materials on the
Great Devon Mystery of 1855**
by Mike Dash
- Introductory Essay. 71
- Contemporary Sources 90
- Secondary Sources. 104
- Other Tracks 119
- Selected Essays. 125

**Joan Petri Klint:
A Proto-Fortean of the 16th
Century**
by Sven Rosen. 151

Strange and Wonderful News
by Michael Goss. 182

The Leopards of the Great Turk
by Michel Meurger. 198

The Case for the Giant Octopus
by Michel Raynal. 210

A Belfry of Crypto-Bats
by Karl Shuker 235

Lake Constance Phenomena
by Ulrich Magin 246

**Paul Kammerer
and the Law of Seriality**
by John Townley & Robert Schmidt . . 251

**Optical Illusions:
A Brush with the Aliens**
by Anne Silk. 261

A Chinese Collection
by Steve Moore
- Introduction 269
- Ancient Chinese Automata 270
- Strange Stories
  of the Sleeping Dragon 290
- Parallel Arrays. 293
- Some New Evidence
  for Dating Trigrams. 300
- The Ma-Wang-Tui Trigrams . . . 303

Index of Fortean Times – 1993
by Steve Moore & Bob Rickard
- Topics 309
- Names: People Mentioned 319
- Names: Contributors. 328
- Names: Fictional 330
- Names: Organisations 331
- Names: Animals & Plants 333
- Articles, Features & Series. 335
- Books Reviewed, by Title 337
- Books Reviewed, by Author . . . 338
- Places. 340
- Dates 347

SUBSCRIBERS TO THIS VOLUME

Mr Ian Abel
Mr John Anderson
Mr P Baker
Mr Jeremy Beadle
Mr K A Beer
Mr R Begg
Mr T Bell
Mr B H Birch
Mr Ronny Blomme
Mr D J Bonney
Mrs Janet Bord
Mr Graham J Breach
Mr Denis Browne
Mr R Burton
Mr R Cameron
Miss Rosamunde Cashen
Mr Peter Christie
Mr N Clarke
Mr Finn Clark
Mr Leslie Clark
Mr David Coe
Mr Jim Darroch
Mr Dascombe
Dr Mike Dash
Mr John Degenhardt
Mr Scott Dent
Mr L W Duthie
Mr Michael Eaton
Mr D R Edwards
Mr Harry S T Fearnham
Mr George R Featherston
Mr Michael A Ferrier
Mr Richard Furlong
Mr Roland Givan
Mr Stephen Gledhill
Mr M Goodman
Mr Stephen A Graham
Mr Chris Green
Mr Howard J Greenhalgh
Mr Kerry Greenwood
Mr Michael R Haigh
Mr Paul Haines
Mr Kim Moller Hansen

Mr Steve Harcourt
Mr Jeremy M Harte
Mr Alan J Heath
Mr Peter Hebblethwaite
Mr Paul Henderson
Dr R J Hetherington
Mr G Holder
Mr Peter Hope-Evans
Mr A J Howe
Mr Thomas P M Jackson
Mr M F Jenkins
Mr Jason John
Mr D Johnson
Mr J F Jones
Mr C S Kershaw
Mr C J Kneebone
Mr William A Knight
Mr Walter Jorg Langbein
Mr Rolf Lovstrom
Mr Ewen C MacLean
Mr Paul Mangan
Mr Jeff Marriott
Mr Steve Marshall
Mr Clive J Martin-Ross
Mr Peter T Massaro
Dr Alaistair McCall
Mr Gordon J L McLellan
Mr J Middlebrook
Mr R D Murrell
Mr S Nixon
Mr Michael Oates
Mr Patrick O'Halloran
Mr Michael J O'Regan
Mr S J Osborne
Miss S C Parsons
Dr Hugh Pincott
Ms Jean Plantin
Mr Colin Potter
Mr John Powell
Mr Clive Prince
Mr Proffit
Mr Terry Pyle
Mr R Record

Mr Danilo Restani
Mr Barry J Reynolds
Mr John Ries
Ms Heather T Rodgers
Mr Peter Rogerson
Mr P J Rogers
Mr Robert Romelli
Mr John Rowe
Mr Colin Ryan
Mr A Sawford
Mr Bruce A S Skeer
Ms Linda Smith
Mr Mark Smith
Mr Graham Spackman
Mr John Sproull
Mr G Stewardson
Mr P L Stiles
Mr R M Stock
Mr Alby F Stone
Mr David Sutton
Mr Clas Svahn
Mr Lars Thomas
Mr Paul R Thomas
Mr Barry Thompson
Mr D C Thompson
Mr H E G Thompson
Mr P G Thompson
Mr Brian Tolley
Mr M Toy
Mrs K Tulley
Mr Geir Uldal
Mr L M Vandenborn
Mr Eddy van Wouwe
Colonel Leen Verhoeff
Mr Paul Viney
Miss Jane Wardale
Dr A Whitehouse
Mr Owen T Whiteoak
M Alvin R Wild
Mr David S Williams
Mr Robert Anton Wilson
Mr Peter Woodin
Mr A J Youde

EDITORIAL

The first volume of a new series would seem to require a few opening words, if only to explain the reasons for its existence and to give some inkling of its intentions.

Since its inception 21 years ago, *Fortean Times* has naturally grown and developed, from a small amateur journal intended primarily for researchers in the field to a large news-stand magazine with a much broader readership. Obviously, this has brought numerous advantages in the quality of presentation, the amount of material published, and the greatly expanded audience reached; but, equally obviously, it has also meant that on occasion the material has had to be tailored to a more commercial and popular market. As a result, *FT* now finds it difficult to publish articles of excessive length or carrying detailed references and annotations, and the same can be said for material delving into the more obscure minutiae connected with the field, with working methods rather than the phenomena themselves, and so on. Naturally, we feel that such material, crucial to the development of research in our field, should not be neglected, so *Fortean Studies* is intended to provide an outlet for the more scholarly and in-depth treatments that complement the wider coverage of *FT*. Amongst such necessary research material we intend to carry an annual index to *FT* (a preliminary step toward a comprehensive index to the complete run of the magazine), the first of which is included here. *Studies* will also absorb and replace the series of *FT* Occasional Papers, which have been unfortunately slow to appear in recent years. Two of these papers are included here.

But what *are* 'Fortean studies'? In a narrow sense, they consist of studies of the life of Charles Fort himself, his works and sources, those subjects which would particularly interest him were he still with us, and the exploration and development of his philosophy in general. We're pleased to say that such material is well represented in this first volume, and delighted to be able to present the remains of Fort's previously-unpublished autobiography. Yet, important as such material may be, contemporary Forteanism has become a much broader discipline. Over the years, we've noticed that *FT* has gathered readers beyond the purely Fortean field, whose interests lie not only in such 'near-relative' subjects as ufology and cryptozoology, but also in folklore, mythology, Earth Mysteries, fringe science, occultism, alternative cosmologies, and so on. In a spirit of inclusion rather than exclusion (for who knows where insights and answers are to be found?), *FT* has never sought to close the door to such interests; and there seems no reason why *Fortean Studies* should seek to exclude them either. So if 'guidelines' were to be set down for articles published here, they would rather be in terms of depth and quality of research than of 'strictly Fortean' subject matter. We should never forget our roots, of course, but surely it would seem better to widen our outlook than narrow it, and let our researches lead us where they will.

On the subject of a broad outlook, it's very gratifying to find that, rather than being just a parochial product of 'British Forteanism', this volume presents a wide spectrum of international interests, with contributions from Canada, France, Germany, Sweden and the USA, besides those from our own shores. Forteanism should, after all have global (if not universal!) interests, and this sense of internationalism is something we hope to develop in future volumes.

Still, regardless of where the material originates, *Fortean Studies* is, essentially, intended to provide a forum to promote and publish further research. And if it achieves no more than that then I, as editor, will be more than satisfied ...

SM

MANY PARTS

REMNANTS OF AN AUTOBIOGRAPHY BY CHARLES HOY FORT

Edited and Expanded Upon by Mr X

Lost for decades and never before seen in print, Charles Fort's autobiography *Many Parts* was written c.1900 and provides many insights into his youth and development as a writer. The manuscript was already fragmentary when it came into the hands of Tiffany Thayer of the Fortean Society, who intended to use it as source material for a never-completed biography, *The Forts of Albany*. We are immensely grateful to Canadian researcher Mr X (his legal name) for rescuing these remnants from obscurity and providing the additional material presented here, including a recollection by Raymond, Fort's younger brother..

INTRODUCTION

In my search for documents relating to Charles Hoy Fort, I found it very difficult to locate a copy of *Many Parts*; and, once having found it, I scattered a few copies among Forteans, so that it might be read and preserved from obscurity. By its inclusion in *Fortean Studies*, I believe far more readers will have the opportunity to examine this work and learn more about Fort's youth and development as a writer.

The only book referring to *Many Parts* was Damon Knight's *Charles Fort: Prophet of the Unexplained*, published by Doubleday & Co. in 1970; but it was offered only in fragments in a chapter on Fort's childhood. Hoping to examine this autobiography, I sought a copy of it without success after contacting Damon Knight and Aaron Sussman, examining several boxes of the Tiffany Thayer Papers in the New York Public Library, and making numerous queries to other Fortean researchers. The whereabouts of the original copy had been forgotten. Fortunately, I also examined the Damon Knight Papers in the George Arents Research Library at Syracuse University in Syracuse, New York. On a second visit, in November of 1989, I located a photocopy of Thayer's typescript copy in Box 3 under 'Xeroxed articles'. With Knight's permission, I obtained a photocopy of this Thayer copy in January of 1990 and copied it again with relatively little editing and the addition of some material to provide some further insights to the reader.

One should keep in mind that Fort's autobiography was written when his family was still alive, and Fort's exercise in autobiography was not considered successful by his own opinion. In a memorandum dated 'November 6, 1929' (which apparently was typed out later by Thayer), Fort reviewed several aspects of his work, his health, and finances, in what was undoubtedly a bout of depression. He wrote of his emergence as "a metaphysician from a story writer". This also gives some evidence as to when he was writing *Many Parts*; for, he writes: "From Sept. 1899 until Sept. 1904, the metaphysician had interfered with and held back the story writer. My book *Many Parts* was simply the work of an immature metaphysician psychologist, sociologist, etc. trying to express [himself] in a story. Also individualism, or stylism, not only interfered and made me not easily readable, but gave me a satisfaction or elation that held back development."

Fort wrote in the plural as 'We', and his references to other members of his family were guised in vague terms. 'They' was Fort's father Charles Nelson Fort; the 'stepmother' was Blanche Fort (née Whitney); the 'other kid' was Raymond Fort; the 'little kid' was Clarence Fort; the 'grandfather' was Peter Van Vracken Fort; the 'other grandfather' was John Hoy; 'Nick' would appear to have been a maternal uncle, John S. Hoy. Fort's mother, Agnes Fort (née Hoy), was the first wife of Charles N. Fort and died shortly after the birth of Clarence Fort; but she makes no appearance nor is she mentioned in the surviving copy. I would suspect that the 'great aunt' in Saratoga (mentioned on page 79 of the manuscript), is either a sister of J. Hoy or, more likely, Peter

V.V. Fort; and, the 'aunt' who saw nothing wrong in gambling may have been a sister to John S. Hoy and Agnes Fort, and may possibly have also been identified herein as 'Martha'. And, the *Democrat*, mentioned herein as being the first newspaper for which Fort worked, was undoubtedly the Albany *Argus*.

Tiffany Thayer made many rash and erroneous identifications regarding these characters; but I would credit him for recognizing two episodes which illustrated Fort's break from his family in Albany, being: his brother Clarence's stealing cake for him during his visit to the 'Industrial Farm', and being denied cake in his Albany home, which was recounted by his wife, Annie Fort, after his death. Thayer apparently never made the journey to Albany to conduct further research into Fort's early life nor finished his attempt at publishing his history of Fort's family and early life.

Fort's childhood home in *Many Parts* still stands in Albany, but the memories of places and people from a century ago have nearly faded away into obscure maps and occasional entries in city directories. The characters, disguised by false names, have long ago left the stage; the scenery has been changed as old houses, schools, and stores have been torn down, new buildings erected, and streets expanded.

Fort was not so much concerned with the elements of true biography as he was in recollecting his own youth in his own literary style. What follows is an account of the early stages of his youth, written before his brief career as a short-story writer, his one novel,

Charles Hoy Fort in 1893, aged 19. The manuscript of *Many Parts* was finished in 1900, when he was 25.

and the world-renowned iconoclastic books. Fort's selection of the title may have been taken from Shakespeare's *As You Like It*, (Act 2, Scene 7, Line 142): "And one man in his time plays many parts, his acts being seven ages;" but I would incorporate the 'many parts' of what fragments remain of Fort's story with other material, to give a fuller understanding of Fort's early life.

THE MANUSCRIPT

[Note numbers (in bold) refer to Thayer's footnotes, on p.45.]

CHAPTERS ONE TO THREE

[Pages 1 to 11 are missing.]

... thought that Law School was built for a large number of serious-looking young men, who left with still more serious-looking books under their arms, and then went over to the "Cottage". But it wasn't; it was built with steps for us to play on and stone blocks for us to jump from. All along were houses built with windows, not to look from, but for us to climb to. Gates for us to swing on, hydrants for us to leap over, fences and stoops for us to hide behind. Why things were could be of no interest to us. For we know: everything was for us.

We a mile away from everything familiar: the witch and the crazy man and the two old maids. Wondering what we should do to be acquainted. Wondering which families had boys in them. Interested in one family, which had a doctor and a dress-reform advocate in it. Advocate coming out in an awful, old rig; that was more dress-reform. We learned something new every day. And across the street was a family even more interesting. For it had not only a General but an Irish setter in it. We could never be so important as all that, but some day we might be a Colonel and own a pug. And there were little boys up and down the street; but none of them was friendly. We taking a sleigh away from a little girl, just to be acquainted. Trouble. Pushing another little girl into a snow pile; perhaps she'd speak to us. More trouble. Knocking a little boy's hat off; that might lead to acquaintance. Little boy beating us fearfully. Oh, we'd just have to go away and be a hermit somewhere!

But allowed to play in the street very little. Spending a good deal of the time in the top floor, which had been fitted up with swings and a see-saw for us. Hurrying home from school, avoiding bad, little boys, going to the park every sunny afternoon with Katie Rooley, the little kid in the baby carriage, we on one side and the other kid on the other side. Collecting pebbles from the gravel walks and listening to the gossip of a dozen nurse girls all in a row. Then walking through the grass on our way home to brush the dust from our shoes, looking creditable to any household, as Mrs. Lawson kept us looking.

And in the yard we played, interested in the plants, which were thinking, feeling, little creatures in the world that Mrs. Lawson lived in and had us, too, live in. Coming home from School [*capitals as per manuscript*] in an Autumn afternoon. Piles of flower pots and window gardens scattered around. Mrs. Lawson calling for us to help for all we were worth; for Jack Frost was coming. Digging and transplanting for all we were worth, helping to get our friends into the house before Jack Frost could catch them. Speaking to geraniums, telling them to have no fear, for we were taking them to a place where they'd be safe all Summer. Of course they could not understand us, you know; but at the same time, they could understand us. Then great excitement! Mrs. Lawson telling us that Jack Frost was only a mile away. All four of us working desperately, getting all the plants in, just as Jack Frost peeked around the church

steeple. All but the sunflower stalks, this discriminating worrying us so that we'd dig up at least one monster of a sun flower, and smuggle it to the top floor to save it too.

Taking turns reading aloud with Mrs. Lawson every afternoon. The Old Boy looking in through the window now and then, but seldom really getting in, for we, too, would seize a broom to help drive him away. We'd rather read than climb fences except, of course, when we really had to climb fences. But arithmetic! It seems fixed in our mind that the multiplication table did not extend beyond twelve times twelve; thirteen times anything was something else. A teacher told us to multiply sixty by ... [1]

[Pages 14 and 15 are missing.]

... to shoot wads of paper around the congregation; a bald head would count fifteen; ears, ten, and so on. It was a very amusing, little game. But we almost liked Sunday school, especially as there were some very good books in the library. Religion as an emotion, was strong in us, though, quite as strong, was a resisting of this emotion. Sometimes, all that wanted to be Christians were called upon to raise their hands. A throbbing and an urging would almost overcome us with a seeing of beauty in what we were called upon to be. But our hand would never go up, as if a feeling of sternness withheld us from what seemed to us an indecent advertising of feeling.

And in the kitchen we spent a good deal of time, except in the reign of Ella, who would chase us into the street, hopping the length of the house on one foot, waving a slipper. Then came Katie, which made two Katies in the house. Mrs. Lawson thought this over, and decided that one should have another name. She was pleased with "Myrtle". And you should have seen big, fat Katie turn purple with indignation when called "Myrtle". Each Katie admitted that two Katies made confusion, but each insisted that the other was Myrtle, so that Mrs. Lawson would call, "Myrtle! Myr-tle! Myr-tell!" and no one would answer.

But we liked to peel apples, trying to peel as well as Katie could, making long spirals, throwing them over a left shoulder for good luck. Turning the ice cream freezer, getting what was left on the dasher for our work. Baking bits of dough, which, if made to look remotely like a man or a cat, seemed different. They were accomplished girls in our kitchen; they spoke Latin fluently, which awed us a good deal. But then we picked up a little Latin ourself, learning that some Latin words are much like English words. We might have picked up a good deal of interesting gossip, were it not that our conceit made us cry that we, too, understood. The cook would say, "Isery yourery ...

[Page 17 is missing.]

Then the boy next door told us that there is no Santa Claus; he had pretended to sleep, and had seen his father arrange gifts around him. We had never thought to doubt Santa Claus before, but had a feeling that, doubt as we might, the boy was right. Then torments like religious unrest. Kind, jolly, old Santa Claus coming down chimneys was too beautiful to give up. But no one could possibly come down our chimney. Then the reindeers, Prancer, Dancer, and all the rest, skimming from roof to roof. We could not give it up; it was too beautiful. But we had to; reindeers can not skim from roof to roof.

Oh, don't take from us any more of our beliefs! Perhaps heaven and the angels, too, were only myths. But, though we had never seen an angel, we knew the Old Boy was real, for we had seen him. We were not quite sure just when, but one, cold gray day, he had looked in through the window, and then, St. Dunstan had caught and held his nose in red hot pinchers. Heaven and angels were true: we were sure, because the sky was so blue. Looking down, knowing whenever we were untruthful, because everytime we told a white lie a little white mark appeared on a finger nail. We often desponded; our finger nails were full of them. And for worse lies, a canker would appear upon our tongue.

Looking down, seeing everything we did except when we went into a dark room and closed the windows before eating anything stolen.

And there, too, was Conscience. Sometimes at night, may be as late as ten o'clock, Mrs. Lawson would look up and see us stepping on our feet in the door way. She'd say, "Why, I thought you were asleep hours ago."

We'd say, "Conscience is pricking me." Confessing some fearful crime. Faltering and writhing, but feeling that every word lessened the burden. Mrs. Lawson taking us in her arms, softly singing tearful, penitent us to sleep with the psalm about green pastures.

[Pages 19 and 20 are missing.]

... not even picking out offenders, sobbing and shouting, loyalty flaming in us, fighting for our own. These seizures or rags were common with us. On our way home from school, older boys would tease us, just to see us run frantically around the street searching for cobble stones to throw. But there was always an underlying self control, for we'd hurl a cobble stone awry, if an enemy should be too near. It was a pose, delighting us to show how awful we were. Only causing entertainment, but thinking we were striking with terror. And during recess, the older boys would rally with the smaller boys. Other, small boys running away, but we standing where we were, in our sobbing, hysterical rage, with its underlying posing. Floundering in the snow, snowballs rattling against our face, handfuls of slush thrown down our neck. Staggering and fighting, calling to the other, small boys, "Come back, ye cowards!" Very much liking the "ye"; it seemed as if right out of a story book. Crying things we had read, our mind filled with much reading. But it was not courage; it was our joy in the picturesque, we seeing gallantry and romance in our defiance. And we had a mania to fight with larger boys, because of the glory that would come to us if we should triumph. There were boys of our own size that we were afraid of, but any larger boy bullying or boasting would possess us with our mania, and we fought continually on the way home from school. Often beaten, but not caring; a larger boy had done it and there was no disgrace. And often winning, for we were strong and chunky. Then the cries from the others would be exalting music, and we'd tingle as we'd see some other boy glad to carry our books home for us. Then we'd want to be chivalrous and forgiving the next day, offering the enemy candy, encouraging no references to our victory, though we longed for references all day long, walking home with the enemy to help him if anyone should taunt him.

[Page 22 is missing.]

... wings. Catching a wasp and learning our first truth in natural history. Holding him by the head, and starting to laugh at him, because then he could not bite us. Only starting; then pained to learn that wasps back up to sting. Holding our breath for a while, and then running into the house to tell everyone our astonishing discovery that there are creatures with the habits of a coal cart. A new world over there in the club grounds; there were grasshoppers in the lawn, a nest of big, black ants in the hollow, pear tree, and in a corner lurked a red-legged spider with a green body as large as a hen's egg. We remember him very well, though of course there never has been such a spider. But there was a new world, and we felt a necessity for strange inhabitants and horrible creatures in it. No snakes and no dragons; so with spiders we created the elements of horror. Wanting to know all about everything; exposing our ears to "darning needles" as we called dragon flies, feeling that it is untrue that they sew up little boys' ears. Digging unsightly holes in the club grounds embankment, not knowing why, but feeling that if we should dig down a foot, we should learn something. Digging down two feet would be twice as interesting; picturing ourself digging to the very center of the earth. Unearthing bits of china such as you will find in all filled-in ground. Having an impression that we had dug down to China, not meaning a pun, not knowing really what we did mean, except that China was somewhere under our feet. We were so much interested in geography that it seemed not a study but a pleasure, but still we had a good many impressions foreign to facts. North America was a stern, rugged creature with a head and a long bill; South America was feminine, gentle and softly rounded; Asia was flat and light yellow.

But Mrs. Lawson would call us from the digging to tell us that we were making extra work for some poor man with a large ...

[Pages 24 to 27 are missing.]

... bare tree; seeing a bunch of straw and horse hair. An old nest. We climbed to it. Putting the old nest in our pocket; birds had built it; once birds had lived in it. But we wanted a nest with eggs in it; had thought that out in the real country, there were nests in almost every tree. Then running from tree to tree, searching for a nest with eggs in it. Splashing mud over ourself; not seeing the mud in our excitement. Then someone came to us, and led us back to the hotel, where our grandfather, though kind, reproached us, and feared that we should never be a good, business man. We wanted to be a good, business man; in our atmosphere, we had a belief that doctors, lawyers, all in other callings are lower in the scale of importance than those that sell groceries though only wholesale of course. We expected to be a partner some day, as They had become, or, even better, to travel for the firm. But all around were hintings and whisperings of something that seemed wondrous and better and meant for us. We heard and felt in that first orchard and in our remembrance of the orchard. Strange things were told us in every picture of a lake or a bit of meadow land. We should not have expressed the heresy, but felt that there was some kind of a life higher than that of a dealer in groceries. Though we knew not quite what, there was something that we wanted in things that have nothing to do with cities and good, business men. [2]

CHAPTER FOUR

Someone discovered that our eyesight was poor. It was explained that we had injured our eyes with too much reading. This was not true, but then it seems more creditable to injure eyes or lose a leg in an accident than to be born with defects. So They sent us to have our eyes examined. An arrangement like automobile goggles on our eyes; we looking at large letters and small letters astonishingly black and clear. We were a spectacle-wearing boy and despised ourself, for the boys that we knew that wore spectacles seemed generally weak and not the kind that our general strength made us of. We told ourself that we should wear the spectacles only when watched. But when out in the street, we knew that the spectacles had come to stay. For we had lived in a fog and had not known it. We were in a different world; trees were not the blurs we had thought them; every leaf was outlined sharp and distinct; objects at a distance were smaller, because blurring had distorted, but again was clear, clean outline; everything was as different as is a photograph from a rough sketch.

But about collecting. We bought birds' wings from a boy living out in the country but coming to school every day. Finding an old store where, for very little, we could buy dried star-fish, sea urchins, shells, and sea beans, little red sea-beans with a black speck, big, gray ones and brown ones. Stories of wideness and remoteness; stories of storms, or palms on coral beaches, ocean depths and strange lands; all told in the rumbling of shells and the odor of brine by these things from the sea. Then we'd look at our geography, picturing ourself some day crossing the ocean to see the wonders of Europe; whispering galleries, old castles, and leaning towers. Turning the pages, until we'd get as far away as the South Sea Islands. Marking a dot on a South Sea Island; the dot would be far-away, adventurous we; other dots out in the ocean would be savages approaching in canoes. Remarkable adventures; remarkable heroism. And then traveling on the point of the pencil to Madagascar, searching along the shore for a dodo to add to our collection.

Spending a good deal of time in reading, going around in the afternoon to see our relatives, because we liked to read, and because they had books. Our grandfather was a man of little education, but he had, somewhere in him, apart from all that made him a "good, business man" an interest in books. Next to the dining room, he had his library, with books such as the works of Carlyle and Ruskin. These books were bright and new-looking. In the store, he had two private offices; one, where he attended to his own affairs, for he owned many houses, and loaned money, usuriously, we learned when we were older; and his really private office upstairs, where, with his friends, he invented and drank strange drinks in vast quantities. Here were the books that he did read; biographies and histories, but books of travel

in the greatest number; at least half a dozen dealing with Arctic exploration; dictionaries, paintings of value on the walls, demijohns all around. We were sent up to get him one afternoon; he was reading a heavy book, a pink drink on one side of him, a yellow drink on the other side. Asking us what we knew about the aurora borealis. And we were eager to tell, but he had to go ... [3]

[Pages 31 to 33 are missing.]

All ready! Other kid snickering. We'd think of a boy we hated or of our troubles in school; then we'd look grave. But the little kid shaking all over. Photographer trying again; all three shaking all over, each blaming the others for making him laugh in this nervous way that had nothing of merriment.

"Now, steady, and you'll see the little bird." Then he'd have two of us looking serious, but upon the little kid a smile was always flickering.

We'd look over our geography, and we'd wish we could have a stone or leaf or anything else from the strange countries, until we found that collecting stamps was what we wanted. Sending to New York for a thousand, assorted stamps. A bulky package came; the faces of kings tumbled to the floor in a shower of color. We were in France with the French stamps; Napoleon, the Bastille, the Revolution in the air about us. We were amid castles and battle scenes in Germany and England. Here was a stamp that had really been in vast, tropical, barbaric India. Then a stamp that expressed the marvels of long travelling in the mystery and romance of Australia. Life was meaning more and more.

In the top floor, we had many amusements, playing stories most of the time. We were three brothers, early settlers, and killed more Indians than were ever heard of by Carson or Boone. And we had a "good, business man" game; with great bargaining and traveling for the firm. In this game, the other kid dominated; we could not bargain with him; we'd have to sell at his price, and buy when he wanted to sell. And sometimes we three got along very well, and sometimes we hated one another. Always telling on one another. Telling every little thing, pleased to see another punished, so virtuous would it make us feel. Why, we'd do detective work to catch the other kid stealing cake so that we could tell, and the others, seeing us in wrongdoing, would cry together, ''I'm going to tell!'' And blackmailing one another. Saying, ''If you don't give me your candy, I'll tell what you did the other day.'' Having notebooks with charges written in them. Sometimes each would have a long list of offenses; then the offenses would cancel off; for if the other kid would tell that we had played with Biff Allen, we should tell that he had uprooted plants in the yard.

''I'm going to tell,'' the other kid would say; and we'd look at our note book to see whether he could afford to tell.

And fighting often. Once we went to Poughkeepsie, very glad to get away, we did hate those others so. Visiting a family with a boy named Artie in it. Artie urging us to buy candy; we clinging to our spending money. Suggesting soda water; we holding back as long as we could. But nickels and dimes slipped away, and we desponded. You see, we wanted to take back something for the little kids. Artie telling of a merry-go-round. Then we just went right into a store and bought two boats for a quarter apiece, beautiful gifts; all blue with yellow stripes around, and pretty white sails.

Artie wanting us to sail the boats. We refusing; Artie sulking. So we sailed the boats in the bath tub that there should be no sulking. Then Artie wanted a storm. We protesting. A terrific storm; boats tossing wildly. Blue paint coming off; yellow paint on the sails. We almost tearful but making feeble, little waves that could do no harm, just to have everything pleasant. Artie sending a tidal wave; a bowsprit knocked off.

In the cars, we unwrapped the boats to see whether they were so awful-looking; paint all patchy; no longer pretty, white sails. Nothing but old, second-hand toys for the little kids. Trying to persuade ourself that something could be done. Perhaps with a little mending or some rubbing of the paint. Nothing could be done. Just throwing the spoiled, old boats from the car window. Oh, big, grown-up persons, don't tell us any more of the happy time that childhood is!

Unhappiness a good deal of the time. The unpleasant things they made us take. We had to eat oat meal in the morning before having anything else. We detesting oat meal, making a fearful time over it, but Mrs. Lawson firm. One time it was spoiled a little, and we were in a frenzy, thinking it the most awful tyranny that could be thought of that we should have to eat spoiled oat meal, Mrs. Lawson declaring that it was good, we crying and wailing in revolt. Then we'd play little games to make the eating easier; irregularities would be mountains, milk, the sea, and sugar glaciers and ice fields, taking a spoonful, the sea rushing in, inhabitants engulfed. Emptying a whole dishful into our pocket now and then. In fact, so strong was our dislike, that we have detested ''breakfast foods'' ever since. And besides the goose grease, the sulphur and molasses, these things that we had to have were the things that we could not have. But some day we'd be a man; looking forward to that far-distant, twenty first birthday. Then we could have all the Chili sauce that we should want. We had some sort of an idea of a Chili sauce spree. Celebrating with our friends; opening bottle after bottle. Awful debauchery; more bottles. On our twenty first birthday, there would be little heard but the popping of Chili sauce bottles.

Paper soldiers had marched into our lives. We and the other kid would drive away the little kid, and he'd walk around the yard while we would drill our soldiers. And then have battles. Each would want the blue-coated soldiers, for they were the Americans. The red-coats were the British. We'd be violent; but then we'd have to give in to the other kid or there'd be no battle. Reasoning that, though we were the British, we were, in some way not clear but satisfying, not the British.

Slinging book covers at each other's army, taking as prisoners all we'd knock down. Feeling a desire of individuality among our soldiers, remembering and following the careers of certain ones, promoting and exalting them whenever they deserved to be honored. We wanted them to seem real; so we wrote names on their backs to make them characters in the great, military story they were living. Giving them marks, which were medals, whenever they'd do remarkable things such as landing on their feet when knocked across the room. But the other kid was sterner with his heroes than we were with ours; whenever his would fail to live up to their records, he'd degrade them, have hangings, burn them at the stake. We could not bear to see our heroes made of common paper like the rest; when they'd disgrace themselves, we'd pretend not to see, though displeased with ourself for favorites.

There was General Burgoyne, who was British, yet was not British. The General was getting old, and we always saw pathos and an appealing in anything old. The General had someone else's head, no spine, and a bad case of wrinkles in the chest. We'd brace him up with cardboard, pasting on a standard a foot long, which was not fair, causing the other kid to protest and defer to our international law. Then he captured the General. Had a court-martial, courteously inviting us, each holding a white handkerchief of truce. But the court-martial was a farce; it was plain that the General was a doomed man, we looking on, offering all kinds of ransoms that we could offer, though having little, for marbles, tops, everything that was ours was the other kid's and everything that was his was ours, except the soldiers in times of war. Other kid firm, pointing out that we were present only as a matter of courtesy and had no voice. Sending the old General to the rack to make him confess, having respect for neither his honors nor his years. Other kid uttering outrageous confessions for the prisoners. We, despairing and excited, crying, "It isn't true!"

General Burgoyne saying, vicariously, "I admit there is not one medal on me that I deserve." Indignation bursting from us.

"I'm a low, common favorite, and I admit I've made my way by sneaky work. Spare me! I'm afraid to die! I'm a coward, and I admit it!" We so indignant that we would have rescued the general by force, only we could not, for there was the white handkerchief in our hand.

Last awful scene. Gallant, old hero dying like a man, we telling him that we knew very well the cries and groans and appeals for mercy were not from him. And we mourning, unable to understand how the other kid could be so mean. Then declaring personal war, beating him up and down the top floor room until he remembered that we had "sassed" a neighbor the day before.

And parades. All three of us lying on the floor in front of the soldiers to have them denser to our view. Enjoying the martial vista, helmets and horses' head sticking up, thick and jagged from a mass of color. More than a thousand, covering most of the long floor; for ours was a spirit to make as important as we could anything that interested us. Pleased with uniforms but more pleased with uniformity. Our eye traveling along a line of helmet tops, along a line of epaulets, along belts or boots. Just as ten men abreast are not attractive, but let each wear a blue badge or a white hat, something for the eye to travel along, and the effect is pleasing.

And when we were asleep, would see them, regiment after regiment go by, our own soldiers and others in fantastic uniform not in our army at all. We interested and then wearied. An interminable army marching by, we so tired that we'd want to see never another soldier. Trying not to look but having to look. We'd say, "Oh, if someone would only wake me up!" But we'd sleep on, having to review the parade, grown monotonous and tormenting. Wishing we could arouse ourself, but unable to, repeating, "Oh, if someone would only wake me up!"

Nevertheless, all three would run up to see the parade in the morning. Mrs. Lawson pouncing in, angry that we should not have waited to put on our clothes. Dashing through cavalry, swishing through infantry, kicking over bands and drum corps. We pretending great distress that she should be satisfied and should not take our soldiers away. Really, we'd be pleased, for she would be a hobgoblin attacking the allied forces. And we'd go back to look for survivors. Finding one standing under the see-saw. Delight. Another kicked to the window sill, and standing. Crying our admiration, giving them medals.

But there was wildness in us, so that Mrs. Lawson could not restrict us to the top floor or to playing in front of the house. When we played in the yard, we wondered what lay beyond the high fence two yards away, and whether an explorer could get around the church to the strange land on the other side. We and the other kid became explorers. The little kid following over our fence; we chasing him back. Starting off again; little kid, too, starting. We scrambling over fences to leave him far behind; little kid far behind, legs too short, but still coming. Then we'd wait and box his ears, sending him back, leaving him crying. Going on to explore; little kid still coming. The only way we could get him back was to go back with him, lift him over the fence, and then run, he not knowing in what direction.

In one yard, we'd find a heavy growth of weeds; that would be a jungle, and every beetle or spider would be a tiger or some other creature of the jungle. A high shed would be a mountain, Mt. Everest. We'd climb Mt. Everest and get into a yard with trees. That would be the Black Forest. A dragon or two lurking around. We'd get twenty yards away; that would be real remoteness, we making maps in our mind of the strange lands we had passed through, we on the steppes of Siberia, looking at all the world around. A little head just appearing over Mt. Everest; little kid still coming. Then we'd be good to him, and all three would steal grapes in Egypt.

CHAPTER FIVE

Neighbors complained to Them about us. Just because in our travels we would tear down a vine or two. Or only break a trellis in scrambling away from the inhabitants. Or maybe only shout impertinent things at savages looking from wig-wam windows. For these offenses They punished us, beating us with a strap or a whip. Striking us in passionate outbursts.

In Mrs. Lawson's room one day. She was teaching us our Sunday school lesson; it was about Moses and the rock. They strolled in, brushing their hat, looking into the mirror to see that the necktie was all right, very particular with every detail of their appearance. Then Moses smote the rock. But they flurried us; we could not pronounce "smote". An easy word, but we said, "smut". Told to read it over; again we said "smut". More flurried; unable to use our brain; saying "smut" still again, because our lips formed that way and we had no brain. To them, we were showing dogged meanness. They struck us in the face.

"That's smote," They said. "Now do you understand what smote is? Say smote."

We whimpering, "Yes, sir; smote." Our brain had cleared; perhaps something had

flashed into it to make it work. Probably not; it was right to beat us when we were bad.

But They often beat us with a dog whip, thinking well of using the butt end. And the butt end seemed to us to be going just a little bit too far; it interfered with our belief that ... [4]

[*Page 42 is missing.*]

... for fun." Couldn't explain that we didn't mean it was for fun to burn the fence, but that the fence had been burned while we were having fun.

But they were gentle enough for us. "Why do you do these bad things?"

"Just for fun." Our stiff body was there; we were somewhere else, or had ceased to exist.

But, even though we weren't there, we could feel that they were trying to hold back. Their hand was on our shoulder. We, who had done wrong, should have blubbered, because of their kindness, only, we weren't there.

"Now, tell me; try to think and don't be afraid; why do you do these bad things?"

Our lips formed, "Just for fun." They struck us savagely; blood gushed from our nose. Then we were there.

Said Mrs. Lawson, "Toddy's nose bleeds so readily."

They went away; but we were there. A wild, mad we. Running up the stairs, blood all over us. Running into the spare room, throwing ourself upon the bed, rubbing our nose all over the counterpane. A dirty, grovelling, little beast, crazed to get even, and doing damage was the only way to get even. Rubbing our nose on the lace curtains, making the room a horror room. Gurgling hysterically and then just sodden, not caring what should be done with us. In fact, wishing they would kill us, for suicide had been in our mind from the earliest days. Trying a sharp rap on our nose to renew the supply; for the truth is that nose-bleeding was an ailment of ours, as were head aches and oppressed breathing, all outgrown one by one.

At the dinner table, we were not allowed to speak; They could not bear to hear our voices. Once, feeling the restraint, we giggled nervously. They looked over the newspaper, saying, "Who's that!" The little kid started to tell; he kept quiet. The other kid answered that he had heard nothing. We said, "I did it." Mrs. Lawson would have told anyway; we wanted credit for truthfulness.

"Go upstairs!" We rising slowly, eating pie as we rose. We going up inch by inch; pie going down inch by inch. Couldn't bear to leave that pie. And this was defiance to them. Jumping from their chair, catching us by the collar, hitting us in the face with their open hand.

We running up the stairs, striking at figures in the wall paper, butting our head against the bannister, trying to kill ourself, biting our arms, running up and down the hall in frenzy. They went out, and, when the other kids came up, we were leaning over the bannister, letting blood drip into the lower hall to do damage. We knew it was dirty work; had as much sense of decency as a grown person; only, just then we were a little beast. The other kids cursed their father. All three chanted the vilest oaths to be thought of. Praying that death in most horrible form should overtake Them.

We were often deeply religious. Often in anguish as we thought of our sins, getting down on our knees to say our own prayers, not waiting for the formal prayers said with Mrs. Lawson in the evening. Often keeping track of our behaviour by marking on a wall the length of time we had been able to be good. There were many quarter days, some half days, and long blanks were encouraging, and we'd try for whole days or even two days for a record. But with our believing, there was incredulity too.

When a small boy, we puzzled over inconsistencies in the Bible, and asked questions that could not be answered satisfactorily. Sometimes puzzling right through a game of baseball.

[*Pages 45 and 46 are missing.*]

Wouldn't know. Knocking us down, we curling up on the floor, keeping our head under, trying to chew the carpet, or biting our own fingers, or just sodden.

We had found our way to the country; we and the other kid and two or three others almost every afternoon. Liking to have favorite haunts, where we'd make believe we were camping. Discovering a malarial, little pond in the Boulevards woods, seeing little, black creatures, which we recognized as real pollywogs. Taking the pollywogs home, watching their legs come out, interested in the marvel of their turning green. Pollywogs losing their tails; we never able to find any. Wanting to have more creatures in our aquarium, trying to make them by soaking horse hairs in a bottle. Horse hairs remained horse hairs, and we exposed another fiction.

And having trouble to start to the country; that little kid always tagging on behind. The best runner would hold him, little kid struggling, the rest of us running until several blocks away, then the best runner following. Little kid starting after; none of us in sight. Little kid wailing on the corner; a fist in each eye.

And then we bought no more birds' wings, for we made a sling shot, searching a whole afternoon for just the right kind of a crotch, shooting our own birds. On a lone tree with low branches we saw our first blue bird, we underneath, aiming with fierce excitement. A fluttering amid leaves, and we could not have been more amazed if a bit of blue sky had fallen at our feet. Then shooting our first woodpecker, dressed in polka dots and a red hood, running up and down a tree, tapping like Mrs. Lawson on a window pane.

But it seemed shamefully wasteful to cut off wings, scalp, and tail, though they looked very neat mounted on white cards. Ours was a spirit to go on and do better, so we tried to stuff birds, making them long-necked things, rumpled and stiff-legged. But practicing with many sparrows, becoming so expert with the sling shot that we could bring a little ball of feathers tumbling from a telegraph wire almost every time. Beaks opening helplessly at us; useless wings spread out, feebly beating the ground, we fiercely exulting, knowing nothing of pity, though to end suffering, we would break necks without injuring the skin.

Learning to leave in the skull after cleaning it and filling it with cotton, making eyes like the eyes of statuary, filling sockets with cotton, learning to cut the skin under one wing, so as to preserve the breast. Finally, we could stuff a bird as big as a pigeon, so that the feathers would be smooth and the form would be its own, though in mounting birds with wires we succeeded less well. Neglecting our school studies, unable to center our mind on them, but spending much time studying natural history, having many books, learning Latin names and the classifications under which all creatures are arranged, reading the lives of the great naturalists. Having every specimen labelled, as in a real museum, a boy with a printing press printing the labels. In the mineral world, we could find few specimens, not much more than clay formations and pieces of cobble stones, ugly outside but beautifully white or pink inside. For ours was a city paved with jasper; only the jasper did not show. Nothing showing but yellowish brown; but the tints of the rainbow underneath. Then, in our remarkable city, other streets were studded with precious stones; for out of granite blocks, we would dig minute garnets now and then. Nevertheless, we had a large collection of minerals, acquired by buying or trading. All kinds of iron ore; the crumbling, black kind, red hematite, and iron pyrites looking like gold; copper ore in many shades of green; crystals, spar, agates; many petrifications, ...

[Page 49 is missing.]

... dandelion.

Often going shooting alone, pleased with ourselves that we should roam alone, seeking ourself in earnest pursuit and not in mere pastime. Wishing we were far away somewhere, and could not see the city from every hill and the vast Capitol everywhere. Feeling marvels of romance and imagining in the mere names of Sumatra, Orinoco, Ceylon. Our desire for remoteness offended by papers scattered around or tin cans every now and then.

Liking to get into the woods, imaging ourself in a real forest. Seeing the remains of a pic-nic. Or we were out on a prairie. A few, old cows coming along; well, they were buffalo. But then the fluttering of a morning newspaper. If we could only be away off and uncivilized somewhere! Then we would get as far away as a large pond, where even the Capitol could not be seen, having told Mrs. Lawson that a boy had invited us to dinner to account for our staying away till night. Having dinner all alone, digging up pota-toes, roasting them in the woods. In a camp fire. We were a pioneer! May be a gypsy or an Indian. We had not learned to swim yet, but we'd paddle around the pond on a shaky raft we had made, liking to stand on one end until it would sink, we to our knees in water, enjoying the feeling of a little danger. Paddling around with our sling shot ready, looking for red-shouldered black birds in the bushes along the bank. And their eggs, all scrawled over with mysterious figuring, as if the black birds had been taking first lessons in writing on them. Shooting our first king bird, thinking him some kind of a bee martin, until we saw his covered-over crown. Crowned with a flame and the rest of him sober and modest. Bringing down cedar birds, stuffing them with their crests standing, trying to preserve their jauntiness of manner, pleased with the splashes of red-sealing wax on their wings. Now and then shooting a strange bird, going home to search through natural histories to find out what he was, going back next day to hunt for his mate, for we had male, female, young, nest and eggs of every species, if possible.

And dreaming, as we tramped over hills and through woods, for the delight in birds, shells, and minerals had become ambition. We wanted to be a naturalist. Seeing ourself in a canoe in strange South American waters. Luxuriance of life around, palms waving, a python swinging from overhanging branches, a jaguar lying at our feet. Or collecting shells on West Indian sands. Or away off in our cabin in the Rocky Mountains; traps, skins, guns around. Everything that is of pictur-esqueness, poetry and soft music playing to us in these imaginings, satisfying because at last we knew what we wanted, and tormenting, because it seemed that things dreamed of could never come true. Still, we'd be twenty some day.

Our grandfather often asked us what we should like to do when we should grow up. Which annoyed us, for we felt that we could not tell him. Asking, "Fell [sic], have you decided yet?" We stupidly answering, "I don't know." But once coming right out with it. Saying that we should like to be a naturalist. Our grandfather looked puzzled; he went away, to his dictionary, we think, between a demijohn and a jug, with a painting of the Grand Canal over it. He came back, looking more puzzled. Evidently the definition did not please him; naturalists deal with birds and animals but not in canned form. Our grandfather looked pained, for he had his own dreams, and ours startled him. Which were of a great grocery house founded by him, going down the generations, his eldest grandson some day the head of the family and important among things in barrels, things in bottles, and things in cans. But not things in cases with ... [5]

[*Pages 52 to 58 are missing.*]

CHAPTERS SIX TO EIGHT

When we weren't running around the streets or reading serious books, fighting and thieving or going to a prayer meeting, with Mrs. Lawson, we were pottering with our collections, taking inventories, making catalogues, arranging and improving. Taking a partner now and then when there was a boy with curiosities that we coveted. But uneasiness; we could not bear to have any one share with us the wonderful things we wanted all our own. We'd have to pick a quarrel just to get rid of the partner, glad to see him go away with his curiosities under his arm. Then we got an air gun; when that air gun was in our hands we had no civilized instincts and our mind could hold nothing but intent to kill. Seeing a fine robin on a lawn, hopping around gravely, throwing out his chest. There were people on the piazza, but we jumped the fence, and kneeling, aimed. A woman screaming; a gardener starting toward us; another woman imploring us not to shoot. We killed the robin.

Mounted this bird, and his appearance filled us with admiration for him and for ourself. A little weak around the knees perhaps, but that fine chest was thrown out magnificently. Dissecting the rest of him, for we no longer threw bodies away, having become interested in mysteries inside. Dissecting all kinds of creatures; had a noose on the cat path under the fence, catching cats to see how everything was with them inside. Opening a department of anatomy, mounting skeletons, preserving specimens in alcohol.

And getting into trouble right along, because we'd return late to supper from our expeditions. We and the other kid together all afternoon; we late; the other kid just in time. Having had the same experiences; we all over with mud; he with only a little mud here and there. And he could explain, having a boyish kind of suavity unlike our fits of stupidity.

Sometimes, down in the store, They would say, "Put this letter over there." We starting toward the door.

"Over there!" We going somewhere else.

"Over there!" We standing, looking at them helplessly, brainless, until They would snatch the letter from us. Often in trouble for obstinacy, whereas we were not there.

The little kid was punished oftenest of all. He'd do outrageous things. Indifferently and without much interest in what he was doing. Mrs. Lawson would make him stay in the yard to play, to keep him off the streets, and because she liked to look out at him. He was her favorite, because he had been so very little when she had come to us. Sitting at the window, sewing, looking out at him. The little kid would want to do something wrong. He'd do something a little wrong, such as stepping among the plants to find out whether he was watched, knowing by the tapping of the thimble on the glass. No tapping; Mrs. Lawson having a caller. Little kid luring the very little kid next door to the fence. Reaching under, starting to pull his neighbor through a space about big enough for cats. Very little kid screaming; little kid pulling away on a very little leg. Parents crying to him; little kid pulling away without excitement; very little kid coming through with a jerk, most of his clothes scraped off.

The little kid would reach over and cut clothes lines just ...

[*Pages 61 and 62 are missing.*]

... and for a few cents something from Africa would be sent to us; little square bits of Japan; trifles that seemed a part of Peru, entrancing us with suggestions of Pizarro, the Incas, llamas, and scenes in the Andes with great condors sailing overhead. Blank spaces in our album filling little by little, for once in the album no stamp would be sold, our trading done with duplicates only. A stamp dealer's catalogue would inflame us with desire, and then They would wonder where all the envelopes were going, we and the other kid, sometimes with a corps of assistants, busily spoiling away. No one at the post office seemed to notice unusual numbers of envelopes from Their store, but once a clerk asked us, for we had torn a package in halves, in such a hurry that we could not wait for something from Cuba or China to arrive. Sometimes we were stupid, but often we were sharp enough. Saying, carelessly, "Oh, the office boy did that just out of meanness when he was fired." And both of us knew not to spoil envelopes too often; we had the wisdom and self control that the true criminal has not; so we were never caught.

Sometimes we'd do very good business. We'd come home at night with a dozen dead birds, some of them rare, a scarlet tanager and a Baltimore oriole and a bobolink among them. We skinning and stuffing until late at night, the other kid "travelling" for us, going to the collectors having them on hand to see our goods the next day, for of all the boys we knew only Mac Dobson could stuff birds as we could, and he had outgrown his interest in collections. We'd sell eighty cents' worth perhaps; forty in cash, twenty sure and the rest in bad debts.

We'd want something from Hong Kong; and the other kid would want something from Hong Kong, a catalogue before us. We'd hesitate; then one would say, "Let's treat the little kid." Not ...

[Page 64 is missing.]

... had not its usual interest, for our own little kid was in the boat. And then on the sands up on the island with an ice house at its end, for all up and down the river were ice houses which burned down now and then. Which seemed as strange to us as the having of chilblains in a hot house. Little kid sitting at the tide line, but we making him sit still further back. Then away back. Really, it was a fearful thing we were doing, taking a boy with us so; Tykesy and Rusty could enjoy themselves, but our feeling of responsibility was too great. Little kid wanting to look for shells; we watching every step he took. Wanting to go in wading. Both of us horrified, but then letting him go out as far as up to his knees. Then showing him how wonderful we were. We swimming out at least ten strokes; the other kid really sitting down with his head under water. With his head under water! Why the little kid just gave up; he had the most extraordinary brothers in all the world. No wonder he "sassed" Rusty and told Tykesy to attend to his own affairs.

But we never took the little kid to the river again; with every tug boat seeming to bear down upon us and every drop of water causing us to fear a leak, the strain was too great. The next time we treated him we took him to the park, and even there the swings went too high.

Back in the business world again, expecting to sell a dollars' worth but realizing ten cents; just nothing but worriment and planning that would not come true. Then going to the park, one of us watching and the other climbing tree after tree, getting a few cat birds' eggs, eggs of robins, and many sparrows' eggs. Every egg delighting us as if a great colored pearl. Disappointed with the result but then advertising a consignment of choice eggs, running from blotched all over to almost pure white, that customers did not know. But in our collection, we had not one falsely labelled thing. In that we were honest and earnest and true.

Partners making a very good deal in grosbeaks' eggs that were sparrow eggs or in counterfeit oriole eggs, though one collector did come back and protest. Partner saying, "Baltimore or orchard oriole? Who said it was? It's a Bizzingum Oriole, which is very rare north of Central America. Why don't you study up?" Collector going away to boast of his Bizzingum egg.

Then, with a whole pocketful of pennies, the partners would have to get away from business cares. Just letting everything go and having an outing, going to the theatre. Up in "nigger heaven". It was beautiful to be partners, brothers, and friends. Both pushing back, if anyone should jostle one, sitting together on the bare bench, may be the bigger arm around the smaller shoulders, enjoying some fearful play, which had been rightfully earned by hard scheming. Just as if there were no such things as anxiety, poor markets, and unmarketable goods.

And then stringency again. With our relatives, the little kid became our rival. We on a corner, waiting for Nick to come home; little kid on the corner below; first one to meet Nick would get more. We going two corners down, going around the block, so that the little kid should not see. Little kid always seeing everything. We laughing, thinking we had fooled him. But then aware of signs of a disturbance farther down the street; a woman looking from a window, complaining that stones had been thrown at her. Little kid not in sight, but we very well knowing that he must be there. Going a block below. And then Nick coming along; little kid with him.

But we were displeased with ourself because of this begging; liking to call on our other grandfather just to talk and see ... [6]

[*Pages 67 to 71 are missing.*]

We liked to throw stones, liking the feel of a round stone fitting in our fingers, or a scaler that would go up and down, skimming a long distance. But we'd not throw stones at Chinamen, nor would we take part in annoying peddlers. To us, every foreigner was a poor man working hard to save enough to bring his old mother from a land of poverty and tyranny. We felt nothing of the hatred other boys had for foreigners. Seeing boys rob the ferocious-looking but mild dwarf's candy stand; for a month we'd think of it. Unable to drive the remembrance from our mind. Mourning over some poor, old mother kept just so much longer away from this free land, which was our land, which was open to any foreigner, and we'd wish we could be in Castle Garden to welcome every one of them and wish every one of them good luck. Except the British. We liked to be forgiving, but we could, never, never forgive the British for what they had done to us.

Trying again to study. Impossible. Going around for horse chestnuts. Every tree filled with stiff, little, Christmas trees with blossoms instead of things all tinsel; then prickly little balls coming out. Slinging up sticks, then slinging sticks for sticks, favorite stick always getting stuck. Liking to have chestnuts just to have them or to throw, for they would bound along a long distance. Then we had a game with them; fighting chestnuts on strings.

When one broke another, the winner was one year old. Breaking a chestnut three years old, the winner would take his record. Having a champion several centuries old, a mean, battered, little lump, blackened in bonfires to harden him, hanging on by a thread, but smashing all the plump, young amateurs. Some other, withered, old veteran killing our champion; then we'd lay away the remains to be honored forever. Always honored things. Placing sticks on car tracks; just to record them as heroes for being run over. Putting a book on the roof, leaving it there all Winter. Just to have it have experiences, picturing its hardships when the snow was falling, pleased with it in the Spring, all faded, with leaves undulating and cover warped. Having a kite caught on a wire to look out now and then and seeing it falling apart, bedraggled and buffeted in stormy weather, we waiting for the frame to drop so that we should have another hero.

Biff Allen was an old kind of youngster, he liked to be with grown men. We liked to be with grown persons, and talk seriously with them; but Biff spent much of his time in the police station, putting on boxing gloves with us, a dozen policemen in shirt sleeves looking on. Pounding each other, getting so tired that we could only lift our hands, pushing out weakly, policemen crowding around, urging us on. But we did not like this; we liked the excitement of fighting and were proud of our reputation as a fighter, but deliberately to fight for the enjoyment of others made us feel a loss of dignity so that we never went back to the police station. In Snyler's stable we had cock fights; Biff holding a "banty" and we holding a "banty" knocking their heads together to make them fight. We liked cock fights very much but there was something about hanging around a stable that we did not like. We'd not go to Snyler's, even for a cock fight, but, when we really had to have a little fighting, would shake up two cats in a bag.

As we were partners with the other kid in collecting and in business we were partners with Biff in enterprises that attracted him, making a bob, then building an ice boat. The ice boat would not go through the door, to be sure, and the river was a mile away, and it was not completed until June, but as a specimen of the ship-builder's art it caused us great pride.

[*Page 74 is missing.*]

... of invented words and then of foreign words found in the dictionary. Forming a polyglot language of French words, Latin words, Arabic words, all kinds of words. Once, when we were the excluded one, we spent a whole afternoon under the dining room table, where the others sat, searching for words to mystify and make us miserable. We making a note of every word they settled upon.

Then in the evening, the little kid chuckling and winking, saying, "Let's go in the domus."

We saying, "Yes, we might as well go into the house now."

Little kid amazed and crestfallen.

"Well then, let's go on the toit. Do you know what that means?"

"Oh, you're going on the roof?" We pretending that we knew simply because we knew just about everything. But both kids crying, "Oh, he was listening! Come on; we don't want anything to do with him anyway. We're enemies with him anyway." And all evening they would have nothing to do with us, just because it was pleasing to be mean. Little kid showing signs of weakening, the other kid saying, sharply, "Come away; don't have anything to do with him." Little kid snatching a book from us, throwing it on the floor, running up the stairs. We'd look at the book unhappily and say something forlornly to the other kid. But the other kid would turn his back and mutter; nothing could be done with him when he had one of his mean streaks. A shower of birds coming down the stairs; little kid destroying the collection. And we rushing up the stairs, positively to kill him. And the other kid very angry, for the birds were his too. Rushing after us, but jumping on our back, for no matter what the cause might be he and the little kid would side against us. All three thumping and wrestling and hating.

But saying next morning, "Is it friends or is it ...

[*Pages 76 to 78 are missing.*]

... the waiters would have style. [7]

Congress Park with a fence all around it and a trout pond inside; tally ho's, with the horn starting behind but reaching well up in front, a burst of brazen sound, and then a rattling on in what seemed a noisy silence; the club house, outside a little ball playing around and around. Going out to the Geyser and down to the Champion Spring where yellow encrustations formed on the earth.

Sometimes, They would come up from the city in the evening. Dancing in the "hops", our great aunt, who was in the next hotel, probably leaning out the window, with a spy glass levelled. And girls! Though that does seem a disrespectful way of speaking of the beautiful, young women that would be pleasant to us, and call us dear little boys.

Sometimes taking all of us driving to the lake, They cheerful and light-hearted, letting us hold the reins. No newspaper in front. And taking us around to the springs, seeing which could drink the more spring water. Asking us about our studies, we switching away from our school studies to talk of our own studies; telling him the difference between a moth and a butterfly, one having coloring matter in scales and the other furry. Telling what we knew about the planets; about Saturn's rings and Jupiter's moons. Or history and mythology. They asking whether we knew the story of Proserpine. We delighted to tell, telling about Hercules as well, though always with our halting and floundering among words.

Taking us to the Indian Encampment, buying us a bow and arrows. Putting us on a merry-go-round, just as if we could not have climbed all over a merry-go-round while they were putting us on one wooden horse. Watching us with a smile. We fascinated, ...

[*Pages 80 and 81 are missing.*]

... expected to tell everything, but just to find out for him. And then our new mother won us as really and truly our new mother by getting scissors and trimming the little kid's hair so that no one else should ever know.

But we knew, and felt disgraced. Shaking our fist at him; digging our fist into his back to let him know what to expect when we should get him home. And the little kid suffered in silence, too polite to let family troubles be known.

22

"You collect stamps?" our new mother asked. "If you'll tell me where to get them, we'll go now." And all together we cried where an old collector of stamps lived. And to the old collector we went, trying not to be too greedy, making our new mother's admission fee into the family as reasonable as we could. And then walking back with her, thinking it would be very bad manners to leave her in the street, though we very much wanted to get back to the album with our new stamps.

And on our way back, the first thing we said was, "She's all right!" Denouncing all that had lied about her. And we'd defend her; and we'd do everything chivalrous. We all excited. Just what wouldn't we do!

The other kid had not our rashness and enthusiasm, but he nodded and said, "She's all right."

"She's all right," said the little kid. "Just the same, she'll tell." And we shook our fist at him.

Boxing the little kids ears when we got him home. Hitting him until the other kid interfered; then we fought them both. Then miserable because they would not speak to us. They would not be friends again; so then we beat them for that. We all alone with no one to play with us. A cruel, hard world, where everything is not forgiven right away. Why, so worked up were we, thinking of uncharitableness and hardness, that, because they ... **[8]**

[*Pages 83 to 89 are missing.*]

... young persons there, for They were still a young man, and our new mother was younger. Progressive euchre in the afternoon, and, in the evening, bright dresses, bright talk, everything of brightness and pleasure, They easy and gracious in way that made us wistful, for we felt that such ways could never be our ways.

They and our new mother going to the theatre, whenever there was anything worth seeing. We three sent early to bed. We and the other kid had one room, and the little kid had a room next door. The other kid seemed to rule us; whenever we wanted to do anything at all illicit we'd have to suggest and await his decision. We'd want the little kid in with us. Sometimes the other kid would be sleepy or irritable or just mean or wanting the little kid

but keeping him away to be the ruler. Then sometimes we'd have business matters to talk over, liking to go over a good transaction in stamps, recalling the steps in our bargaining, debating a purchase thought well of by one but not advised by the other, deploring the lack of capital, which kept us back a good deal.

Then casting off business worries; whistling a bugle call for the little kid. A thud on the floor next door. Might have taken half an hour in our consulting and planning; perhaps a whole hour. No matter how long, the bugle call would be followed by the soft thud of little, bare feet.

Pattering feet; little kid fluttering through the beams from the sky light getting into bed with us, while we played stories. You see, we and the other kid had a game, which had gone on for years. We were the leaders in a military community away off somewhere, though Americans of course. Having many characters among our followers. Our enemies were the Hobgoblins, who looked like pictures of the dodo to us, though we don't know what they looked like to the others.

[*Page 91 is missing.*]

... Ausable Chasm?" giving the hard "ch" sound. With them, mispronouncing was humor; and again everyone would laugh. Labored and primitive humor, but we'd think it very funny to be asked about the Hebrew children.

But about our stories. Warfare not all the time; developing our country in times of peace, sometimes farmers, trappers, business men, having the elections, detecting crime, punishing the wicked, and rewarding the good. But the other kid sitting out on the stairs. A battle begun; little kid quaking. Awful carnage; little kid gasping. Becoming so terrified that he would have to run in to us for protection. And the other kid sternly pitiless. We pleading with him. No; not another word would he play until the little kid should leave. Then we'd hit him. Other kid fighting back and the little kid piling in, siding against us of course. All three rolling and fighting in the dark.

Other times, when They were out, we'd light the gas, and get a remarkably big ironing board from a room used as a storage room. Tobogganing down the stairs, going at fearful speed, knocking all to pieces the base board at the bottom. Or having theatrical performances when we were supposed to be fast asleep. Our favorite play was the "Gunpowder Plot". We'd often write a little play patched up from our reading, giving parts for the others to learn. We were King James sitting on his throne, which was a chair on the bed, and the other kid was Guy Fawkes, looking very wicked in burnt-cork whiskers. The ignorant, little kid not knowing much about the part he was playing, but thinking he knew, which seems to be enough for any actor.

And then other things. We had left the Academy and were going to Public School, Number Two, with a girl's head carved on one side of the doorway and a boy's head carved on the other ...

[Page 93 is missing.]

... the Hickeys at play in their yard. It pleased us to throw a lot of tin cans into the yard. A dead cat was lying near by. It seemed pleasing to have a dead cat thump down among the Hickeys. Dead cat thumping. We were all insolence and vanity, feeling ourself quite as strong as the whole tribe. And there was Harry Hickey, running down the alley. We waiting with our shinny held back. And we struck him calmly, viciously under the eye. But he pounded us, knocked us down, rolled us in the mud. Big chieftain mauled; mud rubbed in the big chieftain's face.

Left to sit on a big stone and think it over. We felt no particular resentment; we had deserved every bit, and recognized a thoroughness of treatment that we could not but admire. Rather humiliating; still, the enemy was bigger after all. Then we wanted to shake hands and be friends, never preying upon the Chesnut Streeters again. May be we might have some little ceremony of signing a treaty. Who'd have thought that a quiet boy, who went around with girls, could be so strong!

Four bits of stick sailing though the air. He had taken and sawed our shinny! We picked up the bits. There was the handle, worn in battles and games to fit our hands, as if it had grown that way. It was a part of us. Covered with notches that we had cut for all kinds of adventures that it had taken part in. Marks in the middle pieces; we remembering what each mark recalled, every mark with meaning. The battered knob was a diary of scratches.

Oh, raging and wildness! Running from the alley. Running back to shout a challenge in story book language. And then going home with the remains of our sacred shinny, putting them under the roof, where our treasures and our heroes were kept.

Then war! Declared by us and declared by the other kid and cried for by the little kid, too. Little kid running out with the fiery cross, though the fiery cross was only imagined. Up and down the street, pausing in front of houses with boys in them, with the whistle that meant to meet on the corner. And then to Washington Avenue, for we were friends with Crousey since we had left the Academy, and Crousey would bring not only his own crowd but the Spruce Streeters, too. Going down to the corner with the other kid. He swinging his shinny bravely; we tossing our new shinny high in the air. Admiring a warlike gallantry in his appearance, martial feeling overflowing in us. All our own "fellers" on the corner. All the good fighters and even Whitey, who was not much good, but had responded just the same. It stirred us that our own should be waiting to fight for us, just as we had often fought for them. One mending his sling shot, another practicing on a hydrant with his shinny. Some excited over the war cloud, others sitting on the curb stone, showing their indifference. One of the Robinsons wanting to know whether we were in the right. Biff Allen saying, "That don't matter; anyone hits him hits me!" And a chorus, "Me, too!" It was our own gang; we cried aloud in eagerness and pride.

And excitement down the street; the allies coming in a straggling band, whooping and waving sticks. Why, no wonder we were moved; old feuds forgotten and former enemies hastening to fight side by side. Then the Spruce Streeters under Limpy Bowen, with their whooping and their waving of sticks. Grown people stopping to look at a swarm of bad, idle boys. We seeing a band of brave, faithful warriors, giving power to our challenge and meaning to our boast. A picture that filled us with the romance of glory of victory and vengeance.

Everyone shouting, forming in the middle of the street, running ... **[9]**

[*Page 96 is missing.*]

... raging half in the street and half in the alley.

Old Harrigan, the fat cop, calling upon us to desist in the name of the law, throwing his club at us, nearly catching our wobbling kid, still hugging his paving stone, saying not a word, all his battle fever hugged into his burden.

And then, when safely away from the law, what bragging! "Did you see me! Yes, but did you see what I did!" Little kids chattering, our own, little kid saying never a word, going away to hide his paving stone. Under a stoop or in a vacant lot, or wherever he did hide it, for he was fond of mysteries, and would never tell anything.

And then going home. Knowing we were in disgraceful condition. Triumphant in our own world, but with adjusting called for in the grown-up world. Walking along a curb stone, feeling that if we could walk a certain distance without falling off, we should be able to get into the house without being seen. Feeling that if our toes should come exactly to cracks in the sidewalk five times in succession, we should have good luck, making sure of good luck by touching every stoop and every other railing. But our new mother was home. Hearing us creeping up the stairs in a way too unlike our own noisy way. Calling us into her room, and looking at us.

"Stand there in a row, until your father comes home," said our new mother. And we stood, obedient, feeling the effect of the commanding appearance, as she went on working butterflies into some kind of a hoop arrangement. The one nearest a table reached over for an ink bottle. Rubbing ink on the white showing through a torn stocking. Passing the bottle down the line; all the torn stockings mended. Rubbing against one another's shoulders to get dirt off; pointing to own faces to show dirt on other faces. Cleaning shoes on the under side of a rug; combing hair with fingers, working collars and neckties into ...

[*Pages 98 to 100 are missing.*]

About this time, Biff Allen told us that he should put up with his mother's impertinence no longer. Proposing that we should run away. Biff knew a sailor, who had been to India, and learned that we could get jobs in Upper Burma, driving elephants for eighteen dollars a week. Then our mind could hold nothing but thoughts of elephants, waving palms, natives in turbans. The other kid, too, wanted to be an elephant-driver. So we sold our stamps for fifteen dollars, Biff contributing a pile of dime novels, which we did not read at the time, telling us that his contribution was quite as good as ours, as we'd find out during lonely watches by the camp fire. But Biff was not satisfied with the fifteen dollars, which he could not touch anyway, for we cast our lots for the other kid as treasurer in every enterprise. Biff wanted us to go down to the store every day. Relays of boys. Bumpy Driscoll carrying sardines to Eagle Street and turning them over to Tykesy. Returning for stuffed olives, and back in time to meet one of us waiting with canned peaches.

And we wanted to take along the little kid; he might get a job driving baby elephants for nine dollars a week. But thinking that, whereas there seemed no room at home for three of us, there might be room for one; so, though we carted away loads of only the best groceries, we left enough for the little kid to carry on business with them when he should grow up and be a good business man.

Little kid very much wanting to go, though never really pleading; we thought it unwise. Coming to us one day when we were in Biff's garret, looking at more groceries than we could possibly have carried. Handing us a parcel. Saying, "It's provisions." We unwrapped a big pickle; wicked, little kid had dipped into a corner grocery barrel. We told him that he was a good, little kid, and we should always remember him when away off in foreign climes. "Foreign climes" too much for him; making awful faces, trying not to cry.

All unhappy, because he was going to lose his two, big brothers, very likely forever. Running down the stairs; going to tell. Going no farther than the bottom step; no more telling among us three. Thinking it over; fists in his eyes. Oh, he'd just have to tell! Little kid saying never a word.

We were to start at four o'clock in the

25

morning, and meet Biff on the corner. Eight o'clock would have done, but four o'clock was more interesting.

Four o'clock. We up and ready to start for India, having said goodbye the evening before to the little kid, who had given up talking of going with us. We went to his room to see him once more. Fast asleep, but all his clothes were on, and he hugged a bundle under one arm. We wavered at this; but India is no place for small boys. So we kissed him goodbye; and the other kid kissed him goodbye. We wanting to have some kind of a ceremony over the little, sleeping kid. Wanting to pray that he should be happy and should be the good, business man that we could never be.

But the other kid said, "Come on."

Creeping down the stairs, passing Their hat on the rack in the gray hall. Wanting to be mournful and sentimental over the hat, going away forgiving everyone for everything.

But the other kid said, "Come on."

Lingering in the street to take a last look at our home. And the other kid said, "Come on."

But Biff was not on the corner; it was nine o'clock before he came, we berating him, wearied and much of our enthusiasm gone. Biff telling a story of being unable to sleep and wandering to the river, where he saved a man from committing suicide.

[Page 103 is missing.]

CHAPTERS NINE AND TEN

The other kid said that Biff had schemed to help the family with the Winter's provisions, for the Allens, on a small income, lived in a large house. At first, we could not believe such scheming and ways so old possible in a boy of our age. But pickles on the table whenever we went through Biff's dining room. Playing in the yard, and embarrassed by stumbling over lobster cans. Soup cans everywhere, we pretending not to see.

What was done to us that night, we do not remember; bread and water probably, as a punishment for staying away all day, for the little kid had not told. For, though They continued to beat the others, They struck us no more after the time we had forced them almost to the floor.

And for a long time we sighed for our camp fires down along the Hudson; the stolen rides on freight cars; battles with tramps; and then the sea, we a sailor, and the other kid a cabin boy, we protecting him from brutal captains. Always protecting someone in our dreams. There was a little girl on the next block; we had saved her many times from wolves, tigers, Indians, and she saying not even, "Thank you," the next time we'd meet her. She in a white dress and blue sash; we all mud and very likely with a black eye. Trying to talk with her now and then, feeling awkward because of her self-possessed ways, but feeling that she must admire us because we were an outlaw in the neighborhood. We marvelled at little girls, and had little ... **[10]**

[Page 105 is missing.]

... beat him into insensibility; no, we'd have the little kid of a big, noble-looking man do the beating, for three against one would not be fair. Anyway, all our dreams seemed to end in violence in some form.

Then in real life again, and, hearing their voice, we would scowl or would try to be very quiet to please them.

Playing ball in the big lot on Hudson Avenue, with wagons of a stranded circus all around, or in the Capitol Park, with its earth worn hard and stony, the remains of an iron fence on a base of crumbling marble, and the ruins of the old, brown-stone Capitol. We interested in all buildings half torn down, liking to see the kinds of wall paper people had, tracing staircases by streaks on walls where people would not keep to the bannister, as we were taught to at home. Sent to church every Sunday morning, we, the other kid, and the little kid, too. Sent over to the Dutch Reformed Church, where there were inclined planes of stone by the stoop, which were very good to slide down. But going to Mason's with our ten cents, buying contrabands, wandering during church hours. Going to the river to marvel at the high water mark on a corner building, the normal surface far below. Looking at a grain elevator. Why should grain be elevated? We often hoisted things. But why should grown people elevate grain? Then all three holding hands, the one in the middle shutting his eyes, the others leading him in devious ways to have him guess what part of the city he was in. He'd guess "Post Office", and there he'd be in the lumber yard. Which was almost as interesting and astonishing as it would be to take a balloon and guess, "Maryland" and find Labrador.

Always wanting something; and not a cent from Them. Hearing that we could get a stuffed penguin for a dollar, a quarter down and the rest in easy payments. Our mind could hold nothing but ...

[Pages 107 to 112 are missing.]

... arms offensively. A dime off for shovelling snow when he was told to shovel snow, sitting down, looking on, making a good bargain, as a good business man should, having ten cents worth of work done, and having twenty cents worth of pleasure seeing us do it. Fearful humiliation at times, but we were willing to do anything to make the collection wholly ours.

At the table. They saying, "Who's making that noise?" The other kid guilty; looking significantly at us. And we, in a tired kind of way, feeling the awfulness of slavery, would answer, "Me."

"Say 'I.' Go upstairs."

We going; the other kid crossing off another dime. He's a good, business man now; he was then.

Trying to study, hating arithmetic except cancellation, which seemed like a game. Trying to understand decimals, then running to the street. Spending much time in new buildings, climbing ladders, sliding down ropes. And liking old buildings, coming down, making believe they were ruins, living many of the Waverly novels in an old frame house that had never held anything more romantic than two old maids. It's queer; there were old maids up the street and down the street, and we thought them creatures pitiable, contemptible, ridiculous, but nowadays there are no such old maids.

And in the Capitol a good deal, daring and "stumping" one another to walk over beams high in the air; crawling through a long tunnel, filled with air almost suffocating. There was a flaw in the reputation of every boy that had not crawled through this tunnel,

coming out gasping at the other side, stuck now and then, if he should be too fat a boy. Going down to the dynamos to have our knife blades magnetized. We had little red horse shoes, but it was more interesting to pick up tacks with a knife blade that we, ourself, had magnetized.

[Page 114 is missing.]

... five more went out of sight. All taking turns in rowing except Billy Robinson, who played the mouth organ, which he thought should exempt him. Playing with hands caving around, "bringing in the bass" as giftless we longed to do, tried to do but could not do. Going in swimming and then running up and down the sands trying to be sunburned. Tortured with blistered backs, but proud of blistered backs, hoping the fiery red would turn brown. Having blisters on our hands from rowing, proud of the blisters, wanting them to become calluses right where the fingers begin.

Every other Sunday morning, They would send us to the Post Office, a big building with a little street all its own beside it. White granite above but worn all discolored from the ground to the height of a man's shoulders. Loungers could sit or stand anywhere else but every unoccupied person in that vicinity had to lean against the Post Office. Granite blocks an ugly brown and shiny, a man with nothing to do, if as far away as Eagle Street, having to go and lean against the Post Office. City Hall, fine, restful churches, other broad walls attracting no one; men that had never written a letter having to lean against the Post Office.

Sending us every other Sunday morning for the mail, for in assigning all tasks They were strictly impartial. Frowning and warning us, for we always took an hour longer than necessary. Punishment and warning were useless; we'd be certain to take that hour. Causing them great annoyance, but never causing them to swerve from their impartiality. We displeasing them, then the little kid displeasing them, then the other kid pleasing them, because he was less often bad. But in all the years of our boyhood never once did they show favoritism. We had to take that extra hour, for every string of snow ...

[*Pages 116 and 117 are missing.*]

Then trouble with Washington Av'ners. We invaded and defeated. Falling back, each unable to see much more than was occupying him, but feeling a spirit of general defeat. Breaking gradually and then giving away all at once. Each fearing to separate from the main body, for that might single him out for pursuit, or darting away anyway, hoping the enemy would continue after the rest. Panic-stricken, picturing far worse than wolves after us, bunching at the corner fence, in a scramble to get over, the strong pushing the weak. But, even in these moments, though hopping in nervousness, Crousey's fierce band almost upon us, we and the other kid would wait to lift the little kid over the fence; that little kid always tagging on behind. Then we'd be safe. Knowing just where barbed wires were torn down, just where fence boards were loose, where a tree would make climbing easier. Into the next yard; woman scolding. Over a shed; an indignant, old man threatening to shoot. Going on to a vacant lot; a trail of heads out windows. Then playing "Follow the leader," chasing away all the little kids except our little kid, who would sit apart, saying nothing, his eyes wide-open, seeing again the wonderful things we had done to the enemy.

It was very good of the little kid to admire us but often we'd wish he'd tone down just a little of the admiration he felt. A taciturn, little kid, but sometimes talking recklessly. Taking a little walk, urged to have some excitement in his dark, uninteresting world. Throwing stones at a big boy. Then saying, "My brother can lick you." Positive we could lick grocery boys, messenger boys, all kinds of boys, and all kinds of boys at once. We were not positive of this; but then we'd rather die than lose anyone's admiration.

And then the next day we'd meet the big boy. He'd say, "Do you want to make anything out of that?" And the little kid, ...

[*Page 119 is missing.*]

... because we could resist nothing that we thought funny, always feeling this inability to conform with discipline and rules. But in geography, when told to draw a map, we would not make merely a scrawl, as would many pupils; we'd get a large sheet of drawing paper, and would trace squares so to enlarge; with a shader, shading lakes and seas, pausing to imagine ourself on them; making mountains that looked like wooly caterpillars, pausing to fight bandits or hunt a panther. And in our compositions, we'd bring in facts from histories other [than] our school history, using the big words that we met with in our reading, proud of our compositions, sometimes having them read aloud, having the fact that we used our own words pointed out.

After school, we'd run around in the streets, annoying people, climbing fences and ringing door bells, and would go home to read Greek and Roman history, French and German, and especially English history; mythology, biographies, and dime novels. We read hundreds of dime, or rather, half dime, novels, going with Whitey to a little, old store to exchange them. Slipping dime novels under our coats, when the little, old man in the little, old store was not looking. Whitey was a thoughtful boy, interested in chemicals and given to stealing.

Our school reports were so bad that often we dared not show them at home. We learned forgery from Whitey, who had very good reports, but dared show only the very best. Taking an old signature, placing it over a report, tracing, rubbing hard, then going over what we pressed into the report. And, at home, it seemed as if nothing They could do could make us better. No longer beating us, but locking us in a little, dark room, giving us bread and water, sentencing us to several days or several weeks in solitude. Three times a day the door would be opened, and bread and water would be thrust into darkness. Three times a day a bundle would come down the air shaft. At the table, the other kids would sit with handkerchiefs on their knees, clipping in things when no one was looking. So well did we take care of one another that when two were serving terms, the free one would be the starved one.

Books coming down the air shaft, and matches to light the gas with. We sitting in the little window, writing our name and date on the white wall, adding, "Imprisoned here for doing nothing," which, we believe, is the view of most criminals. It would please us to write these things, feeling that many years later we, then a great, famous man, should like to come back and look at them. Often we'd have this feeling that the great, famous man would like to see relics of his childhood. Raising boards and nailing them down with paper soldiers or heroic marbles down under; slipping treasures down cracks between walls and floors. Our mind was filled with our reading of great men; positively we should be one of them.

We in prison, and They turning the gas fixture so that we should be in darkness. A monkey wrench coming down the air shaft. Sitting sometimes with the gas burning but oftener in darkness, we a lazy kind of boy but tortured with the awfulness of doing nothing. Then singing to make the time hasten. Melancholy songs, we an unfortunate, little boy, persecuted for doing nothing, crying a little in sympathy with the poor, little boy, who had never done anything wrong. Then singing patriotic songs, half defiantly because of the noise we were making. About "Let freedom ring." Adding, "Freedom don't ring here." Hearing our new mother, under the air shaft, laugh at this. Then we, too, would laugh; for we could never be mean when others were not.

Days seeming to go by, but only half a morning. We pacing ...

[Pages 122 to 132 are missing.]

And then they told us to go to the store Saturdays as well. Worse was to come. They made us work! Sent us up in the loft to scrape old labels off cans and paste on new labels of their own. They made us work!

We were unhappy and the other kid was quite as unhappy. We scraping in resentful carelessness; the other kid scraping as well as he could. We rebelling and grumbling and shirking; the other kid rebelling and grumbling but scraping as well as he could. We sat in a corner; the other kid worked on. Then he refused to speak to us, because we made him do all the work. But why should either of us do any work except just enough to keep out of trouble? How lazy we did hate work! Other kid scraping as well as he could, refusing to speak. So we had to give in; anything, even work rather than not to be spoken to.

Then both of us lazy. Sliding down the elevator cables, exploring from loft to loft, for the store was of two buildings with the elevator running between and landing broken through the walls. Exploring through dark canyons of boxes piled high, every floor a labyrinth of things good to eat. Breaking into cases, taking out cans. Eating a few cherries, then having a light lunch of peaches; trying a little asparagus, going on to apricots. Hammering cans flat so that we could take them out in our pockets. Then lazy and not bothering; just throwing the cans out on the roof. They'd be seen sometime, but we seemed to care nothing for detection so long as detection should not be right away.

Throwing a plum pudding can with too much force. It rolled. It would fall into the street right by the side door. We ran back to our scraping; but the elevator cables were moving. Scraping furiously, but hoping anyway; cables glimmering up, and then the rust spot that meant that the elevator was a floor away. Tall hat appearing. Their face, chest, arms; still, we hoped. [11]

[Pages 134 and 135 are missing.]

CHAPTERS ELEVEN AND TWELVE

We were almost fifteen years of age, and were to take the examinations for High School. We had been taught physiology only in a general way, but had dissected a good deal and had clumsily articulated many small skeletons. But as we read with the underlying desire to be thought remarkable, and as we fought upon the slightest provocation, for glory, we made our collection much larger than that of any other boy we knew, to be thought interesting. Behind everything that we did that was not of shiftlessness and indolence was the animating desire to be thought picturesque or interesting. Once we took Bob Pavey as one of the many partners that we could bear to have share wonders with us from one week to two weeks. In the physiology class, Miss Williams produced a number of phials of alcohol with specimens in them. Handing them out to have them passed from one to another. A toad's heart, a blue bird's liver, the alimentary canal of a lizard; all neatly labelled. We were furious; they were ours, and Bob had brought them to school. Then all the credit was his. Miss Williams saying, "Where is the heart?" We had put it in our pocket. "Where is that lung?" It was in our pocket. "I see there is still a liver missing." In our pocket. Oh, fearful that credit for our work should go to another!

"You have a queer way of acting with the property of others," said Miss Williams, sharply.

We wanted to denounce our partner passionately. "They're mine," we said, sullenly. We were a forgiving kind of a boy, but, though that was fifteen years ago, we have not spoken to Bob Pavey since. He took credit that was our credit.

Roman history, we had not studied in school at all. But we went to the High School, and taking examinations in Roman history and physiology, passed the Regents in both. But our regular examinations! We had kept just barely up with the class in grammar, and in arithmetic we were floundering as if something had been clipped from our mind. We knew; we could not pass. Then truly we should have to go and be a hermit away off somewhere.

The afternoon of the day before examinations. The other kid was waiting outside school for us. Doing a little business in the meantime by trading cigarette pictures to our common advantage. Making the best bargain he could, for we liked to surprise each other. Dear me, how we liked surprises! We'd put candy away and pretend to forget it, just so that we could run across it some time and be surprised to find it. Telling ourself we had thirty cents in our bank, when we very well knew we had fifty cents, then trying to lose track. Just to surprise ourself. One of us telling the other of a very poor bargain, when he made a very good bargain; just to surprise the other a few minutes later.

The cigarette-picture business was the best line that our firm had been in. Both partners thoroughly business-like, keeping books and balancing accounts to see whether they were prospering. Narrowly watching the market, keeping track of quotations during recess or trading hours after school. [12]

[Pages 138 to 147 are missing.]

And behind the things that we dreamed of and the things that we did there was a new instinct, though really only our old posing to be picturesque in a further-on form. We no longer caring for glory as a fighter; all pleasure in the picturesque had settled in our diary. Finding interest in every happening, because it was something to write about. We, who were a collector of curiosities were a collector of incidents also. Trying to write about a hare and hound chase; our mind filled with impressions all mixed up. The start; the thundering of a score of feet on the park lake bridge; the lawlessness of running up the terrace, following paper strewn by lawless hares; the mystery of where we should end up, and a far-away pleasure in the marvel of following a trail that anyone but a blind man could have followed. Scenes changing swiftly; through a barnyard, over a lawn, through ploughed fields, over a fence, torn down in a rush and a scramble.

Then trying to write, laboring with incidents, feeling an impression of force in the pack of hounds rushing together; or of mystery when at the foot of the hill and the hares may be just over the top or miles away. With these impressions, we could do nothing. But telling particularly about some of the boys, having an instinct to bring characters into our story, like recurring mention of them, drawing a map of the course, marking every road and every field, trying to keep every feature within the scale of two inches to a mile.

Or. Five of us out shooting; three of us our rival collectors. A black speck in a distant field; a dead crow. Then all five running. Three rivals passing us; we too heavy. And we were without a crow in our collection; we, who would stuff him; they, who would cut off wings, head and tail. Then the other kid bounding on ahead, stopping to trip the nearest rival, pouncing on the crow. Crow ours; but, quite as delighting, we had the race to write about. [13]

[Pages 149 to 151 are missing.]

"We are indeed three brothers—" It was too much for the little kid. He leaned against a fence post, and put up his arm. He didn't want us to see him cry.

And it was too much for us, for we were

30

looking at the little kid, with his little arm up.

Our same old madness; some of it because we were seized upon, some of it to impress the others. Crying that we should kill Them. Butting our head against a post. Knocked flat. Butting and falling in frenzy, trying to kill ourself or whatever the post meant to us. The other kid looked on, disapproving; the little kid stood erect, not a sign of anything at all on his face.

We said no more. Covering the jars with earth; marking the place with pebbles for grave stones. All three sat on the piazza, saying very little. They took the little kid away.

Evening. Going to the dining room. We had been crying all afternoon, and felt that if there were the slightest reference to the little kid we should break down. And we and the other kid paused in the doorway. For we saw something. What the other kid saw was a smaller table; a leaf had been taken out. This was sensible to the other kid; the table had been too large anyway. He went to his chair to eat his supper, which was what he had gone down to do.

What we saw was the meaning of a vacant chair in the leaf that had been taken from the table. Littleness there brought to us littleness that was no longer there. We could not move and we could not speak. Just standing there, the other kid looking at us as if wondering what new flightiness could be the matter with us.

They looked from the newspaper; we had feared that look once.

We said, "Oh!" Just softly, because we were choked and quivering ...

[Pages 153 to 155 are missing.]

... three found an old revolver of large calibre; snapping the rusty old revolver at one another. Just happening to aim at something else when it went off; nothing left of the something else. Slipping on roofs, but catching a projection just before going over. Beams and stones falling in the Capitol just where we had been a second before. Run over more than once, we lying quiet between wheels or runners. Breaking through the ice; someone throwing a skate strap to us. Here we are still. That in all this world there should be more than two or three grown men seems remarkable.

Our first day in the High School. Boys everywhere; or, not boys everywhere, for girls everywhere. Girls with arms around one another; would have fallen; could not have walked without those arms around. Girls tottering and timid when alone; girls brave enough, chewing gum, afraid of no one when arms were around. Teachers bustling, trying to get things in order for the new year, bustling two minutes, and then taking twenty minutes to tell about their vacations, some of them tanned, a great degree of credit seeming to reflect from a great degree of tan. Older pupils coming in, looking curiously at us first years. Second years, juniors, even seniors coming in. We heard it whispered around when a genuine senior came in. He looked it; we marvelled. Genuine senior talking with a teacher; talking with another teacher; genuine senior talking actually with three teachers. Oh, never again would there be any running around the streets for us; no more peppering of windows with sling shots; we wanted to be a genuine senior and talk with three teachers. Or four teachers; we were always ambitious. We sitting there of no importance; no one paying us any attention. Well some day!

There was one teacher that attracted us. There were three or four, or, rather, one or two that we liked to look at because they were pretty; we liked to see them fluttering around, but they did not attract us as did this teacher. She came in in a great rush, an old hat on one side of her head. Old hat on the other side; then over one eye. Grabbing the old hat, slinging it away anywhere. Getting right down to business, enrolling the first years. We liked the way she made the other teachers skip around; we liked her good humor and her quickness to anger; there was sympathetic gentleness with firmness behind. Theatric in her ways, rolling her eyes, making astonishing faces. We liked everything about her. Near by there was a boy that knew all about the High School; his sister was a teacher; his knowledge made him important among us. A bell ringing; boy whispering what it meant. Someone looking into the room; boy whispering just what celebrity. We asked him who this teacher was, and he was very glad to tell us and all others around that she was Miss North, who knew everything that had ever been heard of, and taught elocution in hours after school.

And as Miss North attracted us, she seemed to notice us. For she sauntered down the aisle, singled us out, and took our hand without asking for it.

Sitting in the seat in front; getting a stronger grip on our hand; and then;

"Little boy, who are you? Who are you, serious-looking, little boy, with your great, big eyes, just like a great, big, solemn owl?" Awful faces made at us; eyes rolled at us; kindness and gentleness too. We wondered whether this were a little elocution for only unimportant us. We told her our name.

Miss North said, "Oh!" She dropped our hand. "Oh, you're one of those cherubs, are you?" She rose and sauntered away.

The boy that knew everything said, "Must know you. If you ...

[Pages 158 and 159 are missing.]

... a bony part anyway." Waiting for an appreciat[iv]e laugh. Then saying sharply, "Do not be simply amused."

We were not simply amused; we were interested, and had little experiments of our own at home. We'd look at clouds; we'd think. Or we'd look at water power; we'd think. And there was a strain of doubting in our thinking. There was the theory that one sees things really upside down; does in infancy, but by experience turns around. Proved by lines and angles. We wanted to argue. Putting the supposition of a man blind from birth; operated upon, then able to see. Would he see things upside down? It seemed to us pretty poor science not to know; there must have been such cases. Professor Overbunk answered unsatisfactorily, we thought, but he seemed pleased again. Still, we accepted almost all truths, though there did seem to be something wrong with about every experiment. Professor Overbunk demonstrating that in a vacuum a bullet and a feather fall with equal speed. The bullet falling first. Teaching us that black is the absence of color and white is all colors. Mixing colors. Producing a brownish gray. Putting a black cloth and a white cloth out in the sun on window sill snow. As black absorbs heat, the black cloth would sink in the snow. White cloth making a

decided impression; black cloth showing not a trace that it had been there. Very hard to teach truths when truth won't come right.

Beginning our study of algebra, with the idea that letters are used instead of numbers, wondering how much "a" time[s] "b" could be. Learning definitions, learning that "x" is the unknown quantity and that the little, top-knot numbers are exponents, having none of the trouble we had expected, Miss Alberts sending us to the black board, then forgetting all about us, reading *Puck* and *Judge*.

[Pages 161 to 170 are missing.]

CHAPTERS THIRTEEN AND FOURTEEN

They would not leave us behind this Summer. We and the other kid were pretty poor property, something like waste property that, if cultivated, might after a while pay its own taxes. They arranged to take our new mother and their really valuable property, the commanding appearance, to a fashionable resort, and then arranged for us. They arranged generously enough, having us join the Y.M.C.A. to send us for a month to the Y.M.C.A. camp on Lake Champlain. And we were so pleased that we were friends with them again, both of us going around to get fishing tackle and everything else that would be needed. No more sullenness, we going down to their room where we had not been in a long time, to play chess, just as we had long before, talking about fishing and hunting, very good friends, everything forgotten and forgiven at last.

A score of us in the train; train seeming to make up its mind never to start, then starting in fits and jolts. Passing many familiar scenes on the way to Saratoga, we pleased now and then to see something that we remembered having seen in former years. Getting to the tail-end of Lake Champlain, narrow and marshy with its log-choked stream leading to Lake George. Gradually widening, broken rocks scattered on the steep banks, as if waiting for a chain gang to come along to get to work. Small towns with circus posters all over walls and fences. Black and white desolation, where forest fires had raged. Farm houses, brooks, ponds, just the places where we'd like to get off, but the train rushing on.

The rattle and blinking of windows when other trains passed, rails clicking, telegraph poles looming and passing in all the majesty of tallness speeding silently by. The whole morning gone, and still whirling Northward. Past Port Henry. Westport! All off!

Piling into carts, seven miles along a road, and all off on a beach with a flock of sheep around, we marvelling that anything white and soft could be made from fleece of creatures so dusty and unkempt. And there was the little island. High and wooded against wideness and blueness. Older boys, who had gone ahead to build and prepare, waiting in boats. We admiring them, for they were pioneers, wondering whether we could get so brown and disreputable-looking, resolving to wear no hat. And there was Harry Hickey, our old enemy, who had continued his enmity in school. But this was not in school; this was out in wideness and blueness with greenness all around, where we'd have grub together and bunk together and be all of one "crowd".

Harry put out his hand. He said, "How are you?" We shook hands, and we, too, said, "How are you?" He taking our baggage, carrying it to a boat. Once we had hit him in the eye, but he was carrying our baggage, and everything was all right. Little waves tapping on big rocks there away up North made us feel that it was very pleasant to be friends.

Wonderful things for us to write about in our diary, we breathing picturesqueness as well as air, trying to impart some of the picturesqueness, but lamely recording only bare facts.

Going on a tramp through wilderness and over mountains to Old White Face. Twenty of us, with blankets in army rolls, under one arm and over the shoulder on the other side, as good as uniforms, feeling that the blankets were interesting because they were "army rolls" and not just common rolls. A real guide in front. Getting all played out; the other kid looking tired, but keeping up bravely, paying not much attention to each other at first, but drawing together when tiredness came. Then running in advance to wait, doing a good deal of work for only a little rest. Stopping to cook dinner in a real camp-fire, finding the joy in remoteness that we had longed for when tin cans or piles of ashes had been always near.

Wading in a stream, finding that in a few minutes our feet were as good as ever. Falling in smartly, and off again. Passing through small villages, bracing up to make a fine appearance, wishing we had a fife and drum corps in front, but pleased with our own banner carried by one of the big boys. We were soldiers or explorers; we were whatever it pleased us to be; mountain peaks, sunshine, brooks, and trees telling us in chorus but each with the charms of its own voice that in all life there is nothing like this nearness to life.

Leaving the road, which had dwindled to ruts with grass between. We were in the North Woods! Where the Deerslayer had followed trails, where the French and the Indians had fought the Colonists. Struggling through underbrush, and then on sunny slopes snatching at wild, little strawberries as we tramped on. Among tall trees, softness underfoot. Into an upright fringe of the blotchy whiteness of birch. Peeling off white bark, pink inside, looking like a page from our diary, with dashes along in lines. A brown forest in front and behind a forest green on its weather side. The startling of things hidden and then suddenly seen. Far enough away to satisfy anyone.

But then picking up an old envelope. Someone had been there before. Annoyed with the envelope, but keeping it to send to the man it was addressed to; he'd be pleased to have something of his that had lain in the North Woods; he'd marvel that it should be sent back to him after the experiences of all that time.

Kicking the leaves that had been green, were brown, and would be soggy black mass underneath, hoping to stumble across Indian relics. Wishing some Indian had been so thoughtful as to leave lying around a few old relics that he did not want. But we'd be thoughtful; stealing away during a rest, to bury whatever we could find in our pockets, even pennies, for someone to find maybe a thousand years later and be pleased with.

In density, in tallness, and then coming out into openings, all openings looking much alike; rolling ground, clumps of bushes, and bare spots of rock poking through. Straight over, as if directed by sign posts, into the forest again, Old Dug, the guide, going on in an unhesitating line, following a trail that we could not see but were pleased with, because it was not a path but a trail. Old Dug knocking over a woodchuck. A real guide shooting with a real Winchester. Giving us the woodchuck. Woodchuck becoming heavier and heavier, we clinging to it, feeling that we should throw away our blanket first, only the blanket was an "army roll", and our interesting appearance would be marred without it. Skinning the woodchuck while going along, other kid holding the fore feet, we stumbling and jabbing dangerously.

Mistiness of coming evening; clumps of spectral pines and the unknown all around; whisperings and sighings. Loneliness that could not be loneliness with twenty in the band. The horrors of a night in a forest diluted into pleasure, as some thing repulsive may be a perfume when refined.

Leaving the woods at New Russia, right on schedule time, we marvelling that there should be anything of schedules and regularity where all was wilderness to us. We in the Keene Valley, the wonders of everything we had read of valleys crowding around. Sleeping in a barn; just like tramps; jumping into hay, expecting to sleep right away, astonished to learn that one may be too tired to sleep right away.

Off next morning; up the mountain, coming to a little lake, stowed away in a pocket in lofty rock. Finding an old scow, and paddling out, perch swarming so that with several hooks on a line we could catch two at a time. Nothing but a drop of depth and clearness with bushes in a fringe around, caught there on the mountain side. We poking through the tangle, thinking it a likely place for curiosities. Fallen trees, depths of old leaves, the wonderfulness of everything as everything had always been. And then a pile of fish scales! Someone had been there before. The old scow had seemed as if belonging to the scene. But fish scales! Always someone there before.

We on a mountain summit, looking down into the valley, and away off at another mountain; patchwork of different-colored farms, clouds casting fantastic shadows here and there. We feeling high and god-like; the man in the dark-green farm was in sunshine, not knowing that the man in the light-green farm could see nothing but clouds. But we knew. Farms struggling up just so far, and then again everything just as it had always been; trees seeming uniform in bushy greenness, and not some tall, some stunted, some fallen, as on our mountain.

Climbing on a boulder to get to the very summit and feel exalted. Initials cut in the rock. Someone there before. And no place on top for our name. We were half playing and half in earnest; we wedged in a stick with a bit of writing floating out in space above all initials. We would have our name highest of all!

Camping out in a tent; everything we had longed for. Stiff and chattering in the early morning fog; just as we had often wanted to be. Off again. Tramping back, singing songs that made the tramping easy. "John Brown's Body" alone was good for almost a mile. His body a-mouldering in the grave; we and his soul marching on.

Evening on the island. All of us around the fire. Urging Old Dug to tell us stories. Old Dug with long legs in long boots, long body and long face, seeming mostly longness and the rest Adam's apple. Telling his experiences in New York. Yes, that was interesting, but had he ever shot a bear? Tell us a story. Oh, yes, he knocked over a bear now and then or caught one in a trap. We wanted a story? Well, there were his troubles with furniture on the installment plan. But had he ever seen a panther? Do tell us a story! Oh panthers were common enough in his early days. A story? Well, his wife had a tea party now and then, but after all there was never very much going on where he lived.

Why, he never said "b'ars" for bears. It seemed wrong. A panther was only a "cat" and not a "painter." That seemed very wrong. Old Dug would have been much more interesting, if he had read of fishing and hunting instead of having fished and hunted all his life.

Around a real camp fire, shooting sparks making the pine needles crackle overhead, the older boys with banjos and guitars, singing songs we had never heard before. They were songs that breathed something new into our life, or breathed upon and aroused something that had always been. Singing, "My Bonnie Lies Over the Ocean," and "Goodnight Ladies." We wanted someone in a white dress and a blue ribbon to sing "Goodnight

Ladies'' to, and then go away ''o'er the deep, blue seas.''

We'd think of the little girl in the next block; that next block so many miles away. Wishing she could see us with our broad, cowboy-kind of a hat. Wishing she could hear us sing, though we could not sing as the older boys sang. They had a strange, wonderful way that moved us, made us feel gentle and want to be good, filling our mind with pictures of our comradeship out there among pines with water all around, then thrilling us with ambition to be famous and do wonderful things some day. It was singing that was new to us; not singing straight alone, all the same way, but one going down and another going up. We learned that this was bass and tenor; couldn't understand how it was done, but wished that little girl in that far away block could hear us, not knowing but what we were singing that way. If she could only see us, we were sure she would be quite stupified with admiration, for we had walked where Indians had walked, we were on familiar terms with a real guide, and we had seen bear marks on a tree. We trying to sing tenor. Bill, a big boy we admired very much telling us to shut up and stop screeching. Then we were unhappy. Bill hitting us a fearful blow in the ribs. Then we were happy. Because he meant he was sorry he had spoken sharply.

And these young fellows made us feel like just a little kid, we with capabilities for admiring quite as strong as our desire for admiration. Bringing out sort of a feminine attitude in us. We becoming drowsy, leaning against big Bill's shoulder. Bill saying, ''Go to sleep, kid.'' Gentle pleasure upon us that he should call us ''kid.'' Listening to his voice rolling away down deep. Some day our voice would be deep; some day everyone would be proud of us; some day– Oh, some day!

Knowing not much about ideals those days, but feeling a dozen around us. How we wanted to be like Bill and Harry and Jimmie ...

[*Pages 178 and 179 are missing.*]

... Statue of Liberty, her torch drooping, knowing not what to do. For what can even Statues of Liberty do when boys are bold?

We wishing that we, too, had the courage to talk and laugh around the fire; there was a girl of about our own age with whom we should very much have liked to talk and laugh with. We were afraid. All we could do was to sit on a log and look noble, and then, feeling too young and an outsider, went down to look after the boats.

Then everyone was ready to leave, promising to call again, at which the Statue of Liberty's torch flared. Rowing away. Singing, ''Good Night, Ladies!'' And we thrilled with something new in our life. It was romance. Feeling it in the voices on the water, feeling a possession of meaning in our being in darkness with the light on shore left slowly behind.

These are the things that made us go away somewhere to write in our diary. Urged to write of darkness and light left behind. Unable to; writing instead, of filling a fish with a pound of shot and betting it would weigh more than a larger fish. Having an impression of the way singing made us feel; writing of pouring molasses into Crayley's shoes.

Rowing, we with little liking for the labor of rowing. Playing baseball as well as the others but excelling in swimming. In fact, they called us ''Froggy.'' Which we did not resent, though all other nicknames had enraged us, for ''Froggy,'' seemed an honorable title. Diving with our hands behind us, going down like a pointed stick; someone throwing in clam shells, fluttering in all directions, we getting every one on our way up. Liking to swim under water in the creek, drifting with the current, seeing weeds and pebbles on the bottom go by. Lying lazily in the water, three hundred feet deep, our arms folded, our legs idle, going almost to sleep, a small surf playing on our island of a face. Rising and falling in the rollers of a steamer, waiting for the second set of rollers long afterward.

Now and then we would leave the camp fire, and row away alone. To be horrified. Water by night would make us shrink and shudder, though not in physical shrinking and shuddering. Not open water, we paddling along, liking to trail our hand in the warmth of cold water under still colder air. But when we were alone on water dark in the shadow of rocks or trees. Feeling treachery and awfulness; ripples glittering in an evil gleaming at us. Or in a patch of weeds. Floating foulness;

all the mystery and fearfulness of the Sargasso Sea condensed there for us; squirming tentacles, alive and writhing to clutch and drag us down. The superstitious part of us would be frightened; the intelligent part of us would be pleased with the unrealness of awfulness only imagined. Rowing away alone at night deliberately to be horrified.

Just loafing around on the sands, trying to be tanned as much as the pioneers; sharp lines on our arms, where sleeves ended. Burying oneself in the sand, all dry on top, and all moist an inch or two down. Stretching out a set line at night. Mr. Roberts telling us that this was against the law. That was interesting; so in the evening we would stretch out a line to a float, having many pendant hooks. Going in the morning to see what we had caught; really expecting to pull up uncouth, fantastic creatures, if not monsters, just because they were caught in the night.

Wandering around in a meadow, trying to follow a bee; turning over stones to see the beetles and the pale grass in dampness underneath; lying along the branch of a tree overhanging the creek, reading novels or dreaming of the extraordinary things we should do some day.

Westport station again. "All aboard!" ...
[14]

[Pages 183 to 185 are missing.]

... others with his sense of wonderfulness and difference. We wanted to walk home with her, but, hearing another boy tell her about his toboggan and invite her to go tobogganing with him, we lost courage. We had no toboggan; we had nothing. Feeling that it was disgraceful to let him cut us out. We let him; we had nothing.

What we wanted was a good suit of clothes to go to school in. Many of the boys had suits of black cheviot, which distinguished them as being of what seemed to us the black cheviot caste. That was the caste we wanted to be of. We knew that They were prosperous, and it seemed natural that we should have wants in proportion; but one of the "boys" in the store had a son dressed better than we and the other kid.

And then our first whole suit with long pants in it. It was dark brown with faint,

yellow stripes. The menagerie that was we then included a zebra. Suit so tight that there we were with big, fat legs again, and the brown came off on our hands; still, at last we were homogeneous. It was not altogether pleasing to be a zebra, but then that was better than having the hybrid's lonely, unclassified feeling. A few weeks later, and there we had gone through the brown and yellow-striped seat of our trousers. No one mending us; we walking down a class room, with our back to the black board. One does feel so conspicuous when without a seat in one's trousers.

Up in our room, looking at thread and needle, but feeling it beneath us to do any sewing. Progressive euchre down stairs; costly prizes; everything always done on a scale that was costly. We upstairs trying to sew rags together. And succeeding very well, we thought. Sitting down. Swish! Worn out cheapness could not keep those big, fat legs in. So we pounded a chair, just as, when a little boy, we pounded chairs ...

[Page 187 is missing.]

... it was our own work. Dreading to get into trouble; still, we would not.

And this flattering seemed to gather impressions from away back to our very-little-boy days. When books in their own shelves, apart from the pleasing of their stories, had mystic charm so that we would sit and gaze upon shelves of volumes. When names of authors had meaning that no other names had in our seeing. We had always placed writing as the highest of gifts, thinking that only an author could be a genius, rating the inventor and the painter and the orator far below. Impressions gathering into idealizing and marvelling. Strengthened by our study of English literature. We looked upon suicide as wickedness; but the suicide of Chatterton was pathos, causing vividness of picturing that could never be forgotten. The misguided ways of doctors, lawyers, or business men were not to be tolerated, but the improvidence of Goldsmith was picturesqueness. We'd picture the days of Grub Street, admiring every character except Boswell. Boswell was a "supe"; "supes" we hated. But above poets, historians, lexicographers, we rated writers of fiction. Others were plodders; writers of fiction were magicians in our seeing.

A teacher would ask some simple question in geometry; there were we silenced as if with a mind darkened. Asking about some perplexing kind of an accusative; we without a sign of intelligence. Teacher asking some question with the answer not in our school book, such as, ''What great author once submitted drawings to Dickens, who rejected them?'' Turning instinctively to us, for our hand would be sure to be up, we all eagerness, no lack of intelligence and no mind darkened. Obscure and trivial questions; we with the facts in our storehouse; our hand waving excitedly.

Going over to the ''club'' in the afternoon. Up in the wrecked, top floor; no carpet left, nothing but barrenness, but new chairs and something new on the mantle piece to make wreck and ruin less uninviting. Having a little football or a little wrestling, but turning to other amusements. Matching pennies; losing all ours, and going to our aunt for more, she seeing nothing wrong in any kind of gambling. Then Mookey taught us poker. Mookey, who had spent a cent once, having no lack of money for poker. Not teaching us the finer points, but the other kid instinctively figuring out stratagems, teaching us. Then we knew as much as Mookey. Then Mookey came around with a faro board. Soon we learned too much of the law of average. Mookey bringing a roulette wheel of card board.

But something was slipping from our life; it distressed us. A football knocked over some of our choicest livers; we were uninterested. Minerals and sea curiosities were covered with dust; we meant to spend a whole Saturday in house-cleaning. But didn't. And then spasms of renewed interest. We'd try to bring back all this that was slipping away. Forcing ourself to go shooting. Hearing a hidden bird whistle; no longer any thrilling. A glimpse of brilliant plumage; no exciting. We'd force ourself to the dreary work of making out a new catalogue; we'd have new labels printed, not liking to pay for them. Minerals and eggs had lost their special interest, which had made them seem far more than only minerals and eggs.

We turned, in a way quite desperate to a new collection to bring back the wonders of the old collections. Our aunt had many valuable autographs, some of which had once been in a famous collection; letters from Franklin, Byron, Scott. We, too, collected autographs, sending to Amiens, France, asking Jules Verne for his. Jules Verne sent us a little letter in a hand so minute that we could get no one to translate it. And we sent to Oliver ... **[15]**

[*Pages 190 to 210 are missing.*]

CHAPTER FIFTEEN AND REMAINDER

The end of our second year in High School was not far away. The other kid managed just to pull through everything, though he had seemed to study very little, but not ending in our disgraceful, conditioned way. He joined the other literary society, though, unlike us, he could have joined either at the first election.

There was not, and it seemed to us there never could be, any improvement in our school work. Nick was interested in our writings for the literary society, and often asked to see what we had written, showing us where we had labored around and around a point expressible in a few words. Just before school closed, he sent for us. Saying, ''How would you like the newspaper business?'' We answering, ''Oh, all right,'' by which we meant that nothing could be more attractive to us. It would be useless for us to wait for the examinations, as Nick knew, for we had always told the truth about our worthless self when he had asked us.

Nick said, ''Well, go around to the *Democrat*; Standish is editor there now, and he will put you on. There won't be much of anything in it for you at first, but it will give you an idea, and some day we may get you down in New York. Just keep your rubbers on, and you'll not slip up.''

Standish was his best friend. They had been kids together, and in the High School together, having had some renown giving ''Brutus and Cassius'' in small entertainments, Standish taking ... **[16]**

[*Pages 212 and 213 are missing.*]

And Mr. Standish calling us. Saying,

"Ministers? Directory!" Rattling papers, slamming down his blue pencil. But we did not understand.

"Look in the directory!" Grabbing and crumpling a handful of papers.

We standing stupid. Oh, yes, the directory! Going to the directory and opening it to search through for all the clergymen in the city. A day's work of a task, but we began with the "A's", glancing along patiently. We'd do it no matter how tiresome; we'd work in the office all afternoon, and, as there was a directory at home, we'd go through that all night if necessary. Then we'd start out early in the morning. Searching for ministers among housepainters, blacksmiths, widows.

Mr. Standish grabbing the directory, opening it in the back, showing us a list of churches and the addresses of the clergymen. We made out the list; we went out on our first assignment. Just think of our being a reporter! Going to see cutthroats, thieves, and assassins. Going to see and write about things that only ordinary people can only read about. And we supplying this reading. We'd see lunatics! Oh, hasten the day when we could chat with maniacs!

We did not go home, and we did not go to see Nick, though he was only a few doors away. We wanted him to think we had gone home, and then surprise him by showing that we had started right away with the work, with all our heart in it. Truly, at last we might have everybody pleased with us. And we did go from minister to minister; all afternoon, until we found we were taking our subjects from supper. Then going home late to our own supper, feeling that we had the right to be late; we were working for our living. To be sure we had seen only ministers, but soon maniacs would be common enough.

[Page 215 is missing.]

... after having related marvelous and impossible experiences himself, that he offered to put in two cents if we would give eight for soda water. But we let him go no more; he had taken half an hour that time, just revelling in being a reporter before the minister, minister's wife, minister's daughter, and two ministerial cats on the piazza.

And then we wrote out our interviews, finding a vast difference between impression and expression, conscious of too many "ands," but unable to get along without the "ands"; with a horror for repeating words, but unable to think of synonyms. And feeling that we should have a variety of forms in the interviews, but not knowing just what we wanted. We had worked hard from early morning until late at night, and next morning handed in what we had written.

Half amused, half friendly Mr. Hamilton handed it back. Saying, "The puzzle-editor isn't in just now. Perhaps you'd better write it over." For our handwriting was the handwriting of the unschooled, and the copy reader had refused to bother with it. We were downcast; writing again, glancing at Mr. Standish, leaping from his chair, dashing back again, glad that he was so very busy and would not know of our disgrace.

Mr. Standish was quite unoccupied, just leaping and dashing anyway; calling us into his office, saying that we could never succeed with our kind of handwriting, advising us to cultivate a large, round hand, remarking that he had known poor writers to produce legible work in that way. We rewriting, making each letter as large as a bean, finding that we smoothed many irregularities with the rewriting.

Of course, when our assignment was over, we knew that we could not very well have distinguished ourself with such work. But how we did long to do something remarkable! Passing vacant ... **[17]**

[Page 217 is missing.]

... we could lounge on a park bench, but were lounging professionally, reporting a tennis tournament. Bound-down clerks and bookkeepers seemed very inferior persons; we saw in our calling the attractiveness that all but actors see in the actor's calling. Describing scenes and conditions in the park; making the weatherman the object of old-time pleasantries; finding material in the incidents in a badly paved street.

Why, at home, our new mother was afraid to speak, we turning her gossip into "copy," though trying to disguise so as to get her into no trouble.

"What was said?" We with ears wide-open. Our new mother glancing from them to us meaningly. They irritated and scornful, refusing to believe that we could write anything, thinking, when they could trace about-town gossip to us that someone else had patched it up for us.

They repeating, "What was said?" Our new mother gossiping; we with note book, scrawling on it in our pocket.

And we had a reaching-out feeling, wanting to write more important, little stories. If we could only produce something with a plot in it, and with characters that we could make speak and act, as if we had created them! There were luring and wonderfulness in this feeling of creative instinct, of which we had only desire for it; seemed godlike to take a pencil, and then let things happen.

Writing half a column about reading character by the way people tore tickets from strips of tickets in the street cars; some grudgingly, some nervously, some cheerfully. We thought this strikingly original. We had read many articles upon the telling of character by simple acts, but because we turned to tickets instead of ways of carrying a cane or opening an umbrella, we thought ourself strikingly original. Above all things we did ...

[Page 219 is missing.]

... work. We'd say, in the evening, "Well, I had a pretty hard day to-day," whether we had or not; just to draw a little sympathy from our new mother, whom, because of the ways that were our ways, we had long before lost as a friend.

We'd long for encouragement; we'd want to be told that at last we were doing creditably. They'd shake the newspaper at us; just as when a little boy talking was forbidden at our table. In fact in their seeing, we were only an experiment of Nick's, They sneering at anything undertaken by "that young Nick" as they called him.

We went to the camp, and Standish told us that, if we should get up a good story, he should be glad to have it.

Swimming and boating again. The year before, we had had pleasure in discovering new places; this year ours was pleasure in revisiting old places. Delighting in a rock if we had only scaled fish on it; pleased with any tree that we could remember anything about, if only that once we had leaned against it. Picturing Northern bleakness and the darkness of white snow and ice in these sunny scenes of trees, grass, and blue water gently rolling pebbles on its edge. Trolling for pike and pickerel, lazily rowing, but the little spoon working furiously on the other end of a line that connected us with unknown depths. Painting on a rocky stretch our name in letters three feet high, people in steamboats wondering who could be as important as all that. Just wouldn't they know some day!

On our way back in the cars, writing our story, with desire to see it in print greater than we had felt for anything we had ever written before. But our mind was in confusion; incidents, characters, scenes were all mixed up, we not knowing where to begin, trying to force a connected story from these things all mixed up. Making our most pretentious effort in writing, trying to tell not only what we had seen but what we had felt. Settling upon a night trip over the lake in the big war canoe; feeling the picturesqueness of a band of us, each with a paddle, skimming over dark waters; unison and rhythm thrilling us. Just like the Indians, who had gone over the same waters in the same way a century before.

Mr. Standish said, "Execrable!" Looking at us in a wild way of his. We thought "execrable" a good word, and used it in our next writing. But he meant our handwriting for the story was printed with only a few sentences made smoother. Which, however, we were sorry to see, for we wanted every word of it to be our own.

Real reporters saying that we had done well. Even Gresham, who seemingly had never before been aware that we existed, was so kind and flattering as to ask us for a match. Nick cut out the story to paste in his scrap-book, saying, "You keep your rubbers on, and we'll have you down in New York yet."

It was only an ordinary, little story, using "story" in the newspaper sense, but it was wonderfulness to us. Because we saw not what it was but what it was meant to be, and not what was in it, but a thousand times as much as was in it; all Lake Champlain, and all the history of Lake Champlain; suggestions of rocky shores and sandy beaches; pictures of rain storms far off in Vermont hills, their coming then seen in roughness advancing over smooth water; the splashing of rain drops sweeping from blots and swirls down upon us, waiting on a point of land to feel force and fury; impressions of deepness, blueness, romance, comradeship.

Wanting to know what They thought of our story, most of which we had tried to have humorous. Not really asking our new mother, but trying to find out.

[Pages 222 to 231 are missing.]

... were only neatly folded documents couched in intricate, unintelligible language.

Going to the Surrogate's Court every morning. Uneasiness. We knew not how to address the Surrogate. We very much disliked to call any fellow-citizen "Your Honor." It seemed un-American. But we wanted to do what was proper, so we'd say, "Good mornin', M-m-m," which might mean, "Your Honor," "Judge," or "Mr. Bonway." And we had this feeling about taking our hat off in offices. Wanting not to appear ignorant, but feeling that we could not take our hat off except in a court, in houses, theatres and such places and to women. It was very trying to be a stranger in this grown-up world we were in. So much world we let trifles distress us that we would pause and linger before a door, trying to decide whether that hat should come off or should stay on. Getting into trouble with the County Clerk, because of our assuming of the briskness we admired so much. Saying, "Ah! Fine morning! How's everything this morning, old man?"

"Don't you get so fresh!"

All the briskness knocked out of us. Called "fresh," and all we were doing was trying not to show our feeling of strangeness.

We'd see the Mayor now and then, and the "boss" often. A great, terrific creature, a Judge, a ruler; it would seem strange to us to look at him now and then and know that once he had been the other little boy that Mrs. Lawson had brought up.

But with all our stiffness we had an easy way too, and made friends wherever we were, clerks here and there explaining and helping

us. And Surrogate Bonway helped us, because it was his way to be kind to everybody. Were it not for him, we should have been arrested once. He was Police Justice then, and Old Lewis had gone to him to get warrants for us and the other kid. We had tied his door knobs together, ringing ...

[Pages 233 to 237 are missing.]

... mischievous as a little boy. Childish we sent in disgrace to stand in the hall, as if we had never seen a bridge-tender or a dock-watch-man. We had to be laughed at; it was our craze to be amusing. Pretending to hang things on a remarkable projection from the German professor's bald head; anything foolish and silly to have us noticed.

Studying at home, studying with Miss North, and then geometry in the evening. Walking home with the bookkeeper, very much liking to discuss grave subjects with him; such as whether opportunity makes the man. Having no gift of language, staggering around in vagueness, searching for words, feeling our instinctive delight in words used not commonly. To say "pristine" or "salutary" or "paradoxical" almost thrilled us.

And going down to Rizzer's house to play poker, having to be home by nine o'clock. The other boys drank now and then, and now and then we would go into a saloon with them. They'd order beer and order beer for us; we would refuse to touch it. Having a scuffle now and then; we would not touch it. Just as with smoking we had held away until desire had come, we could seldom be tempted unless we felt inclination.

Walking down Pearl Street one day. And a feeling came over us. That we should like a comfortable evening at home, with a book in which we were interested in, smoking our pipe, and our feet up on something, with something by our side to pour out now and then. We went into a store and bought a bottle of cheap claret, quite without reasoning.

Waiting until the other kid had gone to sleep; opening the bottle, pouring out until we poured all over ourself. Falling about the room; just sense enough to turn off the gas and make no noise.

Then we drank little glasses of port every now and then, not liking beer, knowing better than to drink whiskey, liking ...

[*Pages 239 to 241 are missing.*]

... at the head of the troops, medals all over us, fellow townsmen shouting our name, flags and handkerchiefs waving, everyone saying, "May be he was bad, but there is good in him after all. Hooray!" Fifes and drums intoxicating us with their music, the bass drum beating like the very heart of it, and our own heart beating so that we should have burst into crying were it not that we despised the showing of emotion.

The banjo was taken from us, our new mother said that the other kid should take music lessons, because he had long fingers.

The music teacher went down to the store for payment; he didn't know Them. Then he did know; however, he was paid long afterward.

We went with Rizzer to Johnnie Whack's one afternoon. Several of the boys had gambled there, and had told us about it. And we wanted to be a "sport." Being a "sport" might win us a little admiration. We were unable to catch up with studies that we could not have kept up with, but admiration we had to have for something; we'd be a "sport."

There was truth in what we felt; all the boys admired a "sport." There was Teddy Higman, one of the great unmarked, a studious, mild boy, but without even exceeding studiousness and mildness to mark him. He'd say, "I saw you coming out of the Delavan yesterday." Not for the world would he go in the Delavan; but he'd look at us as if we had explored a new continent.

"Do you really drink beer?" He'd not drink beer, but there were his eyes as if looking at some superior person carelessly tampering with peril.

"Did you ever gamble?" Why, there were dozens of boys like Teddy, all of them good boys; largely for their admiration we took to badness.

So we went to Johnnie Whack's. Going through the pool room, meeting Mr. Ex, tearing up a slip of strangely marked paper, tearing excitedly, then scattering carelessly. And Mr. Eye, talking in a group about "past performances," "weight for age," and other things that we knew nothing of. To think of Mr. Eye in such a place. And Mr. Zee! Mr. Zee looking at us as if indignant to see us there. Starting toward to speak severely, seeming suddenly to remember something, turning abruptly away.

Going up the stairs, for we had little interest in racing, as imagined in a pool room, wanting to have some action before us. Having no difficulty to get in, for our slow, old city was a "wide-open" town. Glancing indifferently at everything, trying to appear accustomed to things we had never seen before, but astonished to see there young fellows that we had known as quiet, good boys.

Taking a place by the roulette table; Mrs. Lawson had given us a dollar; so we bought a stack of white chips, asking for "checks" which we had learned is more "sporty" than "chips." Very attractive chips with stars or crescents on them and not the plain ones we had played with. Learning the gossip of the place from young fellows, with whom we talked in low tones, as if in a place where we should be very respectful. There was near us a man that had been playing two days without sleeping; he was eight hundred dollars ahead of the game we learned. To us he was the extreme of everything daring, playing whole stacks at a time on whole numbers and on corners, we risking only a little, white chip at a time on colors. Then feeling mean with our one, little, white chip. Putting on a dozen; surely the other boys would recognize "sportiness." And winning right along, as, it seems, is a beginner's way. Losing and then doubling, protecting ourself on the "0's" and the "eagle". Down to the last doubling, losing on black, but the banker saying, "Eagle, the bird!" Which seemed tautological but meant that we had won after all.

A whole stack on black; winning; leaving the two stacks. Little ball circling swiftly, then jolting, falling into a black compartment. Oh, the admiration we felt for ourself!

Piles of white chips around us, built in a castle with towers and turrets that would keep us from ever again wanting anything we could not have. Shoving on a whole tower, trying to shuffle chips with one hand, just as the banker was doing, only, the chips wouldn't shuffle for us. Paid in red chips!

Feeling as if we had been promoted into the class of the man that had played two days without sleeping. And Rizzer digging his fingers into our back, trying to make us cash in. Losing a whole tower; losing a whole wing of the castle. Rizzer trying to drag us away, braving the contempt of the banker.

So we cashed in eleven dollars, and went with Rizzer to Keeler's.

Fried oysters and bottles of beer! That's what we had. Why, it beat Surrogates and dock loungers! Leaning back, smoking cigars. Two for a quarter! And we tipped the waiter! Waiter holding our overcoat, reaching under to pull down our under coat. We had tipped a waiter! There was nothing left except to walk out, chewing a tooth pick, and then have our shoes shined outside.

Didn't go to school next morning. Were in Johnnie Whack's as soon as the place opened. Awfulness.

We spent most of our evenings with Nick, who had moved to our other grandfather's house, because our other grandfather wanted all his children with him. And there, good-natured Martha quarrelled with our other grandfather frequently. This bright, ... **[18]**

[*Pages 245 to 252 are missing.*]

... an orchard had radiated special meaning to us; this meaning had been whispered by shells, sea beans, postage stamps. We had gone on from life in grass, trees, water to marvelling and passion for all life. We were bad, there was weakness in us, there was meanness in us, clumsiness, stupidity, self-ishness, wildness in us. But surely there was something else in us, for any little story that was of the greatness of life exalted us so that our excitement would have burst from us quite in the form of sobbing were it not for our contempt for emotional surrender.

Oceans, strange lands, strange peoples we would surely see some day; phases, degrees, conditions of life would surely be our study some day, if we should have to lose every friend and every prospect.

We would be the great and famous man of our little-boy dreams. We would be a great writer.

Some day.

[*End of a chapter.*]

[*Pages 254 and 255 are missing.*]

... State Line, pleased with changing cars, because that complicated our trip and made our responsibilities greater. And then we had no sense of responsibilities, for, while waiting for the train, we went into the hotel, which, like every building anywhere near a state line, was half in one state and half in the other. Shooting pool with country, young fellows, wanting them to recognize the vast difference between them and a city, young fellow. Drinking port, but then checking ourself, feeling the lowness of drinking too much only once in our life, and would not repeat the experience. Borrowing a fish pole to try a little fishing while waiting. Tripping into an icy stream; perhaps we had taken a little too much port after all. Having to dry by a fire, thus missing several trains. Which would make it difficult to get back by evening. We didn't care.

"All aboard!" We hastening to the train; or, no, we "bustled" like a traveling man.

We were in the Berkshires, familiar ground, because we had been there with our grandfather, yet strange and interesting, for this time we were traveling alone. Little hills piled on big hills, looking like shop-worn chocolate drops, with their brown patches and snow-covered spaces. Sitting out on the steps, where we always sat, even if going only to Troy, to have everything closer to us. Rocks, trees, everything filling us with ambition, making us think of our latest Madeline, wishing we were wandering through the hills with her. Interested in everything; seeing the footsteps of a giant in the snow, tracing them to a shuffling, little boy a moment later; telegraph wires that were white cables with a break here and there where sparrows had rested. Whiteness weighing down greenness, as snow-covered evergreen boughs hung low.

The conductor coming along, not quite liking to see us there, but allowing us to stay, then inviting us into the baggage car. Offering our flask of port. Just weren't we grown-up and experienced! Conductor raising the flask, lowering it and handing it back, explaining that he never drank when on duty. What could be the matter with that flask anyway!

Our station. But we had a ticket for a station three miles farther on. You see, we wanted to do some real detective work. Wanting a feeling of strategy and machinations and skillfulness in what we were doing. No one expected us; there was no one that knew us; but we seemed to think it clever to go into the village not from its station but from the station three miles away. So it was night by the time we had walked back; thus far we had done everything wrong, for we should have to wait until the next day to see the little kid. And very likely there would be the worst trouble of our life at home. We didn't care. We wanted to stay all night in a hotel; all by ourself; no one arranging for us; away off from everything familiar. It would be very pleasing to stay all night in a hotel.

Landlord handing us a pen. We were about to sign in a register! What remarkable experiences! We must have thought we were John Hancock signing the Declaration of Independence, for the landlord looked at his book and then at us reproachfully.

But we made friends with him, wanting to start right away with our detective work, and find out where the little kid was. Sitting before a grate fire, pleased with the landlord partly because he was a landlord and partly because he wore boots. Pleased with the burning logs, pleased with a farmer, because he wore red mittens each on the end of a cord around his neck. "Local color" you know, though we had never heard of "local color" then. **[19]**

[*Page 258 is missing.*]

You see, we could not tell what we might do when we should see the little kid after having not seen him in such a long time. In our hip pocket there was a revolver. We had always felt contempt for auxiliary weapons, but Biff Allen, who does appear again after all, had pressed this revolver upon us. And the little kid was brought to us. Just as little as ever, but sturdy as ever, showing not a sign of ill-treatment except his twitching eye caused in his own home.

All we said was, "How are you?"

All the little kid said was, "Pretty well, I thank you," just as if I were a stranger. But he sort of leaned toward us. And we were seized upon because of that sort of leaning. Our arm

around him, having him sit beside us. Littleness seeming to send a sense of bigness tearing through us. And our flightiness was upon us; we wanted to shout and to struggle. In our mind, we were already in the doorway, our arm around this little kid, battling with the whole village.

Said Mrs. Dean, "I quite envy you your trip through the Berkshires; at this time of the year they must be beautiful."

Said we, "Yes; but I'd like to have come earlier; I'd like to see the maple leaves in Autumn."

Mrs. Dean discussing Autumn leaves with us; asking about the city.

Then we were a reporter again. We were conscious of this peculiarity of our mind running on one subject, but just had to tell some of Gresham's more respectable stories. We had had few experiences; Gresham had had so many; surely he would not resent our piracy.

After a formal call, we said we should have to go. Little kid asking that he might walk to the station with us. Mrs. Dean fearing not; he had lessons to make up. Little kid saying nothing, never pleading for anything denied him. We telling him to be a good boy and study hard, and then going away. But with a depressing, outclassed feeling. How easily Mrs. Dean had made nothing but a formal call of our detective mission, easily turning us from battles to Autumn leaves.

We lingered in the village, dissatisfied with tameness instead of adventure, more and more displeased with the uneventfulness of everything. We would see the little kid alone; we would find out how he was treated. So we waited until dark, then went again to the house. Looking at the lights, wondering which light he was near. And then we saw him. Up in his room; a trellis underneath; moving around in lamplight.

We crept over the lawn. And threw pebbles at the lamplight. Little kid opening the window, making not a sound. He knew; this little kid always knew. Whispering down to us, "Wait a minute."

But we wanted a picture. We climbed the trellis, thinking that climbing this trellis was the most interesting picture we had ever been in.

Little kid coming back, greeting us at the

window. He handed us a piece of cake. Why, this poor, foolish, little kid thought we were hungry! And that did move us. His going down to steal for us, as we had so very often stolen for each other. We wrapped the piece of cake in a paper to keep always.

Little kid wanting to go to China, Singapore, anywhere with us, whispering that two miles down the track we could catch a freight car without trouble. But we thought the hotel would do. Both of us stole down the trellis.

Up in our room. Little kid's head showing not much more than just over the high table we were sitting by. We ordering drinks, soda for him and port for us. Feeling that it was wrong to have him see his big brother drinking, but quite unable to resist having him see his big brother drinking. And smoking a big cigar, murmuring something about "the beastly quality of these country weeds."

The little kid hinted that he smoked cigarettes, having learned to smoke in the Industrial Farm, as he would never have learned at home, for we and the other kid would have trounced him well for it. Then we were severe with him. Little kid very respectful, pleasing us that he should recognize the vastness of difference between seventeen and just only thirteen.

And now tell us about everything; you must not be afraid, for you know whom you're talking to and everything will be used in your favor and against our common enemy. Is anyone ill-treating you? If there be? Great excitement! Pounding of the table. By this and by that if anyone's unkind to you there'll be - - Dear me, a whole massacre in five minutes.

Little kid unmoved. What does he care for Mrs. Dean or young ... [20]

[Page 261, the last page, was torn in half.]

THAYER'S COMMENTARY AND NOTES

PROLOGUE TO
THE FORTS OF ALBANY

As nearly as I can piece it together without going to Albany, the founder of this prosperous line was Peter Van Vranken Fort, of Dutch extraction. He may have had a sister, whose name does not appear. She is deduced from two items in Fort's writings, mention of a great-aunt who lived in a hotel in Saratoga, where Charles was taken to visit her as a child. Reference is made to her fondness for gambling. On the other hand, this belle could have been a Hoy, but I rather think not.

Peter married twice, as appears, but his first wife is not named. Whoever she was, she bore him two children, "Lil" and "Will".

According to my correspondent, Lil married John Delehanty, also of Albany, "under very romantic circumstances at the Church of the Madeleine, in Paris. One child resulted from this marriage, Ethel. The marriage ended unhappily, Lil tossed her bonnet over the windmill, and later divorced her husband."

This is probably the same John Delehanty, an attorney, who was named executor of the estate of C.N. Fort, the father of Charles. We have two letters written by Delehanty in 1913.

The same correspondent states that Will Fort married Anna Baillie, of Albany, and died a few years after marriage, survived by his widow and one child, Marian.

Just when is not stated, but Peter Fort was widowed of the mother of Lil and Will, and took a second wife, one Catherine Farrell of Brooklyn. Upon her also Peter Fort fathered two, one Frank and one Charles N.

Frank married Margaret Downey or Dowling - or something similar - of Baltimore. "Two children resulted from this marriage, Mortimer and Pauline. The family lived in New York, on West End Avenue, about forty-five years ago (that is about 1910)." Indeed, we have a letter to our own Charles (Hoy) Fort, dated Nov 20/1910, written at 823 West End Ave., signed "Your ancient unckle (sic) Frank."

Our good correspondent quoted above, one Mrs. Laurence T. Cashman, née Mary Lowe, who is a grand-niece of Catherine Farrell, was under the impression that her mother's "Aunt Kitty" was the mother of our Charles, but Kitty was in fact his grandmother.

Charles N. Fort was the youngest of Peter's children, but when old Peter V.V., came to die - apparently early in 1896 - Charles N., was running the wholesale grocery.

Charles N. Fort - like his father - also married twice. His first wife was _____ Hoy. His second is not named.

Charles N., fathered upon his first wife - Charles Hoy, Clarence N., and Raymond V. Fort, in that order, beginning with our Charles, Aug. 6, 1874. Internal evidence indicates that Raymond was an infant - certainly no more than two years old - about 1880, and the same evidence indicates that the mother of those three boys was dead at that time, when Charles Hoy was about six *ans*. Not a vestige of memory of his mother remains in the documentation. His step-mother is prominently mentioned, well re-membered, and tragically, for she lost the sight of both eyes. She is nowhere named.

MANY PARTS

As it has been said, these raw materi-als for a life have been "edited" - not to say censored - by several other hands before mine, and the most drastic of all his editors was Fort himself. His first book-length MS - written by him about 1900, was more than 261 pages long. We know that because the last torn page of it in our possession is numbered "261", and it is incomplete. It is a sort of reminiscence cover-ing the years of about 1880 to 1891, while Fort was growing from *ca* 6 *ans* to the age of 17.

Probably what follows here was first entitled MANY PARTS, taking its name from that remark of Shakspere which runs: *All the world's a stage — and one man in his time plays many parts.*

We have that source in Fort's own hand, and shall advert to it shortly. First let us consider the fragmentary MS for its autobio-graphical value.

Of the (at least) 261 pages, only 76 remain. In other words, the maturer Fort (or who else?) has extracted 185 pages of MS from the 261: and who can guess how many pages followed?

We begin with the page numbered "12"

because any that ever preceded that are now missing.

NOTES

The following notes were included within Thayer's copy of the *Many Parts* manuscript.

1 - Perhaps Charles is as old as 8 or 9 at the opening above. If so, the year is 1882 or 1883. Observe, however, that "the little kid" is still in a baby carriage, and that is Raymond Fort, only 4 years young[er] than Charles. The character called "the other kid" is Clarence N. Fort, of an age between Charles and Ray.

2 - That is the end of Chapter Three, on p.28. The grandfather referred to is Peter Van Vranken Fort, and "They" is the term invariably applied to the writer's father, Charles N. Fort.

3 - In the margins of this MS, Fort has made a few pencil marks at a much later date, mostly to identify the characters. Against the above mentions of his grandfather he has twice written "P.V." in the margin. Observe also the beginnings of Fort's interest in the Arctic and the aurora.

4 - In the margin just above, opposite "They", meaning his father, Fort has written "C.N." three times.

The observations upon numerousness of the soldiers, and the practice of marking them for honors for their inanimate achievements, are echoed in Fort's later years by his invention of Super-checkers and his practice of so marking the "men" in that game. I shall advert to this at an appropriate time.

5 - One wonders if the word "Fell", above in the direct quote of the grandfather, indicates that P.V. spoke with a Dutch accent. Probably not. More likely it is Fort's typographical error.

6 - The above mention of "Nick" arouses the question if the father of the three boys may not have been named Charles Nicholas Fort, and the "Nick" adopted as our Charles grew up.

The "other grandfather" mentioned in the last line above is J. Hoy.

7 - In the margin Fort has written "Saratoga".

8 - Above is the first mention of the second wife of Charles N. Fort, the stepmother of the boys. One estimates that Charles Hoy was about 13 at the time of her coming, the year about 1887.

Apparently the lady came on the scene willing

and trying to make friends with her young charges, but it is significant that the next seven pages of MS - 83 to 89 incl. - are missing.

9 - p.96 is missing - with its details of this Nineteenth Century rumble by teenagers.

10 - That is the end of p.104. Probably the altercation between Charles N. and Charles Hoy was described earlier, on pages now missing. Here, however, we observe that enmity between father and son has been growing.

In the third paragraph above, we probably have our first glimpse of Anna Filan who became Fort's wife. She has said she met him when he was 13, so this maiden in the blue sash is very likely she.

11 - Reader's of Fort's *Wild Talents* will recall that in this relabelling process, described above, he pasted peach labels on other fruits and vegetables, "like a scientist".

12 - The year must be 1889.

13 - "The little kid" - that is Raymond Fort - is sent away, and one would like to know why, but we are not likely to learn. All three brothers - indeed all these principals - are long since dead.

14 - Observe, above, Fort's early awareness of his bent for humor, here stated with regret. He wished to record genuine emotion in his diary but ended up recounting practical jokes.

15 - That is the end of p.189, and Fort has begun to foreshadow himself. At age 15 or so, already bookstruck and trying to write, the first famous author he asks for an autograph is Jules Verne.

One wonders what became of that precious letter. It is not here. Probably Fort sold it one stony day.

16 - That is the end of p.211. It verifies the use of "Nick" as a nickname for Charles N., and we see that Fort's first job on a newspaper - the Albany *Democrat* - was obtained by his father's pull, not by the writer's compulsive energies or by any specific triumph.

17 - Some examples of Fort's handwriting clearly demonstrated the temporary effect of the editorial regimen mentioned above. Alas, the effect was all too ephemeral.

N.B. Select examples for facsimile reproduction.

18 - There ends p.244, and it is slightly confusing. "Our other grandfather" was J. Hoy, whom I have assumed to be Fort's maternal grandfather. Perhaps this old man's eagerness to have "all his children"

with him applied equally to his son-in-law, Nick.

We have just one fragment of a letter signed by J. Hoy, and since it is undated and unrelated to any other event known to me, I insert it here as possibly apropo[s] to the above.

The message is written in pencil on both sides of a piece of "tablet" paper ruled in light blue.

(p.) 3) It's getting a little too warm already (.) Write to me immediately on receipt of this letter and tell me you're coming (paper torn off at this point...on the reverse side -)

Will you write me and tell me what you are doing, and how you are getting on / Your Grand-father / J. Hoy (could be "I." Hoy).

19 - So, Charles, at 17, is paying a secret visit to his brother Ray, at an unnamed village upstate. On the way, the passing landscape, as viewed from a seat on the day-coach steps, causes him to write the sexiest line he ever penned as long as he lived. " - - making us think of our latest Madeline, wishing we were wandering through the hills with her."

Obviously our hero is going the way of all newspaper men, drinking, gambling and flirting from Madeline to Madeline. One is pleased to learn that Charles has lost his virginity - perhaps on some of those missing pages - but the intelligence is startling, coming, as it does, so casually. And what has become of Anna in her pretty blue sash?

The year is 1891.

Page 258 is missing: pages 259, 260, and what is left of 261 - torn in half - follow.

20 - That is all.

EPILOGUE

F ort rewrote the book, *Many Parts*, more than once, and we shall follow its career as his stock in trade when that time comes. The portion reprinted above is tendered as so much auto-biography.

Perhaps it was the result of Fort's visit to his brother Ray that caused him to leave home. Several statements of his indicate that he was living in New York City in 1892. On the other hand, two years after Fort's death his widow, Annie, told Theodore Dreiser this anecdote which was taken down by Dreiser's secretary, Evelyn Light, in September 1933.

A.F.: "Charles was a wild kid. He could not bear to be told he must do anything ... They had a stepmother, and lived in a beautiful home in Albany ... Charlie came home one night at 10 o'clock, and found he was locked out. The house had a big red glass door, and he took a stone and smashed every bit of the glass. They made him sleep in the basement with the servants, and when he came up, they would not let him have breakfast with the family for a week. The servants were forbidden to pass him anything, but when the cake came around one day, he made a grab for the plate, and the stepmother tried to grab it away from him. Charlie took the cake and threw it at his stepmother. Then there was a fight. Charlie went to his grandfather's, where his father had to pay board for him until he was of age, and then Charlie went abroad. That is how he broke away.''

Which grandfather that was is not indicated, and the term "of age" may be used loosely. If 21 *ans* is indicated, Fort did not attain that majority until 1895, but if 18 *ans* will suffice, he had barely a year to wait after his visit to Ray which he knew was going to cause a storm.

Later in the same interview Annie told Dreiser that Fort was 18 when he came to New York City.

Annie was not a very reliable witness, but this latter statement is borne out in one of Fort's letters written in 1915, reproduced in full farther along in this volume. Fort's assertion there is that he sold things to a N.Y.C. syndicate "when I was 17 in Albany," and at 18 (1892) was a contributor to "the Brooklyn edition of the *World*," and at 19 (1893) became "editor" of a new paper, the Woodhaven *Independent*, published in or near Jamaica, Long Island.

Now, the contributions to the N.Y.C. syndicate and even those to the Brooklyn edition of the *World* might have been made by

Charles Fort c.1889, aged 15. He wrote to Jules Verne for his autograph.

mail, but to edit a Long Island newspaper - even a weekly - Fort must have been living in the vicinity.

The earliest acceptance we have is on the stationary of the New York *Journal*, April 27, 1897, but earlier ones surely have been lost, because Fort was a going concern by that time, and known to have been living in New York City for more than a year. He received mail at 170 East 32nd Street, dated July 21, '96. It is a postcard, which reads: "Fort:- we are at 322 Columbus Ave - Cor 75th. Stay away - Christopher."

I have no idea who Christopher was but suspect he was a kinsman or friend from Albany.

OTHER MATERIAL

DAMON KNIGHT'S FOOTNOTES

As the only publication to refer to *Many Parts* previous to now, I would offer the following table of references from Damon Knight's biography, *Charles Fort: Prophet of the Unexplained*. The pages that can be positively identified from the manuscript Thayer was copying are in italic, and those which appear near a page break would be good estimates in the absence of the actual manuscript. I would add that: regarding footnote #15, Knight has "of solitude" in his quote, whereas Thayer's copy gives "in solitude," and, Knight has "slipping" in his quote, whereas Thayer's copy has "clipping"; and regarding footnote #17, Knight's quote does not include Thayer's "may be," which I have edited as "maybe." Also, Knight refers to Fort's constructing a bobsled citing his footnote #19, and Thayer's copy identifies it as a "bob."

47

Knight's Footnote	Thayer's Page	Manuscript
4	23-24	*41*
5	25	43
6	25-26	
7	35	63
8	37	
9	34-35	63
10	43	82
11	33-34	60
12	55	*106*
13	56	113
14	53	*104*
15	60-61	120-121?
16	46-47	*92*
17	75	
18	39	72-73?
19	40	73
20	52	102
21	36	65
22	67-68	152
23	72	171
24	80-81	180
25	83-84	*186*
27	84-85	188
29	89	*216*
31	105	259
155	68	*156*

TABLE OF CONTENTS FRAGMENT

A fragment of a table of contents under the title *Many Parts* may represent an earlier version of Fort's manuscript, which may no longer exist. Its pagination is different from the manuscript copied by Thayer and reproduced here. The fragment (torn in the middle, leaving the titles of chapters 13 and 14 incomplete), is as follows:

MANY PARTS

One - The Tramp 1
Two - Seeking An Excuse 12
Three - Anti-fat And Anti-lean 13
Four - Blubber And The Beanstalk 26
Five - Mimicry 41
Six - Public Eye 49
Seven - To Train Up And To Train Down 57
Eight - In Flight From Adoption 66
Nine - An Unpleasant Authority 74
Ten - The Spite Party 82
Eleven - Realization 92
Twelve - Universality 96
Thirteen - The To*** 103
Fourteen - Making An E*** 114
Fifteen - The Family 125
Sixteen - The Character 131
Seventeen - Schemes 142
Eighteen - Slabbic Justice 151
Nineteen - The Artists 159
Twenty - The Author And His Biographer . . 165
Twenty One - Tempting And Resisting 177
Twenty Two - The Turning Of Bardoozer . . . 183
Twenty Three - The Extinction Of The Unfit . 192
Twenty Four - Making Her Debut 196
Twenty Five - Identifying A Demon 199
Twenty Six - The Return Of Ambition 206
Twenty Seven - A Concert Garden Failure . . 214
Twenty Eight - The Opinion Of Critics . . . . . 22[?]
Twenty Nine - The Green Goods Man 228
Thirty - To Invest Her Capital 237

EXTRACTS FROM 'WILD TALENTS'

From the Start of Chapter 3

In days of yore, when I was an especially bad young one, my punishment was having to go to the store, Saturdays, and work. I had to scrape off labels of other dealers' canned goods, and paste on my parent's label. Theoretically, I was so forced to labor to teach me the errors of deceitful ways. A good many brats are brought up, in the straight and narrow, somewhat deviously.

One time I had pyramids of canned goods, containing a variety of fruits and vegetables. But I had used all except peach labels. I pasted peach labels on peach cans, and then came to apricots. Well, aren't apricots peaches? And there are plums that are virtually apricots. I went on, either mischievously, or scientifically, pasting the peach labels on cans of plums, cherries, string beans, and succotash. I can't quite define my motive, because to this day it has not been decided whether I am a humorist or a scientist. I think that it was mischief, but, as we go along, there will come a more respectful recognition that also it was scientific procedure.

From the Start of Chapter 4

Not a bottle of catsup can fall from a tenement-house fire-escape, in Harlem, without being noted–not only by the indignant people downstairs, but–even though infinitesimally–universally–maybe—

Affecting the price of pajamas, in Jersey City: the temper of somebody's mother-in-law, in Greenland; the demand, in China, for rhinoceros horns for the cure of rheumatism–maybe—

Because all things are inter-related–continuous–of an underlying oneness—

So then the underlying logic of the boy–who was guilty of much, but was at least innocent of ever having heard of a syllogism–who pasted a peach label on a can of string beans.

All things are so inter-related that, though the difference between a fruit and what is commonly called a vegetable seems obvious, there is no defining either. A tomato, for instance, represents the merging-point. Which is it–fruit or vegetable?

RAYMOND FORT'S RECOLLECTIONS

The following fragment appears to have been a pencilled draft of a letter written by Raymond N. Fort, sometime after Annie Fort's death in 1937, and was made available with some clarifications of the writing by his granddaughter.

"I have not got any of my brother's notes, manuscripts, or data, as he left these to the Fortean Society upon his death several years ago and his widow, who died recently bequeathed what was left of them to Theodore Dreiser.

"I don't think that I can be of much assistance to you as we did not keep in very close touch with one another. However I might help you out a little in regard to his early life.

"My brother was born August 6, 1874 and was the oldest of three brothers. His father and grandfather were in the wholesale grocery business, an old established firm of P.V. Fort & Son.

"The early life was uneventful, and he passed through the grammar and high school as the other boys of his age. In the later years at high school he showed marked ability in writing and was considered to be quite a wit among his friends. While in high school he wrote numerous stories and sent them to various magazines and they were accepted and published. These stories were all based upon some actual happening, some school boy prank or an expedition in the country. He would take some little incident and embellish it and make a story of it and then we would all have the pleasure of reading about ourselves in a magazine. He always used our real first names.

"After leaving school he obtained a position as a reporter on the Brooklyn *Eagle* and was with this paper a while, when he and another employee of the same paper started a newspaper of their own somewhere on Staten Island but after a while they ran afoul of some of the local big shots and that ended that venture.

"Then my brother got the wanderlust and for a number of years traveled all over the globe paying his fare on slow coasting boats when he was able to and working his way at other times. In this way he saw a large part of the globe, most of the countries in So. America and also Europe and Africa. He was in South Africa for quite a while and I remember him telling of one incident that happened there. He said or did something to a Frenchman who did not like it and immediately he was challenged to a duel. As my brother had never handled a sword and was not very expert with fire arms, he did not know just what to do but accepted the challenge anyway. As he was the challenged party he had the choice of weapons and after giving it a good deal of thought he decided upon fists and so informed the Frenchman's seconds. Of course they objected very strenuously but my brother would not move from his position or would he let the challenge be withdrawn. The fight came off, and the Frenchman was pretty well battered up as my brother knew how to use his fists and possessed unbounded courage. After this he wandered around a while longer and then came back to N.Y., where he met a girl who he knew in his younger days in Albany and married her. He then settled down and started to write but it was hard going and he worked at most anything that he could get in order to live and write. He endured all the hardships that are coincident to getting a foothold.

"You probably know the rest. He spent years abroad studying in all the big libraries of Europe and England and then settled in N.Y. again where he wrote several books and had them published.

"I wish that I could help you out more but as I said before I can only help you about his early life. If there is anything else that you would like to know. I will be glad to be of assistance to you."

THE LUMINOUS OWLS OF NORFOLK

David W. Clarke

Briefly covered by Charles Fort in chapter 10 of *Lo!* (*Complete Books*, pp625-627), the 'luminous owls' of Norfolk have long deserved a fuller treatment. Journalist and author David Clarke has returned to the original sources, uncovering much fresh material about the subject and the conjectures surrounding it.

> Lead kindly light amid the encircling gloom,
>   Lead thou me on.
> The night is dark and I am far from home,
>   Lead thou me on.
>
> *Norfolk folk-tune.*

In the year 1897 a gamekeeper named Fred Rolfe was employed at West Bilney Hall, near King's Lynn in West Norfolk. One very dark night he was out stopping up fox-earths in the grounds when he saw a very bright blue light pass close to his face, startling him as it passed away into the night. As he had been a shepherd for most of his life, and was used to unusual occurrences at night, he did not pay much attention to it, putting it down to some insect; but shortly afterwards he saw the same light again in the distance while walking in the High Plantation. He returned for several nights afterwards with his gun in order to shoot the light and thus solve the mystery ... "at last I saw the light skimming over the ground, I waited till it came within a few yards of me, and then fired at the light. It being dark, you may fancy my surprise when I found a poor old, half-starved barn owl dead on the ground. I thought he had been gathering glow-worms, as it was getting late in the winter; but I have seen a great many owls since then, but I never saw one before give out any light." [1]

Rolfe came forward with this story during January 1908, when the whole of Norfolk was intensely interested in stories which had been circulating for several months in relation to sightings by reliable observers of strange moving lights at night, flitting and hovering over fields and hedgerows. The matter was first brought to the attention of the public through the letters column of the prestigious London *Times* [2]. According to a naturalist, T. Digby Piggott, the lights were supposed to emanate from barn owls which had become luminous through a fungus disease of their feathers or from coming into contact with luminous touchwood from their nesting place.

Piggott obtained his information firsthand from a naturalist and writer upon biological subjects, R.J.W. Purdy of Foulsham, Norfolk, who had observed this unusual phenomenon himself.

In the first published accounts, Purdy took the step of deleting locations and the names of witnesses from his reports, in order to preserve the natural habitat of the owl from would-be curiosity seekers. This precautionary measure had led people to believe that the whole thing was a practical joke, and so he endeavoured to set the record straight at a lecture he gave to the Norfolk and Norwich Naturalist's Society in Norwich on 25 February 1908 [3], in which he recorded all the names and details he had collected in connection with the phenomenon, and so hopefully set at rest any doubts as to its reality.

He stated that the phenomenon was first observed by himself and his son at 7:10pm on the evening of 3 February 1907, a calm, mild night, whilst returning from a long walk from Guist Hall to Foulsham, in Norfolk. They had just crossed one of the shallow valleys which abound in the district, and upon reaching the top of Twyford Hill they noticed a moving light in the sky about a quarter of a mile to the north of them, in the direction of Wood Norton. The light began to move horizontally backwards and forwards, then began to move rapidly vertically to a height of 50 to 60 feet, jumping around erratically upon reaching the highest point of its ascension. They watched it perform these manoeuvres for 20 minutes, and were quite at a loss to ascertain the cause of the light. It looked like a carriage lamp, slightly reddish in the centre [4].

He saw the light, or another like it, next on the night of 1 December 1907. At 7:45pm he was again walking on Twyford Hill, on his way to post some letters on a dark and misty

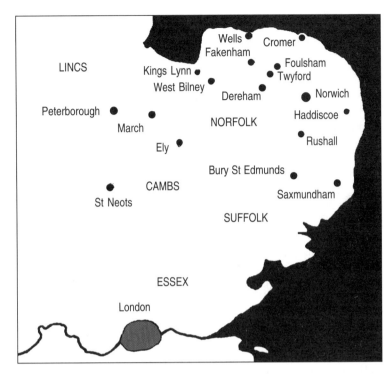

Map of East Anglia, showing locations of places mentioned in the article.

night with fog hanging over the ground, when he saw what he took to be the lamp of a motor-car rushing along the Bintree Road to the south. It suddenly stopped and rose 20 to 40 feet into the air, stopped, and then rose again. He called the attention of some country-men to it, but they only remarked that it "looked funny". His groom's cottage was only a few minutes' walk from the area, so he called out the groom and his wife, with whom he watched as the light performed its aerial manoeuvres.

He walked the half-mile home, where he watched the light with his son and three servants through the attic window. Soon after Purdy, his son and a labourer named Brownwell set out to Twyford Lane, which adjoined the field where the light was still hovering. It was moving to and fro over the field in which were a number of turnip heaps covered with straw. It approached to within 200 yards of them, but then turned back and disappeared in a meadow by a stream, as if frightened when they began to move towards it. They negotiated a nasty fence into the meadow with a ditch of water on the other side, making some noise in doing so, it being pitch dark. The noise evidently disturbed the

light, as it moved off rapidly, vanishing into a plantation near Twyford Church. At one point they distinctly saw two moving lights.

At 10:30pm the same night, Purdy returned to the same field on his own with a telescope. After waiting for about 10 minutes, he saw the light emerge from a covert about 200 yards distant, flying backwards and forwards across the field and at times approaching within 50 yards of where he was standing. It then alighted on a ploughed field, but took off before he could cover it with his telescope. After a few seconds it alighted again in the same field some 100 yards away.

"It remained more than five minutes," said Purdy, "during which time it passed twice across the field of my telescope, or rather the glass passed across it, only to magnify what looked like a large lamp surrounded with mist. The light suddenly disappeared, and I saw it no more." It should be noted that Purdy became convinced during this second sighting that what they had seen was a bird of some kind, most probably a white owl (*Strix flammea*), even though only the light was visible.

Purdy saw the strange light again at 7:00pm on 22 December 1907, whilst walking along the Fakenham Road near Chop Lodge, Twyford, next to the home of the squire to whom the adjoining land belonged. He called at Twyford Hall and called out Mrs Hamond, the squire's wife, and his daughter, to watch as the light moved over meadows to the south. They had an excellent view as the light moved along the valley, but then it seemed to become alarmed by something which caused it to rise high into the air, disappearing about half a mile to the west, towards Guist Church.

On 25, 26 and 28 December it was seen again by Purdy, Twyford school-master L.E. Leary, stationmaster L. Allen, W. Palmer, PC Bird, E. Girling and others at Foulsham. However, it was on the 29th that Purdy obtained a view of what he considered to be "the best display". Whilst on a tour of inspection at 8:00pm with Dr Herbert of Foulsham, and his son "the bird issued from the covert I have before mentioned. Its luminosity seemed to have increased, and it literally lighted up the branches of the trees as it flew past them, occasionally mounting over their tops. After watching it for about half an hour, it was joined by a companion bird hardly so bright. This kept about 100 yards behind it, but not constantly. As they appeared one on each side of a copse it was one of the most curious and pretty sights we ever beheld. They finally disappeared in the trees surrounding Twyford Church, near which, I believe, is their diurnal abode. The same evening it was seen by Mrs A. Digby of Fakenham, her daughter, and Miss Lee-Warner.

"The night following it was seen by Mrs Chas. Hamond of Twyford Hall, Miss Lee-Warner, Mr Philip Hamond of the Norfolk Regt. and Mr E. Hamond, Lieut. R.N., in the Station Meadow, where it alighted on a post by the stream. I saw it hawking along the bank of this brook about 11:00pm the same evening." [5]

At around the same time that the lumi-nous owl was entertaining the inhabitants of Twyford and Foulsham, if we can believe J.H. Gurney of The Zoologist, another one was making night excursions to Haddiscoe marshes, nearly 30 miles away. It was seen by L.C. Farman, "an observer not likely to be mistaken", flitting across the marshes near Haddiscoe Dam at about six paces from the ground, on the night of 25 December 1907. It showed very bright at times, and then frequently vanished (he thought this was due to the breast and head of the bird being turned away from him), but soon it was seen to appear again in the distance, sometimes showing up exceedingly bright. On the two following nights Farman had the opportunity of seeing the light again in the company of others. Gurney noted that "[as] Haddiscoe is thirty miles from where the other luminous pair were seen, it could not have been one of them, though the same causes, whatever they were, may have operated to produce it." [6]

The mysterious lights showed up next back at Foulsham, at 8:30pm on 7 January 1908, when Purdy, his wife, Mr and Mrs Hamond, their son and daughter, and two friends saw them hawking over Palmer's Field for 20 minutes. This display was just as bright as the previous occasions. Eventually one of the lights flew off to the south towards the station, the other one took off in the opposite direction, passing over their heads at 60 feet and rising rapidly toward the plantations. "It seemed far brighter as it approached than after it had passed," said Purdy. "They were seen the same evening at 11:30 by Mr Cyril Morton, Mr Harold Morton of Foulsham Rectory, and Mr H.W. Pallatt, of The Green, Banbury, Oxon., hawking along Blyth's Stacks south of the station." [5]

By this time Purdy's reports were causing much consternation and puzzled interest within zoological circles, and as with all scares various inter-ested people began arriving at the quiet Norfolk hamlet of Twyford in the hope of seeing 'the luminous owls' for themselves. One of these hopefuls was J.H. Gurney of The Zoologist, who arrived over the New Year, spending some time in the company of the squire, Mr Hamond, on whose grounds the 'birds' had made their home. He was not so lucky as to see the light for himself, but was rewarded for his efforts when a gentleman resident of the district showed him a lumi-nous tree! "It was the stump of an ash," wrote Gurney, "which, when he found it, had a phosphorescent superficies of several feet on the decayed side; but the glow was not very bright, and there certainly was no hole which could have held an owl." [6]

Another arrival at the parish was Mr Digby Piggott. He arrived for a two-day visit on 5 January. He did not see the lights himself, but interviewed "ten trustworthy witnesses", mostly those persons already mentioned. Further weird stories began to circulate, including one that on 16 January at 6:00am, the son of Mr W. Palmer saw the owl pass within a few yards of him whilst in Adam's ground. He claimed there were two intensely bright spots on its head, and that it uttered a 'chuck-chuck' noise, supposedly distinctive of the White Owl, as it flew towards the Twyford Plantations.

The village schoolmaster stated that he had seen the light swoop down to the ground one night, which was immediately followed by what he believed to be the shriek of a young rat. Mr Hamond's bailiff stated that he saw one of the lights, which he had been watching for some time as it hunted round a wheat stack on a very dark night, fly off and land on a tree, which he pointed out to Piggott, on the other side of the field; the light it gave out was so strong that he could see distinctly the outlines of the branches round it. [7]

Purdy gave his opinion that the luminosity of the owl was not altogether as rare a phenomenon as had been previously supposed, only that such events were not recorded because people who saw them feared ridicule. He believed that the occasional luminosity of owls who often hunted over areas of marshy ground probably gave rise to the many stories will-o'-the-wisps, Jack-o'-Lanterns, corpse-candles and Lantern-men. He made enquiries with the local farm-people and elicited several remarkable stories of moving lights:

"A groom when in his former employ often saw two lights moving over a pond and going up and down. An old soldier while in some meadows one evening saw a bright light moving along a line. It then came towards him, and when a few yards off went high up into the air and away. His wife when a young woman saw a 'lantern-man' moving down a meadow; it stopped in a tree overhanging a pond and quite lit up the tree, and she could see it moving from branch to branch, but it so

scared her that she gathered up her skirts and ran home. A servant at the rectory states that luminous owls are sometimes seen in the woods about her house not far from Cromer. The old people call them 'lampmen' and are afraid of them. A lane there is called Lampmen Lane, from the frequent occurrence there. Not long ago her brother was walking out at night with a friend and saw a bright light on the road, which he took to be a bicycle lamp. On approaching it it went into a covert close by." [4]

As the local East Anglian newspapers began to feature the story, many letters began to appear from others who had observed mysterious lights and 'luminous owls'. An old labourer living at Fakenham, near the border of the Fens, came forward to relate that he had once seen a will-o'-the-wisp that "flew like an owl". A Fenland clergyman stated that in the 1860s he was often out in the area at night, and that he often saw "the ignes fatuui come down long, dim lines of water, swimming towards one in the air, as it were, to make a sudden upward movement and vanish before they had approached clearly enough to intimate inspection." [8]

At around the same time, in 1866, according to a Mr J.A. Harvie-Brown, a luminous barn-owl was reportedly seen in Cambridgeshire, whilst Mr H.D. Rawnsley related that a similar phenomenon, nicknamed 'the boggle', had aroused much excitement at Greystoke and Skelton in Cumberland during the summer of 1898 and the autumn of 1899. This appearance took the form of "a dazzling light as large as a table lamp". The light appeared to move in undulating curves, flew over hedges and soared over a fir plantation. One witness went out to see it two or three times and though he could never get near it, he was sure it was a bird of some kind because of its distinctive bird-like movements. [9]

Mr B.B. Sapwell, a squire from Aylsham in Norfolk, related that on 24 December 1905, one of his bailiffs had watched a light "as if from a lantern" come down a lane and fly backwards and forwards across a field in which he was standing. It then took off up a lane on the opposite side of the field. He was laughed at when he told his story, but now he believed he may have seen "a luminous owl". [10]

W hen the matter was again a topic of interest in the press, during the winter of 1912-1913, a witness came forward with a story similar in many respects to the tales related by Purdy. Joseph Trumper of Carshalton related that whilst living in the neighbourhood of the Thames in south Buckinghamshire during the winter of 1879-1880, he "continually saw them, and on two or three successive occasions followed them a long distance, hoping to get near them, but never succeeded. They generally went in pairs, one very bright and the other a sort of reflection of it, but much less brilliant, and they invariably kept just the same distance apart - say, apparently, about 50 yards; they would sometimes rise up above the tree-tops, then sink slowly towards the earth, but were nearly always on the move." He noted that the wind did not seem to affect them: "rain also made no difference, as one night, while I was watching the two mysterious illuminations a heavy shower came on, but they shone with undiminished brilliancy through it." The old familiar description occurs again: "they appeared similar to a motor-lamp, yet there were never any rays from them, but solely a globe of brightness ... my brother and a friend spent hours in the pursuit of one, and after a long chase the light crossed a lane in which they were. Although they made a hard run to interrupt it, they were apparently a hundred yards away as it darted over and eventually disappeared." [11]

The above descriptions seem to fit in well with both descriptions of ghost-lights within the annals of folklore and with the elusive antics of the nocturnal hunting habits of the barn owl. The population of the barn owl in rural Britain has been steadily declining since the 19th century along with the increased use of pesticides, reduction of rough grassland, the loss of old barns, derelict houses and breeding sites, deaths on the roads and the toll taken by increasingly severe winters. It is still thinly distributed across the country; in 1982 there was somewhere between 4,500 and 9,000 pairs remaining [12], but no instances of luminosity have been recorded in recent years. Indeed, during 1908 many ornithological authorities as well as laymen, despite the evidence, refused to believe it was possible for birds to assume such a brilliant light as had been reported.

However, the naturalists who believed the 'luminous owl' was a proven fact discovered sufficient evidence to prove that such luminosity was indeed possible. A writer in Harmsworth's *Natural History* (1912) stated: "Barn owls are sometimes more or less distinctly luminous, owing probably to the presence in their plumage of phosphorescent bacteria derived from the rotten wood of the trees forming their dwelling places." In his *Introduction to the Study of Fungi* (p.89), M.C. Cooke stated: "Several Agaries have this property [relating to luminous mycelium-forming fungus], of which the largest number for any locality have been met with in Australia. All of them are species found growing upon dead wood, and all have white spores. Nearly the same story is related of all of them - to the effect that they emit a light sufficiently powerful to enable the time on a watch to be seen by it."

Were these luminous bacteria discovered upon the bodies of owls at the time in question? Other than the story told by Fred Wolfe, another person did come forward to say that he had captured a luminous owl. He was Edward S. Cannell, an engineer at Norwich City Asylum (he was, however, described as "a trained and highly responsible man known to nearly everybody") who lived at Lower Hellesdon in Norwich. He stated that between 6:00 and 6:30 on the morning of 25 February 1908, when it was still dark, he was out in his back garden with his dog when he saw something shining on a grass bank which startled him. It fluttered down across a path and up against a grapevine, whereupon he caught hold of it. "It was an owl, and it was bright and luminous," he said. "I carried it indoors, and put it on a stool, and went out in the garden again - I do not think the dog saw the bird at all. When I came back into the house the bird was dying. It was still luminous, but perhaps the glow was not as strong as when I saw it first. It was the diffused light which first attracted my attention. The luminosity appeared to me to be phosphorescent in nature." He added: "There are a number of owls that fly about the trees at the asylum every night, but I have never seen a luminous one before." [13]

The owl was sent by Cannell to Messrs.

Roberts & Son, taxidermists, of Norwich. They stated, in an interview, that the bird was a fine specimen of a female barn owl. It was well-fed but slightly 'flabby' as though the bird had been ailing for some time. Parasites were found on the body, though they were to be found on all wild birds.

Asked as to whether the body of the bird was still luminous, Mr Roberts replied: "I have seen nothing luminous about it." Indeed, to adapt the language used by Mark Twain with respect to his celebrated jumping frog: "There ain't no difference between the points of this owl, and the points of an ordinary owl." The body was prepared to be stuffed, and that was the last that was heard of it. [14]

The reference to the owl ailing in some way, however, may be relevant as Rolfe's owl was "a poor old, half-starved" specimen. 'A Country Teacher', writing to the Times [15] during 1907 in reference to a pair of luminous barn owls he had observed repeatedly whilst living in Shropshire during February 1892, noted a similar effect. They were living in a barn near his school, but were not as bright as that reported of them by Purdy and others from Norfolk. "I could observe nothing to indicate that the luminosity was under the control of the owl," he wrote. "It always appeared when the birds were in poor condition, and not at other times."

Of course, if the body or feathers of the owls were infected by the dust of some kind of poisonous luminous fungus, the owl would eventually die ... but not before appearing as a moving light to various puzzled observers.

Of the various types of fungus which could produce such effects, the most widespread is the Honey Fungus, *Armillaria mellea* (a white-spored Agaric). This fungus will attack a large range of plants, and can cause widespread damage to fruit and forest trees. Wood which contains growing mycelium of *Armillaria mellea* is luminous and can be seen clearly in the darkness, especially when it infests moist, decaying bark (a fact noticed by Francis Bacon). During the Second World War air-raid wardens during the blackout were often surprised when they were fooled into believing the glow emitted by wood in timber-yards was caused by German incendiary bombs! [16]

Another fungus, *Clitocybe olearia*, is also luminous at night. This species is poisonous and grows around the bases of deciduous trees and stumps. The fungus is nick-named 'Jack o'Lantern fungus'. A barn owl, living in the stump of a tree infected by this fungus could conceivably become infected itself. Birds often develop fungal infections within their lungs, and it was often noted that the phosphorescence seemed to emanate from the breast of the bird.

That some kind of luminous dust-like substance was blowing around in the air at this time in Norfolk is indicated by the following letter, written by a fisherman to T. Digby Piggott:

"On December 12 [1907] several of us fishermen were standing on Wells-bar between 2 o'clock and 6. It was a very dark morning. About 4 we were all surprised to find something blowing about just like blue fire. Our mittens and the edges of our sou'westers were soon full; it hung to them like cobwebs, and some parts of it were very bright. I thought you would like to know about this, as it would be about the same time the luminous owl was seen, and I do not see why it should not hang on a bird's feathers as well as it did on us. There were about ten of us, so I do not think we were deceived in what we saw." [15]

Late in May 1908, Gurney of *The Zoologist* was informed by Lord Linley that there was an ash-stump in his grounds which was displaying a superficies of about eight inches of luminosity. "Sufficient evidence has been brought forward to prove that luminosity in nocturnal birds is after all not so very rare a phenomenon," he wrote, "though seldom approaching the exceptional brilliancy of these Norfolk owls, but often enough to be the origin of a good many will o'the wisp stories ... that there is some connection between luminous trees and luminous owls is the general opinion here, and is highly probable. The fact that it was the owl's breast which emitted the chief glow would be thus accounted for, as that part would come most in contact with the decaying wood of a hollow tree." [6]

Whatever the explanations, the mysterious lights continued to haunt the quiet country lanes and fields of northern Norfolk. Mr Cannell's capture of his 'luminous' owl did not seem to put an end to the mystery, as on the same night (5 February 1908) the two lights were again seen over Foulsham by Mrs Maddison, wife of the village chemist. On the following night, at 10:00pm, Purdy and a friend saw 'the owl' again, and on the 9th Edward Keeler of Paradise Cottages, Foulsham, saw one flying round a spinney at the end of the common. Purdy also recorded observations of the light/s in his log on 17, 19 & 24 January, as well as 4 February.

At around the same time, the flying light reappeared yet again over Haddiscoe. It was seen on 12 and 19 February, hawking over the marshes. "It was on a marsh where I first saw it," wrote Mr L.C. Farman. "I endeavoured to get to it, but the ditch was wide, and whilst going round to the gate it moved off across the marshes. The light was exceedingly bright, resembling an electric light, but of course more dim as the distance widened, but even at a great distance at times it showed very bright." [17]

The light was still going strong in March. One was seen during this month by Mr H. Wormald at East Durham, "glowing with exceptional brilliancy." Purdy recorded observations on the nights of 1, 2, 5 and 10 March. On the 12th two were seen hawking along the valley between Twyford and Guist. It was also seen over land between Paradise and Kendle's farms, along a stream in the direction of Bate's moor. Soon after this its appearance became more sporadic, being spotted only on the nights of 26 and 28 March, and on 28 April.

Purdy obtained his final view of the mysterious light at 11:00pm on the night of 3 May 1908, in the company of police constable W. Palmer. It was "hunting for fieldmice" over Mr Hegg's grazing meadows near Twyford. [5]

It was not seen again during 1908, though searched for by Purdy and others. He was of the opinion that the owl had moulted its feathers, and with them its luminosity disappeared, and "the same was doubtless the case with the one at Haddiscoe, of which no more has been heard." It seems unlikely, however, that a bird could assume such a

brilliant phosphorescence for such a short time in a small localised area, appearing to many observers many miles apart, often on the same evening, and then disappear with equal suddeness.

The phenomenon made a brief, fleeting revisit to the neighbourhood of Twyford during February 1909, when it was seen hovering over Hamond's property once again, but this time no longer as bright as before [18]. Soon after the 'luminous owl' mystery was forgotten in favour of another nocturnal luminous apparition; this was the much heralded German invasion of our shores by 'the phantom airship', which began making night-time sorties over the Norfolk Broads and the Fens during the spring of 1909. The old mystery of the luminous barn owls was dug out to account for many of the strange sightings related by puzzled watchers of the night sky. Several of the observations bore a striking resemblance to the owl stories ... perhaps suggesting that a similar phenomenon was being interpreted in a different way.

It was perhaps coincidence that at the same time the 'luminous owls' were the subject of press investigation in East Anglia, other mysterious flying objects began to be reported from the same area. The *Eastern Daily Press* (Norwich) of 29 January 1908 carried the following story, under the headline "Airship seen over Norwich. Travelling fast over Mousehold":

About 4 o'clock yesterday morning the moon was shining from a cloudless sky. The night was bright enough to enable one to distinguish objects at some distance, more especially if they happened to be in mid-air. Some employees of the Norwich Tramway Company were at work in the tramsheds at the Magdalen Road terminus. Among them was a man named William Moore, who at the time mentioned happened to be stargazing. He was looking over Mousehold way when suddenly there crossed the line of his vision a dark, globular object travelling at a great pace. He rubbed his eyes and looked again. It was coming from the direction of Lakenham and over St. James' Hill towards the northeast. As we have already remarked, it was 4 o'clock in the morning, and possibly Mr Moore was inclined to disbelieve his own eyes. At any rate, he called one or two others, who were also able to distinguish the object. It appeared too large for a kite or a small balloon, and besides its movements seemed to be under human control, for it was travelling against the wind. To the men it looked as if the airship (for which they believed it to be) was globular, and there appeared some structure attached to the side of it. It was at a height of some one thousand feet, and soon disappeared from view.

The marshy bogs of Ireland are renowned for the appearance of the mysterious will-o'-the-wisp. During the winter of 1912-1913, mysterious moving lights, as large and bright as car headlights, were seen by numerous people moving over Lough Erne, County Fermanagh, Lough Beg in County London-derry, Bally Bay in County Monaghan and the Port Rush area of Belfast. In the latter case, people living in the neighbourhood gave their opinion that the many owls which inhabited the area were the cause of the strange lights. The mystery was 'solved' when a young man, out with a shotgun one dark night saw the light, shot into it, and found he had killed an owl! It seems, if his testimony can be believed, that the phenomenon was not confined only to mainland Britain; indeed, in September 1909 two luminous barn owls were reported to have been seen in Spain. [19]

The mystery made its final bid for fame during the early 1920s. On 15 February 1921 it reappeared again over the Haddiscoe marshes, according to our old friend L.C. Farman. He was out duck-flighting, and saw the light, which was not as bright as on the previous occasion he had seen it, flitting over the marshes, frequently alighting, and passing close by him.

On 3 February 1922 several observers at Rushall, a village in West Suffolk, reported seeing what they called "a luminous barn owl". Mr George Sanders obtained the best view of this, and described its light as falling with some brilliancy upon a straw stack when the owl flew round it. Another witness, Mr Dunnett, said anyone might have mistaken it for a distant lamp, while a third compared the light to that of a pale star! [20]

Another luminous mystery began to haunt the hills around Burton Dassett and Fenny Compton in South Warwickshire, starting during Christmas 1922 and continuing through to well into 1924, and causing much interest within the villages and local news-papers [21]. Of the many explanations put forward by would-be 'ghostbusters' the luminous or phosphorescent owl was one of the most favoured. It was reported that a "slightly phosphorescent owl" was seen in the belfry of Burton Dassett church (one of the main focuses of the light-haunting) during 1921, and that the area abounded in owls.

A writer at the time reasoned that an owl infested with phosphorescent bacteria upon its breast and face would account for the sudden appearance and disappearance of the light, and for its strange undulating flight: "in short, the case for a luminous owl or night-hawk is complete in every detail except one - no owl could give off so brilliant a light. If he could, would the phosphorescence last for his nightly appearances during a whole winter, the period during which this ghostly light has been seen? If it were not for the fact that a phosphorescent night-bird would need more phosphorus than it could carry to give such a brilliant and well-defined light - would need, in fact, to grow a several candle-powered arc-lamp out of its head - one might lend an ear to those theorists who pin their faith to a luminous owl." [22]

The luminous owls were not heard from again, though they are occasionally mentioned in zoological journals and the like [23]. It is sad to conclude that if the mysterious lights reported by so many observers were such a novel and rare phenomenon as a phosphor-escent barn owl then science has now lost forever any chance of studying it as the bird that was once such a common resident of our countryside slides helplessly towards extinction.

NOTES AND REFERENCES

1 - *Eastern Daily Press* (Norwich), 16 Jan 1908.

2 - *The Times*, 14 Dec 1907.

3 - *Transactions of the Norfolk & Norwich Naturalists Society*, Vol. 8 (1908), pp.547-552.

4 - *ibid.*, + *The Field (Country Gentleman's Newspaper)*, Vol. 3 (No. 2872), 11 Jan 1908, p.70.

5 - as note 3 above, pp.549-552.

6 - *The Zoologist, Ornithological Report for Norfolk* (1907), p.15.

7 - *The Times*, 7 Jan 1908.

8 - *Enniscorthy Guardian* (Co. Wexford, Ireland), 12 April 1913.

9 - *The Times*, 14 Jan 1908.

10 - *Eastern Daily Press*, 16 Jan 1908.

11 - *Daily Mail*, 26 Dec 1912.

12 - Ian Prest, *British Birds*, Batsford, 1982, p.195.

13 - *Eastern Daily Press*, 7 Feb 1908.

14 - *Eastern Daily Press*, 8 Feb 1908.

15 - *The Times*, 26 Dec 1907.

16 - W.P.K. Findlay, *Wayside & Woodland Fungi*, Frederick Warne, 1967, p.99.

17 - *The Zoologist, Ornithological Report for Norfolk* (1908), p.5-6.

18 - *The Zoologist, Ornithological Report for Norfolk* (April 1910), No. 826.

19 - *The Northern Whig* (Belfast), 26 April 1913; and see note 18 above.

20 - *The Zoologist, Ornithological Report for Norfolk* (1922), 29th Annual Report; *British Birds*, Vol. 16, No.9, 1 Feb 1923; B.B. Riviere, *History of the Birds of Norfolk* p.105.

21 - For further details of the Fenny Compton lights, see David Clarke & Granville Oldroyd, *Spooklights: A British Survey*, privately published, 1985.

22 - *Birmingham Gazette*, 20 Feb 1923.

23 - See, for example, Donald Menzel & Ernest Taves, *The UFO Enigma*, Doubleday, 1977, p.58; Count de Sibour in *Knowledge*, September 1913.

ACKNOWLEDGEMENTS
Grateful thanks must go to the staff of the British Library (Newspaper Library), Norwich Library, Sheffield Library and Mr Granville Oldroyd, without whose help this article would not have been possible.

THE NEW ENGLAND AIRSHIP INVASION OF 1909

Joseph Trainor

The 'mystery airships' seen over New England in 1909 have been covered, relatively briefly, by both Charles Fort and John A. Keel, but mostly making use of distant newspaper sources. Joseph Trainor has, instead, searched the files of local newspapers nearer the site, concentrating on the month of December 1909, and uncovered a great deal of fresh material, both on the airships and a number of other Fortean events besides.

During the month of December, 1909, the New England states were inundated by the most massive UFO wave in their history. Thousands saw the mysterious lights in the evening sky. Indeed, on one day alone, 23 December, UFOs appeared simultaneously in no fewer than 29 communities in Massachusetts, Rhode Island and Connecticut.

Since few are left alive today who remember this remarkable flap, the Fortean researcher is forced to consult the numerous newspaper accounts of the period. Reading these old stories, one cannot help but be struck by the similarities between the 'airship' invasion of 1909 and the UFO phenomenon as we know it today.

It was not until Wallace E. Tillinghast, vice president of the Sure Seal Manufacturing Co. in Worcester, claimed to have flown to New York in an 'airship' that people actually came forward to reveal that they had seen unknown objects in the sky. The self-proclaimed inventor called a news conference on 12 December and told reporters that he had flown his machine from Boston to New York, circling the Statue of Liberty at the conclusion of his trip. Several hours earlier, people in Litchfield, Conn., had reported the presence of "an air machine with a lantern which whined above in the air and was seen by several people." (*Milford Daily News*, 13 December 1909).

However, UFOs were seen in Massachusetts as early as July. According to the *Leominster Enterprise* of 14 December 1909, "there are people in North Leominster who declare that they have seen this machine high in the air, with a lantern attached, in the summer. It is thought that he has been keeping his machine within a few miles of Leominster and that he has done a few nocturnal stunts."

On 18 August 1909, an odd-looking UFO was seen over Fisher's Island, N.Y., by four men of the U.S. Lifesaving Service, forerunner of today's Coast Guard. One of them was Edward N. Knapp of North Attleboro, Mass., whose story was told in the *Attleboro Sun* of 18 December 1909. Knapp said the men "saw a brightly-lighted aeroplane with two dark figures amid the great white wings which whirled rapidly through the darkness at 2:30[am] ... Upon glancing heavenward they saw the airship. It was an eighth of a mile above the flagpole, in front of the lifesaving station, and from their quick observation they thought it was about 60 feet in length and 20 feet in width. It was flying at the rate of about 80 miles an hour, with a brisk northeast wind. The engine was evidently muffled, they said."

The surfmen's description, however, does not match that given by Tillinghast. He said his invention was a 1,550 lb. monoplane with a 72 foot wingspread "capable of carrying three passengers with a weight limit of 200 pounds each, a distance of at least 300 miles ... at a rate of 120 miles per hour." Of course, this description is utter nonsense. No airplane in the world was capable of such performance in 1909. In fact, the first plane to come close was the British Handley Page bomber of 1918. And no plane could have performed some of the feats achieved by the 'airships' of New England, as we shall see.

Public interest in the 'airships' began with a widely publicised report by William Leach, a surfman at Fire Island, N.Y., who heard an object pass overhead the night of 12 December 1909.

According to the *Pawtucket* [R.I.] *Times* of 13 December, Leach "heard an airship pass over ... while he was doing beach patrol work at 7:15 o'clock last night. Leach said he heard a buzzing sound in the air and that whatever made it passed directly over his head, but at a considerable height. He said the noise was like that made by a swiftly running motor ... Whatever made the noise was going out to sea in a southwest direction, apparently heading for the New Jersey coast. Leach said he looked over his head and tried to follow the course of whatever made the noise but could see nothing. The weather was overcast and therefore there was no star that he could watch to see if anything passed before it."

Leach's report encouraged a Mr E.H. Hanna of South Windham Road, Willimantic, Conn., to come forward. Hanna reported that he had seen an 'airship' during September. According to the *Hartford* [Conn.] *Daily Courant* of 15 December, "Mr Hanna saw something that he thought at the time might be an airship of some description and while he did not obtain a very satisfactory view of the contrivance, owing to darkness, he is able to say that ... his attention was attracted by a bright light in the east, beyond Windham. The light was high in the air and appeared to be moving rapidly, coming toward him. It swayed back and forth and had the appearance of a travelling searchlight, but it was so far away that Mr Hanna could not get a very good idea of either the shape or the size of the machine." Hanna watched the UFO "until it had disappeared behind the hills between South Windham and Lebanon, being at that time moving in a southerly direction, going towards the coast."

Hanna's sighting is interesting because it shows the UFO performing an intelligent manoeuvre. First it flew westward towards him; then it veered to the south. In addition, the Windham area has long been Connecticut's 'saucer corner', with UFO sightings dating back to the 18th century.

While public attention was focused on the Connecticut coast, strange events were taking place elsewhere in New England. There was a 'wildcat sensation' in Springfield, Mass., at this time, according to the *Springfield Daily Republican* of 21 December. But the main 'phantom panther' action took place in and around Templeton, Mass. This is the notorious 'Montachusett'

region of the Bay State, the home of many inexplicable events, such as the Andreasson affair of 1967, the UFO flaps of 1973 and 1975, and the Philipston 'fireball' of 1976.

On 26 November 1909, Joseph Chandler of Fitzwilliam, New Hampshire, took his dog rabbit-hunting in the Greenwood section of Winchendon, Mass. "He was making his way over some undergrowth when he was attracted by the howling of the hound. Hastening in the direction of the noise, he saw the dog being pounced upon by an animal resembling a panther or a wild cat, but before he could get a shot at the animal, it disappeared in the woods. The dog was badly bitten on the front legs, besides having several deep gashes down his back, caused evidently by his opponent's claws." (*Gardner News*, 27 Nov 1909)

The panther turned up again in East Templeton on 14 December. "Mrs George Wheeler reports the latest known haunt of the animal. She was driving on Otter River Road ... when near the junction of Baptist Common Road her attention was attracted to an animal standing between two houses there. It evidently saw Mrs Wheeler's carriage about the same time that she observed the stranger, and it bounded across an open patch of field and disappeared from sight in the woods ... Mrs Wheeler described the animal as being about the size of a shepherd dog and [it] had a long tail." (*Gardner News*, 15 Dec 1909)

Hunters in the Templeton area cleaned their rifles and shotguns and turned loose their dogs, but it was all in vain. The panther struck with impunity on 17 December in downtown Templeton itself. "It was about 6 o'clock Friday night when one of the employees of the Brown-Hadley Co. was driving home from his work in that factory when he heard some indescribable bloodcurdling scream issuing from a swamp beside the road. He hastily held up his horse for a moment, but soon plied the whip as a large, dark-bodied animal crept stealthily toward his wagon. Later in the evening, the animal was chased by an unterrified employee of Eugene Griffith, just south of the village. Saturday forenoon [18 December] tracks which were not made by any known human habitants of the vicinity were found back of the houses on the South road. All day yesterday [19

December] various veterans of the chase were in pursuit of the animal but to date his pelt does not adorn the side of any barn in the vicinity." (*Gardner News*, 20 Dec 1909)

While the panther was prowling the streets of Templeton, another uncanny entity was raising havoc in Old Orchard, Maine. He was a 'wild man', described as "six feet tall, dark complexioned with several months growth of beard on his face and as lank as a greyhound."

On 8 December, the wild man "was chased by I.F. York and others for half a mile through the campground, but he escaped into the woods. Mr York was coming along Fern Avenue where he was met by the stranger, who pelted him with stones. Mr York had a soldering iron in his hand and started after his assailant. He was no match for the man, who left him far behind." (*Pawtucket* [R.I.] *Times*, 15 Dec 1909)

Curiously enough, a UFO was seen in Leominster the night of 15 December, in the middle of the Templeton panther flap. Leominster is ten miles south of Templeton and also part of the Montachusett region. According to the *Leominster Enterprise* of 17 Dec 1909, "people have been watching the clouds every night in hope of seeing the phantom ship. Some declare they have seen its big red headlight, or some other light, which they accredit to the aeroplane but are not positive in regard to it. Others have seen something and when asked what it was could not describe it but do tell of seeing it for many minutes."

On 16 December, the scene of UFO action suddenly shifted 30 miles to the south, to the city of Marlboro in central Massachusetts. UFOs first appeared in Marlboro on this night, but it was not until the following week that they were reported in the local paper. Then the newspapers in nearby Worcester picked up the tale and created a national sensation.

According to the *Marlboro Enterprise* of 24 Dec 1909, "One of the most positive proofs of the existence of the airship comes from ex-councilman B.W. Johnson who says he saw the airship Thursday evening, Dec. 16th, in the southwestern part of the city and that it came down so low that he could hear a man talking from the craft."

The *Marlboro Enterprise* also refers to ten other UFO sightings in the city that week, including this tantalising item: "A young man named Beauregard is an authority for the statement that on the same night [16 December], the airship landed on the southern side of Lake Williams."

Wallace Tillinghast may have been a wonderful inventor, but not even he could have been in two places at once. Yet, on 17 December, we apparently have 'airships' in Leominster and in Warwick, R.I., over 90 miles away, at the exact same moment. The Leominster UFO was red; the one in Warwick, blue.

"Charles J. Greene, who is head gardener at the estate of Col. Robert H.I. Goddard at Potowomut Neck noticed a moving light in the sky somewhat north of the Goddard place. He and other employees watched the light until it was out of sight to the southwest. According to Mr Greene, the light was of rather a bluish tinge. The framework of an aeroplane was not discernible at that distance ... Had the night been darker with less interference from the moon and stars, Mr Greene thinks it very likely that he could have satisfied himself that it was an airship ... He judged that it crossed the west shore of the [Narragansett] bay at a point above Old Warwick." (*Providence* [R.I.] *Journal*, 22 Dec 1909)

The next UFO sighting took place in Taunton, Mass., about 15 miles east of Providence. "A local city official says that it is his belief that the mysterious airship which has been seen flying over Worcester passed over this city a few nights ago. This gentleman states positively that he saw something in the air that was moving at a rapid rate, and he also claims that he saw the searchlight used." This sighting would have taken place on 19 December, as it was reported in the *Taunton Gazette* of 23 Dec 1909 at the height of the airship flap.

On 20 December the celebrated Hoe incident took place in Boston, first chronicled in the books of Charles Fort [1]. According to the *Pawtucket* [R.I] *Times*, "Another fly-by-night airship story made the rounds of the local newspapers yesterday, with Immigration Inspector Hoe as its sponsor, but, like the previous tales, it was impossible of verification. All that Mr Hoe could say was that at 1:00am yesterday [20 December] he saw a bright light passing over the harbour and came to the conclusion that it was an airship of some kind."

Two inexplicable events occurred during this period, just prior to the main UFO flap. The first was the appearance of a butterfly in Pepperell, another town of the Montachusett region. Although it was the coldest winter since 1898, a butterfly was captured by Thomas Aiken on 17 December. "While he was at work in the woods of Amory A. Lawrence near the Nashua River, he noticed a large yellow and black butterfly flitting about, apparently unaware of the season. Mr Aiken succeeded in capturing the pretty creature and now has him alive and happy in his possession at his house on Farmer's Row." (*Pepperell News*, 23 Dec 1909)

The second event was the death of a man calling himself 'Edward E. Courtenay' in Taunton on the morning of 21 December. Courtenay's death is truly odd. He stood in the middle of the Hart Street railroad crossing, gaping at a freight locomotive as it bore down upon him, and made absolutely no effort to step out of the way. It was almost as if he had never seen a railroad train before. He was "struck and hurled to one side by the fender of the locomotive." (*Taunton Gazette*, 21 Dec 1909)

His death was investigated by Officer P. Henry Galligan, who uncovered a mystery. At first, police believed that the dead man was Arthur Letourneau of Middleboro Avenue, East Taunton, but further investigation revealed that Courtenay had merely boarded with Letourneau for a few days. According to Letourneau, Courtenay gave the impression that he was from Fall River. However, when Galligan checked with the Fall River police, they noted that 'Edward E. Courtenay' was not listed in the city directory. (*Fall River Herald*, 22 Dec 1909)

The curious thing about 'Courtenay' is his costume. He was dressed completely in black. "The dead man was about 60 years of age; height five feet, six inches; weight 140 lbs; had grey hair, partly bald, with grey moustache ... wore a black overcoat, dark clothes with a

black derby hat size 6 3/4 inches." (*Taunton Gazette*, 22 Dec 1909)

Whoever the 'man in black' may have been, he carried on him a kit of weaver's tools and cheques for $200 and $500 made out to 'E.E. Courtenay'. Galligan traced the cheques to a bank in Springfield and made enquiries to police there. But the mystery was never solved.

Beginning with the evening of 21 December, the UFO flap shifted into high gear. There were two theatres of UFO action that night, the central Massachusetts region and Rhode Island. It appears that there were at least three UFOs involved, for UFOs appeared simultaneously over Marlboro and Southbridge, Mass., communities 40 miles apart.

In Marlboro, crowds of people, whose curiosity had been stimulated by the Johnson and Beauregard stories, gathered at the Civil War monument on Main Street to watch the skies. "They saw an aerial craft shooting along the southwestern heavens at a good rate of speed ... At the city hall ... crowds formed and about 7:45 what looked like a comet showed up and rapidly steered to the southwest and disappeared. Among those who saw it was Officer J.J. Buckley but he would not talk for publication on the matter." (*Marlboro Enterprise*, 22 Dec 1909)

And 40 miles to the west, "many residents of Southbridge are positive they saw an airship hovering over the town ... between 7:30 and 8:00 o'clock. It had a bright headlight on it and would circle around, finally going westward at about 8:00 o'clock." (*Southbridge Herald*, 30 Dec 1909)

The best description of a UFO during this period came from Rhode Island. A massive object flew over the cities of Providence and Pawtucket at 1:15am. The witnesses were Mr and Mrs William S. Forsythe of 85 Evergreen Street, Providence, R.I. The couple were up late, making preparations for Christmas, "when Mrs Forsythe looked out of the windows. Her attention was attracted by two red lights in the sky which were different from anything she had ever seen before. She called her husband to the window and both watched the strange spectacle. The lights appeared to be covering a course that was varied, now rather close to the earth and then soaring upward, but always making towards the south. They were able to make out an object which appeared to be in front of the lights ... It was moving at such high speed that they could get little more than a superficial view of the appearance of the object, although what they saw was enough to satisfy them as to the identity of the contrivance. The Forsythes watched until the lights faded out in the haze on the southern horizon. When they arose in the morning, they promptly told all their friends of what they had seen." (*Providence* [R.I.] *Journal*, 22 Dec 1909)

Late night workers in Pawtucket, R.I., also witnessed the passage of the UFO. Before passing the Forsythe house, on the Providence-Pawtucket line, the object had put on a brief display. People were alerted "by a whirring noise in the heavens above Pawtucket, and those who looked upward beheld a dark object which was easily discerned by the presence of two red lights. It moved gracefully away in a southerly direction, crossing the city over Woodlawn as if bound for Newport." (*Pawtucket* [R.I.] *Times*, 21 Dec 1909)

The following evening, 22 December, J.C. Worcester, the principal of Springfield High School, received several telephone calls from anxious people, asking about the 'astronomical phenomenon' outside. "They said they could see flashes of light in the northern sky. Some described the light as like that of a fire balloon." That is, a red or reddish-orange light. (*Springfield Daily Republican*, 25 Dec 1909)

At approximately 5:40pm, a second UFO made its appearance over Worcester, the second largest city in Massachusetts. "The light was first seen by a squad of policemen leaving the Central Station on Waldo Street at 5:40 o'clock. At about the same time, a patron of a restaurant on Main Street saw the light. He called to the proprietor and soon fifty patrons of the place were on the sidewalk looking at the light. It was about twice as bright as the moon, which at one time broke through the clouds but not clearly enough to make possible to see what the light was attached to. Persons standing in front of the State Mutual, the highest building in the city, said the light was fully 1,000 feet in the air." (*Pawtucket* [R.I.] *Times*, 23 Dec 1909)

Another description of the UFO was given by John B. Goodell, a local merchant. Goodell said, "I was standing in the street, talking to a party of friends, when I saw what seemed to be a peculiarly bright star shooting towards us across the sky. Soon the appearance became that of a broad bar of light and then in a few moments I could make out the framework of the airship and clearly see the two men perched just behind the headlight. It wheeled and circled about the city and for a time remained almost but not quite stationary." (*Taunton Gazette*, 23 Dec 1909)

The UFO first approached Worcester from the direction of Millbury. It moved across the central portion of the city, then reversed direction and drifted over the State Mutual building. Then it speeded up and zipped away to the southwest.

Its next appearance was in Spencer, a neighbouring town. The report is very sketchy: "What is thought by some to be the Tillinghast airship was seen here last night in the sky over this section and also on the previous night. As a matter of fact all that can be seen is a very bright light in the heavens, which moves about in various directions, sometimes with considerable speed." (*Spencer Leader*, 24 Dec 1909)

The UFO then turned east and headed for Marlboro. Here it chased a train, for the first of many such times during the flap. "Among those who got a good look at the ship as it swiftly speeded along was Motorman Gary Lane of the Boston & Worcester Street Railway. He saw it about 6:20 between Marlboro and Hudson as he was driving his car, and the ship kept ahead of him all the way to Marlboro. It then turned back, according to other witnesses. The ship carried a bright light and attracted the attention of large crowds of people as it passed along." (*Marlboro Enterprise*, 23 Dec 1909)

After pacing Lane's streetcar to Marlboro, the UFO flew west towards Clinton. But halfway there, it suddenly veered southwards and returned to Worcester. Since its first appearance over the city word had spread, and now 2,000 people stood on Main Street, hoping for a glimpse of the 'airship'.

This time, the UFO "travelled from 800 to 1,000 feet above the earth, for a time passing up and down over the centre of the city from east to west, and later describing circles nearly over City Hall. When the light appeared, there was a slight fall of snow, and the moon and the stars were not visible. These conditions remained the same up to about 9 o'clock when the light disappeared to the southwest." (*Pawtucket* [R.I.] *Times*, 23 Dec 1909)

By now, the newspapers were well aware of the crowds that had turned out in Marlboro the previous night. When word arrived of the appearance of an 'airship' over Worcester, New England reporters hurried to the home of Wallace E. Tillinghast. The self-styled inventor was not home, however, and his wife turned aside all questions, saying "My husband knows his business. He'll talk when the proper time comes."

While the Worcester UFO was making its celebrated flight to Spencer and Marlboro and back, another 'mystery light' was active up north in the Montachusett region, putting on a show for the inhabitants of Leominster. A 'red light' was spotted over Monument Square in downtown Leominster by several witnesses, including a reporter for the *Leominster Enterprise*. This object was stationary.

Elsewhere in town, "George Pratt, employed by the Upham Clothing Store, says that as he alighted from a car at Nelson Street Wednesday night on his way to supper, he saw the 'red light' but would not say it was a flying ship, only that it appeared 'six times as large as a star.' He said he went to George A. Allen's to tell him about it. Mr Allen was not at home, but Pratt says Mrs Allen came out and she too saw the peculiar light. Pratt walked home and told his father, the latter going to the top of Nelson Street Hill where he says he was able to pick out the luminous orb from among the stars. Mr Pratt said the light went [south] in the direction of Princeton." (*Leominster Enterprise*, 23 Dec 1909)

These widespread 'airship' reports were featured in virtually every major New England newspaper the afternoon of 23 December. People began scanning the skies in earnest. And when the sun went down that day, the stage was set for the most spectacular UFO outbreak in the region's history.

When the conductor pulled out his watch and bellowed "All aboooooard!" for the Evening Limited at Boston's North Station, he had no idea that his train was going to make UFO history. However, as the train approached the town of Ayr, 30 miles northwest of Boston, it encountered some unexpected traffic. A cigar-shaped UFO, with a dazzling white light in front, came down from the clouds, hovered over the train and followed it all the way to Miller's Falls, a total distance of 100 miles. The UFO was observed by the train's passengers for over three hours.

"A messenger on a train westbound out of Boston first saw the airship at Ayer, when it came down from the west to meet the train. The messenger is a violent convert to the airship theory. He says the powerful light of the ship was played upon the cars of the train, and it followed along until this city [Fitchburg] was reached. Then it temporarily disappeared and was not picked up again until the train got up the line, and for some time the light played over and around the cars." (*Fitchburg Sentinel*, 24 Dec 1909)

This account is corroborated by "Inspector Frank Metcalf of the [Springfield] police force [who] claims to have seen the mysterious airship last evening. He was coming from Boston on the Fitchburg division of the Boston & Maine Railroad, and said that after leaving Athol his attention was called to the airship, although all he could see of it was the searchlight. The machine kept ahead of the train from Athol until near Miller's Falls, when it shot off to the side and went away. The machine was driven ahead of the train and then would wait until the train caught up and would go ahead again. It seemed to be a good height in the air, and all he was able to see was the light from the searchlight which it carried. He thought the airship was up at least 1,000 feet in the air and kept at about the same height during all the time it was following the train. Considerable interest was manifested among the passengers, and a closer view of the flyer would have been welcome. Some of the passengers saw the light when the train was as far east as Ayer Junction." (*Springfield Daily Republican*, 25 Dec 1909)

During the early evening hours, the entire Montachusett region was abuzz with UFOs. At 4:30pm, the enigmatic 'red light' made a return visit to Leominster. "The headlight of the airship which has been soaring above the town upon several occasions after dark was observed last night by a number of persons." (*Leominster Enterprise*, 24 Dec 1909)

Five miles to the north, in Fitchburg, a dazzling white light appeared on the western horizon. "Soon after 6 o'clock, like fire the word went around that the mysterious airship that startled Worcester the night before was hovering over the city. Over the peak of Rollstone Hill a wonderfully bright light glowed, and hundreds watched it with wonder, not unmixed with awe ... Before 7 o'clock, the light in this city disappeared." (*Fitchburg Sentinel*, 24 Dec 1909)

The editor of the *Sentinel* assured his readers that it was only Venus, then prominent on the horizon. Yet, at the same moment the UFO appeared over Rollstone Hill, another aerial light approached the town of Clinton, 25 miles southeast of Fitchburg.

"When the car came in from Worcester at 5:40 o'clock, the story that there was visible a real ship of the heavens spread rapidly ... The first view of the heavens at once revealed a tremendously bright light in the southwest, and because of its exceptional brilliancy, the very first thought was that it could not be a star. It was carefully watched as to its progress ... and there were many who would declare today that it cut up various capers. Telescopes and field glasses were ranged at it, and some declare that the light was this side and others that it was the other side of the clouds. People gathered on the corners, went into vacant lots and until 8 o'clock when it disappeared in the southwest the craning of necks continued without abatement." (*Clinton Daily Item*, 24 Dec 1909)

Here we have two distinct UFOs. From the *Sentinel*, we learn that Venus set at 7:00pm. Yet the Clinton UFO was visible for an hour after that.

UFOs were also seen in other Montachusett towns, such as Gardner, Athol and Orange. "The mysterious airship ... was seen in Gardner last night at 7:30 o'clock, and those persons who witnessed its flight are positive that it was not Venus ... Hector Jalbert, a clerk at the Griese Pharmacy at 224 Parker Street had his attention directed to the light in the sky and watched its movements for one-half hour when it disappeared at a point southwest of Gardner. He said 'I went out of the store last night about 7:15 o'clock and upon

looking up saw a light, which seemed to me to be too low in the sky to be a star. I watched it for some time, and at different intervals it seemed to flash just as a searchlight on a trolley car will do when it is coming towards a person at a considerable distance away. I'm convinced that it was an airship that has a powerful light...'." (*Gardner News*, 24 Dec 1909)

"Henry Melancon, who works at the Transcript office [in Athol] states he believes he saw the Worcester airship ... between 7 and 7:30 o'clock. He had just come out of his house on Maple Street when he noted the bright white light in the west. It was not like a star but rather more like an electric-arc searchlight, and it shot from one side to the other. The object was moving to the west all the time and finally, according to Mr Melancon, passed out of sight." (*Springfield Daily Republican*, 25 Dec 1909)

"An airship was seen flying above the southern part of Orange at 7 o'clock ... When it was first discovered it was supposed to be the evening star, but as the light gradually moved along in a westerly direction it was believed that it was the light of an airship." (*Greenfield Gazette and Courier*, 25 Dec 1909)

Fifty miles further west, a UFO was reported crossing the town of Shelburne Falls. "A mysterious lighted air craft is reported as having been seen gliding through the air by several Thursday evening. No one has been able to furnish any identification of the strange ship, but the few who were privileged to witness the sight are convinced it was a real airship." (*Springfield Daily Republican*, 25 Dec 1909)

From the timing of the reports and the consistent direction of flight, it appears that this was the UFO which first appeared over Fitchburg at six o'clock. It flew west over Gardner, Athol and Orange, and was last seen in Shelburne Falls. However, this was not the same UFO as the one which paced the Evening Limited from Ayer to Miller's Falls. That UFO passed through Fitchburg much later in the evening.

Although the newspapers of the time insisted that only one UFO made the trip from Worcester to Boston, it is clear from studying local reports that several flying objects were involved. The 'airship' in Milford, for example, did not conform to the newspapers' insistence upon an alleged west-to-east flight pattern.

"Last night both of the Milford and Upton [Street Railway] crews running cars on the Grafton division, Motormen Casey and Richards and Conductors Hoey and Droney, saw it near Grafton and even nearer to Milford. Harry R. Rogers, foreman of construction to the Milford & Upton, saw it also, while a passenger on Conductor Droney's car. The machine was said by some to have circled about in the air over Grafton about 7 o'clock and then to have been steered along the car line south toward Hopedale, skirting along south of that town and then to have darted away [northeast] in the direction of South Framingham, its searchlight plainly visible ... Conductor Droney said he saw the light but could distinguish little else, so great was the height at which the flying machine was being operated. That it was piercing the air at a rapid rate he judged from the fact that his attention was called to it first when at the front of his car, the light being then far off, but before he could run to the rear platform, it appeared to be miles in front of the speeding electric." (*Milford Daily News*, 24 Dec 1909)

This UFO turned south before reaching Framingham and zoomed instead over the town of Ashland, doubling back the way it came. "The supposed air ship light was viewed by many Thursday evening between 6:30 and 8 o'clock ... What people hereabouts saw was a very distinct bright light or star in the southwest sky. Nothing more than the light was seen to indicate what might be the cause of its movements, but it did move and faster than is often noticed in any of the regular heavenly bodies. It seems improbable that a light of that magnitude would be maintained on any air-ship as the power for its generation would be considerable weight and of no use except for display." (*Ashland Advertiser*, 31 Dec 1909)

As with the previous night, the big show was in the Worcester area. The first sighting was in Marlboro. "About 6:45, strange lights were seen in the southwest, and many were willing to stake their reputations on it being an airship. There seemed to be a strong searchlight in front and a dim outline following it. There is no question, however, that the light seen Thursday night was of a different order from that seen here Tuesday and Wednesday nights. Some said it was Venus, which at that time is shining at her prettiest. The naked eye was not trusted by many people, who used telescopes, marine and field glasses to see the piece of brightness." (*Marlboro Enterprise*, 24 Dec 1909)

From there, the UFO flew southwest to Worcester. "When the light appeared, it was little more than a pinpoint to the naked eye but gradually grew larger until it was plainly visible ... The light appeared shortly before 7 o'clock to the people of Worcester, where fully 50,000 people thronged the streets and all points of vantage waiting for the spectacle. The light was smaller and less brilliant than on Wednesday night ... It remained in view of the Worcesterites for ten minutes, then it disappeared to the southwest, moving rapidly." (*Providence* [R.I.] *Journal*, 24 Dec 1909)

The papers believed that the UFO seen in Worcester and Marlboro was the one which later appeared in Grafton, North Grafton, Ashland, Hopedale and Northboro. But as we have seen, this was more likely the UFO which buzzed the Milford & Upton trolley. Instead of one 'airship' moving from west to east, what we actually have is a number of localised flaps, all taking place between 6:00 and 8:00pm.

In the south, UFOs were reported in Taunton, Mass., and Central Falls, R.I. (*Attleboro Sun*, 24 Dec 1909)

One of the best UFO descriptions comes from Pawtucket, R.I. "It was about 9 o'clock that people beheld in the heavens two lights, one much larger than the other ... Persons passing down High Street noticed the lights but could not make out any form of airship as it was too high in the skies ... Among those who had the view were Miss Charlotte Delaney, daughter of ex-senator Lyons Delaney, Jesse Barber, Samuel Kyle and Major George S. Tingley of South Union Street. Major Tingley says that, in his opinion, the ship was moving in the air at the height of fully 1,000 feet from the earth. The big light was very prominent, and the smaller one was easy to discern ... It seemed to Major Tingley that the course of the lights was toward Providence and after watching them awhile, they took a change, suddenly veering, as it appeared to him, in the direction of East Providence. He and his family watched the lights until they disappeared from sight, and all the neighbours within earshot were invited to join the scene." (*Pawtucket* [R.I.] *Times*, 24 Dec 1909)

Another UFO was seen in Willimantic, Conn., where E.H. Hanna had made his sighting the previous September. "About 7:30 o'clock, a bright light was seen in the sky to the southwest, a little to the west of Norwich. Various people on the streets saw it, stopped and commented on it. At the corner drug store near Mayor Dunn's emporium, there were at one time 50 to 60 people gazing at the light and wondering what it was. It moved like a searchlight, the rays pointing at one time in one direction and then changing to a different point on the compass. Mayor Dunn was one of those who saw the light, and he said it looked to be 20 to 30 miles away. After about twenty minutes the light was no longer to be seen." (*Hartford* [Conn.] *Daily Courant*, 24 Dec 1909)

A t the same moment the Willimantic UFO appeared, pedestrians strolling the concrete walks of the Public Gardens, between Boylston and Arlington Streets in Boston, paused to stare at a sudden dazzling light in the sky.

"At first, those who saw the lights took them for some unusually bright star, shining through the hazy atmosphere. The two strong searchlights were distinguished from the blurred outline as they flashed among the buildings on Beacon Street. Visible for a few minutes, the lights disappeared again and shortly after were seen above the Common, crossing over the Charles Street Mall. Many of the skaters in the Public Gardens were attracted by the lights and left the ice to join the throngs of Christmas shoppers who forgot their errands to watch the strange sight. The lights moved so quickly that they soon outdistanced the following crowd and served to put to rest the belief that they might have come from a large balloon. At times, when seen from what was taken to be the side of the machine, the lights had the appearance of automobile headlights, casting a bright glow as from a reflection. Then they were seen head on and the vague outline of an aerial craft was barely discernible between the two lights, which seemed to be on either end. At the height of 600 feet, which the airship maintained, the lights looked scarcely a fathom [6 feet] apart, shining with a brightness greater than that of the moon.

"Long shadows were cast by the lights as they floated for a moment and then quickly dimmed. Above the Common the lights remained apparently stationary for somewhat less than a half hour, in evident contravention of the popular belief that an aeroplane can remain in the air only when in motion ... A little before 8 o'clock, the lights disappeared in the direction of Lynn. So rapidly did they move that those who attempted to keep the machine in view saw the lights for only a few minutes as they faded into the distance." (*Boston Herald*, 24 Dec 1909)

However, the UFOs had already been to Boston's North Shore area. At 7:00pm, James Duffy of Silsbee Street, Lynn, was walking down Union Street in that community when "his attention was attracted by a swishing sound similar to that made by a flock of wild geese directly over his head. Gazing upward, he said he saw four bright lights and a big black object which was travelling at such a high rate of speed that he was able to obtain only a fleeting glimpse of it." (*Lynn Evening News*, 24 Dec 1909)

In Revere, "Alexander Rampell ... alleges not only to have seen the lights but the framework of an aeroplane as well. He describes the airship as having wings with a sweep of about 70 feet and a propeller about 45 feet in length ... Chief Arthur L. Kimball of the fire department, Samuel Gilby of the sewer commission, Fireman Arthur Marden and George Pratt are some of the other Revere citizens who are convinced that it was an aeroplane." (*Lynn Evening Item*, 24 Dec 1909)

The same paper reported a "bright white light" over Natick at 7:00pm. After an absence of 15 minutes, the UFO returned to Boston. "Coming over the Common and proceeding in the direction of Copley Square, the lights were again visible a little after 8:15. This time they passed quickly over Rack Bay, followed by a detail of patrolmen from Station #18 in case the operator attempted a landing, and disappeared in the direction [west] of Brookline and Chestnut Hill." (*Boston Herald*, 24 Dec

1909). The final sightings of the day occurred in Cambridge, over Harvard Square at 10:30pm, and in Framingham, shortly after 11:00pm.

The climax of the flap was certainly on 23 December, with UFOs appearing in 30 New England communities. But they weren't finished with the area yet. UFOs made several more appearances the following evening, in Boston, in Providence, and in several Massachusetts towns in Essex County.

At approximately 4:25pm on 24 December, a UFO entered Providence's airspace. "The visitor appeared from the northwest, passing over the centre of the city in a southerly direction to a point over the Providence River, then swung around and circled several times around the big chimney, nearly 315 feet high, of the Narragansett Electric Lighting Company's plant. Then it started off towards the southwest, rising higher and higher in circles and then stood nearly still, as if just drifting on the wind for quite a while. Then it started off again, making side movements to the right and left. It remained over the city about an hour and then disappeared in a northwesterly direction." (*Boston Herald*, 25 Dec 1909)

A Boston policeman reported seeing an 'airship' at 7:00pm. "Off to the southwest near the roof of Steinert Hall could be seen a clear violet-tinted light 'half the size of a bowl' travelling towards the west and finally sinking behind the Back Bay building skyline. At least a dozen observers had seen the light in the west or southwest, and all agreed that it moved slowly toward the west, disappearing from sight about 8 o'clock. It was generally described as the colour of an arc light and about half the size of an arc light globe." (*Boston Herald*, 25 Dec 1909)

Another UFO put in an appearance at Newton, seven miles west of Boston, at the same moment the violet UFO was over the Hub. "The first appearance was at 7 o'clock and people said it was plainly visible until 7:45 o'clock. Among those to make out the light of the supposed airship were W.E. Mars, A.W. Rees and Daniel O'Connell. They said the light was first seen in the west and that they came nearly over the town, circled round several times and disappeared in the west." (*Boston Herald*, 25 Dec 1909)

As with the previous nights, a UFO buzzed a streetcar, this time in Waltham. According to the *Boston Herald*, "At 7:30 o'clock, an electric car bound from Waltham to West Newton was stopped to allow the passengers to alight and get a view of the mystery. The car was in the charge of William Galway, a motorman, and Otto Rowley, conductor. The passengers said they could hear the noise of the engine of the airship."

The same issue reports sightings in Essex County, near the New Hampshire border, in Rowley and Newburyport. "About 7:40 o'clock, Thomas P. Hale of Rowley, on leaving the Boston train at the Rowley station, saw a bright white light in the sky that seemed to travel ahead of him as he went towards his house some distance from the depot. The general direction travelled by the light was northward and it moved with a noticeable speed."

Further north, in Newburyport, "thousands of people observed the mystery that has excited so much attention of late. The bright light, which at times presented different colours, circled over Newburyport and finally disappeared in a westerly direction."

The final UFO sighting of the 'Flap of 1909' took place on Christmas Day in Fall River, Mass., 17 miles southeast of Providence. "Two moving lights were in sight from the streets of this city early Friday morning and those who observed them feel sure it was Wallace E. Tillinghast of Worcester and his flying machine. William Purdy of Hillside Street ... pointed out two lights plainly visible in the heavens. Mr Purdy, the *Herald* man and the group gathered about them on the street watched the phenomenon. Beyond any question there were two lights in the sky. They were due west of the city and about 70 to 75 degrees up from the horizon towards the zenith. They were brighter than any of the stars which were visible at the time and much nearer together than any familiar bright stars; in fact, they seemed to be almost touching. They were in an almost horizontal line but not entirely so, one being the least bit lower than the other. They kept this relative position and plainly moved about in the sky, as all in the group could see. No one could see any form or framework or other evidence of an airship or anything else but the moving lights." (*Fall*

And so ended the great airship invasion of 1909. But what of Wallace E. Tillinghast, the man who claimed to have flown from Worcester to New York?

The night of 23 December, reporters laid siege to his house. Tillinghast was not airborne and neither would he discuss the issue. He said, "I was out of Worcester last night. Where I was is my own business. It may be that I flew over the city, but that is my own business, too ... When I get ready, I shall speak fully and not until then." (*Providence* [R.I.] *Journal*, 24 Dec 1909.

In his book, *Operation Trojan Horse* **[2]**, author John A. Keel calls attention to a UPI dispatch of the period which mentions that Tillinghast was in close contact with Paul B. Morgan, head of the local phone company, and John B. Gough. The dispatch claimed that Gough had a 100 foot shed on his estate in West Boylston, six miles north of Worcester, where 14 men were supposedly at work on an airship. Keel asserts that Tillinghast was a front for an unknown group. He cites a *Providence Journal* article which stated, "Tillinghast is absolutely incommunicado ... He is not permitted an hour's peace. At his office there are constantly two or three persons who want to know something. At the door of his place of business and at his home he is closely watched by mysterious men."

Mysterious, indeed! The Gough property was under tight security that week. A UPI correspondent was unceremoniously ejected. However, a local man did manage to get inside the shed. What he saw merely adds to the mystery.

H.A. Brigham was an assessor for the town of Boylston. He also held the contract for garbage collection in Clinton. Sometime during May 1909, he wandered onto the Gough place looking for the foreman, Mr Bigelow, and came upon the large shed.

"I went inside and was looking about a bit and saw what I thought at first was a new-fangled windmill. I believed that Mr Morgan was getting up some new scheme in a windmill and that it was being assembled in the barn. Suddenly a man spoke up and asked me if I had any particular business in the barn. I told him I had not, but that I was looking for the foreman. The man suggested that what was in progress was of rather a private nature and that perhaps I had better retire. I did so but later I guess Mr Bigelow told them I was all right and could be depended upon not to say anything and I was given an opportunity to inspect the 'windmill'. It turned out to be an aeroplane, and I would say it was a dandy, so far as I can judge. There seemed to be a lady who was considerably interested in the whole matter. She drove up in an auto with others while I was there. They were in a big rush to get an incline built that day. The incline was afterwards built on the sidehill near the barn where a fine starting place was afforded. It was of chestnut planks and was a hundred feet in length. The sidehill affords a fine starting place for an airship. They were planning to make the first trial very early the following morning. I never heard anything more directly as to what success was had ..." (*Clinton Daily Item*, 24 Dec 1909)

There are many intriguing questions concerning Mr Brigham's adventure into the Gough shed. There is the sudden mysterious appearance of the guardian, for one. In addition, how did the airship people know how to find Brigham? He left the shed hurriedly and did not stop to give his name.

Note how the airship people went to the trouble of bringing him back to the shed. When Brigham returned, men were feverishly at work on an incline. Why?

I believe that somebody was putting on an elaborate show for Mr Brigham's benefit. In those days, airplanes often used ramps or inclines to take off. The men built just such an incline, then told Mr Brigham that the contrivance in the barn was an aeroplane.

At first, Brigham didn't know what the object was. It struck him as a 'new-fangled windmill'. It was only after he was shown the 'aeroplane' and the newly-constructed ramp that he accepted it as such. I submit that H.A. Brigham wouldn't have known an aeroplane from a giraffe. He saw an unusual object and described it in terms that he was most familiar with.

Reading the phrase 'new-fangled windmill', I am inescapably reminded of the object with the 45 foot propellor seen by Alexander Rampell in Revere on 23 December and the 20 foot "great white wings that whirled rapidly" about the object seen by Edward N. Knapp at Fisher's Island, N.Y., on 18 August. The concept of a helicopter keeps coming to mind. But who could have had a helicopter in 1909? Extraterrestrials? Time travellers from later in the 20th century? The questions are endless.

The UFO reports of 1909 reveal a certain consistency. Few witnesses saw an actual vehicle. The most commonly reported UFO was a 'bright white light' or 'a searchlight' attached to a dimly-perceivable object. Another common UFO was the dark object with two red lights.

In terms of behaviour, the 1909 'airships' exhibited characteristics comparable to the post-1947 UFOs. New Englanders reported objects that moved in the traditional 'falling leaf' motion, porpoising in the air, moving jerkily from side to side, and so on. Note also the presence of 'airships' hovering over rail-road trains, especially electric trolleys. Another UFO was seen hovering above Rhode Island's largest electric plant. Finally, it should be noted that, in the only known landing of a UFO in 1909, the object set down on the shore of Marlboro's Lake Williams.

Clearly, then, we are dealing with a continuing phenomenon. UFOs behaved back then as they do today. And, as was true in 1909, they are still a mystery.

REFERENCES

1 - *The Complete Books of Charles Fort*, Dover Publications Inc, NY, 1974, p.509. (See pp.507-511 for Fort's summary of the New England airship flap [*New Lands*, chapter 34]).

2 - John A. Keel, *Operation Trojan Horse*, Manor Books, NY, 1970. Keel's summary of the New England scare, and the case of Wallace E. Tillinghast, appears on pp.101-109.

THE DEVIL'S HOOFMARKS

SOURCE MATERIAL ON THE GREAT DEVON MYSTERY OF 1855

Edited by Mike Dash

The 'Devil's Hoofmarks', mysterious snow-prints appearing across Devon in February 1855, have been the subject of considerable speculation ever since Charles Fort revived modern interest in it in his *Book of the Damned* (1919). Mike Dash, contributing editor to *Fortean Times*, has spent many years collecting the original source material, the explanations and theories, presenting here a selection of original documents and an assessment of the evidence.

INTRODUCTION

AN ASSESSMENT OF THE SOURCES AND THE EVIDENCE

On the night of 8-9 February 1855 (and on one or two nights thereafter [1]) trails, resembling those of a donkey, were laid across large areas of Devon. They appeared in shallow snow, between half an inch [2] and four inches deep [3], meandering through villages and gardens [4]. Sometimes, it was said, they did 'impossible' things, such as crossing roofs [5], leaping tall walls [6], disappearing through small holes in hedges [7], or stopping dead on one side of a haystack, leaving its sides and top undisturbed, and commencing abruptly once more on the other side. [8]

The trail itself was equally mysterious. It was ubiquitous - there were villages where hardly a home had not been visited [9], and the marks were reported from more than 30 locations across the county, as well as one or two in Dorset [10]; if the tracks had been left by a single creature, it would have had to have travelled a distance variously estimated at between 40 [11] and 100 miles [12] in a single night. The marks, which were almost all four inches long by three broad or rather smaller [13], appeared to have been left by a biped, although the prints were almost always in a single file [14], rather than alternating to right and left as most tracks do. Sometimes the prints appeared cloven [15], sometimes not [16], and the stride was tiny, almost mincing, at between eight [17] and 16 inches. [18]

The circumstances were unusual. Devon, and indeed much of Britain, was in the grip of an especially severe winter, one so fierce that "the thermometer was one degree lower than has ever before been known by the 'oldest inhabitant' [19]" and the rivers Exe and Teign froze over for part of their length, allowing games and on one occasion a feast to be held on the ice [20]. Snow fell heavily at about midnight on the night of 8-9 February [21], but towards dawn the temperature rose and there was rain [22]. The thermometer then fell once more, and there was a frost at dawn [23]. These are circumstances in which trails and footprints can be considerably distorted by the processes of thawing and refreezing, but one local source asserted that many tracks left by common animals remained easily identifiable in the morning [24], and on the whole it appears that a considerable majority of the inhabitants, most of whom were country people who might have been expected to be familiar with all manner of trails left by the local wildlife, were puzzled and in many cases scared by these tracks and by the places in which they were discovered.

The first traceable report of the mystery, which appeared on 13 February 1855, mentions that some locals were already inclined to ascribe the hoofmarks to a visit from the Devil [25]. The same article also gives the first of many less exotic solutions to the mystery, suggesting that the tracks may have been made by a monkey which had escaped from a menagerie; in coming weeks and years, it was variously proposed that the 'Devil's Hoofmarks' were made by the Great Bustard [26], heron [27], badger [28], mouse [29], rat [30], otter [31], swan [32], kangaroo [33], donkey [34], cat [35], wolf [36], and hare [37], or by flocks of birds. [38]

Within a few hours of the first discovery of the prints, a number of attempts were made to track down whatever had made them. A number of parties traced the prints for miles

[39]; in Dawlish, an armed group of local tradesmen followed some tracks from the local churchyard to Luscombe, Dawlish-water and then Oaklands, a total distance of around five miles, without discovering anything material [40]. At Clyst St George, on the other side of the river Exe, two villagers following a trail through a field discovered four oblong globes of whitish excrement, the size of a large grape, alongside the tracks [41]. Others from the same area remarked on how the tracks had stopped and started suddenly, in the middle of fields [42] - as though they had been left by a bird, or something more mysterious, that had then taken wing.

Recollecting the events of 9 February from a distance of 40 years or more, several witnesses added further details, which might or might not be accurate. One heard how the hoofprints had been discovered to alternate, "at huge but regular intervals", with a mark like that left by the tip of a crutch-stick. The same gentleman was also spun a scary yarn about an attempt by a local hunt to corner the beast that had made the prints, which was cornered in a wood near Dawlish, but left unharmed by hounds that "came back baying and terrified" [43]. (The Reverend Rowe, of Marychurch, retained a distinct recollection of the latter event [44].)

On the day that the trails were first discovered, several people had the idea of making tracings of the strange footmarks, which showed that broadly similar tracks had been left in a variety of locations. However, no one person, nor any group, tracked the mysterious prints for more than a few miles in order to see whether the trail was single or multiple, ascertain how varied were the footprints themselves, or to check the apparently reliable reports that they had been found in the most anomalous of situations. In the absence of this information, and in the presence of a proliferation of contradictory theories each based on the same scant evidence, it seems unlikely that the mystery of the Devil's Hoofmarks can now be solved.

The Sources

The primary sources for the story of the mysterious footprints are comparatively few, and those that remain are sometimes more or less direct copies of each other. The most valuable evidence, contemporary manuscripts and letters from witnesses to the phenomenon, are scarcer still, though they are supplemented by perhaps inaccurate recollections set down many years later, and by local newspaper reports.

The only known surviving manuscripts dealing with the Devil's Hoofmarks are a collection of papers assembled by the Reverend H.T. Ellacombe, who was vicar of the parish of Clyst St George from 1850 until his death in 1885 [45]. They were kept in the parish box in the church. In 1952 the local historian Major Antony Gibbs, of Pytte, a hamlet close to Clyst St George, drew the papers to the attention of the folklorist Theo Brown, who printed extracts from them in the *Report & Transactions of the Devonshire Association* for 1952 [46]. The papers include a number of letters addressed to Ellacombe by friends, including the Reverend G.M. Musgrave of Withecombe Ralegh, the draft of a letter sent to the *Illustrated London News*, marked not for publication, and tracings of hoofmarks which, Brown concluded, were probably made on the spot. Included among them are references to tracks found in the outskirts of the city of Exeter - a 'furthest north' for the hoofmarks. Ellacombe also notes that the marks were similar in shape while 'varying some little in size', records the weather conditions on the night they were made, and notes that his dog was disturbed, and barked, during the hours of darkness.

Ellacombe was well-placed to observe the prints; a number were found in the grounds of his rectory. He spoke to some of the people who had attempted to track whatever had made them, and even obtained samples of the excrement found alongside the trail, which he forwarded, without receiving a reply, to the noted naturalist Richard Owen. The tracings preserved among the Ellacombe papers double the number of representations of the hoofmarks known to have survived, and include marks that the vicar believed were left by claws.

Equally valuable, perhaps, are a series of letters written to, and published by, the *Illustrated London News*. The first of these, by a correspondent signing himself 'South Devon', is certainly the most influential piece of evidence concerning the tracks. It forms the

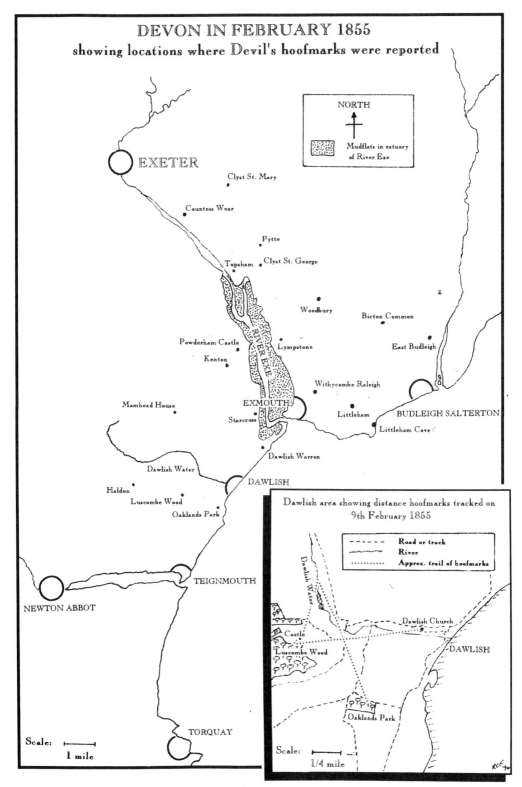

DEVON IN FEBRUARY 1855
showing locations where Devil's hoofmarks were reported

NORTH

Mudflats in estuary
of River Exe

EXETER

Clyst St. Mary

Countess Wear

Pytte

Topsham   Clyst St. George

Woodbury

Bicton Common

Powderham Castle   Lympstone

Kenton

East Budleigh

RIVER EXE

Withycombe Raleigh

Mamhead House

EXMOUTH

Starcross   Littleham   BUDLEIGH SALTERTON

Littleham Cove

Dawlish Warren

Dawlish Water

DAWLISH

Haldon

Luscombe Wood

Oaklands Park

TEIGNMOUTH

NEWTON ABBOT

TORQUAY

Scale:
1 mile

Dawlish area showing distance hoofmarks tracked on
9th February 1855

- - - - Road or track
———— River
+++++++ Approx. trail of hoofmarks

Dawlish Water

Dawlish Church

Castle

Luscombe Wood   DAWLISH

Oaklands Park

Scale:
1/4 mile

RCF. 194

basis of almost all later accounts of the case, and features all the principle anomalies associated with the 'Devil's Hoofmarks'.

To begin with, 'South Devon' gives a list of some of the principle places where footmarks were discovered, including Torquay and Totnes, some way to the west - so far (six and 12 miles) from the principle scene of action that G.A. Household, a local historian whose useful booklet *The Devil's Footprints* [47] reprints a number of contemporary press accounts, queried the accuracy of the suggestion [48]. He was also responsible for putting into print the suggestion that the marks 'in every parish' were 'exactly the same size and the step the same length', two influential statements that are not, in fact, quite true. The writer, or his informants, also noted that the prints at one point appeared to have vaulted a 14-foot wall, and appeared on the roofs of houses. He dismissed the idea that thawing and refreezing could have distorted the marks, noting that other animal prints remained perfectly recognisable. Finally, he claimed that the marks formed a trail at least 100 miles in length, were in a straight line, and had at one point crossed the two-mile wide river Exe. Again, each of these latter assertions can be challenged.

Most later commentators, up to and including Rupert Gould [49], remained ignorant of 'South Devon's' identity. He appeared, on his own evidence, an experienced countryman with 'much experience in tracking wild animals and birds upon the snow', who had once spent five months hunting in the Canadian wilderness. Thanks to Theo Brown's rediscovery of the Ellacombe papers however, we now know that the author was 'young D'Urban' [50], 19 years old, of Newport House, Countess Wear.

D'Urban was evidently an able man - he later became the first curator of the Royal Albert Memorial Museum at Exeter [51] - and there is no reason to doubt that he had hunted and knew animal tracks. It is, nevertheless, reasonable to wonder how far youthful enthusiasm may have coloured his telling of events. Certainly his letter is quite dogmatic in rejecting possible explanations for the prints; equally, his drawing of the prints, showing a curving line of uncloven hoofmarks, is the least detailed, and least ambiguous, of all the surviving sketches [52]. Another contemporary witness, the Reverend G.M. Musgrave, immediately wrote to the *ILN* to point out: 'The outline accompanying your intelligent Correspondent's recital of the circumstances hardly conveys a correct idea of the prints in question.' [53]

Musgrave's letter goes on to give a more detailed list of locations where the tracks had been reported and to set out his own observations on the phenomenon. He had been told, by a 'scientific acquaintance', of the discovery of the haystack through which the mysterious trail-maker appeared to have walked. He also recounts how he encouraged one congregation to whom he delivered a sermon to believe the explanation that the tracks werre those of an escaped kangaroo - this became one of the most widely-circulated 'explanations' for the events of 8-9 February. But, as Musgrave admits, he himself had little faith in the theory and advanced it in preference to leaving his congregation to believe that the Devil had strolled through their parish.

The letter following Musgrave's in the *ILN* is anonymous, but it appears to have been written by a doctor living in Topsham [54]. He and a friend had closely examined tracks found in the neighbourhood and, having discerned the marks of claws, were inclined to believe that the trail had been left by an otter - this despite the fact that, as the author admitted, 'I am not familiar with the otter myself'. In fact the suggestion appears to have been advanced principally to explain the men's important direct observation that the trail passed under low branches, and apparently through a 6" diameter pipe.

This, the evidence of two clergymen, a doctor and a young gentleman, is *all* the direct, first-hand evidence we have of the Devil's Hoofmarks. Of our remaining sources, the accounts published in the local press are at best compilations of what was being said of the marks in the area (Exeter) in which the papers were being published. There was, in the provincial press of the 1850s, little conception of what we today would call 'reporting'. Each title was run by a proprietor, perhaps alone apart from his printer, perhaps with a very minimal staff. There were few resources for news-gathering other than conversation and the occasional letter from a correspondent 'on the spot'. The reports should therefore be treated with some caution. They are certainly valuable for indicating the main areas in which the hoofmarks were seen, and in giving an impression of the general consternation which their appearance caused. It should, however, be remembered that all their descriptions of the prints themselves are second-hand at best.

The story of the hoofmarks was carried by many papers throughout the UK, and no attempt has been made to scour the archives of the Newspaper Library at Colindale for any and all accounts. Nevertheless the rediscovery in the course of this research of two hitherto unknown reports from an Exeter paper called the *Western Luminary* [55], one of which is the earliest known record of the 'Devil's Hoofmarks' and the other of which confirms the previously doubtful existence of tracks in Newton Abbot, suggests it is not impossible that further important contemporary evidence could still be unearthed.

Not every eyewitness to the hoofmarks put their experiences into print in 1855. There was correspondence on the subject in *Notes & Queries* in 1890 [56] (by which time, evidently, the tracks had already been forgotten by many Devonians, and mythologised by others), and as late as 1922 further eyewitness accounts were still being published [57]. These later sources, though, need to be treated with caution. The passage of years is likely to have rendered them inaccurate and, as will be argued below, they contain many folkloric elements which have tended to add mystification to the mystery.

Finally, we have sources that tell of similar occurrences, and sources that seek to explain the 'Devil's Hoofmarks'. The former are vital to a proper understanding of the phenomenon, since they challenge the notion that the Great Devon Mystery is unique and, therefore, particularly mysterious. The latter are merely a selection from the many thousands of words that have subsequently been written upon the subject. We have had to restrict ourselves to extracts from the most influential or the best informed, and to passages setting out the main theories explaining the phenomenon of the hoofmarks. Very many accounts, particularly popular accounts, have been excluded.

But, since each is based (so far as it is accurate at all) on the evidence of the same four eyewitnesses, the same press accounts, and the same recollections, they rarely have much to add to the debate.

Anomalies Associated with the Devil's Hoofmarks

The mystery of the 'Devil's Hoofmarks' is mainly concerned with the anomalies reported by their discoverers and by commentators on the case. But just how inexplicable were these peculiarities?

The ubiquity of the prints

First, the marks were ubiquitous. They were 'vast' [58] in number; 'there was hardly a garden in Lympstone where these footprints were not observable, and in this parish he appears to have gamboled with inexpressible activity' [59]. In Dawlish, 'his footprints were traced through the greater part of the town' [60], and in other parts of the county prints were found in 'fields, gardens, roads, house-tops, & other likely and unlikely places' [61]. In all, the tracks 'extended over a tract of country of 30 or 40 miles, probably more ... Now, when we consider the distance that must have been gone over to have left these marks - I may say in almost every garden, or doorstep, through the extensive woods of Luscombe, in enclosures and farms - the actual progress must have exceeded a hundred miles.' [62]

This, if executed in a single night, by a single animal, was certainly a feat worthy of the Devil himself. Indeed - as Rupert Gould pointed out - to cross even 40 miles, supposing steady progress and a generous 14 hours of darkness, with the generally-reported stride of around eight inches, would require the perpetrator to move at the rate of six steps per second [63]. But the supposition that the hoofmarks were the work of one creature is a dangerous one. The greatest distance we can say with confidence that a set of tracks was followed was about five miles - a long way, particularly if the marks were made by a fieldmouse or a small bird, but not an impossible journey for some animals to make in a night.

Several accounts make it clear that the trail was *not* continuous. H.T. Ellacombe wrote: 'At

Exmouth I have been informed by those that saw them there were marks in the middle of a field, insulated - without any apparent approach or retreat' [64] - while - also in Exmouth - one W. Courthope Forman recalled that 'the footprints came up the front garden to within a few feet of the house, stopped abruptly, and began again at the back within a few feet of the building' [65]. Some tracks, at least, did not lead into thin air; in Torquay, a gentleman followed a trail from his garden to a tree stump, under which he discovered 'a very large toad'. [66]

The length of time it took to lay the trail is also open to serious question. While it appears that the great majority of the tracks were first seen on the morning of 9 February, several accounts suggest that some were discovered at other times. The *Western Luminary*, writing perhaps three or four days afterwards, noted simply that the prints had been made 'since the recent snow storms' [67], while more explicitly the *Western Times* referred to the appearance, in Topsham, of tracks laid on 13 February. [68]

Prints found in anomalous locations

The alarming ubiquity of the Hoofmarks was not the most puzzling feature of the phenomenon. Their appearance in many bizarre and unlikely places aroused even greater comment. Prints were said to have appeared on a second-floor window sill [69], in a garden guarded by a 14-foot wall [70], and, as we have seen, on either side of a foot-high hole in a hedge [71], of a drainpipe [72] and a haystack [73]. In addition, several reports refer to the appearance of tracks on rooftops. [74]

While these apparently well-attested reports [75] allow us to assert that a few of the main animal suspects - notably the donkey - could not have made *all* the prints, a surprising number of animals can climb well enough to have been responsible for the bizarre trails. These include cats, rats, and mice. Birds are even more obvious candidates, if one assumes that their feet could have iced up into horseshoe shapes.

Taken together, the reports of prints found in anomalous locations suggest that a very small animal - one small enough to enter a 6" pipe or pass through a foot-high hedge-hole -

made *some* of the prints. Alternatively, it is of course possible that these marks were made by human hoaxers anxious to make it appear that only a devil could have been responsible. The discovery - reported by the Reverend Musgrave - of prints which led to a haystack which had no marks on its surface, and commenced again on the other side, is perhaps the most difficult incident to explain using an animal hypothesis. However, we have it only at second hand and it is impossible to know how carefully the surface of the haystack was examined.

Indeed, the problem with assessing all the reports of prints found in strange places is a lack of full descriptions of their precise situation. It is not at all clear, for example, how carefully witnesses checked the alignment of hoofmarks leading to high walls with any trail found within them. It is therefore still possible that the marks found outside a wall were made by one animal and those discovered inside by another. Similarly, the suggestion that the trail crossed the river Exe and began again on the other side [76] is nowhere supported by evidence that anyone tracked the hoofmarks right to the shore on one bank and then located the point at which they emerged from the river on the other; on the contrary, the fact that no report mentions investigators following a trail across the iced-up river strongly suggests that no-one tried. All we can say with certainty is that hoofmarks were found on both sides of the Exe estuary.

The similarity of the prints

Perhaps the most peculiar of all the mysteries associated with the Devil's Hoofmarks is the suggestion that prints found in many different locations were absolutely identical both in size and stride. The Reverend Musgrave, for example - on the evidence an exceedingly careful observer - wrote that he and a fellow-clergyman measured the distance between hoofmarks found in Withecombe Raleigh with a ruler, and 'the interval between each impression was found to be undeviatingly eight inches and a half. On the same day a mutual acquaintance ... measured the intervals between similar prints in his garden, above a mile and a half distant from the rectory, and found it to be exactly eight inches and a half. This, in my opinion, is one of the most remarkable and confounding circumstances we have to deal with' [77]. In addition, 'South Devon' gives the measurements of the hoofmarks themselves as four inches by 2 3/4, and asserts that 'the foot-marks in every parish [were] exactly the same size and the step the same length. [78]

Unfortunately, most of the other surviving descriptions of the hoofmarks are not as precise as these. Where measurements are given, however, they often differ considerably, as the table of descriptions – see page 76 – shows. The prints themselves varied in size from 3½" to 4" long and from 1½" to 2 3/4" wide, and the stride from 8" to 16".

In my opinion, these variations strongly suggest that the great majority of the Devil's Hoofmarks were made by animals, rather than by human hoaxers for whom a uniform shape and stride would have been important. The difference in the reported size of the hoofmarks themselves further suggests that a number of different animals were responsible for the tracks.

Nevertheless, it still seems remarkable that the size of the prints should vary so little while the distance between them varied so much.

The sharpness of the prints
An associated puzzle, which attracted a fair amount of comment at the time, is the question of whether or not the marks really were those of hoofs.

Several of the more careful witnesses thought they saw the marks of claws within the prints [79], and one of Ellacombe's drawings shows them quite clearly. Richard Owen used these accounts to conclude that the 'hoofmarks' were actually the footprints of a badger [80]. Other authorities, such as 'South Devon' and *The Times*, assert the prints were clearly made and showed no sign of claws. [81]

Similarly, many of the footprints appeared whole while others were cloven. There is some suspicion - supported by a comparison between the sketches made by 'South Devon' and the Reverend Musgrave - that on occasion the identification of cloven prints depended on the quality of the observer as much as on the prints themselves, but other documents make

it fairly clear that in many places cloven marks were interspersed with perfect prints [82]. Again, this suggests that many of the prints were made by small animals - whether they were mice, squirrels or even badgers - either hopping or moving along with fore and hind legs held close together, the appearance of cloven prints marking spots where the left and right legs were placed slightly further apart. It may also be that a number of cloven prints were made whole by the process of thawing and refreezing.

The latter suggestion seems at odds with the curious insistence of several sources that the hoofmarks were astonishingly clearly cut. 'South Devon' noted: 'The most singular circumstance connected with [the mystery] was, that this particular mark removed the snow, wherever it appeared, clear, as if cut with a diamond or branded with a hot iron' [83], but he was not alone in making the observation. The businessman Mr Wilson [84], who found a similar trail on a Devon beach in 1950, told Eric Dingwall the prints 'were clearly impressed on the sand almost as if cut out by some sharp instrument', while Lynda Hanson's hoofmarks, appearing in a Humberside garden in the 1950s [85] were odd in that 'at the bottom of the print, dry concrete could be seen, not compressed snow as is normal when a person or animal treads on snow.' The significance of these peculiar observations remains obscure, though they certainly look anomalous; there seems no reason to assume that the witnesses were exaggerating, even unconsciously, for effect.

Finally, there is the matter of the 'undeviating line'. Certainly later writers, such as C.O. Burge and Manfri Wood [86] obtained the impression that the Devil's Hoofmarks followed a dead straight line across villages and fields, climbing any obstacles in their way. This is far from the truth; contemporaries reported meandering lines of prints crisscrossing gardens and churchyards [87]. The myth seems to have its origins in accounts which stress that individual hoofmarks appeared in a straight line, one directly in front of another. This greatly puzzled most observers, and led to the common observation that the footprints must have been made by a biped [88]. However, it is also possible that they were the work of small animals hopping

TABLE OF DESCRIPTIONS OF THE 'DEVIL'S HOOFMARKS'

LOCATION	SIZE	SPACING	DESCRIPTION	SOURCE & DATE
Dawlish	c. 3½ x 2½"	12"	"like a donkey's hoof"	Western Luminary, 13 Feb 1855
Lympstone	1½-2½" wide	8"	"Closely resembled a donkey's shoe" Not cloven	Times, 16 Feb 1855
Not specified	1½-2½" wide	8-14"	"Closely resembled a donkey's shoe ... Not in a straight line, but track deviated not more than 6" on either side of a line."	Exeter & Plymouth Gazette 17 Feb 1855
Dawlish	? x ?	16"	Some whole, some cloven	Exeter & Plymouth Gazette 17 Feb 1855
Exmouth	? x ?	9"		Western Times, 17 Feb 1855
Newton Abbot	? x ?	?	"About same size and shape as others"	Western Luminary, 20 Feb 1855
Topsham, Lympstone, Exmouth, etc			Cloven. Like a donkey's	Exeter Flying Post, 22 Feb 1855
Ditto	4 x 2.75"	8" "or more"	"The perfect impression of a donkey's hoof"	Illust'd London News, 24 Feb 1855
Withecombe	? x ?	8½"	"undeviatingly, in two locations a mile and a half apart"	Illust'd London News, 3 Mar 1855
Near Withecombe	? x ?	?	Claw or toe marks	Illust'd London News, 3 Mar 1855
Topsham	? x ?	?	Marks of toes and pads	Illust'd London News, 3 Mar 1855
Weymouth	? x ?	line	"Like cloven hoof of calf"	Notes & Queries, 25 Jan 1890
Dawlish	"In single file, in the shape of a small hoof [containing] marks of claws"			Devon & Cornwall N&Q, 1923
Clyst St George	Size varies...like a donkey shoe, sharply defined...single line..excrement found near tracks ... in one place tracks were double...dogs barked in night			Ellacombe papers, in Trans. Devonshire Assoc, 1952

with their feet held together, or indeed of larger creatures. The donkey, cat and fox, among other animals, can leave trails that look very much like a single line of tracks. [89]

It should also be pointed out that 'South Devon', again, stresses a point that other accounts do not support. Musgrave's drawings show a slight side-to-side variation (perhaps of the order of an inch or two) in some prints [90], while the *Exeter & Plymouth Gazette* reported that the prints 'are alternate like the steps of a man, and would be included between two parallel lines six inches apart.' [91]

The reactions of animals
Sherlock Holmes' 'dog that did not bark' was equally conspicuous on the night of 8-9 February. The thousands of hoofmarks that appeared during the night appear to have been made without alerting the local dogs, let alone their human masters. Only the Reverend Ellacombe [92] seems to have possessed a guard dog that barked in the night.

This absence of warning again seems to suggest a natural explanation for the mystery. Certainly domestic animals - particularly cats - are traditionally thought to be sensitive to the presence of the supernatural, while one would have expected the local dogs to react to an invasion of hundreds of gypsies. [93]

The only other report we have of animal reactions to the hoofmarks comes in a decidedly folkloric tale heard by R.H. Busk, who wrote of a hunt that set to pursuing a trail of Devil's marks 'till at last, in a wood, the hounds came back baying and terrified' [94]. If this is merely a tall tale, it had the backing of the Reverend J.J. Rowe of Marychurch (Torquay), who recalled: 'The episode of the hounds, &c., I well and distinctly remember.' [95]

An unexpected (and unreferenced) possible explanation for the above tale appears in John Godwin's *This Baffling World* [96], which tells how Daniel Plummer, the village idiot of Woodbury - a man given to 'decking himself in layers of chicken and goose feathers' and wandering through the woods making animal noises - was nearly lynched by a 30-strong hunting party from Topsham, which flushed him out of a thicket and then gave chase.

The Uniqueness of the Prints

When the inhabitants of Devon peered from their doorways at the mysterious prints that had appeared during the night of 8-9 February, they appear to have been uniformly convinced that they were witnessing an unprecedented phenomenon. No-one - at least no-one known to the newspaper-writers and the correspondents of the London papers - had seen their like before, and this was a principle element of their mystery.

Yet, while the hoofmarks were undoubtedly unusual, they were far from unique. Twenty-one known cases bear comparison with the Great Devon Mystery, and it does not seem outlandish to suggest that hundreds, perhaps thousands, more are now lost or were never reported [97]. Taken together, these supplementary cases suggest a natural, rather than human or supernatural, explanation for the phenomenon.

Least useful are a number of brief, unreferenced asides likening the 1855 prints to poorly-remembered, second- or third-hand reports. Thus the *Western Times*, writing of the Devil's Hoofmarks [98], remarks: 'It is said a similar occurrence took place about five years ago', while the *Illustrated London News* [99] notes the tradition that a single line of regular hoofmarks, ascribed to the devil, appear annually on a hill in Galicia. These cases are of minimal value because they contain so little detail, or are reported on such doubtful authority, that it is impossible to tell how closely the prints resembled those found in Devon.

More interesting are accounts such as that from the *Inverness Courier* of 1 March 1855 [100], which show that cloven tracks apparently similar to those found in Devon were discovered in the snow elsewhere in Britain that same winter. (The Inverness tracks were said, on examination by a local naturalist, to be 'those of some animal, probably a hare or a polecat.') The *Daily Mail*, in 1922, printed a brief correspondence concerning tracks, ascribed to the devil, which had appeared on rooftops in both Norfolk and the Cotswolds in 1852-53 [101], and there is also an intriguing report, discovered by Fort in *The Times* of 14 March 1840 [102], which predates the Great Devon Mystery by 15 years but refers to prints, resembling those of a pony, appearing in snow in several areas of the Highlands. On this occasion, however, the mystery prints do not appear to have followed the alarmingly regular patterns seen in Devon.

In the Black Country around Wolverhampton, in January 1855, cloven hoofmarks, similar to those of a deer, were found on the vertical walls and roofs of a number of pubs, starting with The Cross at Old Hill in Rowley Regis. Elizabeth Brown, landlady of The Lion pub, suggested a supernatural explanation for the mystery, telling a public meeting that 'her house was mainly frequented by quarrymen and the tracks were nothing new to them. Similar hoofmarks were to be seen burnt into the rock at Pearl Quarry, on Timmins Hill, and trails of them led from that place to the Hailstone.' Since the Rowley hoofmarks appeared nowhere but on the walls and roofs of pubs, however, it seems at least as likely that the Lion marks were made by local chapel 'ranters' who wanted to make a point about the pernicious effects of alchohol [103]. It is now impossible to say whether news of the Black Country hoofmarks reached Devon by early February - if they did, the case for human hoaxers would be considerably strengthened.

Strange hoofmarks are by no means an exclusively 19th century phenomenon. In 1957, Mrs Lynda Hanson of Hull saw footprints matching the dimensions and stride of the Devon prints in her Humberside back garden. They were cloven, four inches across, and spaced 12 inches apart. The prints were made in an inch of snow and, like some of the Devil's Hoofmarks, appeared exceptionally sharply defined. They stopped dead in the middle of the garden. [104]

Of even greater interest is the British Fortean Eric Frank Russell's careful account of some mystery prints discovered in the snow in Belgium during the closing days of World War II. The marks were somewhat smaller than those found in Devon, being 2½ inches long by 1½ inches wide, but they ran for two miles in 'dead straight line', between nine and 15 inches apart. Russell was familiar with the details of the Great Devon Mystery and conceded that his prints 'weren't as dramatic as Gould's - they didn't hop across rooftops', but he still felt he had 'seen the inexplicable'. [105]

Finally, and most mysterious of all, is the story told by the respected psychical researcher Eric Dingwall in the middle 1950s [106]. He had the details from a Mr Wilson who, on an October 1950 visit to the Devon seaside he remembered from boyhood, discovered a single line of hoofmarks leading from a deserted beach straight into the sea.

On this occasion the marks were of whole, not cloven, hoofs. They were six feet apart, and so deeply impressed in the sand that they were significantly deeper than the footprints left by Wilson himself, who weighed 16 stone. Like Mrs Hanson's prints, they appeared strangely cleanly made, 'as if each mark had been cut out of the sand with a flat iron,' yet a hoax appears unlikely, since the beach was locked and deserted, and Wilson had not announced his intention of visiting it to anyone.

Suppositions and Theories

What made the Devil's Hoofmarks? There is a short answer to this question, which is that we shall almost certainly never know. It is, nevertheless, possible to venture a few general comments.

Firstly, as both Rupert Gould and Theo Brown suspected, the cause of the prints was almost certainly multiple. There were simply too many prints, in too many locations, for any one entity - except, perhaps, Milton's Satan - to have made them. Nor, given the observed differences in the shape and spacing of the prints, and the dates on which they appeared, need we assume that all the marks were made by the same type of animal, the same mechanism, or the same group of human hoaxers.

Nevertheless, the considerable similarities between the various prints, and the existence of comparable reports from other areas, does seem to suggest that *most* of the Devil's Hoofmarks were made by a single type of animal, or group of humans.

Before summarising the main theories put forward to explain the marks, it may be worthwhile considering briefly the degree to which the special circumstances of February 1855 contributed to the mystery of the hoofmarks. The weather was certainly unusually cold, though perhaps not unprecedentedly so - we are told it was so severe that flocks of birds were driven ashore in Norfolk, and they also appear to have been present in Devon [107]. Very few people, other than farmers, would have ventured out overnight, so the number of potential witnesses was limited. The ground was hard, and the duration of the cold snap could have driven even shy and nocturnal animals to travel considerable distances, and perhaps venture into villages and towns, in search of food. The long winter night may also have played a part, giving whatever laid the tracks that much longer to make them. And, of course, it had been snowing, so any tracks that did appear were far more apparent than they would normally have been [108]. In short there are good, natural reasons why the hoofmarks should have appeared, and been noticed, in the Devon winter rather than in summer.

Whether the thaw that occurred during the night of 8-9 February contributed to the mystery is more difficult to say. Certainly it is a suspicious circumstance, since it is well known that animal tracks that partially melt and are then refrozen can become considerably distorted. The anthropologist John Napier, in his work on Bigfoot and the Yeti, devotes considerable attention to the manner in which thawed bear or yak prints can be taken for those of an Abominable Snowman [109], and one of the very few witnesses who was out and about during the night in question commented on the peculiar way in which his cat's prints were turned into something very like hoofmarks by the thaw [110]. Against this we must set 'South Devon's' insistence that the trails left by men, cats, dogs, rabbits and birds were still clearly identifiable in the morning [111]. On balance, and taking into account my reservations about William D'Urban's reliability as a witness, I am inclined to think that the thaw and subsequent frost of 8-9 February may well have played a significant part in the appearance of the Devil's Hoofmarks.

The location of the prints can also give valuable clues as to what made them. In Lympstone, for example, the hoofmarks wandered up and down gardens and criss-crossed the whole town promiscuously [112]. This seems more typical of the behaviour of animals foraging for food than it does of human hoaxers; why multiply the risk of discovery by leaving such a meandering trail, when a single line of footprints would have done at least as well? On the other hand, 'South Devon' notes that, to the north, 'this mysterious visitor generally only passed once down or across each garden or courtyard,' which, if true, sounds much more like the action of a hoaxer. Similarly, the prints found at Exmouth were noted 'particularly in many of the garden paths', an unproductive place for animals to search [113]. In Topsham the likelihood of human involvement in the mystery seems even greater; prints there appeared five days later than they did in other parts of the county, crossing the churchyard and leading 'to the very door of the vestibule' [114]. Theo Brown thought that this trail could have been made by Anglican loyalists making a point to the controversial Puseyite, or High Church, vicar of the parish, and she may well have been right. A similar preoccupation with the local church, however, was evident in Dawlish, where something or someone walked 'direct from the vicarage to the vestry door' [115] and 'left marks all over the churchyard and between the graves' [116]; Dawlish was not a Puseyite parish.

Anglicans

It would appear, then, that some at least of the Devil's Hoofmarks may have been left by low-church Anglicans out to make a point. The Topsham prints found on 13 February, as noted above, are particularly likely to have been made in this way.

The notion that the prints were hoaxed would have been strengthened had the marks really been as uniform as tradition suggests. Indeed, one would actually expect the marks in any one area to be identical, since they would presumably all have been made with the same implement. Is is, however, possible, that the thaw distorted what were originally identical marks.

Human hoaxers anxious to make it appear that the devil had walked might well have gone to the effort of making a few marks on rooftops and leaving others leading up to haystacks or impossibly small holes in hedges. It is, however, hard to believe that low churchmen were responsible for all the prints found on 9 February. There were so many that a conspiracy of dozens would have had to be involved - and why go to the effort of spending a freezing night out and about, laying trails across the countryside or through private gardens, to make a point about the local clergyman that could better be made in his own churchyard?

Badgers

It was Richard Owen, one of the great naturalists of the age, who first suggested the Devil's Hoofmarks were made by badgers, and the suggestion thus deserves a careful hearing.

In a letter to the *Illustrated London News* [117], Owen pointed out that badgers are nocturnal and known to venture considerable distances in search of food in winter. However, his choice of the badger as culprit appears to have been based on the fact that it is 'almost the only plantigrade [118] quadruped we have in this island', rather than on a positive identification of the Devon prints.

The theory was attacked by Rupert Gould, who had already tangled with Owen over the latter's 'utterly childish' identification of the sea serpent seen from HMS *Daedalus* as a sea

lion [119]. A badger's paw prints are staggered, as it has rather a wide tread, and the result would be a double line of imprints, he wrote [120]. In addition, a badger could hardly have made the tracks seen on roof tops and probably could not have been responsible for those found in closed gardens.

Balloons

The idea that the Devil's Hoofmarks were left by a balloon does not appear to have been proposed at the time, but it has since attracted some support and the theory is, according to one astrologer, supported by the celestial alignment on the night in question. [121]

The suggestion is that the hoofmarks were made by a rope left dangling from a balloon as it passed slowly overhead. However, even supposing that a horseshoe-shaped grapnel had been attached to the rope, it seems unlikely in the extreme that such a random action would have left marks in almost-straight lines, let alone have left trails leading through pipes and hedges. And while at first glance the balloon theory could account for the tracks seen of roofs, it does not explain why no scuff marks from other trailing portions of the rope were found - nor indeed why anyone would have been so suicidal as to

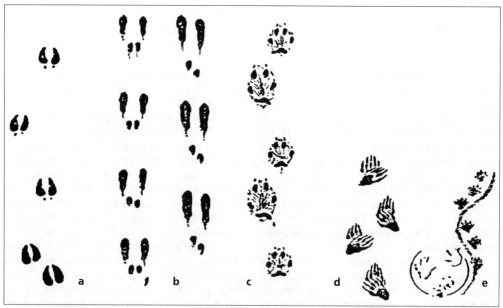

Fig. 1 - Known animal prints, for comparison with the 'Devil's Hoofmarks': (a) Whitetail deer; (b) Cottontail hare; (c) fox; (d) badger; (e) otter, with circular boundary marking.

be aloft in the middle of the night and in such immediate danger of being blown out to sea. Really it is a hypothesis that could only be advanced by someone largely ignorant of the complexity of the case.

Birds

At first glance the theory that birds made the Devil's Hoofmarks appears to explain many of the anomalies of the case, and several different species have been suggested as culprits.

Certainly birds could have left trails on roofs, in walled gardens, and on either side of haystacks, and it also seems possible that some species could have proceeded along pipes and through small holes in hedges. We know that large flocks of sea birds were driven ashore by the severe weather, so it seems there might well have been enough animals of the same species around to leave many similar trails in different parts of the county.

The hypothesis seems to fall down, however, when the shape of the hoofmarks is compared to that a bird's foot, whether it be clawed or webbed. Proponents have had to suggest either that the animals' feet were swaddled in some sort of cloth [122] or that they were iced up [123]. Whether ice could have formed in hoof-like shapes on the feet of many different birds seems unlikely, and though there is at least one recorded instance of a flock of iced-up gulls leaving lines in the snow in their attempts to take off [124], the witness did not examine the resultant trails sufficiently closely to state whether they bore any resemblance to the Devil's Hoofmarks.

The observation that icing up made it difficult for the gulls to fly at all also counts against this otherwise attractive theory, although the Reverend H.T. Ellacombe did observe that some of the tracks were surrounded by flurries of snow that might have been made by the beatings of an iced-up bird's wings as it struggled to take off. [125]

Cats

Cats have not traditionally been linked to the hoofmarks, but the idea that domestic tabbies left the trails is supported by the only eyewitness we definitely know to have been out and about on the night of 8-9 February - the tenant of Aller Farm in Dawlish. He noted that the thaw and rain which occurred during the night half-melted his cat's tracks, and then froze them 'into the shape of a small hoof, with still the impression of a cat's claws enclosed', and reported this observation to the Reverend Edward Fursdon, vicar of Dawlish. [126]

If the villages of Devon contained anything like the number of domestic cats that would nowadays be found in similarly-sized communities (and, given the great prevalence of rats and mice, there may well have been more), and if they were allowed out to wander, cat tracks may well have been responsible for many of the hoofprints, including those found on roofs. There must, however, be some doubt as to whether the actions of thawing and refreezing could have so uniformly turned the trail of any cat into that of a devil over five or more miles.

Donkeys and ponies

'Like a donkey's hoof' [127]. 'Closely resembling a donkey's shoe' [128]. Many of the primary sources for the Great Devon Mystery draw attention to the considerable similarity between the Devil's Hoofmarks and the prints left by donkeys or ponies.

The general supposition at the time was that this resemblance was purely superficial and that the straight lines in which the tracks appeared meant they could only have been left by bipeds. However Theo Brown discovered in the course of her researches that 'donkeys are the only animals that plant their feet in an almost perfect single line' [129], which convinced her that a stray had probably left at least some of the tracks found in exposed locations. Needless to say, another explanation must be sought for the trails found in walled gardens and on roofs.

Gypsies

The suggestion that the Devil's Hoofmarks were made by entire tribes of Romany gypsies acting in concert has the great attraction that it seeks to explain the entire mystery, including the anomalous location of some of the tracks and the problem of how so many miles of similar prints could have been made in a single night.

The theory has only recently come to light,

having been first suggested by Manfri Wood in his autobiography *In the Life of a Romany Gypsy* (1973) [130]. According to Wood, the Devil's Hoofmarks were the result of at least 18 months of careful planning by seven Romany tribes who used more than 400 pairs of specially-made 'measure-stilts' fashioned from stepladders to leave the trail in an attempt to scare away rival tribes of Didekais and Pikies - pagans who were fervent believers in devils. The scheme depended on making it appear that the prints could not have been left by humans or animals, and as such special efforts were made to leave tracks in inaccessible and bizarre places.

We have a similar story from another source, one 'Graham', who wrote to the *Daily Mirror* in 1983 [131]. He was backed up by a 'travelling gentleman' named Danny Smith [132], but though neither refers to Wood's book their letters cannot be regarded as definite confirmation for the story.

It is certainly possible that between 400 and 500 gypsies *could* have left all the trails found in Devon, though they would have done well to have traversed so many gardens and roofs without being spotted. However, the Romany theory does have significant weaknesses.

Firstly, the traditions recorded by both Wood and 'Graham' do not accord to what actually happened on 8-9 February. Both place events in Somerset, and Wood, who is much more detailed, states that the hoofprints were made with 'size 27 boots', each with a stride of 9 feet. He also notes that 'the devil was supposed to walk right across Somerset in as straight a line as possible - he was not supposed to make any detour around houses or churches or barns or so on, but his footsteps had to go straight up one wall, over the roof and down the other wall.'

What happened in Devon was very different. The tracks often meandered wildly, and, as was observed above, there would seem to be little profit to a hoaxer in risking discovery by walking many times up and down a garden, particularly as the idea of a single undeviating line of tracks is so much more sinister. In addition, the prints that were made were much smaller than those that would be left by 'size 27 boots' and, crucially, often had a stride of only eight inches.

While it might be possible for gypsies to manufacture 'measure stilts' with a three yard stride, the idea of balancing a pair of stepladders while taking such tiny paces seems absurd.

Finally, there seems to be no tradition that the Romanies used similar methods to mark out other territories, even though similar tracks have been found elsewhere.

One possible confirmation for the gypsy theory was noted by a correspondent to *Notes & Queries* who wrote of the discovery of impressions 'of the point of a stick' left at huge but regular intervals alongside the hoofmarks themselves [133]. These, Ray Manners has suggested [134], may have been made by Romanies attempting to balance on their ladders. However, the *N&Q* reference is far from contemporary and there is no evidence from 1855 to back it up. In addition, the idea that the stick-marks were 'regular' does not accord with the theory that they were made by a gypsy occasionally in danger of overbalancing.

All in all it seems to me more likely that the Romanies appropriated the idea of the Devil's Walk to their traditions than that they were responsible for the event themselves.

Hares
The hare theory was suggested by a reporter from the *Inverness Courier*, who noted that tracks similar to those found in Devon had been traced up a hillside near the town and had been judged to have been produced by either a hare or a polecat. [135]

It certainly appears that the Scottish tracks were produced by an animal of some kind, but since the identification of the creature remains far from certain the hare theory is unproven.

Kangaroos, monkeys and wolves
Perhaps the most unlikely of all the theories proposed as a solution to the Great Devon Mystery was the notion that the hoofmarks were made by a kangaroo. Though propounded from the pulpit by the Reverend G.M. Musgrave [136], there is almost nothing to be said in its favour. It seems that a pair of kangaroos were kept at a private menagerie in Exmouth, but there is nothing to suggest that either or both escaped. The absence of either

would surely have been noticed given the publicity accorded to the theory. Kangaroo prints do not resemble hoofmarks and the adult animal's tread considerably exceeds the maximum 16 inches attributed to the hoofprints. In addition, even two kangaroos could hardly have left all the prints found on the morning of 9 February.

The sheer exoticism of the idea aside, the only apparent virtue of the kangaroo theory is that it might explain how some of the prints found in walled gardens came to be made. Even a kangaroo, though, might have trouble bounding a 14-foot wall.

Even less need be said about the suggestion that the marks were left by a monkey escaped from a travelling menagerie [137]. While an agile monkey might conceivably have clambered over walls and onto roofs, a single creature could not have left all the marks - and there is, again, no evidence that any animal had escaped from a menagerie, travelling or otherwise.

Still graver objections can be made to the idea that the trail was left by a wolf, since this animal has long been extinct in the UK. It is true that there have occasionally been modern sightings, but these are generally accompanied by reports of extensive depredations among local livestock.

Meteorological phenomena
One of the most remarkable contributions to the lore of the Devil's Hoofmarks came from a Scotsman, J. Allan Rennie, who claimed to have found, on at least five separate occasions, tracks very similar to the Devon prints which had been made by a mysterious weather phenomenon. Once he actually witnessed them being made. [138]

Rennie's first encounter with the puzzle came in northern Canada in 1924, when he twice saw a line of tracks on a frozen lake. His companion on the first occasion, 'a French Canadian dog skinner', was so scared by the trail (which he attributed to the semi-mythical 'Windygo' [139]) that he deserted Rennie's expedition, while on the second occasion Rennie himself was terrified to see a line of tracks approach him, though no creature appeared to be making them.

'The tracks were being made within 50 yards of me - 20 - 10 - then, smack! I shouted aloud as a large blob of water struck me in the face. I swung around, brushing the moisture from my eyes, and saw the tracks continuing across the lake.'

Rennie attributed the phenomenon to 'some freakish current of warm air, coming into contact with the very low temperature [which] had set up the condensation', and said he had seen similar trails in Kent, in 1939, and in Strathspey on 2 December 1952 and 9 January 1953. He took some photographs of the trails made on 2 December 1952, but these do not appear to have been published.

It is evident that this phenomenon could leave marks on roofs and in walled gardens, though it seems much less likely that it would form the sort of meandering tracks found in Lympstone. The chief drawback to Rennie's theory, though, is that he did not see tracks much like those found in Devon. The Canadian trails looked as though they had been made by snowshoes, while the Strathspey prints, though they appeared in a single straight line, were 19 inches by 14, and seven feet apart. 'In shape and size they have not always been uniform, varying from the bilobal to tracks which looked as though they had been made by a gigantic rabbit or mole,' Rennie wrote.

It would thus appear that the phenomenon is unlikely to have left the closely-spaced, regular trails found in Devon. In addition, we have the problem that Rennie himself is the only person to have claimed to have seen it [140] and that naturalist Maurice Burton, on consulting meteorologists, was told that it was 'impossible' for a known weather phenomenon to have produced such tracks. [141]

Otters
The otter theory appears to have been put forward principally to explain how a line of tracks could pass through a narrow pipe, but it does have the additional virtue of introducing an animal which, even in the 1850s, would not have been well-known to many countrymen. It might be possible for otters to be driven ashore from their frozen rivers in search of food, and every place where the footprints were seen was within half a mile or so of a stream or river. However, if otters *were* involved, it seems extremely unlikely they could have been responsible for all the prints,

particularly those that appeared in walled gardens and on roofs.

Rats and Mice

Thomas Fox, one of the many correspondents who wrote to the *Illustrated London News* in March 1855, appears to have been the first to suggest that the Devil's Hoofmarks could have been made by rodents - specifically rats. [142]

Fox and his brother had found tracks in the latter's garden very like those described from Devon and - more than one hundred years later - similar trails were discovered in Epping Forest by the zoologist Alfred Leutscher, who subsequently delivered a lecture on the subject to the Zoological Society [143] and wrote up his theory for the journal Animals. [144]

A number of animals, Leutscher pointed out, including the hare, rabbit, squirrel and rat, are known to leave hopping tracks in which all four feet, held together, can form a pattern similar to a hoofmark. The effect can be enhanced if the marks are left in snow which melts and then refreezes. However, only one animal - the woodmouse - is small enough to leave the eight-inch tracks found in Devon, and its tracks, found in Epping Forest, closely resemble the Devil's Hoofmarks.

There are, nevertheless, drawbacks to the rodent theory. Proponents have to explain why large numbers of mice or rats hopped such very long distances, rather than walking or scurrying about, thus leaving a more readily identifiable mixed trail. There must also be some doubt whether a single mouse or rat could really cover the distance of almost five miles (from Dawlish churchyard to Luscombe, Dawlishwater and then Oaklands [145]) which one party claimed to have traversed in following a single trail. And while it would seem possible for rodents to climb onto roofs, there seems no good reason why they should want to hop so singlemind-edly over them. Finally, rats and mice are so common that one would expect trails similar to the Devon marks to be reported far more frequently than they actually are.

Toads

Toad-tracks were proposed as a solution to the Great Devon Mystery in the *Exeter Flying Post* of 8 March [146] on the authority of a gentleman from Torquay who had followed a trail from his garden to a tree-stump, under which he discovered a large toad.

The drawbacks to the theory are that it does not appear adequately established that the toad in question made the trail, and that it is not quite certain that the Devil's Hoofmarks extended so far west as Torquay, which is six miles to the south-west of Newton Abbott. In addition, it would seem that a toad, with its webbed feet, would be unlikely to leave horseshoe-shaped tracks unless its prints were very considerably distorted.

UFOs

It would, frankly, be surprising if the Devil's Hoofmarks had never been linked to the UFO mystery, and indeed George Lyall, writing in *Flying Saucer Review* [147], suggests the prints may have been made by a laser beam used as some sort of measuring device by a flying saucer.

It is impossible to prove or disprove this kind of claim, though again it seems worth noting that the meandering, regular tracks found in parts of Devon do not sound as though they were produced in the manner suggested.

In any case, while the possibility of animal or human causes remains, the UFO theory can safely be put to one side.

Water monsters

Rupert Gould, a former naval officer with a particular interest in the mysteries of the sea, was the first to point out the proximity of the Devil's Hoofmarks to the sea, and to draw attention to the parallel Kerguelen case in which hoof-shaped tracks would also appear to have been left by something that came from the sea [148]. The same theory was also proposed by the ghost-hunter Elliott O'Donnell in his account of the mystery. [149]

The suggestion that an unknown sea animal made the Devon tracks is lent some support by the strange account given by Eric Dingwall's informant, 'Mr Wilson', who found a straight line of hoofmarks proceeding down an empty Devon beach and entering the water [150]. However, even Gould conceded that no known sea animal could have left the trails; nor is there any obvious reason why such an animal should have evolved hoofs or wished to venture quite so far inland as the Devon tracks suggest.

Summary

No one theory entirely explains the appearance of the Devil's Hoofmarks and the apparently related tracks that have occasionally been seen elsewhere over the years.

While there is some reason to believe that a few of the tracks found in 1855 were made by humans, there is no good evidence to suggest that all were, nor can the proponents of the ingenious Romany theory explain either the close grouping of the prints or the appearance of similar trails in other parts of the country.

The meteorological theory, which also has something to recommend it, again fails to explain the extremely short distances between the hoofmarks. In addition, only one witness has ever claimed to have seen marks definitely attributable to a meteorological phenomenon, and the precise mechanism which allows the weather to produce a trail of markings is not at all understood.

On the other hand, it appears that the reservations of those who dismiss the various animal hypotheses may have been over-stated. In particular, the variations in the exact shape of the prints, and the lack of evidence to support the popular idea that they were invariably found in a dead straight line, suggests that it is possible that the Devon prints were left by common quadrupeds.

The hoofmarks bore so close a resemblance to those made by donkeys and ponies that it is surely possible that some trails were left by these animals. Many, however, cannot have been.

Only one other animal has been definitely shown to leave prints closely resembling the Devil's Hoofmarks in the snow, and that is the woodmouse. It therefore seems quite likely that a number of the prints found in 1855, including some of those seen on rooftops, were made by rodents. In addition, this theory can explain how the trail could lead through pipes and small holes in hedges or fences.

Presuming that the observations made in 1855 were accurate, however (which we can never now know), it would appear that even the woodmouse could not have left all the Devil's Hoofmarks. It is also difficult to see how the scurryings of such a common animal have failed to cause similar panics whenever hard winters occurred before or since. The mystery remains.

Acknowledgements

Grateful thanks are due to the many people who have contributed towards this paper - to colleagues who have sent clippings to *Fortean Times* over the years, and, particularly, to those who have corresponded with us on the subject of the Devil's Hoofmarks themselves:

Paul Begg, Peter Christie, Collectors of Unusual Data - International, Penny Dash, R.G. Easter, Robert Forrest, Ray Manners, Bob Rickard, Peter Roberts, Doc Shiels, Karl Shuker, Caryl Sibbett, Bob Skinner, Paul Thomas, Paul Willis and Gerald Wood.

In addition, I owe a considerable debt to earlier researchers, particularly Theo Brown and Rupert Gould.

NOTES TO THE INTRODUCTORY ESSAY

1 - Document 8.
2 - Document 7.
3 - Document 3.
4 - Document 2.
5 - Documents 2, 11
6 - Documents 1, 2.
7 - Document 11.
8 - *Ibid.*
9 - Documents 3, 7.
10 - Document 17.
11 - Document 39.
12 - Document 7.
13 - See table of descriptions.
14 - Document 23.

15 - Documents 6, 17.
16 - Document 3.
17 - Documents 2, 7.
18 - Document 6.
19 - Document 3.
20 - See *Western Times*,
    17 February 1855.
21 - Documents 2, 3, 7.
22 - Documents 3, 21.
23 - Documents 3, 25.
24 - Document 7.
25 - Document 1.
26 - Document 11.
27 - Documents 14, 17, 23.

28 - Documents 11, 16.
29 - Document 45.
30 - Document 14.
31 - Document 11.
32 - Document 39.
33 - Documents 2, 4, 5.
34 - Document 21.
35 - *Ibid.*
36 - Document 3.
37 - Document 29.
38 - Document 34.
39 - Documents 1, 3, 11.
40 - Document 3.
41 - Document 23.

42 - *Ibid.*

43 - Document 15.

44 - Document 17.

45 - Anon, *H.T. Ellacombe*, a pamphlet available to visitors to the parish church at Clyst St George.

46 - Document 23.

47 - G.A. Household, *The Devil's Footprints: the Great Devon Mystery of 1855*, Exeter 1985.

48 - *Ibid* p.11.

49 - Document 39.

50 - This is probably the William D'Urban mentioned in the pamphlet on the Rev Ellacombe (see note 45) as a friend of the vicar's. He lived to be 96 and left a daughter, with whom Theo Brown corresponded in 1951.

51 - Document 25.

52 - Document 7.

53 - Document 11.

54 - *Ibid.*

55 - Documents 1, 5.

56 - Documents 15-19.

57 - Documents 20-21.

58 - Document 2.

59 - *Ibid.*

60 - Document 3.

61 - Document 6.

62 - Document 7.

63 - Document 39.

64 - Document 23.

65 - Document 18.

66 - Document 13.

67 - Document 1.

68 - Document 8.

69 - Document 23.

70 - Document 7.

71 - Document 11.

72 - *Ibid.*

73 - *Ibid.*

74 - Documents 2, 3, 6, 7, 11.

75 - The *Exeter Flying Post* (Document 13) dismisses the idea that prints had appeared on roofs, but on no discernable authority.

76 - Documents 7, 22, 39.

77 - Document 11.

78 - Document 7.

79 - Documents 11, 23.

80 - Document 11.

81 - Documents 2, 7.

82 - Documents 2, 3, 6, 11.

83 - Document 7.

84 - Document 36.

85 - Document 37.

86 - Document 20, 46.

87 - Documents 2, 3.

88 - Documents 2, 3, 4, 6, 7, 8.

89 - Documents 11, 23.

90 - Document 11.

91 - Document 3.

92 - Document 23.

93 - Manfri Wood (Document 46) states that special parties of Romanies were charged with keeping any guard dogs quiet, but this does not seem to explain why animals kept indoors were also silent.

94 - Document 15.

95 - Document 17.

96 - John Godwin, *This Baffling World*, London 1971, p.42.

97 - Our data covers only the years 1840 to 1957, is significantly biased towards British cases (16 out of 21 reports) and is the result of a gradual compilation over 20 or so years rather than a sustained trawl through the archives.

98 - Document 4.

99 - Document 30.

100 - Document 29.

101 - Documents 31-32.

102 - Document 38.

103 - *Black Country Bugle*, nos 67 and 108, October 1977 and March 1981.

104 - Document 37.

105 - Documents 33 and 44.

106 - Document 36.

107 - Document 23.

108 - Of our database of 21 cases, no fewer than 14 concern prints found in snow, while one set of tracks appeared in sand and another case concerned prints discovered in snow and sand.

109 - John Napier, *Bigfoot*, Abacus 1972 pp.47-8, 106-07.

110 - Document 21.

111 - Document 7.

112 - Document 2.

113 - Document 4.

114 - Document 8.

115 - Document 21.

116 - Document 1.

117 - Document 11.

118 - An animal that walks on the soles of its feet.

119 - See his *The Case for the Sea Serpent*, London 1930 pp.108-120.

120 - Document 39.

121 - Document 47.

122 - A notion proposed by one W.W. in his *The Swan with the Silver Collar*. See Document 39.

123 - Document 34.

124 - Document 34.

125 - Documents 23 and 25.

126 - Document 21 - and see also Document 3 for a comment on this theory.

127 - Document 1.

128 - Document 2.

129 - Document 25.

130 - Document 46.

131 - Document 27.

132 - Document 28.

133 - Documents 15 and 38.

134 - Document 48.

135 - Document 29.

136 - Documents 2 and 11.

137 - Document 1.

138 - Documents 40 and 43. Rennie first wrote of his experiences in a letter to the *Glasgow Herald* published on 11 December 1951. Another letter from him on the same subject was published on 9 February 1953.

139 - In Canadian folklore, the windigo was the possessed body of an Algonkian indian. It preyed on men. Carole Carpenter, 'The cultural role of monsters in Canada', in *Manlike Monsters on Trial*, Vancouver 1990.

140 - Document 3.

141 - Document 43. However, Michael T. Shoemaker reports finding irregularly-spaced hoof-mark-shaped prints, apparently formed by falling blobs of water, in a layer of snow thinly covered with ice in Shenandoah National Park. *Fate* April 1986 p.128.

142 - Document 14.

143 - *Journal of Zoology* vol 148, 1966 p.381.

144 - Document 45.

145 - Document 3.

146 - Document 13.

147 - Lyall, George, 'Did a laser create the Devil's Footprints?', *Flying Saucer Review* vol 18 no 1, January/February 1972.

148 - Document 39.

149 - Elliott O'Donnell, *Great Sea Mysteries*, London 1929.

150 - Document 36.

TABLE OF LOCATIONS OF TRACKS

'DEVIL'S HOOFMARKS'

	SOURCE & DATE
Dawlish	Western Luminary, 13 Feb 1855
Topsham, Lympstone, Exmouth, Teignmouth, Dawlish.	Times, 16 Feb 1855
"Both sides of the River Exe"	Times, 16 Feb 1855
Exmouth, Littleham, Lympstone, Woodbury, Topsham, Starcross, Teignmouth, Dawlish-water, Oaklands	Exeter & Plymouth Gaz.ette 17 Feb 1855
Exmouth	Western Times, 17 Feb 1855
Newton Abbot.	Western Luminary, 20 Feb 1855
Topsham, Lympstone, Exmouth, Teignmouth, Dawlish.	Exeter Flying Post, 22Feb 1855
Exmouth, Lympstone, Woodbury, Dawlish, Torquay, Totnes, Luscombe Woods.	Illust'd London News, 24 Feb 1855
Topsham	Western Times, 24 Feb 1855
Mamhead, Starcross Tower, Powderham Castle, Kenton, Dawlish, Newton, Exmouth, Withecombe Ralegh, Lympstone, Woodbury, Topsham, Bicton, Budleigh	Illust'd London News, 3 Mar 1855
Dawlish	Times, 6 March 1855
Exmouth, Weymouth.	Notes & Queries, 25 Jan 1890
Bideford, Torrington	Devon & Cornwall N&Q, 1922-1923
Torquay, Barton, Walcombe, Dawlish	Trans. Devonshire Assoc., 1950
Clyst St George, Teignmouth, Exeter, Marley, Littleham Cove, Warren, Clyst St Mary, Haldon, Lympstone, Luscombe	Trans. Devonshire Assoc., 1952
Teign Valley, Haldon, Powderham, Lympstone, Exmouth, Topsham	Trans. Devonshire Assoc., 1954
Dawlish, the Warren, Exmouth, East Budleigh	Manchester Guardian, 16 Mar 1955
Bolt Head, Watcombe, River Dart	Devon Ghosts, 1982

OTHER MYSTERIOUS TRAILS

Glenorchy, Glenlyon, Glenochay, Scotland	Times, 14 March 1840
Kerguelen, 1840.	Oddities, 1929
Devon, c.1850.	Western Times, 17 Feb 1855
Galicia, c.1850	Illust'd London News 17 Mar 1855
Cotswolds, c.1852.	Daily Mail, Dec 1922
Inverness, Feb 1855	Inverness Courier, 1 March 1855
Old Hill, Black Country, 1855	Black Country Bugle, March 1981
From Dorset to Lincolnshire, c.1855	Devon Ghosts, 1982
From North to South Devon via Dartmoor, date uncertain	Devon Ghosts, 1982
Lincolnshire, date uncertain.	Notes & Queries, 25 Jan 1890
Unknown, 1870s.	Devon & Cornwall N&Q, 1922
New Jersey, 1908	Tomorrow, Autumn 1987
Northern Canada, 1924	Chambers' Journal, 1953
High Weald, Kent, 1939	Chambers' Journal, 1953
Near Everberg, Belgium, 10 Jan 1945	Great World Mysteries, 1957
Devonshire coast, 1950.	Tomorrow, Autumn 1957
Cromdale, Scotland, 2 Dec 1952.	Chambers' Journal, 1953
Isle of Wight, 1954	Jour. Bombay Nat. Hist. Soc., 1954
Ipplepen, Devon, 1955	Devon Ghosts, 1982
Hull, Humberside, Jan or Feb 1957.	Daily Mirror, 7 Feb 1983

CONTEMPORARY SOURCE MATERIALS

Document 1

The Western Luminary & Family Newspaper for Devon, Cornwall, Somerset & Dorset.
13 February 1855

DAWLISH. MYSTERIOUS. - Since the recent snow storms, some animal has left marks on the snow that have driven a great many inhabitants from their propriety, and caused an uproar of commotion among the inhabitants in general. The markings, to say the least about them, are very singular; the foot print, if foot print it be, is about 3½ inches long by 2½ inches wide, exactly, in shape, like a donkey's hoof: the length of the stride is about a foot apart, very regular, and is evidently done by some two-footed animal. What renders the matter more difficult of solution is, that gardens with walls 12 feet high have been trodden over without any damage having been done to shrubs and walks [1]. The animal must evidently have jumped over the walls. It has also left marks all over the churchyard and between the graves [2]. Many parties have traced the prints for miles, but as yet, without any solution to the mystery. Several of the very superstitious draw long faces, and say it must be the marks of old _____ : others conjecture that it must be some monkey which has escaped a travelling menagerie [3], with something on its feet; but all wish the enigma unravelled.

Document 2

The Times.
16 February 1855

EXTRAORDINARY OCCURRENCE. - Considerable sensation has been evoked in the towns of Topsham, Lympstone, Exmouth, Teignmouth, and Dawlish, in the south of Devon, in consequence of the discovery of a vast number of foot-tracks of a most strange and mysterious description. The superstitious go so far as to believe that they are the marks of Satan himself; and that great excitement has been produced among all classes may be judged from the fact that the subject has been descanted on from the pulpit.

It appears that on Thursday night last [4] there was a very heavy fall of snow in the neighbourhood of Exeter and the south of Devon. On the following morning the inhabitants of the above towns were surprised at discovering the footmarks of some strange and mysterious animal, endowed with the power of ubiquity, as the footprints were to be seen in all kinds of unaccountable places - on the tops of houses and narrow walls, in gardens and courtyards, enclosed by high walls and palings [5], as well as in open fields. There was hardly a garden in Lympstone where these footprints were not observable. The track appeared more like that of a biped than of a quadruped, and the steps were generally eight inches in advance of each other. The impression of the foot closely resembled that of a donkey's shoe, and measured from an inch and a half to (in some instances) two and half inches across. Here and there it appeared as if cloven, but in the generality of the steps the shoe was continuous, and from the snow in the centre remaining entire, merely showing the outer crest of the foot, it must have been convex. The creature seems to have approached the doors of several houses, and then to have retreated, but no-one has been able to discover the standing or resting point of this mysterious visitor. On Sunday last, the Rev. Mr Musgrave alluded to the subject in his sermon, and suggested the possibility of the footprints being those of a kangaroo [6]; but this could scarcely have been the case, as they were found on both sides of the estuary of the Exe [7]. At present it remains a mystery, and many superstitious people in the above towns are actually afraid to go outside their doors after night.

Document 3

Woolmer's Exeter & Plymouth Gazette.
17 February 1855.

THE MYSTERIOUS FOOT-PRINTS
To the Editor of the Exeter and Plymouth Gazette
SIR - Thursday night, the 8th of February, was marked by a heavy fall of snow, followed

by rain and boisterous wind from the east, and in the morning frost. The return of daylight revealed the ramblings of some most busy and mysterious animal endowed with the power of ubiquity, as its foot-prints were to be seen in all kinds of unaccountable places on the tops of houses, narrow walls, in gardens and court-yards enclosed by high walls and palings, as well as in the open fields [8]. The creature seems to have frolicked about through Exmouth, Littleham, Lympstone, Woodbury, Topsham, Starcross, Teignmouth, &c, &c. There is hardly a garden in Lympstone where his foot-prints are not observable, and in this parish he appears to have gamboled with inexpressible activity. Its track appears more like that of a biped than a quadruped, and the steps are generally eight inches in advance of each other, though in some cases twelve or fourteen, and are alternate like the steps of a man, and would be included between two parallel lines six inches apart. The impression of the foot closely resembles that of a donkey's shoe, and measures from an inch and a half to (in some cases) two inches and a half across, here and there appearing as if the foot was cleft, but in the generality of its steps the impression of the shoe was continuous and perfect; in the centre the snow remains entire, merely showing the outer crust of the foot, which, therefore, must have been convex. The creature seems to have advanced to the doors of several houses, and then to have retraced its steps, but no one is able to discern the starting or resting point of this mysterious visitor. Everyone is wondering, but no one is able to explain the mystery; the poor are full of superstition, and consider it little short of a visit from old Satan or some of his imps. On Sunday last [9] the Rev. Musgrave, of Exmouth, delivered one of his usual eloquent discourses in Lympstone Church, and in speaking of Satan as a tempter, who was continually besetting our path, though invisible, aptly alluded to this mysterious visitor who had left behind him visible evidence of his presence and expressed it as his opinion that the foot-prints were those of the kangaroo; but it must have been a busy animal indeed to have played up such pranks as this creature has done. I observed the impressions of my horse's foot made on the same night, and found they measured more than six inches across, whereas the real measurement of the foot was four and a half. This, no doubt, arose from the foot-print forming a nidus for the rain, which, by thawing, expanded the foot to its exaggerated size [10]. I think it therefore difficult to arrive at the precise size of the animal's foot, which would, doubtless, be influenced by the same cause. What can the creature be? The kangaroo has claws four in number in the hind foot, and one of them peculiarly elongated. Surely the impression from this would not so exactly resemble the donkey's shoe. From its universality and vicinity to houses, is it possible that it may be the foot-print of the domestic cat, which always moves about at night? I think it very likely that the combined impression of a hind and fore foot in the thawing snow may have produced the mystery [11]. I merely offer this as a suggestion. If any of your numerous readers can throw any light upon the matter they will gratify the minds of many wondering people, and set at rest the perplexity of the timid and superstitious.

Yours, obediently,
Spectator

[*same paper*]

DAWLISH
The weather during the past week has been intensely cold, and on Sunday morning the thermometer was one degree lower than has ever before been known by the "oldest inhabitant"...
THE MYSTERIOUS FOOT-PRINTS. - Under this head our Dawlish readers will find in another column many curious particulars relating to the extraordinary footmarks which have caused so much excitement on both sides of the Exe.

In connection with the above "mysterious" occurence, we have received the following particulars from our Dawlish correspondent: 'Considerable excitement has been caused among the inhabitants of this place since Friday last in consequence of a report that a strange animal, whether natural or supernatural is not known, had paid us a visit. His foot-prints were traced through the greater part of the town. They resembled somewhat those of a donkey, but, to add to the effect of the mystery, it was rumoured that in some instances they were "cloven". So great was the excitement produced by the reports which got abroad that a party of tradesmen and others armed themselves with guns and bludgeons, and spent the greater part of the day in tracing the foot-prints. From the church-yard they proceeded to the grounds of Luscombe and Dawlishwater, and thence to Oaklands [12]. At length, after a long and weary search, they returned as wise as they set out. Some considered that the foot-prints were those of a large bird from a foreign shore, and others believed that they were those of a kangaroo or wolf, or some other beast escaped from a travelling menagerie. The greatest mystery was that in no place could there be traced more than two impressions, which were about sixteen inches apart. It will be remembered that we had a heavy fall of snow, about four inches deep, on the previous evening (Thursday), and that shortly after eleven o'clock the weather becoming a little milder, it changed into sleet and rain [13], and in the morning the ground was covered with a thin sheet of ice.'

Document 4

Western Times
17 February 1855

EXMOUTH. A MYSTERIOUS VISITOR. - On Friday morning last, this place was thrown into a state of alarm, in consequence of a report that the town and neighbourhood had been visited in the night by no less a person than His Satanic Majesty, and that the marks of his feet were distinctly to be seen imprinted on the snow, particularly in many of the garden paths [14]. In the course of the morning groups of persons were to be seen congregated together in parties of six and a dozen, all busily engaged in examining the marks. Whatever it might have been, it appeared to have two feet, and the foot steps were about nine inches apart. Some gave it as their opinion that they could not have been the Old Gentleman's foot-steps, as he was bound, the term not having expired when he was to be set at liberty [15]; others maintained that he was now enjoying his freedom, and could go where he liked and come where he pleased, but which of those were right there

was no means of deciding. Some said it must be a donkey, but he happens to have four feet, others that it was a bird which is only to be found in Australia [16]. The most puzzling part of it was no-one could see where this visitor had gone into the gardens, or where it had come out, the gate being locked during the night, and some of the walls being seven feet high. It is said a similar occurrence took place about five years ago. All we can say up to the present time is that it still appears a mystery, no one having been able to throw light upon the subject.

Document 5

Western Luminary & Family Newspaper for Devon, Cornwall, Somerset & Dorset.
20 February 1855

NEWTON ABBOT. THE MYSTERIOUS FOOTPRINTS. - The mysterious foot-prints have been seen near this town as well as other places, during the past week, and some of the inhabitants appear quite astonished, while others appear to laugh at the matter. No one can think or tell what these foot-prints are. They appear to resemble those observed in other places, being about the same size and shape. [We have heard: but do not know whether it is the fact, that a kangaroo has escaped from some private menagerie, and is the author of the mysterious foot-prints. We rather suspect that it is the result of natural causes. Ed. W.L.] [17]

Document 6

Trewman's Exeter Flying Post.
22 February 1855

"MYSTERIOUS FOOTPRINTS." - An excitement worthy of the dark ages has prevailed in Topsham, Lympstone, Exmouth, Teignmouth, Dawlish, and, for ought we know to the contrary, in many other places, caused by "foot-tracks of a most strange and mysterious description," as the local penny-a-liners to the London papers have described them. These are to be found in fields, gardens, roads, house-tops, & other likely and unlikely places, deeply embedded in snow. The shape was a hoof, and as the Devil is supposed to have a cloven foot, why of course the impressions were Satanic, at least this was the suggestion of the intelligent mind who does the correspondence for the *Times*. It happens, however, that *both* foot-tracks are cloven, so that old Harry must have disguised his sound foot to escape detection [18], although, singularly enough, according to "our own correspondent," the steps he took to elude the vigilance of the police have led to his discovery. The following is the account sent to the *Times*: ... [19]

We can't pretend to give an explanation of this "mysterious affair", but all we know is that if this Devil has taken it into his head to have a steeple chase in Devon, he has manifested very peculiar taste in choosing such an inclement season for his sport.

Document 7

The Illustrated London News.
24 February 1855

FOOT-MARKS ON THE SNOW
IN DEVON (From a Correspondent) [20]

As many of your readers have perused, I have no doubt, with much interest, the paragraph which appeared in several of the papers last week relative to the mysterious foot-marks left upon the snow during the night of Thursday, the 8th, in the parishes of Exmouth, Lympstone, and Woodbury, as also in Dawlish, Torquay, Totnes, and other places on the other side of the estuary of the Exe, in the county of Devon, extending over a tract of country of thirty or forty miles, or probably more; and as the paragraph I allude to does not fully detail the mysterious affair, it may probably be interesting to many to have a more particular account - which I think this unusual occurrence well deserves.

The marks which appeared on the snow (which lay very thinly on the ground at the time), and which were seen on the Friday morning, to all appearance were the perfect impression of a donkey's hoof - the length four inches by two and three-quarter inches; but, instead of progressing as the animal would have done (or indeed as any other would have done), feet right and left, it appeared that foot had followed foot in *single line*, the distance from each tread being eight

inches or rather more - the foot-marks in every parish being exactly the same size and the step the same length [21]. This mysterious visitor generally only passed *once* down or across each garden or courtyard and did so in nearly all the houses in many parts of the several towns above mentioned, as also in the farms scattered about; this regular track passing in some instances over the roofs of houses, and hayricks, and very high walls (one fourteen feet), without displacing the snow on either side or altering the distance between the feet, and passing on as if the wall had not been any impediment. The gardens with high fences and walls, and gates locked, were equally visited as those unprotected. Now, when we consider the distance that must have been gone over to have left these marks - I may say

Fig. 2 - Drawing of the Hoofmarks accompanying 'South Devon's' letter to the *Illustrated London News*, 24 February 1855. (Document 7.)

in almost every garden, or doorstep, through the extensive woods of Luscombe, upon commons, in enclosures and farms - the actual progress must have exceeded a hundred miles. It is very easy for people to laugh at these appearances, and account for them in an idle way. At present no satisfactory solution has been given. No known animal could have traversed this extent of country in one night, besides having to cross an estuary of the sea two miles broad. Neither does any known animal walk in a *line* of single footsteps, not even man. [22]

Birds could not have left these marks, as no bird's foot leaves the impression of a hoof, or, even were there a bird capable of doing so, could it proceed in the direct manner above stated - nor would birds, even if they had donkeys' feet, confine themselves to one direct line, but hop here and there, but the nature of the mark at once sets aside its being the track of a bird. The effect of the atmosphere upon these marks is given by many as a solution, but how could it be possible for the atmosphere to affect one impression and not affect another? On the morning that the above was observed the snow bore the fresh marks of cats, dogs, rabbits, birds, and men clearly defined. Why, then, should a continuous track, far more clearly defined - so clearly, even, that the raising in the centre of the frog [23] of the foot could be plainly seen - why then should this particular mark be the only one which was affected by the atmosphere, and all the others left as they were? Besides, the most singular circumstance connected with it was, that this particular mark removed the snow, wherever it appeared, clear, as if cut with a diamond or branded with a hot iron; of course I am not alluding to its appearance after having been trampled on, or meddled with by the curious in and about the thoroughfares of the towns. In one instance this track entered a covered shed, and passed through it out of a broken part of the wall at the other end, where the atmosphere could not affect it.

The writer of the above has passed a five months' winter in the backwoods of Canada, and has had much experience in tracking wild animals and birds upon the snow, and can safely say, he has never seen a more clearly-defined track, or one that appeared to be less altered by the atmosphere than the one in question. Marks left upon thin snow especially may after a time blur a little, but never lose their distinctive character, as every one will know who has been accustomed to follow the track of the American partridge.

Should you think the above likely to interest your readers, or draw from any of them a better solution of this most singular occurrence than has at present been given, perhaps you will allow it a place in your most interesting journal. I send you a copy of the foot [24], taken from the snow, and also a succession of the steps, to show you the manner of progressing.
South Devon

Document 8

Western Times.
   24 February 1855

TOPSHAM. THE TWO-LEGGED WONDER. - The same excitement prevails here as at Exmouth and other places relative to the "Satanic Hoof". The track has been seen here in great perfection, and some people say it was sent as a warning to the Puseyites [25] - hence it is that the "phenomenon" has visited the Puseyite parishes of Woodbury, Topsham, and Littleham-cum-Exmouth [26]. In this place it has traversed the churchyard - and even to the very door of the vestibule. The "sombre perpetual" [27] has not, it is said, exhibited a pleasant countenance since the occurrence. Its first appearance here was on the eve of Saint Valentine. [28]

Document 9

Brighton Guardian.
   28 February 1855

Letters to the Editor
THE MYSTERIOUS FOOTSTEPS IN DEVON
SIR - Is it not possible - nay, probable - that these are the footsteps of that animal so accurately described by Biom Heriolfson, the Icelandic navigator, who visited the coasts of Labrador, A.D. 1001, and to whom, with Lief, Baron Humboldt, in his "Cosmos," [29] attributes the discovery of America? The

records of this event are both numerous and authentic, and have received ample confirmation from the researches of Rafn, the greatest Northern scholar of our times. Biom Heriolfson describes an animal, which he terms the Unipede, or Uniped, as having a foot similar to that represented by the copy given in the *Illustrated London News*, with the exception of an almost imperceptible division in the outer and inner circles of the hoof. The character of the limb was, in his opinion, a stranger phenomenon than its singleness, for it partook rather of that of a quadruped than of that of a bird. He informs us that the wings appeared to radiate from the middle of the back with the feathers spreading out in a manner similar to those in the tail of a peacock; but they were slightly divided into two equal parts when the bird was in motion. Moreover, the uniped had the power, when alarmed or excited, of erecting a single crest of feathers above the head so peculiar and striking that an opinion prevailed among the learned of Iceland that this animal was the unicorn, hitherto considered fabulous. Let it be remembered that the inhabitants of Iceland, during the eleventh, twelfth, and thirteenth centuries, created and maintained, amidst its snows and volcanic fires, a literature which would have honoured the happiest climes of Europe. Biom Heriolfson, in completing his description of the uniped, states that the organs of vision approximated so closely that they had the appearance of a double eye. This bird, he affirms, flew, or rather ran, with incredible swiftness, touching the ground frequently and at equal distances. Thus the footsteps would be in a direct line.

The cry or note of this animal was something hideous, unlike that of any other bird or beast. The learned Gardner [30] in a late edition of his great work on the music of nature would seem to imply that Wagner, Schumann and other celebrities of the modern German school have borrowed their notions of music from the peculiar tones of the uniped; but, Sir, I entirely dissent from their opinion, as these masters have repudiated any such association by affixing Dueped [31] to their compositions.

In conclusion, your readers may rest assured that the dimension of the *tail* of the uniped is just one half of a great dodo.

S.K.E.
North-street, Brighton, February 26th

Document 10

Trewman's Exeter Flying Post.
1 March 1855

A GHOSTLY VISITOR. - The mysterious foot-marks which have so puzzled the people of Exmouth have been likewise traced at Woodbury; and, as these foot-prints first appeared in the morning snow, after a most bitter freezing night, the farmers have little doubt that the impressions must have been made by the tread of a warm footstep - which inclines them to think that the ghost of St Wenceslas is troubling them because they would not sing his saintship's glory and honour in the parish church [32]. There are some persons, however, who supposed the mysterious footprints to give evidence of the cloven hoof, and they wished the patron of the parish, Mr Custos Corfe, to be consulted, as they thought, with his experience in Puseyism, he might know something of the measure of a cloven foot. The more knowing ones, however, still cleave to the Wenceslas hypothesis, deeming it unreasonable to suppose that Satan would disturb a state of things that empties the church and keeps ill-feeling and discord constant residents in the once united parish of Woodbury.

Document 11

Illustrated London News.
3 March 1855

PROFESSOR OWEN ON THE FOOTMARKS IN THE SNOW IN DEVON [33]
(To the editor of the *Illustrated London News*)

An esteemed zoological friend has submitted to me a carefully-executed drawing of one of the more perfect impressions left in the snow at Luscombe, South Devon, on or about the 8th of last month. It was of the hind-foot of a Badger. This is almost the only plantigrade quadruped we have in this island, and leaves a foot-print larger than would be supposed from its size. The Sketch, of which you have given a Cut in p.187 (Feb.24th), gives a correct general idea of the shape and proportions of these footprints, but without the indications of the pad on the sole, and the five small claws, which the drawing sent to me exhibited. Such perfect foot-prints were rare, because those of the fore and hind-foot are commonly more or less blended together, producing the appearance of a line of single footsteps; which appearance, if a bear had been abroad in the five winter months spent by your Correspondent in Canada, would have shown him was not peculiar to the foot-steps of man, but characteristic of other plantigrade mammalia, though they may be quadrupedal. The badger sleeps a good deal in his winter retreat, but does not hibernate so regularly and completely as the bear does in the severer climate of Canada. The badger is nocturnal, and comes abroad occasionally in the late winter, when hard-pressed by cold and hunger; it is a stealthy prowler, and most active and enduring in its quest of food.

That one and the same animal should have gone over 100 miles of a most devious and irregular route in one night is as improbable as that one badger only should have been awake and hungry out of the number concealed in the 100 miles of rocky and bosky [34] Devonshire which has been startled by the impressions revealed by the rarely-spread carpet of snow in that beautiful county.

The onus of the proof that one creature made them in one night rests with the assertor, who ought to have gone over the same ground, with a power of acute and unbiassed observation, which seems not to have been exercised by him who failed to distinguish the truly single from the blended foot-prints in question.

Nothing seems more difficult than to see a thing as it really is, unless it be the right interpretation of observed phenomena.

Richard Owen

We have likewise received communications upon the above subject from A.B.P., Ipswich; A CONSTANT READER, Burgh; A.A.; I.S., Jersey; K.L.M., Clifton. W.W., Somerset, will perhaps state the authority for the statement of the strayed swan [35]. The following are ingenious attempts to explain this remarkable appearance:-

I have read with great interest the paragraph in your last publication giving an account of the most extraordinary prints in the snow, which have occasioned such excitement and fomented so melancholy a mass of superstitious folly in the villages lying southward of Exeter, on either side of the river Exe. Permit me, however, to state that the outline accompanying your intelligent Correspondent's recital of the circumstances hardly conveys a correct idea of the prints in question. As an amateur accustomed to make most accurate drawings from nature, I set to work soon after these marks appeared and completed the accompanying exact fac-simile of those that were visible on the lawn of our clergyman's garden in this parish [36]. He and I traced them through a low privet hedge, by a circular opening of one foot diameter. On applying a rule, the interval between each impression was found to be undeviatingly eight inches and a half. On the same day a mutual acquaintance, familiar with natural history, and not long since returned from the Pacific Ocean, measured the intervals between similar prints in his garden, above a mile and a half distant from the Rectory, and found it to be exactly eight inches and a half. This, in my opinion, is one of the most remarkable and confounding circumstances we have to deal with. In the course of a few days a report was circulated that a couple of kangaroos had got loose from a private menagerie (Mr. Fische's, I believe) at Sidmouth. Few of us had had opportunities of seeing the impression made on sand or loam by the hinder feet, or hocks rather, on which this animal sits; and we were not unwilling to give credence to the suggestion that the exotic quadruped (walking, when it does walk, as a biped; but bounding over vast lengths of space more like a chamois) might have been loose and vagrant in the neighbourhood, and left the strange impress here referred to. Still, it was quite inexplicable that the animal, considering the scale of the foot, should leave, in single file, one print only, and, as has been already observed, with intervals as exactly preserved as if the prints had been made by a drill, or any other mechanical frame. A scientific acquaintance informed me of his having traced the same prints across a field up to a hay-stack. The surface of the stack was wholly free from marks of any kind, but on the opposite side of the stack, in a direction exactly corresponding with the track thus traced, the prints began again! [37] The same fact has been ascertained in respect of a wall intervening.

No animal with cushion paw, such as the feline tribe - diminutive or large (cat or tiger) - exhibit, could have made these marks; for the feet of most quadrupeds tread in parallel lines, some widely divaricated, others approximating very closely. The ass, especially, among the animals daily seen, approaches the single line. The fox leaves round dots in a single line; the stoat two and one alternately. Moreover, the feline tribe leave concave prints; whereas, in each of these mystic prints, the space enclosed by the bordering line was convex, as in the print of a patten.

Early in the week we were informed that two cranes had been shot at Otterton, below Budleigh Salterton, and that these were the mystical printers; but the well informed in zoology at once rejected this offered explanation [38]. Within the last four-and-twenty hours, a very shrewd and intellectual neighbour of mine, about six miles distant, wrote me word that a gentleman in the parish adjoining his own had traced these peculiar prints through his garden-walks into a six-inch gutter, and there he saw the marks of *claws*. This has induced some to suppose them to be the track of a catamountain [39]. Two other gentlemen, resident in the same parish, pursued a line of prints during three hours and a half, marking their progress under gooseberry-bushes and espalier fruit-trees; and then, missing them, regained sight of the impression on the roofs of some houses to which their march of investigation brought them. These gentlemen "swear to claws." Upon which my correspondent (a member of the Society of Antiquaries) observes, "We incline to believe they must be otters, driven out in quest of food [40]. Our friend felt toe-marks at the contracted part of the print, though they were not discernible by the eye."

Some "chiel amang" [41] the congregation where I was discoursing three Sundays since had evidently been "taking notes, and, faith! he presented them" (as Burns would say); and though, without incurring the charge of the slightest approach to irreverence, I found a very apt opportunity to mention the name of kangaroo, in allusion to the report then current. I certainly did not pin my faith to that version of the mystery, nor call upon others to receive it *ex cathedra* [42]; but the state of the public mind of the villagers, the labourers, their wives and children, and old crones, and trembling old men, dreading to stir out after sunset, or to go out half a mile into lanes or by-ways, on a call or message, under the conviction that this was the Devil's walk, and none other, and that it was wicked to trifle with such a manifest proof of the Great Enemy's immediate presence, rendered it very desirable that a turn should be given to such a degrading and vitiated notion of a superintending Divine Providence; and I was thankful that a kangaroo was "in the wind," as we should say, and serving to disperse ideas so derogatory to a christianised, but assuredly most unenlightened, community. I was reminded, nevertheless, by one pertinacious recusant, that it is written that Satan should be unchained for a thousand years, and that the latter days are at hand. Still, mine was a word in due season, and did good.

The generality of such of us as can reason dispassionately on view of a phenomenon which seems, as yet, to be without precedent or parallel, incline to believe it must be a bird of some unfamiliar tribe, wandering and hopping over this region; but all inquiry seems to be fruitless. I have addressed communications to the British Museum, to the Zoological Society to the keepers of birds and beasts in the Regent's Park menagerie; and the universal reply is, they are utterly unable to form any conjective on the subject, however correctly the impressions had been copied.

I am emboldened to address you with more than the ordinary confidence of a correspondent "well up on his facts" inasmuch as I am living in the centre of the district where the alarm, so to speak, was first given. Sir L. Newman's Park, at Mamhead, is exactly opposite to my own residence. Starcross Tower is an object of the picturesque, and beautiful to gaze upon from my study window; and Powderham Castle gleams in the sunshine, half a mile further up. These are on the other side (west) of the river Exe, two miles in its breadth; and the marks were as abundant throughout the places just specified, and their neighbourhood - Kenton, Dawlish, Newton, &c - as here at Exmouth, Withecombe Ralegh, Lympstone, Woodbury, Topsham, and the vicinity of Bicton, and Budleigh. There are many "travelled men," and deep thinkers too, among us, far from being

Credulous to false prints

(as *Isabella* says to *Angelo*) **[43]**; but - eager as we are to ascertain the exact point of knowledge in natural history at which the elucidation of this unprecedented mystery might commence - our anxiety as zoologists, or as students or connoisseurs in any one of the sciences, is a feeling of apathetic indifference in comparison with our regret for the prevalence and evil working of that gross and incredible superstition which is raging like an endemic disease among the lowest class in every direction; and I shall have every cause to rejoice, if, on view of what has now been laid before you by pen and pencil, any one of your numerous readers and abler contributors should succeed in solving the difficulty, and remove thereby a dangerous, degrading, and false impression.

Withecombe, near Exmouth.
G.M.M.

As much interest has been excited by these extraordinary foot-tracks, I beg to offer you a few remarks in explanation of what I have observed in this neighbourhood (Topsham). Myself and another medical friend bestowed considerable time in endeavouring to discover the peculiarities of this most singular impression. The outline, certainly, in all cases resembles that of a hoof which has given rise to the idea of its supernatural origin among the ignorant; but, on more minute examination of the tracks, we could distinctly see the impressions of the toes and pad of the foot of an animal; a rough draft of which I showed to a friend of mine in Exeter, and, without any comment on my part, he recognised it as that of the otter, being well acquainted with that animal and its habits.

I have enclosed you a rough Diagram of the impressions which we observed within the hoof-like tracks; the outside toes were larger than the rest. I am not acquainted with the otter myself; but of this I am fully convinced, that the animal, be it what it may, is of low stature, from the tracks having shown it to have passed uninterruptedly under the branches of shrubs, &c., not more than eight or nine inches from the ground; and in a neighbouring village it went through a six-inch pipe drain. It must be borne in mind that most rivers have been frozen over for some weeks, and therefore the otters have thus been prevented from obtaining their usual food - namely fish; and when such is the case, they ramble many miles in search of other food.

The otter is not a rare animal in this neighbourhood, and frequents the streams near Exmouth, Lympstone, Woodbury, Budleigh, Topsham, Clyst, the river Exe (in all which parishes tracks have been seen), as well as Dawlish, Torquay, Totnes, &c. The tracks in this parish we observed going in contrary directions; we did not notice any in a direct line, but in alternate steps, forming two parallel lines of steps. We also saw tracks on a low wall, and over the tiles of a linhay **[44]**, and in several instances it had visited the summer-houses and tool-houses of gardens; in all of which portions of the same characteristics were more or less traceable, the ball or pad in the centre being more frequent than the others. Its visits have been repeated in some localities of this town.

Topsham, Feb. 26th, 1855.

Let your Correspondent, "South Devon," who furnished the accounts of footmarks published in your Number of Feb. 14th inst. know that if he, on any future occasion, should see such footmarks, he may, on accurate examination, discover a heelmark and three toemarks - made probably by the foot of the Great Bustard (*Otis tarda*). The two ends of the asinine shoeprints in your Number of last week are probably those of the two outer toes; and the upper rounded end, the cushioned junction of the toes at the heel end. I saw marks of this sort on Saturday, the 24th inst, after the commencement of the thaw on the Friday, and do not doubt of their being such as I have named. What I saw had evidently (although the thaw had partially obliterated them) a central third linear impression.

Ornither

Document 12

The Times. [45]
6 March 1855

THE MYSTERIOUS FOOTPRINTS IN DEVONSHIRE. - The interest in this matter has scarcely yet subsided, many inquiries still being made into the origin of the footprints which caused so much consternation on the morning of the 8th ult. In addition to the circumstances mentioned in *The Times* a little while since, it may be stated that at Dawlish a number of persons sallied out armed with guns and other weapons for the purpose, if possible, of discovering and destroying the animal which was supposed to have been so busy multiplying the footmarks. As might have been expected, the party returned as they went. Various speculations have been made as to the cause of the footprints. Some have asserted that they are those of a kangaroo, while others affirm that they are the impressions of the claws of some large bird driven on shore by stress of weather. On more than one occasion reports have been circulated that an animal from a menagerie has been caught; but the matter at present is as much a mystery as it ever was.

Document 13

Trewman's Exeter Flying Post.
8 March 1855

THE 'MYSTERIOUS FOOT-PRINTS'. - A gentleman, residing at St Mary Church, Torquay, has given us the following and most probable cause of the mysterious footprints seen in different parts of this county. He says that, whilst the snow was on the ground he observed one morning some very curious marks in his garden. He traced them for a considerable distance, and ultimately into a shed or linhay, and from thence under the stump of a tree, when, on examining the place closely, he soon discovered a very large toad, lying closely against the bank. He states that the impression left on the snow exactly corresponds with the woodcuts given in the *Illustrated London News* of March 3rd. Can anyone afford a better solution of this "mystery"? As for the impressions being seen on house-tops - that's all moonshine. [46]

Document 14

The Illustrated London News.
10 March 1855

THE FOOT-MARKS IN THE SNOW, IN DEVON.
(We select the following from several additional communications upon this inquiry):-

In addition to what I said in my letter of the 28th ultimo [47], relative to the "Footmarks in the Snow in Devon," it appears to me that, as the "snow lay very thinly on the ground at the time," as stated by your Correspondent, such was the reason why the inner part of the tracks was not so clearly defined as the outer part of them; therefore the outline reversed would look like a donkey's track, as stated in my previous letter; and I presume the heel of the tracks has been taken for the forepart of them.

If birds made the tracks, they probably were either web-footed ones or waders - most likely the latter, as they could run much swifter and better across the country. Dr Buckland, in his "Bridgwater Treatise," vol.ii p.39 [48], in speaking of tracks in new red sandstone, set forth in plate 26A of that work, says - "None of the footsteps appear to be those of web-footed birds; they most nearly resemble those of Grallae (waders), or birds whose habits resemble those of Grallae. The impressions of three toes are usually distinct, except in a few instances; that of the fourth or hind-toe is mostly wanting, as in the footsteps of modern Grallae."

Now, if the foot-marks in the snow were made by waders, the shallowness of the snow is a sufficient reason why the impression of the fourth or hind-toe was not made (as in the cases noticed by Dr Buckland), and with respect to web-footed birds their hind-toe is very small.

The size of the tracks in the snow - namely four inches by two inches and three quarters - shows that they must have been made by very large birds (if they are attributable to them), and the probability is that some waders were frozen out by the severity of the weather from the shores of the rivers or estuaries of the sea, and that they ran over South Devon in the night of the 8th ult. in search of food, and afterwards mounted aloft, as cranes do, before the dawn of day.

If the bird theory is correct, perhaps some one skilled in ornithology may, from the size of the tracks, and the distance (eight inches) of the stride between them, give some idea of what species of bird it was.

Jabez Allies

Tivoli House, Cheltenham, 3rd March 1855

Saint Mary's Church, Torquay, Devon, 3rd March 1855

Having seen in the *Illustrated London News* sketches of the foot-prints made in the snow in this neighbourhood by some animal unknown, and as various conjectures are made as to what animal has thus travelled over fields and gardens, and after going clean over housetops has not been stayed by a tidal river two miles wide, I send you an attempted explanation of the affair. There are certain times and seasons for the pairing and breeding of animals accurately fixed by Nature. The green plover is frequently caught in the snow in Scotland after his arrival in that country, and he must bear it as best he can, and why should not other animals have to face the snow-flake in the breeding season, and have to travel a weary way before they can make their beds and lay them down in peace? This, I am persuaded, is the hard fate of the animal who has caused such unwonted prints upon the snow in Devon; as I infer from the simple fact of finding the marks of the animal first, and then finding the carcass with the evident marks of a violent and sudden death in the track. It was neither bird nor beast that made the marks, but a reptile; not only putting his feet and claws (for he had claws) to the ground, but his belly too; hence the puzzle of the large print made in a line by his four feet and his belly all at once, every time he hopped. At the twenty-first milestone from Exeter, and third from Torquay, a large toad was found by me in the turnpike-road, crushed to death by a carriage-wheel; the track of the same was well defined for some distance along the road, and was exactly as described by your Correspondents and illustrated by you. [49]

The time for frogs and toads to spawn in Devon is rather earlier than in the north. Frogs are scarce here, but toads are not; and as Shaldon village lies against a steep hill, the houses admit toads to travel over them easily; and all toads that are to breed must travel to the water to do so, be the distance more or less; and as nobody turned out this unfortunate toad to seek his mate and meet his death, it has no doubt been the fate of others like him to have had a trip on the snow-flake.

Alex. Forsyth

BALLINGDON, near Sudbury, Suffolk, March 3, 1855.

The foot-marks described by your Devon Correspondent are made, in my opinion, by the poor despised and insignificant rat [50]. My brother lives in a house a quarter of a mile from Sudbury, surrounded by fields and gardens; he called my attention to the foot-marks of rats about his garden, and we found they had laid siege to his potato clamp. Tracing the depredators, he exclaimed, the Devonshire donkey has been here! and, on examination, I found the foot-marks exactly to agree with those described in the *Illustrated London News* for last week. We found the marks of no other mammalia, except of the rabbit, and no one would suppose they could all be made by the same kind of animal. The snow being drifted, and, consequently, of varying depths, afforded me an opportunity of observing the cause of the variety of the foot-marks. Where the snow was only one inch deep, marks were very distinct: in one they were caused by the rat walking slowly on all his toes; in another track he is evidently trespassing on the heel, as does the bear, the rabbit, and the squirrel; in another track the donkey shoe-form is more clearly defined, which is caused by the snow being deeper. The rat is an expert climber, though far inferior to the squirrel, whose conformation his greatly resembles: they are provided with a very powerful but short forearm, the muscles of which are strongly developed.

It is well known that when these little animals leap or bound along they alight upon their four feet very close together, and the large muscles of their short arm cause the *ulnae* to be far apart and nearly touching the ground, and in their descent form in the snow

100

the semi-circular part of the donkey shoe; and the toes of the hind-feet approaching near to the *ulnae* or, elbows of the forearm, complete it by forming its two sides. The impression between the heels and the shoe is made by the rat's tail. I should have said the distance from the toe of one impression to the heel of the preceding line was eight inches.

Thomas Fox

We agree with a Correspondent that the following attempted solution, from the *Brighton Guardian* of Feb.29, between its jest and earnest, is calculated to envelop the subject in deeper mystery:–

[Here the *ILN* inserts a letter from the *Brighton Guardian*, 29 February. See Document 9.]

[Next the *ILN* inserts an article from the *Inverness Courier*, 1 March 1855, concerning mysterious footprints found in the Highlands. See Document 29 - ed.]

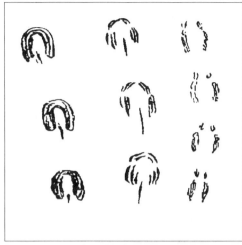

Fig. 3 - Drawing of the Hoofmarks by Thomas Fox from Document 14. See also Fig. 9a.

NOTES TO CONTEMPORARY SOURCES

1 - This sort of obstacle should have proved impassable even to a stilt-walker, so supporters of the Romany theory must assume that their gypsies sat on top of the walls and swung their stilts over the obstacle. One wonders if anyone inspected the snow-covered tops of the walls for the marks of such a passage.

2 - If, as the writer of this passage apparently suspected, there is some significance to the track-maker's prediliction for the churchyard, a human or supernatural agent would appear more likely than an animal.

3 - The 'travelling menagerie' theory is, of course, a familiar motif in 'out of place animal' stories - see, for example, Mick Goss, "The Crocodile of Cefn Caves", in *Fortean Times* 51:52-6. In fact, escapees from circuses and menageries rarely fare well in the wild; they are unused to fending for themselves. Nor was any evidence ever produced to prove that a travelling show had

lost one of its animals in the vicinity on the night in question.

4 - i.e., the night of 8/9 February 1855.

5 - Pointed fencing.

6 - The suggestion that a kangaroo was responsible for the hoof-marks probably owed more to the animal's rarity in Victorian England, and to ignorance as to its precise habits, than to any real similarity between its footprints and those found in the snow.

7 - The apparently impassable barrier of the River Exe is mentioned by the *Illustrated London News* in its influential description of the mystery [document 7]. "No known animal could have traversed this extent of country in one night, besides having to cross an estuary of the sea two miles broad," its correspondent noted. In fact, at low tide the river is as little as a couple of hundred yards wide in places, and is only four feet deep at one

point. In addition, within a week of 8 February it was reported that the intensely cold winter had frozen the estuary. At Exeter a party was held in mid-river, with food provided by a gas stove set up on the ice, while further south the iced-up Teign estuary was reported to have been crossed by a boy pushing a wheelbarrow. It is not clear whether the river Exe had already frozen by the night of 8/9 February, though a correspondent to the *Illustrated London News* (3 March) hints that it was. (See *Western Times* 17 Feb 1855 + *The Devil's Footprints: The Great Devon Mystery of 1855*, ed. G.A. Household, Devon Books, Exeter, 1985, pp.6,8.) There is, I suspect, no need to suppose that any mystery animal must have flown or swum the river; it could simply have walked, or hopped.

8 - From the close similarity in the phrasing of these details and the equivalent passage in *The Times*, and the proximity of their publication dates, it would appear that the accounts in both papers were supplied by the mysterious 'Spectator'.

9 - 11 February 1855.

10 - This process of thawing and refreezing has been known to produce other anomalous footprints, particularly in the Himalayan stronghold of the Yeti, where distorted bear footprints have been taken as the spoor of the Abominable Snowman. See John Napier, *Bigfoot* (Abacus 1972) pp.41, 47-8, 106-7, 110, 117, 165, 169. However, as the *Illustrated London News*'s correspondent 'South Devon' pointed out [see Document 7], the tracks of 'cats, dogs, rabbits, birds' left that night remained distinct and recognisable.

Had the mysterious tracks been enlarged to the same degree as those of the author's horse, it is possible they were originally as small as 1 2/3 inches wide. See also Document 21.

11 - The 'cat' theory was also advanced by Henrietta Fursdon in *Devon & Cornwall Notes & Queries*. See Document 21.

12 - This, a distance of about 8 miles, could be the furthest the tracks were followed by any one person or group. It is important to remember that speculation about a trail 100 miles long or more is based on the estimate of the *Illustrated London News*'s 'South Devon' [see Document 7]. Rupert Gould linked, by the shortest possible route, the main sites at which hoofmarks had been reported, and calculated the minimum distance travelled as 40 miles. There is, as Gould recognised, no evidence that a continuous track actually existed; indeed there are a number of references to sudden stops and starts [see Document 25]. The marks could have been made by two or more animals, devils or indeed parties of gypsies.

13 - It would appear from this statement that thawing and refreezing of the mysterious tracks may well have taken place.

14 - Tracks sticking to paths may well have been left by humans; there seems no reason why animals should favour paths, and if they were hunting for food one would expect them to prefer gardens.

15 - Satan having been bound, to be unleashed only after the fulfilment of certain prophecies in the Book of Revelation, according to the New Testament. See also note 18.

16 - Probably a reference to the kookaburra.

17 - This is the first suggestion that not all the prints were made on the night of 8 February.

18 - Most authorities represent Satan with two cloven hoofs, not one. However, *Brewer's Dictionary of Phrase and Fable* is equivocal, observing both that the Devil is "represented with a cloven foot" and that "however he might disguise himself, he could never disguise his cloven feet."

19 - See Document 2.

20 - Identified by Theo Brown as William D'Urban of Newport House, Countess Wear, who was 19 years old at the time of the incident. See document 23.

21 - This, apparently one of the most mysterious aspects of the case, is not actually true. See the table 'Descriptions of the Devil's Hoofmarks'.

22 - Again, these three important and influential statements may be doubted. See notes 7 and 12 and, for deviations in the straight line of prints, Document 3.

23 - A horny but elastic material

in the centre of the sole of a horse's foot.

24 - Not printed in the *Illustrated London News*.

25 - This is a reference to a contemporary clash between High and Low Church Anglicans in the Devon area. The High Churchmen, or Puseyites, were nominally members of the Church of England, but alarmed their more puritan brethren by their suspiciously Popish sympathies [see note 32]. They followed Dr Edward Pusey, a tractarian (that is, a contributor to Cardinal Newman's influential *Oxford Tracts*).

26 - It seems worth pointing out that the prints also appeared in many Anglican parishes, including those of Exmouth, Clyst St George and Lympstone, where the local clergymen took a keen interest in the phenomenon.

27 - Possibly a reference to the church warden.

28 - i.e., 13 February. Here we have a definite statement that some tracks appeared several days *after* the first prints were found on the morning of 9 February. This appears to contradict the idea that the trail was laid in a single night by bands of gypsies, though of course it may be that the scale of the operation was such that the Romanies had to complete it in stages. It has also been suggested that the Topsham prints were a hoax. Probably, though, the appearance of hoofmarks on a number of nights suggests an animal or natural expanation for the mystery.

29 - Baron Alexander von Humbolt (1769-1859) was a leading German explorer and scientist. *Cosmos*, his most popular work, was a multi-volume treatise on natural history published between 1845 and 1862 - 'a profound and moving statement of our relationship with earth' (*Hutchinson Dictionary of Scientific Biography*).

A further reference to the Uniped(e) may be found in *Eirik's Saga* (Magnus Magnusson & Hermann Palsson, trans.: *The Vinland Sagas*, Penguin, Harmondsworth, 1965, pp.101-102). There, however, it is Thorfinn Karlsefni and his crew who encounter the Uniped, rather than Bjarni Herjolfsson ('Biom Heriolfson').

30 - It has not proved possible to identify this volume.

31 - Meaning obscure.

32 - A reference to the Puseyites' willingness to venerate saints as well as God - for example, by permitting the singing of the famous carol 'Good King Wenceslas' at Christmas. Woodbury was one of a number of Puseyite parishes in the district. See Document 22.

33 - Richard Owen (1804-1892), founder of the Natural History Museum and all-purpose Victorian scientific expert, was perhaps the leading naturalist of the time. Few non-scientists cared to take issue with him, though his reputation suffered in later years after he opposed Darwin's theory of evolution. See Nicholaas A. Rupke: *Richard Owen: Victorian Naturalist*, Yale University Press, 1994.

34 - Wooded.

35 - Having failed to interest the *ILN* in his letter, W.W. proceeded to publish his own pamphlet on the mystery. *The Swan With the Silver Collar* (Wells Journal Office, 1855) suggested that the marks had been made by a swan, wearing protective pads in the shape of hooves, that had crossed the channel from France. The Journal no longer has a copy of this pamphlet, though Rupert Gould possessed one [see document 39].

36 - The author of this letter was himself a clergyman: the Rev. G.M. Musgrave, vicar of Exmouth.

37 - It is a shame this observation is at second hand, since it is so obviously anomalous.

38 - The shooting of mundane animals alleged to have been behind mystery animal flaps is another commonplace of the literature. Fort, for example, observes sceptically that a 1905 case from the north of England, where a wolf was thought to be on the loose, ended with the shooting of a large dog. See *Complete Books*, pp.649-661.

39 - A leopard.

40 - While the otter theory neatly explains some of the more mysterious tracks left on the night in question, the *ILN*'s correspondent does not dwell on how an otter could walk through a haystack.

41 - Scottish: 'person among'.

42 - With authority.

43 - Measure for Measure, Act II Scene 4.

44 - A farm outbuilding with an open front.

45 - The influence that *The Times* enjoyed in mid-Victorian Britain is not always appreciated by modern readers. While it had both competitors and detractors, it stood far above the former, while the latters' criticisms meant little to most of its readers. Its articles were frequently taken up and reprinted by the provincial press, and it also enjoyed substantial prestige overseas. Thus, while the material it published on the Devil's Hoofmarks was largely a rehash of what had been said in the local papers, it had a substantially greater impact on the way in which the story was remembered than did the more detailed coverage of the *Illustrated London News* and the Devon press.

46 - It is hard to know how seriously to take this no-nonsense statement, but as it is a casual throwaway, and also unreferenced, we cannot really use it to dismiss the testimony of witnesses who claim such tracks *were* seen.

47 - This letter does not appear to have been among those published in the *ILN* of 3 March.

48 - Buckland, William (Dean of Westminster), *Geology and Mineralogy Considered with Reference to Natural Theology*, 2 vols., London, 1836.

49 - Reptiles, of course, are active mainly in warm sunlight - certainly not on bitterly cold February nights. However, Victorians commonly grouped amphibians and reptiles together under the latter name.

50 - In more recent times, Alfred Leutchser and Maurice Burton both put forward the suggestion that the tracks were left by field mice. See introductory essay.

SECONDARY SOURCE MATERIALS

Document 15

Notes & Queries.
7th Series volume viii, 28 Dec 1889 pp.508-509.

PHENOMENAL FOOTPRINTS IN THE SNOW, S. DEVON.

- Staying recently in S. Devon, I was asked what solution *N&Q* had supplied for a phenomenon which seems to have convulsed England in general, and S. Devon in particular, some five-and-thirty years ago. I remember nothing about it myself, but I am told that on occasion of a deep fall of snow somewhere in the years 1852-4 an extraordinary track, consisting of a clawed foot-mark of unclassifiable form, alternating at huge but regular intervals with (seemingly) the point of a crutch-stick [1], and vaulting over walls, hedges, rivers, even houses, and obstacles of every sort, appeared over a surface of 35 miles, all produced in one night; that the track was followed up by hounds and huntsmen, and crowds of country folk, till at last, in a wood (I think it was said over Dawlish), the hounds came back baying and terrified. This was the moment when one would think the real excitement would begin. Nevertheless no one seems to have had the courage to rush in where the dogs feared to tread, and the matter ended in a battle of conjecture on paper. The most general local impression seems to have been that it was the devil put his foot in it, though so widespread a belief in so useless and partial a manifestation of a personal devil seems incredible. Now what did *N&Q* contribute to the inquiry? I have looked in the general index under all the headings under which I can conjecture that the matter might have been classified - "Fantastic", "Phantom", "Phenomenal", "Mysterious", "Footprints", "Snow", "Devon", "Devil's Walk", "Diable boiteux", "Hooky Walker" - but all in vain. Can any contributer better versed in back numbers assist me?

R.H. Busk
16, Montagu Street, Portman Square

Document 16

Notes & Queries.
7th S. ix, 11 January 1890, p.18.

PHENOMENAL FOOTPRINTS IN SNOW, SOUTH DEVON.

- The beast was discovered to be a common badger, and the storm that the foot-prints had caused dropped to dead calm in a single day.

D.

[Many similar replies are acknowledged.]

Document 17

Notes & Queries.
7th S. ix, 25 Jan 1890 p.70.

PHENOMENAL FOOTPRINTS IN THE SNOW, S.DEVON.

- Your anonymous correspondent at the last reference falls into the common error of "playing dominoes" instead of giving a reply. The query I reported from my Devonshire friends was, "what *N&Q* had said on the subject at the time". D., instead of supplying a reply, sends a *rechauffe* [2] of an exploded theory.

Some one, I am told, repeated my query in the *Western Morning News* (published at Plymouth but circulating over the whole of S. Devon) of the 31st ult. [3] A large number of answers were elicited by this, some of which have been forwarded to me, as well as a number of private communications. From all these it appears that the exact date was February, 1855. Mr David Kemeysa-Tynte, Balnageith, Torquay, partly from childhood's memory and partly from a book called *Country Essays* [4], supplies an account very similar to my first report. Mr E. Spencer, dating from Tavistock, disposes thus of the badger theory:-

"For years I had a tracing of the footprints taken by my mother in her garden, Montpellier House, Exmouth. It represented half a dozen hoof-like marks, such as would be made by a small donkey, only they were those of a biped; moreover, after reaching the gate of the garden, which was of close wood, they continued in the road outside. Prof. Owen, on being consulted, assuming that they must have been made by a quadruped, replied that it must have been a badger, which places its hind foot exactly where the fore-foot had stood, and so left a trace like a biped. But, unluckily, he had not been told that the same tracks were found on the flat tops of some buildings, and on that of a church tower [another correspondent adds "hayricks"]."

Mr Spencer goes on to suggest ingeniously that the tracks might have been caused by herons driven from their usual haunts by strong frosts, "a slight thaw having obliterated the thin wedges of snow in each footstep, and given it the rounded, hoof-like form." He adds that he was led to this guess by seeing on a subsequent occasion some marks like a heron's track on a snowdrift over the Bransen Tor Brook. But I think it is difficult to imagine that the "slight thaw" - if there was one at all, and there is no contemporary evidence of the fact, but rather the contrary, as many speak of the snow remaining firm all the next day - could have so uniformly, over such a large tract of country as thirty or forty miles, transformed the appearance of a claw into that of a hoof.

Mr Charles Taylor, dating from Tavistock, is one who points this out. He has also taken the trouble to collect from the *Illustrated News* [5] of the moment various accounts, which exactly agree with that I sent you, supplying the further detail that the hoof impression measured 4 in. by 2 3/4 in., the distance between each tread being rather over 8 in., exactly the same in each parish, and that one wall the track passed over was 14 ft. in height. He goes on to quote that, besides the badger theory, the otter, bustard, and crane were all guesssed at. It was also adduced that two kangaroos had escaped about that time from the Sidmouth menagerie. Mr C.B. Mount, Norham Road, Oxford, also supplies the reference to the *Illustrated London News*. But all fail at some point or another.

Another correspondent writes:-

"I addressed communications to the British Museum, the Zoological Society, the keepers in the Regent's Park, and the universal reply was that they were utterly unable to form any conjecture on the subject." [6]

My friend the Rev. J.J. Rowe, Marychurch, writes: "The episode of the hounds, &c., I well and distinctly remember."

Christopher Foddard, Willow Bank, Paignton, writes:-

No allusion has yet been made to the mysterious footprints having extended into Dorsetshire. We were at Weymouth at the time, at Gordon Place, on the Green-hill. I remember a creepy feeling on seeing the hoofprints in the snow, which passed from Green-hill over the high wall of our garden ... I have a very distinct recollection; it was like the cloven hoof of a calf, one immediately in front of the other. I remember also the theory of their being caused by a badger ... But be it bird or beast ... why should these marks have simultaneously appeared over so wide an area, and never been observed before or since?

G.E. Garvey, 23 Walker Terrace, Plymouth, writes to similar effect, but apparently it was in Lincolnshire that he observed them.

R.H. Busk
16, Montagu Street, Portman Square.

Fig. 4 - Drop capital 'S' from *Punch*, vol. 28, No 29 (1855), illustrating a piece entitled 'A Wonder at Wolverhampton', which mentions in passing a ghost, a sea serpent and the Devil's Hoofmarks - the Devil here played by Punch himself. Could this be the origin of the 'crutch stick' marks associated with the prints in later lore? (See Document 15, Note 1.)

Document 18

Notes & Queries.
7th S. ix, 1 Mar 1890 p.173.

PHENOMENAL FOOTPRINTS IN THE SNOW

- My attention has been called to the discussion on the above subject. I do not know whether the matter has been threshed out to the satisfaction of your correspondents, so cannot say whether the following remarks will be of interest. At the time of this occurrence, Feb. 7, 1855, I was living in South Devon, and was seven years old. The impression made upon me was deep and lasting. The excitement and, among some classes, the consternation was intense. Devonshire was, and is, a superstitious county, and the ignorant unhesitatingly believed the footsteps to be those of his Satanic majesty. Many educated people, no really satisfactory explanation ever being forthcoming, retained the idea that there was something uncanny about the whole affair. My most vivid recollection of the matter is in connexion with the home of friends living at Exmouth. Here the footprints came up the front garden to within a few feet of the house, stopped abruptly, and began again in the garden at the back within a few feet of the building, just as if the animal, bird, or, adopting the popular idea, demon had made a gigantic leap. The only record I have of the affair consists of cuttings of the *Illustrated London News*, which give the accounts no doubt alluded to in your valuable paper. The issues of Feb. 24, March 3, 10 and 17, 1855, contain many most descriptive and entertaining letters, but the explanations and suggestions do not appear to me either satisfactory or conclusive.

W. Courthope Forman
35, Medora Road, Brixton Hill
[Innumerable replies on this subject are acknowledged.]

Document 19

Notes & Queries.
7th S. ix, 29 Mar 1890 p.253.

PHENOMENAL FOOTPRINTS IN THE SNOW.

- Mr F.B. Bingley, of Guildford, writes to the *Daily News* of March 7:-
    "Kangaroos were kept, or perhaps still are, by a gentleman at Sidmouth. One escaped when a slight fall of snow was on the ground. The footprints, being so peculiar and far apart, gave rise to a scare that the devil was loose."
    L.L.K.

Document 20

Devon & Cornwall Notes & Queries.
Vol.12 (1922-3) pp.197-8.

The Devil In Devonshire. - The following story in C.O. Burge's *Adventures of a Civil Engineer* (1909), p.72, dates, he thinks, from the forties of last century, but well within the range of his memory: "One cold winter's morning when Devonshire lay deep in snow, it was found, by prints left distinctly in it, that some two-legged creature, taking enormous strides, had travelled the county from sea to sea. Each point was distinctly that of a hoof, and one followed the other at distances apart of from twelve to fourteen feet. But for one fact the track might have been made by a man on an enormous pair of stilts suitably shaped at the foot; this fact was that the course taken by the gigantic being, which was straight, never deviated where houses, barns, or other large obstructions crossed its path, but apparently went right through them, the snow being entirely untouched all round them. The distance covered in one night rendered the stilt theory also untenable, and the mystery, which was much written about in the few newspapers of the time, has never been cleared up to this day."

Can any reader supply exact references to contemporary accounts, or give further details? It would be interesting to have the exact date and route of His Satanic Majesty's visit. I have a vague recollection of hearing about a similar mysterious visit in the seventies, when people were so terrified that they were afraid of venturing outside their doors after dark.

R. Pearse Chope.

Document 21

Devon & Cornwall Notes & Queries, Vol.12 (1922-) pp.265-7.

The Devil in Devonshire. - As a living witness to the footprints in the snow in 1855, I am writing my remembrance of them. I was a child myself, but my father, the Rev. Edward Fursdon, was the Vicar of Dawlish at the time, and, although there may have been other places where the footprints occurred, Dawlish was certainly the centre of interest, and where the footprints were most defined. It was late in the winter, either February or March, when the snow fell: the date could be ascertained from the *Illustrated London News*, of those months in 1855; where it was certainly reported and illustrated.

The footprints occurred in the night, and owing to my father being the Vicar he was immediately visited by curates, churchwardens, and parishioners to ask him his opinion of the footprints, which were all over Dawlish. They were in single file, in the shape of a small hoof, but contained in the hoof were the marks of claws. One track especially attracted attention, which went direct from the Vicarage to the Vestry door [7]; other tracks were found leading straight up to dead walls, and again found on the other side, many were found on the roofs of houses; and in all parts of Dawlish. All sorts of suppositions were raised as to the possibilities of its origin - escaped kangaroo or tiger from a travelling wild beast show, a donkey, and lastly, his Satanic Majesty - and from that supposition my father had letters from all parts of England inquiring for details.

I myself remember distinctly seeing the footprints, and my terror as a child of the unknown wild beast that might be lurking about, and the servants would not go out after dark to shut outer doors. The solution my father considered of this mystery was given to him by the tenant of the Aller Farm, Dawlish. My father was visiting him, and they spoke of the footprints; and he said he was quite sure they were the marks of cats. On the night they occurred he went out to tend his lambs between three and four. The house cat followed him, making the usual footprints in the snow. Whilst he was with the lambs, there was a slight thaw, and a shower of rain; and he saw the cat's footprints had been half-melted, and washed by the shower, and a frost coming on immediately, had frozen them into the shape of a small hoof, with still the impression of the cat's claws enclosed. [8]

I do not think there can be many eye-witnesses of the footprints left, and the information may be valuable to you.

Henrietta E. Fursdon.

The Devil In Devonshire. - An aged lady, now resident in my house, was living in North Devon at the time of the startling occurrence, and remembers it distinctly, and how alarmed people were in the Bideford and Torrington districts. Few were courageous enough to be abroad after dark. From a menagerie an animal had escaped. The terror-spreading creature was a kangaroo.

T. J. Joce.

The Devil In Devonshire. - ['J.S.A.' summarises the evidence given in the *Illustrated London News* of 17 and 24 Feb 1855. See Documents 7 and 11.]

Document 22

Report & Transactions of the Devonshire Association.
Vol.LXXXII (1950) pp.107-12.

Forty-Seventh Report on Folklore
By W.F. Jackson Knight, Recorder

No new observations concerning folk-lore have been submitted during the period covered by this Report. Certain members of the Association have, however, reported the outstanding questions of the mysterious occurrences in Devonshire during 1855 and 1921 [9]. Some account of them should clearly be presented here, and sooner rather than later. Therefore, with the approval of the General Editor, Miss Theo Brown was asked to compile an account, as far as possible up-to-date. This Report is followed by what she has written. The Report itself ends here.

THE GREAT DEVON MYSTERY OF 1855 or "THE DEVIL IN DEVON"

No account of this extraordinary affair has hitherto appeared in the *Transactions of the Devonshire Association*, although the centenary of the event will be upon us in another five years. The best known account was given in the *Illustrated London News* of 24th February,

1855, p.187, as follows:-

[See document 7]

It is a pity that the "copy of the foot" was not reproduced; the accompanying wood-engraving showed only the trail, as a series of donkey's hoof-marks.

The account should be compared with the contemporary Devon journals; for instance, that given in Woolmer's Plymouth & Devon Gazette of 17th February, 1855, p.5 [10]. This states that the night of 8th February was marked by a heavy fall of snow (as opposed to the thin layer described in the other notice), and this was followed by rain, boisterous wind from the east, and, in the morning, frost. These sound like the conditions which produce an ammil frost, such as we experienced in February 1947. All the weather reports of early 1855 indicate an exceptionally severe winter: the Morning Chronicle of 22nd February mentions skating on the Serpentine and ice on the Thames thick enough to walk across. The Devon papers paint a gruesome picture of the privations of the poor at this time, hundreds out of work in Torquay alone, bakers unable to get through to Lustleigh, benighted folk frozen to death; and editorials make eloquent appeals to the rich to subscribe generously to the many soup-kitchens and coal-funds. The Saturday before the trail was laid, the road between Exmouth and Exeter was frozen over and the regular coach service had to be suspended (Western Times, 10th February). A few days later the Teign was frozen over in several places (Western Times, 17th February), and on the 16th the sea-wall at Teignmouth collapsed taking with it a section of the railway.

In Woolmer's Exeter & Plymouth Gazette, 24th February, it was stated that the River Exe had been frozen over for more than a fortnight, and was now safe for skating from the Exe Bridge to the Salmon Pool. In the issue of the 17th, it is stated that on the Tuesday last (five days after the "mystery") the ice was so thick at St Thomas's, that, besides skating, gas was laid on from the main street, and a gas stove, placed on the ice, cooked a huge dinner! Did the mysterious creature swim or walk across the Exe? Incidentally, at no point till it reaches the coast is the Exe two miles across,

as stated by the Illustrated London News correspondent. Woolmer's Gazette adds to the list of places visited: Teignmouth, Starcross, Topsham and Littleham; one is inclined to believe that the creature did not swim the estuary at all, but may just have walked across the river at some point above Topsham.

Now, as to "South Devon's" point about the footsteps being in a single line which has given rise to so much excitement, and which has been quoted again and again, I would like to say that this is the only contemporary account I have met with that makes any such claim. The Western Times of the 24th gives the headline: "THE TWO-LEGGED WONDER"; Woolmer's Gazette states that the steps are generally 8" in advance of each other, but sometimes 12" or 14", and are "alternate of each other like the steps of a man and would be included between two parallel lines six inches apart." The marks look like donkey's shoes, but they varied in thickness from 1½" to 2½" across. They sometimes looked cleft, but were usually "continuous and perfect". In the centre of the shoe the snow remained intact, and only the outer edge was clearly marked. A Dawlish correspondent corroborates that the mark was rumoured to be cloven. On the Friday, people armed themselves with bludgeons and guns to try and follow up the tracks. "In no place could be traced more than two impressions which were about sixteen inches apart." There was hardly a garden in Lympstone where the footprints were not to be seen, even on top of houses, narrow walls, etc.; they appeared often to approach doorways and then to retreat. They went right through the middle of Dawlish. I have not so far been able to discover any account of the trail further west to Totnes. My father used to speak of it - he was born only 10 years after the event, and the track had passed near our place as it proceeded from Torquay, through Barton and Watcombe towards Dawlish.

Explanations suggested in 1855 ranged from: "The poor are full of superstitions, and consider it little short of a visit from old Satan or some of his imps," to hints given from the Lympstone pulpit by Rev. G.M. Musgrave to Exmouth, who considered the marks were made by a kangaroo!

Since that period, the mystery has offered

much scope to many kinds of investigators. The zoological theories varied unconvincingly from a bird carrying a donkey's shoe to Prof. Owen's hind leg of a badger. Commander Gould notes the proximity of the sea; as also does Elliott O'Donnell who included the story in his *Strange Sea Mysteries*, 1926, on the grounds that the monster started from Totnes, the highest navigable point of the River Dart, and followed the coast, roughly to Exmouth, where presumably it disappeared into the sea. The late Mr Harry Price in *Poltergeist Over England* mentions this phenomenon among the many inexplicable happenings which might be due to poltergeist activity.

A possible parallel case has occurred in Devon, which is mentioned in the *Transactions of the Devonshire Association* for 1876 (Vol. VIII, p.659). R.J. King quoted a story from Kemble's *Saxons*, vol. i, p.351 [11], about the Dewerstone on Dartmoor. Here, after a heavy fall of snow, were found the print of a naked human foot *and* the print of a cloven hoof, both ascending towards the highest point...

In 1840 little horse-shoe tracks were found in the snow of uninhabited Kerguelen Island in the Antarctic (Lt.Comr. R.T. Gould, *Oddities* pp.20-1) [12]. Will each of these occurrences be eventually attributed to "natural causes" with the advance of scientific knowledge? Or should they all be studied together as a group? If so, the "Abominable Snowman" of the Himalayas is the best-known modern example and it should be carefully investigated. The "Snowman" may be bears or giant yogis, as hinted by various correspondents in *The Daily Telegraph*, January to February, 1950. Mr Ward Price, writing from Tibet in the *Daily Mail* of Tuesday, 14th March, 1950, said that his muleteers "declared they had seen them quite near the rest-house where I passed a night. Much bigger than ordinary men, they are said to have had their heads and feet turned backwards."

As regards our own case, *The Western Times* raises three interesting points which should be carefully borne in mind. First, in the issue of 17th February, 1855, regarding the Exmouth tracks: "It is said that a similar occurrence took place here about five years ago."

Secondly, on the 24th, writing of the tracks

at Topsham: "Its first appearance here was on the eve of St Valentine." This is the only indication so far that the track was not made overnight on the 8th. Was it perhaps started on the 8th and continued by purely human agents as the idea spread?

Thirdly, in the same issue one reads of the footprints: "Some people say it is sent as a warning to the Puseyites - hence it is that the 'phenomenon' has visited the Puseyite parishes of Woodbury, Topsham, and Littleham-cum-Exmouth. In this place it has traversed the churchyard - and even to the very door of the vestibule. The 'sombre perpetual' has not, it is said, exhibited a pleasant countenance since the occurrence." And in another place we find the headline, "SATAN IN THE DIOCESE OF HENRY EXETER". [13]

This sounds too absurd. But *Trewman's Exeter Flying Post*, which has no space for mysteries of any kind, devotes most of its correspondence columns from 11th January onwards to the enormities of the dreadful incumbent of Woodbury. His crowning profanity appears to have been the introduction at Christmas of a new book of carols which expressed most unseemly sentiments: the doings of a certain King Wenceslas were extolled, one carol stated that ox and ass bowed down at the Nativity of Our Lord, while some carols even inclued a line or two of Latin! It is hard to understand, after all these years, the bitterness of these letters.

However, it does seem to be a line worth following up, when studying the Devon Mystery, though if the trail was started by anti-Puseyite practical jokers, we need not expect, necessarily, to find this motive in every parish concerned. Incidentally, there was another fracas in full swing at St Marychurch. Church funds were low, and the vicar and his wardens had concocted a deed authorising themselves to levy a church rate of 2½d in the pound! (*Western Times*, 17th February.)

At this point the discussion must be left for the time being. Further information may still be obtainable from family papers, diaries, contemporary letters, etc., and would be most welcome. Meanwhile, we heartily thank Mr L.C.W. Bonacina, F.R.Met.S., whose enquiries reopened this problem.

Document 23

Report & Transactions of the Devonshire Association.
Vol. LXXXIV (1952) pp.163-171

A Further Note on the 'Great Devon Mystery'
By Theo Brown

I

Following the previous note (*Transactions*, vol.lxxxii (1950) pp.107-12), more research has been undertaken, and some information has come to light, which, though it does not "solve" the mystery, does introduce some evidence hitherto unpublished which qualifies the previous picture.

First, as regards the physical limitations on the "monster" which perpetrated the long trail, over roof-tops, etc.: a letter in *The Illustrated London News* of 3rd March, 1855 [14], says that pad-marks were visible under bushes with branches 8" or 9" from the ground, at Topsham, and at a nearby village the trail passed *through* a 6" drain pipe.

Then, a comment on the *length* of the trail, from Totnes to Exmouth, which was reported in the account quoted in the previous note from *ILN* 24th February, 1855. I can still find no supporting evidence that the track started so far west, except that one letter, *ILN* 3rd March, says "...Dawlish, Newton, etc.", and the fact that the man who wrote the first statement is known to have been an exceptionally careful observer. *The Torquay Directory* of 21st February, 1855, uses an account common to *Woolmer's Exeter & Plymouth Gazette*, 17th February, *The Times*, 16th February, and the *News of the World*, 25th February; it adds nothing to associate the tracks with Torbay or with Totnes. I have made a number of fruitless enquiries; South Devon is an expanding area in which traditions are hard to trace. Most contemporary accounts begin the trail "from the cutting at Dawlish", etc., or from Teignmouth.

At Teignmouth, there is a tradition that the footprints came *across* the beach, through the town, past the present gas works, and on up the lane called The Lea, towards Bishopsteignton. I was told this by an old fisherman, Mr W Hook. I am again indebted to the Harbour Master, to Mr C.J.R. Gilpin, Mr E.G.C. Griffiths and to Miss R.I. Thomas of *The Mid-Devon Advertiser* who drew my attention to the tradition, also to the Editor of that periodical who kindly published a letter for me on the subject.

Other people who have made enquiries for me are: Mr D. Fletcher of the Totnes Antiquarian Society, Mr Edward F. Burt of the Torquay Borough Library, Mr A.G. Madan of the Torquay Museum, and Mr C.E. Hicks of the Torbay Branch. I am very grateful to them all, and it is possible that we may yet unearth something positive.

II

Immediately after the first note was published, a member, Maj. A.H. Gibbs of Pytte, Clyst St George, informed me that he held a large quantity of letters and drawings in the parish box of his church, all collected by the Rev. H.T. Ellacombe, who was Rector of Clyst St George from 1850-1886, and is well known as the author of *Church Bells of Devon*. Maj. Gibbs has very kindly allowed me to make extracts and to quote from these documents.

The letters are mainly addressed to Mr Ellacombe from various friends and authorities whom he had consulted. These include: the Rev. G.M. Musgrave of Withecombe Raleigh, W.I. Brodrip and Prof. (later Sir Richard) Owen, the well-known naturalists, and Dr I.A. Ogle of Oxford. There are also traces of drawings, made on the spot (I conclude), a MS poem of great length by Musgrave and a still longer one by him, in print: "Valentine's Day, the Tale of a Griffin", - which poor creature had started out from Dawlish, got lost around Topsham (note the statement in *The Western Times*, quoted in my previous paper [15], that the tracks did not appear at Topsham till St Valentine's Eve). There are also some more recent letters and cuttings.

The most interesting item, however, is the rough copy of a letter which Ellacombe sent to *The Illustrated London News* with the request that it should not be published. The copy was evidently made in haste and the writing, in places, is extremely difficult to read. He states that he saw the marks at Clyst St George "tho' not till two or three days after they were first seen," and his letter, dated 13th March, 1855, continues:-

"There is no doubt as to the facts - that thousands of these marks were seen on the snow on the morning of the 9th ult. extending over many miles on either side of the Estuaries of the Exe & the Clyst - even to the suburbs of the City. All agree in form - *varying some little in size* - but the general appearance was the same - that of a Donkey's Shoe - such is the answer given me by my parishioners & other neighbours who saw them on that morning - they seemed - to use an expression of a statement which appeared in the *Illustrated News* [sic] Feb.26 - 'as if the snow had been branded with a hot iron' - or the form of such a shoe had been cut out with a knife - to the ground - which was everywhere visible, tho' the snow in the middle part did not appear to be touched! - the depth was about 3/4 of an inch - it fell at midnight - when there was a sleet & a *thaw,* and after that a *freeze* **[16]** - the night was not dark, the marks, as of one creature were on my own premises - across a Lawn round the house to a Pump Shed - these were visible three days afterwards. My Dog barked that night and so did the dogs of my neighbours where marks were seen. There is scarcely a field or an orchard or Garden where they were not - all in a single line - under hedges - in one field near me; a turning round and doubling appeared - (two neighbours who followed the tracks thro' the same field in the snow [? hand writing almost illegible here] met with Excrement (and there the tracks were spread [?]... doubled: but afterwards, single.

"The same was observed more or less in all the adjoining parishes.

"At Exmouth (distant 5 miles) I have been informed by those who saw them there were marks in the middle of a field, insulated - without any apparent approach or retreat - and all in one direction - & so they were in many gardens closed with high walls - in one the marks appeared under a wall to the end of a garden - & then turned round & returned *half the length.* At a house at Marley near Exmouth, marks were seen on the Cill of a window two stories high. From all these and much more information which I have gathered from credible eye witnesses, one would suppose that some winged creatures alighted from above - traversed a certain space - & then

Fig.5 - The Rev. H.T. Ellacombe (1790-1885). From Theo Brown, *Devon Ghosts* (Document 25).

soared on high & away - it is very well known that many flocks of wild Fowl visit these Estuaries during the severe weather - "

He concludes by saying that perhaps the tracks may, after all, be those of a two-footed entity hopping, and that the donkey's shoe appearance is due to atmospheric conditions. He adds a drawing of the mark showing what some observers call claws. A footnote says: "A Note on the Excrementa. Four oblong lobes of a Whitish Colour - the size and shape of a large grape." Yet another addendum remarks that he had obtained samples which he had forwarded to Prof. Owen, with what result I do not know. Neither of Owen's letters mention them.

Another place visited at Clyst St George was Pytte, where Maj. Gibbs lives. In 1855 a Mr Doveton lived there, and Mr Ellacombe said that the trail led up to a garden door, which was closed, then appeared the other side of it and ran all round the garden. To do this, Maj. Gibbs tells me, it must have hopped an eight-foot wall!

A letter from the Rev. George Musgrave (dated 21st February) states that the prints were made by a crane which was shot at Otterton, thereby recanting his previous opinion of a kangaroo, which escaped from Sidmouth and was shot near Teignmouth. He adds: "The sages of Lympstone pronounced the *vestigia utiorsum* [17] to be decidedly Satanic: and an Exmouth old woman has taken occasion to remind us that Satan was to be unchained for a thousand years."

A further letter from him, dated the 26th February, states that "young D'Urban" wrote the article in the *Illustrated London News* but that his drawing of the trail is not quite accurate, and gives drawings of six prints. However, I give copies of all the known tracings. The difference between the various marks is so great that I still believe the cause to be multiple - in which case Mr d'Urban's drawings stand and we have no reason to doubt their accuracy.

There is also the MS copy of a long poem by Musgrave - thirteen verses of it, each containing eight lines, to the effect that people tended to blame each other's animals for the marks: a neighbouring parson had a dog's paw-marks all over his roof and accused the author's Newfoundland, now dead these seventeen years; other suspect agents include: a grandmother's pattens [18], a donkey, a kangaroo, a badger, an otter, a duck, cat and gull. The route is said to run "from the cutting at Dawlish to Littleham Cove", crossing the sand at Warren.

III

The "young D'Urban", mentioned by Musgrave, was the grandson of the founder of Durban. He lived to the age of 96 and left a daughter, Mrs R. Coates, now living at Bronte House, Lympstone. She writes of the 1855 visitation (letter dated 27th September, 1951):-

"My father was 19 and my mother 16. My father lived at Newport House, Countess Wear, and my mother at Winslade, Clyst St Mary. The marks were all along the high garden wall and over the roof at Winslade; both my father and my mother saw them and often talked to me about them. As you know, the marks were all over Haldon and I have been told they came down to the water's edge opposite Lympstone and appeared again this side."

IV

From Professor Owen's two letters to Mr Ellacombe, it is evident that he had been sent two drawings of the track as it appeared at Luscombe and Clyst St George. Figure [6b] almost certainly depicts *one* of these. He was dubious as to the accuracy of the drawings, but, assuming that they were correct, he ruled out the theory of otter or bird and decided, rather dogmatically, in favour of a badger, saying that badgers roamed far in snow conditions, and could, moreover, *climb*. Mr Brodrip seems to have agreed with this.

The drawings of the track, by Ellacombe, do resemble the shoe-marks of a donkey, and it is quite obvious that the supposed "claw marks" are simply snowed up "feathers" at the rear of the foot, familiar to all hunting people. And therefore, where "claws" were seen, the track must have been read backward! The donkey does place its feet almost in

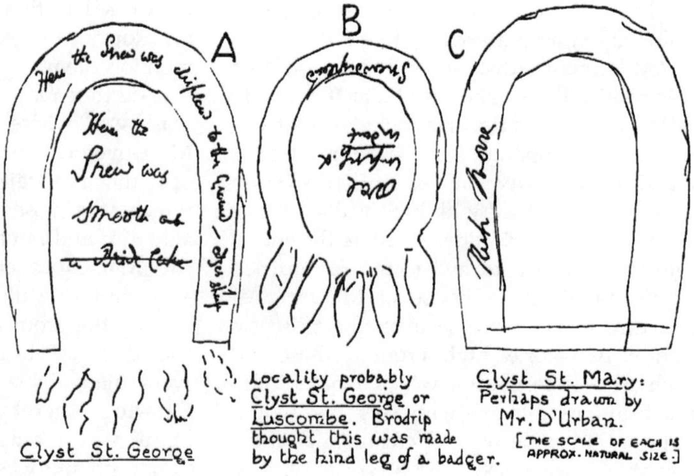

Fig. 6 - Facsimilies of drawings from among the Ellacombe Papers. From Theo Brown, 'A Further Note on the Great Devon Mystery' (Document 23).

Clyst St. George

Locality probably Clyst St. George or Luscombe. Brodrip thought this was made by the hind leg of a badger.

Clyst St. Mary: Perhaps drawn by Mr. D'Urban. [THE SCALE OF EACH IS APPROX. NATURAL SIZE.]

a straight line as in Mr D'Urban's drawing in the *Illustrated London News* of 24th February, 1855. The marks depicted by Mr Musgrave, from Exmouth, look more like pony shoes which have broken in half - it even seems possible to identify the feet in the six examples shown. Another explanation for the broken shoes has been suggested by Mr Irish, the well-known Sidford blacksmith; when I showed him the Musgrave drawings, he said they looked much like old oxen "cues", which were of course made in two pieces to fit the cloven hoof. But only the hind feet were shod.

Of course, neither oxen nor donkeys could hop over roof-tops or crawl through a 6" drain; but they may have accounted for some of the tracks.

I have consulted Mr H.G. Hurrell on the matter. He says that the badger does make a straight track, but the spoor is quite different and shows two claws, and although thawing might enlarge the marks even to the size of a man's boot (as it sometimes does) the characteristics would be constant. The description of the excrement is nothing like that of a badger or a bird of any kind, and of course no bird makes a mark anything like a donkey's shoe. However, as he points out, the sudden appearance of the track in the middle of a field can only point to a bird, and,

similarly, the ability to leap walls, etc. He makes three interesting points:-

"(1) In the isolated field they were found in the middle ... and they were all facing the same way; against the wind.

"(2) The excrement may well have been the *castings* or undigested pellets of birds. They are about grape size and are sometimes whitish in many good-sized birds.

"(3) The outlines of the tracks are so irregular that it looks as if the feet had been frozen up."

With these points Mr R.G. Adams, the well-known ornithologist who lives at Lympstone, concurs. The shape of the prints baffles the naturalists, who say that if it is due to the ice freezing on birds' feet, then it may happen again! Mr L.C.W. Bonacina remarks that in a "glazed frost" birds stick to snow and that if anything like this happened in February 1855, it is curious that no-one seems to have mentioned the fact; Ellacombe expressly mentioned the flocks of birds taking refuge in the estuaries but did not seem to have noticed anything peculiar about their feet.

V

Finally, a brief note on parallel occurrences. Mr R. Waterfield has noticed a reference to Borley Rectory in *Unbidden Guests*, by Wm. O.

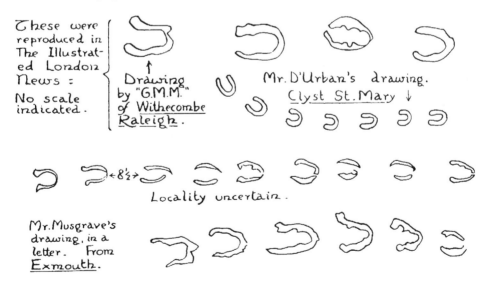

Fig.7 - Drawings from the *Illustrated London News* (above), compared with those from the Ellacombe Papers (below). From Theo Brown, 'A Further Note on the Great Devon Mystery' (Document 23).

Stevens (1949), p.79, who says that Capt. W.H. Gregson observed "...a track of blurred, formless, but distinct footprints in new-fallen snow that trailed along the garden and ended abruptly. They could not have been made by human being [sic] or by any other known form of life, and they stopped in a way that defied explanation."

Montague Summers, in *The Vampire in Europe* (1929), mentions an odd case in his introduction. In June, 1918, a lady took a small house "at Penlee, South Devon, not far from Dartmouth" (there is no Penlee that I know of in South Devon; either Penlee is not the name, or Cornwall must be intended). The house seems to have inspired awful nightmares, and one morning, the mark of a single cloven hoof was found in the middle of the parquet flooring; there being no means of entrance for anything so large.

Two interesting cases should be quoted from the correspondence which followed the Great Devon Mystery, in *ILN* of 10th and 17th March, 1855 [19]. Near the Galician border of Russian Poland there is a hill, called Piashowar gora, which is said to mean Sandhill. Every year, footprints similar to those in Devon are found, running round the side of the hill. And even where there is no snow, the marks are seen on the sand. It is hardly necessary to add that the cause was locally reputed to be a supernatural one!

Labrador is the scene of yet another phenomenon. When Biorn Heriolfson, from Iceland, discovered Labrador in AD 1001, he is supposed to have found there a bird with only one foot which was shaped like a hoof, slightly divided. He named this strange object a "Uniped". [20]

VI

Besides these, other cases of strange footprints crop up in various parts of the world from time to time. Hence, it has seemed worth while to study carefully the example on our own doorstep. There is so far no one explanation that can fully fit all the known facts, but two new points emerge from the Ellacombe collection of papers and drawings:-

(i) The trail is now *known* not to have been continuous, since it appeared suddenly in the middle of fields around Exmouth.

(ii) The print varied considerably in size and shape, judging by the tracings of drawings made by contemporary observers living on the east side of the Exe (though Y may possibly have been collected at Luscombe).

Thus it is fairly evident that the cause was a multiple one. If one bird with frozen feet could have been responsible, then probably a number were involved, and these might account for the straggling marks like those shown from Exmouth, and those on roof-tops, etc., but I do not believe that any bird, however strangely frozen up, could possibly have produced all the Clyst marks, so exactly resembling those of a donkey. I still feel pretty confident that some of the tracks may have been "assisted" by humans with the aid of a hot donkey's shoe or even a man's heel-iron (i.e., a "stook" shaped like a small horseshoe), after the surface of the snow was frozen hard so that it would not show ordinary footprints. This, if true, demonstrates the well-known tendency to improve on a story, aided by wishful thinking by human agency.

The motives might range from practical jokes to fanatic zeal associating burning hoofmarks with the "Puseyite parishes"!

Document 24

Report and Transactions of the Devonshire Association.
Vol. LXXXVI (1954) pp.295-6.

Fifty-First Report on Folklore
by Theo Brown, Recorder

THE GREAT DEVON MYSTERY
I am indebted to Captain E.C. Brent, RN, DSO, and to Mrs Meredith Williams for some further useful references to the Mystery. These references are to be found in a short correspondence in *Notes & Queries*, 7th Series, Vols. VIII and IX, December 1889, pp.508-9, to January 1890, pp.18 and 70 [21]. One tradition in South Devon described the track as a "clawed foot mark of unclassifiable form, alternating at huge but regular intervals with (seemingly) the point of a crutch stick" and adds "that the track was followed up by hounds and huntsmen, and crowds of countryfolk, till at last, in a wood (I think it was said over Dawlish), the hounds came back baying and terrified." Montpelier House,

Exmouth, is added to the list of private gardens visited by the "monster" who appears to have left donkey-like prints inside and outside the closed gate. A cloven hoof appeared at the same time at Weymouth in Dorset, and a further memory extends the path of the track across England to Lincolnshire, but the year cited is circa 1853. So it may refer to a different occasion.

An interesting theory, which hands the problem to the meteorolgists, is given in an article by J Allan Rennie in *Chamber's Journal*, December 1953, p.745. [22]

Mr Tom Pym has given me a folk memory of the visitation. He says that the Devil walked from the Teign Valley, down over Haldon into Powderham, past the church. He then got over the river Exe into Lympstone, and came up the main road from Exmouth to Topsham. He came up the hill from Lympstone. He (or rather, I suppose, his footprints) was seen by the pub on Bridgehill, "and there was the last track of 'un."

Document 25

Extract from *Devon Ghosts*, by Theo Brown (Norwich, 1982) pp.47-53.

The Great Devon Mystery

The winter of 1854-5 was a hard one; judging by the contemporary newspapers the 'Crimean winter' was decimating our troops far from home who already had enough to endure from wounds, disease and shortages of all kinds due to lack of organisation. Here at home weather conditions caused widespread unemployment and hunger; horse-drawn supplies could not get through to the villages and old folk were known to drop dead in the streets. In the West Country soup-kitchens and other hastily organised charities offered scanty palliatives. The better-off sat by their firesides and composed furious letters to the press inveighing against the goings-on of the Puseyites who were infiltrating the Church of England, dressing their choirs in surplices and using J. M. Neale's 'Popish' book of carols. All too soon their fears would appear justified, with headlines in the local press about the Devil visiting Devon in person in order to embarrass the Bishop of Exeter.

The night preceding 8 February there was a light fall of snow, followed by what in these parts we call an 'ammel frost' - i.e. a slight thaw and a very sharp frost which means that the snow becomes ice, particularly treacherous if the layer of snow is shallow as this was. The next morning when the honest Devonians looked out of their houses they were amazed to find a seemingly endless track of what looked like donkey's hoofmarks, zig-zagging across gardens and fields.

Some of the more curious followed the tracks a little way. Apparently every mark was exactly the same, and they proceeded in a dead straight line keeping the exact distance of 8½ inches apart. What was even odder was that no obstacle made the slightest difference. The creature (whatever it was) on coming to walls simply continued the other side as though it had walked straight through. A shed would be entered at the back wall and the footsteps emerge again the other side. Houses were walked over - you could see the marks going over the roof-tops. Low bushes were walked under, and a six-inch drain pipe passed *through*.

People quickly compared notes and journalists started to try and collate the reports and rumours. The first of these was a young man, called D'Urban, aged 19, who was later to become the first Curator of the Royal Albert Memorial Museum at Exeter. He listed the places where the track was observed, starting at Totnes and travelling eastwards. They included reports from Torquay, Dawlish, Luscombe and places the other side of the Exe estuary: Woodbury, Lympstone, and Exmouth. This account was published in *The Illustrated London News* of 24 February. *Woolmer's Exeter & Plymouth Gazette*, however, had reports in their 17 February issue, naming Teignmouth, Starcross, Topsham and Littleham as well, but not mentioning Totnes. How the tracks crossed the Exe is not discussed, but as the river was thickly frozen, no doubt that presented no difficulty. The previous Sunday the Vicar of Exmouth, the Reverend George M. Musgrave, had used the occasion to warn his flock that Satan is ever ready to cross our path, though in his opinion these particular footprints were not made by the Devil but by an escaped kangaroo. However, it does not look as though many heeded his cautious words, for the paper remarks: 'The poor are full of superstition, and consider it little short of a visit from old Satan or some of his imps.' An editorial comment bewails the 'vast amount of ignorance and superstition which still lingers in the rural districts of the county', remarking that in his town some of the prints were said to be cloven, and a Dawlish correspondent wrote:

'So great was the excitement produced by the reports which got abroad that a party of tradesmen and others armed themselves with guns and bludgeons, and spent the greater part of the day in tracing the footprints. From the church-yard they proceeded to the grounds of Luscombe and Dawlish-water, and thence to Oaklands. At length, after a long and weary search, they returned as wise as they set out.'

A generation later, a Londoner who was visiting South Devon in 1855 added: '...The track was followed up by hounds and huntsmen, and crowds of country folk, till at last, in a wood (I think it was said over Dawlish), the hounds came back baying and terrified.' [23] Some people even reported that the footprints they investigated showed clear evidence of claws, thus increasing the horror of the incident.

An editorial comment in the *Western Times* (24 February), discussing the 'Two-Legged Wonder', the 'Satanic Hoof' at Topsham and Exmouth, commented: '...and some people say it is sent as a warning to the Puseyites, hence it is that the "phenomenon" has visited the Puseyite parishes of Woodbury, Topsham, and Littleham-cum-Exmouth. In this very place it has traversed the churchyard - and even to the very door of the vestibule. The "sombre perpetual" has not, it is said, exhibited a pleasant countenance since the occurrence.' [24]

This account, appearing beneath the famous headline 'Satan in the Diocese of Henry Exeter', says that the footmarks were first seen on St Valentine's Day, but I think that the tracks were not all laid on one night but, first appearing on the night of 8 February, were found over a period of some days or even weeks.

Of course at that time - and ever since - people have discussed this mystery, and all the great naturalists have been consulted. However, it can safely be said that no one

has ever propounded a solution that covers all the points. There is a vast amount of paper in journals and letters that one can consult; above all if one follows the track all the way from Exmouth to Torquay one can still find family memories, oral traditions of the event, but little solid evidence. Every kind of animal from rats to a kangaroo has been proposed. A Mr Fish [25] at Sidmouth kept a wallaby at Knowle, Sidmouth, and this having escaped was thought by some to be the answer; Professor Owen offered a badger, but neither of these could have jumped a fourteen-foot wall or squeezed through a six-inch drain pipe, let alone have left clear marks on the sill of a second-story window!

There is little evidence that the tracks started further west than Teignmouth, though an item in my grandfather's scrapbook makes one wonder. The Barton Hall estate used to extend to the coast at Watcombe till about 1848 when this portion was sold to Isambard Kingdom Brunel in order to build his great house. The quotation goes: 'On a winter's morning the men on the estates were startled at the discovery of strange footprints in the snow; the "cloven foot" was the general remark along the countryside.' My father, who often told us the old story, believed that the creature had crossed the Dart at some point and started as far west as Bolt Head. In any case the mysterious creature that hopped on one leg the best part of a hundred miles in one night was the basis for a favourite yarn.

Here opinions differed sharply. Had it one leg or two? If two they were not directly in front of each other. In fact the first point I spotted was that no one at that time and in those weather conditions could follow the tracks far enough to be certain they were continuous. Then the churchwarden of Clyst St George, the late Major A. H. Gibbs, who lived at Pytte, his family home, contacted me and most generously allowed me to consult a dossier on the mystery which was kept in the parish chest. This had been meticulously compiled by the famous church bell expert, the Reverend H.T. Ellacombe, who had been the vicar in 1855. He made careful drawings of the tracks and had found that the marks were *not* continuous, but appeared sporadically, e.g. suddenly in the middle of a field, with flurry surrounding them, as though made by a large ice-laden bird struggling to take off. It was noticed in the Exe estuary that many of the birds seeking water were liable to become frozen into the water, as has happened in some more recent frosts this century. So birds with ice on their feet seem part of the solution, but not all.

The detailed drawings of the hoof-marks were most revealing. They varied greatly; from some sectors came hoof-marks plainly made by a pony-shoe, again some were broken and vaguely looked cloven. Some were certainly made by a stray donkey (donkeys are the only animals that plant their feet in an almost perfect single line). Some showed iced-up 'feathers' at the back, forming the supposed 'claws' that had excited a lot of people - though this meant the trail had been read backwards.

However, though we can reconstruct much of the mystery (and the marks at Woodbury were obviously manufactured by practical jokers with a hot shoe, since they were said at the time to look like this, the shoe pressed cleanly down to the ground as if made by a hot iron), yet no one explanation will cover all the reported factors.

Other mysterious tracks are reported from all over the world, and England is full of its share. About the time of our 'visitation' it was said that another track was laid from Dorset right across England into Lincolnshire; attempts have been made to link up the two, but not convincingly. Furthermore, a Dartmoor man has told me that there is a tradition of another track coming down from North Devon across Dartmoor to the southern side.

In 1955, I was talking to a group at Ipplepen and mentioned our famous mystery, and they at once told me there had been footprints seen that February at a house in the village. So I looked in. It is a very old house, said to have been a meeting house for Orange supporters. It is L-shaped and thatched. One day in February, the lady of the house saw it was snowing very heavily; she was a little anxious, as the roof timbers were none too strong, so she went out to see how thick the snow was lying. It was about four inches thick, and across the roof appeared a steady single track exactly like that made by a woman's shoe, going up to the ridge and over. She went indoors, not wishing to get wet, and to her astonishment found her two dogs, a Golden Labrador and Staffordshire Boxer, were looking frightened and refusing to enter the kitchen. After two hours the dogs relaxed and all was peace. Two other people saw the footprints. A hundred years, almost to the day...

Finally, one last mystery. After I had written two papers for the Devonshire Association, and quoted the careful reports of the Reverend H.T. Ellacombe, I was told that the dear old chap had been seen in the vicarage drive. I asked, rather sceptically, how in the world he could be recognised a hundred years later and was assured that the percipient had his portrait and knew just what he looked like! I have not heard that he has been seen around since.

Document 26

Daily Mirror.
   17 Jan 1983

OLD CODGERS [Letter column]

R.C. Hope, Avenue Mansions, Blackheath Grove, London SE23, writes:

The other day you re-published the old story of the "Devil's Hoofprints" - the single line of hoofprints which appeared in the snow in South Devon in 1855 - and commented that it is one of your favourite mysteries.

But there is no mystery. It never happened. It was merely a story in a newspaper, that is, a pack of lies. Standards of journalistic integrity were not as high then as they are, I hasten to add, now.

Who could possibly have followed such a trail in the snow over a hundred miles? It would have been obliterated within three hours by traffic of people and animals.

Oh, certainly there was a single line of prints - on the front lawn of a town-bred parson.

A naturalist identified one of the prints as that of the hind foot of a badger - and that is what it was. Other "reports" from other townies in the circulation area of the paper were probably of other animals.

The explanation is that most animals when walking on a yielding surface such as snow instinctively place each foot in line with their nose, carefully testing each step.

They then place the rear paw in the print of the opposite forepaw as it is raised. It is beautiful to watch.

I feel sure the naturalist who identified the print would have mentioned this fact, but, of course, it didn't get into the paper.

Well, it's got into this one now, friend - thanks for spoiling a good yarn!

Document 27

Daily Mirror.
2 February 1983

Graham (full name and address supplied) writes from Slough, Berks:

Allow me to offer an explanation of the single trail of hoofprints which mysteriously appeared in the snow one February night in 1855. The answer to the mystery can be found in the lore of the true Romany gypsy.

For many reasons the Romanies do not like to be associated with those we know as Didikais or Pikies and at that time, 1855, the latter had usurped an area of Somerset formerly used only by Romanies. Didikais are highly superstitious, part of their belief being that at certain times the Devil walks abroad.

It was this belief that the Romanies used to frighten off the Didikais. That trail of hoofprints indicated that something had been "out and about" the previous night.

Was it the Devil? Well, all the Didikais and Pikies in Somerset thought so, and promptly left the area.

In fact the prints had been made by Romanies. Attaching some sort of shoe to the base of ladders, after much practise they got a uniform length of stride and by extending the ladders were able to get the prints over roofs and haystacks.

The whole exercise had been planned for some time and involved fifteen different Romany camps.

This idea of using the Devil to clear an area of Didikais has been used since, but never on such a large scale. [26]

Granted such a ruse would have put the fear of the Devil into the Didikais, Graham. But how the Devil did the Romanies manage it without leaving tell-tale marks of human handiwork in the snow?

Document 28

Daily Mirror.
18 Feb 1983

Danny Smith, who describes himself as "Travelling Gentleman, County of Hertfordshire", writes:

Graham, the reader who suggested that the mystery footprints which appeared in the snow one February night in 1855 were the work of gypsies, was right. As he said, Didikais and Pikies had been giving the true Romanies a bad name in the area.

So a meeting of seven Romany tribes was called and they drew up a plan to teach the Didikais a lesson.

The whole operation took fifteen months to prepare - walking over the route, getting to know the local people and their habits, allotting various jobs to different Romany camps and so on.

Came the night of February 8, 1855 - the Night of the Mulo (Devil). The first Romanies to go out were the look-outs. Then came the stilt-treaders.

There were 400 pairs of stilts and each had a pair of hoofprints at the base. Every stilt-treader had to be fit and athletic. Each was told how far to go before handing over to the next and so on until all 400 stilt men had done their part.

After that, a clean-up team went out, to make sure there were no tell-tale marks left to show what had gone on.

As a result of the prank neither the Didikais nor the Pikies went near that part of the country for years and February 8 was known to them as "The Night of the Mulo's Walk".

Thanks, Danny. Four hundred sets of hoofprints not only kept the Didikais on their toes - the making of 'em must have kept the petulengroes busy, too!

NOTES TO SECONDARY SOURCES

1 - Mention of the mysterious 'crutch stick' markings was noted by Fort [Document 38], but does not appear in contemporary reports. Its significance was obscure until the advent of the theory that the tracks were made by gypsies, at which point the *INFO Journal* drew attention to the possibility that the marks were left by stilt-walkers balancing precariously [see introductory essay and Fig. 4].

2 - Stale. (Literally, reheated food.)

3 - At the time this paper was being researched at the British Newspaper Library, Colindale, the relevant volume of the *Western Morning News* had been sent to be rebound.

4 - It has not been possible to identify this volume.

5- *Sic*. Ed.

6 - Given the similarity in phrasing with an 1855 letter to the *Illustrated London News* [Document 7], it may be that the author of this letter was the Rev. G.M. Musgrave.

7 - Again, the report of such purposeful tracks suggests a human or supernatural agent, not an animal in search of food.

8 - This important piece of evidence, albeit second hand, seems to be the only account by someone actually out and about during the night on which the footprints appeared. It seems to confirm that, in some parts of the county at least, there was indeed a thaw capable of distorting existing trails.

9 - This reference, apparently to other mystery tracks in Devon, is never elaborated on. A detailed search of the local press for 1921 might be rewarding, but has not been attempted for this paper.

10 - See document 3.

11 - John Kemble, *The Saxons in England*, 2 vols., London, 1849. This report has obvious folkloric overtones and probably little in common with the "Devil's Hoof-prints".

12 - See document 39.

13 - This headline appeared in the *Western Times*, 24 February 1855, according to Theo Brown. See document 25.

14 - See document 11.

15 - See document 22.

16 - Further evidence of a thaw, followed by more freezing weather - this time first-hand; see note 8.

17 - Roughly, 'the manner of the footprints'.

18 - Wooden-soled overshoes.

19 - See documents 14 and 30.

20 - See document 9.

21 - See documents 15-19.

22 - See document 40.

23 - See document 15.

24 - See document 8.

25 - Or Fische; see document 11.

26 - See also document 48.

OTHER MYSTERIOUS TRACKS

Document 29

Inverness Courier.
    1 March 1855

MYSTERIOUS FOOTPRINTS IN THE SNOW. - Some curiosity and superstitious alarm were felt here before the thaw commenced by the discovery of foot-prints in the snow, exactly resembling those described to have been seen in Devonshire, as if some unknown animal with a single foot and cloven hoof, had traversed in a straight line miles of hill and dale, deterred by no difficulties of ascent, declivity, or hedges. *The Illustrated London News* devoted a long description and an engraving to the foot-prints. Those seen in this neighbourhood were traced for a considerable way across the fields, and at the Longman [1], and again at the Crown, near the house of Abertarff [2]. Many of our townsmen went to see the phenomenon, and one brought home a lump of the snow in which the footprints were strongly impressed, exhibiting it as a very curious and mysterious occurrence. The cloven hoof had an ominous and by no means prepossessing look! Fortunately, however, an observant naturalist had already examined the foot-prints and decided the point. Some animal, probably a hare or a polecat, had traversed the field at a gallop with its feet close together. The paws had become slightly filled with snow, so that only the round form was impressed, and the open space between them left a slightly-raised and pointed mark like the centre of a cloven hoof. This gentleman followed a track till on an ascending slope the animal appeared to have slackened its pace to a trot, and then left upon the snow distinct impressions of its four feet. Further on, the animal seems to have sat down on the snow, and again its four feet were distinctly traced. Nothing more was desired - the mystery was solved.

Document 30

The Illustrated London News.
  17 March 1855

FOOT-PRINTS IN THE SNOW
(To the editor of the *Illustrated London News*)

I beg the favour of you to insert in your newspaper the following fact, upon the authority of a Polish Doctor in Medicine living in the neighbourhood:- On the Piasho-wa-gora (or Sand-hill) - a small hill on the borders of Gallicia, but in Russian Poland - every year are to be seen in the snow the same foot-prints as those seen in Devonshire, in a single line round the hill, at a few inches and regular distance from each other; no mark of a beginning or end being distinguished. It is universally attributed by the inhabitants to supernatural influence. The same foot-prints are occasionally visible in the soft sand with which this bare hill is covered.
  C.C.C.
  Heidelberg, March 12th, 1855

Document 31

Daily Mail.
  13 December 1922

A TEST FOR ELDERLY READERS
To the Editor of the *Daily Mail*.

Sir - I was living in the Cotswolds with my father during the years 1852-3. A prolonged frost and very deep snow occurred in one of those years and strange tracks were seen in the snow, passing over the roofs of houses. I remember seeing the weird spoor.

Various opinions were given, as the marks were seen in various parts of England. The local bucolics said the devil made them. Can any of your elderly readers tell me if the matter was cleared up?
  SEPTUGENARIAN

Document 32

Daily Mail.
  15 December 1922

MYSTERY FOOTPRINTS OF LONG AGO
To the Editor of the *Daily Mail*.

Sir - I was much interested in Septugenarian's letter regarding the mysterious footprints seen in the snow in the '50s, as I distinctly remember, when I was a little girl of about six years of age, my father coming in one day and telling me that the devil was about, as the marks of a cloven hoof had been seen in the snow in various parts, including the roofs of houses.

I was a very nervous child and it made a great impression on me. We were then living in a little town in Norfolk. I never heard if these marks were explained.

I was born in 1846. [3]

Document 33

Doubt [4]
  No. 15, Summer 1946

Our Cover

The "devil's hoofmarks" on our cover come from HFFS Russell ... He observed them at first-hand, and this is the way he tells about it, in his letter of 2-9-16 FS: [5]

"Wonderfully, they were first seen by me, and I could hardly believe my own eyes. They were spotted on a snow-covered hill behind the Chateau de Morveau, near Everberg, which is partway between Brussels and Louvain, Belgium, at 10pm on January 10th, 1945. The snow varied from two to four feet in depth [6], and I traced the prints for half a mile in a north-westerly direction until they entered a tiny wood, or copse, where abruptly they disappeared. A thorough search of the site of the copse revealed no hole, lair or tree where anything might have concealed itself without leaving some evidence in the snow. I then traced the prints in the opposite direction, south-easterly, for nearly two miles, crossing several fields and a small stream, until they faded out on a hillside thick with windblown snow which had drifted over the prints for an unknown distance. But the footprints didn't reappear on the crest of this hill, nor was there any sign of them on the opposite sheltered side.

"The prints measured about 2½" in length by 1½" wide, were spaced in pairs directly one behind the other (see sketch), the distance between prints of one pair being about nine inches, and between two pairs twelve to fifteen inches. They ran in a dead straight line, one print immediately behind another, without slightest misplacement to left or right. Judging by their depth, whatever made them was at least the weight of an Airedale dog, a good medium-sized creature of some sort. [7]

"Due to frost, and lack of further snow, the prints remained visible for two days, during which time I drew the attention of several people to them, including one Arthur Davies, of Sheffield, Victor Beha, of London, and some local Belgians. Unfortunately, all were singularly lacking in curiosity, Beha suggesting that they'd been made by a gyroscopic rat - which is probably as good a guess as that of any dogmatic scientist. Local Belgians couldn't think what they might be, never having seen the like before. Three cameras were available, but not a film to be got for love or money, otherwise I could have got several good photographs of this phenomenon. (Films were hell on the continent - the number of useless cameras being toted about would break your heart.)

"Looked to me somewhat like the prints of a goat, and there were odd goats in that part of Belgium - but goats don't step leaving single-line spoor. Unfortunately, the prints weren't as dramatic as Gould's - they didn't run for miles over several counties, and they didn't hop across rooftops. I remain firmly convinced that to me has been vouchsafed a sight of a typical piece of Forteana and that I've seen the inexplicable. But I wish I'd been able to photograph them as Smythe did those prints of the Abominable Snowman in the Himalayas. Anyway, there's the data, for what it's worth."

Document 34

Journal of the Bombay Natural History Society.
     Vol.52 p.666, 1954

Not the Snowman?

Sir,
During the hard frost at the beginning of February, publicity was given to reports of giant footprints, some 20 inches long [8], found crossing deep snow in various parts of the Isle of Wight. At the Needles they were said to lead to the edge of the 200-foot cliff with no sign of any return tracks, while at Bembridge they appeared to come from the direction of the sea and disappear inland. [9]

Reference was also made to one of the world's most baffling mysteries, recorded in February 1855, from South Devon, where similar, though much smaller, footprints said by some to be those of Satan himself, were observed covering a large area and crossing inaccessible places like the tops of houses and narrow walls as well as in open country.

I venture to put forward an explanation of their origin. During the recent heavy snowfall, and while walking about the Yarmouth-Freshwater road where the high tide had

Fig. 8 - Eric Frank Russell's drawing of the tracks he saw near Everberg, Belgium, in January 1945. From the cover of *Doubt* No. 15, Summer 1946 (Document 33).

covered the mud-flats above Yarmouth harbour, I caused numerous seagulls to take flight at my approach. As they rose from the water several of these made sudden crash-dives, repeating the performance over a considerable distance. It seemed that this was due to the frozen state of their feathers, which prevented them making any balanced or sustained flight.

Similar attempts to fly over deep snow instead of water would, I suggest, produce the effect of a series of giant footprints. A large flock of smaller birds, such as starlings, may have given rise to the Devon footprints under similar conditions. These, be it noted, were described as occurring in straight lines, unlike the tracks of a four-footed animal. [10]

I should be most interested to have the views of more experienced bird-watchers.

J.A. Douglas
Yarmouth, Isle of Wight

Document 35

Report and Transactions of the Devonshire Association.
Vol.LXXXVIII (1956) pp.251-2

Fifty-Third Report on Folklore
by Theo Brown, Recorder

... Footprints in the Snow, 1855.

At Ipplepen, during a fall of snow in February, a trail of footprints was seen on the thatched roof of Penrae. This is a very old house, formerly a farm, and, traditionally, said to have been a meeting-place of Orange supporters. It is L-shaped, the short arm running back contains the kitchen, and, over it, a bedroom, with plaster-work round a bricked-up fireplace. The moulding includes the legend W M 1704 R, but the 7 and the 4 are of later date than the 1 and the 0. This is called the William and Mary Room.

One day in February, Mrs Hall went out of the house and looked up to the roof to see how thick the snow was lying on it, as the timbers were not too strong. Up the slope, over the William and Mary Room, was a track, as of a woman's shoe, about size five, heel and sole quite distinct, each print a step apart, leading up to the top of the ridge. Unfortunately, Mrs Hall did not go round to see what happened on the other side of the roof, as it was snowing hard. It was then that she observed the strange behaviour of the dogs, who normally hang around the kitchen when she is cooking. They are: a Golden Labrador and a Staffordshire Boxer. On this occasion they refused to enter the kitchen and hung about the threshold in a frightened manner for two hours, nor would they enter by the door on the other side. After two hours the spell suddenly lifted.

There is no tradition of a ghost at Penrae, although the Labrador has been seen to mark a corner of Mrs Hall's bedroom with acute apprehension, some years ago, hackles up, and so forth.

Besides Mrs Hall, two other witnesses saw the footprints.

Document 36

Tomorrow.
Volume 5 Number 3, Spring 1957

Did The Devil Walk Again?
by Eric J Dingwall

Of all the strange stories to which I have listened for so many years, that told by Mr Wilson was one of the oddest and the most inexplicable. Indeed, Mr Wilson himself was so completely bewildered by his extraordinary experience that he had only confided it to three highly trusted friends, a canon of the Church, a doctor and a customs officer. The thing was impossible. It could not have happened. And yet Mr Wilson knew that it had happened and that it had happened to him.

One day when Mr Wilson was quietly reading his newspaper by the fire his heart began to beat more quickly. So he had not been the only one! Others had had the same strange experience and could no more explain it than he could. Now at least people could not say that he was lying, mad or suffering from delusions.

So it happened that he wrote off to me, since my name was mentioned in the article he had read, and in careful, soberly-phrased terms he told me his story. I confess that my own interest in it almost exceeded his own and so at the first opportunity I hastened down to the little village where Mr Wilson carries on his business.

I found him in a little office. He was a tall, well-built man with a kindly smile and an assured manner, obviously no imaginative dreamer of tall stories.

When we had made ourselves comfortable Mr Wilson began to tell me something about himself and his history. He had not always lived in a village, where he had now built up for himself a neat little business. Years before he had been the proprietor of a flourishing concern in New York, but after the Wall Street crash he had lost a good deal of money and decided to return to England. At first he found himself working for others but, being a man of sturdy independence, he finally set up on his own. And it was when taking a short holiday at a West coast watering place where he had spent his childhood that *it* happened.

It was in 1950, Mr Wilson said, that he went down to the West country to stay in the Devonshire coast town where he had spent so many happy days of his youth. Never could he forget that holiday as long as he lived, for it was on the last day of his stay that he decided on impulse to go and look at his old home and walk again on the beach where he had played in his childhood years. This little beach is entirely enclosed by rocks and steep cliffs and is invisible from above. The only trace is by a passage through the cliffs which is closed by a tall iron gate. This gate is used as a pay gate in summer and is locked up in winter. On that October afternoon the gate was locked, but Mr Wilson's old home was almost opposite the gate and he remembered that it was possible to get round the gate by going through the garden of the house. So he did this, and was soon on the sands of the beach, which was deserted and gloomy on that autumn day [11]. The sea had been to the top of the beach but now the tide had gone out, leaving the sand as smooth as glass. Mr Wilson looked at the sand and could hardly believe his eyes. For starting at the top of the beach and just below the perpendicular cliff was a long single line of marks, apparently hoof-marks of some biped, which were clearly impressed upon the wet sand almost as if cut out by some sharp instrument. The marks were about six feet apart and led from the cliff in a straight line down the centre of the narrow beach [12] and into the sea. [13]

Mr Wilson's first reaction seems to have been intense curiosity. He approached the prints and examined them with the most careful attention. He tried to jump from one mark to another and then, removing his shoes and socks, tried to see if he could match them with his own stride. But they were so far apart that he could not reach from one to the next, although he was a tall man with long legs. The hoof-marks which were not cloven, resembled those which might have been made by a large, unshod pony, and the impressions were deeper than those which he himself made with his shoes on, even though he weighed some sixteen stone. What he particularly noticed at the time was that no sand was splashed up at the edges: it looked as if each mark had been cut out of the sand with a flat iron. [14]

Totally Inexplicable

After Mr. Wilson had told me his story and had seen that I treated it seriously, as the three others had, and showed no inclination to disbelieve him, he went on to tell me how, after examining the footprints, he had realized how totally inexplicable they were. For here was a biped with a track shaped like a hoof, starting immediately beneath a perpendicular cliff on a closed beach and ending in the sea. There was no returning track. I asked if it were possible that the animal, or whatever it might have been, could have turned right or left in the sea and regained the land at some other point. But Mr. Wilson produced photographs which showed that the beach was a comparatively narrow space completely enclosed by rocky headlands on either side. What possible creature, from land or water, could have made such footprints as these? And what size could it have been to have so long a stride? What kind of hoof could make so clear-cut an impression? As Mr. Wilson said, what might he have seen if he had arrived a little earlier, for the receding tide was only just beyond the last print of the line? After asking himself questions such as these, Mr. Wilson wondered if perhaps there was something uncanny about the footprints. For were it a sea animal why should it be provided with hard hoofs? If it were a land animal why should it walk into the sea and where did it go when it got there?

Or did it have wings? In any case, what known animal could make such a track?

Questions very like these had been asked before, and it was just because Mr. Wilson had accidentally come across a reference to another case of mysterious tracks that he had written to me. For just over a hundred years ago - in 1855 to be precise - there had been a night of heavy snow fall in the neighbourhood of Exeter and southwards into Devon, and when the countryfolk awoke a strange sight met their eyes. For there upon the snow were odd foot-tracks resembling hoof marks, which seemed to be those of a biped rather than those of any four-footed creature. Each mark was about eight inches ahead of the next and the prints were so widely distributed over a large area that it seemed that more than one creature must have been involved. But what was still more mysterious was the route taken by this animal. The prints were not only on the ground but also on the roofs of houses, on the tops of walls and even on enclosed areas like courtyards.

The prints caused the utmost concern and consternation and discussion about them raged in the press for several weeks. Every kind of animal was suggested and then rejected. Some thought the tracks were made by badgers or by birds; others thought that an escaped kangaroo was responsible, or possibly a racoon. Gradually the excitement died down and the villagers were no longer frightened to come out of their cottages for fear that Satan himself would again be walking. And so the devil's hoofmarks remained an unsolved mystery.

It was not till 1908 that the strange footprints were seen again, this time in the United States, from Newark to Cape May in New Jersey [15]. Here again were reports of marks like the hoofs of a pony in the thick snow, and again we have the story of how the tracks led up to wire fences and then continued on the other side, even when the uprights were only a few inches apart. No solution seems to have been reached and eventually the New Jersey Devil was forgotten, just like his predecessor in the Devon country-side.

What are we to make of these stories and what was it that made the strange prints that so astonished Mr. Wilson on that October afternoon? The more questions one asks the more baffling does the case become. There may be a simple explanation for this experience, just as there may be for the two or three previous cases reported, of which Mr. Wilson knew nothing. So far no one has thought of one. If anyone does, no one will be more happy than my friend Mr. Wilson, and those who hear his story will not be tempted to think that, on a Devon beach in 1950, he had all but seen the Devil walking again.

Document 37

Daily Mirror.
  7 Feb 1983

  OLD CODGERS [Letter column]

Chilling

  Mrs L[ynda]. Hanson, Desmond Avenue, High Road, Hull, Humberside, writes:

  The theories about the mystery footprints in the snow in 1855 have been of great interest to me because similar footprints appeared in our garden when I was a child, in the 1950s.

  The prints were some 4 inches across, shaped as a cloven hoof, and appeared 12 inches apart in a single line - stopping in the middle of the garden [16]. No snow had been disturbed anywhere.

  What was also interesting was that at the bottom of the print, dry concrete could be seen, not compressed snow as is normal when a person or animal treads on snow. [17]

  This has intrigued our family for years.

* *We're not surprised, ma'am - reckon we'd 'ave made tracks ourselves next day.*

[Responding to a personal letter from Bob Rickard, editor of *Fortean Times*, Mrs Hanson added:]

"The hoof-marks appeared in my parents' garden in January or February 1957. It had snowed about 1" deep during the night and in the morning the marks were discovered.

"They were shaped as a cloven hoof, 4" across, approx 12" apart in a straight line and stopping in the middle of the garden... At that time we had a very good house dog, but he never even barked."

NOTES TO OTHER FOOTPRINTS

1 - Now Inverness industrial estate.

2 - A residential area close to Inverness Royal Academy.

3 - This puts the date of the incident at c.1852.

4 - The sporadically-published journal of the Fortean Society, edited in New York by Tiffany Thayer.

5 - Or 9 February 1946. Thayer's Fortean Society adopted a 13-month calendar dating from the group's inception (1931), and with the 13th month, Fort, slotted between August and September. HFFS, a title awarded to Russell, stands for "Honorary Fellow of the Fortean Society". The author's actual full name was Eric Frank Russell, the noted science-fiction author; he was for many years British correspondent of *Doubt* and was author of the book *Great World Mysteries* (1957), in which another account of these prints appears. See document 44.

6 - Compare this with the very thin covering of snow - ½ to 4 inches - in Devon on the night of the Devil's walk.

7 - This compares with Devon's single track left by a foot approximately 4 inches by 2 3/4, 8½ inches apart.

8 - A size that puts one in mind more of an Abominable Snowman than a devil. For another size comparison, see Document 36.

9 - Rupert Gould [see Document 39], himself a naval officer, was among the first to draw attention to the possibility that the Devil's Hoofmarks were made by a sea creature. Those left in Devon were generally within easy reach of the coast, while whatever made the prints on Kerguelen island, Gould believed, must have come from the sea. This datum lends slight support to what otherwise appears a peculiar theory.

10 - However, one would expect the take-off attempts of a flock of stricken birds to leave a much less regular trail than that reported in Devon.

11 - The isolation of the beach, and the unplanned nature of Wilson's visit, appear to make a hoax unlikely.

12 - The implication is that the

prints were in a single file, as were the Devil's Hoofmarks.

13 - The possibility of a link between Devon's hoofmarks and the sea was pointed out by Gould. See Document 39.

14 - Compare this with reports that the Devil's Hoofmarks were so clear they appeared to have been branded with a hot iron [Document 7], and with Eric Frank Russell's 1945 report of the mysterious displacement of snow in the hoofmarks he examined in Belgium [see Documents 33 and 44].

15 - These marks were associated with the fabulous Jersey Devil - a bat-winged, horse-headed and hooved improbable reported in New Jersey's Pine Barrens at the time. See James McCloy and Ray Miller, *The Jersey Devil* (Wallingford, Pennsylvania 1976); Loren Coleman, *Mysterious America* (Winchester, Mass., 1983).

16 - A very fair approximation of the prints in Devon a century earlier, with the exception of the slightly longer stride.

17 - See note 14.

SELECTED ESSAYS AND THEORIES

Document 38

THE BOOK OF THE DAMNED
   by Charles Fort
   pp.305-310 of the Dover collected edition (New York 1974)

Notes and Queries, 7-8-508:
   A correspondent who had been to Devonshire writes for information as to a story that he had heard there: of an occurrence of about thirty-five years before the date of writing:
   Of snow upon the ground - of all South Devonshire waking up one morning to find

such tracks in the snow as had never before been heard of - "clawed footmarks" of "an unclassifiable form" - alternating at huge but regular intervals with what seemed to be the impression of the point of a stick - but the scattering of the prints - amazing expanse of territory covered - obstacles, such as hedges, walls, houses, seemingly surmounted -
   Intense excitement - that the track had been followed by huntsmen and hounds, until they had come to a forest - from which the hounds had retreated, baying and terrified, so that no one had dared to enter the forest.
   Notes and Queries, 7-9-18:
   Whole occurrence well-remembered by a correspondent: a badger had left marks in the snow: this was determined, and the excite-

ement had "dropped to a dead calm in a single day."

Notes and Queries, 7-9-70:

That for years a correspondent had had a tracing of the prints, which his mother had taken from those in the snow in her garden, in Exmouth: that they were hoof-like marks - but had been made by a biped.

Notes and Queries, 7-9-253:

Well remembered by another correspondent, who writes of the excitement and consternation of "some classes." He says that a kangaroo had escaped from a menagerie - "the footprints being so peculiar and far apart gave rise to a scare that the devil was loose."

We have had a story, and now we shall tell it over from contemporaneous sources. We have had the later accounts first very largely for an impression of the correlating effect that time brings about, by addition, disregard and distortion. For instance, the "dead calm in a single day." If I had found that the excitement did die out rather soon, I'd incline to accept that nothing extraordinary had occurred.

I found that the excitement had continued for weeks.

I recognize this as a well-adapted thing to say, to divert attention from a discorrelate.

All phenomena are "explained" in the terms of the Dominant of their era. This is why we give up trying really to explain, and content ourselves with expressing. Devils that might print marks in snow are correlates to the third Dominant back from this era. So it was an adjustment by nineteenth-century correlates, or human tropisms, to say that the marks in the snow were clawed. Hoof-like marks are not only horsey but devilish. It had to be said in the nineteenth century that those prints showed claw-marks. We shall see that this was stated by Prof. Owen, one of the greatest biologists of his day - except that Darwin didn't think so. But I shall give reference to two representations of them that can be seen in the New York Public Library. In neither representation is there the faintest suggestion of a claw-mark. There never has been a Prof. Owen who has explained: he has correlated. [1]

Another adaptation, in the later accounts, is that of leading this discorrelate to the Old Dominant into the familiar scenery of a fairy story, and discredit it by assimilation to the conventionally fictitious - so the idea of the baying, terrified hounds, and forest like enchanted forests, which no one dared to enter. Hunting parties were organized, but the baying, terrified hounds do not appear in contemporaneous accounts.

The story of the kangaroo looks like adaptation to needs for an animal that could spring far, because marks were found in the snow on roofs of houses. But so astonishing is the extent of snow that was marked that after a while another kangaroo was added.

But the marks were in single lines.

My own acceptance is that not less than a thousand one-legged kangaroos, each shod with a very small horseshoe, could have marked that snow of Devonshire.

London *Times*, Feb 16, 1855:

"Considerable sensation has been caused in the towns of Topsham, Lymphstone [2], Exmouth, Teignmouth, and Dawlish, in Devonshire, in consequence of the discovery of a vast number of foot tracks of a most strange and mysterious description."

The story is of an incredible multiplicity of marks discovered in the morning of Feb 8, 1855, in the snow, by the inhabitants of many towns and regions between towns. This great area must of course be disregarded by Prof. Owen and the other correlators. The tracks were in all kinds of unaccountable places: in gardens enclosed by high walls, and up on the tops of houses, as well as in the open fields. There was in Lymphstone scarcely one unmarked garden. We've had heroic disregards but I think that here disregard was titanic. And, because they occurred in single lines, the marks are said to have been "more like those of a biped than of a quadruped" - as if a biped would place one foot precisely ahead of another - unless it hopped - but then we have to think of a thousand, or of thousands.

It is said that the marks were "generally 8 inches in advance of each other."

"The impression of the foot closely resembles that of a donkey's shoe, and measured from an inch and a half, in some instances, to two and a half inches across."

Or the impressions were cones in incomplete, or crescentic basins.

The diameters equalled diameters of very young colts' hoofs: too small to be compared with marks of donkey's hoofs.

"On Sunday last the Rev. Mr. Musgrave alluded to the subject in his sermon and suggested the possibility of the footprints being those of a kangaroo, but this could scarcely have been the case, as they were found on both sides of the Este [3]. At present it remains a mystery, and many superstitious people in the above-named towns are actually afraid to go outside their doors after night."

The Este is a body of water two miles wide.

London *Times*, March 6, 1855:

[Here Fort quotes at length from Document 12.]

In the *Illustrated London News*, the occurrence is given a great deal of space. In the issue of Feb. 24, 1855, a sketch is given of the prints.

I call them cones in incomplete basins.

Except that they're a little longish, they look like prints of hoofs of horses - or, rather, of colts.

But they're in a single line.

It is said that the marks from which the sketch was made were 8 inches apart, and that this spacing was regular and invariable "in every parish." Also other towns besides those named in the *Times* are mentioned. The writer, who had spent a winter in Canada, and was familiar with tracks in snow, says that he had never seen "a more clearly defined track." Also he brings out the point that was so persistently disregarded by Prof. Owen and the other correlators - that "no known animal walks in a line of single footsteps, not even man." With these wider inclusions, this writer concludes with us that the marks were not footprints. It may be that his following observation hits upon the crux of the whole occurrence:

That whatever it may have been that had made the marks, it had removed, rather than pressed, the snow. [4]

According to his observations the snow looked "as if branded with a hot iron."

Illustrated London News March 3, 1855-214:

Prof. Owen, to whom a friend had sent drawings of the prints, writes that there were claw-marks. He says that the "track" was made by "a" badger.

Six other witnesses sent letters to this number of the *News*. One mentioned, but not published, is a notion of a strayed swan. Always this homogeneous-seeing - "a" badger - "a" swan - "a" track. I should have listed the other towns as well as those mentioned in the *Times*.

A letter from Mr. Musgrave is published. He, too, sends a sketch of the prints. It, too, shows a single line. There are four prints, of which the third is a little out of line.

There is no sign of a claw-mark.

The prints look like prints of longish hoofs of a very young colt, but they are not so definitely outlined as in the sketch of February 24th, as if drawn after disturbance by wind, or after thawing had set in. Measurements at places a mile and a half apart, gave the same inter-spacing - "exactly eight inches and a half apart."

We now have a little study in the psychology and genesis of an attempted correlation. Mr. Musgrave says: "I found a very apt opportunity to mention the name 'kangaroo' in allusion to the report then current." He says that he had no faith in the kangaroo-story himself, but was glad "that a kangaroo was in the wind," because it opposed "a dangerous, degrading, and false impression that it was the devil."

"Mine was a word in season and did good."

Whether it's Jesuitical or not, and no matter what it is or isn't, that is our own acceptance: that, though we've often been carried away from this attitude controversially, that is our acceptance as to every correlate of the past that has been considered in this book - relatively to the Dominant of its era.

Another correspondent writes that, though the prints in all cases resembled hoof marks, there were indistinct traces of claws - that "an" otter had made the marks. After that many other witnesses wrote to the *News*. The correspondence was so great that, in the issue of March 10th, only a selection could be given. There's "a" jumping-rat solution and "a" hopping-toad inspiration, and then someone came out strong with an idea of "a" hare that had galloped with pairs of feet held close together, so as to make impressions in a single line.

London *Times*, March 14, 1840:

"Among the high mountains of that elevated district where Glenorchy, Glenlyon and Glenochay are contiguous, there have been met with several times, during this and also the former winter, upon the snow, the tracks of an animal seemingly unknown at present in Scotland. The print, in every respect, is an exact resemblance to that of a foal of considerable size, with this small difference, perhaps, that the sole seems a little longer, or not so round; but as no one has had the good fortune as yet to have obtained a glimpse of this creature, nothing more can be said of its shape or dimensions; only it has been remarked, from the depth to which the feet sank in the snow, that it must be a beast of considerable size. It has been observed also that its walk is not like that of the generality of quadrupeds, but that it is more like the bounding or leaping of a horse when scared or pursued. It is not in one locality that its tracks have been met with, but through a range of at least twelve miles."

In the *Illustrated London News*, March 17, 1855, a correspondent from Heidelberg writes, "upon the authority of a Polish Doctor of Medicine," that, on the Piashowa-gora (Sand Hill) a small elevation on the border of Galicia, but in Russian Poland, such marks are to be seen in the snow every year, and sometimes in the sand of this hill, and "are attributed by the inhabitants to supernatural influences."

Document 39

ODDITIES
  A Book of Unexplained Facts
  by Rupert Gould
  (London 1929, 1943)

THE DEVIL'S HOOF-MARKS

A Scottish minister once preached a sermon upon the text "The voice of the turtle is heard in our land" [5]. He was literally-minded, and unaware of the fact that the "turtle" referred to is the turtle-dove, and not that member of the Chelonia which inhabits the ocean and furnishes the raw material of such "tortoise-shell" articles as are not made of celluloid. In consequence, the deductions which he drew from his text were long remembered by such of his hearers as were better-informed.

"We have here", he is reported to have said - "we have here, my brethren, two very remarkable signs and portents distinctly vouchsafed to us. The first shall be, that a creature which (like Leviathan himself) was created to dwell and abide in the sea shall make its way to the land, and be seen in the markets and dwelling-places of men; and the second shall be, that a creature hitherto denied the gift of speech shall lift up its voice in the praise of its Maker."

A visitation of a somewhat similar and hardly less startling kind occurred in Devonshire on February 8, 1855. The following account of it was published in *The Times* of February 16th.

[See Document 2]

So far and, unfortunately, no further - *The Times*. The *Illustrated London News*, however, took up the question, and opened its columns to what proved to be quite an extensive correspondence, which I have used as the source of most of the information here given. In the West Country the affair gradually blew over - although I believe that it is still well remembered. There was no repetition of the occurrence, but it took a long time for the "excitement" and "superstitious folly" to die down. One correspondent [6] speaks of "labourers, their wives and children, and old crones, and trembling old men, dreading to stir out after sunset, or to go half a mile into lanes or byways on a call or message, under the conviction that this was the Devil's walk, and no other, and that it was wicked to trifle with such a manifest proof of the Great Enemy's immediate presence..."

The correspondence presents, as might be expected, a curious medley of additional facts and half-baked theories. I will first summarise the facts, premising that *The Times* account, while giving a good outline of the events, necessarily omitted one or two very curious details.

An eye-witness, signing himself "South Devon", sent in an able account, from which the following extract is taken.

128

[See Document 7]

Another correspondent, signing himself "G.M.M.", also afforded a good deal of supplementary information, as the following extracts will show.

[See Document 11]

In view of the very remarkable facts detailed in these letters, it will be admitted that the Devonshire rustics had every excuse for indulging in what their betters were pleased to term "superstitious folly". A natural explanation of the facts seemed impossible to find, and difficult even to suggest; while any explanation certainly postulated the visit of something very un-canny - something which walked upon small hooved feet with a very short, mincing stride, which sought darkness and solitude, which had never rested, which had crossed a river two miles wide, which had hung round human habitations without daring to enter them, and which had on some occasions walked up walls and along roofs, while at other times it had passed through such obstructions as if they did not exist. Assu-redly the peasants were not to be blamed if their minds went back to such grim texts as Isaiah xxxiv.14:

"The wild beasts of the desert shall also meet with the wild beasts of the island, and the satyr shall cry to his fellow."

Of course, many naturalistic explanations were offered, but none can be regarded as satisfactory. In the words of Maginn's Aun-ciente Waggonere,

Somme swore itte was ane foreigne birde,
Some sayd itte was ane brute....

The various candidates who, by their "next friend", claimed the authorship of the marks comprised (among birds) cranes, swans, bustards, and waders; and (among beasts) otters, rats, hares, polecats, frogs, badgers, and - *mirabile dictu* [7] - kangaroos.

The theory that a bird made the marks is obviously untenable, as "South Devon" pointed out. But an anonymous writer, one "W.W." [8], made a pathetic attempt to evade the various fatal objections. By his account, five days after the appearance of the Devon-shire hoof-marks a swan turned up, alive but exhausted, at St. Denis in France, wearing a silver collar "with an inscription engraved on it, stating that the bird belonged to the domain of Prince Hohenlohe, in Germany". "W.W." maintained that this bird, whose feet had probably been "padded in the shape of a donkey's hoof or shoe" by its owner, to prevent damage to the garden in which it was normally kept, had no doubt made the mysterious marks!

Some of the other theories were ingenious. For example, one Thomas Fox sent in a very clever drawing to support his view that the marks had been made by the four feet of a leaping rat [see Fig. 9a]. There was a good deal, too, to be said for the otter theory. But the opinion most generally accepted was, of course, that put forward by the famous naturalist Richard Owen.

Here is his letter.

[See Document 11]

In the mid-Victorian era, that "period of digestion", the authority of an established name counted, in scientific as in other matters, for more than it does now. Probably all but a very few, such as the unfortunate observers who saw something different from what Owen so clearly tells them they ought to have seen, regarded this letter as absolutely decisive.

Nowadays, we know a little more about scientific dogmatism - and we also know a good deal more about Owen himself. He was, undoubtedly, a very able man; but on several important occasions he showed himself cap-able of making dogmatic assertions, in defiance of fact, which proved him to be possessed of a singular and not entirely "scientific" type of mind.

A good example of this tendency is his controversy with Huxley, in 1857, over the *hippocampus major*. Owen, coming forward "on the side of the angels" as the great scientific gun of the anti-Darwinians, committed him-self to the dogmatic assertion that there were certain anatomical features - such as the above singularly-named structure - which were peculiar to the brain of man, and afforded ample ground for classifying him as a genus apart from all other mammals. Actually, as Huxley soon afterwards showed, such structures are common both to man and to all the higher apes, as well as many of the lower ones.

Proxime accesserunt [9] may be placed Owen's exploded theory that the adult skull is a modified vertebral joint - a theory originally suggested by Oken - and his utterly childish "explanation" of the "sea-serpent" seen by H.M.S. *Daedalus* in 1848: an explanation flatly contradicting the observed facts, and postulating that the naval officers who observed them were, one and all, half-witted.

His explanation of the Devonshire hoof-prints is more plausible; but it does not fit the facts - nor is he fair to "your correspondent". "South Devon" nowhere stated, as Owen asserts, that man is the only creature which makes single foot-prints in snow - he said that no creature, not even man, makes a single line of prints: and this is generally true [10]. It is quite possible that the prints of a badger's hind-foot might be superimposed on the last impression but one made by the fore-foot on the same side of the body, and so produce an apparently single foot-print. But such prints would undoubtedly be "staggered", for the badger has quite a wide "tread", and the result would then be a double line of imprints, not a single one. Badgers, also, are not commonly credited with the ability to scale walls and walk along roofs. As between the claims of the badger and the otter, the latter certainly seem better founded.

In [Figure 9] I have drawn foot-prints of a badger and an otter for comparison with the Devonshire hoof-marks. It will be admitted that the resemblance is not striking. It is only fair, however, to say that one or two of the writers to the *Illustrated London News* stated that faint traces of claws had, as Owen remarks, been seen, or imagined, at the edges of the hoof-marks. [11]

And Owen was entirely right in questioning the assertion that one creature had made all the marks. If, as alleged, they extended for something like a hundred miles, it is in the last degree unlikely that this track, while it endured, could have been traced throughout its whole extent by a competent observer. And even if we reduce its length to a minimum of some forty miles only, the application of simple arithmetic is still fatal to the hypothesis of a single creature. Allowing this

fourteen hours of darkness in which to make a 40-mile line of hoof-marks 8 inches apart, it must have kept up an average of more than six steps per second from start to finish! [12] And that is the absolute minimum - an addition of 30% for loopings and turnings, which seems reasonable enough, would necessitate the creature's taking ten steps per second for fourteen hours continuously. This, I submit, is simply unthinkable. The conclusion that more than one creature made the hoof-marks naturally follows - a conclusion, unfortunately, which neither explains the marks away nor identifies their authors. And it is worth noting that, on this supposition, "South Devon's" estimate of 100 miles for the total length of the track may easily have been below the truth.

Another naturalist, Frank Buckland, in spite of being one of Owen's disciples and admirers, rejected his "badger" theory - going further and faring worse. Writing long after the event he gravely asserted (in his *Log-Book of a Naturalist*) that the hoof-marks had been *proved* to be the track of a racoon! He must have been grossly misinformed. Besides possessing all the physical handicaps which put Owen's badgers out of court, the racoon adds one of its own - it is not a native of this country. In effect, Buckland was informing his readers that a pack of escaped racoons, arriving and departing with utter secrecy, had wandered singly, for one night only, over a large area of Devonshire - acquiring, during their excursion, the difficult and previously-unsuspected accomplishment of walking up vertical walls and through haystacks.

But, putting aside the reported facts which are inexplicable on any naturalistic theory (such as the unobstructed passage of the tracks through walls, etc.), there is a crucial objection which appears to me to dispose of the claims not only of the badger and the otter, but of all the birds and animals supposed, by someone or other, to have made the mysterious marks. I except the kangaroo - that theory does not require serious discussion. It was only mooted, originally, because the private menagerie of a Mr. Fishe, at Sidmouth, contained a couple of these animals.

The objection is this. We can be quite certain, from the alarm the hoofmarks occasioned among the rustics, that they were most

  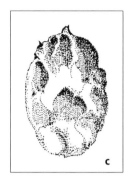 

Fig.9 - Illustrations from Rupert Gould, *Oddities* (Document 39), comparing (a) Thomas Fox's rat tracks, (b) an otter's hind foot, (c) a badger's hind foot, and (d) one of the Hoofmarks.

unusual - that nothing like them had ever been seen within living memory. It is therefore indisputable that they were not made by any common, well-known, creatures [13]. If such had been the case - if, for example, they had been the foot-prints of badgers or otters - they would have been seen in Devonshire every winter. Instead of being a nine days' wonder, and scaring the feebler brethren into fits, they would have been looked upon as a perfectly familiar sight, not worth a second glance. Yet, with one exception, there is no record of such marks having been seen on any other occasion before or since. [14]

Unbeknown, apparently, to the correspondents of the *Illustrated London News*, a very similar case had occurred some fifteen years earlier, in a very different part of the world. The story had been published for eight years; but it is a curious fact that while the authority for it, Captain Sir James Clark Ross, R.N., was in England in 1855 and must, one would think, have heard of the Devonshire hoof-marks, he did not, apparently, direct attention to the very similar incident which was within his own knowledge.

The following is an extract from Ross's *Voyage of Discovery and Research in the Southern and Antarctic Regions*, vol. i. p. 87. His ships, the *Erebus* and *Terror* [15], were then at Kerguelen Island, a large subantarctic island in the Southern Indian Ocean. The date is May 1840.

"Of land animals we saw none; and the only traces we could discover of there being any on this island were the singular foot-steps of a pony or ass, found by the party detached for surveying purposes, under the command of Lieutenant Bird, and described by Dr. Robertson as 'being 3 inches in length and 2½ in breadth, having a small and deeper depression on each side, and shaped like a horseshoe.'

"It is by no means improbable that the animal has been cast on shore from some wrecked vessel. They traced its footsteps for some distance in the recently fallen snow, in hopes of getting a sight of it, but lost the tracks on reaching a large space of rocky ground which was free from snow."

One wonders, if they had "got a sight of it", what they would have seen. [16]

It is scarcely a far-fetched conjecture to suppose that the creature which made the "singular foot-steps" seen by Ross was akin to those whose tracks were observed in Devonshire. If we accept this, one or two conclusions seem to follow.

The Kerguelen creature was not a denizen of Kerguelen itself - at least, what we now know of the fauna of that island makes this exceedingly improbable. Presumably, then, it made its arrival from seaward. Either, as Ross suggests, it was a survivor from some wrecked vessel, or it was a sea-creature which, for some reason, had made an excursion on land. As to what manner of sea-creature it may have been, if it was one, I offer no opinion. The available selection is wider than might be at first supposed - it may be recalled that some years ago a seal was found halfway up a Scottish mountain, and miles from the sea. The locale of the Devonshire hoof-marks points to a similar conclusion. All the places mentioned by name lie close to the sea-coast or to the estuary of the Exe.

On the other hand, it is possible that in both cases the agents were land animals - presumably tropical land-animals [17]. The appearance of their foot-prints in snow would normally be a matter of inference, rather than observation, while they would never, except by a rare accident, be observed in either of the temperate zones. Land-animals swimming ashore from a ship would naturally seek for food - and, if timid, might easily cover a very considerable distance in a single night, and hang round buildings without daring to enter them.

On either supposition, it is possible that there is some quite simple solution of the Devonshire hoof-marks to be found, if one knew where to look for it. But there is a caveat to be entered. If land-animals made the marks, the available data are probably sufficient to enable a competent zoologist, with an un-biased mind, to make a reasonable suggestion as to their identity. But no authority on earth - not even the Ministry of Agriculture and Fisheries - can set limits to the number and variety of the creatures which, even though unknown to science, may yet live and move and have their being in the sea.

Document 40

Chamber's Journal.
    December 1953, pp.745-6

Last Run
New light on the Abominable Snowman

J. Allan Rennie

The mysterious Abominable Snowman keeps well his hold on public interest. As far back as 8th February 1855 we find a great old stir being caused by the appearance of his tracks at Dawlish and Teignmouth, in Devon. These were bilobal, in the shape of a large cloven hoof, and they negotiated roof-tops and high walls with a complete contempt for obstacles of any form. *The Times* featured the occurrence, the *Illustrated London News* published sketches and eye-witness accounts, while the local pulpits thundered that Satan was abroad, on the business of claiming his own.

All sorts of weird theories were put forward as an explanation for these tracks, the blame being laid on creatures ranging from a kangaroo to some gigantic bird hitherto unknown to science, but the fact remains that not a single one of these solutions was other than ridiculous, and even less worthy of credence than the views of those who held the tracks to be of super-natural origin.

In my own part of the world, the Cairngorm country and Strathspey, there is a tradition of long standing concerning a local Abominable Snowman called the Bodach Mor MacDubh, or 'Giant Old Man of MacDuff's Mountain' [18], and I was reminded of the many tales I had heard relating to him when, on 2nd December 1952, while walking about a mile from the village of Cromdale, I came across tracks every bit as mysterious as those observed almost a hundred years before in Devon.

They were running across a stretch of snow-covered moorland. Each print was 19 inches long, by about 14 inches wide, bilobal in shape, and there must have been all of seven feet between each 'stride'. There was, however, no differentiation between a right and left foot, and they proceeded in more or less a single line.

I followed the tracks for about half-a-mile, until they terminated at the foot of a pine, for all the world as though the strange creature making them had climbed up into the foliage of the tree. Yet they did not end here, for about 20 yards further on, in the adjoining patch of arable, I picked them up again. They traversed the little white field, plunged down the hill to the river's edge, and disappeared directly opposite the village churchyard. What a perfect point of vanishment for an Abominable Snowman!

The sun was dipping low towards the horizon, and I took to my heels and ran, not, I am almost ashamed to admit, from any superstition, but because I wanted to get a camera and take a picture of those tracks before the light went. In this, I am glad to say, I was successful, and as soon as the pictures were printed I showed them to several local people, including gamekeepers and ghillies. I noted the light of uneasiness in the eyes of some as they studied the photographs, and the puzzlement in others. One ghillie stated bluntly that they were *Bodach* tracks, while others could not make any guess as to their origin.

I will confess that I should have been equally baffled but for a rather unique experience that came my way about thirty years ago.

In 1924 I was working with an exploration party in Northern Canada. One day, when snowshoeing across a frozen lake, I came across tracks in the snow which mystified me and reduced my companion, a French-Canadian dog-skinner, to a state of gibbering terror.

The tracks, somewhat oval in shape, looked at first glance as though they had been made by snowshoes of the 'bear-paw' type, except that they had two toe-like impressions sticking out from the main print, and ran in an almost straight single line. Their most unusual feature, however, apart from their great size, was the distance between each imprint - more than the length of a tall man. What sort of creature, I asked myself, could have been responsible for such giant strides?

My companion was only too willing to enlighten me. Crossing himself and praying in voluble French, he interspersed his supplications with remarks about the 'Windygo', insisting that we get back to camp without delay.

Of course, I knew all about the Wendigo. He is the dread monster of the Canadian wilderness. In the far North-West of Canada the Dog-rib Indians call him the 'Weetinoe', and among the Montagnais Indians of the Mistassini region he is known as the 'Atecheme'. In Britain he would be called simply the 'Abominable Snowman'.

I examined the tracks more closely. To me they were completely inexplicable, and I will admit I was somewhat disturbed as I gave in to my companion's pleading and continued towards camp.

Next morning we found that our dog-skinner, together with the French-Canadian cook, had deserted down-country, and I shall always remember that first encounter with Wendigo tracks because of the inconvenience these departures caused us. But the winter survey went on, and the incident had almost faded from my mind when, a few weeks later, I again had occasion to cross the same lake, this time alone.

It was a day of brilliant sunshine, with the white expanse of the snow-covered lake gleaming brightly in the frosty air. All the world was silent and still, except for the crunching of my raquettes in the deep snow. A few small scatterings of cloud suggested that a fair breeze might be blowing upstairs, although nothing of this could be felt at ground-level. I was within half a mile of the shore when I saw the mysterious tracks for a second time - on this occasion, while they were actually being made. There on the flawless, smooth white of the snow a whole succession of tracks in line astern were appearing miraculously before my eyes. No sign of life anywhere, no movement even, other than the drifting clouds overhead and those tracks springing suddenly into being as they came inexorably towards me.

I stood stock-still, filled with reasonless panic. The tracks were being made within 50 yards of me - 20 - 10 - then, smack! I shouted aloud as a large blob of water struck me full in the face. I swung around, brushing the moisture from my eyes, and saw the tracks continuing across the lake.

In that moment I knew that the Wendigo, Abominable Snowman, *Bodach Mor*, or what have you, was for ever explained, so far as I was concerned. Some freakish current of warm air, coming into contact with the very low temperature, had set up condensation which was projected earthwards in the form of water-blobs. When these landed in the snow, they left tracks like those of some fabulous animal. This time they were a little smaller than those I had seen on the previous occasion, nor were the prints so far apart, but in form they were pretty much the same.

Since then, on a few rare occasions, I have encountered what I call 'blob-tracks' in the Arctic and other parts of the world. I even saw them in the High Weald of Kent during the severe winter of 1939. And this very year I found them here on my own doorstep, in Strathspey. In shape and size they have not always been uniform, varying from the bilobal to tracks which looked as though they had been made by a gigantic rabbit or mole.

It is an uncongenial task extracting the wonder from old beliefs and tales, nevertheless the natural reason for them can also prove of interest and should not be withheld so long as the debunking is based on a sound premise.

Water-blobs can perform every trick accredited to the Abominable Snowman. They can leave their tracks over the roofs of houses, leap high walls, or cross ravines. They are, in other words, a matter for study by the meteorologist rather than by the zoologist or demonologist, and are only encountered in conditions of low air temperature.

If I am wrong, there is but one alternative. Those latest tracks I found *must* have been made by the *Bodach Mor*.

Document 41

Manchester Guardian.
16 March 1955

MISCELLANY
"The Devil's Footprints"

The story of "The Devil's Footprints" is still current in these parts (writes an Exmouth reader), although no one has mentioned it to me personally during the last 10 years or so. No one ever produced a rational explanation of these marks, which were of a cloven hoof and which went up and over the roofs of houses where these lay in the path of the line [19]. They were reported to have started somewhere in Dawlish, whence they went over the sandy peninsula known as the Warren, crossed the river to Exmouth, and ended up somewhere in the region of East Budleigh.

I have heard tell of a man who tried to frighten his neighbours some time after this happening by climbing to the skylight of his house after a snowfall with a goat's foot on the end of a long pole.

Document 42

Manchester Guardian.
22 March 1955

MISCELLANY
The Devil's Footprints

In "Miscellany's" notes about the mysterious footmarks which appeared in the snow one night in the region of the River Exe a hundred years ago it was said that no satisfactory explanation has been produced. I suggest (writes "P.J.") that the marks could only have been made by the trailing rope of a balloon. The rope, probably with a grapnel attached, would leave a mark in the snow on descending to earth; then, released of the weight of the rope, the balloon would rise and continue on its way for a few yards before again descending and repeating the process. The marks were in a single file; they were found on rooftops and other inaccessible places; they took a very erratic course and crossed a river estuary two miles wide. In all probability the balloon eventually floated out to sea, unless, of course, the whole affair was a superb practical joke. [20]

Document 43

ANIMAL LEGENDS
by Maurice Burton
pp.197-207 (London 1955)

PROBLEM PRINTS IN THE SNOW

Certain things make me feel I am in touch with something more vast than the world of men. Holst's "Music of the Planets" is one; but that may be auto-suggestion springing from the composer's title. This same feeling, induced also when gazing into a clear, starlit sky, comes to me from hearing certain passages in Vaughan Williams' "London Symphony", but I would hesitate to attribute this last to any influence the title may exert. The sight of a beech wood on a clear sunlit morning in October, a red sunset at sea, church bells on New Year's Eve, carol singers - in the distance - on a frosty night, and the picture conjured up in my mind by the story of the footprints in the Devon snow, all have this mystic quality. It is easy, therefore, to sympathise with the Devonians who, nearly a century ago, were afraid to leave their houses. If the tracks in the snow had appeared at Christmas instead of in early February, their mystical quality would have been enhanced, but they would have permitted of a more easy explanation, except that a reindeer does not have a hoof like a donkey.

In spite of this quasi-poetic start, it is my purpose to deal prosaically with animal tracks, in the snow or mud, as the case may be. Before doing so, it is fitting to recall briefly the Devon affair. In the past few months I have asked a number of people for details, but whereas all knew the story, all were very uncertain on its finer points.

The first report was in *The Times* for February, 1855. Heavy snow had fallen on the preceding Thursday night in the Exeter area. In the morning a vast number of prints, as of donkey shoes, were found in the snow, with a mound in the centre where the frog should be. Each print was directly in advance of the other, at regular intervals of 8 ins. They went from Topsham to Lympstone, Teignmouth and Dawlish. They ended abruptly on one side of the estuary of the Exe and started again on the Exmouth side, two miles across water from where they had left off. They went across fields and gardens, along the tops of flat walls, over roofs, over haystacks. They were seen in courtyards surrounded by high walls or high fences. They would go up to a 14 ft. wall, and start again on the other side, as if whatever had made them had gone straight through the wall. In places, they went up to the door of a house and backed away again, but for the rest the line of advance was straight. According to *The Times*, each print measured 1½ by 2½ ins. According to *The Illustrated London News* of February 24 of the same year, they measured 4 by 2 3/4 ins. The line of tracks started suddenly and ended abruptly.

I have no intention of attempting an explanation, for two very good reasons: that I have none to offer, and that I should be sorry to see the mystery solved, just as I would prefer not to analyse too closely Holst's ''Music of the Planets'', or any other of the things I have mentioned. But snow, for me, is an opportunity to study animal tracks, and animal tracks are, for me, even now, more of a mystery than otherwise.

Chard wrote a book, lavishly illustrated, entitled *Animal Tracks*, in which he surveyed the marks made in the ground by British mammals. It is an excellent survey. It shows the different impressions left by each animal walking, trotting, running and galloping. In it, we learn, too, that the tracks of a young animal register more accurately than those of an old animal; that a female tends to walk in a

less direct line than a male; and other basic principles. What we cannot learn, and the book cannot possibly give, are all the abnormal tracks, the evidence of unusual tricks of behaviour, often combined with unusual conditions of the ground. These can only be learned by long experience and, what is more important, by linking them with what is already known of the animal itself. We are told of the remarkable way an experienced tracker will deduce from its tracks the age and sex of the animal that has passed by, how long ago since it passed, whether it was tired or well-fed and so on. From my limited experience I suspect the tracker, consciously or unconsciously, used much more than appearance of the tracks. There are such things as scats, a knowledge of the weather during the preceding days, the appearance of the surrounding vegetation, even the smell of the beast left on the trail. Moreover, a tracker can do these, to us, wonderful things, only for the beasts with which he is fully familiar. Give him a drawing or photograph of the tracks of the animals with which he is not familiar, and it is by no means certain that he would show quite the same skill. With only pictures of the tracks of some animals he had never seen, he would be as mystified as any one of us.

Over and above this there are freak tracks. For example, we found, on a patch of mud in an opening between two meadows, a few tracks that looked exactly like those of a small deer. There was no possibility that they could have been deer, and sheep and pigs were even more unlikely. After close scrutiny we came to the conclusion that they were made by the fore-paws of rabbits or hares, running at full speed, so that all other tracks were on grass-covered firm ground. A more mystifying set of prints were those found on the roof of a shed recently during a period of intense hoar frost. At least they would have been mystifying had we not seen our cat sitting there earlier on. Or, again, a weasel crossing a muddy road in front of me a few months ago, suddenly leaping in the air, in a curve that carried him fully 3 ft. on to a grass slope. The recognisable weasel tracks ended abruptly, where the animal, a few inches long in the body, had taken its surprising leap. Had I not seen the leap take place, I might have presumed from the tracks that a hawk had swooped and carried off the weasel...

[Discussion of alleged Yeti footprints omitted]

The phenomenon of the devil's hoof-marks appears not to have been confined to Devon. I have had a few reports of similar occurrences in other parts of the country, but because these reports are at second-hand and not very fully documented nothing more will be said of them here. They are, however, sufficient to suggest that the devil's hoof-marks may have occurred in England on more than one occasion but the trails, not having the length of the Devon phenomenon, aroused little interest. They add interest, on the other hand, to an account published in the *Glasgow Herald* for 11 December, 1951. The writer told how, when "working as a timber cruiser with a winter exploration party (he) was carrying out a strip survey in Northern Quebec." He continues: "One day, when snow-shoeing over a snow-covered lake, I came across tracks which puzzled me and reduced my companion, a French Canadian dog-skinner, to a state of gibbering terror."

[Burton gives a summary of Rennie's Canadian experience. See Document 40]

On 9th February, 1953, this same correspondent returned to his subject again in the *Glasgow Herald*, with the surprising news that he had seen this phenomenon again in Scotland after a lapse of fourteen years. Moreover, he had had the opportunity of photographing the tracks.

[A further summary follows of Rennie's Scottish experience. See Document 40]

Then comes the long arm of coincidence, for this writer continues: "I encountered the second lot of tracks on January 9. On this occasion I was walking through dense woodland and found them in a forest clearing. This time I was unable to fetch a camera before darkness fell, but I managed to make my way back to the locality two days later.

"When I first saw these second tracks they could not have been more than an hour or two old, and were made in deep, soft snow. During the next twenty-four hours there was some fine, misty rain, followed on the succeeding night and morning by severe frost [21]. This had had the effect of crusting the snow so that while I myself did not sink into it the tracks retained their original depth and were clearly defined.

"These second tracks were slightly smaller than the first, and the distance between each print was shorter - only about 4 ft. 6 in. - but they were of extreme interest in that they bore a remarkable resemblance to the pictures I have seen of Yeti tracks sent back by the Himalayan Reconnaissance Expedition in 1951. They were very definitely bi-lobal and, at a point where they leapt across a sunken roadway for a distance of about 20 ft. the likeness to the published Yeti pictures was most marked."

I have discussed these observations with meteorologists and the consensus of their opinion is that there is no known meteorological phenomenon that could account for the Strathspey trails. One, indeed, said - "It is impossible." As I have suggested, if we take the Himalayan tracks as a separate phenomenon it presents a close parallel to the hedgehog story and its non-acceptance by the experts. If we take devil's hoof-prints, and their alleged repetition elsewhere, the windygo and the Strathspey tracks, there is a closely similar parallel. And all these snow-tracks may be related, a wide-spread phenomenon occurring sporadically and possibly due to the same cause or group of related causes. As with the hedgehog and apples, the rats and the egg and the rest, the experts will have none of it.

Document 44

GREAT WORLD MYSTERIES
by Eric Frank Russell
(London 1957) pp.28-45

SATAN'S FOOTPRINTS

In the mid-nineteenth century there occurred a remarkable phenomenon that aroused widespread curiosity, much excitement and a little fear in the British Isles. This was the sudden appearance in the county of Devon of a long trail of mysterious footprints the like of which no man had seen before. First report of them was given in *The Times*, February 16th 1855, reading as follows :

[See Document 2]

Having said that much, *The Times* lost interest, perhaps thinking it beneath its dignity to have anything to do with the night-time gallivantings of Satan. It gave no more space to the subject. The *Illustrated London News* promptly chipped in by inviting first-hand reports from its readers and was swamped with correspondence. A witness on the spot, signing himself 'South Devon', gave the facts as he saw them:

[See Document 7]

At this stage the astute reader may be ruminating on a couple of contradictions in the preceding accounts. Noting the raised crest of snow in the middle of each print, *The Times* says that the mysterious foot or feet must have been convex. But a convex foot would have left a hollow in the centre of each print. The evidence is that the foot was *concave*. *The Times* also starts off its account by saying that 'there was a very heavy fall of snow'. Just how deep it was depends upon what one calls 'very heavy'. As the man on the spot, Mr. South Devon reports that 'the snow lay very thinly on the ground at the time', so thinly that the prints went right through it and left it looking 'as if cut with a diamond or branded with a hot iron'.

Another writer to the *Illustrated London News* asserted that local labourers, their wives and children, old crones and trembling old men, dreaded to stir out after sunset or to go half a mile into lanes or byways on a call or message, 'under the conviction that this was the Devil's walk, and no other, and that it was wicked to trifle with such a manifest proof of the Great Enemy's immediate presence'.

Yet another correspondent, 'G.M.M.', said that he had personally examined the prints in company of a local clergyman on whose lawn they had appeared:

[See Document 11]

There followed a welter of guesses naming half the living creatures known to the British scene, each correspondent writing lengthily and sometimes passionately in support of his particular candidate, and each seemingly convinced that the unrecognizable was merely the recognizable somehow made unrecognizable to any but himself. Swans, moorhens, cranes, seagulls, bustards, turkeys and others were offered. Those who scorned the birds and preferred the beasts 'proved' to their own satisfaction that the marks had been made by otters, frogs, polecats, mice, rabbits, hares, badgers and almost everything but tomcats.

One or two backed up the Rev. Mr. Musgrave's theory concerning kangaroos for no other reason than that a Mr. Fische, of Sidmouth, Devon, had in his private menagerie a couple of kangaroos both of which remained firmly caged throughout the entire ruckus. [22]

A certain Thomas Fox, writing in the *Illustrated London News*, March 10th 1855, 'proved' that the prints were caused by a rat jumping repeatedly and landing with all four feet close together to form an impression of single prints. If this were true, the creature had leaped at accurate intervals of eight and a half inches for a total distance of about one hundred miles, hopping up one side of rooftops and down the other, clearing haystacks and fourteen-foot walls *en route*, and managing to teleportate [*sic*] itself across an estuary two miles wide.

Some rat!

Excited and argumentative laymen were silenced when suddenly Authority stepped in and made its pronouncement. This came in the form of a letter to the *Illustrated London News* from Richard Owen, then a famous naturalist whose views were regarded with proper awe.

[See Document 11]

This represents the dogmatic mind in its most pompous mood. From the heights of his allegedly coldly scientific and purely objective wisdom Mr. Owen asserts that his solution is the one and only correct one. And that is in bland disregard of the fact that he never actually observed the phenomena he interprets, whereas those he criticizes had done so at first-hand.

A good deal of intelligent interest in this mystery was taken in modern times by the late Lieutenant-Commander Rupert T. Gould, R.N., a shrewd if somewhat irascible author who devoted much of his time to analysing such puzzles, collecting and overhauling ancient typewriters and - to judge from his many letters to me - gathering odd-shaped scraps of writing paper from heaven alone knows where. In his book *Oddities* he takes a dim view of Owen's opinion, pointing out that in Victorian days people tended to be over-awed by well-known names and had not acquired the modern habit of reaching for the salt. Therefore Owen's statement was accepted without argument by all save those who had failed to see what Owen said they should have seen.

Nowadays, continues Gould a trifle acidly, we know a lot more about scientific dogmatism and a good deal more about Richard Owen. As a naturalist, Owen was esteemed a very great man but, like many such, was not above occasionally making bald assertions in defiance of facts. This weakness became most evident in 1857 during a controversy with Huxley on the subject of *hippocampus major*, Owen assuming the leadership of the anti-Darwinians and advancing the since exploded theory that the adult skull is a modified vertebral joint.

Possibly influenced to some extent by the fact that he was once a naval officer himself, Gould also damns Owen for his 'utterly childish' explanation of the sea-serpent seen by H.M.S. *Daedalus* in 1848; pointing out that the said explanation flatly contradicts the observed facts and postulates that the naval officers who observed them were, 'one and all, half-witted'.

Owen's theory, disguised as an incontrovertible statement of fact, does not stand up under serious examination by anyone with enough gumption not to be influenced by a big name. For an animal of its bulk and build the badger has a fairly wide stance. It is quite true that the prints of its hind-feet may be impressed upon and blend into those of its fore-feet. But not in single line. They form two distinct lines staggered with respect to each other.

And while a badger might conceivably swim an estuary two miles wide, or while one or more badgers might prowl one side of a broad river while a second group foraged the other side, no badger ever heard of has the agility to mount house-tops, stroll with neat precision across sharply sloping roofs, jump high walls, or surmount haystacks without leaving a print thereon.

The most noteworthy and the most important feature of the whole affair, as detailed by eye-witnesses, is that feelings were stirred across the entire range from curiosity to open alarm, because the prints *were unfamiliar*. They were strange. They were new, unrecognizable, incomprehensible, even to old inhabitants who had lived through many a snowfall in company with all the local lifeforms. Indeed, it was these older ones, who could tell a badger from an ox, who got the biggest scare.

The Times, after apparently deciding to have nothing more to do with the matter, weakened enough to give it small mention in its issue of March 6th 1855.

[See Document 12]

The late Charles Fort, by far the most redoubtable digger-up of peculiar data, also turned his attention to this mystery, and found concomitant items that had escaped Gould's notice. I quote from his omnibus volume, *The Books of Charles Fort*.

[See Document 38]

Since Fort never gained either time or space for the full expression of his ideas concerning these and numberless other more baffling incidents, even in a volume of greater than a thousand pages, it is futile to attempt to summarize his expressions in a page or two of this book. All that may be offered, for the reader's edification, is his satirical comment: 'It is my own acceptance that not less than a thousand one-legged kangaroos, each shod with a very small horseshoe, could have marked that snow in Devonshire.'

Rupert T. Gould also sought elsewhere for similar prints but seems to have found only those discovered on Kerguelen Island, as mentioned on page 27 [of *Great World Mysteries*]. The original account was written up in May 1840, by Captain Sir James Clarke

Ross, when his ships, the *Erebus* and *Terror*, were lying off Kerguelen.

[See Document 39]

Kerguelen is a large, sparse, sub-antarctic island with little enough flora and fauna. One thing seems fairly certain: whatever hoofed creature was native to the place or 'had cast on shore from some wrecked vessel', it was anything but a badger.

The general agreement in areas so dispersed as Devon, Scotland, Poland and Kerguelen Island is that whatever makes mysterious, single-file tracks is hoofed or has feet the treading-surfaces of which leave hooflike spoor. Witness after witness compares the marks with those of a foal, donkey, pony or ass. Though spread apart in space and time the phenomena have the puzzling aspect of prints left by a junior member of the equine species making short hops on one leg.

On January 10th 1945, when Rundstedt's push through the Ardennes had failed to reach its objectives, snow lay in Belgium at depth varying between two and four feet. And it was there that this writer discovered strange prints very similar to but not identical with those already described. A drawing of the phenomenon, complete with measurements, was used as cover illustration for the fifteenth issue of *Doubt*, the magazine of the Fortean Society. Details published therein enable me to have the peculiar experience of quoting myself. All that is omitted from the following description is the harrowing tale of what I suffered struggling in rubber thigh-boots through that depth of snow.

[See Document 33]

At that time the evidence definitely created the impression of small hoof-marks, though at this date I do not know why I thought of a goat rather than a pony or donkey. There was nothing to show that the hoof was cloven. Possibly my thoughts were influenced by the local multiplicity of goats. All I do know is that I witnessed something baffling and sufficiently like earlier phenomena to be worth noting and recording.

To return to the prints seen in Devon; eye-witnesses confessed themselves mystified not only by the one-legged appearance of the tracks but also by the way they jumped 'unsurmountable' obstacles. The line of prints, they declared, meandered through or over all sorts of 'inaccessible' places such as rooftops, haystacks and enclosures surrounded by high walls. But had the witnesses seen sparrow-tracks doing the same they would have thought nothing of it. Any bird could do it with no trouble at all. This phase of the matter is mystifying only if it be assumed that the track-maker is an animal.

Some years ago a Shropshire friend of mine followed a single file of bird-prints across the snow in his paddock, through a hedge and into a field where eventually he caught up with a lame jackdaw which was hopping on one foot and fluttering its wings. He took the bird home, tended to it. In the end it became the family pet and something of a household tyrant.

This petty incident, plus consideration of the real 'unsurmountability' of obstacles in Devon, moves me to suppose that the Satanic footprints could have been made only by one or more winged creatures either hoofed or having strong, heavily webbed, concave feet that in given circumstances - such as presence of snow -'leave prints deceitfully like those of hoofs. Creatures that waddle as they walk, placing one foot before the other.

If this none too satisfactory theory should happen to be correct it will prove difficult to gain positive identification of the culprit or culprits until such time as it or they may be caught red-handed doing it again. But it would be a mistake to place the blame on life-forms native to the localities in which strange prints have appeared. The quality of this mystery is that the prints are unfamiliar.

Given that some kind of bird is responsible for such tracks, we must accept that it may have been a rare visitor of a kind·not yet known to science. One from anywhere in the world, from Poles to Equator, inexplicably transported hundreds or thousands of miles from home.

The mysterious misplacement of living creatures is nothing new. Time and again they have turned up far from natural habitat, appearing as incongruous in their surroundings as would a hyena in the Isle of Man.

Daily Telegraph, July 9th 1938 - TROPICAL

SNAKES IN POND. 'Water snakes of a kind found only in tropical regions have been discovered in a lake covered with lilies and iris in the grounds of the home of Miss A. Bevis, Sarisbury Green, Hampshire.'

A six-year-old bear was shot near Oloron Sainte-Marie, France. Ribbon fish were found hard aground in Scotland and South Africa. Turtles native to the Gulf of Mexico, known as Kemp's Loggerheads, ambled along beaches of the English Channel and Ireland. Nick, a brindle bullterrier, vanished from New Brighton, Cheshire, swam, flew or walked across seventy-five miles of ocean and blandly popped up at Groudle, near Douglas, Isle of Man. It is a wonder he did not encounter an out-of-place hyena there. There is an irresistible theory to explain this dog-feat, namely, that Nick was in league with Old Nick.

Daily Telegraph, June 28th 1938 - AFRICAN TURTLE IN KENT. 'While working on the Royal Military Canal, at Kenardington, Kent, Mr. F. Gill saw a turtle basking in the sun and managed to catch it. Measuring eleven inches from head to tail, it is similar in appearance to a tortoise, but much faster in movement.' The thing was identified as an African mud-turtle.

In 1931, according to the *New York Times*, the police of Mineola, Long Island, mustered their resources and set up a hue and cry after a hairy ape, four feet tall, seen wandering loose by several people. Armed citizens joined the hunt, poked and pried all over the area. Apelike footprints were found, complete with the offset thumb characteristic of the species. This was in June and the pursuit continued unabated into mid-July when several more startled folk reported seeing the creature. No ape was found.

Data of this description can be piled up to formidable proportions but it might be fitting to terminate the subject with the statement that a queer skull was dug up in the Isle of Man. It was sent to the Department of Vertebrate Zoology of Liverpool Museum, where Douglas A. Allan, Ph.D., D.Sc., identified it as the skull of an adult hyena.

The complete unfamiliarity of prints found in Devon and elsewhere points directly to something that had strayed far from home, some creature or creatures whose spoor may have appeared quite commonplace to Naga headhunters or Eskimos or even the penguins at the South Pole.

Evidence suggests that the print-maker was bipedal and put one foot directly before the other, leaving a single line of prints. It was winged. And it had splayed, concave feet as perfectly adapted to its own harsh environment as are those of the camel.

It is this writer's suspicion that in the north or south polar regions, or both, lives a rare bird not yet known to science. Like the albatross, it has powerful wings and is capable of long, sustained flights. But like the road-runner of the Great American Desert, it prefers to walk.

Normally, this bird forages through polar wastes, chasing surefootedly across fields of snow, scampering up the rooflike tilts of glaciers, flapping over walls of ice and haystacks of bare rock. Once in a blue moon it is swept far from its usual hunting grounds or is enticed abroad by the spread of snow. Then it lands, mooches around a while - and scares hell out of every decent Christian for miles and miles.

This is all theory, of course, backed by nothing save that it fits the facts. I offer it mostly in the hope that some day ornithologists may discover my bird, give credit where credit is due, and graciously name it 'Russell's snowrunner'.

Document 45

Animals.
Volume 6 Number 8 (20 April 1965) pp.108-09

The Devil's Hoof-marks
Alfred Leutscher

Readers of *The Times* opening their papers on the morning of 8th February, 1855 [23], must have been startled, or perhaps amused, by the account of a strange happening. The *Illustrated London News* took up this story, and invited eye-witness accounts, and explanations, from its readers. A spate of letters followed, including some vivid descriptions such as this one sent in by 'South Devon':

'When we consider the distance that must have been gone over to leave these marks - I may say in almost every garden, on door-steps, through extensive woods, upon commons, in enclosures and farms, over houses, hayricks, and very high walls (one 14 feet) without displacing the snow - the actual progress must have exceeded a hundred miles. No known animal could have traversed the extent of country in one night, besides having to cross an estuary of the sea two miles wide. Neither does any known animal walk in a line of single footsteps, not even man.'

These tracks became known as the 'Devil's Hoof-marks'. Authorities such as the London Zoo and the Natural History Museum were consulted, but the whole affair remains a mystery to this day. A whole list of animals was suggested, such as the otter, badger, hare, polecat, frog, kangaroo, rat, and various birds. From the size of the tracks, the least likely would be the kangaroo, although some were in the area at the time, on a private estate.

One ingenious suggestion was an escaped balloon which had dragged its mooring ring on the end of a rope. It is a little hard to imagine how it managed to keep at a steady height; bobbing up and down at regular intervals to mark the trail, yet obligingly drifting along the tops of walls, and over houses without waking the inmates.

The insistence in many letters that no animal can walk in a straight line must be challenged. This is precisely what some can do, and in two ways. The cat and fox, for example, have a way of walking in a tight-rope fashion, one foot in front of the other, in a clean 'register': that is, the hind foot placed in the track of the opposite fore foot. The result is a very neat line of tracks. One only has to watch a cat as it walks along a fence top to appreciate its powers of balance. This fits in very well with the Devon trails, except that each individual track would show toeprints instead of the curious 'U-shaped' hoof-marks.

Other trails which are made in a straight line are those of an animal which hops. All four feet land in a bunch, in a leap-frog action, so that the hind tracks are leading. When this happens in a soft medium like snow, especially when it begins to melt, the tracks become blurred and run together. The result is a 'U' or 'V-shaped' impression. Examples of such leap-frog hoppers among British animals are the hare, rabbit, squirrel, rat, and mouse.

The drawing submitted by 'South Devon'

shows a trail of clear hoof prints, each an exact facsimile, as if made by some tiny animal whose feet were shod. Such clear and regular prints seldom occur, since irregularities in the ground or snow cause variations in size and shape. One is tempted to think that the observer in this instance did not draw what he actually saw, but rather what he wanted to see - the hoof-marks of Satan [25]. This is understandable, since a common human failing in most of us is to let a preconceived notion mar our judgement.

Another drawing which I examined, by a correspondent signed 'GMM', has given me a clue to a possible solution to this mystery. It shows a carefully drawn set of tracks, each of irregular shape, and roughly 'V-shaped' in contour. This is precisely what a small hopping animal would produce in snow, and there is only one British animal small enough to fit the Devon trails - the wood mouse (*Apodemus sylvaticus*).

It was during a search for snow tracks in Epping Forest, in the severe winter of 1962-3, that I came across dozens of trails of the wood mouse, each consisting of small 'V-shaped' marks regularly spaced out and conforming to the measurements which were given a hundred years ago. When I found them I was totally unaware of their significance (*Animals*, 18th February 1964).

In the intense cold and silence of the forest,

Fig. 10 - Illustration from Alfred Leutscher, 'The Devil's Hoof-marks', in *Animals* (Document 45), showing wood mouse tracks.

what could have been a better setting for the return of the mysterious Devon visitor. In this case, however, the mischievous little rodents were playing the Devil at his own game!

Wood mice are very common in Devon, nocturnal by nature, energetic leapers, and agile climbers [26]. In accepting this earthy little creature, two questions have to be answered. Why did this only occur in Devon and why only on that one occasion? Firstly, snowfall is an uncommon event in South Devon, so that these mouse trails would seldom be noticed. Secondly, once a lead was given that a tiny devil had been abroad, who among the Devon folk would have dared to deny his presence. Everyone knows that 'there are Piskies up to Dartymoor, and tiddn good you zay there baint'. Better let sleeping dogs lie. And what a cheeky little devil it was, for every footstep it took was in a backward direction!

This theory was first expressed in a paper delivered by Mr Leutscher to the Zoological Society of London. [27]

Document 46

IN THE LIFE OF A ROMANY GYPSY
  by Manfri Frederick Wood
  (London, 1973)

THE MULO

In the old days before most of the Romanies became Christians they all believed in mulos, which were Romany dead men before they were finally allowed to the land of the dead. How long they haunted their particular part of the country depended entirely on how wicked they were in their lives. A good Rom that died was never supposed to become a mulo at all but went straight to the land of the shadows. The mulo was supposed to live inside the body of a dead man lying in his grave, but he came out of the tomb every night as the dead man's double and at cock-crow he returned to his grave until high noon when he came out for half an hour. If you got in his path you would have a terrible vengeance on your head - you would commit suicide or commit some terrible crime or if you were a woman, the mulo would rape you and you would give

birth to an idiot child. Some said that the mulo was not a dead man at all but the devil in the guise of a dead man. But whichever way you looked at the mulo they were afraid of him and made a point of stopping at a camping site in time to get out of the mulo's way inside their tents or wagons. So the old gypsies years ago never travelled at noon and were out of sight by dusk.

Whenever a tribe took to religion - that is, when they became Christians - they dropped most of their older beliefs, and anyone who kept on worrying about mulos was in great danger of being turned out of the tribe. So it turns out that most of the pure Romanies in this country no longer bother about mulos and travel at any time of the day or night if they have to, while a good many of the Didekais and Pikies [28] are still very particular about keeping out of the mulo's way. In our family the belief in mulos was a very useful weapon for clearing an area more or less permanently of Pikies. One of the first tricks of this nature occurred well before my time - well before the general use of the motor car in fact. I am not sure about the exact area or even the approximate date when this occurred - but it is a true story as I got it from one of my uncles and it filled the newspapers at the time and caused a great sensation. As far as I can recall, it happened in the county of Somerset.

That night, as everybody in the area found first thing in the morning, the devil walked right across the county of Somerset. Only it wasn't the devil at all but some seven Romany tribes using over 400 sets of measure stilts with size 27 boots at their base. The whole operation took over 18 months to plan out and prepare, and the reason for it was that on a particular stretch that had always been a Romany drom [29] as far back as anyone could remember a lot of Pikies had drifted in and caused a lot of trouble for the Romanies.

Now I don't know exactly how a measure-stilt was constructed, but I do know that it consisted of a pair of step-ladders that could be lengthened or shortened by means of slides and hinges. They were joined on top by a wheel. The bottom of each step-ladder stood in the great big boot and the man operating the stilts stood on one of the ladders and joggled about on it to make as deep a foot impression as possible. Then he would either swing the second ladder over the top by the wheel - if there was enough head room - or, if there was not enough room, he would raise the ladder by the slide and move it forward by one 'devil's stride'. Either way he got an exact measure of a stride, as the measure-stilts were constructed so they could not over- or under-stride the three yards it was meant to do. [30]

When the second ladder had been shifted to the front, the 'stilt-treader' stepped onto it and shifted the first ladder in front of it again. Then he joggled about on the second ladder to make a deep impression and stepped forward onto the first ladder again - and so he went on without ever stepping off the measure-stilts for the whole operation. This was straightforward enough while striding over open country, except that it was done on a dark night and required skilful balancing all the way - but going over hedges, ditches and country lanes posed a serious problem as people might be using the highways and lanes and see a man working the measure-stilts. So when he worked his way over and along a public right of way he had to throw a sheet over the whole works so that the devil would be seen walking rather than a man with ladders on boots. Walking with that cloak over the top he saw even less of what he was doing than when he walked over the fields.

The devil was supposed to walk right across Somerset in as straight a line as possible [31] - he was not supposed to make any detour around houses or churches or barns and so on, but his footsteps had to go straight up one wall, over the roof and down the other wall. The stilt-treader could not walk up walls - he had to straighten out his stilts to turn them into a long ladder and then make a muddy line [32] of 'devil's strides' with a spare set of 27-size boot-seal impressions; halfway over the top he had to hoist the ladder up and swing it the right way round and without too much noise over to the other side of the building. This was the snaggiest part of the whole business as it required exceptional physical strength and poise. Also, dogs were bound to bark in some of the farm buildings that were being boot-marked and if any of them brought a farmer out of bed the cat would have been out of the bag.

If any man tried to play this trick on his own he would do well if he managed to cover two miles in one night. It would be quite a feat if he managed to cross two cottages or one village church - but that night the devil walked the breadth of Somerset, because there were seven Romany tribes in this and between them they used well over 400 measure-stilts. The route was planned very carefully and every part of it studied over a period of about 18 months. When the plan was put into operation it went off without a single hitch. After the men got back with their measure-stilts, a party made their way over the devil's trail from each of the camping sights and busied themselves with obliterating the tracks made to and from the devil's strides by the 'stilt-treaders'. The next day the devil's footprints could be clearly seen along the whole route. It put the fear of God into all the locals - but that was not the point of the exercise. For the next few years it kept the area free from Pikies and Didekais who swore blind it was a mulo that had crossed and they were not going to take any chances.

Document 47

Prediction.
March 1981

The Walker on The Wind
by Madeline Montalban

It is strange that so many people with an occult bent seem to prefer to turn their attention to the so-called mysterious East for the inexplicable. Perhaps it is a case of distance lending enchantment to the view; or what is comparatively unknown heightening credence. Whatever the cause, it does seem that the genuine mysteries of one's own country often arouse less interest than those of faraway places.

This is a pity because there have been so many strange occurrences in England alone that they must surely be worthy of further study. For instance, there is one event that seems to be aptly summed up by the well-known quotation: 'Who shall know the mysteries hatched in the depths of the sea, and who shall know the name of the Walker on the Wind?'

This true tale originated in Devon and was vouched for by the people in Lympstone,

Exmouth, Dawlish and Teignmouth - not forgetting Topsham and lesser-known villages. Most people in agricultural areas rise with the sun and, on one particular snow-bound morning - February 9th, 1855 - the early risers were baffled to see what appeared to be footprints in the snow: all in a straight line, going up the sides of houses and farms, over the roofs and down the other sides of the buildings.

These odd tracks appeared in several towns, and baffled their occupants greatly because two-footed creatures don't normally place their feet exactly in a straight line; neither, of course, do they walk up the side of a house, across the roof and down the other side. Come to that, quadrupeds don't walk in a straight line except for members of the cat family (including domestic ones).

However, there were no reports of missing lions or tigers with a penchant for long-distance walks - and house moggies don't travel in that fashion either! Yet there was no denying the fact that odd footprints did appear in the snow over a distance of more than 100 miles. Each print was about four inches long and nearly three inches wide; the prints were approximately eight inches apart and shaped like hoof-prints.

This latter point was enough, of course, to get the tracks dubbed as 'the Devil's hoof-prints' - though what the Lord of Evil was doing wandering about so aimlessly was never explained. However, these mysterious tracks caused a sufficient sensation at the time for the London *Times* to print a report about them; laying much emphasis on the fact that the tracks did not swerve at all. **[33]**

The tracks appeared on the top of 14 ft walls; up and over roofs and snow-covered piles of hay; some even appeared on the tops of farm-wagons which had been left out overnight. The footprints were evenly spaced and indented, therefore evidencing no change of speed (which would have altered the depth of the snowy depressions).

This particular mystery has never been satisfactorily explained. Yet every mystery does have some solution, so let us try to find an explanation before labelling the matter as an occult mystery, because a true occultist strives to exclude what cannot be possible before accepting what might be. Firstly then,

we will try to find a solution using simple astrology: bearing in mind that the sign placements of the planets and lights are more important than the house positions when trying to unravel a mystery. Also, it is more than likely that two signs - Scorpio (signifying hidden mysteries) and Pisces (strange events) - are likely to figure largely in any mystery.

Here, then, are the placements of the appropriate planets (without benefit of the rising sign, of course, as we do not know at what time the footprints were made during the dark hours of February 8th and 9th) to the nearest degree, taken from an aged ephemeris which, of course, does not include Pluto. Dawn indicates sunrise and, on February 9th, 1855, this was at 7.27 a.m.

It seems quite feasible to suppose that these mysterious tracks were, in fact, first noticed at that hour as there is no indication in any reports of the incident of anyone being wakened during the night. So, at that time the placement of the planets and lights was: Sun at 20° Aquarius; Moon, 9° Scorpio; Neptune, 14° Pisces; Uranus, 12° Taurus; Saturn, 9° Gemini; Jupiter, 12° Aquarius; Mars, 3° Pisces; Venus, 5° Pisces; and Mercury, 5° Pisces.

A pattern begins to emerge: Neptune, Mars, Venus and Mercury were all in Pisces and the Moon in Scorpio, which means that five powers were in Water signs. Also, if one uses the simple but useful mundane map placement (beginning with Aries and ending with Pisces ruling the 12th House), one finds the Scorpio Moon afflicting Uranus - planet of the future and of things new - and in conflict with Jupiter - representing long distance travel - with Uranus and Jupiter also adversely aspected.

This can be interpreted to mean that someone (or something) travelled. Also, as Jupiter was in an Air sign (but a 'friendly' sign), this indicates that whoever, or whatever travelled had no malign intentions. At this same time, the Moon had been in good aspect to Mercury, Mars and Venus; and was about to make a good aspect to Neptune - so, again, there is no indication of any evil intent.

Remember, too, that these four planets (Mercury, Mars, Venus and Neptune) were all occupying Pisces, the sign of mystery and concealment, and the Moon was in the secretive sign of Scorpio. Mercury in Pisces denotes forgetfulness or muddle, and was near to Mars; Saturn in Gemini can represent a delayed journey when badly aspected with Mercury; also, Saturn rules the metal lead, and was in good aspect to Jupiter in Aquarius.

Further, the Moon was in the House of Secrets and opposing Uranus - ruler of Aquarius - and Aquarius was occupied by the Sun and Jupiter. Jupiter is lord of long-distance travel and the Moon in Scorpio indicates secret travel; Mercury signifies forgetfulness and all those planets occupying Pisces indicate a mystery - so what is the solution? Did something or someone sail overhead (Jupiter and the Sun in an Air sign) and forget (Mercury) something which not only delayed the journey but also involved the metal lead?

Is it possible that someone, through forgetfulness, left a measure-marker outside an aircraft, so that it dangled from its rope and made that mysterious, single track in the snow - up walls and over roofs and haystacks? If so, the Devil can be exonerated from this particular mystery. Or can he? After all, 1855 was certainly not the age of the aeroplane: so we appear to be back at square 1 again ... or are we?

Well, as long ago as the 15th century, Leonardo da Vinci designed an aircraft that could (and did) fly; although, of course, air transport did not start getting seriously under way until the 1900s. But wait, what about the Montgolfiers and their air balloons?

Air balloons (and their ascents and landings) were familiar sights in Victorian London. Little children were taken to see them start their flights from Hyde Park.

The early balloonists must, presumably, have had to make practise flights. And it isn't impossible, I suppose, that an air balloon crossed Devon on a dark and snowy night with its measure-marker out. After all, this could account for those mysterious tracks; that is, of course, if balloonists of that era did undertake night ascents. Alternatively, perhaps a balloonist was blown off course, let the measure-marker down in order to find a safe place to land, then forgot about it.

Either of these alternatives seems to offer at least a *possible* solution to the mystery which would also fit in with the astrological data. The Moon is an indicator of travel and, when

in Scorpio, can be interpreted to signify a 'secret' trip. Jupiter, lord of long-distance travel, was in Aquarius, one of the Air signs, with Saturn afflicting Jupiter (denoting a delayed journey). Saturn was in Gemini (another Air sign) and afflicting Mercury, another planet of travel. Mercury in Pisces suggests forgetfulness leading to delay, muddle and mystery. And, finally, the Moon, Jupiter and Uranus were all in mutually bad aspect - suggesting a troubled, secret air journey.

So, did early balloonists make the Devil's footprints?

Trying to solve ancient mysteries by using simple astrology can be a fascinating pastime ... so let's just leave it at that.

Document 48

INFO Journal.
October 1982

The Devil'd Hoof-marks
A Possible Solution
by Raymond D. Manners

The mystery of the Devil's Hoof-Marks has been written about many times with explanations varying from extraterrestrials to wood mice. We appear to be no further toward a solution of this enduring mystery than were the naturalists and others who wrote to the papers in 1855. It is time for a re-examination of the evidence, to throw away all the previous theories, and to examine the possibility that the Devil's Hoof-Marks were not formed by a strange and unknown animal, but by men. In fact, by tribes of Romany gypsies.

The basic details of the event as recorded by newspapers of the time are repeated here for the benefit of those who are not completely familiar with the details of that snowy night in Devonshire a hundred and twenty-seven years ago.

The London *Times* for February 8, 1855, reported the following extraordinary occurrence:

[See Document 2]

A further report appeared in the *Times* for

March 6th, 1855:

[See Document 12]

Additional discussion appeared in the pages of the *Illustrated London News*. The following is taken from the issue of February 24th, 1855:

[See Document 7]

In the issue of March 3rd, 1855, the following details were provided by a correspondent signing himself as G.M.M.:

[See Document 11]

5Naturally people were not slow in coming forward with explanations. The famous naturalist Richard Owen suggested that the tracks were made by a badger. A swan with padded feet was also suggested. Other candidates included otters, leaping rats, a hare running with its legs held together, polecats, frogs, cranes, bustards, and the inevitable kangaroo. As Charles Fort says [34], "My own acceptance is that not less than a thousand one-legged kangaroos, each shod with a very small horseshoe, could have marked that snow of Devonshire".

A thoughtful review of the Devil's Hoof-Marks was provided by that talented and entertaining writer Rupert T. Gould [35]. He concludes his review by writing: "it is possible that there is some quite simple solution of the Devonshire hoof-marks to be found, if one knew where to look for it. But there is a caveat to be entered. If land-animals made the marks, the available data are probably sufficient to enable a competent zoologist, with an unbiased mind, to make a reasonable suggestion as to their identity. But no authority on earth ... can set limits to the number and variety of the creatures which, even though unknown to science, may yet live and move and have their being in the sea."

When we return to *The Book of the Damned* we find that Fort had been much more thorough in uncovering references to the occurrence, and some of these provide important clues that were missed or ignored by Gould. Thus, in *Notes and Queries*, 7-8-508:

[See Document 15]

Impressions of the point of a stick? This is only mentioned by Fort and immediately brings to mind someone balancing on something and occasionally supporting himself or saving himself from falling by thrusting the end of the balance pole in the ground. Is it remotely possible that the Devil's Hoof-Marks could have been made by someone balancing on a pair of stilts with the foot pads shaped like a donkey's hoof?

Consider the facts:

1. The tracks extended for at least a hundred miles and were made in the course of a single night.

2. The only marks were the tracks and the impressions of the point of a stick. There were no marks of any other kind.

3. There were no unusual noises during the night; no dogs barked and no one saw or heard anything unusual.

4. All the marks were apparently identical in size and were regularly spaced about eight-and-a-half inches apart.

5. The prints continued over the roofs of some houses and apparently went straight through objects such as walls and haystacks, appearing on the other side.

6. The prints stopped at the estuary of the River Exe, continuing in the same straight line on the other side (some two miles across the water).

The above facts, taken singly or together, mitigate against the prints having been made by someone on stilts. In addition to making many thousands of eight-and-a-half inch steps over a distance of in excess of a hundred miles, the person would have had to swim across the estuary carrying the stilts and continue making the prints on the other side. Swimming across two miles of open water in the dark in a snowstorm is no mean feat in itself, but carrying a pair of stilts as well - and walking on those stilts for over a hundred miles - would require a superman. No wonder those people of Devonshire in 1855 thought it was the Devil!

But now we come to a story submitted to INFO several years ago by Raleigh M. Roark, and extracted from the book *In the Life of a Romany Gypsy* by Manfri Frederick Wood.

[See Document 46]

Now this story is placed at an undefinable date in an area of Somerset. But surely this is exactly what happened that snowy night in Devonshire? Not one man on stilts but literally hundreds!

We can well imagine the gypsy tribes planning this operation for several months, taking careful notes of the exact track they were to follow while engaged in selling clothes pins from door to door in the towns. They would be certain to note the presence of dogs, ditches, haystacks, fences, and houses that could be easily surmounted. Perhaps they would have erected sighting marks in open country, or across the estuary of the River Exe, or perhaps they would have simply stationed men with lanterns as guides in the open countryside.

But the most difficult aspect of the story is the measure stilts. And in Devon, the prints were not spaced three yards apart but 8½ inches! A pair of step ladders attached to a wheel at the top with an 8½ inch stride, with one leg being swung over the other at every step would require incredible skill to operate. A unicycle would be child's play by comparison. Whatever the construction of the stilts, some accessory means of balancing such as a pole would have been necessary. If the measure stilts used in Devonshire were simply normal stilts with a restricting linkage between the two legs, the treader would still have been required to walk in a straight line.

However, we do know from the above story that they probably spent over a year in making the measure stilts, and a good part of this time was probably spent by the men of the tribe in becoming proficient in their use. Naturally, each treader would have carried a spare hoof-mark to make the impressions on the roofs of houses, in culverts, under hedges, etc.

If we assume that 400 pairs of stilts were used in Devon, then each treader had to cover about ¼ mile of ground. No-one had to swim across tbe estuary of the Exe, the line of prints was simply picked up by Romanies on the other side, commencing from a pre-arranged point [36]. It is conceivable that the entire operation was completed in a couple of hours, including brushing away the tracks of the treaders as they approached and left their line of prints. This would possibly have been the job of the women and older men, who were probably also employed to keep the dogs quiet. The entire operation does not appear to be difficult for the determined yet secretive Romanies who had well over a year to prepare for it.

Some credence can also be given to the measure stilt theory for the simple reason that gypsies are traditionally uncommunicative with non-gypsies and extremely close mouthed regarding their private affairs. If any word of the intended operation had got out either before or after the event, the element of superstitious fear that they planned to impart in the Didikais and Pikies would have been lost. And by maintaining secrecy, they were free to use the same strategy another time in another place. No doubt the hundreds of sets of measure stilts were broken up for clothes line poles and clothes pegs and sold in the same towns and villages where the inhabitants firmly believed that they had been visited by the very Devil himself!

As Gould said, "...it is possible that there is some quite simple solution of the Devonshire hoof-marks to be found, if one knew where to look for it." The solution outlined above is certainly more credible than jumping wood mice or one-legged kangaroos!

NOTES TO ESSAYS AND THEORIES

1 - Fort was unaware that claw marks were also mentioned by the Reverend Ellacombe in his papers [see Document 23]. They were identified as "feathers" of snow, so - while it may well be that the marks were real - Fort was probably right to suggest they were seized on by the superstitious.

2 - Lympstone.

3 - Exe.

4 - See Document 35 for a similar anomaly of snow displacement.

5 - Canticles ii.12 [Footnote by Gould]

6 - He signed himself 'G.M.M.' [*Illustrated London News*, 3.3.1855. [Gould] See section one, note 35.

[Ed].

7 - Amazing to say.

8 - His letter to the *ILN* on the subject was considered (3.III.1885) but not printed. So he published a small pamphlet - *The Swan with the Silver Collar* (Wells, *Journal* Office, 1855, price 2d.) - of which I possess a copy. [Gould]

9 - Next in line.

10 - Mr Musgrave's letter, already quoted, indicates one or two exceptions. He might also have instanced the camel. [Gould]

11 - See Document 11.

12 - I am indebted to Mr. H.V. Garner for drawing my attention to this point. [Gould] The same objection, incidentally, does not appear to apply to the theory that Romany gypsy 'stilt treaders' were responsible for the trails. 'Well over' 400 gypsies were said to have been involved, manipulating clumsy 'measure stilts'; assuming 500 Romanies were present, their rate of progress would have had to be from 43-56 steps per hour, depending upon whether the trail was a mere 40 miles long or, as Gould postulates, 30% longer. If the trail was 100 miles long, the progress would have had to be a more impressive 108 steps per hour, or 1.8 steps per minute. All these calculations, of course, assume a more-or-less continuous trail, whereas there may well have been very considerable gaps. [Ed.]

13 - But see the section "Other Mystery Footprints", the evidence in which suggests that the phenomenon may not be as rare as Gould thought.

14 - But for this, and the fact that the hoof-marks were found on walls and roofs, a candidate whose qualifications were not put forward at any time - the common rabbit - would seem as good a claimant as any. In snow of a certain depth, a leaping rabbit *does* leave a track not unlike a series of hoof-marks. But it is clear, from "South Devon's" letter, that he saw, and examined, rabbit tracks made at the same time as the hoof-marks, and did not associate the two. [Gould]

15 - These ships were later themselves the subject of a famous mystery, written up by Gould in the same volume as his essay on the Devil's Hoofmarks. Having been made available to Sir John Franklin's disastrous naval expedition in search of the North-West Passage, and having apparently vanished along with both their crews, they were reportedly seen stranded upon a giant iceberg spotted off the Canadian coast. See "The Ships Seen on the Ice" in *Oddities*.

16 - Dr. R. M'Cormick, R.N., who was supposed to be the official zoologist (and geologist) of Ross's expedition, does not refer to these marks in the account of the voyage given in his *Voyages of Discovery in the Arctic and Antarctic Seas, and Round the World* (London, 1884). It is probable, however, that he never saw them himself (his journal at Kerguelen is mostly devoted to a trivial and querulous account of his teal-shooting expeditions): and he was not the man to give prominence to the work of others. His book, also, was published forty years after the voyage. [Gould]

17 - It was not, obviously, a common denizen either of the British Isles or of Kerguelen; localities whose climates are respectively temperate and sub-Polar. [Gould]

18 - Better known to Forteans as the Big Grey Man of Ben MacDhui. See Affleck Grey, *The Big Grey Man of Ben MacDhui* (Aberdeen, 1970).

19 - It is interesting to note how the passage of time has changed the original meandering wander of the tracks to a more single-mindedly diabolical single line.

20 - The "balloon theory" is hard put to explain the reported tiny distance between the "hoof-marks" as well as the extreme regularity which most observers found the most puzzling thing about them. In addition, one might have expected to find drag marks left by a rope, particularly when the distance from balloon to ground was effectively shortened as the craft passed over a house.

21 - This sounds very like the conditions in Devon on the night and morning of 8-9 February.

22 - This does not appear to have been definitively established.

23 - This reference is incorrect. The correct date is 16 February. See Document 2.

24 - This is a very loose 'quotation' from Document 7.

25 - See the introductory essay for comments on the character and expertise of 'South Devon'.

26 - Nevertheless, the presence of tracks on rooftops would still appear more than a little mysterious.

27 - See *Journal of Zoology* vol.148 (1966) p.383 for a reference to this meeting. Leutscher's paper was not reprinted in the *Journal of Zoology*.

28 - Pagan travelling tribes.

29 - Area of influence.

30 - Note the considerable discrepancies between the Romany tradition and the events reported in 1855: the 'walk' took place in Devon and Dorset, not Somerset; the prints were of small hoofs rather than giant boots; and the length of stride was generally well under a foot, rather than 9 feet. Incidentally, the idea that even the most practised stilt-operator could balance on the two narrow feet of one ladder while swinging another over his head, at one point with that whole ladder at 908 to the vertical, and presumably extending more than six feet ahead of him, seems improbable.

31 - While suitably diabolical, the idea of a straight march across a county does not accord with the remarkable meanderings actually noted in Devon. See note 19.

32 - This, and the previous description of 'joggling', suggests there is no Romany tradition that the trail was laid in snow.

33 - This is incorrect. See Document 2.

34 - See Document 38.

35 - See Document 39.

36 - There is in fact no contemporary evidence that anyone established that the prints went up to one shore of the Exe, and began anew on the opposite shore.

A PRELIMINARY BIBLIOGRAPHY

[This is only a partial listing of the material published on the subject of the Devil's Hoofmarks. It does not include the documents cited in the main text, nor has any definitive effort been made to track down all references in the Fortean literature.]

Anon - 'Devil's Hoofmark - By a Mouse?', *The Times* 16 January 1968 [*An article on Leutscher's woodmouse theory.*]

Anon - 'Devil's hoof prints', *Western Morning News* 15 February 1982 [*A brief summary of the mystery and the main theories.*]

Anon - 'Devon Case of 'Devil's' Footprints', *Western Morning News* 4 January 1940 [*Summary of the 1855 case prompted by a heavy fall of snow in the area.*]

Anon - 'Footprints in the Snow', *Western Morning News* 14 August 1937 [*Compares the Devil's Hoofmarks to some recently-discovered alleged Yeti prints in the Himalayas.*]

Anon - 'The Mysterious Footprints', *Reynolds' Miscellany* 28 April 1855 p216 [*A sceptical note based on the* Illustrated London News' *accounts.*]

Anon - 'Mystery of the Devil's Hoofprints', *National Enquirer* 1 April 1986 [*An article alleging similar marks had been found in the US and UK. Includes a distorted account of Mr Wilson's 1950 Devon report and several American stories linking hoofmarks to the occult, based on an interview with Brad Steiger.*]

Anon - 'Mystery that Made its Mark', *Express & Echo* (Exeter) 27 February 1986 [*Brief newspaper comment on the mystery.*]

Anon - The Reverend H.T. Ellacombe, Devon nd [*An 8-page Gestetnered biographical pamphlet available at the parish church of Clyst St George. It includes a section on the Devil's Hoofmarks.*]

Anon - 'The Riddle of Satan's Spoor', *Black Country Bugle* no 67 (October 1977) [*An article about the appearance of hoofmarks in Rowley Regis, near Birmingham, in January 1855.*]

Anon - 'The Riddle of Satan's Spoor', *Black Country Bugle* no 108 (March 1981) [*An article about Elizabeth Brown, landlady of the Lion pub, who saw marks similar to the Devon prints on the wall of her tavern. Refers to another article on the same subject, published by the Bugle in 1978, which may be a mistaken reference to the article noted above.*]

Anon - 'Still They Puzzle Over This Mystery', *Express & Echo* (Exeter) 28 November 1968 [*A brief editorial comment.*]

Anon - Article in *Wide Awake*, 1855 [*While searching an index of Devon oddments, Peter Christie came across a reference to the above article (personal communication). It has not proved possible to locate a copy of the publication.*]

Anon - 'A Wonder at Wolverhampton', *Punch* vol 28-29 (1855) p112 [*Mentions the Devil's Hoofmarks in the context of a number of recent wonders, including the apparition of a ghost and a sea serpent sighting.*]

Arnold, Larry - 'Has the Dover Devil visited South-Central Pennsylvania in March 1978' in *Pursuit* vol 11 No. 3 p121 (1978). [*A Fortean investigator photographs a curious track of 'prints', rendered unidentifieable by melting, that cross a snow-covered roof in a rural area.*]

Bailey, Steve - 'Was it the Devil Who Left His Calling Card?' *Sunday Independent* 26 February 1978 [*Short account based on Michell and Rickard's* Phenomena.]

Beadnell, Charles - 'The 'Marks of Satan'', *The Times* 5 August 1937 [*A letter, from a Surgeon Rear Admiral, comparing the Devon mystery to 'Yeti' footprints found in the Himalayas.*]

Brown, Theo - 'Strange Footprints in the Snow Which Baffled South Devon', *Western Morning News* 15 January 1951 [*An article* summarising the mystery, based on Brown's early research.]

Brown, Theo - 'Devil's Footprints', *Western Morning News* 8 July 1963 [*A letter criticising simplistic versions of the mystery and pointing out the lack of evidence for a uniform and unbroken trail.*]

Buckland, Frank - *Logbook of a Fisherman and Zoologist*, London nd, c1870 [*Includes an account of the Devon mystery asserting that the tracks were made by a racoon. Sometimes referred to as* Logbook of a Naturalist *in the literature.*]

Burton, Maurice - 'Nature Notes', *Daily Telegraph* 2 January 1965 [*Discusses Leutscher's wood mouse theory.*]

Country Essays [*A nineteenth century work which supposedly contains an account of the mystery. It has not been possible to locate a copy.*]

Coxhead, J.R.W - *Legends of Devon*, London nd [*Includes a chapter on the Devil's Hoofmarks reprinting some contemporary press reports.*]

Fate - Article on the Devil's Hoofmarks in August 1952 edition [*It has not proved possible to locate a copy of this issue of the magazine.*]

Fort, Charles - Notes, *Doubt* vol 25 p391 [*Reprints Fort's note of the Cotswold prints.*]

Fort, Charles - Notes, *Doubt* vol 27 p421 [*Reprints Fort's original notes on the Devil's Hoofmarks.*]

Gaddis, Vincent - 'The Devil Walks Again', *INFO Journal* vol 1 no 2 [*Draws attention to the Wilson case (document 36)*]

Godwin, John - *This Baffling World*, London 1971 [*Includes a good chapter on 'The Devil in Devonshire' giving facsimiles of a number of contemporary press reports.*]

Household, G.A. (ed) - *The Devil's Footprints - the Great Devon Mystery of 1855*, Devon Books, Exeter, 1985 [*A booklet reprinting contemporary press reports with a brief commentary and some illustrations.*]

Kemble, John - *The Saxons in England*, 2 vols London 1849 [*Includes mention of a Saxon tale of a miraculous footprint found on Dartmoor.*]

Koopman, M. - 'Meteorological Cause', *Prediction* ?July 1981 [*Letter commenting on Madeline Montalban's article (Document 47) and mentioning some other printed sources, including Rennie's meteorological hypothesis.*]

Lyall, George - 'Did a Laser Create the Devil's Footprints?', *Flying Saucer Review* vol 18 no 1, January/February 1972. [*An article suggesting the marks were made by a laser mounted in a UFO.*]

McLeod, Penny - 'Did the Devil Walk Again?', *Titbits* 9 February 1980 [*Mentions the sea monster theory and alleges that small hoofed sea creatures were washed up on Canvey Island, Essex, in 1953 and 1954.*]

Michell, John, & Rickard, R.J.M. - 'Unreasonable Footprints' in *Phenomena*, London 1977 pp.76-7. [*An essay linking the Devil's Hoofmarks to other mysterious footprints.*]

O'Donnell, Elliott - *Strange Sea Mysteries*, London 1926 [*Includes a chapter on the hoofmarks, noting their proximity to the sea.*]

Price, Harry - *Poltergeist Over England: three centuries of mischievous ghosts*, London 1945 [*Suggests the hoofmarks may have been the result of poltergeist activity.*]

Reader's Digest - 'When the Devil Walked in Devon', in *Strange Stories, Amazing Facts*, London 1979 p.377 [*A short standard retelling.*]

Rickard, R.J.M. - 'If You Go Down To The Woods Today' in *INFO Journal* No. 13 (May 1974). [*Although about British mystery cat reports, it mentions in passing the overnight appearance of large "bear-like" tracks in snow in a garden in Farnborough, Hampshire, on New Year's Eve 1970, with photographs. Among explanations proposed were gull prints enlarged and distorted by melting edges.*]

Shoemaker, Michael - 'Devil's Footprints', *Fate* April 1986 [*A letter written in response to Gordon Stein's article (below), correcting some errors and adding material to support the meteorological hypothesis.*]

Smith, Caron - 'Devilish Deeds Down at Eerie Bridge', *Middlesbrough Evening Gazette*, 26 March 1992 [*Notes a tradition that a line of 'Devil's Hoofprints' once passed under Newham Bridge, known locally as 'Devil's Bridge'.*]

Stein, Gordon - 'The Devil's Footprints', *Fate* August 1985 [*A summary, in a leading American Fortean magazine, of the events of 1855, based on the usual sources.*]

Willis, Paul - 'The Devil's Hoofmarks: an unsolved enigma', *INFO Journal* vol 1 no 1 [*A summary, with bibliography, drawing attention to Charles Fort's contribution to the mystery.*]

JOAN PETRI KLINT
A SWEDISH PROTO-FORTEAN OF THE 16TH CENTURY

Sven Rosen

While early historical sources must be used with care (for the author's concerns are rarely the same as our own), there are some that remain vast treasure-houses of anomalistic data. Sven Rosen reviews the work of the 16th century Swedish scholar Joan Petri Klint, whose illustrated book of prodigies exists only in manuscript, and uncovers a systematic compilation of wonders that suggested, to its author, the imminent end of the world.

Although Forteanism derives its name and philosophy from Charles Fort (1874-1932), he was obviously not the first to interest himself in anomalies and their interpretation. His forerunners may have differed in their purposes, methods of collection and treatment of the material, yet they have left us valuable compilations of data, and their interpretations, produced in specific historical and conceptual circumstances, remain of interest in themselves. As an independent field of study, Forteanism should of course have an independent history: and Joan Petri Klint of Sweden belongs firmly in that history.

The date of Klint's birth is unknown, but he died on 21 October 1608, at Östra Stenby in Östergötland. In 1558, Klint became a university student at Uppsala; he was ordained as a minister in 1564, and obtained a benefice at Östra Stenby in 1568. He was considered a very learned scholar in his day and when he died he left his successor a wife named Karin (at the time it was customary for the successor to a benefice to marry his predecessor's wife) and several unpublished manuscripts. Among these was a chronicle of the bishops of Linköping and a chronicle of King Gustav Vasa's reign, which contains many items about human folly, cruel punishments, strange behaviour and disappearances, and so on. He also left a book on portents and wonders, which is what mainly concerns us here.

The book is usually referred to by the name *On Meteors*, although the original title-page is lost. It seems originally to have been called *Om the tekn och widunder som föregingo thet liturgiske owäsendet* ("On the signs and wonders preceding the liturgic broil"). The book is now in the Stifts- och Landsbiblioteket library (Box 3085, S-580 03 Linköping, Sweden) and carries a new title-page crediting the work to *Jonas* Petri Klint, a 19th century librarian's mistake for 'Joan', the 16th century spelling of 'Johan' (John). Klint also used the dialect versions 'Joen' or 'Jon'.

Unlike his near-contemporary Olof Månsson Svinefot (better known under his pen-name of Olaus Magnus), who belongs more to the history of ethnology and dealt with Forteana only in passing, Klint became engrossed in the subject. His collection of anomalies is perhaps a little antiquated, but the book has 199 folios (398 pages) and also numerous pictures drawn in black, red, green, yellow and brown ink. Klint was no great artist, but his naïve pictures suit the content very well.

On the face of it, the book is a jumble without any real ordered treatment of the subject. However, parchment was expensive, and Klint may well have felt obliged to write down the cases very much in the same order that he learned of them. Even so, the cases are generally divided into different types, which are described on separate pages (although due to faulty binding the current sequence of the pages has become disordered). The contents include: swarms, comets, mock suns, auroras, visions and apparitions, earthquakes, volcanoes, falls, coincidences, strange animals, strange births and monsters, unusual behaviour, compulsions (e.g., odd kleptomania), instant retribution, folklore and so on.

Klint believed that the universe obeyed a divine order. Everything had a purpose, and the purpose of unusual things was to attract attention. Thus anything unusual could be interpreted as a portent, a sign from God pointing out the shape of things to come.

Of course, Klint's tales may not all have emanated from reliable quarters. At least some of them were, literally, old wives' tales.

Fig. 1 - The calf born near Örebro in 1588.

For example, there is a note that in 1504 a cow in Finland gave birth to two male children (folio 76, with a picture of the cow and her sons). They were "in all their shape like humans, except for their slight inclination to slobber as cattle do". The regent Svante Sture took care of the children but slaughtered the cow. They were brought up, but were never allowed to marry, or even to come close to women. Klint heard the story from Henrik Mattsson of Rananäs in 1569, and he was a reliable man ... but he had the story from his mother!

There are stories of crossbreeds between animals and men (accompanied by grotesque pictures), and more likely tales of monstrosities. Geographically closer to Klint's home territory than the last example is a story that in 1575 at Gränna a woman bore a dead child "like the Devil, just a lump of flesh, with no joints ... its thighs were straight, it had a big belly and no skin on its body, only red flesh." By accident the woman had, a few months earlier, trodden on a big toad and flattened it, whereupon she became afraid and gave a loud cry (fol. 63). There may well be a believable basis to the story of the defective birth, although the tale of the toad may have been coincidental or an embroidery. Nonetheless, it is a typical explanatory tale of the time.

Also doubtful or just on the line can be placed a case from 1588, in Martio: "Near Örebro in the parish of Svensta, in a croft called Kalkaboda just outside Stenkulla, a cow gave birth to a calf with the appearance of a human head and human feet, but without forelegs. The calf seemed to be a half-man, half-calf. He had big eyes, stretched out his tongue and wanted to get at the people who were watching him; [he] rose bellowing and off he went, but he was slain" (fol. 128B). Perhaps the face of a malformed calf without a nose could look human?

There are several accounts (with pictures) of animals and men born with two heads, heads grown together, and more (or less) limbs and tails than nature should provide. Such things do occur in the natural run of things, of course; to Klint, though, they were portentous.

Generally, it seems that Klint's data grow more likely and acceptable the closer the occurrences were to himself in time and space. Here, then, I will try to focus mainly on what happened in Klint's neighbourhood, although first the material must be set in context.

THE HISTORICAL BACKGROUND

Klint appears to have begun his collection of portents in 1587. In that year a colleague of his, Nicolaus Ringius (a native of Småland) published a book entitled *Prognosticon Theologicum*, which contained 'incontrovertible' proof of the imminent destruction of the world. There were also 'latter day prophets' printing apocalyptic predictions and revelations, such as Georgius Olai, L.E. Swart, and others. It appeared that the world was scheduled to end in 1588: and the years 1587 and 1588 were plague-stricken famine years, with wars and rumours of wars.

The political situation was rather tangled. After the final breakdown of the union in 1523 Scandinavia was divided into two kingdoms, Sweden (with Finland) and Denmark-Norway, and these states were continuously warring with one another. In Sweden the three royal brothers Eric XIV (reigned 1560-68), John III (r.1568-92) and Charles IX (r.1599-1611) were fighting against Danes, Russians, aristocrats, one another, and others. Eric was declared insane in 1568 and was later murdered by his sane brother John, a very religious man and a crypto-Catholic plotting against the Lutherans. His Catholic son Sigismund (r.1592-99) whose mother was a Polish princess, was elected king of Poland and inherited Sweden from his father, but was dethroned in the latter country after a religious war in which Polish armies were involved. At the borders of Finland and in Estonia, there was a permanent state of warfare with the Russians.

Klint's only involvement in politics seems to have been a spiritual support for the Lutheran struggle against King John's Catholic liturgy. And at least in Klint's view, God seems to have been rather upset because of that liturgy, too.

COMETS

Klint describes some 30 or more comets (most of them 'stolen' from other books) and Wilhelm Norlind has attempted to identify some of these [1]. This is Klint's account of Halley's comet, appearing in 1607 (exactly as predicted by an almanac in 1605, Klint remarks):

"Anno 1607: in September, on the eve of St. Matthew [21 September] a tail-star was seen in the northwest, standing under Charles' Wain [the Plough], directing her tail over herself eastwards, and she was visible after Michaelmas [29 September]. Sometimes

Fig. 2 - Halley's comet, 1607.

Fig. 3 - The 'meteor' of 28 November 1569.

she was clearly visible but sometimes dusky, and she went her way in a southerly direction. ([She] did not have a very big tail)." (fol. 22B).

It was a she-comet, and her tail was up. However, she was a normal comet. Not all of them were: Klint also describes some comets looking like swords and crosses.

METEORS(?)

Some of Klint's meteor reports are curious as well. "Anno Domini 1569, on 28 November. In the evening a light suddenly appeared in the sky, as if a star had fallen down, and [it] shone so that one could have seen to thread a needle, and emitted a very hot light, burning the faces of those who were out of doors. The horses perspired white lather, and this light was seen all over Sweden, in Norrbotten as well as in the Åland islands." (fol. 62)

Perhaps Klint does not mean that people outdoors got burned, but that they could feel the heat radiating from the meteor, and that the horses were all in a lather. Norlind explains this simply as an exceptionally brilliant meteor. The distance between Norrbotten and the Åland islands is about 420 miles.

Showers of meteorites appear to have struck Sweden in the 1560s. Klint summarises as follows:

"From anno 1560 until anno 1570, sounds have been heard from within the ground like neighing horses and rumbling armies, riding in rattling armour all through the night. Item [2]: the din of mill-wheels and grinding millstones has been heard from the sky, and when the noise was at its height it stopped dead. Item: things like pots have fallen from the sky, glowing in the same way that pottery

Fig. 4 (above) - One of the 'pots' that fell in the 1560s, and the 'pit' it made.

Fig. 5 (right) - The 'night sun' of 1581.

does when just taken from the fire, when it is red hot. Item: big pits have been made with large walls of earth surrounding them." (fol. 95)

The word Klint uses for 'pit' can also mean a 'grave', and his drawing in the margin shows both a pot and a grave. Klint's account of these showers of meteorites is supported by an account by the learned scholar Petrus Pauli Gothus (1550-1593), who gives a very dramatic account of how people fled in panic, believing that the Judgment Day had come, when on 6 January (the 'Thirteenth Day', a festival equivalent to Twelfth Night in England; the event was probably in 1569) glowing pots fell in showers from the sky, breaking against outcrops of rock, knocking holes in the ice of lakes and striking deep pits in the frosty ground, where turfs, half an *aln* thick (12 inches), were thrown up into mounds two fathoms (12 feet) high all around the craters [3]. The 'pots' may have been iron meteorites, but the scope of the bombardment is sensational, unless the story was exaggerated on the way to Professor Gothus's study.

NIGHT SUNS

Klint also records a curious incident when the sun appeared to return after dark. "Anno Domini 1581, on the night of Candlemas [2 February], at a very late hour, the sky opened three times, and the first time a blue smoke and a flame came from the opening. The second time the sun

appeared alone. But the third time when the sun appeared she emitted a [hot] glaring light, which singed the hair of the horses and the clothes of those who were outdoors, so that they had to [quickly] protect their faces by drawing their clothes over their heads, and white lather dripped from the horses." (fol. 119)

In Klint's terminology, "the sky opened" refers to the sudden appearance of a bright light; Klint often uses the same phrase when, for example, describing auroras. This light, which he twice calls a 'sun', is here likened to an opening in the black vault of heaven. Here we have a feminine sun, and of a very brilliant kind; so brilliant that the observers had to hurriedly protect their faces.

Klint's picture of the event (figure 5) shows the sun against a background of stars, indicating the late hour. The sun is drawn in a conventional way with a face, as in the almanacs of the period. The 'spirals' around the sun may be conventionalised clouds, here used as an embellishment. Klint often framed his pictures with similar 'spirals', especially when depicting visions or things seen in the sky, but this does not necessarily indicate that the clouds were actually present; he also drew such spirals when he says that the sky was clear. The picture shows the first phase of the sighting, when "a blue smoke and a flame came from the opening", and also the sun, the presence of which in this phase is implied by the text, rather than overtly stated. The smoke

Aerial apparitions at Törnevalla. Fig. 6 (L) - Soldier with fasces and drums, 1577. Fig. 7 (R) - Bells, 1577-80.

and the flame are directed obliquely downward. (The number 89 may refer to some previous binding of the book; the picture is now on folio 119).

As the sun appeared three times, Klint gave several interpretations. The significance of the omen was, he says: "great trouble with the liturgy, item drought, item storms, item great distress for women in childbed." If the above phenomenon had happened today, it would undoubtedly have been labelled a 'UFO' [4].

AERIAL SOUNDS

I would not suggest that the 'pots' mentioned previously were abortive castings by Someone Up There making bells ... but bells were heard from above in the late 1570s:

"Anno Domini 1577 at Linköping, the sky appeared open and a big tolling bell was seen ... one man held the bell-pull and tolled, and the sound was heard. Item: King Eric died at Nörby that year. Item: King Stephanus was crowned king of Poland that year. Item: the Russians besieged Reval and suffered great injury, and their commander Ivan Wasiliewitz was slain there." (fol. 94B)

"Anno Domini 1577 and [also] until 1580 two bells, one big and one small, were heard tolling in the sky. The bells were first heard on St. Barbara's eve on the 3rd of December at Törnevalla at Linköping. At that place they

were heard most often, most distinct and best, and Herr Sven who was then a vicar there often heard them, and many others who visited the place heard them as well. Also the Bishop of Linköping, who was then 'Master' Mårten, heard them. Item: tolling bells were heard in the sky at Söderköping and at Linköping. Item: the sky seemed open and soldiers were seen in the sky on both sides of the opening, and they carried fasces [5] in their arms. The vision lasted more than an hour, then it disappeared. And the sky was blue-black until dawn. This is verily true. [Interpretation:] Yes, observe how many thousands of men were slain in the Danish and Russian wars, and in the civil war between King Sigismund and Duke Charles, not to mention those who drowned at sea [i.e., in the naval battles]." (fol. 135B)

The happenings at Törnevalla (which is where the vision of soldiers mentioned above occurred) are better described on folio 94. It appears the tollings always occurred at night. The first time it happened the vicar sent his men out to see what was going on. They returned and said that the tolling came from above: "... Herr Sven went out and heard the same thing; it was a distinct, sonorous sound. He then summoned all his household to listen, and they all heard it. And the tolling continued until the cocks crowed. But it often happened that when two men were listening for the sound only one of them could hear it,

155

Fig. 8 - Above, the supposed cannon which caused an aerial explosion in February 1593, and below it mock suns and halo, 2 March 1593.

while the other one could not. And when the tolling ceased drum-beats were often heard from the sky until the third cock-crow, when it stopped." (fol. 94). Figure 6 shows one of the soldiers with fasces seen at Törnevalla in 1577. The objects to the right of the soldier are drums, which sounded like drums of copper, according to Klint, though there is no mention that the drums were actually seen.

Figure 7 shows the large and small bell in the sky at Törnevalla in 1577-80. In the upper margin is a later addition (possibly written by Samuel Ungius, Klint's successor): "the bells of Kalmar tolled in the night, all of them together, Anno [15]97". This refers to an incident during the civil war which has nothing to do with the bells in the sky. The occurrence is recorded by the vicar Nicolaus Magni in the church register of Lönneberga: "Anno 1597, in the night of St. Andrew [30 November] all the bells of Kalmar were tolling but no man caused it. The same thing happened at Dörby and at Kläckeberga. And while the bells tolled two men appeared in the sky, and both of them carried a birch-broom or a fasces, and they were fighting between themselves. Thereafter a disease arose, which caused shooting pains in the limbs, in the

fingers and toes, and the nails partly fell off before the victims died." The symptoms suggest poisoning by ergot, which perhaps could also cause hallucinations; and indeed a lot of strange things were seen and heard in Kalmar during the years 1597-98.

Further aerial sounds were reported during the 1580s, including trumpets and an angelic choir. Possibly they are to be accounted for by some meteorological or atmospheric phenomena. The fact that not everyone could hear the sounds does not necessarily suggest anything 'paranormal': possibly the sounds were sometimes very faint, or the pitch touched the limit of audibility. Klint also recorded aerial explosions, such as one (fol. 154), which occurred in the evening of the 4th day of the Distinget (a fair in Uppsala) in February 1593. A sound like a tremendous cannon being fired in the sky was clearly heard over a distance of 14 old Swedish miles (98.2 English miles). A similar incident occurred on 2 January 1601. Figure 8 shows Klint's drawing of the cannon, while on the same page below appears a yellowish ring that was seen around the sun on 2 March 1593, with two mock suns appearing on either side of it. Both the noise of cannon-fire and the mock suns were associated by Klint with the Diet of Uppsala in 1593, where Luther's catechism was accepted. Although Klint was not involved in politics he did participate in the Diet of 1593 as a member of the ecclesiastical estate [6].

OPTICAL PHENOMENA

There seems to have been some sort of meteorological commotion in Klint's time, as he devotes an entire little treatise to mock suns and similar phenomena (and their political connections). Sometimes several suns were seen in the sky, and there were also strange circles, arches and rays, with the sun occasionally appearing to have horns. Strange as these stories may be, they can probably be explained as refractive phenomena, so only one example is given here (figure 9). In 1491 there appeared to be two burning horns (Anti-Christian symbols) standing on either side of the sun (fol. 9B) and before the Reformation Christ (the sun) was hard pressed between Catholics and Mahometans. In the 1490s a Turkish army again

156

tried to invade Europe, and the portent was also connected with King Hans of Denmark's invasion of Sweden in 1497.

Refraction phenomena or not, this accumulation of mock suns and rings in the sky during a few years seems odd. Klint drew charts where, almost month by month, he records such phenomena over a number of years [7], with pictures to explain what they looked like.

Fig. 9 - Two 'burning horns' bracket the sun, 1491.

BLOOD RAINS

Rains of blood make a couple of appearances in the book (including a rain where the streets were flooded with blood, one *aln* (23 inches) deep, in 158-? (the last figure is missing because the upper part of the page is torn; Petrus Pauli Gothus gives the year as 1588). According to Klint these rains selected the little town of Söderköping, to which they returned again and again in the 1560s [8], and they seemed to be connected with the war. Klint himself lived in Söderköping in 1566-68.

"Anno Domini 1562, on the day of St. Barbara [4 December] there was a rain of blood at Söderköping." This seems to be the first case mentioned from the town. The rain was repeated in 1565, but no date is given. In 1566, from 17 to 22 September, another rain of blood: "The clouds drifted away with the west wind." Also on the day of St. Barbara in 1567 Söderköping was raided by the Danes, and its castle burned down. In 1568, on 27 and 28 August, another rain of blood at Söderköping (fols. 62, 155).

Varberg was a castle on the Danish side of the old frontier between Sweden and Denmark. "Anno Domini 1569, in October, a rain of clotted blood at Varberg. 14 days thereafter the Danes took [i.e., recaptured] the castle by treachery after Bo Grip had been shot ... Item: at the same time the Swedes infested Scania, ravaging and burning. Item: Anno 1569, a rain of blood at Söderköping." (fol. 62B)

Blood also appeared in many other strange ways, such as in the following case of a 'phantom hitchhiker'. It happened in February 1602, Klint says (naming his informant in the margin as a man called Eskil Larsson), when people were returning from the Candlemas (2 February) fair in Västergötland. Among them was a vicar on his way home, with two farmers as passengers in the sleigh (I assume it to be a sleigh, although Klint doesn't say what kind of vehicle they were in). There was a lone girl, described as a servant, on the road to Vadstena, and she asked for a ride. She was very good-looking, so they stopped and picked her up. After a while they came to a halting-place where they decided to get something to eat, and the vicar and the farmers kindly offered her some pieces of bread, but she asked for something to drink. The vicar asked the woman of the house if he could buy a jug of beer, but when it was brought to them the jug contained malt. A second time the woman went for beer, but this time the jug was full of acorns. Now the woman of the house begged them to follow her and see for themselves that she was, in fact, drawing *beer* from the barrel. Yet when they returned to the table the jug was full of blood. "They were now terrified and confused. The servant girl [i.e., the hitchhiker] said: 'Are you not going to ask what it means?' The vicar asked, and she said: 'I know. There will be good crops this year. There will be enough fruits of the trees. But there will be many wars and plagues.' Then she vanished." (fol. 115) [9]

RAINS OF FIRE

Blood was not the only thing raining from the sky. "Anno 1597, on 18 October, during the night, fire was seen falling down from the sky on to the water, and it burned in three big blazes on the surface, causing steam to rise from the water; and there was a gruesome din, noise and turmoil caused by the fire from the sky, which ceased towards the dawn. It lit up all the mooring places like the bright sun; and although the sky was clear one could not see it because of the burning and floating fire in the air. And verily, it looked like three big

Fig. 10 - Rain of fire, Bräviken, 18 October 1597.

fires were made on the water. Item: the same thing was seen at this place as well as in Bråviken on that very night; fishermen saw it. The noise and thunder were not so terrible here, however, as the fire floated down onto the earth and into the water, glaring all through the night like bright day, and it was seen towards the east." (fol. 176B)

Something made the night so bright that the stars were not discernible. Fire floated in the air, fell into the water without apparently being extinguished, and also fell on the earth. The phenomenon occurred at Bråviken, which is a mysterious bay where, in recent years, the Swedish navy spent some time chasing 'Unidentified Russian Submarines'. It was also visible from Östra Stenby, a little south of Bråviken, where Klint lived, but evidently the noise was much lower there.

Klint mentions several rains of fire, but usually the accounts are very brief. For example: "Anno D. 1585, on ... a rain of burning fire and brimstone in Stockholm and in the country around Roden [the coastal area of Uppland], and between Stockholm and Uppsala; the fire lay there burning in the streets singeing the clothes of those upon whom it fell, and it smelled of pure brimstone." (fol. 125) [10]

RAINS OF RYE AND BARLEY

There are several other rains mentioned, of worms, slugs and almost-things. There was a rain of peas in 1571, round about some Danish towns ... "Item: small turnips and beans also fell from the sky." Not a very substantial datum, that one, perhaps (Klint drew a picture showing the fall). However, in 1571 there was also a rain of rye at Söderköping, "item wheat", which was collected by German merchants (fols. 64b, 65)

Also, Anno 1580, evidently at the same place, another shower of rye - or almost-rye. "The grains looked like fine flax-seed; they were dry and hard like the seeds of juniper berries, they tasted like juniper berries, and they did not smell like rye." This case is described twice in the book. (fols. 64B, 65, 110B)

1590 was one of a succession of bad harvest years. Klint reports another rain of grain - almost-barley this time. It was used for sowing. "Many persons sowed of it five or six barrels ... The grains looked like wheat, very ripe, but the plant looked like barley when it grew, and most of the crop supplied tasty flour used as porridge." In the margin, Klint has written: "I, Jon Petri K., sowed a quarter of a barrel of it myself." (fols. 64B, 65)

Although this report reads as if the grain fell in Klint's own parish, a simpler explanation seems more likely. German merchants in those years were trading in grain with the selling-point that it had fallen from the sky, and thus had a divine origin. Klint probably bought his barley from these men. That the seeds didn't look normal suggests that they were a (genetic) variant unknown to the locals.

Bad rains: "From 1580 and almost every year, the earth has been swarmed with slugs, as they [evidently the parishioners] call them, eating up the rye in the autumn." These slugs (or almost-slugs?) were covering the ground in 1586, 1588, 1596 and 1597. In 1596 worms and slugs "came down with a south wind and rain, and the night after Michaelmas (29 Sept) they consumed all the rye." (fol. 3)

Fig. 11 - A sketch of one of the slugs that swarmed (or fell) in the 1580s and 1590s.

Fig. 12 - Woodcut by Lemberger in the Swedish Bible of 1541, showing the rain of fire from the sky mentioned in Job 1:16.

AURORAS

The Northern Lights should not be much more common in southern and central Sweden than, for example, polar bears. Yet in the late 16th century the sky seemed ablaze. These ghostly lights were interpreted as divine fires and portents, with Biblical authority (Habakkuk 3:3-4: "[God's] glory covered the heavens ... And his brightness was as the light").

Klint says: "The first time these lights were seen was in 1538, on the day of St. Thomas [21 December]. Then what happened? Anno Domini 1538: soon Dacke's rebellion started and lasted until 1544. Anno Domini 1540 a peasant called Lars Joansson departed to Östergötland to raise an army of Huns [i.e., bandits] and slay the lords and all the nobility, but he was soon discovered and stopped, and broken upon the wheel..." (fol. 35)

If there should be a connection between solar activity (sun spots), auroras and the spirit of unrest, then perhaps Klint's approach was right. There seem to have been three main 'outbreaks' of auroras (in 1538 - ?, in the 1560s, and in the 1590s), and they all coincided with wars (Dacke's war until 1544; war between Sweden, Denmark and Lübeck in 1563-70; war between Sweden and Russia in 1563-81 and 1590-95; and civil war in 1597-99).

Fig. 13 - The black-green bear-like cloud seen in the sky on 22 September 1593.

As always, the accounts of these portents run parallel with political notes. For example: "Anno 1563 at Ronneby in Scania a red cloth was seen hanging in the sky for several days, looking as if it were drawn out of a tub full of blood. Item: Anno 1564 the Swedes raided, burned the town to the ground and slew all the people they could find, and the Finns horribly murdered wives, men and children." (fol. 51B, with a picture of the cloth). The red cloth was an aurora, a very rare sight in Scanialand. It coincided well enough with King Eric's 'victory' there a year later.

Sometimes Klint's observations are in diary form. "Anno Domini 1593, on 28 August and 15 September: the light glared greatly in the sky. Item: now and then the sky became black below the light, darker and darker.

"A.D. 1593, on 21 September, i.e. on the eve of St. Matthew: the light burned brightly in the sky; towards it were turned black rays and teeth; then more blackness passed over the light, and the black rays disappeared. Much blackness gathered under the light.

"A.D. 1593, on 22 September. The light burned greatly in the sky all night through, and beneath the place where the light was flaming and dancing, the sky was surely black. Even so, stars were seen, but in the middle of the light a black-green cloud was standing like a bear, its head facing south-east [in the direction of Poland] for a while, then it dispersed like a cloud. Some time passed and it vanished, still in the same spot. This happened in the evening at about 8 or 9 strokes [8:00 or 9:00pm]. Yet the light was

burning intensely all around the cloud. Item: on 27 September, the light burned fiercely blood-red. Item: at that time King Sigismund arrived before Stockholm, and he marched into Stockholm on Michaelmas [29 September]." (fol. 34, 34B)

Now followed rumours of civil war. "Anno D. 1593, on 21 November: the light flared violently in the sky as it had previously done, jumping like flails across the sky, except that now it passed over the whole sky like a log-fire. It blazed and glared to and fro, and the sound of its flames and flares was heard. Thus it continued all the night through." (fol. 35)

In the manuscript there now follows a lot of similar descriptions, all heralding political change. Klint's impressionistic notes of these lights often convey a very direct sense of awe.

"Anno D. 1597, on 31 August: much burning upon the sky; it burned together like bloody armies, on one side it was red, on the other blue."

Now civil war was unavoidable. Kalmar was a key fort. "Anno D. 1599, on 6 March: the sky burned greatly until midnight when Duke Charles' men managed to capture the town of Kalmar."

It is noteworthy that Klint (in August 1597) saw the auroras cluster like bloody armies. There are several reports of such aerial battles, but people not only saw auroras that *looked like* armies, they sometimes saw the actual armies themselves, and in detail as well, with armour, horses, guns, swords, banners, and so on. Not many such battles are recorded from Sweden, however. By far the most spectacular aerial battles seem to have occurred in Germany and Italy (especially the latter), which would be strange if auroras *were* the cause. Perhaps the Italians had a greater imagination.

Even so, Klint records an aerial battle seen in Östergötland in 1565 (figure 14). Two armies were seen fighting a battle in the eastern sky in the evening. Above the armies stood a sword turning its sharp point upwards, i.e., westward (fol. 155B). Significantly, in 1565 the war between Sweden and Denmark reached its climax. In Klint's drawing the sword is red, the armies are red and green. To the left is a Danish flag (red and white), but the flags to the right are green. If

Fig. 14 - The aerial battle seen in Östergötland in 1565

they are supposed to be Swedish flags, they should have been blue and yellow, but auroras are mainly red and green.

VISIONS

It appears that an unusually large amount of visions were seen in the sky in the late 16th century. Klint describes many of those seen in Sweden, as well as elsewhere. Common elements of the Swedish visions were shining clothes, soldiers (with shining armour), swords, rods, fasces, rays, and such like. This suggests that the visions may have originated as auroras, but then perhaps evolved into something else. Klint was extremely interested in visions, so some of them are described in great detail, and we also get a glimpse of the circumstances in which such visions were seen. "The sky opened", Klint often says, meaning that a part of the sky was lit up (the appearance of an aurora?); then awe-stricken spectators stood and watched the light for hours. Klint often says they watched the sky until dawn. Around them was, I imagine, a complete darkness, as there were no street-lights in those days. Perhaps there is a parallel here with crystal-gazing where, after prolonged staring, visions appear to the viewer in the crystal ball. Some similar process might be involved with the spectators staring at the bright, shimmering auroras, eventually leading them to have visions.

Many visions (especially the foreign ones) are rather lengthy and elaborated, but a few of the shorter ones can be quoted here. First are three visions which could have been illusions created by auroras.

"Anno 1568, on 21 January. In the evening after darkness the sky opened in the south, and inside the opening stars were moving to and fro; then a sudden light struck downwards and the stars were pulled out with it, and a violent storm arose in the north-west. Item: in 1568 King Eric married Karin Månsdotter ... if the Dukes John and Charles had arrived at the wedding they would have been murdered. But the more they sensed that, the more they deprived him of the kingdom." (fol. 56, with picture)

It would perhaps be possible to elaborate on that interpretation. King Eric was a highly gifted man, a dreamer and a musician (the moving stars) who, because he suddenly developed schizophrenia, was overthrown by his brothers (the sudden light); the brothers spent years trying to hunt down his followers, and some of them were executed (the falling stars). Klint appears to have connected the moving stars with the wedding, and the sudden light with the deposition of the king.

"Anno 1569, on 6 June, at Rönö, during the night the sky seemed open and two hands were holding a blood-stained fasces. Item: on 10 July 1569, John was crowned king ... [Klint also says that Danish ships looted Reval, and an attempt on 'King' Eric's life was made] ... Item: Anno 1569, on the day of John the

161

Fig. 15 - Woodcut from the Swedish Bible of 1541. A wildman and wildwoman stand to either side of the royal coat-of-arms. At the centre of the shield is the symbol of the Vasa dynasty, which, although looking like a crossbow, is actually a sheaf.

Baptist (24 June) a horrible thunder and rumbling occurred in Stockholm, the whole city shook, and many people fainted with fright." (fol. 56B; also fol. 65, with pictures)

The thunder on King John's name-day is understood as referring to him being an obdurate Catholic, while God was not. The fasces was, of course, a transformation of John's coat-of-arms: a sheaf.

"Anno Christi 1592, in the sky above the cathedral of Linköping what seemed to be three standing fasces were seen, at 11 o'clock and until 2 o'clock, when they disappeared. The bishop Per Benedicti saw them, item Johannes [who was then] the head of the cathedral, and others. Then what happened? Anno [15]92, on 17 November, His Majesty King John III departed this life in Stockholm. Almighty God have mercy upon his soul for ever, Amen." (fol. 152)

Not only was the sheaf transformed here, but the aurora also tried to mimic King John's

number; although on the other hand, John was succeeded by his son Sigismund, who was already King Sigismund *III* of Poland, and an even more inflexible Catholic than his father.

Finally, a short vision of the eschatological kind: "Anno Domini 1588, in October, the sky above Stockholm was cloudless. On the stroke of nine in the evening the sky opened, and in the opening stood a man with a crown of thorns on his head, so that the thorns were seen, with a bloodstained face and wearing a long robe of silk. He rapidly stepped out, but quickly returned into the opening. Immediately another man stepped out, having a lantern crown on his head, shining like the sun, and he had a big grey beard and wore a shining robe like a golden star reaching to his feet, and he walked to and fro for more than an hour, and then he returned again, and the sky was once more as it was before. Matt. 24:30 ['And then shall appear the sign of the Son of man in heaven: and then shall all the tribes of the earth mourn, and they shall see the Son of man coming in the clouds of heaven with power and great glory']. Now is fulfilled what St. Matthew wrote and nothing remains, but one thing: Matthew 25 [i.e., the Last Judgement]." (fols. 127B, 128)

The shining robe and the silk suggest an aurora, but the religious content seems to have developed further than this, perhaps. A different version of what might have been the same event (or the same story) is given by Petrus Pauli Gothus in his *Een rett Christeligh Vnderwijsningh*. On 8 August 1588 in Stockholm, at about 7:00pm when the sky was clear and cloudless, Christ was seen in the sky like a 12 year old boy, dressed in a golden robe and wearing a crown of gold, standing in the silent summer evening with one hand outstretched

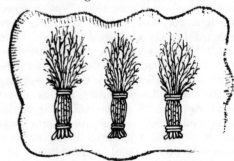

Fig. 16 - Three fasces seen above Linköping, 1592.

162

Fig. 17 - The vision in the sky at
Stockholm, October 1588.

towards the spectators, as if he wanted to say
(Petrus interprets) "The day is gone, the
evening has come ... the End is near." The
young Christ had a 'naked' (beardless) face,
and bare hands and feet. The vision was
immobile.

The foreign visions described by Klint do
not seem to be based as much on auroric
elements as the Swedish cases are, and they
were often more complex with 'scene-shifting'
as if in celestial movies. What all of the visions
had in common was that they reflected
current political or religious ideas (like the
vision of 1588, just mentioned, which reflected
the prophecies of Nicolaus Ringius, and
others). Foreign cases were often more
fantastic - probably because no firsthand
accounts were available; also perhaps because some visions were used in Lutheran
propaganda, in which the Germans were
specialists.

ON THE CRUDE AND
UNDERDEVELOPED STATE
OF SCANDINAVIAN VISIONS
COMPARED WITH THOSE
OF CONTINENTAL EUROPE

If Klint's collection of visions is representative, the most developed visions seem
to have been those of southern Europe.
For example, in Rome, on the eve of St.
Laurentius (9 August) in 1580, a huge army
marched across the sky. They were Turks with
stars and crescents painted on their banners,
and they fought a gigantic battle against a
Christian army. It lasted for six hours, and the
struggle is nothing that can really be described

in brief. The Moslem army covered an area of
49 English miles in the sky, Klint says. Drums
were heard, and there were cries and turmoil.
Finally the Turkish horses waded in blood up
to their knees, and so did their emperor, who
held a scimitar in his hand (fols. 104, 104B,
105, 108, with a picture of horses wading in
blood on 107B) [11]

The visions of Northern Europe appear to
have been less developed. For example, one
Moslem-Christian battle was fought in the sky
at Rosenberg, Germany, in 1597, but on a far
smaller scale. Some deformed humans were
also seen, and a procession of men in black.
While the vision contained a few shifts of
scene, there is *no mention of sound*. Klint copied
this case from a printed notice posted on the
gate of the town church in Söderköping. (fol.
147, 147B, with picture)

Another case occurred when Duke John
(later King John III of Sweden) married the
Polish princess Katarina Jagellonica, and the
vision shown in figure 18 was seen in the sky
on 4 October 1562 (fol.50). Later, in 1563, on 24
June, the day of John the Baptist (note the
beheaded man in the vision), Duke John was
imprisoned at Åbo by his brother, King Eric
XIV, who feared that John was taking over
Sweden's foreign policy. Klint adds that six
years later John's turn came to imprison King
Eric, "but in the days of King John's reign
thousands of men got their heads chopped off,
and he was a *fasces* [i.e. 'a rod'] to Sweden". So
the bier, the head and the fasces were also a
general omen of the reign of King John. The
vision contains several 'aurora elements'
(sword, fasces, blood), although it was seen,
not in Sweden, but at the town of Wilna in
Poland (now Vilnius in Lithuania).

Fig. 18 - The vision at Wilna, Poland, 4 October 1562.

163

Fig. 19 - The vision at Prenzlau, Germany, 1 September 1554.

At Prenzlau in Germany on 1 September 1554, "a thick and dark cloud appeared in the sky, and in the cloud was seen a clear image of the crucifixion" as it had taken place "1522 years and 157 days before". The vision was very detailed, but it was no 'movie'; rather a kind of celestial 'snap-shot', which would appear to be less advanced. (fol. 37, 37B)

The technically most perfect Scandinavian vision mentioned by Klint occurred in Denmark on 15 August 1570 (figure 21). Regrettably, the name of the town where it happened cannot be read, as Klint's handwriting is illegible here; but he says that a full account was written down by a duke named Augustus and sent to the king of Denmark. A battle between two armies was seen and drops of blood rained to the ground. Then both armies fell down as well, and there was a change of scenery. A large cross appeared, and above it was written "Jesus Nazarenus Rex Judeorum". On the cross itself was written "Finis", and below it "Venite ad Judicium", and some other divine remarks. It was a dumb vision, without sound, but can perhaps be classed as rather advanced since explanatory texts appeared in the sky. (fols. 60, 60B, 61B)

Except for the bell at Linköping (which was seen *and* heard), the visions of Sweden were primitive and seem to have contained neither sound nor text (a few aerial battles were heard, but then they were not seen). Usually the visions contained only one scene (for example, a man with a sword, or someone, such as God, walking to and fro). A few battles were seen in the sky, but nothing to compare with the aerial battles seen further south in Europe. Very often the Swedish visions were immobile, containing only a single image, such as a sword or fasces.

Even so, there were occasionally more complex Scandinavian visions and one occurred in Stockholm on 13 March 1567, between 11:00 and 12:00pm. The moon suddenly became as red as blood (a characteristic of several visions recorded by Klint) and four hands were seen around it, one hand extending from its 'mouth'. After that three tall knights were seen walking in the sky, and they appeared to enter a gateway. The knights were interpreted as representing the three royal brothers, Eric, John and Charles (named on the manuscript folio (134) shown in figure 21 as Erik, Johan and Carl).

INTERPRETATIONS AND ANIMAL PORTENTS

Klint interpreted most omens in accordance with a rather obvious symbolism in which parallelism is a fundamental idea. For example, mock suns signify the appearance of traitors, rebels, impostors or false prophets. Like the mock suns, they will try to 'replace' or 'darken' the true ruler but, in the same way that the true sun will always regain its power, so the changes they bring about will be no more than passing. Thus failure is inherent in the portent. Klint has a more elaborate and less obvious system for interpreting the details, but that is perhaps best shown by the examples illustrated throughout this article.

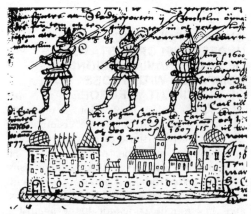

Fig. 20 - The vision of three knights at Stockholm, 13 March 1567.

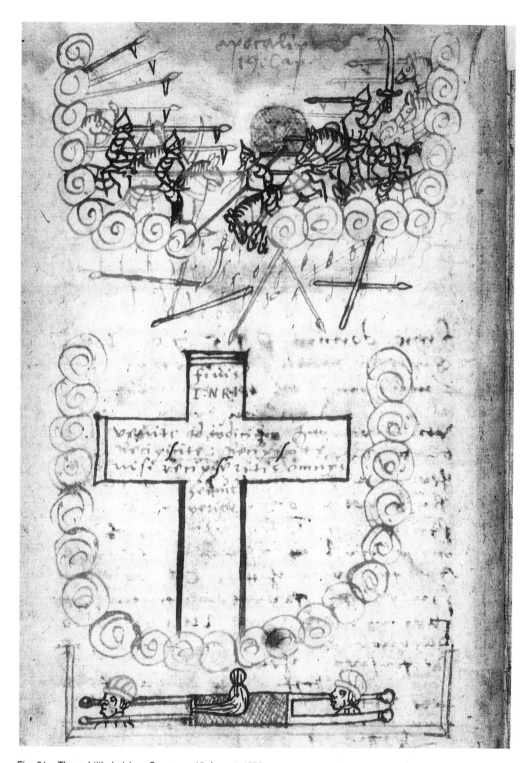

Fig. 21 - The subtitled vision, Germany, 15 August 1570

Fig. 22 - The monster of Fribourg, 1523.

To modern eyes, portents connected with animals often seem extremely amusing, particularly those dealing with the 'misshapen' Catholic church, its Popes, legates, monks and Jesuits, since the Lutheran God (who was of course responsible for the marvels) here emerges as a great Cosmic Cartoonist who, with a few strokes of his divine pen, is able to give, say, a perfect "figurative representation of the Jesuitical religion" through the creation of a "pug-nosed" something with the appearance of "spectacles on its nose" [12], and a greenish spotted bag of skin shaped "like a monk's robe". This calf-like thing emerged from a river at Fribourg in 1523, and also had two spots on its forehead, two horns, pointed ears and a hare-lip. The skin was green with darker green spots, and it shone; the animal had a belly like that of a human being, and it stretched out its tongue. It portended the coming of the Society of Jesus. (fol. 17B)

When the Catholic diplomat Samuel Laski, "an ill-tempered and horrible man", arrived in Stockholm on 12 July 1599, God made a marvellous caricature: a pig born in the Södermalm quarter of Stockholm at about the same time, "with only one eye in the middle of its forehead" and "its snout bent upwards like a horn". Laski was a one-eyed man, and the resemblance was striking

according to Klint, who humbly perpetuated the masterpiece on folio 188B (figure 23): "the birth of that monstrous pig was the *significationis*" of Laski.

The pictures are carelessly drawn and, although supposed to be the same animal, show differences: the animal was said to have hooves bent like buckhorns, but this is only apparent in the left-hand image. It had one large eye in the centre of its forehead, with something like an elephant's trunk hanging down over this (thus the appearance in the right-hand image that it may have had two eyes; however, Klint's text is quite clear as to the number, and he makes the same statement twice). It had a wide mouth and its snout was bent upwards like a hard, sharp horn. It was hairless and had a lion-like tail. To Klint, of course, the horn was a devilish symbol, thus symbolising Laski even more closely.

When the pig tried to suck the sow she could not stand its pointed snout, and finally she bit the little monster to death. That was the end of Laski's fortune: he could derive no advantage from Sweden and was soon expelled. Such a cyclopean malformation is apparently created when the two eyes are so close that they have grown together, and Klint records a similar account (fol. 47B) of a lamb born in March 1559 at the parsonage of Hegersta. It had "one head and only one eye in the middle of its forehead, but it had two bodies and eight feet, and it was black" [13]

DRAGONS

The incidents discussed in this section are largely connected with the Lutheran struggle against Catholicism in Sweden (which is, after all, the over-riding theme of the book). King John, his Polish wife Katarina, and their son Sigismund were Catholics (while, in Klint's view, God was not), and they were backed up by such

Fig. 23 - Two views of the one-eyed pig born at Södermalm in 1599

166

Fig. 24 - The dragons named after Herbestus, 1570, and Possevinus, October 1572.

intriguers as the Pope, the Devil and the Jesuits. During this struggle many dragons appeared in the sky, usually flying in a south-to-north or north-to-south direction. North and south symbolised the religious antipodes according to Klint, who named most of the dragons after their spiritual allies, the cardinals and Jesuits.

"Anno 1570, a big red dragon was observed flying from the south to the north. Shortly thereafter a Jesuit monk called Herbestus arrived in the country to become Queen Katarina's confessor. He left the country as soon as the Queen died in 1583, but he caused much evil while he was here." (fol. 74B)

The dragon was called Herbestus, but Klint's picture of the beast seems to be copied from a bestiary. Is this how dragons were described by the people who actually claimed to have seen them? I think not. The flying dragon of the reports usually looked like a kind of wooden steelyard known in Swedish as a *besman*, consisting of a heavy round or oval lump of wood with a graduated arm attached. The dragon was said to have a large head and a thin tail or body; it flew low, on a level with the tree-tops, and it emitted sparks. It was often black as soot, was thought to belong to the element fire, and could appear fiery. This is, in fact, how Klint describes most of his dragons in the text, in spite of his elaborated drawings.

"Anno 1579, another Roman legate called

Antonius Possevinus arrived in Sweden; he was sent by the Pope to propagate the Jesuitical religion ... but while he was here such a storm arose that all the crops blew down, and we got a bad harvest that year. The clerics of Sweden were now in great tribulation, and they were being persecuted for the sake of their true religion..." (fol. 70B). The persecution was caused by the so-called Red Book, with which King John tried to impose a new liturgy. That the Catholics got the blame for the crop failures is an interesting, but predictable, change of viewpoint; when the Reformation was new it was the Lutherans who were blamed [14].

Possevinus also seems to have got a dragon named after himself, a beast looking like a falling star, which as early as October 1572 dashed out of a black cloud shaped like a black man ("a black man" here implies the Devil).

After the death of King John III in 1592, Luther's catechism was accepted by the Diet of Uppsala, which was a victory for the ecclesiastical estates over the throne, and many portents were seen in connection with it. For example there is the following, notable mainly because it was almost witnessed by Klint himself.

"Anno 1593, on 5 February, the first day of the Distinget [fair at Uppsala], in the evening the sky opened in Uppland, and a sudden great light burst through the opening two or three times, like broad daylight, and in the opening stood a man with a blood-stained sword ..." [Here Klint interprets: "Here God threatens with a sword if we do not reject the Catholic faith."] "... At that very moment I, Joen Petri Klint, was riding my sleigh on the east gorge near the hamlet of Mulaboda, and thus when I was driving and I could hardly find the road because of the darkness, the sky suddenly lit up three times, and once the light was so bright that I could have threaded a needle, but it went quickly away. Yet the sky was somewhat cloudy, and to the south in the forest a little ahead of me, a wind, like witches are in the habit of making [a whirlwind]

passed through the tall trees." (fol. 153B)

The victory at Uppsala had to be defended, as a multitude of omens predicted. For example: "Anno 1593, on 21 August, in the week of the 10th Sunday after Trinity, a Tuesday evening about one hour before sunset there was a sudden light in the south, like a big star, and she gave out sparks and shone, and then she disappeared. At that very moment there came from the spot something like black smoke or a black cloud, stretching itself out straight in the sky. Then it coiled up like a curve or half a barrel-hoop, and its front end grew large while its rear part grew thin;

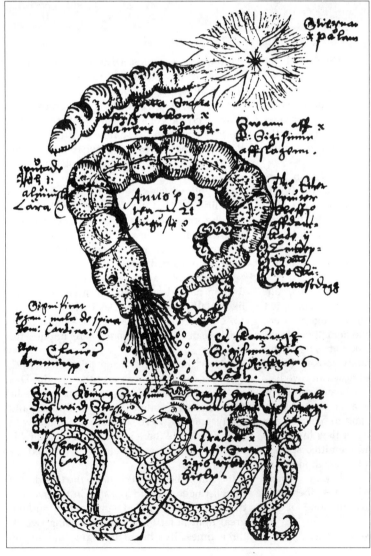

Fig. 25 - At the top, the dragon of 21 August 1593; below it, the two warring serpents seen in Uppland that same day.

Fig. 26 - The dragon Samuel Laski of 18 October 1598.

and then it twisted into a linked shape, becoming like a row of [large] balls of many colours, and it grew a large dragon's head; the whole looked like a dragon or a fierce-looking serpent, and he slowly drifted northwards like a cloud. Arriving in the northwestern sky near the sunset, he descended southwards, so that many people [felt alarmed], some of them thinking that he had fallen to the ground, and they were confused and struck with horror, because he then looked mightily fierce and horrible, and he stopped and spat forth fire down on to the earth, as from a dragon's mouth. And then he rose again into the air and disappeared in the direction of the northwest, towards the sunset, so that he was hardly visible an hour after sunset. [A note in the margin of folio 165B places this sighting at Söderköping]

"But at the same day and hour in Uppland, in Stockholm and its surroundings, and in Uppsala, two serpents were seen fighting in the sky, and one of the serpents tore the other serpent to pieces, and the victorious serpent had recourse to a tree and grasped it with its tail, and above him was a crown." (fol. 166, 166B)

The apparent change of sex here, from she to it to he as the phenomenon transforms from star to cloud to dragon, is the result of word-gender in old Swedish: 'star' was a feminine noun, 'cloud' neuter, and 'dragon' masculine. At the top of the page shown in figure 25, Klint quotes Isaiah 30:6 on "the viper and the fiery flying serpent".

What happened following this portent? In September 1593, King Sigismund of Poland arrived in Sweden as the heir to the throne. The star was Poland, Klint says, but it expired, signifying the defeat of the king. The trail of smoke coming from the spot where the star disappeared was the pack of Catholics in the king's train. The dragon was named Malaspina after one of the worst of the lot, a papal legate called Johannes de Malaspina who, besides being a cardinal and a prince, was also a thorn to the Lutherans. He demanded their submission and wanted Catholic churches to be opened in Stockholm, Uppsala and Kalmar. ("The dragon gave out sparks", Klint reminds us). The churches were denied him, so he then renewed his demands, this time for Jesuit schools to be founded in Stockholm, Uppsala, Kalmar and Växjö ("The dragon belched fire"). God and the clergy were not very keen on that idea either, so "when that was denied him he called us Swedes crude *barbados*". (fols. 159B, 167, 167B)

That was hardly diplomatic. On 14 July 1594, when Malaspina tried to leave the country, lightning struck his war-ship in the Stockholm archipelago. Klint drew a picture of the event, showing the red fire of heaven striking the mast. The cardinal himself seems to be climbing the bowsprit. "Johannes de mala spina male spiritus," Klint remarks, apparently punning on Johannes' name, difficulties and evil soul. (fol. 168)

The second vision, of the two warring serpents, was fulfilled during the civil war (which, of course, was presaged by a multitude of other portents). The two serpents were Sigismund and his Lutheran uncle, Duke Charles. The serpent Charles, supported by the tree (the people) won the crown. During the war itself there were also hundreds of portents, many of them centred round the key fort of Kalmar, where bells tolled in the night, drums and trumpets were heard, the earth seemed to quake, and much noise, turmoil, cries and shooting occurred in the sky. After one such nocturnal battle in the air in 1598 bloodstains were found everywhere on the snow, but no other marks were seen. Before the battle at Stegeborg, on 8 September 1598, fire floated over the town and shone through the windows. Finally, in the night of 18 October 1598, "a big dragon was seen, like a big star, flying from the north to the south. It hummed a great deal, surrounded with flames and shining, and a great light came after it." (fol. 181B) On 13 October the defeated Sigismund broke his oath and escaped, a traitor to the last, to prevent his troops from complete surrender, so the directions in the portent five days later are important. This time the dragon flew from the north to the south: Sigismund was defeated and running. The dragon of 18 October is shown in figure 26, but although it symbolised the defeated Sigismund, Klint named it (true to habit) after Samuel Laski, Sigismund's Jesuit diplomat, who did not appear until 1599.

A few other dragons are mentioned, such as the one that appeared in 1595: on "22 December, there came over Söderköping a great darkness and a terrible hailstorm lasting about half an hour. And as the hailstones fell a clearly shining light was seen right over the town church, like a lantern; and from it came a sparkling dragon which flamed from the mouth and around about itself for a while, and then it disappeared as the dark hailstorm went away. But out there in the bay a northwest wind was blowing, and it was raining." (fol. 169)

Klint's drawing actually shows a dark dragon's head inside a dark cloud from which hailstones are falling. The story is discussed further on fols. 169B and 171B. There is mention of the "sowing of dragon's

ice" over the church, which seems to refer to the hailstorm. Klint connects this with the story of 'Bror Måns' (Brother Magnus), a lewd monk from Vadstena who was expelled from Sweden in 1596 "together with a flock of pregnant nuns, who one and all gave birth to children as soon as they had crossed the border". Klint says some of the nuns murdered their babies as soon as they were born. This, of course, is a piece of anti-Catholic propaganda: the nuns were, in fact, a group of screaming and fragile old ladies in their 60s or 70s who were thrown out of their nunnery into the street by main force. The recruiting of new nuns had become illegal as soon as Sweden became a Protestant country.

There then follows an account of bad weather, which appears to connect this dragon-portent with the hard winter of 1596. "In March the weather was like summer during the day, with bright sunshine, but like the severest winter at night. There was drought, and many people were sick with the cough for a long time." Lakes were frozen to the bottom, the sowing was delayed because the fields were frozen and could not be ploughed, and so on. It is obvious that, although he does not say so explicitly, Klint saw a connection between the dry winter and the dragon's hailstones (dry rain), and between the sunny days and cold nights and the brightness and darkness of the dragon.

The wholeness of Klint's world-view is hard to show in full, and perhaps even harder to understand. History to him was a cosmic drama where every important scene was being rehearsed again and again in the sky,

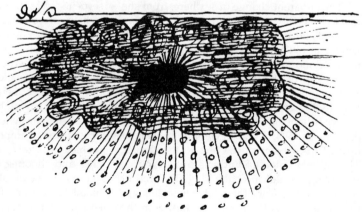

Fig. 27 - The head of a dragon and the hail at Söderköping, 22 December 1595.

among the stars, by the elements and in the animal kingdom, until finally it was staged as real events in the real world. Most important was the accumulation of portents: the whole of Nature pointed out the direction.

Klint, of course, only cared about what the portents *meant*, not what they were. One can suppose that some of the 'dragons' were meteors, but it is pointless to speculate since there is no such thing as 'pure observation'. Our brains interpret our observations at the same instant that we observe, so our inter-pretations are also part of our observations. Dragons do not belong to our present world-view, so naturally we do not see them. If a 16th century dragon were to appear in our skies, we would not be able to see it in the same way that our ancestors did. To us it would be a UFO, perhaps, or something else that belongs to our cultural framework. But if some day UFOs go the same way as the dragons did, we wouldn't be able to see UFOs either. Other things will appear in the sky, strange things to be sure, but we cannot imagine now what they might be.

FASHION

Nothing of importance is foreboded only once, so it is in the nature of portents that a certain theme will prevail for a while until its meaning is fulfilled. This is, according to Klint, what would be expected since God, if He wants to tell us something, or if He gets upset (as He frequently appeared to do), will use every conceivable means to convey His message. For example, in the 1590s God stated His views on the latest fashion in clothing. His message was that it was ridiculous and, furthermore, that

Fig. 28 - One of the birds at Vadstena, February 1592.

since vanity is a sin one should not be too well-dressed.

"Anno 1592: birds of a strange species recently arrived and settled, especially at Vadstena, where some of them were shot or captured. They had the most gaudy feathers which, most notably, looked like starched frills around the neck. They were just as wide and stiff, and stood out around their necks. They had two big ears and a square, stubbed tail. And these same birds were shot in the month of Candlemas [February] in 1592 at Vadstena. Item: from anno 1580 until the present day a dreadful fashion arose: awful, large and wide ruffs around loose shirt-collars, starched so the frills protruded far and wide around the neck like half a barrel-hoop fastened together with a piece of iron."

(L) Fig. 29 - The Danish mackerel, 23 February 1599.   (R) Fig. 30 - The Näcken at Norrköping, 15 June 1599.

171

Fig. 31 - The child of Erfurt, born 15 February 1596.

(fol. 141)

These strange birds were almost certainly the wading bird, *Philomachus pugnax*, known in English as the ruff precisely because of its frill of neck-feathers. They have ear-tufts, but only in the mating season. Their natural habitat is in Lapland, but occasionally they appear in southern parts of the country, although not very often. What is perhaps most curious is that they appeared so early, in February.

The waters also brought the message. On 23 February 1599, a mackerel was caught in the Great Belt outside Nyborg (Denmark) and it was sent to King Christian III, arriving in Copenhagen on 25 February. It had a deformed mouth and its dorsal fin looked like a sheaf or fasces, red and bloody. A white frill (of scales?) surrounded its neck, protruding as if fastened with a piece of iron (fol. 185B). As the sheaf was the symbol of Swedish royalty, the portent obviously referred to the wearing of ruffs in that country.

The Devil endorsed the style: "Anno [15]99, on 15 June. For a good half hour the Näcken [15] was sitting on a stone below the big bridge at Norrköping in the middle of the stream. He was bald, wore a ruff round his neck, a blue coat with buttons and black trousers. A blue coat ... at the time when so many people used that [blue] Oriental broadcloth. Afterwards: two men and three maids drowned at Fiskeby, one girl at Norrköping, and two fishermen at Hendely, almost on the same day." (fol. 185B)

"Anno 1596, on 15 February, a child was born in Erfurt in Thüringen [Germany]. Its father was a man called Hans Dolck and its mother's name was Malin Hans Dolck. When it was born it had a white ruff around its neck, and a glutton's belly, but it only lived for three months." (fol. 173)

MISCELLANEOUS PORTENTS

Klint records many other events which are not so easily classifiable. "Anno Domini 1566, on 2 July: some people saw the Man with the Scythe walking in a cabbage-patch at Söderköping, and as he cut down the cabbage heads each stroke was heard, and they saw how the heads fell, but in the morning the cabbages were unharmed. Item in 1566 the great plague struck Söderköping and the whole of Sweden." (fol. 59)

Fig. 32 - The man with the scythe lops cabbages at Söderköping, 2 July 1566.

172

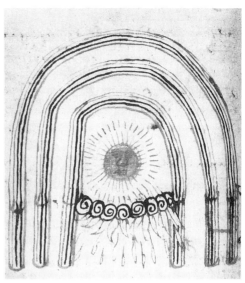

(L) Fig. 33 - Thor's wedges or sky-axes fall during a storm. (R) Fig. 34 - Premature sun, nocturnal rainbows and a fiery cloud, 9 March 1583.

Figure 33 shows Thor's wedges or sky-axes falling to the ground **[16]**. The text (fol. 170) deals with strange thunderstorms at particular times of the year, especially Christmas and Easter, causing such bad weather for lady aviators "that the witches presumably were prevented from going to the Blåkulla on those nights." Blåkulla means 'The Blue Hill', and is the Swedish equivalent to the German witch-mountain, the Brocken. Folklore is not unanimous as to which 'Blue Hill' was the right one, as there are many in Sweden, but the most well-known Blåkulla is situated in Kalmarsund, the narrow sound between Öland and the mainland. I have no doubt that this island-hill was the Blåkulla Klint had in mind. Otherwise the most famous Blåkulla in Scandinavian lore was Hekla, or Heklafjäll, in Iceland, named after Odin's blue mantle. Heklarin (mantle-wearer) was one of Odin's names.

The first case in the book is also about lightning. "A.D. 1546, on 6 August, at about midnight, a mighty storm with claps of thunder and lightning passed over Mecheln in Brabant, and the flashes of lightning struck through the windows of the castle and set fire to 600 barrels of gunpowder, causing 70 houses in the neighbourhood to collapse and more than 300 people to be blown to pieces. The gunpowder was intended to be sent to Germany for use against the Lutherans, because the Emperor Charles V had started a war against the Duke of Saxony, the Margrave of Hessen, and other princes" (fol. 1). Klint also associated this big bang with the Council of Trent and the death of Martin Luther in 1546, who thus received a suitable salute from God.

A couple more cases of aerial phenomena: "A.D. 1587, on 10 January, one hour after sunset, when the moon rose he was as red as copper, and two brooms or branches were sticking out of his mouth, and they were there for two hours. Then they disappeared, and the moon was as bright as usual." (fol. 127). There are several similar accounts. It should perhaps be noted that the moon was masculine, the sun feminine, in Scandinavian tradition.

"A.D. 1583, on 9 March two hours before sunrise, the sky was clear and three rainbows were visible in the east, standing on the earth, and inside them a dark sun with a black cloud appeared, and beneath it a red cloud was dripping down on to the earth. Then it all disappeared, and the sun rose as bright as usual, and she radiated a hot light." (fol. 112B)

In January 1568, in general Daniel Rantzau's camp outside the town of Skänninge in Östergötland, a huge flock of crows was seen, seeming very upset and making a horrible noise. Then four crows flew at a fifth one and pecked it to death, so that blood and feathers fell to the ground. Then with a horrible noise the flock left and flew eastwards. The case was reported by the vicar of Veta, Herr Per, who

Fig. 35 - Warring crows at Skänninge, January 1568.

meaning of the portent was that the true nature of the Pope and his power was soon to be exposed, and so it was, "by St. [!] Luther in 1517."

"In 1532, on the very day and hour that the Margrave Joachim went forth to meet the Turks in Austria, little new-hatched chicks, only two days old, crowed loudly during the whole day and all through the following day and night, which is not usual. Sabinus interpreted the portent as favourable to the Margrave against the Turks." (fol. 19B, with picture of a chick)

During the first day of the peace negotiations at the castle of Padis in Estonia on 1 September 1575, a huge flock of sea-birds settled on the castle and covered the roofs, towers and battlements. They stayed there all through the night but flew away in the morning. No one had ever seen such birds before, and no one knew where they came

himself witnessed the incident. The same year King Eric XIV was dethroned and imprisoned by his brothers and succeeded by his brother John (the duke of the east); some years later Eric was murdered with a plate of pea soup laced with arsenic. (fol. 57)

"Anno 1574, when Wesenberg in Estonia was besieged the general Claus Åkonsson sent some of his soldiers to Tolsborg, three miles [21.5 English miles] outside Wesenberg, and they stayed there from 5 March for 14 days afterwards, having their camp on the shore of a lake. A few evenings thereafter a tremendous number of wolves appeared before the camp; they stood there leering at the men and howling a great deal, and when they arrived they were as thickly packed as if an army had arrived with clamour and tumult, but a moment later they left. On 17 March 1574 there was a fracas in the camp at Wesenberg between the Scotch and German [mercenary soldiers], and in the tumult 1500 of the Scotch were slain, and the Germans lost 30 men. The Swedes had to raise the siege." (fol. 74, 74B)

In 1496 the strange 'monstrum' shown in figure 37 was found in the River Tiber at Rome. It had the head, ears and mane of an ass. In its right hand, which looked like an elephant's foot, it carried a banner with two crossed keys (the papal symbol) painted on it. Its left hand and arm were human, but scales covered the arms, the neck and the legs. Its left foot was like that of an eagle, but it's right foot was like that of a bull. At its anus appeared "a mouth surrounded by a shag or beard, and flames of fire belched out of it." (fol. 199B) The

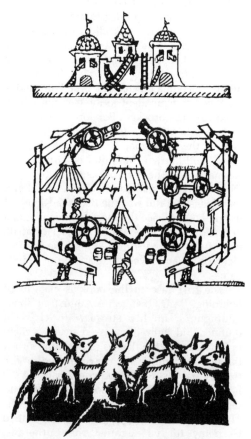

Fig. 36 - The wolves at Wesenberg, 1574.

174

Fig. 37 - The River Tiber monster, 1496.

from. Some of the birds were shot, but no one recognised their species. The negotiations fell through. (fol. 73)

In October 1587, in a small lake at Tryserum, near Lake Ronnen, a strange animal was seen, looking like a big ox or horse. Klint's illustration shows *both* alternatives, ox and horse, but only one monster was seen. It rushed to and fro, hissing and groaning, causing the water to heave, and it threw dead fish up on the shore. Of these, a man who lived nearby salted down half a barrel of eels. The whole night after the monster was seen the water continued to boil and whine; and finally the water rose high and violently belched fish far up on land, with a great noise. Many sea-birds arrived and cried and fought among themselves. This happened in calm weather, and many people watched it in a great agony of fear (fol. 92, 92B, with a picture of a water-horse). One witness, mentioned in the margin, was the owner of the lake, Baron Nils Gyllenstierna, who later became Lord High Steward. On folio 127 is added that the monster killed all the fish in the lake.

Tryserum is in Småland near the east coast, a little south of the border with Östergötland, but it belongs to the diocese of Linköping, so Klint may have been able to get first-hand information. Only one actual eye-witness is named, however: Baron Gyllenstierna.

To conclude this section, a ghost story: "Anno 1580 in May: a party dressed in white and mounted on white horses was seen during the night riding along the Spettalsgatan [a street] in Söderköping. The watchmen and other people saw them through their windows, and heard the horseshoes beating on the paved street. Item in June people began to die in masses from the plague, and it lasted until the end of the Dog-days. Item these phantoms were also seen by dominus Bergeus Petri, who was the late queen's priest, and the priest of the poor." (fol. 107)

A SUMMARY, AND THE END OF THE WORLD

There are many independent sources supporting Klint's general claim that an unusual amount of strange phe-

Fig. 38 - The flocking at Padis, 1 September 1575.

175

Fig. 39 - The lake monster at Tryserum, October 1587. Although only one monster was seen, it was said to look like an ox or a horse, so Klint drew both. Dead fish can be seen on the lake shore at the bottom of the picture.

nomena occurred in Sweden in the latter part of the 16th century. Historians are also amazed at "the sudden increase of superstitiousness" that occurred during that period. "More than ever before menacing portents and wonders were seen on earth and in the sky. Church registers, which previously were reporting important events in the country, now became filled with memoranda on such wonders." [17]. Even the government got carried away. For example, in 1588 King John III promulgated Royal Instructions as a result of the critical portents of that year when, among other things, rains of worms ruined the crop. King Charles IX issued similar Instructions. There was an 'undergrowth' of End-Time beliefs that sometimes reached the 'treetops'.

I am inclined to believe that some of these superstitions were based on facts, and that something very real and very threatening was going on. Bloody snow, blood rains and haloes may have been caused by volcanic dust, or some other dust from other sources. It is a well-known fact that the climate got colder at this period, resulting in famine years; and Klint also complains about the worsening weather. Climatic change could also be at the root of other changes as well. This could explain, perhaps, the swarms or 'falls' of insects, larvae, worms and slugs, although it may not explain the falls of 'almost'-rye and barley. Also, the tolling and noises from the sky could perhaps have been due to strange atmospheric disturbances. Meteors were le-

gion, and we might even speculate that the disturbed weather was caused by the Earth passing through some thin cloud of cosmic dust, containing a few bigger iron 'pots'. These speculations aside, the behaviour of the sun seems to have changed and auroras were seen at latitudes where, in common decency, they had no right to be. Finally, there were the noises in the ground, and earthquakes shook Sweden, especially in 1593 and 1601 (fol. 45B). As for the many ghosts and visions that were seen, they may have been influenced by starvation and malnutrition [18].

Klint accumulated a lot of data pointing to 1588 as a fateful year, or even the Year of Doom. Yet the eschatological atmosphere cooled down somewhat after the Doomsday prophecies had 'failed' (as historians of religion put it). There are some data, however, suggesting the possibility that *attempts*

Fig. 40 - The ghostly riders at Söderköping, May 1580.

176

(L) Fig. 41 - The storm over Münster, Easter 1588.

(B) Fig. 42 - Three corpses rise from the churchyard, Münster, 1588.

were actually made to create a veritable Judgment Day in about 1588.

As an example, on Easter Sunday in 1588, at 4:00 in the morning, it was said that God had a go at Münster, Germany. A great darkness enveloped the city, so black the sky and earth could not be told apart. Then a thunderstorm arose and lightning crisscrossed the atmosphere so that the sky looked like a burning oven (figure 41). The earth quaked, the church bells fell from their towers, two long streets were rent apart and five houses sank into the ground with men and livestock inside. Three corpses woke up in the cathedral and another three dug themselves out of the churchyard. Figure 42 shows the corpses in the churchyard: one with a pious appearance, one aflame who did nothing but scream, and a soot-blackened one (who had perhaps spent time in Purgatory) who appeared to be in a state of shock (Klint also has a picture of the corpses from the cathedral). Some of them seemed utterly confused, however, and did not speak coherently, but Klint says that one of them praised God. Then there was an anti-climax. The storm died down, no general resurrection occurred, and those corpses that did wake up returned to their graves. In all, the balance sheet was negative: six resurrected, while 44 others in the city were killed, along with many domestic animals. Klint interpreted the incident as a most gruesome portent predicting the end of the world; but it seems to have been more of a technical mishap. (fols. 131, 131B, 132, 132B) [19]

Klint lived in a smaller universe than we do. The Earth was the only planet of importance, and it was about 5,000 years old. God lived in the sky, and He was like a peasant chief. He supervised his subjects, and if He didn't like what He saw, He tossed pots around in wild bursts of fury. Hell was a horrible place in the underworld, but it had ventilation shafts which opened out in Iceland, for example, where wailings and groanings were reported coming from volcanic craters.

But Klint's world may also have been a lot larger than the world we live in, because it was not so thoroughly mapped. Almost 70 per cent of Sweden and Finland was uninhabited territory, wasteland and virgin forests, where trolls and dragons had plenty of room to exist. The church did not deny these beings, but saw it as one of its tasks to incorporate them into a Christian belief system. Klint's book, then, covers some of the last decades of the Fabulous Age.

NOTES & REFERENCES

1 - Wilhelm Norlind: "Astronomische Streifzüge in Joen Petri Klints 'Om Meteorer'." in *Dragma (Festskr. t. Martin P. Nilsson)*, Lund, 1939, p.334-345.

2 - Klint frequently uses the word 'item' in its archaic sense of 'likewise', 'also', to introduce separate entries in a list.

3 - P.P. Gothus, *Een rett Christeligh Vnderwijsning...* (etc), Stockholm, 1590. The book has no pagination, but the story is told in the introduction.

A similar case is mentioned in the popular science magazine *Forskning och Framsteg*, July 1994. A rain of black stones fell from the sky at Hessle in Uppland on New Year's Day in 1869. Coincidentally, this 'rain' also occurred on a festival at the beginning of January, and took churchgoers by surprise on the slope down from the church, as they were returning home from morning service. A meteor exploded in the sky and threw hundreds of meteorites to the ground: "...[it] looked as if one had been standing in front of the mouth of a cannon which had been fired". The stones were apparently small, but easy to find since they burned holes in the snow. A book was written about this event, *Om Meteorstensfallet vid Hessle den 1 Januari 1869*, by K.A. Fredholm, Uppsala, 1869.

4 - A very similar phenomenon was reported at Norra Kvill in Småland on 17 April 1982. The eyewitness, Anna Karlsson, woke up in the middle of the night because a strong light was shining in through her window. When she moved the curtain aside she felt considerable heat. "The window, the curtain, and the wall were really hot, and you could almost burn yourself on the window-pane." In the east she saw an egg-shaped UFO, as large as the full moon. It moved to and fro under some thin clouds. "From the right side of the object came something like a welding flame of many colours; it was directed obliquely downward." After a while the UFO disappeared, then returned, before disappearing again; thus it seems to have appeared in the sky twice.

The incident took place at the spot where the oldest oak-tree in Sweden (the so-called 'Kvill oak') is growing, and for several days afterwards the witness suffered from the after-effects of her exposure to the intense radiated heat (*UFO-Aktuellt*, issue 2, 1982).

5 - Essentially, 'fasces' describes the bundle of rods, surmounted by an axe-blade, which was carried by a Roman lictor as a symbol of a magistrate's authority. The fasces described by Klint, and shown in figures 6 and 16, appear to be similar, though lacking the axe-blade and frequently trailing unbound and unshaped twigs bearing thorns or sharp points. Klint's fasces appears to combine elements of rod- bundle, sheaf, besom and whip or scourge. As there seems to be no direct English equivalent, 'fasces' has been left untranslated.

6 - Throughout the centuries strange 'claps of thunder', similar to the ones mentioned by Klint, have been reported from the Stockholm-Uppsala region. The most spectacular of these is described in Bishop A.O. Rhyzelius' book *Brontologia*, 1721, p.89:

"In 1697, on Dominica Quasimodogeniti, or Low Sunday, the day when the sad news of the death of King Charles XI was to be announced from the pulpits ... at 4 o'clock in the morning as the bells rang for matins, one tremendous bang was heard in the sky over Uppsala: such a clap of thunder that it sounded as if some 1,000 cannons were simultaneously fired. Not only did many doors and windows in the city break, but some old houses fell down, and piles of timber here and there in the city tilted over. In his sermon for the morning service Dr Jesper Swedberg interpreted the occurrence as a miraculous intimation relating to the death of such a great king."

The king who now seized power was Charles XII, the warlord who in popular lore was to be called 'The Thunderer'. In a letter to the king Dr Olof Rudbeck wrote: "On this day, when the sun rose, such a thunder-peal was heard, that never within living memory, no, I think, not ever before, was anything like it heard: not only the windows shattered but the houses and the very earth trembled, and afterwards came a rapid torrent, whereupon the sun rose very bright, and we got a fine, warm day." The torrent suggests that it was indeed a thunder-clap, but no doubt an unusual one.

The most recent bangs that I know of occurred on 26 August 1985, a Monday, when three loud explosions in the sky caused the ground to shake and smashed windows, glasses and china, from Saltsjöbaden to Nynäshamn. However, nothing was heard in the central parts of Stockholm. According to *Arbetet*, 27 August, and *Sydsvenska Dagbladet*, 27 + 29 August, the bangs were quite inexplicable and did not have a seismic origin, nor were there any aircraft in the area. But on 29 August the sounds were suddenly explained by H.G. Wessberg, press officer of the Defence Staff, who claimed that they were either caused by two Swedish military airplanes over Nyköping (where no bangs were reported), or by two Soviet planes west of Ösel in Estonia, in which case the sound must have travelled across the Baltic to select two Stockholm suburbs without being noticed anywhere else. Unfortunately, after the bangs were explained, no one bothered to explain the explanations.

7 - In the years 1580, 81, 84, 87, 88, 91, 92, 93, 98 and 99.

8 - One infers that the blood-rains were concentrated mainly at Söderköping, as Klint has no data on similar rains elsewhere during that period (except at Varberg), even though the book is loaded with other strange data from numerous other places.

9 - As American folklorists would have us believe that the 'Phantom Hitchhiker' story originated in the USA in the 1920s, this much earlier story seems worth further comment. It is interesting that the driver of the sleigh is a priest; this points to a possible origin of the story.

From the earliest times until the Reformation, there was a religious custom with a very similar 'motif': the circuit of the Spring Chariot. The custom is best described in the 14th century Icelandic *Flateyjarbók* (a collection of sagas of the Norwegian kings), although it was first mentioned by Tacitus (55-120 AD) in his *Germania*, chapter 40.

A chariot was driven along a certain route through the tribal lands. At one or more halts along the road the chariot was stopped by a divine hitchhiker. In those regions where the driver was a priest, the hitchhiker was a goddess, Freya (The Lady). Where the driver was a priestess, the hitchhiker was a god, Freyr (The Lord). The hitchhiker was invisible, of course, but his/her presence became apparent as soon as the deity had entered the chariot, which now became so heavy that it would not move. The hitchhiker's place was in the back seat. [That the deity sat behind the driver is also verified by the ceremonial chariots found at Dejbjerg in Denmark, dating from the 2nd century AD; there the goddess had actually left some of her personal belongings (clay vessels and a piece of a loom) in the back-seat for the archaeologists to find. Amongst others, see H.R. Ellis Davidson, *Gods and Myths of Northern Europe* (Pelican, Harmondsworth, 1964, p92-96)]. He or she predicted the future, using the vocal chords of the driver, who was in trance. Nobody could fail to notice the drastic transformation of the driver's sex. A priest possessed by the goddess spoke in a female voice; a priestess possessed by the god behaved in a very masculine fashion. The bystanders could also ask questions about the future, which were answered. When the final prediction had been made the hitchhiker vanished, and the chariot drove on.

The circuit of the chariot seems to have been performed as early as possible in the spring (*Flateyjarbók* even mentions one case when the chariot got stuck in a snow-drift), which ties in with Klint's story, occurring as it does in February. On occasion it seems that the part of the divine hitchhiker was acted by a human stand-in, giving the deity a most

Fig. 43 - A deteriorated page which mentions a rain of crosses "everywhere in Germany" in 1501.

physical presence; *Flateyjarbók* mentions one such case.

In later times the custom changed, of course. In Catholic days the chariot contained holy relics and the priest, or priests, used to bless the land. When the Lutherans rose to power the custom was abandoned.

If Klint's story was modelled on some religious custom of the above kind, it is not surprising that the hitchhiker was female: Västergötland, where the scene is laid, was a stronghold of the pagan Freya cult.

The transformation of the beer may be a 16th century addition, perhaps influenced by Biblical thought (Luke 24: 15, 30-31). Still, the 'beer miracle' may reflect some knowledge of who the hitchhiker 'really' was:

Freya was the goddess of prophecy, and one of her names was Heidr (Clairvoyant). She also brewed beer: good beer in fact. In Klint's story the beer transformed into malt, and Freya was the goddess of the harvest. Then it transformed into acorns, pig's food, and Freya was a goddess of pigs. One of her names was Syr, which means the Sow. Finally the beer transformed into blood. Freya was the goddess of life and death, the giver and the destroyer, and the name of her celestial residence was Folkvangr (Battlefield). A Swedish postage stamp shows Freya riding across a battlefield in her chariot, with a horn of cooling beer in her hand.

Of course I am not suggesting that I have here traced the 'origin' of all Vanishing Hitchhiker legends. My point is simply that the theme of such a story is very old, and that such stories may therefore have been around a lot longer than is usually thought.

10 - This rain of fire and brimstone occurred in May 1585, according to a manuscript now in the National Library, Stockholm (D 562, "Thenne öfuerne Gudz retferdige wredes teeckn...", 1585). Twice in May it

rained fire and brimstone, according to this narrator, and the brimstone lay thick in the streets; then came a rain of hailstones, big and small, which ignited if fire was brought to them, and burned with a crackling sound like sulphur.

On 4 June an unnamed fire-and-brimstone prophet appeared, who attracted crowds of people in Stockholm and said he was sent by God to preach the End of the World. He walked up to the castle and called to the king and his court, and when they appeared he openly revealed their sins and ordered them to repent. He preached with a drawn sword in his hand, but was not arrested because the authorities feared his fearlessness.

Then on 6 August, a Sunday, at 9:00 or 10:00 in the morning, darkness settled over the city and there was thunder, and "the fire of heaven" suddenly appeared inside a church (the name of which is not mentioned), dancing under the vaulted roof, causing such panic that people cried to heaven and the parson ran terrified from the pulpit. Yet the fire caused no harm, except to some 'wives' whose clothes were burned. Many poor and weak people were trampled, however, and some may have died afterwards.

There are several other accounts of similar rains of fire in old Swedish books. In his *Memorabilium Sveticae gentis exempla* (1671), Professor Johannes Schefferus gives the following account, which I have translated from the Swedish edition, *Svenska folkets ärominne*, printed in 1733:

"In the evening of the 3rd day after Whit Sunday in 1629, some fishermen of Lyckås in the countship of Visingsborg went to a nearby lake, called Landsjö, to set fishing-nets. While they were engaged in this, black clouds and a fog appeared from the north and caused a sudden and heavy shower of rain. Together with the rain-drops fell a lot of glowing

fire, and it extended over the entire area of the lake. The fire falling into the lake was extinguished, but the fire that stuck to the fishermen's clothes burned holes and left ashes behind. The fishermen were so horrified by this that they were taken ill, and hardly managed to return home. Some of them died shortly thereafter." It appears that if these old claims are to be trusted the fire-rains often occurred in the vicinity of lakes and bays. One wonders whether opposites (fire and water) attract?

A modern explanation of rains of brimstone is that the 'brimstone' was pollen from pines, while rains of fire have been explained as auroras, lightning, or sparks carried on the wind from distant fires used in forest-clearance. Yet if the clearance-fire was so distant one wonders how the sparks could still be so hot. It is often mentioned that they burned holes in clothes.

"In 1705, in the parish of Grängie in West Dalarna, at a lake called Vässman, one day in the evening at about 10:00 fell, no doubt from a heated and lightning-prone atmosphere, a rain of fire, like burning sparks, which fastened on to clothes and burned holes in them. More than 100 people witnessed the event." A.O. Rhyzelius, *Brontologia*, 1721, p.97.

The fire-rain is a phenomenon which now seems to have ceased.

11 - The aerial battle over Rome in 1580 is doubtless a fabrication but (like some other cases mentioned by Klint), it may save the reputation of those British ballad writers and pamphleteers who are accused by Leslie Shepard (in *Fortean Times* 29, p.15) of making up their stories out of whole cloth. Klint's account of the vision in 1580 seems identical with the aerial battle at Carlstadt in 1606 mentioned by Shepard. According to Klint, the details are:

a) The moon was as red as

blood for nine nights, and on the right side of the moon was seen a glowing sword, while on the left side was a fasces.

b) A Moslem and a Christian army paraded in the sky and fought a horrible battle, as described above.

c) For the nine nights when the moon was red the 52 year old wife of an alderman in Rome was in labour, and during the battle she gave birth to three sons. The first one had four heads and four arms, and the first head cried and prophecied the downfall of the papacy and the death of the Pope. The second head prophecied a Moslem victory near Cologne, on the Rhine. The third prophecied a Christian union against the Turks. The fourth prophecied another Turkish victory over the Christian kings. The second child was as black as a Moor and predicted great calamities during the Moslem occupation. The third child was as pale as Death and urged the people to repent, otherwise "before 1588 all these prophecies will come true". After that the three children died and were buried.

This is obviously the same story as that recorded by the English pamphleteer, who, equally obviously, did not invent it himself. The original story may well have been a complete fabrication, but it was only *adapted* in the English pamphlet.

12 - Although early, the reading 'spectacles' or eye-glasses is certain. See N. Jacobsson in *Julhalsningar*, 1915, for further discussion of the case.

13 - See George Ives, *Man Bites Man* (ed. Paul Sieveking), Jay Landesman Ltd, London, 1980, p.38, for two very similar cases: "One-eyed pig has trunk" and "Lamb with cyclops eye".

14 - See, for example, Peder Svart's *Krönika* (Chronicle): chapter on the year 1527.

15 - The Näcken or Neck is a Scandinavian water- spirit, often identified, particularly by churchmen, with the Devil.

16 - Thor's axe or hammer was associated with the thunderbolt.

17 - Prof. Hjalmar Holmqvist, *Svenska Kyrkans Historia* [History of the Church of Sweden], 1933-34, vol. 3, p.185.

18 - That 'starvation and malnutrition' make people more prone to see ghosts seems to be a standard explanation. Be this as it may, ghost sightings seem to have peaked during the plague years, to judge from the accounts of Klint and Petrus Pauli Gothus.

Petrus Pauli's book of 1590, *Een rett Christeligh Vnderwijsning...* [etc.], was prompted by the author's harrowing experiences during the plague in 1588, which also convinced him that the End of the World was near. One thing that interested Petrus was how people changed when facing death in the plague. Some became pious, and their speech was prophetic; most victims spoke 'strange words' and raved incoherently about the Second Coming, Petrus tells us. Others went raving mad and had to be tied down hand and foot with ropes before they died (personality changes also seem to have been a symptom of the disease). Yet even those who were neither mad nor ill "saw strange rooms [i.e., places or scenery] and horrible ghosts", and they fell into sudden trances and were transported to strange places in their sleep. And the dead were seen dancing in the wind at night, face to face or whirling round each other in a playful dance of death, over the roofs and chimneys, up in the air and down again to the earth, causing great fear and alarm among the living, who didn't know where to run or what to do. And there are other similar observations.

It is, of course, impossible to really understand historical accounts of this type. Terms like 'mass hysteria' or even 'mass psychosis' are simply labels to avoid the problem. Petrus offered seven causes for the plague, as follows:

a). Astrological causes (a recent(?) conjunction of Mars and Saturn is mentioned).

b). Eclipses of the sun and the moon.

c). Damp weather; mists, fogs and poisonous winds and miasmas coming from the earth (fens and swamps are mentioned, as well as smoke from volcanoes, and other strange mists).

d). Unsettled or unusual weather, such as warm winters and cold summers.

e). Green fruits and unripe grain; "all kinds of food and drink that is raw or unripe".

f). Infection "caused by breath, clothes, and bodily contact ... so that one man will moisten or poison another with his company; his breath, clothes or touch".

g). The seventh cause was God, who used the other six causes to punish all mankind, or single nations, for their sins.

Apart from God, who was the 'motor', Petrus stressed damp weather as the main cause, and also quoted Martin Luther on that point. It was thought that dry or aromatic smoke might keep the plague at a distance, and some people probably started to burn incense as soon as the first rumours of the plague were whispered. It is probably idle to speculate whether that incense may have contained hallucinogens.

19 - For further discussion of the Münster case, see Michael Goss, *Strange and Wonderful News*, in this issue, at note 33. There the case is dated to 20 September, 1616.

"STRANGE AND WONDERFUL NEWS..."

BROADSIDES, TABLOIDS, FOLKLORE AND FORTEAN PHENOMENA

Michael Goss

Author of *The Evidence for Phantom Hitchhikers* and many articles on folklore and the paranormal, Michael Goss explores the world of the 17th century broadside ballad, its usefulness (or lack of it) as an information source, and its similarity to modern tabloid newspapers ... and has a few cautionary words to say about the relationship between 'hard news reports' and 'contemporary legend'.

Spontaneous atheistical combustion! Such was the fate of Jasper Conningham, "A Scotsman lewd of life,/ That long had liv'd/ Unlawful from his wife". We encounter him in a broadside ballad of c.1600 entitled *A Wonderful Example of God's Justice* [1] and simultaneously in an Aberdeen garden, where he is first shown trying to entice his sister into an act of incest. Being "Godly, wise, and vertuous", this sister not only negates the proposition but warns (at some length) that righteous God has a Hell "with quenchless flames of fire" waiting for the wicked. And, as a matter of course, she urges him to repent.

Jasper won't. He doesn't. Instead he cynically accuses her of having told him "a tale of Robin Hood" - a fable, that is:

You are deceived
  Fair Sister, then, said he,
To talk of Heaven's Glory,
  or Hell's plagues unto me:
They are devised Fables,
  to keep poor Souls in fear...

because in his considered opinion there is no God, no Devil - no heaven, no hell - no afterlife, neither of pleasure nor of pain.

Practically any 17th century reader or listener could have predicted that Jasper Conningham was about to be instantaneously and terribly proven wrong. So he is:

For in the Garden,
  whereas he did abide,
Suddenly a Fire,
  sprang up on every side;
Which round about inclosed
  this damned wretch that day,
Who roar'd and cry'd most grievous,
  but could not start away.

While the divine fire rises to his knees, "Burning blew like Brimstone,/ in most outrageous wise," earnest attempts are made to prise Jasper free with long staves and pitchforks - the blaze being too intense for anyone to get closer to him than the length of a wooden-handled implement. But all in vain. Now Conningham acknowledges there *is* a God and also a Devil; in effect, he is suffering the fabled torments of the damned (specifically, the aforementioned quenchless flames in which he professed not to believe) but here and now on Earth. He does so with admirable sincerity; still more remarkable is the manner in which, despite his understandable pain and terror, he manages to conform with the ballad's metre and rhyme-scheme. At last, after four stanzas totalling 32 lines:

...with these speeches,
  his Eyes fell from his head,
And by strings hung dangling,
  below his Chin stark dead.

The eyes may be dead, but Jasper isn't. He retains consciousness even when "from his mouth there fell/ his foul blasphemous tongue", undergoing a sort of progressive rot until:

By lice and filthy Vermin
  he was consumed quite.

In fact, he takes two hours to die, at which the fire from heaven ceases as abruptly as it came. Merciless in condemnation of the victim to the end, the narrator adds that Conningham's "Carcass stunk more filthy/ than any Carrion Beast" - so much so that:

No man was able
  for to endure the smell,
Nor yet to come to bury him,
  as true Reports doth tell.

All that remains for us is the inevitable last-stanza moral, without which this text would feel oddly incomplete: let blasphemers take warning by this tale - let all Christians think seriously about it as well.

Let's leave aside the possibility that we have here a Wonderful and Early Example of the phenomenon we all recognize as spontaneous human combustion, not to mention a Wonderful Example of God's Justice expressed through that medium. As I hope to indicate, there are grounds for thinking that the balladeer was perfectly justified in constructing a title which placed as much emphasis on the religious implications of the story as the text does on the actual phenomenon. What interests me more, I think, is that Jasper Conningham patently and indubitably should have known better.

He lived, or is alleged to have lived, in an age where Sin was rigorously and unfailingly punished; the broadside ballads were firm on that point. Tempt not the Lord, whose ability to inflict instant or near-instant judgement on the flagrantly blasphemous - likewise his permanent disposition to inflict such - was a matter of record in this kind of popular literature.

More certainly still, the incestuous Aberdonian got what he was asking for. A central irony operates in these verse-tales of divine judgement/punishment: the Sinner is condemned out of, or according to the terms uttered by, his or her own mouth. Dorothy Mat(t)ley, engulfed quite literally by "A most wonderful and sad judgement", stood as testament to that. A Derbyshire woman too fond of swearing her innocence by means of that popular formula "and may the ground open up and swallow me if I'm lying", Dorothy reacts to what proves a just accusation of having stolen tuppence by uttering her pet phrase; moments later she vanishes into a deep, voracious and apparently custom-made hole and is "buried in the ground so deep/ which would have made the hardest heart to weep" [2]. Staffordshire could tell of a similar case concerning a Bible-thief who expressed the pious hope that his hands would rot off if he had stolen the sacred tome - which, as he *had* done, so they commenced to do, and other parts of his body besides [3]. In a variation upon the theme of moral dereliction, verbal expression and punishment of both, we learn of *Terrible News from Brainford* involving a drinker so foolish as to offer a toast to the Devil [4]; moments later he slumps forward dead and, worst of all:

His nose upon the Table hung,
a ghostly sight to see.

The Devil, by the way, is a not-uncommon frequenter of 17th century broadsides, where he acts against sinners by Divine permission - as God's agent, no less. So when Gabriel Harding lies strenuously about having killed his wife in *Strange and True News from Westmorland*, he is confronted jointly by an angel in green *and* by the Devil: the first denounces and exposes his covert crime and the second breaks his neck [5].

Supernatural judgements are a not-negligible subdivision of the anomalous events which populate 17th century broadside ballads. Or, to put it another way, the great broadside collections - those of Pepys in Magdalen College, Cambridge, Wood (Bodleian, Oxford), Roxburghe (British Library), Euing (University of Glasgow) *et. al.* - are awash with the kind of material which Fortean researchers love to collect. And to put it yet another way, there is scarcely a class, category or type of 'Fortean' phenomena *not* represented somewhere or somehow in these versified 17th century narratives.

We find ghostly apparitions: a great many of them, most often purposeful ones which return to this earthly plane to redress legal or moral issues left unresolved by their death; they reveal the whereabouts of missing deeds, buried treasure, corpses (their own or those of victims whom they secretly and foully murdered). Poltergeists ravage houses and consciences; witches perform their nefarious magic until haled off to stake or gallows. There are sideshow spectacles: carcases of beached sea-monsters and pig-faced women who seem marginally happier than the females credited with having given birth to Siamese twins, reptiles or (in one extreme case from Henneburg) 365 children all at one go (yes, one for every day of the year, perhaps making appropriate the ballad's title: *The Lamenting Lady*).

Then there is the Devil - everywhere: punishing sinners who range from corn-hoarding profiteers to Dirty Doll Winterbottom, the covetous tallywoman of Horsleydown, or else masquerading as a hackney-cab passenger simply to terrify its driver. Look up

Fig. 1 - The Devil appears out of thin air to spontaneously rot off the hands of a Bible thief. From *Strange News from Staffordshire*, (1677).

above: the sky rains down showers of wheat, thunderbolts which set towns ablaze, giant hailstones which destroy cattle. The sky clears - only to prepare for a parade of bloody or double suns, phantom armies, battalions of birds (starlings at Cork, unidentifiable species at Dole in France) which engage in hideous mortal combat to the consternation of all onlookers [6].

Part if not most of those onlookers' consternation arose from the belief - amounting to sure knowledge - that prodigies did not manifest without purpose. In this they almost anticipated Charles Fort's speculation that a relationship existed between human action and phenomenal event, a hypothesis which suggests that a certain course of action can unwittingly create a suspension in the laws of Nature. "And what this mighty wonder means", wrote the balladeer-chronicler of the dreadful storm that hit Shrewsbury on 4 May 1681,

> there's none can tell but God alone;
> 'Tis he that sends things in extreams,
> 'tis he that makes such wonders known. [7]

The exact meaning was open to debate - fruitless debate, in this writer's opinion - but not the moral import. These things were signs, omens, warnings. The broadside ballads which canvassed acceptance for them were couched as warnings as well.

I don't think it realistic to set aside the ballad's moralizing tendency: to treat broadsides as a source of useful Fortean data which has unfortunately become encrusted with naive, irrelevant slabs of sermonizing which must be pared away for us to get at the *genuine* content, the Phenomena. Moral intention and cautionary message were not subsidiary or presentational features of the text. To some extent, they *were* the text. They are recognized as determining characteristics of broadside ballads regardless of actual content or informational focus. We may suspect that an ambition to edify was not the real motive behind the publication of these ballads and still less the reason that people bought them. Sermonizing by custom and justification (because the audience expected it, because the licensing authorities which oversaw the printing of ballads from the mid-1500s demanded it) were almost certainly lesser selling points than sheer entertainment - or amazement - value. But the essential 'moral thrust' of broadsides needs to be acknowledged. It is stereotypical - in the title, in the (often lengthy) subtitle, in the opening and closing stanzas and at all points convenient, or even inconvenient, in between.

And yet, if ballads resembled versified sermons for simple folk, they were also about *news*. There is critical consensus that, however feeble broadsides' claims might be as poetry - however dubious their claims to factuality - they were sold as topically-relevant news media. After examining some thousands of them, Hyder Edward Rollins could write that:

> They were, in the main, the equivalent of modern newspapers, and it cannot well be denied that customarily they performed their functions as creditably in verse as the average newspaper does in prose. [8]

Not all broadside ballads set out to be journalistic, of course. Flicking through the large representative sample found in Pinto and Rodway's *The Common Muse*, we find a huge number with little or no 'news value' as such: ballads which pretend to be nothing more than love lyrics, social commentaries or satires, religious meditations and jocular tales (including quite a few notably smutty ones). Even so, the editors have included almost as many which, in their opinion, stand for "the popular journalism of the day", and they add:

> Every important or exciting event, from the defeat of the Spanish Armada down to the latest robbery, rape or murder, was recorded in ballad form, and the balladmonger ... combined the functions of the journalist who wrote and the newsagent who distributes the cheap sensational newspapers of our own day. [9]

If the ballads' content seems fabulous - if it seems 'folkloric' in a sense that I hope to explore presently - we are responding to the fact that they belonged to a tradition of 'told as true' stories which, wholly or partially, were fictive. This brings them into line with the branch of folklore tagged for convenience as 'contemporary' or 'urban legend', but also into line with modern newspapers, which sometimes report rumours or disputable allegations in the context of factual news. I hope to explore these dimensions as well.

The accent of the journalistic broadside - which, Rollins notes, outnumbered all other types in the 17th century - was consistently on truth and reliability. Prodigies and anomalies relied on this impression of factuality for their impact; hence broadsides echo to the refrain of the balladeers' favourite tag, *"though 'tis strange, yet 'tis true"*. Elsewhere the title/headline or subtitle presents truth and reliability as a sales-point, as in *A true and perfect Relation from the Faulcon* (a scarcely-credible account of a spectacular haunting centred on the putative restless spirit of a departed baker), or in *A true relation of a Notorious Cheater ... Robert Bullock*, and again in *True Wonders and Strange News from Rumsey in Hampshire* which relates how a woman gave birth to a toad, a dead child and a serpent - in that order. [10]

The balladeer made no compromise on this issue. Nor did the sales-teams which hawked broadsides through town and country, as Autolycus can be seen to do in Shakespeare's *The Winter's Tale*. When a potential customer seems inclined to question the literal truth of a ballad which deals with "how a usurer's wife was brought to bed of twenty money-bags ... and how she longed to eat adders' heads and toads carbonadoed", Autolycus has a readymade retort:

> "Here's the midwife's name to't ... and five or six honest wives that were present. Why should I carry lies abroad?"

And in corroboration of a narrative concerning a fish that sang a ballad critical of the hard hearts of maids, he can point to the signature of five justices on the printed page [11].

Aside from the signed statements from witnesses/authority figures, other forms of corroboration might appear. In an equivalent to our "It was in the papers ... It was on the TV", the writer might generously refer his audience to more comprehensive treatments available in book (pamphlet) form, thereby using one anomalous account to support another [12]. Less practically, you might receive an invitation to proceed to a certain address where the chief witness (often the chief sufferer) featured in the ballad could be found, ready and willing to repeat the contents from his or her own lips. As, for instance, was Thomas Cox, the hackney-cab driver assaulted by Satan in the guises of a bear and a shower of fiery flashes. Though incapacitated and prostrate on his sick-bed, he had happily retained the power to talk about his harrowing experience:

> There's many hath seen him from both far and
>   near;
> From whose just Relation the truth did appear,
> Now in *Baldwins* Gardens there in Cradle
>   Court,
> This man is living as hundreds report,
> And those that will take but the pains for to go
> A further Account of the truth you may know,
> Yea from his own mouth he will freely unfold,
> The sum and the substance of what I have
>   told. [13]

As conveyors of news, as vehicles for ostensibly reliable information, broadsides tempt Fortean researchers to treat them as data-bases - that is, to treat them in a way appropriate to that other and more familiar point of reference, the newspaper. In fact, and even without the hint thrown out by Rollins, Pinto and Rodway just now, it seems fair to say that the 17th century broadside's closest living relative is our oft-castigated tabloid.

Of course, there are differences which should not be overlooked; maybe we should say that the broadside (typically devoted to a solo event or topic) resembles in many respects a single *page* or even a single news-item in one of our tabloids. For my present purpose, the similarities are more interesting than the differences. There are the in-common eye-and-brain engaging headlines, with the broadside's buzz-words, 'Wonder' or 'Strange', parallel to the tabloid's 'Shock' and 'Sensation'. There is the stated or implicit claim to accuracy, veracity and factuality; witnesses are named and perhaps quoted, authority figures likewise. So, tho' 'tis strange, yet 'tis true: broadside and tabloid alike pose as vehicles for 'hard news', upon the factuality of which we may rely.

We like to pretend a cynicism or scepticism for what the papers tell us, not least of all when the papers doing the telling are tabloids. At the same time, we are prone to accept, consciously or not, that *most* of what they tell us is true or (depending on the nature of the news item in question) that it is more likely to be part-true than completely false. If *The Guardian* informs me that Eric Cantona was sent off in the Manchester United/Norwich match, I accept that he *was* sent off, though from the attached description I may not agree with the writer's statement that he deserved to be. If *The Sun* reports 500 dead in a Chilean earthquake, I accept there *was* an earthquake, though it may be that the paper got the number of dead wrong. So to anomalies - news items, though not necessarily considered by most readers to be of the same level of significance as Chilean earthquakes or the doings of Eric Cantona. When I read that a terrible big cat has been seen on the Durham moors, I accept that such an animal *has* been reported. I do not, however, automatically concede that it is or was 'terrible' (an evocative adjective thrown in to heighten the report) nor even that it was in the strictest zoological terms a big cat.

And we all know that newspapers, tabloid or otherwise, occasionally use anomalous events as fillers: as 'human' or 'general interest' stories. We also know that some of these are folkloric. Here I apply that term in its more academic sense: papers sometimes publish as factual news stories which are legends.

One quick example. Tucked away in an odd corner of *The Star* for 12 February 1987 was a nice little report entitled "Snake Bites Shopper". It told of a 24 year old woman rushed from the Army & Navy Store at Victoria, London, to St. Thomas's Hospital after being bitten by a baby cobra "that had escaped detection" in a consignment of rugs from India and Pakistan, one of which she had been examining. The store manager was not only named but quoted, and in a way which appeared to confirm that this incident, or something like it, had indeed taken place.

This pleased me a good deal, for here was a revival of the grand old Carpet (or Rug ... Blanket ... Blouse) Snake, a contemporary legend which achieved a height of popularity or currency in the USA during 1968/69 and which has been spasmodically noted by folklorists ever since. You can read all about this serpent's evolutionary history in many books of urban legends **[14]**. I phoned the store for confirmation of the incident more or less from a sense of duty; Fortean folklorists do things like that. I would have been more surprised to receive such confirmation than to find it not forthcoming; the odds seemed heavily stacked against anything involving a Snake in a Rug (or Blanket ...) having transpired. Sure enough, I was assured that nothing of the kind *had* transpired. It was mildly disappointing to be unable to discuss the story with the store manager named in *The Star's* article, but - again - not *so* very surprising, not least of all because he didn't exist.

The *Star* had published as fact a fully-fledged and vintage urban legend. This, we may concur, is a practice not unknown to the world of journalists. But their counterparts back in the 17th century may have run up against the same sceptical accusation; frequently, and most particularly when the focus is upon some 'prodigy', broadside ballads involve a plot that belongs to the folklorist's concept of modern oral fiction - to legend, that is. However, a 17th century writer would not and could not have gone about the Carpet Snake in so bald a manner as *The Star's* unnamed reporter. Where, he might demand to know, is the moral content? Where is the moral justification, the cautionary message to the audience?

Contemporary folklorists insist that, like most if not all urban legends, the Carpet Snake and its variants or analogues certainly possess cautionary value. Put simply, the tale is a criticism of imported goods, a cautionary tale reinforcing our distrust of the cheap and the Eastern. Also (need I say?), it exploits our fascinated fear of snakes...

Nothing of this steals into *The Star's* version. By and large, while admitting that folklorists often and routinely impart 'meanings' to contemporary legends in print (reinserting or reinstating what may have been lost from the oral originals, perhaps), newspaper versions of such material do *not* indulge in moralistic comment. The story is left to speak for itself. The problem is that *(a)* the story is so briefly rendered that it says very little beyond the purported fact that a particular event took place and *(b)* that the omission makes for its closer resemblance to a 'hard news' story.

Snake yarns are perennially popular and have been since the Serpent's debut in the Book of Genesis. In validated legends *and* in legend-like narratives, the snake is the ultimate invader, a corrupter, a contaminator, a danger. And now, as we follow the process by which the possible meanings assignable to anomalous reports undergo truncation - a process by which such meanings flagrantly expressed in the 17th century ballads are degraded to subtextual hints or disappear completely to leave only curious turn-the-page-and-forget-it little stories - let us consider a narrative familiar both to Forteans and to folklorists. We are looking here at reports of reptiles in the human stomach. We are looking at the Bosom Serpent.

My first piece of source-material (a broadside in the Euing collection) gives away its plot in a 12-line subtitle, so to preserve a little mystery here I will announce it simply as:

A WARNING for all such as desire
to Sleep upon the GRASS:
By the Example of *Mary Dudson* Maid-servant
to Mr *Phillips* a Gardener, dwelling in *Kent*

Street, in the Borough of *Southwark...*
which is, in all conscience, long enough [15]. Moving straightway to the main text, we find that one hot day in July, Mary - "pliant, milde and meek", an asset to the gardening profession - made the mistake of stealing a nap on the grass. She fell into a deep sleep from which she could not be awakened for a considerable time, regaining consciousness only to lie in torment:

... her body was exceeding weak:
It seemed to her great wrong
to sit, to lye, to walk, or speak.
Her thirst it was exceeding strange,
she did drink so abundantly,
Her body all coal black did change,
which seem'd a wondrous Prodigie.

Then on 14 August 1664 in the view of several amazed witnesses, she vomited up 14 young adders (which were promptly destroyed) and an adult female some 14 inches long "with seeming legs exceeding strong" [16], which, being prevented from returning to Mary's mouth, appears to have escaped. At time of writing, concludes the ballad, Mary continues "both sick and weak,/ an Object of true Charity". Then, having told us a story which he claims hundreds can testify to, the narrator signs off with the observation that only God knows what the future holds - "for who knows when that he shall die?" - and commends the reader to Heaven.

We come at the story after a leisurely discursive introduction:

Good Lord, what Age we do live in,
how many Wonders doth befal,
Yet we repent not of our sin,
nor unto God for mercy call.

so that it is only in the fourth stanza and after a link-verse which introduces the idea of snakes through reference to Eve's beguilement by the Serpent, that we enter "a story strange, and yet most true" - not without the reinforcement that it is:

A warning fair to those that sleep
upon the ground, or in the grass,
Lest Serpents into them do creep,
as to this Maid it came to pass.

Yet by comparison with many 'prodigy' ballads, the moralizing element is restrained while conversely the informational content is quite high. Nevertheless, the cautionary effect is important; one feels that the writer would have been unwilling to omit it, even had the chance to do so arisen.

Now contemplate this ballad's modern equivalent. Again the heroine is a 'maid' - is engaged in horticultural work - takes a nap in the sunshine - and apparently swallows a snake.

A Reuter report picked up by several British papers for 20 August 1987 carried *Pravda's* claim that an 11 year old girl (identified only by her first name of Mata-net) from the Caspian Sea Republic of Azerbaijan had fallen asleep while picking tomatoes and (apparently) swallowed a 26-inch snake. She was rushed to a children's hospital where 3.5 pints of saline solution caused her to vomit it out into a wash basin. That much is summarised from the *Daily Telegraph's* "Soviet girl safe after swallowing snake in sleep". There is little to be added from the two other articles that I have seen, beyond the *Sun's* "Girl swallows a 2ft snake" informing us that it was a *poisonous* snake which "crawled into her mouth as she slept" and (a scarcely-necessary explanation, some might feel) that the salt water was administered to make her sick [17].

Finally (but as a result of somewhat casual phraseology?) we read that "the snake slithered out without harming her". *The Guardian* scores no points with a heading like "Salt 'n' snake", but names the species as a Caucasian cat snake [18].

Even when taken in combination, these three news reports reduce the story to a series of minimalist factual statements. There is no moralization. There is no inclination to draw any conclusion whatsoever, no correlation or notice of analogues. The item comes over as a curiosity with no meaning beyond what it has to tell us. If we wish to approach it analytically - if we wish to dwell on the pathos or to 'metaphorize' the snake as a symbol of invidious attack upon maidenly innocence, a theme which I perceive in the Mary Dudson ballad - well, that's our affair.

A Fortean might say that at least this data corroborates the old and scientifically-rejected folktale that snakes can and do creep into the mouths of incautious sleepers or that it offers factual support for the credibility of legend-like narratives about snakes, amphibia, insects and even small mammals in the human stomach: a range of materials which again are not calculated to please the conservatively-minded. And what would a folklorist make of it? Like the Fortean, he or she would add it to a heap of material of the same type. Eventually, but regardless of its literal truth or lack of it, he or she might attempt to find subtextual meanings in it, perhaps.

The Bosom Serpent is "a story-complex rather than a story-type", in the opinion of Dr Gillian Bennett, a leading contemporary 'legendist' who has made it the subject of several years' on-going research [19]. Her approach to it in an introductory paper for *Dear Mr Thoms* 22 is a model of how folklorists process their material. There is a sort of working definition of the narrative and its parameters; a checklist of motifs present in the versions and then (the bulk of the article) comes what may be the most comprehensive collection of versions/variants c.1561-1989 to have appeared in recent years outside book format. Dr Bennett notices a set of variable structural options relative to how the story is told, but also a clear division between versions which have "strong sexual elements and involve women exclusively" and those which have not (and do not). Here Dr Bennett is collecting towards a future and more analytical paper or, it's to be hoped, a series of papers; she is not concerned with examining the literal truth or falsity of the material. On this score, however, I might guess that *most* folklorists (not necessarily including Dr Bennett) would, if pushed, prefer to make the definition that as we are calling the story a *legend*, we are also implying that it is *not* literally true [20].

E vidence of a story-type's survival for almost 500 years ought to be interesting and significant in itself. We ought to be able to talk of narratives without insisting on the primacy of "it really happened/didn't happen".

In practice, though - and, I suspect, because we are chiefly concerned with trying to present anomalous reports in a materialistic-scientific context which necessitates classifying them as authentic 'hard data' on which our arguments can be based - we insist upon this very thing. Problem: the material we handle occupies what Fort called "the hyphenated state of truth-fiction" [21]. There are fictional accounts which mimic fact and factual accounts which resemble fiction to a disconcerting degree. There are 'ostensive' accounts where fiction, perhaps an urban legend, has provided hints or plots which some people have tried to act out in real life, so that the legendary mouse gets into the Coke bottle or the razorblade into the Hallowe'en apple with human assistance.

Most Fortean material can be called 'folkloric' on one level or another. In what we have seen so far throughout this paper, an anomaly may be presented as fact, perhaps with actual or token corroborative devices to incite acceptance (named/quoted witnesses, signatures, etc.) and yet remain fiction. The corroborative device is a ploy common to authenticated account and its fictional counterpart alike. The avowed truthfulness of the narrator is another artefact common to both and integral to the story; as one reviewer remarked, we require that the narrator assumes a firm belief in his or her own (fabricated) ghost story even if in private he or she has it not [22]. The audience has a preplanned part in all this, suspending disbelief for the duration of the narrative or, failing that (as occurs in some legend performances) restricting it to a perfunctory level which does not disrupt the narration or spoil enjoyment of it.

I believe that newspaper editors find this a workable arrangement. Confining discussion to Fortean-style anomalies (which, as I have written elsewhere, seldom rank high in the editorial hierarchy of 'hard news' stories [23]) it is evident that the audience is presented with something that may be believed or disbelieved, according to taste, temperament, education or whatever. Nevertheless, the journalist plays the game strictly according to the rules by presenting the report with every semblance of truth and in a way that might permit the reader to take it at face value - as 'real news', that is.

A majority of anomaly researchers prefer to accept the written or printed word *on some level* as what Charles Fort termed 'data'. And Fort is a good example of a writer who seldom insists on what he has to say being accepted as inherently factual while defying us to dismiss it as fiction. On the one hand, he could with ingenuous charm write "I believe nothing of my own that I have ever written" [24]; on the other he rejects the image of himself as "a benign ghoul, digging up dead old legends and superstitions" [25] and turns down the self-suggested notion of including Santa Claus in his brief because:

> ... I am particular in the matter of data, or alleged data. And I have come upon no record, or alleged record, of mysterious footprints in snow, on roofs of houses, leading to chimneys, Christmas Eves.

Many of us would follow his lead. But suppose such a record of mysterious snow-prints existed: would we not accept it? We accept the published records of the 'Devil's Hoofprints' - snowprints, some of them on rooftops! - from Devon in 1855; Fort accepted them to the point of writing up the case in *The Book of the Damned* [26]. We ransack old journals for material - for data, acknowledging that some kind of distortion may be present in the reporting, yet treating what we find as basically factual. Broadsides and pamphlets become legitimate sources because they contain the historical analogues which create for contemporarily-published data an appearance of greater solidity and credibility.

How far and *to what extent* is this legitimate? Look back at the fiery death of Jasper Conningham. It seems fair to assume that there *may have been* someone of that name (or similar) who lived in Aberdeen (or thereabouts) in or around the 1600s. He *may* have died suddenly and violently. Fire *may* have been involved in his demise. It is *not* safe to assume, despite this paper's opening gambit, that he was a victim of spontaneous human or even spontaneous atheistical combustion. This *may* have been a metaphorical disguise for the fact he was consumed by an incestuous passion that somehow contributed to his death [27].

Anyone who wishes to interpret such material literally and factually has to proceed with major caution. A cryptozoologist might deconstruct Martin Parker's balladic *Description of a strange (and miraculous) fish cast upon the sands ... in the hundred of Wormwell ... Chesshire* (?1636) [28] as a not-inept though accidentally comical impression of a whale, perhaps a sperm or cachalot [29]. But a similar reductive process for *The World's Wonder!* allegedly taken by fishermen in Cucanga Bay "neer the Province and Kingdom of China" in 1664 would be direly misleading [30]. Look at the description: 12 feet long by six feet broad - "A Piece of Ord'nance" mounted on its back - face like a man's, crown on head, fish-like fins, eagle's claws on its legs (!), two crossed flags on its shoulder-blades, three muskets and a sword displayed on its rump ... plus other insignia and artefacts on various other parts of its anatomy. There is no need to try reducing this prodigy to any known or even unknown species: Rollins explains in his introductory note that it "alas, was only a symbol of the triumph of England over Holland and France, not a real fish at all", and the sumptuously-anomalous details all part of an elaborate nationalist allegory.

I'd concede it unlikely that any researcher would persist for long with attempting to find cryptozoological credibility in this instance. But antique materials can be deceptive in other, less obvious ways. What may seem a valid source of 'data' merely flavoured by touches of melodrama or poetic licence may be utterly unreliable - if it is factual data that we look for from it.

Rollins urges caution over *Newes from Hereford OR A Wonderful and terrible Earthquake ... that hapned on Tuesday ... the first of October, 1661*, the work of somebody signing himself 'W.K.' [31], for, as this scholar opines, "in spite of the impressive list of witnesses whose names W.K. adds to the end of his miraculous story, one has great difficulty in believing it." A Fortean raised like Alice's White Queen on believing as many as six impossible things before breakfast might regard this as unadventurous scepticism. And certainly, there are wonders enough in the ballad to make a reader almost want them to be true.

Working through the 26 quatrains, we find the introductory promise of "a most terrible Earthquake ... / And violent storms too by a thunderclap" (stanza 3) more than fulfilled. The prelude to all this came at around 2:00pm when the air darkened and "a high mighty wind" developed, lasting for two hours during which "most vehemently/ It made the tyles from off o'th' housen fly"; in

consequence "people durst not go out of door" and church steeples were blown down (sts. 4-6). This tempest passed: the air seemed to be clearing, only to grow overcast at around 6:00 or 7:00pm (st.9); next came "hailstones full as big as Eggs ... / The like in England nere before hath been" which killed cattle in the fields (sts. 9-10). There followed "a terrible Earthquake" which shook houses for the space of half an hour and "many famous buildings did deface" (st. 11).

With people thinking that the Day of Judgement had come, the sky suddenly became as bright as at noon, but presently thick dark clouds overspread it, "out of which appear'd two arms and hands", the right hand clasping a great broadsword and the left "a cup of crimson blood" (sts. 13-14). The amazed onlookers - numbering a thousand or perhaps thousands - also saw the apparition of "a piece of Corn" grow to maturity, "ready for to mow" with an equally apparitional scythe conveniently placed nearby (st. 15). Then a mighty voice proclaimed: "*Wo, wo to man that draweth breath/ And the Inhabitants of all the Earth*" (st. 16). Many pregnant women went into labour (st. 17) and among them Margaret Pellmore, wife of the town clerk, gave birth to three children with teeth who "spake as soon/ As ever they into the world did come" (st. 18-19). The writer quotes their verify'd words:

> The first did say this day no man can shun,
>   Which is appointed and not yet begun.
> Where will be found the second child it said
>   Sufficient men alive to bury the dead?
> These words did then from the 3rd child
>   proceed
> Where shall be corn enough to satisfy your
>   need?
> These were the words they said at that
>   same tyd
> And presently all these three children dy'd.
> (sts. 20-21)

The rest of the ballad addresses the interpretation of what these things signify (sts. 20-21). In W.K.'s estimation, "It doth betoken anger great from God" (st. 22) and the urgent necessity for prayers of repentance, especially since the aerial cup of blood and sword betokened "great wars" (st. 23), while the children's speeches indicated the advent of sickness (st. 24) and famine (st. 25). "These

Fig. 2 - Woodcut accompanying *A Lamentable List of Certaine Hideous Signes Seen in the Air in Germany, &c.,* (1638).

are but warning pieces to you all", concludes the narrator as he reinforces the call for repentance and readiness to meet Thy Maker (sts. 25-26). But before he goes, there is appended "A List of the names of the persons that witnesseth the truth of this" - two churchwardens, two constables plus five more, though there are "divers others, too many here to be inserted".

Fort deals with the Hereford phenomena in Chapter 29 of *New Lands*, where he credits a pamphlet entitled *A True and Perfect Relation of the Terrible Earthquake* "published by two church wardens in the year 1661" as his source **[32]**. He focuses on the fact that "It is said that monstrous flaming things were seen in the sky" - which in view of what we just heard from W.K. seems a mild way of putting it - and moves directly to Margaret Petmore (*sic*) and her three linguistically-advanced children, though he errs by saying that "it is not recorded what the infants said, and whether in plain English or not..."

Fort is interested in the convention-defying notion "that there could be relation between the abnormal in obstetrics and the unusual in terrestics", but he is still more interested in castigating conventional scientists who refuse to accept the connectedness of "shocks of this earth and phenomena in the sky". Though he expresses a certain uneasiness in making too much of this case ("Mrs Margaret Petmore was too sensational a person for our liking, at least in our colder

and more nearly scientific moments") he shows a readiness to enlist it in the panorama of events which make up his chapter, the main drift of which seems to concern the hypothesis of a meteor stream exploding at or over a window area of England that had Hereford as one of its triangulation points.

It may be as well that Fort's thesis didn't rely too much on this episode. It seems unlikely that any of the events he summarises - and/or the events described by W.K. - took place at Hereford on 1 October 1661, nor at any other time.

Both writers were basing their versions on one of several pamphlets of this date; if Fort transcribed the title of his source wrongly, as he was prone to do from time to time, it may be that both were indebted to *A Strange and true Relation of a wonderful earthquake that hapned at Hereford* which Rollins nominates as a likely inspiration for W.K.'s ballad. The more significant fact is that both borrow wholesale from *another* pamphlet (again, one of several) which appeared as early as 1580, in which the fearful tempest and associated disasters occur *not* in Hereford, but in "Praga, Bohemia". An extract from a summary-version of this year by Anthony Munday shows that W.K.'s borrowings *are* wholesale rather than confined to a few incidentals.

Munday says that the storm hit "Praga" at two in the afternoon (cf. W.K., stanza 4) - that people dare not go out into the streets (st. 5) - that three church steeples were blown down. In the evening: "marvelous thunder", giant hailstones *and* an earthquake lasting "the space of halfe an houre" - cf. W.K., stanzas 9-11. Next came the sword and bowl-of-blood bearing phantasmal arms and hands in the sky, the corn and scythe apparition and a "giant voice" proclaiming *"Wo, wo to the earth and to the inhabitants thereof"* (W.K., sts. 13-16). Women fell into premature labour, including *Margaret* Broboth, the *wife of the town clerk* (W.K., sts. 17-18) who gave birth to three children, "their mouthes replenished with teeth", each of whom uttered an oracular statement: *"The day is appointed which no man can shun/ Where shall we finde living to bury the dead?/ Where shall we finde corne to satisfie the hungrie?"* (W.K., sts. 19-21) [33].

Two accounts: but I feel we've been reading about the same storm - and about the same phenomena. We've been reading the same story set in two quite different places. Or, as Rollins charitably puts it, W.K. "did nothing but give local habitation and a name" to a story that was over 80 years old when he found it; he deleted 'Praga' and substituted 'Hereford'.

I don't think I want to turn all this into an accusation of gross error or misconstruction on the part of Charles Fort. Nonetheless, the validity of treating old and fabulous-sounding material as a matrix of 'data' is very questionable. The real value of W.K.'s ballad (or of Munday's earlier version) does not relate to the recording of wondrous anomalous facts from Hereford or 'Praga'. I'd guess that the balladeer was grandly unconcerned about the literal truth of what he was transcribing; charged with promoting spurious news, he would have replied that he wanted to be considered a moralist, not a journalist, and that a warning was a warning. If people believed enough in the Hereford phenomena to repent and return to God, he might say, the act of fabrication was justified.

Or consider the flamboyant catalogue of Forteana set out in *A Lamentable List, of certain Hidious, frightfull and Prodigious Signes ... seene in the Aire, Earth, and Waters ... 1618 untill this instant. Anno 1638. In Germany, and other Kingdoms and Provinces adjacent* [34]. We are directed to contemplate: a blazing star that hovered over Bohemia for 27 days; water metamorphosed to blood in Hungary; two phantom armies clashing in the air of Brunswick; three rainbows and three suns ("all in one day") at Vienna plus "A noyse like Ordinance" in the air above Lints, also in Austria; blood dropping from trees at Darmsted, "oyle resembling blood by just conceit" oozing from furniture and walls at Tursin, a rain of gore at Wirtemburg; meteoric phenomena over Bohemia; a tempest of hail at Ratisbone; "Strange fruit" near Frankendal, crows locked in "mortall battle" in Silesia. A "monstrous forme" of the sun and "strange Raine-bow" enlivened existence at Hamborow; great bands of horsemen and guns paraded the Pomeranian skies; there was a "monstrous birth" near Strasburg, a sword and rod in the Silesian heavens. At this point I must abort my original plan to summarise *all* the marvels in this broadside, having run out of steam after covering only half of the ballad's 20 verses.

How much of this 'really happened' or was believed to have happened doesn't worry me. The point is: yes, these *are* Fortean phenomena, but they are presented, as per title, as *Signes*. It was in this spirit, as a moralist and not as a recorder of parascientific data, that the balladeer-chronicler of the shower of wheat that fell on Shrewsbury in May 1681 could write:

Let no Strange things forgotten be,
Lest they're the last that e're you see [35].

This paper has wandered - perhaps that should read 'meandered' - from broadside ballads of the 17th century to modern tabloids - from antique anomaly-reports to their modern counterparts - from Forteana to folklore and back again. How might I sum up what is intended to be its theoretical skeleton? I might proceed like this:

1. *Seventeenth century broadside ballads include a wide range of anomalous, 'prodigious' or 'Fortean' events. They do so in journalistic fashion, affirming these events are (were) real - that they took place as described - that the versified reports of them are "true and perfect"; typically, they include perfunctory forms of corroboration (witness signatures, citations of other texts) to promote acceptance.*

2. *On close inspection, the import of these*

ballads is not 'scientific'. Their purpose is to entertain or to amaze while reinforcing certain conventional religious, moral or political lessons. They may (and frequently do) function as cautionary tales.

3. The content or narrative line of such "strange but true" ballads is frequently recognizable in folkloric terms: as legendary. Certain examples are represented today in the form of contemporary or 'urban' legends which also blend the motive to entertain with the (seldom overt) wish to instruct or caution.

4. Fortean phenomena are also presented today in newspapers - again, as facts which amaze by their sensational deviation from normality or from accepted ('scientific') views of Nature. Here their fundamental purpose is to entertain, but by necessity they are presented more or less in line with other kinds of news found in the same papers - that is, as factual occurrences.

5. Those who wish to engage with such disposable news items on a more profound or scholarly level may include folklorists, for whom the reports are not necessarily or literally true, but narratives that duplicate, replicate or otherwise sustain narrative processes wherein the story reflects or encapsulates certain messages, beliefs etc. of an import greater than the mere entertainment or novelty-value these stories possess. Should the story prove to possess a basis of fact - i.e., should there be good evidence that the events described actually took place - this factor may be deemed interesting yet peripheral to the narrative's meanings as narrative.

6. Forteans, though aware of possible non-literal or subtextual meanings in these reports, are more likely to become involved with the literal truth or falsity of the accounts...

And I could add here that for many anomalists this literal truth is of critical importance. The data may become the focus for speculation which invites us to acknowledge powers, properties, phenomena or wild talents outside the accepted realms of Science. It may excuse criticisms of the exclusive, complacent and stereotypically limited status of scientific knowledge. Proponents of that knowledge (scientists - 'experts') may become the enemy, the pretensions of whom the Phenomenon helps to deride and puncture. A zoologist's refusal to admit the existence of a lake monster may become somewhat more important than the lake monster itself.

The Ideal Fortean - is there such a being? and if so, where is the evidence for such a being? - excludes nothing.

But the nature of our society, our education, our conceptualisation of knowledge and also the peculiar materialistic outlook which operates among people who like to dwell on topics characteristically immaterial have tended to exclude the idea of literature whose purpose is non-literal: a literature whose purpose is to convey moral meanings in the guise of entertaining mystery.

It may be time to recall that there are stories whose interest and Truth (with a capital T) reside as much in how or why they are told as in what they have to tell ... and others in which the central event may matter a bit less than how people are invited to interpret it.

APPENDIX
Fortean Phenomena in 17th century Broadside Ballads

This appendix attempts to survey by roughly-acceptable divisions of 'class' or 'type' the contents of the majority of ballads consulted during the compilation of this paper. Full titles and publication details of the sources may be found in the notes to my main text.

GHOST
* reveals buried treasure, etc.: 'Strange & Wonderful News from Northamptonshire'. Rollins, *Pack of Autolycus*, 30 (178-184)

* reveals murder/redresses wrongs: 'The Disturbed Ghost'. Rollins, *Pack of Autolycus*, 29 (172-178)
* purpose ambiguous: 'A true & perfect relation from the Faulcon'. Rollins, *Pack of Autolycus*, 15 (87-92)

POLTERGEIST
'Drummer of Tedworth'. Rollins, *Pack of Autolycus*, 19 (114-121)

'MONSTROUS BIRTHS'

* **Siamese Twins:** 'The Two Inseparable Brothers'. Rollins, *Pack of Autolycus*, 2 (7-14) [Colloretti Bros.] 'Nature's Wonder?' Rollins, *Pack of Autolycus*, 23 (139-146) [Fisherton, Salisbury case]. For another, [Westminster 1687] see Rollins, *Pepys Ballads III*, 150 - 'The wonder of the present age'.
* **giving birth to reptiles:** 'The Wonder of Wonders' + 'True Wonders & Strange News', Rollins, *Pack of Autolycus*, 31 + 32 (185-194)
* **365 children born at once:** 'The lamenting lady'. Rollins, *Pepysian Garland*, 20 (121-131)
* **pigfaced woman:** 'A monstrous shape...' Rollins, *Pepysian Garland*, 79 (449-454). For the story of Tannakin Skinker, Ashton, *Century of Ballads*, (312-314): 'The Long-nos'd Lass'.

DEVIL attacks

* **corn-hoarders:** 'A looking-glass for corn hoarders'. Rollins, *Pepysian Garland*, 65 (370-375). 'A Warning-piece for corn-engrossers'. Rollins, *Pack of Autolycus*, 6 (31-35). Two ballads - the (alleged) incidents are different.
* **tallywoman:** 'Sad and dreadful news from Horsly-down'. Rollins, *Pack of Autolycus*, 37 (215-218)
* **hackneycab driver:** 'Mans amazement'. Rollins, *Pack of Autolycus*, 38 (219-224). Also in Pinto & Rodway, *The Common Muse*, LXXIX.

MIRACLE

* **cure of Maria Anna Mollier:** 'The Happy Damsel'. Rollins, *Pack of Autolycus*, 40 (231-234)

SHOWERS

* **of wheat:** 'Strange News from Brotherton'. Rollins, *Pack of Autolycus*, 7 (36-43). 'A New Wonder'. Rollins, *Pack of Autolycus*, 36 (210-214) and see also material in 'Lamentable List of ... Hidious ... Signes', in same source, 4 (21-25)

PREMATURE BURIAL

* **of Lawrence Cawthorne:** 'Misery to be lamented...' Rollins, *Pack of Autolycus*, 12 (68-74)

EARTHQUAKES/TEMPESTS etc.

* **including giant hailstones, aerial apparitions:** 'News from Hereford'. Rollins, *Pack of Autolycus*, 14 (81-86). See also 'Lamentable List ... Signes' in same source, 4 (21-25).

CRYPTOZOOLOGICAL

* **bird-battle: Cork, 8 Sept. 1621:** 'A battell of Birds'. Rollins, *Pepysian Garland*, 25 + 26 (150-160)
* **bird-battle: France, 26 Feb. 1675/76:** 'The Frenchmans Wonder'. Rollins, *Pepysian Garland*, 26 (161-165)
* **reptiles in human body:** 'A Warning ... by the Example ... of Mary Dudson'. Rollins, *Pack of Autolycus*, 22 (132-138)
* **strange fish:** 'The World's Wonder'. Rollins, *Pack of Autolycus*, 25 (151-155) i.e.: Cucanga 'A description of a strange (and miraculous) fish'. Rollins, *Pepysian Garland*, 77 (437-442). Also in Pinto & Rodway, *The Common Muse*, LXXVII [The Wormwell, Cheshire, whale (?)]

NOTES

1 - The full title of this ballad reads: *A Wonderful Example of God's Justice Shewed Upon One Jasper Conningham, A Gentleman Born in Scotland, Who Was Of Opinion That There Was Neither God Nor Devil*. It appears in the third volume of *The Roxburghe Ballads* (ed. William Chappell & J.W. Ebsworth, 1871-1899) pp.103-110, and is reprinted in John Ashton's *Century of Ballads* (Elliot Stock, London, 1887) pp.94-100. The same story is represented in *The Pepys Ballads* (ed. Hyder Edward Rollins, Vol. III, No. 128) by 'The Punish'd Atheist' - which omits to name the guilty soul, merely assuring us that he "liv'd in the North" and that "The like of him you ne'r did hear". Although this version may seem to deal with a uniquely-appalling episode that took place in or about 1685, Rollins (who remarks dryly that "one would be glad to have further witnesses to its truth") unswervingly identifies it as "only a modernisation" of the Conningham story, which he says was probably published prior to 1600. This would explain the close similarity of the two ballads, with such macabre details as the vain efforts to pull the victim free, the falling out of his eyes and tongue and the stench of the carcase being transcribed from one text to another. For another sponta-neously-combusted sinner, see the following note.

2 - See Rollins, *The Pack of Autolycus* (full publication details given below in note 6), No. 11, pp.62-67. Dorothy shared her unfortunate and dangerous tendency towards perjury with Susanna Brighton of Brampshot in *Eight Dreadful Examples of Gods immediat Judgement on wicked Persons* (Edinburgh, 1710; see Rollins' introductory note to 'The Punish'd Atheist' in *Pepys Ballads*, Vol. III, No.128). Similarly to Dorothy, Susanna was much given to over-emphatically hoping that "God would burn her alive if the things were not true [that] she declared". Also akin to Dorothy, she was justly accused of theft (specifically, of three silver spoons) whereupon - again, like Dorothy! - she uttered "horrid Imprecations" capped with her typical invocation of immolation by the Almighty: "she wished Fire would fall on her, and consume her to Ashes if she was any ways guilty..." The Almighty responded typically as well. Susanna was instantly set ablaze by a flash of lightning and her body reduced to a cinder so that, sure enough, "upon handling parts of her fell into ashes". This episode, as Rollins notices, bears a thematic relationship with the story of Jasper Conningham and/or the unnamed-but-Punish'd Atheist of the later (Pepysian) broadside. Divine combustion of sinners was evidently more common as a 17th century narrative motif than it could ever have been in 17th century real life.

3 - 'Strange and true news from Staffordshire', in Rollins, *The Pack of Autolycus*, No. 34 (pp.200- 205). The same case occurs in a rival broadside, 'A Warning for Swearers' in Ashton's *Century of Ballads*.

4 - Rollins, *The Pack of Autolycus*, No. 13, pp.75-80.

5 - 'Strange and True News from Westmorland' is in the Euing collection at the University of Glasgow. It is conveniently reprinted in Rollins, *The Pack of Autolycus*, No. 27 (pp.162-167) and also in Ashton's *Century of Ballads*, pp.89-93.

6 - I have attempted to support my statement that 17th century broadsides are a treasure-house of Fortean materials by giving fuller citation of the types listed here in the main text - plus a few others - in my Appendix. Beyond that, interested readers might like to consult three books which I have found particularly useful in the way they reprint ballads located in some of the more important specialist collections. Ashton's *Century of Ballads* has already been mentioned above in note 1. Hyder Edward Rollins' *The Pack of Autolycus Or Strange and Terrible News of Ghosts, Apparitions, Monstrous Births, Showers of Wheat, Judgements of God and Other Prodigies and fearful happenings as told in Broadside Ballads* (Harvard University Press, Cambridge, Mass., 1927) deals chiefly with material from the Pepys and Wood collections, though not exclusively. The same author's *A Pepysian Garland. Black Letter Broadside Ballads Of The Years 1595-1639* (Cambridge University Press, 1922) presents a selection from the first folio volume in that noted collection. Finally, he is the editor of Harvard University Press' eight-volume edition of *The Pepys Ballads* (Cambridge, Mass., 1929-1932) and of several other compendia of early ballads besides. Rollins' books are especially commendable for their scholarly introductory notes, carrying full literary-bibliographical information, and also remarks on analogues contemporary with or subsequent to each ballad. Some of Rollins' introductory notes serve as mini- bibliographies in their own right.

7 - 'A new wonder', see Rollins, *The Pack of Autolycus*, No. 36 (pp.210-214).

8 - Rollins, *A Pepysian Garland*, p.ix.

9 - Adrian De Sola Pinto & Allan Edwin Rodway, *The Common Muse. An Anthology of Popular British Ballad Poetry XV-XXth Century* (Chatto & Windus, London, 1957).

10 - See Rollins, *The Pack of Autolycus*, Nos. 15, 21 and 32. I suppose I could have added here his No. 17, 'A sad and true relation of a great fire'. 'True' or 'truth' also features in five of what I call, perhaps innacurately, subtitles in the same source; see Nos. 7, 23, 27, 33 and 38.

11 - *The Winter's Tale* Act IV, scene iv.

12 - The relationship between broadside ballad (a versified story confined by definition to one side of a single sheet) and the contemporaneous pamphlet (a prose account occupying several pages) deserves more space than I can give it here. Regarded as printed news-media, they have much in common, covering the same type of material and not infrequently the selfsame topics or events; as I mention later in the main text, it was not unknown for a ballad to be written directly *from* an already-published pamphlet. However, certain differences existed and it may not be distorting the case to suggest that the 'target audience' of the two forms may not have been precisely identical. The broadside ballad, set in verse and to a tune (albeit this was usually alluded to by reference to some popular melody, not rendered in any notational form!) was at heart a lyric. It scored high in terms of direct impact and memorability and if the demands of rhyme and/or metre imposed a restriction on how the 'message' was expressed, sheer simplicity and economy was responsible for putting that message across. By contrast, prose pamphlets placed more strenuous demands on the concentration, comprehension and general literacy of the reader; they might contain more information, but required more effort and perhaps even education for that reader to get at the information. The difference between broadside and pamphlet may be summed up (again, only roughly) as comparable with the difference between a modern tabloid and a modern 'quality' newspaper. For a readable though selective (?) guide to the precursors of the modern newspaper, see the opening chapters of Mason Jackson's *The Pictorial Press. Its Origins and Progress* (Hunt & Blackett, London, 1885).

13 - 'Man's Amazement...' See Rollins, *The Pack of Autolycus*, No. 38 (pp.219-224). Also in Pinto & Rodway, *The Common Muse*, No. LXXIX. Very similar is the envoi to 'A New Ballad of The Midwives Ghost' in the Pepys collection (see Rollins, *The Pepys Ballads*, Vol. 3, No.95). Aware that sceptical reaction was spoiling an excellent story of an apparition revealing the bones of illegitimate children covertly brought into the world and then helped out of it some 15 years prior, the writer goes on the offensive. You have only to visit the Cheshire Cheese in Holborn to satisfy yourself of the facts, he asserts: the grisly remains are on public display there. No doubt a small admittance charge would have been payable at the door...

14 - I gave the Army & Navy's legendary Rug Serpent (and its many analogues recent or not-so-recent) a reasonably thorough outing in 'Department Store Snakes' for *Fate*, February 1989, p.83ff. More scholarly treatments occur in Jan Harold Brunvand's seventh chapter of *The Vanishing Hitchhiker. American Urban Legends and Their Meanings* (US edition by W.W. Norton, 1981; UK edition by Pan, 1983) which cites Patrick B. Mullen's important paper, 'Department Store Snakes', *Indi-*

ana Folklore 3 (1970), pp.214-228.

15 - Reprinted in Rollins, *The Pack of Autolycus*, No. 22 (pp.132-138). Rollins cites and summarizes several analogues, quoting Topsell on serpents' predilection for sliding down the human gullet when offered the opportunity. Of particular interest is the way he relates the material here to reports based on the well-known Octopus Egg legend in the *New York Tribune* for 28 September 1924.

16 - I can make nothing of the curious reiteration of '14' here; if not merely coincidental, it may represent the writer's attempt at poetic symmetry or something similar. The mention of legs on a snake is curious, too, making the reptile a complete anomaly. Or does the balladeer have in mind a newt rather than an actual adder? Newts ('efts', 'elvets', etc.) frequently figure in narratives of reptiles found in the human stomach.

17 - Perhaps my remark about the lack of necessity for explaining that the salt water was applied as an emetic is a little unfair. In some of the versions given by Bennett (see below) salt water is given to the victim to promote raging thirst in the (swallowed) snake, which is then enticed out by a bowl of water placed cunningly close to the patient's mouth. Usually in these stories, however - and deriving from another popular belief concerning snakes' preferences - the tempting drink is milk. It may be that *The Sun's* journalist felt it necessary to eliminate the impression that Soviet medics gave Matanet salt water because they subscribed to the old folk-belief just mentioned.

18 - Presumably *Telescopus fallax*, which is indeed found in the Caucasus as well as in the southern Balkans, eastern Adriatic and southwestern Asia. The cat snake is small and slender, measuring

75 or exceptionally just over 100 cms. It is also venomous, thus justifying *The Sun's* description of it as a 'poisonous' snake.

It goes without saying that these three news items are duplicated or replicated many times over in the pages of *Fortean Times*. See, for example, issue 70 (August-September 1993) p.16, where a Turkish actor is said to have swallowed a snake while sleeping in a tent; the original report appeared in *Bugun*, 29 July 1991. A particularly interesting discussion on this theme ('Yorkshire's Water-Wolf' by Nigel Mortimer) can be found in *Fortean Times* 51 (Winter 1988-89) pp.48-49.

19 - Gillian Bennett's 'The Legend of the Bosom Serpent' occupies all 22 pages of a special issue of *Dear Mr Thoms* (No. 22, August 1991 - the annotated bibliography of 31 items is more than slightly useful). 'Updates' are included in subsequent issues of this journal, namely: No. 23 (October 1991) pp.4-7 and No. 27 (August 1992) pp.17-21 - the latter including the *Daily Telegraph's* report of the Caucasian case mentioned in my main text. Dr Bennett has also discussed the Bosom Serpent in her inquiry, 'What's 'Modern' about the Modern Legend?' in *Fabula* No. 26 (1985) pp.219-229.

20 - I would infer the same from David Jacobson's *The Affairs of Dame Rumor* (Rinehart & Co., New York/Toronto, 1948, pp.23-24) which treats the belief- report "That snakes and other reptiles also creep into the bodies of people imprudent enough to sleep in open fields" as "a popular rumor theme".

21 - Charles Fort, *Wild Talents*, Chapter 5. See *The Complete Books of Charles Fort*, Dover ed., 1974, p.864. All quotations from Fort's work which follow refer to this edition.

22 - *Athenaeum* review of J.H.

Ingram's *The Haunted Homes and Family Traditions of Great Britain*, 15 March 1884: "The teller of ghost stories must be a believer in what he tells us, at least, ostensibly; he must assume the virtue though he have it not". In this critic's opinion, Ingram had erred in his preface by expressing a measure of scepticism about the stories which composed the contents of his book. Montague Summers also discusses the desirability of believing in ghosts when creating stories about them in the introduction to his *The Supernatural Omnibus* (1931, etc.). In urban legends a compromise is sometimes reached whereby the narrator repeats a story read or heard elsewhere while prefatorily *refusing* to swear to its veracity; nonetheless, he or she proceeds to 'report' it as if it *was* or *is* true.

23 - Michael Goss, 'Alien Big Cat Sightings in Britain: A Possible Rumour Legend?' in *Folklore* 103, 1992, pp.184-202.

24 - Fort, *Lo!*, Ch. 3. *Complete Books*, p.555.

25 - Fort, *Lo!*, Ch. 13. *Complete Books*, p.643.

26 - Fort, Nit>Book of the Damned, Ch. 28. *Complete Books*, p.305ff. See also Mike Dash's paper in this volume.

27 - This metaphorical translation may be supported by the sixth stanza of the Pepysian alternative version of the Conningham story, 'The Punish'd Atheist' (see note 1), which describes the sinning party as "with Lust inflam'd" while later, as part of his seduction speech, he tells his sister: "... if any Hell there be,/ The Flames I will endure for thee".

28 - Rollins, *The Pack of Autolycus*, No. 77, pp.437-442. Also in Pinto & Rodway, *The Common Muse* No. LXXVII.

29 - The dimensions reported by

Parker - one of the most prolific ballad-writers that the 17th century produced - place the fish within the physical range of the sperm whale, *Physeter macrocephalus* as given in Christina Lockyer's contribution on the species for *The Encyclopedia of Mammals* Vol. 1 (ed. Dr David Macdonald. Guild Publishing, London, 1985, pp.204-209). Parker states the head-tail length as 21 yards 1 ft (= 64 ft) which compares well with the length shown in Lockyer (68 ft). At five yards (15 ft) in length, the lower jaw was significantly shorter than the upper ("thrice so much" = 45 ft) and contained 34 teeth, some weighing two lbs; there were "no teeth i' th' upper jaw/ But holes, which many people saw". Lockyer states there are usually 20-25 on each side of the cachalot's lower jaw. Contrary to some descriptions, this species *is* equipped with teeth in the upper jaw, though fewer of them and these do not always erupt clear of the gum - hence perhaps the 'holes' which Parker speaks of. In view of my own criticisms of taking ballads' data too literally, I'd go no further in trying to identify the Wormwell wonder.

30 - Rollins, *The Pack of Autolycus*, No. 25, pp.151-155.

31 - Rollins, *The Pack of Autolycus*, No. 14, pp.81-86.

32 - *Complete Books*, p.475.

33 - Triplicated events are commonplace in folk- narrative. The stylistic trick of incremental repetition (or repetition which introduces a dramatic pause while simultaneously advancing the plot, as when Sir Patrick Spens' ship is described as going a league, a league, a league and barely three) also relies on triplication and it is a standard ingredient of folk poetry, of which the ballad is the prime example. Whether serial utterance of oracular statements by three prodi-

gies speaking in turn (as here) counts as a recognized motif, I am uncertain. But I know of one other example from a 1616 tract reprinted in Mason Jackson's *The Pictorial Press* (publication details in note 12; see pp.26-29). Reversing the idea of truth from the mouths of babes in the Hereford/ Prague story, 'Miraculous Newes from the cittie of Holdt ... Munster [in Germany], the twentieth of September last past 1616' has three dead bodies rising from their graves after a prelude of thunder and lightning. The first, "very white, cleane, and cleere", beat his hands together while proclaiming: "Blessed be God in the highest Heaven, that our release is come, for we have wayted many a hundred yeare for this time". He was somewhat upstaged by his successor, "toppe to toe, like unto a burning fire", who waved his hands and tore his hair as he bellowed forth a call for repentance, promising that the Lord had His chastising rod in hand to punish all sinners, but specifically the wealthy, proud and presumptuous, "wherefore hee will destroy you with a suddaine sicknesses, and fiery Pestilence..." Lastly, the third corpse ground and gnashed his teeth while striking his hands against each other: "Woe, woe to the wicked; this is the time that we have long attended and looked for." The people (perhaps remarkably, by modern standards) were overjoyed at this proof of God's "Fatherly mercy and unspeakable goodnesse" and immediately set aside a day of supplication, prayer and fasting. [For further discussion of this case, see Sven Rosen's 'A Proto-Fortean of the 16th Century: Joan Petri Klint' in this issue, at note 18; there the event is dated to Easter, 1588].

34 - Rollins, *The Pack of Autolycus*, No. 4, pp.21-25.

35 - Rollins, *The Pack of Autolycus*, No. 36, pp.210-213.

LEOPARDS OF THE GREAT TURK

EXOTIC FELINES IN FRENCH CULTURAL HISTORY

Michel Meurger

French folklorist Michel Meurger, author of *Lake Monster Traditions* and numerous articles on the cultural aspects of cryptozoological lore, here examines the feline stereotype as it interweaves between folklore and historical reportage, from ancient times to the present. The cases are drawn from France, but the inferences drawn are applicable over a much wider range.

It was impossible to guess just what made Joe Sam decide the black panther was around again. Only it was always around in the first storm.
Walter Van Tilburg Clark: The Track of the Cat

Michael Goss wrote in 1986: "Ten thousands of words have been written on the 'phantom feline phenomenon', and it is easy to suppose that between them they have managed to probe every conceivable angle on that bizarre topic to exhaustion point. One aspect which tends to receive comparatively little wordage, however, is the history of alien big cat sightings in the UK." **[1]**

Yet Goss's attempt to discover old narratives about mystery felines had meagre results. He had to state that: "Accounts of significantly large felines which cannot be interpreted as unusually developed wildcats or feral equivalents are curiously scarce prior to c.1969." **[2]**

Shall we conclude, then, that elusive felines belong merely to a contemporary bestiary? I hardly think so. Rather I would suggest that researchers, instead of concentrating solely on anglo-saxon sources, should also take a look at the material awaiting them in European archives, for exotic felines are no newcomers to the cultural history of the continent. Lions, panthers and leopards have left their spoor in hagiography, mediaeval romance and Renaissance chronicles, and in the following pages I will attempt to present a sketch of the genesis and evolution of this peculiar motif.

But first of all, a word of caution.

This promising material is not devoid of pitfalls. One error, common enough, would let us take age-old accounts as direct evidence, imbued with our modern sense of factuality.

Cryptozoologists are prone to this sort of anachronism, increased by their selective use of sources.

As the reader will soon discover, my own quest will not provide a hoard of illuminating evidence demonstrating once and for all the survival of *Panthera leo atrox*, or the action of paraphysical phenomena creating tulpoid cats and ghostly leopards. To the contrary, local sources will offer no more than a cluster of soft *identifications*, based on lacunary natural knowledge and folk preconceptions. Therefore, this essay strives only to follow the evolution of a specific kind of *belief*.

CHAPALU AND 'MONT DU CHAT'

Our investigation begins in the cell of an Irish monk of the Dark Ages. In a life of Saint Abban, compiled in the 9th century, the anonymous clerical author relates the damage wrought by an 'inaudita bestia' (an 'unheard of beast'). This monster was formed like a "cat as big as a year-old calf", had a burning breath and blazing tail. Saint Abban seized this beast of prey and threw it into a lake, where the demonic cat appears every seven years **[3]**.

Sister Mary Donatus, discussing this story in her thesis, *Beasts and Birds in the Lives of Early Irish Saints* (1934), compares Saint Abban's cat with the Chapalu or Palug's cat of Welsh lore. This vicious kitten, thrown into the sea at birth, was rescued and reared by the sons of Palug. Grown up, the cat became a fearful plague to mankind. According to a poem from the 10th or 11th century:

Nine score fierce [men] fell for its food, nine score warriors **[4]**.

Mary Donatus shows that Chapalu was originally a sea-monster; Saint Abban's cat is also for her "unmistakably a water-beast", combining cat and dragon. The motif of the seven year period of underwater banishment is recurrent in dragon tales; furthermore, dragons have fiery breath. The locale of the tale leads us to suggest other associations with the dreadful 'peists', or Irish dragons. Saint Abban's cat lived in the river 'Brosnay', probably the little Brosna, a tributary stream of the Shannon issuing from Lough Dearg (the 'Red Lake'). This lake is the site of a well-known dragon legend [5].

Monstrous cats, like peists, were initially conceived as supernatural creatures, that could be exorcised by holy men. Later, such definitions were secularised, and the demon-cat mingled progressively with the image of exotic felines that the crusaders came to know. Due to the close contacts between Ireland and the continent, the Celtic legend of Chapalu found a home in the world of mediaeval romance. The monstrous cat became, with giants and dragons, one of the opponents of gallant knights.

The *Livre d'Artus*, a French romance from the 14th century, shows Merlin explaining to King Arthur the origins of the giant cat. During Ascension Night a peasant, fishing in the 'Lake of Lausanne' (Lake Geneva), promised the first fish he would take to the Lord.

He broke his vow twice, and then the fishing line brought up a coal-black kitten. The fisherman took it home and reared it, but the feline grew to monstrous proportions, tore out the throats of the whole family, and took up its abode in a cavern on a mountain over-hanging the lake. There the cat became the scourge of travellers following the pilgrim road to Rome. Hearing this sinister story, Arthur took himself to Lausanne, climbed the mountain and, after a bitter struggle, cut the cat down with Excalibur.

Here the kitten is clearly represented as a lake creature. Moreover, in a variant to the tale, instead of living underground, the grown-up monster still hides underwater [6].

For the author of the *Livre d'Artus*, the cat is no longer a wholly supernatural creature, yet it has retained its ties with the hellish world; the black cat's emergence is ascribed to the sacrilegious conduct of the fisherman.

Arthur's fight against the big cat was a well-known episode in mediaeval European culture. But the mighty monarch was not always seen as the vanquisher. For example, in the *Romanz des Français*, written before 1204, Arthur is slaughtered by the 'Capalu'.

This unhappy end was represented on the mosaic floor of Otranto cathedral in Italy, built

Fig. 1 - A detail of the mosaic floor in the cathedral of Otranto, Italy, showing 'Rex Artus' being killed by the cat of Lausanne.

199

Fig. 2 - A pilgrim is overwhelmed by a mountain devil. Fresco from Roure church, France, 1510.

between 1163-1165, in the reign of the Norman King William the First of Sicily. The big-spotted cat can be seen springing on 'Rex Arturus', who rides a horned animal and flourishes a mace. Below, the cat of Lausanne has already brought down the king and is killing him [7].

Freymond has demonstrated that the location of the fight near Lake Geneva may be an error. In fact, a passage at the end of the *Livre d'Artus* shows conclusively that the monster's lair was identified with a mountain overlooking Lake du Bourget, in Savoy. Here, since 1232, the summit has been called 'Mont du Chat' ('Cat's Mountain'). In the 14th century *Ancienne Chronique de Savoie*, the place is even designated 'Le Mont du Chat-Artus' ('The Mountain of Arthur's Cat') [8].

Through the ages, the association between the Savoyard mountain and the cat became traditional and passed from learned culture into folklore. The Franciscan Jacques Fodéré, in a book published in 1612, notes of the man-eater that: "The common folk called it a wild cat, but it was of such extreme size that it was verging on a tiger" [9].

At this later period, the famous feline had lost most of its supernatural associations. For mountain-people, the fierce creature was now a giant specimen of an animal from the native fauna, the wild cat. The learned monk, for his part, conjured the image of a feline from distant lands, the tiger. In both cases, the mountain terror had been reduced to the status of a simple *beast*.

In the last years of the 19th century, Freymond made a field study in Savoy, asking local erudites if they had gathered local legends about the ravenous feline. The answer was positive. Abbot P. Jullien told him that old people still remembered the episode and called the cat 'The Beast' ('la Bête'). This 'Beast' devoured travellers. Finally, a 'soldier' put the nightmare to rest [10]. At the end of the line, an anonymous soldier had taken the place of the gallant king.

Freymond shows that the legend of the cat may have been transported from France to

200

Savoy by pilgrims following the traditional road towards Rome. Between Aiguebelette and Chambéry, travellers had then to climb the southern slope of Mont du Chat [11].

One may surmise that the cat initially played the part of a demon of the mountain passes. For mediaeval man, avalanches and robbers were not the only dangers awaiting travellers through the rocky wastes. Mountains were the domain of Satan, the place where witches met demons at the top of jagged crags. In the chapel of Saint-Sébastien in Roure, in the French Alps, a fresco from 1510 shows a pilgrim, walking in high country, overwhelmed by a mountain devil [12]. According to this interpretation Arthur, the champion of Christendom, would have freed the roads to a holy place by killing the monster-cat.

EXOTIC CATS IN EUROPEAN TOPOGRAPHY

The early localising of big cat episodes in the lives of saints gave them the potential for further rationalisation.

According to early mediaeval sources Saint Abban, in addition to the cat-dragon, had also slain a giant *lion* at Padua. Three hundred human beings had already been slaughtered before Abban's intervention [13]. Here the demonic cat, possibly an adumbration of the "huge wild cats of Ireland" [14], had already been replaced by an exotic feline.

Arthurian romances, too, played their part in writing lions and panthers into the familiar European landscape. In the *Merveilles de Rigomer*, written by a troubadour from Tournai in the 13th century, Gawain battles with a ferocious panther from 'la male Gaudine' [15].

Yet literary traditions about alien big cats are even older, reaching back to the very time when pious monks were recording the feats of Saint Abban. In the 9th century Notker the Stammerer, a friar from the Swiss monastery of Saint-Gall, recorded the story of Pépin the Short's fight against a lion. Pépin (715-768) was king of the Franks and father of Charlemagne, and according to the cleric gave a proof of his fighting qualities by challenging a lion and beheading it with a single blow. In a variant, the feline had just escaped from its cage [16].

This alleged occurrence was well-known in learned circles and from this level was integrated into folk-culture. A sculpture from the 13th century in Notre-Dame de Paris shows King Pépin standing on the body of the lion he had just slain. According to Gaston Paris, the sculptor was inspired by oral tradition [17].

A century after the sculpture was made a Flemish chronicler, Jean des Près, retold the story. For him, the great lion came from Tharsis and was on the road to some princely menagerie when it managed to escape in the depths of the Bavarian forest. "The great wild lion inhabited this wood ... No one dared to go through it, since the lion very cruelly devoured the passers-by." Pépin cleared the wood by killing the ferocious beast [18].

From the 9th to the 14th century, the episode had grown and evolved. From a bare

Fig. 3 - A witch rides out on the back of a tiger-cat. Fresco from Schleswig cathedral, c.1300.

201

outline it burgeoned into a full-blown narrative, loaded with precise information about the origin and hiding place of the exotic feline. The claimed event is even commemorated by a monument, the sculpture in Notre-Dame. Such embellishments helped the legend to take root. According to a mediaeval source, the escape of the big cat took place, not in distant Germany but in France, in a densely forested area near Ferrières en Gatinais [19].

Exotic felines from the popular bestiary seem to have borrowed some sulphurous associations from other cats. During the persecution of the Templars (1305-1314) the knights were accused of having worshipped a huge black cat. Later, in cases tried by the Inquisition from 1421 to 1440, poor shepherds from the Alps admitted paying homage to the Devil, and sacrificing black cats to him [20]. Witches were said to ride on big cats as they made their way to their gatherings. This belief is illustrated by a fresco painted around 1300 on the vault of Schleswig cathedral: a woman with a horn in her left hand rides on the back of a giant cat which is striped like a tiger [21].

In Christian symbolism some exotic felines were interpreted as possible embodiments of the Devil. Saint Peter had compared the Devil to a 'roaring lion', and this metaphor helped the great maned cat to enter the twilight world of demonology. In 1542 at Viry, near Geneva, the familiar devil of a sorcerer was called 'lion' [22]. A possessed person, young Laurent Boissonnet, waiting to be exorcised at Soissons in 1582, claimed that a "great white lion" with "eyes as big as salt boxes" was leering at him from the window of his cell [23].

Since Pliny the Elder the spotted leopard had been considered as a *hybrid*, the fruit of the union between the lion and the panther, and thus called 'leo-pardus'; that is, 'lion-panther'. As such it was a symbol for illegitimate unions. People saw it as untameable and extremely fierce. The story was told of the Holy Marcianna, a martyr from Caesarea, who was spared in the arena by a lion, but mercilessly devoured by a leopard [24].

This feline was also related to the 'Beast from the Sea' of the Book of Revelation. A miniature from a Flemish Apocalypse, painted during the 15th century, shows the Beast like a seven-headed leopard, adored by

renegade monks [25].

This eschatological aspect may have played a part in the insertion of the exotic feline into mediaeval demonology. During the 1440 trial of Gilles de Rais, Marshal of France and serial killer, a black magician recalled an invocation of the Devil in a wood near Pouzauges castle, where a "demon in the form of a leopard" roamed around the magic circle [26]. One has to remember that in heraldry leopards and lions were synonymous. For Gilles, warlike knight and faithful comrade of Joan of Arc, the leopard, emblem of the devilish antagonist, may have been mixed up with the heraldic lion, attribute of the English.

LEOPARDS IN THE FRENCH GARDEN

In the chronicle of Saint Vivant de Vergy, a Burgundian monastery, we find this passage: "In the year 1545, Dom Odin Lescrivain, a friar from Saint-Vincent, killed in Chevigny wood, at a place called 'Les Trois Vies', a strange and wild beast called a leopard. The aforesaid animal slew and devoured several people, both men and women, as they were tending their flocks, and caused deep grief and disfigurement to others. Therefore, the local representatives proclaimed that whoever should kill this beast would be rewarded, and the aforesaid Odin received six *ecus* when he shot down this beast with his harquebus. And it was found that the beast was a male wolf, in other words, a werewolf, called in Latin 'Veneficus Anthropophagus'." [27]

Like Darwin's "entangled bank", the various definitions of the beast of Saint-Vincent are "bound together by a web of complex relations" [28]. The chronicler had indeed bestowed three identities on the fierce animal: leopard, male wolf and werewolf.

Today, such terms are distinct, and even contradictory. Yet for the author of the narrative, leopard/male wolf/werewolf were incompletely segregated definitions. This text bears witness to a wavering between nature

(R) Fig. 4 - A page from a 15th century Flemish apocalypsis. Note the depiction, at the bottom, of a cult of the seven-headed leopard.

and culture, with still ill-defined frontiers between magic and exoticism.

The presence of a savage wolf, at this time and place, need hardly surprise us. In 1544, during the invasion of France, the troops of Charles V had crossed Champagne, a bordering province. To slow down the enemy, the French resorted to a scorched-earth policy. Now, as Master of the Royal Hunt Jean de Clamorgan wrote in 1576:

Wars also attract a lot of wolves to a country. Indeed, wolves follow an army, living on the raw flesh of dead men, horses or other cattle that have been killed. Wolves accustomed to men's flesh will hardly choose other food. [29].

The beast of Saint-Vincent may have been one of those wolves nourished on the battlefield and trying to satiate its anthropophagous tastes by attacking shepherds. As I have shown elsewhere, the identification of a ravenous wolf with a werewolf was fairly common in the 16th century [30].

Yet the Burgundian chronicler stated unambiguously that the "strange and wild beast" was called a *leopard*. We can therefore conclude that around the middle of the 16th century the exotic feline stereotype was already known and used popularly, in competition with the enchanted wolf, to describe a beast of prey with unusual characteristics. People around Saint-Vincent *thought* that a leopard or werewolf was depopulating the area. Dom Odin killed a male wolf.

We have to wait some years to enrich our knowledge about bizarre felines from the folk bestiary. In 1556, a venturesome Franciscan friar, André Thévet, published his *Cosmographie du Levant*. The monk remembers that, being at the court two years before, he had taken part in a discussion about 'loups cerviers'. Some of the gentlemen said that such beasts were "extremely cruel and furious". Then Thévet adds the following commentary:

Not so long ago, one of such a sort was seen in France. In the year 1548, this 'loup cervier' emerged from the Orléans forest, in the province of Berry, and devoured several people. The beast was killed by a gentleman usher of the king's house called Sébastien de Rabutin, Lord of Savigny. The aforesaid lord told me at Fontainebleau, in 1554, that this wolf was not the same as

our common wolf, but rather had fur similar to a leopard's. [31]

Jean de Marconville, a compiler of wonders, reshaped the story in his miscellany, published eight years later:

In the year 1547, in Berry, Auxerrois and Orléanais, two cruel beasts were seen; they caused inestimable damage by slaughtering a multitude of men, children and animals that they encountered. No one dared to go out alone or unarmed. In the end, parishes banded together and rose up in arms, and after lengthy hunts they were killed, having caused incredible harm. As told by Thévet, it appeared to be a Holy Scourge sent upon those provinces; yet the story goes that Soliman, the emperor of the Turks, had sent as a great wonder to King Francis I some leopards, ounces and other wild and cruel beasts. While being brought to the monarch, one or two escaped from their keepers in Orléans forest and caused the aforesaid damage. [32]

In eight years folk tradition had blown up the episode to the dimensions of a Great Fear. The original 'loup cervier' with "fur similar to a leopard's" split into two "leopards or ounces". This time, the escaped-feline explanation stood in sharp contrast to the supernatural interpretation.

The process of legend formation had been stimulated by the vagaries of zoological knowledge. During the Renaissance, three names were used to designate *Felis lynx*: 'loup cervier', lynx and 'ounce', the last designation being current [33]. Moreover naturalists, following Pliny the Elder, sometimes described the lynx as a sub-species of wolf with speckled fur, or even as a kind of leopard.

The name 'loup cervier' in Thévet's narrative should not be unequivocally translated as lynx. The identity of the beast(s) from the Orléans forest wavers between the real wolf, the dubious lynx and the exotic leopard. And even this last identification lacks firmness: as Jules Camus has shown, as early as 1476 the kings of France were using *cheetahs* (called 'leopards' in the sources) as auxiliaries in hunting hares and roe-bucks [34]. The Swiss naturalist Conrad Gesner, in his *Historiae Animalium* (1551), shows gentlemen of the French court going to the royal hunt with their cheetahs chained behind them to the saddle [35].

The date advanced by Marconville for the escape of the big cat(s) corresponds better with historical chronology than the one proposed by Thévet. Francis I died in March 1547. One can well imagine that cheetahs were sent to the French king in the last months of his life by his ally, Soliman II (1520-1556).

Still, the relation established between 'leopards' and Turks may have covert polemical aspects. Soliman and Francis had signed a commercial treaty in 1528. Yet for the French people the sultan remained the greatest enemy of Christendom. In 1529, Soliman had besieged Vienna. How long before his janissaries invaded France, turning the towers of Notre-Dame into minarets? Turkish cruelty was also proverbial, and Marconville mentioned it as 'cruauté turcique'. In hostile narratives, Ottoman dignitaries were often shown throwing Christians to the lions in Neronian fashion [36]. The 'cruel leopard' is therefore an appropriate emissary of the 'cruel Turk'. The canine tooth foretold the scimitar.

With time, Sébastien de Rabutin's feat took on epic proportions, and during the reign of Henry II (1519-1559) his fight with the beast of the Orléans forest was immortalised by a painting in Fontainebleau Castle. Here a gentleman is shown putting to the sword a strangely striped wolf [37]. In his *Inventaire des Merveilles de la Maison Royale de Fontainebleau* from 1643, Father Dan writes that the work represents a "nobleman under sentence of death" who was pardoned after having dispatched a fierce 'loup cervier' [38]. More than a century after the event, folklore had reorganised the episode. Like Arthur, Rabutin had been forgotten and the victor is now, like legendary dragon-slayers, an anonymous hero.

If we return to the 16th century, we will discover that 'leopards' had also taken root in popular demonology. A pamphlet from 1574, summing up the misdeeds of Gilles Garnier, a werewolf from Franche-Comté, states that this 'lycophile', wandering "into the woods and wild places", was met by a "phantom in the shape of a man" who told him that: "He would teach him how to change at will into a wolf, a lion or a leopard, and because the wolf is more familiar than the other kinds of wild beasts he chose to disguise himself in that shape." [39]

The identity of the beast of Saint-Vincent fluctuated between leopard and werewolf. Here, in the Burgundian tale, the leopard appears as a disguise available to Satan's servant.

The African big cat reappears elusively in chronicles of the time. In 1584, a priest noted in the parish register of a hamlet near Chartres that a child was attacked and savaged within an inch of his death by a 'wild beast'. According to public opinion, the assailant was "a leopard or ounce" [40]. As in the previous cases, popular designation cannot be equated with zoological identification. We are following the trail of a belief, not of a leopard on the run.

The memoirs of Claude Hatton (1553-1582), a priest from Mériot near Provins, provide precious testimony about rural life during the wars of religion. Hatton's diary mirrors the terror of the countryfolk, pillaged by roaming soldiery. Attracted by unburied corpses, wolves were coming back, their packs harrassing men and cattle. Grim reality led to the focusing of fears on a half-glimpsed, half-imagined beast of prey. Hatton wrote that "a wild and furious beast, unknown to the country" made bloody raids on Mériot's outskirts, devouring people. "This beast was not as big as an old male wolf, but extremely cruel ... it was neither bear, wolf nor lion. Some thought and said it was an ounce, others disagreed." Finally, peasants cornered and killed the voracious animal [41].

The priest briefly alludes to another 'unknown beast' which, in 1577, had eaten a child in the province of Brie. Then, again, Hatton entrusts to his memoirs a record of the havoc wrought on his parishioners by 'unknown beasts' around 1579. One of them haunted the woods and had a liking for tender children's flesh. Ploughmen were afraid to go to the fields, and armed themselves with heavy clubs. "We have heard the opinion that it was a leopard or werewolf, and that this beast was none other than a 'Vaudois' (sorcerer) who, by devilish art, took this shape." [42]

Around Mériot rustics, confronting the seemingly unknown, turned to traditional categories to solve it. By 1579, the out of place feline is a serious rival for the transformed man.

The stereotype of the exotic feline reappeared in the next century. About 1693, for example, according to sketchy sources, no less than 100 inhabitants from the province of La Marche in central France fell under the ravenous teeth of a 'panther' rampaging through woods and moors [43].

But such a hecatomb is overshadowed by the renowned episode of the Beast of Gévaudan. Between 1764 and 1766, three provinces in the centre of the country were made insecure by repeated attacks by predators subsumed under the fabulous identity of a single 'beast'. Young shepherds and shepherdesses were killed, their disembowelled, beheaded bodies strewn over the mountainsides. Observations were shaped by traditional preconceptions, and the folk bestiary was resorted to in identifying 'the' monster. The affair was also one of the first 'scoops' of a nascent press, with portraits of the beast appearing in numerous European countries. The feline stereotype was not lacking in this heap of printed material. In November 1764, a writer for the *Courrier d'Avignon* stated: "many people believe the beast to be a hyena, others see in it a panther escaped from its keeper." [44].

The identification of the scourge of Gévaudan with a hyena was as weak as the one with a panther. Both were traditional. In times of crisis, people revitalised the slumbering array of anomalous creatures, quasi-wolves and felines from outside. This folk-opinion was strong during the Gévaudan affair, as attested by a public announcement made in November 1765 by the powerful Intendant d'Auvergne, Ballainvilliers. In this official document, a giant beat of three

provinces was called for, to subdue an enemy presented thus: "You are not unaware, gentlemen, that for three months a strange beast, *believed to be a leopard*, has roamed through these districts." [45].

Quite recently a bold theorist, gathering all the identifications of 'the' monster as a feline, has suggested that the beast of Gévaudan was "Jack the Tigron", a hybrid of lion and tiger, artifically created by "rivals of Dr Frankenstein" [46]. Alas for this beautiful hypothesis, which is worthy of a science fiction novel, the bodies of the beasts killed in Gévaudan were, as usual, identified as wolves [47]. The hyena and leopard from 1764-1766 were, like dragons, from the stuff of folklore.

The Gévaudan affair left deep gashes in the popular mentality. The beast's iconography, brought to more isolated places by pedlars, helped stereotypes to stabilise and influence later episodes. I have studied this imprint of the Gévaudan model on a more recent 'scare', the Cézallier case, between 1946 and 1956. Here, from the mountainous range of Le Cézallier, a popular panic had radiated through four departments of central France.

According to press articles and interviews from my field study (1983), the main culprit of repeated attacks against horned cattle was generally interpreted as an elusive 'lioness', hiding in the gloomy fir forests and maiming cows in their pasture during the night. The length of the scare (10 years) produced a multiplication and diversification of identities. Witnesses claimed to have seen a whole menagerie: hyenas, lynxes, cheetahs and even bears. The Cézallier social commotion can be read partially as a revival of the Gévauadan stereotype, reorganised to cope with new

Fig. 5 - Two representations of the 'Beast of Gévaudan' from popular broadsheets, c.1765.

Fig. 6 - The author with the 'monster of Valais', at the Sion Museum, Switzerland.

ideological conditions in post-war France [48].

When one of the predators was killed at Grandrieu in 1951, it was only a wolf...

CONCLUSION:
"WOLVES WILL RETURN..."

In February 1994 I was standing in front of a glass case, containing the stuffed body of a beautiful male wolf. The place was the Sion Museum in Valais, where I was interviewed by a reporter from the French-language radio of Switzerland. The wolf was a concrete solution to an enigma and, at the same time, testimony to the gap between the content of reported sightings and naturalistic reality.

Around the spring of 1946, an unidentified predator was running through Valais' mountain pastures, killing and devouring sheep. The Abbot and naturalist Ignace Mariétan interpreted the beast as a *lynx*. This speculation was popularised by the radio and daily press.

Then witnesses came forward, claiming they had clearly seen the lynx. They even described the distinctive pointed ears, but the animal was uncatchable. Next a tamer of wild beasts offered his services to the authorities. He asserted the plurality of the 'monster of Valais': according to this expert, a whole family of panthers was at large in the Swiss mountains. Another specialist, a big game hunter, contradicted him: there was *one* beast, a puma. Accomodating witnesses soon reported having had the privilege of beholding both the awe-inspiring parade of the panther family, and the puma's capers in the mountain's romantic gullies.

Science was also trying its best to solve the mystery. An easy-going zoological institute in Lausanne, after a careful study of the beast's plaster casts, was certain that the predator was feline. Professor Mathey even went so far as to identify the unknown animal as a "lynx from Savoy". Early in 1947, naturalists from the Berne Museum produced their own interpretation. For them, other plaster casts of the monster's tracks showed affinities with lion's paws. Noah's Ark had released its menagerie on top of Mont-Blanc. According to informants and experts, one lynx, five panthers, a puma and a lion haunted the Alps.

Learned and popular consensus united around the feline stereotype. Then, by mere chance, a poacher shattered the dogma. On 27 November 1947 he was lying in wait when a bizarre animal jumped into his line of sight. I was presently gazing at his prey, the mountain terror. Not a lynx, nor a panther, but a strong male wolf [49].

Pondering this very Fortean sequence, I thought that the Valais case offered some points of interest. If the poacher had not shot the wolf, belief in the feline identity of the beast may have lived on for some years, strengthened by experts and public opinion, until a modern legend would have grown: a Swiss equivalent to the saga of the Exmoor Beast. The Valais affair also showed the decisive influence of specialist speculation on the popular mentality. The lynx hypothesis, propagated through press and radio, had moulded the sightings, adapting the actual perception to the feline stereotype; an interesting process that can also play a part in other monster sightings such as lake-monsters and wild men [50].

The big cats of contemporary legend are no longer considered to be anthropophagous beasts. In France today they seem to represent a kind of parable of the encroachment of a new wilderness, invoked by rural exodus and the neglect of the fields. "Wolves will return", embittered countrymen told investigators [51].

But leopards from darkest Africa and pumas from the Rocky Mountains are more adequate metaphors than wolves to express the vanishing of a cultivated space created over the centuries. Lionesses and panthers will continue to appear along brambly tracks because they have a deep cultural function: to symbolise the intrusion of the wasteland.

NOTES

1 - Michael Goss, 'Phantom Felines (4): Folklore and Beyond', in The Unknown, October 1986, p.62.

2 - Goss, op. cit., p.64. On this topic see also, for the U.K., R.J.M. Rickard, 'If you go down to the woods today...' in INFO Journal, Vol. 4, No. 1, issue 13, May 1974, pp.3-18. Janet & Colin Bord, Alien Animals, Stackpole Books, Harrisburg, 1981, pp.44-76. J. & C. Bord, Modern Mysteries of Britain, Grafton Books, London, 1987, pp.93-105. Di Francis, Cat Country, David & Charles, Newton Abbot, 1983. Di Francis, The Beast of Exmoor, Jonathan Cape, London, 1993. Richard Halstead & Paul Sieveking, 'An ABC of British Alien Big Cats (1992-1993)', in Fortean Times, No. 73, Feb 1994, pp.41-44.

3 - Sister Mary Donatus, Beasts and Birds in the Lives of the Early Irish Saints (a thesis presented to the graduate school of the University of Pennsylvania), Philadelphia, 1934, p.203.

4 - Anne Ross, Pagan Celtic Britain, Routledge & Kegan Paul, London, 1968, p.302.

5 - Lewis Spence, The Minor Traditions of British Mythology, Rider, London, 1948, p.126. On the 'Irish Dragon Hunt (1968)', see F.W. Holiday, The Dragon and the Disc, Futura, London, 1973.

6 - E. Freymond, 'Arthus' Kampf mit dem Katzenungetüm', in Beiträge zur Romanischen Philologie: Festgabe für Gustav Gröber, Niemeyer, Halle, 1899, pp.311-396 (p.323).

7 - R.S.Loomis, Arthurian Legends in Medieval Art, Vol. 1, Oxford University Press, 1938, p.36. Walter Haug, Das Mosaik von Otranto, Reichert, Wiesbaden, 1977, p.31.

8 - Freymond, op. cit., p.374-377.

9 - Jacques Fodéré, Narration historique et topographique des couvents de l'ordre de Saint-François, Rigaud, Lyon, 1619, pp.926-927.

10 - Freymond, op. cit., p.386-387.

11 - Freymond, op. cit., p.391.

12 - François Cali, L'Ordre Flamboyant, Arthaud, Paris, 1967, p.141.

13 - Sister Mary Donatus, op. cit., p.214.

14 - Sister Mary Donatus, op. cit., p.204.

15 - A. Micha, 'Miscellaneous French Romances in Verse', in R.S. Loomis (ed.), Arthurian Literature in the Middle Ages, Clarendon Press, Oxford, 1959, p.386.

16 - Gaston Paris, Mélanges de littérature française du Moyen-Age (I), Champion, Paris, 1910, pp.183-215.

17 - Paris, op. cit., p.189.

18 - Paris, op. cit., p.191.

19 - Paris, op. cit., p.189.

20 - Jeffrey Burton Russell, Witchcraft in the Middle Ages, Cornell University Press, Ithaca, 1972, pp.196, 216-217.

21 - F.H. Hamkens, 'Heidnische Bilder im Dome zu Schleswig', in Germanien, 1938, p.178.

22 - César Duval, 'Procès de sorciers à Viry', in Bulletin de l'Institut National Genevois (24), 1882, p.375.

23 - Dom Charles Blendec, Cinq histoires admirables Guillaume Chaudière, Paris, 1582, chapter

14, folio 19A.

24 - Louis Charbonneau-Lassey, *Le bestiaire du Christ*, Desclée de Brouwer, Bruges, 1940, p.293.

25 - Frederic Van Der Meer, *L'Apocalypse dans l'art*, Fonds Mercator, Anvers, 1978, pp.220-221.

26 - Georges Bataille (ed.), *Le procès de Gilles de Rais*, J.J. Pauvert, Paris, 1965, p.307.

27 - Victor Jacquemont du Donjon, *Mélanges*, Garnier, Paris, 1900. See also Michel Meurger, 'Les félins exotiques dans le légendaire français', in *Communications* No. 52, Le Seuil, Paris, 1990, pp.175-196 (p.186).

28 - Charles Darwin, *The Origin of Species*, 1859, chapter 3.

29 - Jean de Clamorgan, *La chasse au loup*, reissued: Bouchard-Huzard, 1866.

30 - Michel Meurger, 'L'homme-loup et son témoin. Construction d'une factualité lycanthropique', in Jean de Nynauld, *De la lycanthropie, transformation et extase des sorciers* (1615), Frénésie, Paris, 1990, pp.143-179.

31 - André Thévet, *Cosmographie du Levant*, Jean de Tournes E.G. Gazeau, Lyon, 1556. Meurger, 'Félins exotiques...', p.187.

32 - Jean de Marconville, *Recueil mémorable d'aucuns cas merveilleux adevenuz de noz ans*, Jean Dallier, Paris, 1564. Meurger, 'Félins exotiques...', p.187.

33 - Hélène Nais, *Les animaux dans la poésie française de la Renaissance*, Didier, Paris, 1961.

34 - Jules Camus, 'Les guépards chasseurs en France au XV et au XVIe siècle', in *Feuille des jeunes naturalistes* No. 214, 1 Aug 1888, pp.129-131.

35 - Conrad Gesner, *Historiae Animalium*, apud C. Froschoer, Tiguri, 1551, Book I, p.938.

36 - See, for example, the anecdote about the Turkish 'Bassa', "thirsty for Christian blood", in Phillipe Camerarius (trans. by Simon Goulart) *Les méditations historiques*, Harsy, Lyon, 1610, p.365. See also the story of the Moroccan king who organised fights between slaves and lions in Father Dan, *Histoire de barbarie et de ses corsaires*, Rocolet, Paris, 1637, Book V, p.460.

37 - Louis Lavauden, *Essai sur l'histoire naturelle du lynx*, Allier, Grenoble, 1930, p.67.

38 - Lavauden, *op. cit.*

39 - *Arrest memorable de la Cour de Parlement de Dôle, du 18e jour de janvier 1574, contre Gilles Garnier, Lyonnois, pour avoir, en forme de loup, dévoré plusiers enfants...*, Savine, Sens, 1574, folio 9; translated in Montague Summers, *The Werewolf*, Kegan Paul, Trench, Trubner & Co, London, 1933, pp.226-228. See also E. William Monter, *Witchcraft in France and Switzerland*, Cornell University Press, Ithaca, 1976, p.147.

40 - Marcel Robillard, *Le folklore de la Beauce*, Vol VIII, Maisonneuve et Larose, Paris, 1972, p.13.

41 - *Mémoires de Claude Hatton*, ed. Bourquelot, Paris, 1857, Vol. II, p.907.

42 - Hatton, *op. cit.*, and original manuscript of Claude Hatton, Bibliothèque Nationale, Paris, MS. 11575, folio 864A.

43 - Michel Meurger, 'Trop humaine Babette', in J.L. Brodu and M. Meurger, *Les félins mystères. Sur les traces d'un mythe moderne*, Pogonip, Paris, 1984, p.28.

44 - Abbé Pourcher, *Histoire de la bête du Gévaudan, véritable fléau de Dieu*, Saint-Martin de Boubaux, 1889; Slatkine Reprints, 1981, p.95.

45 - Quoted in François Fabre, *La bête du Gévaudan en Auvergne*, St. Flour, 1901, p.46.

46 - René de Chantal, *La fin d'une énigme. La Bête du Gévaudan*, La Pensée Universelle, Paris, 1983, pp.275-276, 337.

47 - Abbé Xavier Pic, *La Bête qui mangeait le monde en Pays de Gévaudan et d'Auvergne*, Chaptal, Mende, 1968.

48 - Michel Meurger, 'Félins exotiques...' pp.176-177, 183-184. Michel Meurger, *On the Track of the Beast. Legendary Wolves and Felines in French Folk Culture* (unpublished study).

49 - Michel Meurger, 'Félins exotiques...' pp.180-183.

50 - On the role of cultural stereotypes in the shaping of sea and lake monster representations, see Michel Meurger, with Claude Gagnon, *Lake Monster Traditions. A Cross-Cultural Analysis*, Fortean Tomes, London, 1988. Michel Meurger, 'In Jormungandra's Coils: A Cultural Archaeology of the Norse Sea Serpent', in *Fortean Times*, No. 51, Winter 1988-1989, pp.63-68. 'Naturalisation et factualisation de l'Imaginaire. L'exemple de l'homme-marin', in *Cahiers de l'Imaginaire*, X, 1994, pp.67-77.

51 - Michel Meurger, 'Trop humaine Babette', p.33.

THE CASE FOR THE GIANT OCTOPUS

Michel Raynal

In spite of the fact that a carcass was washed up in Florida in 1896, the existence of the giant octopus as a species is far from accepted by modern science. Michel Raynal, author of several articles on unknown animals, re-examines the 1896 case and evaluates a number of other apparent sightings.

In 1801, French malacologist Pierre Denys de Montfort tried to establish the existence of two large species of cephalopods from in-depth research into old Greek, Roman and Scandinavian chronicles and from eye-witness accounts he collected from sailors and whalers: he named them 'Poulpe Kraken', which has since been demonstrated to be the giant squid *Architeuthis*, only accepted by science in 1852 (Heuvelmans 1974), and 'Poulpe Colossal', the giant octopus, the existence of which is still controversial.

THE FLORIDA MONSTER OF 1896

One of the most incredible of zoological mysteries began on 30 November 1896, when two cyclists, Herbert Cole and Dunham Coretter, discovered a huge mass of rotting flesh, half embedded in the sand on a beach near St. Augustine (on the east coast of Florida). Because of its size, they believed it was the remains of a whale.

Dr DeWitt Webb, a local surgeon fond of natural sciences and president of the St. Augustine Scientific, Literary and Historical Society, came and examined the 'Florida monster' (as it was nicknamed) on 1 December 1896. The mutilated cadaver was of a light pink colour, and so hard that it could not be cut with a knife. It was about 20 feet (6 m) long and 4 feet (1.20 m) high, and Webb estimated it weighed about 5 to 7 tons. But above all, he realised that it was the remains of a gigantic octopus!

On 7 December, Webb came back to the beach with two photographers, Edgard van Horn and Ernest Howatt. The overexposed photographs taken on this occasion were considered lost until recently, and we only possessed drawings made from them by Alpheus Hyatt Verrill for the *American Naturalist* in April 1897: the first drawing (figure 1), from a frontal view, shows Webb standing behind the body of the animal, a pear-shaped bag, with the the stumps of five arms; the second drawing (figure 2), from a side view, looks like an elephant lying on its flank, and shows a tapering cadaver with two or three stumps of arms.

In fact, one of these 'lost' photographs was found by Gary Mangiacopra in 1994: it is quite obvious that Alpheus Verrill - son of Prof. Addison Emery Verrill - made a drawing from this photograph for his father's article in the *American Naturalist* and another drawing for his own article in the *Hartford Daily Courant* of

Fig. 1 - A front view of the Florida monster. Drawing by A.H. Verrill, after a photo taken 7 December 1896. (*Amerian Naturalist*, April 1897. Photo: Bibl. Museum Hist. Nat., Paris.)

18 February 1897.

Meanwhile, a Mr. Wilson wrote to Webb about his own observations:

> One arm was lying west of the body, 23 feet long [7 m]; one stump of arm, west of the body, about 4 feet [1.20 m]; three arms lying south of the body and from appearances attached to same (although I did not dig quite to body, as it lay well down in the sand, and I was very tired), longest one measured over 32 feet [9.75 m], the other arms were 3 to 5 feet [90 cm to 1.50 m] shorter.

Soon after, a storm drifted the cadaver out to sea, and it was then cast ashore again, its arms cut off.

Another witness, Dr Grant, examined the monster in early December, and his account was published in the *Pennsylvania Grit* of Williamsport on 13 December:

> The head is as large as an ordinary flour barrel and has the shape of a sea lion. The neck, if the creature may be said to have a neck, is of the same diameter as the body. The mouth is on the under side of the head and is protected by two tenacle [*sic*] tubes about 8 inches [20 cm] in diameter and 30 feet [9 m] long. These tubes resemble an elephant's trunk, and obviously were used to clutch in a sucker-like manner any object within their reach.
>
> Another tube or tenacle of the same dimension stands out on the top of the head. Two others, one on each side, protrude from behind the monster's neck and extend fully 15 feet [4.50 m] along the body and beyond the tail. The tail, which is separated and jagged with cutting points for several feet, is flanked with two more tentacles of the same dimensions as the others and 30 feet [9 m] long. The eyes are under the back of the mouth, instead of over it.

Grant describes 7 'tentacles' (in fact arms) of the same length: nothing indicates the presence of squid's tentacles. The 'tail' with two tentacles might in fact be a fragment of the umbrella. And the dimensions of the arms of the monster (about 9 m long and 20 cm thick) confirm Wilson's and Webb's figures (see below).

Meanwhile, Webb wrote to several scientists and one of his letters was published in the *Nautilus* of January 1897:

> I have been greatly interested in an immense cephalopod which came ashore about 5 miles south of Jack Mound, Anastasia Island. Only the stumps of tentacles were left, as it had been dead for, perhaps, days. The body proper measured 18 feet [5.50 m] in length, 11 feet [3.35 m] in breadth and 3½ feet [1.05 m] thick above the sand as it lay soft and flattened on the beach. Of course there is no way of knowing how long the tentacles were, but, judging from the size of the body, the arms must have been of enormous length.

The article was headlined as 'a large decapod', suggesting it was a squid. It should be stressed that Webb only spoke of a 'cephalopod', but he was more precise in his letter of 8 December to Mr J.A. Allen:

> You may be interested to know of the body of an immense octopus thrown ashore some miles south of this city [St. Augustine]. Nothing but the stumps of the tentacles remain, as it had evidently been dead for some time before being washed ashore. As it is, however, the body measures 18 feet [5.50 m] in length by 10 feet [3 m] in breadth. Its immense size and condition will prevent all attempts at preservation. I thought its size might

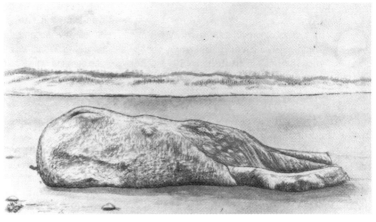

Fig. 2 - A side view of the Florida monster. Drawing by A.H. Verrill, after a photo taken 7 December 1896. (*Amerian Naturalist*, April 1897. Photo: Bibl. Museum Hist. Nat., Paris.)

Fig. 3 - The Florida monster and DeWitt Webb, December 1896. (Photo: Van Norden Lockwood. St Augustine Historical Society.)

interest you, as I do not know of a record of one so large.

The 'width' of 10 feet (3 m) refers to the whole remains (body and stumps of arms), and not solely to the body, as can be seen on the drawings: in the front view, the width of the body is about half that of the total spread of the remains, or about the size of Dr Webb, i.e., about 5 feet (1.50 m). This estimate is confirmed by the other drawing, where the width of the body represents about a quarter of its length, thus 18 feet (5.50 m)/4 = about 4.5 feet (1.40 m).

Webb's letter to J.A. Allen was forwarded to Prof. Addison Emery Verrill, zoologist at Yale University in New Haven (Connecticut) and an authority on cephalopods. Verrill published a first note in the January 1897 issue of the *American Journal of Science*; but considering the impressive dimensions reported by Webb, Verrill (like the editor of the *Nautilus*) thought it was a giant squid rather than an octopus.

Other photographs taken by Mr Van Norden Lockwood between 1885 and 1899 came to light in 1993. The first shows a crowd of about 50 people, who came to the beach to see the cadaver. The second one, overexposed, shows two horses and a carriage, with several people on the left. In the middle lies the mass with a cable around it and a pole on the left. On the right stand Webb and 2 other men.

A third one (figure 3), wrongly dated to 16 January 1897 but taken in December 1896, shows Webb standing near the body of the Florida monster, with the pole and cable. Webb's size giving the scale, one can estimate that the body is 5 feet (1.50 m) wide, which confirms the dimensions claimed by Webb, as well as my own estimates above.

Another photograph (figure 4), taken on 7 December or soon after, shows a part of the body on the right, but a stump of arm is visible lying towards the left. The cable and the pole are again present as in Lockwood's photograph. Using the pole as a scale, and if Webb was 1.70 m high (including hat), the diameter of the arm is about 35 cm, consistent with Webb's statement of a stump 10 inches (25 cm) thick where it was cut.

Soon after, Verrill received from Webb new details and the photographs of which we have only drawings. He commented on them in the *New York Herald* of 3 January 1897, and in the *American Journal of Science* for February:

These photographs show that it is an eight-armed cephalopod, and probably a true *Octopus*, of colossal size. Its body is pear-shaped, largest near the broadly rounded posterior end. The head is scarcely recognizable, owing to mutilation and decay. Dr Webb writes that a few days after the photographs were taken (7 December), excavations were made in the sand and the stump of an arm was found, still attached, 36 feet [11 m] long and 10 inches [25 cm] in diameter where it was broken off distally.

Verrill concluded that Webb was right: it was a giant octopus. He calculated that the weight of the living animal should be about 18 to 20 tons! Its arms should be 75 to 100 feet long (23 to 30 m) - a total spread of 150 to 200 feet (50 to 60 m)! - and 18 inches (45 cm) in diameter at the base, with suckers one foot (30 cm) in diameter! Verrill proposed to name it *Octopus giganteus*: one century after Denys de Montfort, the colossal octopus became a reality.

Verrill did not rule out, however, that this octopus could be related to the genus *Cirroteuthis*: the two lateral stumps on the drawing in frontal view could in fact be fins.

Octopods are divided into 2 sub-orders, cirrates (or ciliated octopuses), which have 'cirri', and incirrates, which have none. The arms of the cirrates have only one row of suckers, fringed by two rows of cirri. The body has two lateral fins. They are said to be short (less than one foot in length), but large specimens have been recorded.

Cirroteuthis magna, described by William E. Hoyle in 1886 from a specimen caught by the oceanographic ship *Challenger* in the Antarctic Ocean, was 1.15 m (4 feet) long. Another cirrate, remains of which were preserved during the same expedition off Patagonia, had suckers 12 mm in diameter, instead of 8 for the previous one: it should be more than 1.50 m (5 feet) long.

In 1932, G.C. Robson mentioned a *Grimpoteuthis* caught by the *Discovery* off South Georgia, which might be 3-4 feet long (0.90 to 1.20 m).

In 1972, Clyde F.E. Roper and Walter L. Brundage Jr. analysed photographs of ciliated octopuses taken by the *Mizar* and the *Alvin* in the Western Atlantic. Of the 24 specimens, eight exceed 50 cm, and the four largest ones are 90, 102, 103 and 128 cm long.

Finally, in 1984, the diving saucer *Cyana* filmed, above a hydrothermal spring of the Pacific rift, a cirrate 2.50 m (more than 8 feet) long, almost as large as the largest known octopus (*Octopus dofleini*, the giant Pacific octopus).

Dr Webb noticed the absence of a caudal fin, like that of squid, but what looks like lateral fins can be seen on the first photographs.

Early in January 1897, Webb wrote to Prof. William Healey Dall, curator of molluscs at the U.S. National Museum in Washington, that the cadaver was so heavy that a dozen men had been unable to move it.

There is an 'unpublished' photograph taken on this occasion. I write this in quotes, because thousands of people have seen it, as it was shown in the British TV series *Arthur C. Clarke's Mysterious World* (about which more later). It shows the cadaver and three workers. A second photograph, from the same series, shows what looks like the stump of an arm.

In his letter of 17 January 1897, Webb wrote to Prof. Dall that he had decided to make a great effort, confirming that the estimate of 5 to 7 tons for the remains was not exaggerated:

> Yesterday I took four horses, six men, three sets tackle, a lot of heavy planking and a rigger to superintend the work and succeeded in rolling the invertebrate out of the pit and placing it about 40 feet [12 m] higher up on the beach where it now rests on the flooring of heavy planks ... The slender part of the body was entirely empty of internal organs. And the organs of the remaining part were not large ...

Fig. 4 - The Florida monster, 7 December 1896. What appears to be an arm extends towards the background from the monster's body at the right. (Photo: Division of Molluscs, Smithsonian Institution.)

Fig. 5 - The Florida monster, Webb and onlookers, 17 January 1897. (Photo: Van Norden Lockwood. St Augustine Historical Society.)

Three photographs were taken on this occasion: one shows Webb and five other people behind the cadaver, with the cable, planks and the four horses behind (figure 5). The other ones show a mass of tissue lying on the planks (figures 6 and 7).

In his letter of 18 January, Webb wrote that the muscular layer, 3 to 6 inches thick (7.5 to 15 cm), was made with outer circular fibres, and inner longitudinal fibres. No caudal fin was present, nor any 'feather': it could not be a squid at all.

These details are consistent with the octopus hypothesis. Webb says that the organs of the back part of the body were not large: kidney, heart, stomach, pancreas, etc., are indeed small in octopuses. On the other hand, eyes, brain, and beak (large in a giant octopus) are in the mutilated part of the body: they had been cut off by waves or even predators.

Regarding the muscular layer, octopuses have longitudinal muscles along the axis of the body, on the outer and the inner faces of the mantle, and circular muscles between them. Webb describes only 2 layers: outer (circular), and inner (longitudinal): the external layer was probably destroyed by the waves and rotting.

Early in February 1897, Webb took samples from the creature, which he sent in a jar of formalin to Dall and Verrill. The samples sent to Yale have been lost, but those sent to the Smithsonian Institution are mentioned in the annual report of this museum for 1897:

Dr DeWitt Webb, St. Augustine, Florida, presented negatives of photographs of a sea monster stranded near that place, named *Octopus giganteus* by Professor Verrill. Portions of the remains, preserved in formalin, were also transmitted.

From his examination of the samples sent to Yale, Verrill changed his opinion, and wrote several letters published in *Science* of 5 March, in the *New York Herald* of 7 March and in the *New Haven Evening Register* of 24 February:

I have just received large masses of the carcass cast ashore in December and described by me as the body of an *Octopus* in the *American Journal of Science* and elsewhere. These masses of integument are 3 to 10 inches [7.5 to 25 cm] thick, very tough and elastic, and very hard to cut. They are composed mainly of tough cords and fibres of white elastic connective tissue, much interlaced. This structure resembles that of the blubber of some cetaceans.

The presence of arms was based on Wilson's and Webb's accounts (and Grant's one, unknown to Verrill), "not confirmed later", Verrill wrote. But the first photographs show stumps of arms, later cut off by the storm; despite this evidence, Verrill claimed in the *American Journal of Science* of April 1897:

Apparently nothing that can be called stumps of arms, or any other appendages, were present. Folds of the integument and mutilated and partly detached portions may have been mistaken for such structures.

Verrill noticed, however, that the samples were poor in oil, so that they did not float on the water, unlike cetacean blubber. Incidentally, cephalopod tissues are poor in fat tissues and are recommended as hypocaloric food.

Verrill finally came to the conclusion that it was a part of the head of a sperm whale, a theory he presented in *Science* on 19 March, and later in the *American Naturalist* of April 1897:

> The structure found is closer to that of the integument of the upper part of the head and nose of the sperm whale than to that of any other structure known to me. It is probable, therefore, that the great bag-shaped mass represents nearly the whole upper part of the head of such a creature.

Verrill thus believed that the Florida monster was mainly the spermaceti tank of a sperm whale, a tissue rich in collagen and which can weigh about 5 tons. He recognized, however, that no whaler could identify the cadaver with any part of a sperm whale. It was also very strange that there was no vent, that is to say a hole one foot (30 cm) in diameter. And how is one to explain Webb's statement about 'organs' (or in another letter of 'viscera'), which are absent in the spermaceti tank?

Yet Dr Frederic A. Lucas, curator of comparative anatomy at the U.S. National Museum, claimed in *Science* of 19 March 1897:

> The substance looks like blubber, and smells like blubber, and it *is* blubber, nothing more nor less.

The affair was forgotten, as buried as the cadaver of the Florida monster. There was a brief note in *Chamber's Journal* in 1897, then in the *Washington Post* in 1909. 20 years after the events, Alpheus Hyatt Verrill, the son of Prof. Addison Emery Verrill, spoke again of them in his book *The Ocean and its Mysteries* (1916):

> Only a few years ago a strange object was washed up on our Florida coast and, as in the case of the wonderful giant squids, photographs of this new 'sea monster' and pieces of its substance were sent to Prof. Verrill. At first it seemed as if this would prove the existence of another unknown and gigantic cuttlefish, but upon examination it turned out to be a portion of some very different creature. Although some 20 feet [6 m] in length and 40 feet [4.30 m] in circumference and weighing many tons, yet this great mass of tough, fibrous flesh was a mere fragment of some titanic marine monster and in its structure and shape so different from any known form of animal that no scientist could even guess at its origin, and it has gone down to posterity as one of the mysteries of the sea.

In 1952, 55 years after the stranding, Alpheus Hyatt Verrill gave a similar version of the affair and its conclusion in his book *The Strange Story of our Earth:*

> Photographs and a description were sent to my father, Professor A. E. Verrill, at Yale, who assumed it to be the remains of a giant octopus ... But when my father studied the specimens he was completely at a loss. The flesh was totally unlike that of any known creature, for it contained neither the fibre of muscles, nerves, blood vessels, sinews nor bones. Probably nine out of ten scientists would have proposed an explanation but my father frankly and freely admitted that he was at a complete loss, that he couldn't even guess what it was, but that it unquestionably was the remains of a part of some totally unknown marine creature.

These versions are in contradiction to the cetacean hypothesis (which is not even mentioned): it seems that Prof. Verrill had more and more doubts about his idea of a cetacean. Dr Frederic A. Lucas, on the other hand, did not change his opinion, when he wrote an article on the errors of zoology in 1928:

> After due study of photographs and glowing accounts by non-scientific observers, the mass was named *Octopus giganteus*. However, some Doubting Thomas put a piece of the animal into a big jar and sent it to the National Museum, where the jar was opened by a member of the staff, who promptly said 'blubber', a remark that was repeated by the friend to whom he showed it. And blubber it was, for it proved to be the wave-worn case of a sperm whale, from which the spermaceti had been taken before it was cast adrift. As an English writer observed, this shows the difficulty of sitting in Connecticut and describing a species in Florida. And now there can never be an *Octopus giganteus*, for by the rule "once a synonym always a synonym", the name has been attached to the sperm whale and can never properly be applied to a cephalopod.

Apart from the personal attacks on Webb and Verrill, Lucas is wrong when he supposes that the spermaceti was lost before the cadaver was cast ashore. There was only the mass of connective tissue from which to explain the shape, size and properties of the Florida monster. If I can copy Lucas, this

215

(T) Fig. 6, (B) Fig 7 - The Florida monster, 17 January 1897.
(Photo: Van Norden Lockwood. St Augustine Historical Society / Ken Barritt Jr.)

shows the difficulty of sitting in Washington and debunking a species in Florida...

Apart from these, nothing but a brief mention from time to time: in 1937, Paul Bartsch alluded to the Florida monster, claiming it was a giant squid, *Architeuthis*. In 1931, in his famous book *Lo!*, Charles Hoy Fort quoted without any comment two articles by Prof. Verrill. Several Fortean authors have copied this passage from their master, for instance John A. Keel in his book *Strange Creatures from Time and Space* (1970), summarizing a summary of the affair...

Science-fiction writer Arthur C. Clarke, who met with F.G. Wood (about whom more below), also alluded to the affair in 1960, in a popular book on the oceans. He summarized the story 30 years later in his novel *The Ghost from the Grand Banks* (1990), where an expedition rescues the *Titanic* in 2012, 100 years after its wreck; among other adventures, it encounters an *Octopus giganteus* (Clarke even alludes to photographs of the Florida monster still unpublished in 1990!).

Even Bernard Heuvelmans, the father of cryptozoology, author of a book on giant cephalopods in 1958 (*Dans le sillage des monstres marins - Le Kraken et le Poulpe Colossal*), did not mention this case, although he was aware of it. As he wrote in the second edition of this book (1974):

> I was so confident in Professor Verrill's authority, who had rehabilitated the legendary Kraken, that I did not mention the incident of the so-called *Octopus giganteus* in the first edition of my book. It seemed to me that it encumbered a file already huge. I was wrong. In Science, you must never trust anybody.

MODERN ANALYSES

Meanwhile, the affair had actually surfaced again. In 1957, Forrest Glenn Wood, a marine biologist then working at the Marineland Research Laboratory (Florida), came across an old clipping entitled 'the facts about Florida', which claimed:

> In 1897, portions of an octopus, said to have been more gigantic than any ever before seen, were washed up on the beach at St. Augustine. Prof. Verrill, of Yale University, who examined the remains, which alone reputedly weighed over six tons, calculated that the living creature had a girth

of 25 feet [7.50 m] and tentacles 72 feet [22 m] in length!

In fact, with a diameter of about 5 feet (1.5 m), the circumference should be 'only' about 15 feet (4.50 m) (diameter multiplied by 3.14); Alpheus Hyatt Verrill, in 1916, gave a circumference of 14 feet (4.20 m), in agreement with my estimates.

Wood decided to check the information. Little by little, he found some more clippings about the monster and several photographs of the cadaver itself; he published a first account of his investigations in 1957, in *The Mariner*. Dr Gilbert L. Voss, a leading expert in cephalopods at the University of Miami (Florida), helped Wood to locate 5 articles published by Verrill, and told him that in the collections of the Smithsonian Institution in Washington, there was (in 1962) a large jar labelled '*Octopus giganteus* VERRILL'.

Harold A. Rehder, curator of molluscs at the Smithsonian, did not want to loan these samples (sent by Webb in 1897, as mentioned above). But he gave Wood new photographs of the monster and copies of Webb's letters to William H. Dall, then curator of molluscs at the U.S. National Museum.

Next, Joseph F. Gennaro Jr., a biologist at the University of Florida, was allowed to take a sample of the Florida monster for histological examination. The jar contained fibrous masses, white, poor in oil, and very tough, corresponding well to Verrill's description. Examination through the microscope did not show any cellular structure, but it was similar to samples of octopus and squid and unlike cetacean tissue: therefore, it was not a sperm whale.

Gennaro then examined the samples through polarised light (Figure 8): the proteins of the Florida monster's connective tissue appeared as bright and dark stripes of the same width, as is the case in octopuses (instead of the wide bright and thin dark stripes found in squids). After 170 years of purgatory, Denys de Montfort's Colossal Octopus was scientifically confirmed. As Gennaro concluded in his *Natural History* article (1971):

> The evidence appears unmistakable that the St. Augustine sea monster was in fact an octopus, but the implications are fantastic. Even though the sea presents us from time to time with strange and

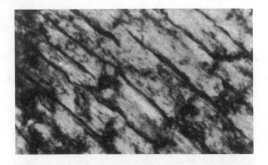

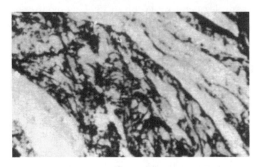

Fig. 8 - Micrographs in polarised light through sections of squid (top), octopus (centre) and the Florida monster (bottom). The lighter bands are connective tissue oriented parallel to the plane of the section; dark bands are oriented perpendicularly. The dark bands of the squid are very narrow. The monster's tissue resembles more closely that of the octopus.
(Photo: *Natural History*, March 1971.)

astonishing phenomena, the idea of a gigantic octopus, with arms 75 to 100 feet [23 to 30 m] long and about 18 inches [45 cm] in diameter at the base - a total spread of some 200 feet [60 m] - is difficult to comprehend.

D ifficult indeed, so that when Wood and Gennaro published the results of their investigations in the March 1971 issue of *Natural History*, some readers thought that it was an April Fool's joke!

It is true that Gennaro was photographed with a skeletal foot. A Mr James Fanning, in a letter published in the May issue, wondered if it was evidence of a physical contact with the late Prof. Verrill, or was Gennaro transforming into an octopod, with his third appendage?

In fact, Gennaro was an authority on the effects of snake venom on the bones, and he had decided to break the ceremonial of these authors' photographs. As Peter Schossberger said in another letter "a touch of humour in these grim times is most welcome" (Americans were still in Vietnam, and even in Cambodia and Laos). In the *Wall Street Journal*, however, Wood did not find this humour appropriate:

> I've written a nasty letter to the editor [of *Natural History*] and I personally think that Gennaro was irresponsible. I don't think he took this thing seriously.

None of the great scientific magazines, *Nature, Science, New Scientist*, spoke of the giant octopus: I am only aware of a brief note in *Sciences et Avenir*, July 1971. Nothing also in the oceanographic magazines: only Willard H. Porter mentioned Wood's and Gennaro's work in *Oceans*, September-October 1971. And the *Oceanic Citation Journal* of September 1971 wrongly summarized the story as follows:

> OCTOPUS: FLORIDA: identification of carcass: 1896: St. Augustine: giant squid.

12 years later, Gerald L. Wood (no relation to F.G. Wood) debunked the giant octopus in the 3rd edition of the *Guinness Book of Animal Facts and Feats* (1983):

> Dr Gilbert L. Voss, a leading American expert on the cephalopods, thinks the remains may have been part of a large mammal - or even a whale shark - the skeleton having fallen out as the floating body rotted. Certainly it is difficult to believe that a *positive identification* could be made of connective tissue after such a long time, and the fact that neither suckers nor a beak, the two characteristics that could have placed this enigma firmly among the cephalopods, were seen or mentioned is another minus ... Another point worth noting is that the soft, gelatinous flesh of these invertebrates is extremely prone to decomposition.

In fact a positive identification *can* be

made after 75 years: there are even such tests on fossil bones several million years old. In 1993, the DNA of a beetle kept in yellow amber for 100 million years was cloned by an American team, whose work gave birth to Michael Crichton's famous techno-thriller novel *Jurassic Park*, later filmed by Steven Spielberg.

Regarding the hardness of the cadaver, F.G. Wood had already answered in his article of 1971. Frederick A. Aldrich, director of the Marine Sciences Laboratory of the Memorial University in Newfoundland (Canada), and an authority on giant squids, wrote to him:

> Frankly, I would tend to favour a cephalopod identification ... Cephalopod tissue, particularly squid tissue in my experience, is firm and does not easily decompose beyond a certain stage, and actually hardens and toughens upon exposure.

The samples of the Florida monster were of connective tissue rich in collagen. Radio-crystallographic studies have shown that the structure of the collagen recalls that of crystals. The molecule is reinforced by many hydrogen bridges, which explains the tough-ness and hardness of this substance. Inciden-tally, anybody who has eaten octopus or squid is aware of the toughness of the flesh of these animals! Collagen also resists most proteolytic enzymes (those which break the protein into its amino-acids), and particularly those en-zymes that cause rotting, explaining why the cadaver remained unchanged for several months.

The head was very mutilated, so it is not surprising if the beak was absent. Neither Webb, nor Wilson, nor Grant mentions any suckers, and there is no evidence of them on the stumps of arms shown in the photographs, but who knows if this kind of giant octopus really had suckers: after all, some squids have no suckers, but true claws (*Onychoteuthis* for instance).

In the popular magazine *Argosy* for March 1973, Gennaro wrote:

> ... it was found that the chemical constituents of the monster's collagen were of the type found in the octopus, and that none of this type of tissue exists in the squid at all.

Gennaro did not publish this analysis, which was repeated by Roy P. Mackal, who is a biochemist at Chicago University (Illinois); the results have been published in *Cryptozool-*

ogy in 1986. The *Octopus giganteus* sample differs from cetacean and squid samples by its low content of glutamic (8.8%) and aspartic (5.9%) acids, and high percentages in proline and above all glycine (34.6%). The latter proportion of glycine is typical of collagen, but how can Gennaro be so affirmative?

The structure of the collagens is: - Gly - X - Y - Gly - X - Y - etc., where Gly is the glycine, X and Y being 2 other amino-acids. Glycine thus accounts for at least 33.3% (for instance, human collagen: 34%).

> The *Octopus giganteus* tissue [Mackal writes] is almost pure collagen, which is precisely what one would expect for an aquatic invertebrate, such as a giant octopus, with a mass of 6000 Kg or more.

Collagen actually takes a part in support (in the vertebrates, it is in the spinal column, and in squids it is in the 'feather', with another protein, elastein). The spermaceti tank of the head of the sperm whale is also rich in collagen, and its shape and dimensions might explain the Florida monster, as suggested by Verrill in 1897. The structure of collagens is almost similar from species to species, but there are some differences in the concentration of some amino-acids: there is an increase of aspartic and glutamic acids from homother-mic (hot-blooded) to poikilothermic (cold-blooded) species, with a decrease of serine and threonine.

Mackal emphasizes that the storage in formalin has modified the content of serine and threonine, but the total of aspartic and glutamic acids is about 15% in the monster, instead of 10% in vertebrate collagens: it thus came from an invertebrate.

I have proposed an iron/copper analysis of the samples. If the Florida monster was a vertebrate, its blood would contain haemoglobin, a protein made with iron. If it was an invertebrate, its blood would contain haemocyanin, made with copper.

Roy Mackal gave me some samples in 1984 at the 3rd Congress of the International Society of Cryptozoology in Paris. Paul Rancurel, a biologist at the University of Aix-Marseille, made the analyses under my direction, and the results have been published by Mackal in *Cryptozoology* in 1986:

Sample	Weight (mg)	Cu (ppm)	Fe (ppm)	Cu/Fe
1M	12.8	300	1600	0.19
2M	29.1	60	200	0.30
4M	5.6	240	560	0.43
6M	10.5	330	470	0.70

(concentrations in parts per million).

1M has a very low ratio (0.19) of copper/iron (Cu/Fe), signifying a vertebrate: it comes from a dolphin. 4M has a relatively high ratio of Cu/Fe (0.43): it comes from an *Architeuthis*. 6M has a still higher ratio of Cu/Fe (0.70), but it comes from a cetacean: it may be due to a difference of solubility in the storage solvent.

2M (*Octopus giganteus*) has a high ratio of Cu/Fe (0.30), consistent with an invertebrate, but the result of 6M should make us cautious.

I have proposed three other tests allowing a precise identification:
1) an electrophoresis of the collagen, compared with known collagens.

2) decoding the sequence of amino-acids of the collagen, compared with known collagens.

3) an immunological test: a collagen solution is injected into a rabbit, which will make antibodies against the monster's collagen. The rabbit's plasma is tested with known collagens through radio-immuno assay (RIA). One would expect the following result:

Vertebrates	Squids	Octopuses
− <<———————————————————>> +

| weak reactivity | high reactivity |

Until these tests are made, I remain convinced that the Florida monster was a giant octopus.

SIGHTINGS IN THE WESTERN ATLANTIC

Where do these giant octopuses live? Prof. Verrill proposed a habitat in the *New York Herald* of 14 February 1897: "Its habitat is probably the broad plateau that extends about 200 miles off the coasts of South Carolina, Georgia and North Florida ... "

This opinion was based on accounts from whalers who had there observed harpooned sperm whales vomiting huge fragments of the arms of cephalopods, with suckers "as large as dinner plates", but they may have come from giant squids rather than octopuses.

F.G. Wood, in his *Natural History* article of March 1971, suggested that these giant octopuses are living off the Bahamas Islands. In 1956, he was at West End, Grand Bahama Island, with a fishing guide named Duke. One day, Wood remembered vague rumours about 'giant scuttles' he had heard in 1950-1951, while working at the Lerner Marine Laboratory in Bimini, Bahamas:

Scuttle is the Bahamian word for octopus - perhaps a felicitous blending of cuttle and a descriptive term for the manner in which octopuses slither across the bottom.

This explanation is quite likely, but one should notice that the word recalls the verb to scuttle, possibly alluding to the attacks on boats by these monsters.

I asked Duke if he had ever heard of giant scuttles around West End. Not surprisingly, he said that he had; then he proceeded to tell me when, where, and by whom they had been seen.

Duke added that the arms of these creatures were 75 feet (23 m) long, that they came into shallow waters if sick or dying, and that they are dangerous to fishermen if they can reach the surface with one arm, while being anchored to the bottom with another. This is true: octopuses are almost harmless when they are not fixed on the sea-bottom.

Wood also asked the Island Commissioner of Grand Bahama, who related his own account. When he was about twelve (c.1925-1930), he was fishing off Andros Island with his father and another man, above 600 feet (180 m) of water:

His father had hooked something - the bottom, he thought at first. The line could be drawn up, but slowly, as if it were hauling up a large object. When the end of the line came in sight, still many feet away in the clear Caribbean water, they could see a very large octopus clinging to it. Detaching itself from the hook, the octopus came up and attached itself to the bottom of their boat, but finally the octopus released its hold and disappeared into the depths.

This incident illustrates what Duke said: this giant octopus could not reach the bottom while touching the boat, so it was less dangerous than its size would suggest.

Gary S. Mangiacopra defended this hypothesis of a Bahamian habitat in several articles published in 1975-1977, in *Of Sea and Shore*. He also noted that the Florida current might bring the cadaver of a giant octopus from the western Bahamas to St. Augustine.

Gary Mangiacopra also suggested that *Octopus giganteus* might live on the coast of Florida itself. Apart from the stranding of 1896, Gary unearthed a clipping from the *New Haven Evening Register* of 22 February 1897, about the fight of judge Theodore Tuttle of New Haven (Connecticut) against a 'huge octopus' off Palm Beach, Florida:

Suddenly, a long quivering tentacle reached up over the side of the boat and atached [sic] itself to his hand. Seizing a hatchet, he severed it. Another shot up beside the first one, and then another over the stern of the boat and two or three by the side. The judge dealt many blows, severing the tentacles as fast as he could.

One caught him around the neck and another around his right arm. Shifting the hatchet to the other hand, the judge managed to cut them both. Then the creature itself appeared, and several other tentacles.

The judge grabbed a fish knife, and plunged it into the monster, and then struck the head several times with the hachet.

The octopus finally succumbed and sank and the judge rowed to the shore, suffering acute pain where the tentacles had touched him. Lotions were applied, and after a few hours he had recovered.

Squid suckers have a kind of teeth, unlike that of octopuses, which could explain this 'acute pain'. But it is also possible that this remark refers to an allergy. Could it be a jellyfish, rather than an octopus? This would explain the numerous tentacles of this monster, which seem to be reborn as soon as cut, like those of the Lernaean Hydra. It should perhaps be emphasized that the newspaper was influenced by the Florida monster, which was mentioned at the end of the article:

A huge forty-foot [12 m] octopus was thrown up on the beach near St. Augustine a few weeks ago and several small ones were seen here lately, but this is the first instance ever known of any one being atacked [sic].

The story of the Florida monster, the size of which was exaggerated, had been related by Alpheus Hyatt Verrill in the same newspaper only eight days earlier: it was 'natural' to refer all the sea monsters reported in this area at the same time to the same creature.

Two alleged 'sightings' located in the same area were reported in the American tabloid *National Examiner* of 5 January 1993. Jean-Louis LaRocque, of Port-au-Prince (Haiti), who escaped from the Haitian dictatorship with 14 other refugees, said that his 17 foot (5.10 m) boat had been overturned by a giant octopus:

Then its tentacles latched onto me, and I could feel its powerful, fleshy suckers trying to pull the skin off my back.

All his friends died in this drama, and only LaRocque was rescued by a tanker.

A diver from Cocoa Beach (Florida), Danny Boerwinkle, explored a wrecked ship in 90 feet (30 m) of water, when he saw a giant octopus. He tried to photograph it, but the flash made the animal furious:

The monster changed colour from a light brown to an irridescent green. Then, he blasted me with an incredibly powerful jet of smelly ink that tore my camera from my hands.

Treasure hunter lieutenant Harry E. Rieseberg described a fight against a giant octopus in the popular magazine *Mechanix Illustrated* of February 1939:

An observation bell with one occupant was lowered 20 fathoms to the bottom of the sea during a treasure hunt 100 miles off the northern coast of Haiti. As the bell reached bottom, a giant 24 foot octopus [7.30 m] was seen crawling along a cleft in the coral reef ...

Rieseberg cut two arms with the snipes of its diving robot.

The grey repulsive mass with its 10 ft [3 m] long snaky arms flayed the water as it swam to meet the invader in its lair. The octopus looked like a gigantic tarantula, circled like a boxer, crouched on its 8 arms ... and lunged at the bell. It struck with terrific force!

Slowly dying after two tentacles had been severed by the steel claws of the robot, the octopus writhed and spewed its defensive fluid to make the water inky black ... Bubbles swirled upward as the sea-dragon died.

100 miles north of Haiti are the Caicos Islands, south east of the Bahamas: why does Rieseberg not say so? The attitude of the octopus, erect on its arms like a spider, is ridiculous. Last but not least, we may recall that an octopus has no lungs (it breathes through branchiae), so it cannot emit bubbles - unless it is nothing else than a balloon, which the photographs confirm!

Captain Jacques-Yves Cousteau speaks in his book *Pieuvres, la fin d'un malentendu* (1973) of incidents which took place off the Bahamas:

> Between Florida and the Bahamas, in the Gulf Stream, fishermen reported having their lines broken by an enormous animal which, when sighted, resembled a squid. Incidents of this kind were so numerous and well attested that an expedition was organized. Its purpose was to photograph the animal in question and, for this, a flash camera was attached to a line in such a way as to be activated by traction. The animal was, in fact, hooked on the line and broke it. When the camera was recovered, it was found that shots had been taken at 300 and 600 feet [90-180 m], but they showed only an indefinable stretch of brown flesh.

As it "resembled a squid", it might also have been an octopus. Gary Mangiacopra was able to find another mention of these incidents in the April 1964 issue of *Fate*, in an article by Curtis Fuller:

> A gigantic something is lurking in deep water near Bimini, Bahamas. It has been suggested that it's a giant squid or a prehistoric form of shark. That's quite a spread, but many fishermen have seen it. One said it has brown and black and brownish-yellow spots.

Burton Clark, director of the Miami Seaquarium, who made an expedition off Bimini in Spring 1964, gave more details to Gary Mangiacopra:

> Dr Herald [in fact Harold] Edgerton, of the Massachussets Institute of Technology, provided a sophisticated submergible camera with strobe lights which could be activated by any creature taking the bait ... Using a sophisticated straightline fathometer, we did determine that at a depth of approximately 1000 feet [300 m] there was indeed some large creature that showed up clearly on the fathometer trace paper.

> ... Speculation is that it is probably a giant squid or perhaps even a giant shark. There are those who claim to have hooked such a creature, usually at night when it was not possible to determine exactly what they had been able to hook.

Dr. Harold Edgerton did not possess the photographs taken during this expedition; and Curtis Fuller did not keep the articles he referred to in his 1964 paper for *Fate*.

The brown and yellow spots of the monster are consistent with the skin of an octopus: in the giant squid *Architeuthis*, it is red, and the sole spotted giant fish is the whale shark (*Rhineodon typus*), a plankton feeder which can be ruled out as far as these incidents are concerned.

There is another allusion in an article by Roy Mackal, published in 1967 in *Oceanology International*, which he curiously failed to mention in his book *Searching for Hidden Animals* (1980), where a chapter is devoted to *Octopus giganteus* Verrill:

> In 1963 and 1964, the famous charter boat skipper Tommy Gifford had several ... experiences off Bimini, in the Bahamas. Using a heavy cable as a line and a series of specially-made giant steel hooks, Gifford latched onto several deep-sea 'monsters' that towed his 40 ft [12 m] boat for hours against the full power of his engines. On one occasion, Gifford's steel 'fishing line' was bitten clean in two.

These lines had been added to Mackal's article by the magazine. Swimming for hours is the behaviour of a pelagic animal, such as a giant squid or a great white shark, rather than an octopus, unless it is a very peculiar octopus...

That this animal might have been an octopus seems to be confirmed by the following report, from the *New Haven Journal and Courier* of 4 February 1880. The crew of captain Léon Saint-Marie's fishing boat *Rinaldo* was trying to salvage cotton from a wrecked ship off Galveston (Texas). Suddenly, its boat was towed by a sea monster for 3 miles:

> The captain expresses the positive opinion that it was nothing more or less than a devil-fish, and says that he is perfectly familiar with the creature and its habits, having met it frequently in the vicinity of Nassau, in the island of New Providence [in the Bahamas], off the Capes of

Florida, and in the Caribbean, but says that he has before never known of any in the vicinity, except small ones ...

Bahamas comes from the Spanish *baja mar*, which means 'shallow sea', which alludes to a vast limestone plateau at a depth of some feet. This plateau contains thousands of caverns and circular openings called blue holes. Having explored several blue holes off Andros in 1970, captain Cousteau writes in his book *Trois aventures de la Calypso* (1973):

> There are many fishes in them, and the natives are usually willing to use their boats at the holes; but they refuse under any condition to dive. They believe that the holes - which they consider to be 'bottomless' - are inhabited by monsters; by evil spirits, known as *lusca*, which are always ready to drag men and their boats down into the bowels of the earth. These monsters resemble giant octopuses; and, if pressed, a native is usually found who can tell the names of the latest victims to succumb to their voracious appetites for human flesh.

The *lusca* of Andros was the subject of a whole article by Bruce S. Wright, for *The Atlantic Advocate* in 1967. Wright was director of the North Eastern Wildlife Station, in New Brunswick (Canada). His native guide asserted that the *lusca* was living in an inland lake of Andros:

> The *lusca*, it seemed, was a large and dangerous beast that appeared from its description to be half octopus and half dragon.

The guide said that the *lusca* had long tentacles tipped with strong suckers. No freshwater cephalopod is known, but the lake communicated with the sea, as sharks and barracudas were found in it. Fluorescein colouration has shown that many blue holes make a true underwater network.

The discovery of skeletons in the inland lakes (called banana holes) was considered to be the remains of the food of the *lusca*. But these people could have died by many other means: hurricanes, pirates, etc. And if they had been eaten by a giant cephalopod, their bodies would have been broken into pieces by the beak of these creatures.

Bruce Wright then relates his own account: in 1947, his team of skin divers was near Nassau, New Providence Island:

> ... I had taken the whole unit out to see one of the most famous of all blue holes. It was the Great Hole in the Ocean, a huge vent in the sea floor 40 feet [12 m] in diameter in 30 feet [9 m] of water about two miles south of Rose Island. We had dived to the rim of the hole ... However, I forbade further descents when we saw schools of large jacks swim into the hole at our approach, but come boiling out in panic as if something much more deadly than ourselves was in the pitch blackness below.
>
> We had no lights and could see nothing, but several of us distinctly felt a strong swirl as if a jet of water was being forced out the hole as the jacks broke clear. On the ascent a remora came up to me and tried to stick to my leg. I showed him what my knife was for - remoras are rarely found far from large sea creatures.

The jet might be a natural phenomenon, but the escape of the jacks and the presence of a remora are fairly consistent with a large sea creature. Bruce Wright, now aware of the *lusca*, wondered if the jet was not made by a giant cephalopod moving by reaction.

Other accounts, also reported by Bruce Wright, come from the eastern coast of Andros, above a submarine canyon called The Tongue of the Ocean, where the depth reaches 5000 feet (1500 m). A diver of Small Hope Bay, Dick Birch, made a curious observation:

> A couple of years ago we had a sperm whale out there that was acting queerly. It was jumping and had something tangled about its head. There was something in the water beside it but we could not get close enough to see what it was.

This sperm whale was certainly eating a giant squid caught in the depths of the canyon, its head tangled in the arms of the mollusc: giant cephalopods found in the stomach of these cetaceans are always squids; if they also ate octopuses, they would be known to science! The reason is that they share the biotope of squids (they are pelagic).

A second sighting, which took place in the same area, might refer to an octopus, according to its native name:

> When we were trolling for dolphin beyond the reef the guide was asked if there were any octopuses thereabouts. He replied: "Just over there I found a big scuttle floating dead last year. My sport took pictures of it."

"How big?"

"I don't know for sure, but it was longer than this boat."

We were in an eighteen footer [5.50 m].

Bruce Wright then mentions a U.S. ship which, east of Andros, caught a giant squid after it had fought against a sperm whale. A fragment was examined by Dr Gilbert L. Voss, who identified it as an *Architeuthis*. This specimen is listed in Gerald L. Wood's *Guinness Book of Animal Facts and Feats*, which gave the year as 1966.

In fact, the capture was in 1958, and the animals eating the remains were sharks, not a sperm whale, as reported by Dr. Voss himself in an article for *Sea Frontiers*, August 1959. It was 47 feet (14.30 m) long, the largest one recorded in the 20th century. A fragment is kept in the Museum of Natural History in Vienna (Austria).

So, Bruce Wright and Dr Voss think that the *lusca* is a giant squid. Gerald L. Wood writes:

Although the so-called giant *scuttle* of the Bahamas is traditionally an immense octopod, Dr Voss says all of the sightings of large cephalopods in the Gulf Stream off Florida have been of the giant squid *Architeuthis*, which are quite common in the area, but are quickly eaten by the rather large shark population when they are disabled and brought to the surface. He also mentioned that the head and brachial crown of one individual collected off Bimini by a charter-boat skipper in the 1960s weighed approximately 500 lb [227 Kg] and must have come from a very big specimen.

Although, in the Tongue of the Ocean east of Andros, we are actually dealing with giant squids, the *lusca* is associated with the blue holes, a habitat of an octopus.

Bruce Wright was also involved in another sighting, not mentioned in his article. It is quoted in a book by Simon Welfare and John Fairley: *Arthur C. Clarke's Mysterious World* (1980) and occurred in 1964, when Wright saw a huge cadaver stranded on a reef off Caicos, south east of the Bahamas:

The wind was blowing right on to the shore and the boat would not land. We had no dinghy and the sight of a big barracuda just before we entered the discoloured water around the carcass discouraged swimming ashore. I observed and

photographed the carcass from our nearest approach which was about 20 yd (18 m). It was simply a cigar-shaped mass of flesh without any mouth, pectoral fins, tail flukes, eyes or a blowhole. It was over 50 ft [15 m] long and about 10 ft [3 m] in diameter.

And Welfare and Fairley added :

It was in the same area off the Florida coast that a seaman, J.C. Martin, at the end of the second world war says he saw an enormous octopus floating right beside his ship.

These accounts had been recorded for a TV series on the mysteries of the world (UFOs, Tunguska comet of 1908, Baghdad batteries, etc. - and cryptozoology). Simon Welfare never answered my inquiries, but I finally found an article by Bruce Wright in *Field and Stream*, December 1965, about his expedition to Caicos:

I asked if any large sperm whales were ever seen in the Caicos area. They are. As a matter of fact, a dead one had recently washed ashore over the northern fringing reef ... The whale lay on a rockbound windward shore, which could be reached only by wading. The water around the whale was a dull red and great swirls showed that it had company. I strongly advised against wading. We photographed the carcass from the boat at as short a range as possible, but we could not examine it in as great detail as I'd have liked. It was all of 70 feet [21 m] long, and the flukes had been removed by the sharks that were working on the whale.

The size (70 feet long, 10 feet in diameter), shape, and red colour of the water round the cadaver are consistent with a large sperm whale: cephalopods have a pale blue blood.

Later I learnt that Bruce Wright himself wrote to F.G. Wood after his 1971 article, and he let him know of his article on the *lusca* of Andros, which he now referred to as *Octopus giganteus*, and his observation of a cadaver off Caicos, for which he made the same linkage, this time wrongly.

Regarding the account of John C. Martin, who had retired from the U.S. Navy: he had also written to F.G. Wood in 1971 about his observation. Gerald L. Wood published a passage from this letter in the second edition of his *Guinness Book of Animal Facts and Feats* (1976):

In 1941 I was a coxswain in the first division aboard the *USS Chicopee* A0-41 ... The ship had departed Baton Rouge, Louisiana, with a cargo of aviation gasoline and fuel oil for Portland, Maine.

It was at the end of March or April that the ship was steaming off the coast of Florida in the general area of Fort Lauderdale and St. Augustine. Dead ahead of our course appeared something on the surface of the water that could not be readily described. The closer we approached it looked like a huge pile of brown kelp seaweed. As it hove into view there was no doubt as to its identity. The coils of its arms were looped up like huge coils of manila rope. However, the coils were over 36 inches [91 cm] in circumference ...

The creature measured an estimated 30 feet [9.14 m] in diameter and its arms seemed about equal length; coiled but moving slowly.

The 'coils' of the arms were 36 inches (91 cm) in circumference, i.e., 29 cm in diameter, the same order of magnitude as the arms of the Florida monster.

I wonder about the meaning of the 'diameter' of the creature, 30 feet (9 m) (Gerald L. Wood converts into metric units with an overprecision of 9.14 m). Certainly it is not the diameter of the body (it would be 6 times wider than that of the Florida monster). Even the length of the latter (20 feet, 6 m) is a third smaller than this 'diameter'. I rather think that Martin alludes to the umbrella.

The length of the coiled arms is difficult to estimate mentally, but a length of 30 feet (9 m) is consistent with that of 36 feet (11 m) given by Webb.

But let us come back to the *lusca* of Andros. George J. Benjamin, of Toronto (Canada), also recorded this tradition for *National Geographic* in September 1970. In the late 1950s, he was above a blue hole, and his guide told him:

"You go down dere and *lusca*, him of de hahnds, sure to catch you", he warned.

The *lusca*, he said, was a terrible creature, like a monstrous octopus or cuttlefish. If you ventured too close to a blue hole, the *lusca* would shoot its tentacles into your boat, and "once the hahnds get hold of you, you dead, mahn !" The holes, the man said, were full of skeletons of the *lusca's* victims.

"I remind de time one stop a two-master dead in de water. He wrap' all around de rudder, and wid de free hahnds he feelin' on deck. Once de hahnd feel a mahn, dey was a flunder in de water, and bot' mahn and *lusca* gone."

Only a few weeks earlier, he said, he had lost a boat and a new outboard motor to a *lusca*. The boat had drifted from its mooring, floated too close to this very blue hole, and the *lusca* had shot out its 'hahnds' and dragged it down.

Benjamin dived, and if he did not encounter the *lusca*, he did actually find the boat half embedded in the sand, in the blue hole.

Marine biologist Kathy Sellers, a member of a blue hole expedition, also heard of the *lusca*, called 'Him of the hairy hands', as reported by Colin Willock:

The Andros Islanders swore that this giant squid-like creature lived in the bottomless blue depths. He not only ate human beings, but had been known to drag down a three-masted schooner and crew.

The *lusca* is generally nicknamed 'Him of the hands', that is to say 'he who has arms', which recalls the French word *poulpe*, from the Greek *polypos*, 'many-footed'. But why 'hairy hands'?

Another biologist, Robert Palmer, also heard of the *lusca*, 'half octopus, half shark', in these words:

"De *lusca*, mahn, dat his hole. He drag our boat down theah. All th' conch, them crawfish, dey his'n now. We jus' lucky he doan' get us. Th' boat too, thas his now. That *lusca*, he bad, mahn!"

In a book called *Grand Bahama* (1972), P.H.J. Barratt describes another blue hole off this island, 10 miles north-east of Hawksbill Creek:

Many kinds of exotic marine life, real or imaginary, live in the hole, among them a giant squid, a patriarchal jewfish, a seacow and (personally observed) a 5 feet [1.50 m] long nurse shark.

Thus huge serranidae, 2 m (7 feet) long or more, are living in the tropical Western Atlantic; the 'seacow' is the manatee (*Trichechus sp.*). The 'giant squid' is again our giant octopus, because of its biotope.

According to Benjamin, Willock and Palmer, the *lusca* is nothing more than the whirlpool associated with the blue holes, but apart from the tradition of this tentacular monster, we also have circumstantial sightings off Andros (the one related by F.G. Wood, for instance). It would also be very strange that such a huge creature would be known only from sightings and not from tradition.

I thus think that the tradition of the *lusca* is a mythical version of the giant octopus *Octopus giganteus*, as the *kraken* of Scandinavian sailors was a mythical version of the giant squid *Architeuthis*.

Rumours about the existence of giant octopuses off the Bahamas are not recent. The oldest and most dramatic report I am aware of is the one related by a French journalist, Bénédict-Henri Révoil, in *Pêches dans l'Amérique du Nord* (1863):

> An American captain, who I knew very well in New York, told me that in 1836, while off the Lucayes Islands [=Bahamas], his ship had been attacked by a kraken which, spreading its gigantic arms, had seized and brought two men of his crew into the sea ...

An arm of the 'polyp' had been cut during the fight:

> This monstrous appendage was 3.50 m [11.5 feet] long and as big as a man. I saw this curious specimen of natural history in Mr. Barnum's Museum in New York, where it is kept, coiled, in a huge jar filled with alcohol.

It is likely that Jules Verne took his inspiration from this story for the passage in *20,000 Leagues Under the Sea*, where the *Nautilus* is attacked by giant cephalopods: the scene takes place off Lucayas, i.e., the Bahamas!

There may be a still earlier account, reported by Italian Pietro Martire d'Anghiera, the author of Columbus' biography. In his book *De orbe novo* (about 1500), he noticed that in the Caribbean islands, the animals were not dangerous to the Spaniards, but:

> One night, one of them was come on land and was sleeping on the sand, when a monster came out of the sea and took him away by the middle of his body, despite the presence of his friends, and came back to the sea with its prey, before this poor man who cried out could be helped.

This monster is not described, but it should be an octopus, the sole big marine animal, apart from pinnipeds (seals), which can venture on land. And this drama certainly took place in the Bahamas, explored by Columbus.

In 1872, the scientific magazine *American Naturalist* referred, under the title 'a colossal octopus', to a letter from a Mr J.S. George, of Nassau (New Providence Island, Bahamas):

> [It] mentions a huge octopus ten feet [3 m] long, each arm measuring five feet [1.50 m]; the weight was estimated at between two hundred and three hundred pounds [90 to 135 Kg]. The monster was found dead upon the beach, and bore marks of injury.

And Mr. George remarked:

> This is the first specimen I have seen during twenty-seven years residence in the Bahamas, but they are known here traditionally as being of immense size."

If a length of 10 feet (3 m) is not 'colossal', the weight (200 to 300 pounds, 90 to 135 Kg) is impressive: the official record for the common octopus (*Octopus vulgaris*) is a specimen also 3 m long, but which 'only' weighed 25 Kg.

This would lead us to think that Mr. George's estimate is much exaggerated, but the relative length of the arms vs body is also strange: 5 feet/10 feet, whereas in large octopuses (*O. vulgaris* and *O. dofleini* for instance), arms represent 4/5 or 5/6 of the total length. Bernard Heuvelmans suggested to me that the so-called 'length' might be the spread of the animal, that is to say an octopus '10 feet long, each arm measuring 5 feet', which is quite logical. But what about the weight? For if Heuvelmans is right, this specimen should weigh not even 25 Kg, but only about 10, and certainly not 90 to 135!

So, I suppose that the arms of this octopus were mutilated, as in the Florida monster: it indeed bore 'marks of injury'. This would explain not only the weight but the proportion of arms/body. We can even calculate the size of the living specimen:

{Length head + body} = 10 - 5 = 5 feet (1.50 m).

Total length = 5 or 6 x {length head + body} = 5 or 6 x 5 = 25 or 30 feet (7.50 to 9 m).

Length of the arms = 4 or 5 x {length head + body}, or total length - {length head + body} = 25 or 30 - 5 = 20 to 25 feet (6.10 to 7.60 m).

Spread = Length of the arms x 2 = 20 to 25 x 2 = 40 to 50 feet (12.20 to 15.20 m).

This spread is thrice that of the giant Pacific octopus, the largest known octopod. An octopus having half that spread (6.10 m), mentioned by McGinittie, weighed 50 Kg. The Nassau specimen, twice as long, would be 2 cubed = 8 times heavier, or 50 x (12.20/6.10) cubed = 50 x 8 = 400 Kg in weight! Mr. George's estimate - 90 to 135 Kg for the mutilated animal - was thus very likely.

French naturalist Roland Heu let me know of another account in a letter to me of 25 June 1982:

> I have read an article, certainly in the early 1950s, in a magazine which might be *Paris Match*, but I cannot assert it; the author described his diving, I believe in the Antillas, but perhaps in the Bahamas. My memory is not accurate, but I am sure that he used the expression 'as big as lorries' to speak of the octopuses he had observed. This article was illustrated by a number of vague and unconvincing photographs due to the lack of comparison with known objects, but ... I remember that the author did not depict these animals as frightening, he did not seem to consider them very dangerous and he explained the bad quality of his photographs by these cephalopods' tendency to escape.

Despite my investigations, I have not found the article in question. Many lorries weigh 13 tons, close to the estimate of 18 tons for the living specimen of St. Augustine according to Prof. Verrill.

One might notice that the famous Bermuda Triangle covers the Bahamas (supposed habitat of these giant octopuses), and Florida (stranded monster of 1896). The craziest ideas have been proposed on this subject to explain why boats have disappeared in this area, including some from Ivan T. Sanderson, one of the pioneers, with Bernard Heuvelmans, of cryptozoological research: abductions by Extraterrestrials from their 'flying saucers', parallel worlds and space-time, Atlantis survivals, and so on. In fact, Lawrence David Kusche showed in 1976 that most incidents occurred in a strong storm, and remains of the boats have been always found later.

Looking through the literature on the Bermuda Triangle, I found some interesting reports. In his book *Without a Trace* (1977), Charles Berlitz writes that in 1968, off Great Isaac (west of the Bahamas), a photographer named Bruce Mounier saw an 'underwater abominable snowman'! I would not mention this report if Berlitz had not added:

> According to Mounier the creature then made for a cave ... perhaps a fortunate circumstance for Mounier in the light of a Bahamian legend concerning such a monster, called the *luska*, with a face like an animal's and a neck like a snake's, living in sea caves and feeding off human divers.

Berlitz alludes to the *lusca* under the name of *luska*. His information come from Dr J. Manson Valentine, of Miami, who wrote to me on 11 April 1982:

> The *luscas* live in caves in the sea but emerge to do their dirty work at night.

It appears that Berlitz mixed Bruce Mounier's 'sighting' and the native tradition of the 'luska'. The "neck like a snake's" of the 'luska' may refer to the arms of the octopus (remember the 'long snaky arms" reported by Rieseberg).

The name *De Lucsa*, dialect for 'the lucsa', slightly different from the *lusca* used at Andros, is also found sometimes. In an article for *Saga*, July 1973, diver Bob Wallace recorded this tradition of *de lucsa* about a blue hole off Eleuthera. Wallace did not see any *lucsa*, but he could observe spiny lobster 4 feet (1.20 m) long, which is significant for our purpose...

Charles Berlitz mentions another report from a shark hunter, captain Joe Talley, off Caicos, south east of the Bahamas:

> We wanted to set deep water lines off the drop-off at Caicos. But the boys wouldn't stay after sundown. They said that some boats were taken right down by giant squids or something like that. The boats are small, about 25 feet [7.50 m] long, and a big thing can crawl aboard very easily. They said that a while ago a giant squid placed a tentacle on the gunnel of a boat and climbed aboard. The boys jumped off and the boat drifted out to sea.

Was it really a giant squid? Its behaviour was more consistent with an octopus. Octopuses can climb out of their aquariums, unlike squids (because of their hard internal 'feather': they are even unable to get back to sea when they have been thrown ashore).

Richard Winer, another writer on the Bermuda Triangle, made a strange observation in November 1969 off Bermuda, while diving in 4000 feet (1200 m) of water, which he relates in *The Devil's*

Triangle (1974):

It was late in the afternoon and the rough seas were distorting the light rays that penetrated into the depths ... How deep it was or its size I couldn't tell. It might have been 100 feet [30 m] beneath us - maybe 150 feet [45 m]. Its size I could only guess at - maybe 100 feet [30 m] across, possibly 75 [23 m], but no less than 50 feet [15 m] in diameter. It was perfectly round. Its colour was a deep purple. It was moving slowly up toward us. At its outer perimeter there was a form of pulsation, but there were no movements of water ...

Pat Boatwright, who was diving with Winer, thought it was a giant octopus, but Winer thought that it was a giant jellyfish, because of the similar movement.

The largest known jellyfish is *Cyanea capillata*, the floating dome of which can reach 3 m (10 feet) in diameter. A specimen found on the coast of Massachusetts and described by Prof. Agassiz in 1865 had tentacles 40 m (130 feet) long: impressive, but still insufficient. Did Winer observe a gigantic jellyfish? Gary Mangiacopra had no theoretical objection, and I agree with him on that point: in the seas, all zoological groups have giants (cetaceans, giant squids, whale sharks, etc.).

Observation conditions were not excellent, however, as noted by Winer himself. Moreover, the animal came from the depths, an even darker zone, and it was deep purple, a colour at the limit of the visible spectrum - or it seemed to be purple, due to the absorption of high wavelengths. The poor available light could not even be reflected by the sea bottom, 1200 m deeper. The dimensions reported by Winer are thus very hazardous.

I n 1984, incidents occurred off the Bermudas Islands, and they have been related in the Fall 1985 issue of *ISC Newsletter*, and by Michael Bright in *BBC Wildlife*.

Fisherman John P. 'Sean' Ingham was fishing for big Geryon crabs, when several crab traps of his 50 foot (15 m) long boat, the *Trilogy*, were lost about 30 miles off this archipelago, in depths of 3000 feet (900 m), after a considerable strain on the cable.

Dr Bennie A. Rohr, a biologist at the National Marine Fisheries in Pascagoula (Mississippi), suggested it was a giant octopus, which ate the Geryon crabs, a hypothesis shared by F.G. Wood.

On another occasion, Ingham could see on the chromoscope (a kind of sonar), "a pyramid shape approximately 50 feet [15 m] high" on the trap. The boat was towed by the animal at a speed of 1 knot, for several hundreds of yards.

In 1985, the same incident reoccurred, but this time Ingham could haul up the trap:

As the trap approached the surface he could see a large mass covering it. It appeared to him to be a very large cephalopod with what he described as tentacles wrapped around the trap.

He tried to hook it but the gaff kept on pulling through the tissue, and ripping it so that the parts fell off. When it was pulled just out of the water, it began to break up on the wire mesh. In the end he only managed to get a relatively small piece in a bucket. Everything else fell into the water.

Ingham was sure that it was an abyssal octopus, the spread of which he estimated at about 30 feet (9 m). Dr. Brian Luckhurst, senior fisheries officer of Bermuda, photographed this 'small piece' which, however, weighed 49 lb (22 Kg), and kept it in his freezer. Photographs were sent to the Smithsonian Institution in Washington, where scientists were unable to identify what it was.

In May 1988, the cadaver of a large unidentified marine animal was found on a beach of Mangrove Bay, Bermuda, by Teddy Tucker, a fisherman and diver. The thing was about 8 feet (2.40 m) long, rubbery, odourless, and very hard - which reminds one of the Florida monster.

Mr. Tucker kept a sample in formalin and took photographs which he sent to Dr Eugenie Clark, a shark expert. She showed them to Roy Mackal, Forrest G. Wood, Clyde Roper (cephalopod expert at the Smithsonian Institution), and James Mead (marine mammalogist at the same institution), who were unable to identify it. James Mead ruled out the possibility that it might come from a cetacean, as it was odourless.

Examination through the microscope, made by Jeffrey K. Taubenberger, of the U.S. National Institutes of Health in Bethesda (Maryland) did not show any cell structure, and he suggested that the sample was collagen. This was confirmed by an examination through an electronic microscope by Tim Maugel, of the department of zoology at the University of Maryland in College Park.

Dr Sydney K. Pierce, of the same department, analysed the amino-acids, and his conclusion is rather puzzling: the 'Bermuda blob', as it was nicknamed, comes from a poikilothermic vertebrate, i.e., a cold-blooded vertebrate, though Dr Pierce emphasizes that the amino-acid content might have been modified by the storage in formalin.

No known fish or reptile has a skin thick enough to possess such a mass of collagen. As I said about the Florida monster, the differences between collagens are not so marked as to be so accurate, particularly with a storage in formalin. That Tucker's 'blob' did not come from a marine mammal is very important, and until new tests are available, I would tend to think that it is a piece of a giant octopus.

Other reports were recorded in the 1950s north-east of Cuba by François Poli. In his book *Les requins se pêchent la nuit* (1957), he relates an incident which occurred at night, similar to those off Bimini in 1964. The fishermen's lines were broken by a huge marine animal, and a fisherman suggested that it might be a giant octopus. Another one, called Sanchez, related his own story:

> One day, he had hooked one, the tentacles of which measured "at least four metres" [13 feet] and he had the greatest difficulty getting rid of it, having realised that he could not kill such a monster and haul it up without overturning his boat.

François Poli also heard 'crazy stories', about much larger specimens:

> They spoke of giant octopuses of the Caribbean sea, the spread of which could reach about 15 metres [50 feet], able to drag down their six metre [20 feet] long boats, and even to seize a fisherman with one of their tentacles and to swallow him. These monsters never came to the surface, they said, except on certain nights of a full moon where they floated for some minutes in the dark, their phosphorescent eyes on the surface. These octopuses moved at the speed of a shark, attacked all that came close to their tentacles and feared only one ennemy: the sperm whale. They also mentioned the case of captured sperm whales which bore on their bodies marks of suckers as large as no-entry signs.

This is the fifth time that nocturnal activity is reported: on 'a certain night' an unidentified sea-monster killed a conquistador in c.1500. Burton Clark, referring to the incidents off Bimini in 1964, said: "there are those who claim to have hooked such a creature, usually at night". Dr J. Manson Valentine, on the *lusca* of Andros, wrote to me: "The *luscas* live in caves in the sea but emerge to do their dirty work at night". And captain Talley mentioned that Caicos natives refused to use their boats "after sundown", for fear of being attacked by giant cephalopods.

These nocturnal habits may be related to the quest for food. It should be remembered that spiny lobsters are also nocturnal, and we have reasons to think that the giant octopus feeds on benthic crustaceans. The luminous eyes might be photophors, often found in squids, but not in octopuses, as far as I know. As I said above, marks of injury on the flesh of sperm whales can only come from giant squids. By the way, as a no-entry sign is about 40 cm (15 inches) in diameter, the monsters involved were about 100 m long! I thus suppose that the Cuban fishermen mixed two different stories: the observation of giant octopuses and the marks on the skin of the sperm whales, wrongly attributed to the same creatures.

Another Cuban fisherman, Torial, reported stories of monsters off Mexico:

> They had a huge cylindrical body with yellow stripes and kinds of tentacles similar to that of octopuses.

Yucatan, in Central America, is similar to the Bahamas, with an immense limestone plateau in shallow waters, with a lot of caverns. The resemblance is not limited to geology, as the same species are found in both places: barracudas (*Sphyraena barracuda*), nurse sharks (*Ginglymostema cirratum*), etc., and spiny lobsters (*Panulirus argus*), which is significant if *Octopus giganteus* feeds on these crustaceans, as I have suggested in a letter to *Cryptozoology*. So, why not *Octopus giganteus*?

F.A. Mitchell-Hedges related a story of a giant octopus precisely off British Honduras (now Belize) in 1938. Two fishermen were missing and only their boat had been found near two islands, Water Cay and Range, separated by shallow water where a blue hole opened itself. Some days later, another fisherman, Gabriel, told Mitchell-Hedges that he had been attacked by a giant octopus in the same area: Gabriel struck the monster, which changed in shape and colour, with his harpoon: "He claimed that its tentacles were as big as his thigh."

This meant that the monster had a total spread of about 20 m!

I t is now the time to conclude. Let us take all the available reports. We can rule out the most obvious hoaxes : Harry E. Rieseberg's one and Bruce Mounier's abominable sea man off Bimini, 1968, associated to the 'luska' by Berlitz. I would not buy Jean-Louis LaRocque's and Danny Boerwinckle's sightings off Florida in 1993, reported by the *National Examiner*, which smell fishy rather than having a whiff of octopus.

We can also rule out the misidentifications: the observation made by Dick Birch off Andros (a giant squid most probably) and the stranded cadaver of Caicos in 1964 (a sperm whale). The 'huge octopus' attacking judge Theodore Tuttle off Palm Beach in 1897 might have been a giant squid or jellyfish, accounting for the 'acute pain' felt where the tentacles had touched him.

Even so, we still have a number of reports allowing us to draw the following identikit picture. The specimen from St. Augustine had a body about 20 feet (6 m) long. Bruce Wright's guide saw a *scuttle* off Andros more than 18 feet (5.50 m) long. John C. Martin mentions a 'diameter' of 30 feet (9 m), which might apply to the umbrella, on a specimen floating dead off Florida. John Ingham speaks of 'a spread' of 30 feet (9 m).

The length of the arms is enormous: Dr Webb dug out a *stump* 36 feet (11 m) long. John Martin estimates their length as 30 feet (9 m), but on coiled arms. Duke claims that the arms of the giant *scuttles* of Bimini reach 75 feet (23 m). The arms would thus be about 4 times longer than the body + head, as in the largest known octopus, *Octopus dofleini* of the Pacific.

The arms were 10 inches (25 cm) thick at 36 feet (11 m) from the root in the Florida monster (one can estimate from the photographs that the thickness is about 36 cm at the base); 36 inches (91 cm) in circumference according to Martin, i.e., 29 cm in diameter; as big as Gabriel's thigh (20 cm ?); as big as a man's body according to an American captain

quoted by Révoil.

There is no detail on the suckers. First-hand witnesses (John Martin for instance) do not speak of them. Webb did not notice them on the Florida specimen, and on the photographs there is no evidence that they might have been present. The only allusion is that of Bruce Wright's guide, who said that the *lusca* had "long tentacles tipped with strong suckers". This would explain their absence on the arms of the Florida monster, as only stumps remained, and that they remained unnoticed in living specimens.

According to the Andros tradition, these creatures have 'hairy hands' (read: arms covered with 'hairs').

The weight would be 5 to 7 tons for the Florida remains, and probably about 20 tons for the living specimen. One also hears of octopuses "as big as lorries".

The St. Augustine specimen was pale pink, but it was probably depigmented. The skin would be brownish, as reported by Cousteau (mentioning photographs showing "an indefinable stretch of brown flesh"), Curtis Fuller (describing "brown and black and brownish-yellow spots"), Martin (comparing the animal with "a huge pile of brown kelp seaweed"), and even Torial (speaking of "yellow stripes").

Although it is not mentioned in the reports, it seems that the animal has lateral fins, as can be seen on the photographs of the Florida monster. They are certainly used for motion, apart from crawling and swimming through jet reaction.

In fact, the aspect of the animal seems rather disconcerting: Cousteau says that it "resembled a squid". About the *lusca*, he says that "these monsters resemble giant octopuses". Captain Talley speaks of "giant squids or something like that" off Caicos. George J. Benjamin describes the *lusca* as "like a monstrous octopus or cuttlefish" and Colin Willock, as a "giant squid-like creature". The explanation of these strange descriptions is that the giant octopus, rather than being a 'simple' huge *Octopus*, is a gigantic cirrate octopod.

So we can explain the presence of lateral fins, which increase the resemblance with giant squids (even if the latter have one single fin at the posterior end of the body), and the mention of 'hairy hands', which alludes to the fringes of cirri of the ciliated octopuses, which indeed look like hairs.

This hypothesis of a species related to *Cirroteuthis* was first suggested by Prof. Verrill, for the Florida monster. I came to the same conclusion in 1986, and consequently the scientific name of *Octopus giganteus* proposed by Verrill in 1896 should be changed, as the Florida monster did not belong to the genus *Octopus*. I thus proposed to change the generic name of *Octopus* into *Otoctopus (gen. nov.)*, from the Greek *oton*, 'ear', the lateral fins making one think of such organs in many cirrates. The name of the species is therefore *Otoctopus giganteus*, which I described in an article for *Le Clin d'Oeil* in 1987.

My hypothesis has since been summarized by Heuvelmans in his checklist of the 140 animals relevant to cryptozoology (*Cryptozoology*, 1986) and by Franco Tassi in the magazine *Orsa* in 1989, and finally by Michel Dethier and myself in 1991, in the *Bulletin de la Société Neuchâteloise des Sciences Naturelles*; but this is the first time that most of the data are published and commented on.

T he species ranges from Caicos to the Western Bahamas and southwards to Yucatan. Its presence on the coasts of Florida is not certain: the Florida monster and the dying specimen observed by John Martin might come from the Bahamas, drifted by the Florida current. Though F.G. Wood suggested an abyssal habitat (at the base of the canyons west of Bimini and east of Andros), it appears that they live at less than 300 m (1000 feet), as shown by the tradition of the *lusca* (associated with the blue holes), the reports by Cousteau, Burton Clark, one of F.G. Wood's informants, etc.

They defend their lair, from which they go out mainly at night: it seems that the animal is searching for food, certainly spiny lobsters (*Panulirus argus*), but also clams, fishes ... or sometimes fishermen! Bioluminescent organs have been reported on one occasion: if they really exist, they would take a part in attracting the prey.

These creatures are known to the Bahamian fishermen as *lusca* (or *lucsa*), or giant *scuttles. Scuttle*, which comes from cuttlefish, sounds like the verb to scuttle, which might allude to the attacks on boats sometimes said to be made by these monsters.

Several other reports come from the Bermudas: Winer's so-called giant jellyfish in 1968; a huge mass of collagen found in 1988, which looks like the Florida monster; and incidents where John Ingham in 1984-1985 lost several crab traps at a depth of 3000 feet (900 m) to a huge octopus 30 feet (9 m) in spread, of which he could take a large gelatinous piece.

This animal is living off a volcanic archipelago at abyssal depths, separated from the limestone plateau of the Bahamas by depths of 3000 m or more (10,000 feet).

The gelatinous aspect, noticed by Ingham, increases the resemblance to a jellyfish. Richard Winer was mystified by the pulsating mass, a behaviour found not only in jellyfishes but also in some cirrate octopods.

It seems to be a distinct form, which I propose to name *Otoctopus giganteus inghami (subsp. nov.)* in Ingham's honour. If it is a new species, it would be *Otoctopus inghami (sp. nov.)*, and if it is a new genus, I propose *Geryonoctopus inghami (gen. nov.)*.

As a conclusion, I would like to suggest additional tests on the remaining samples, indepth research in old archives and field investigations in the Bahamas, Yucatan and Bermudas. It took several centuries before the giant squid *Architeuthis* was accepted by science, despite remains having been kept in museums since the 17th century. Let us hope that the giant octopus, about which the controversy has lasted about 100 years, will be recognized more rapidly...

BIBLIOGRAPHY

*** : 'Among scientists' (*The Tatler*, St. Augustine, Vol.6 [no. 1], 16 January 1897, p.19; no. 2, 23 January 1897, p.7; no. 9, 13 March 1897, p.7).

*** : 'Annual report of the Board of Regents of the Smithsonian Institution, showing the operations, expenditures, and condition of the Institution for the year ending June 30, 1897' (*Report of the U.S. National Museum, Part 1, 1899, pp.22, 47, Washington, Government Printing Office*).

*** : 'Battle with an octopus' (*New Haven Evening Register*, 22 February 1897, p.7).

*** : 'Bermuda blob remains unidentified' (*ISC Newsletter*, Tucson, Vol. 7 [no. 3], Autumn 1988, pp.1-6).

*** : 'Big octopus on the beach' (*Florida Times-Union*, Jacksonville, 1 December 1896, p.3).

*** : 'Biology/Fisheries [ref. 71-4A-2252]' (*Oceanic Citation Journal*, La Jolla, Vol. 8 [no. 4], September 1971, p.31).

*** : 'Fish that are dangerous' (*The Washington Post*, 14 February 1909).

*** : 'Galveston fish story, A' (*New Haven Journal and Courier*, 4 February 1880, p.1).

*** : 'Giant octopus blamed for deep sea fishing disruptions' (*ISC Newsletter*, Tucson, Vol. 4 [no. 3], Autumn 1985, pp.1-6).

*** : 'La pieuvre géante sous le microscope' (*Sciences et Avenir*, Paris, no. 293, juillet 1971, p.605).

*** : 'Last of this sea serpent' (*New York Herald*, 2 December 1896, p.6).

*** : 'Monsters ahoy! - scientists on trail of giant sea creatures' (*National Examiner*, Boca Raton, 5 January 1993, p.39).

*** : 'Not classified yet' (*The Daily Herald*, St. Augustine, 18 [?] January 1897).

*** : 'Scientists say sea creature of 1896 was Monster Octopus' (*New Haven Journal and Courier*, 10 April 1971, p.23).

*** : 'Sea monster that came on the Florida coast, The' (*Pennsylvania Grit*, Williamsport, 13 December 1896).

*** : 'Was not an octopus' (*New Haven Evening Register*, 24 February 1897, p.1).

ALFAYA (Andrés): *Le Triangle des Perturbations* (Paris, Robert Laffont, 1981) [pp.75-80].

BARLOY (Jean-Jacques): *Les Survivants de l'Ombre* (Paris, Arthaud, 1985) [pp.67-74].

BARRATT (P.H.J.): *Grand Bahama* (London, David and Charles Ltd, 1972) [p.25].

BARTSCH (Paul): 'Sea Serpent season brings new crop of incredibilities' (*Science News Letter*, Washington, 26 June 1937, p.403).

BENJAMIN (George J.): 'Diving into the blue holes of the Bahamas' (*National Geographic*, Washington, Vol. 138 [no. 3], September 1970, pp.346-363).

BERLITZ (Charles): *Without a Trace* (New York, Doubleday and Co, 1977).

BLEAKNEY (J. Sherman): 'Gennaro's funny foot' (*Natural History*, New York, Vol. 80 [no. 7], August-September 1971, p.12).

BRADLEY (Kim): 'Monster from deep - Huge octopus washed ashore nearly century ago' (undated).

BRIGHT (Michael): 'The big blob, or what grabbed the crab traps?' (*BBC Wildlife*, Bristol, Vol. 3 [no. 9], September 1985, pp.431-433).

BRIGHT (Michael): *There are Giants in the Sea* (London, Robson, 1989) [pp.120-139].

CLARK (James C.): 'The legendary giant octopus resurfaces' (*Orlando Sentinel*, 6 September 1991, pp.1, 7).

CLARK (James C.): 'Was it a 5-ton octopus? The facts remain inky' (*Constitution*, Atlanta, 15 September 1991).

CLARKE (Arthur C.): *The Challenge of the Sea* (New York, Holt, Rinehart and Winston, 1960) [pp.120-121].

CLARKE (Arthur C.): *The Ghost from the Grand Banks* (London, Victor Gollancz Ltd., 1990).

COUSTEAU (Jacques-Yves) & DOLÉ (Philippe): *Pieuvres, la fin d'un malentendu* (Paris, Flammarion, 1973) [pp.216-217].

COUSTEAU (Jacques-Yves) & DOLÉ (Philippe): *Trois aventures de la Calypso* (Paris, Flammarion, 1973) [pp.167, 215-216].

DENYS de MONTFORT (Pierre): *Histoire naturelle des mollusques*, in BUFFON: *Histoire naturelle générale et particulière* (Paris, Dufart, 1801) [Mollusques, Vol. 2, pp.256-412].

FANNING (James): 'A Touch of Humour' (*Natural History*, New York, Vol. 80 [no. 5], May 1971, p.92).

FORT (Charles Hoy): *Lo!* in *The Books of Charles Fort* (New York, Henry Holt & Co., 1941) [pp.619-620].

FULLER (Curtis): 'A word on monsters' (*Fate*, Evanston, April 1964, pp.24-25).

GENNARO Jr. (Joseph F.): 'The creature revealed' (*Natural History*, New York, Vol. 80 [no. 3], March 1971, pp.24, 84).

GENNARO Jr. (Joseph F.): 'Octopus giganteus, largest creature in the world?' (*Argosy*, New York, Vol. 376 [no. 3], March 1973, pp.30-32).

GNAEGY (Charles): 'Deadly mystery of the Bahama Blue Holes' (*Saga*, New York, July 1973, pp.10, 12-13, 72, 74-76).

GREENWELL (J. Richard):

'Interview' (*ISC Newsletter*, Tucson, Vol. 2 [no. 1], Spring 1983, pp.1-5).

GREENWELL (J. Richard): 'The Bermuda Blob' (*BBC Wildlife*, Bristol, Vol. 2 [no. 8], August 1993, p.33).

HEU (Roland): personal correspondence, 25 June 1982.

HEUVELMANS (Bernard): *Dans le Sillage des Monstres Marins - Le Kraken et le Poulpe Colossal* (Paris, Plon, 1958; Geneva, Famot-Beauval, 1974).

HEUVELMANS (Bernard): 'Annotated checklist of apparently unknown animals with which cryptozoology is concerned' (*Cryptozoology*, Tucson, Vol. 5, 1986, pp.1-26).

KEEL (John A.): *Strange creatures from Time and Space* (Greenwich, Fawcett Gold Medal Pub., 1970) [p.249].

LUCAS (Frederic Augustus): 'The Florida monster' (*Science*, Lancaster, Vol. 5 [no. 116], 19 March 1897, p.476).

LUCAS (Frederic Augustus): 'Some mistakes of scientists' (*Natural History*, New York, Vol. 28 [no. 2], March-April 1928, pp.169-174).

MACKAL (Roy P.): 'Sea-serpents and the Loch Ness Monster' (*Oceanology International*, Beverly Shores, Vol. 2 [no. 6], September-October 1967, pp.38-44) [p.39].

MACKAL (Roy P.): *Searching for Hidden Animals* (Garden City, Doubleday & Co., 1980) [pp.33-49].

MACKAL (Roy P.): 'Biochemical analyses of preserved *Octopus giganteus* tissue' (*Cryptozoology*, Tucson, Vol. 5, 1986, pp.55-62).

MANGIACOPRA (Gary S.):

'Octopus giganteus VERRILL: a new species of cephalopod' (*Of Sea and Shore*, Port Gamble, Vol. 6 [no. 1], Spring 1975, pp.3-10, 51-52).

MANGIACOPRA (Gary S.): 'Monster on the Florida beach' [Parts 1 & 2] (*INFO Journal*, Arlington, [Part 1]: Vol. 5 [no. 1] (whole no. 17), May 1976, pp.2-6. [Part 2]: Vol. 5 [no. 2] (whole no. 18), July 1976, pp.2-6).

MANGIACOPRA (Gary S.): 'The Great Ones' (*Of Sea and Shore*, Port Gamble, Vol. 7, [no. 2], Summer 1976, pp.93-96).

MANGIACOPRA (Gary S.): 'A monstrous jellyfish' (*ibid.*, Vol. 7 [no. 3], Fall 1976, p.169).

MANGIACOPRA (Gary S.): 'More on *Octopus giganteus*' (*ibid.*, Vol. 8 [no. 3], Fall 1977, pp.174, 178).

MANGIACOPRA (Gary S.), RAYNAL (Michel), SMITH (Dwight G.) & AVERY (David F.): 'Update on *Octopus giganteus* Verrill' (*Of Sea and Shore*, Port Gamble, in preparation).

MARTIRE D'ANGHIERA (Pietro): *De Orbo Novo, les huit décades* (Paris, Ernest Leroux, 1907) [pp.127-128].

MITCHELL-HEDGES (F.A.): *Battles with Giant Fish* (London, Duckworth, 1923).

MITCHELL-HEDGES (F.A.): *Mes combats avec les monstres marins* (Paris, Payot, 1938) [pp.120-125].

MOFFITT (Donald): 'A 200-foot octopus washed up in Florida, two scientists claim' (*Wall Street Journal*, New York, Vol. 177 [no. 68], 8 April 1971, pp.1, 33).

PALMER (Robert): *The Blue Holes of the Bahamas* (London, Jonathan Cape, 1985).

PALMER (Rob): 'Ecology beneath the Bahama bank' (*New Scientist*, London, Vol. 111 [no. 1507], 8 May 1986, pp.44-48).

PALMER (Rob): 'In the lair of the *lusca*' (*Natural History*, New York, Vol. 96 [no. 1], January 1987, pp.42-47).

POLI (François): *Les requins se pêchent la nuit* (Paris, Presses Pocket, 1957) [pp.147-156].

PORTER (Willard H.): 'Sea serpents and ocean monsters' (*Oceans*, Menlo Park, Vol. 4 [no. 5], September-October 1971, pp.60-63).

RANCUREL (Paul): personal correspondence, 6 November 1985 and 22 May 1986.

RAYNAL (Michel): 'L'incroyable dossier des Pouples géants' (*Amazone*, Saint-Amour, no. 1, octobre 1982, pp.42-46).

RAYNAL (Michel): 'Poulpes géants: d'autres témoignages' (*ibid.*, no. 2, janvier 1983, pp.29-31).

RAYNAL (Michel): [letter to editor] (*ISC Newsletter*, Tucson, Vol. 2 [no. 4], Winter 1983, p.11).

RAYNAL (Michel): 'Le poulpe colossal des Caraïbes' (*Le Clin d'Oeil*, Nice, no. 16, 1987, pp.21-25).

RAYNAL (Michel): 'Properties of the collagen and the nature of the Florida monster' (*Cryptozoology*, Vol. 6, 1987, pp.129-130).

RAYNAL (Michel) & DE-THIER (Michel): 'Le "monstre de Floride" de 1896: cétacé ou poulpe colossal?' (*Bulletin de la Société Neuchâteloise des Sciences Naturelles*, Vol. 114, 1991, pp.105-115).

RÉVOIL (Bénédict-Henry):

Pêches dans l'Amerique du Nord (Paris, Hachette, 1863) [pp.240-241].

RIESEBERG (Harry E.): 'Octopus, terror of the deep' (*Mechanix Illustrated*, Vol. 21 [no. 4], February 1939, pp.42-44).

SCHOSSBERGER (Peter): 'Gennaro's funny foot' (*Natural History*, New York, Vol. 80 [no. 7], August-September, 1971, p.12).

SPALDING (Franck H.): 'The facts about Florida' (undated).

TASSI (Franco): 'La piovra gigante' (*L'Orsa*, Rome, Vol. 12 [no. 4], 1989, pp.22-25).

VALENTINE (J. Manson): personal correspondence, 22 April 1982.

VERNE (Jules): *20,000 Lieues sous les Mers* (Paris, Hetzel, 1870).

VERRILL (Addison Emery): 'Gigantic Octopus' (*New York Herald*, 3 January 1897, p.13).

VERRILL (Addison Emery): 'A gigantic cephalopod on the Florida coast' (*The American Journal of Science*, New Haven, Vol. 3 [no. 13], January 1897, p.79).

VERRILL (Addison Emery): 'Additional information concerning the giant cephalopod of Florida' (*ibid.*, no. 14, February 1897, pp.162-163).

VERRILL (Addison Emery): 'A sea monster off Florida coast' (*New York Herald*, 14 February 1897, p.5).

VERRILL (Addison Emery): 'What is this creature?' (*ibid.*, 7 March 1897, p.13).

VERRILL (Addison Emery): 'The Florida monster' (*Science*, Lancaster, Vol. 5 [no. 114], 5 March 1897, p.392).

VERRILL (Addison Emery): 'The Florida sea monster' (*ibid.*, [no. 116] 19 March 1897, p.476.

VERRILL (Addison Emery): 'The supposed great octopus of Florida: certainly not a cephalopod' (*The American Journal of Science*, New Haven, Vol. 3 [no. 16], April 1897, pp.355-356).

VERRILL (Addison Emery): 'The Florida sea-monster' (*The American Naturalist*, Salem, Vol. 31, April 1897, pp.304-307).

VERRILL (Alpheus Hyatt): 'Octopus for New Haven' (*New Haven Evening Register*, 14 February 1897).

VERRILL (Alpheus Hyatt): 'An octopus for Yale' (*The Hartford Daily Courant*, 18 February 1897, p.11).

VERRILL (Alpheus Hyatt): *The Ocean and its Mysteries* (New York, Duffield & Co., 1916) [pp.118-119].

VERRILL (Alpheus Hyatt): *The Strange Story of our Earth* (New York, Grosset & Dunlap, 1952) [pp.92-93].

VOSS (Gilbert L.): 'Hunting for sea monsters' (*Sea Frontiers*, Miami, Vol. 5 [no. 3], August 1959, pp.134-136).

WEBB (DeWitt): correspondence to DALL (letters dated early January, 17 + 18 January, 5 + 10 + 12 February, 17 March 1897).

WEBB (DeWitt): 'A large decapod' (*The Nautilus*, Vol. 10 [no. 9], January 1897, p.108).

WELFARE (Simon) & FAIR-LEY (John): *Arthur C. Clarke's Mysterious World* (London, Rainbird Publishing Group, 1980) [pp.74-76]

WILDER (B.G.): 'A colossal octopus' (*The American Naturalist*, Salem, Vol. 6, December 1872, p.772).

WILLIS, (Paul J.): 'An Octopus in the Hand' (*INFO Journal*, Arlington, Vol. 2 [no. 4] (whole no. 8), Winter-Spring 1972, pp.1-3).

WILLOCK (Colin): 'In search of the hairy-handed monster' (*TV Times*, London, 9-15 September 1972).

WINER (Richard): *The Devil's Triangle* (New York, Bantam Books, 1975) [pp.202-203].

WOOD (Forrest Glenn): 'St. Augustine six ton octopus' (*Mariner*, September 1957, p.4).

WOOD (Forrest Glenn): 'Stupifying colossus of the deep' (*Natural History*, Vol. 80 [no. 3], March 1971, pp.15-16, 18, 20-24).

WOOD (Forrest Glenn): 'In which Bahamian fishermen recount their adventures with the Beast' (*ibid.*, pp.84, 86-87).

WOOD (Gerald L.): *Guinness Book of Animal Facts and Feats* (Enfield, Guinness Superlatives Ltd., 2nd edition, 1976) [pp.208-211]; (3rd edition, 1982).

WRIGHT (Bruce S.): 'South to Caicos' (*Field and Stream*, New York, December 1965, pp.49-51, 86).

WRIGHT (Bruce S.): 'The lusca of Andros' (*The Atlantic Advocate*, Vol. 57, June 1967, pp.32-39).

A BELFRY OF CRYPTO-BATS.

Dr Karl P.N. Shuker.

A zoologist with a long-standing interest in the scientific study of unexplained animals, whose books include *Mystery Cats of the World* (1989), *Extraordinary Animals Worldwide* (1991) and *The Lost Ark* (1993), Dr Karl Shuker reviews several cryptozoological reports of mysterious bats from various parts of the world. Large or small, the animals that may lay behind the tales currently remain unknown to science.

From the earliest times, bats have always been viewed as creatures of mystery - as arcane and abstruse as the opaque shadows of night that animate so many of their kind. It is certainly true that during the past two centuries science has succeeded in brushing aside many cobwebs of longstanding confusion and credulity enveloping these winged wanderers, but there are a host of others still to be dealt with. Indeed, as disclosed in this article, there are certain sources of provocative (and scientifically inconvenient?) but little-known data on file that not only question the validity of several fondly-treasured tenets of traditional bat biology, but also provide startling evidence for the existence of several dramatic species of bat still awaiting formal zoological discovery.

THE 'AHOOL' AND THE 'OLITIAU' - OR, HOW BIG IS A BAT?

One evening in 1927, at around 11:30pm, naturalist Dr Ernst Bartels was in bed inside his thatched house close to the Tjidjenkol River in western Java, and lay listening to the surrounding forest's clamorous orchestra of nocturnal insects. Suddenly, a very different sound came winging to his ears, from directly overhead - a loud, clear, melodious cry that seemed to utter 'A-hool!'. A few moments later, but now from many yards further on, the cry came again - a single 'A-hool!'. Bartels snatched his torch up and ran out, in the direction of this distinctive sound. Less than 20 seconds later he heard it once more, for the third and last time - a final 'A-hool!' that floated back towards him from a considerable distance downstream. As he recalled many years later in a detailed account of this and similar events (*Fate*, July 1966), he was literally transfixed by what he had heard - not because he *didn't* know what it was, but rather because he *did!*

The son of an eminent zoologist, Dr Bartels had spent much of his childhood in western Java, and counted many of the local Sundanese people there as his close friends. Accordingly, he was privy to many strange legends and secret beliefs that were rarely voiced in the presence of other Westerners. Among these was the ardent native conviction that this region of the island harboured an enormous form of bat. Some of Bartels's Sundanese friends claimed to have spied it on rare occasions, and the descriptions that they gave were impressively consistent. Moreover, as he was later to discover, they also tallied with those given by various Westerners who had reputedly encountered this mysterious beast.

It was said to be the size of a one-year-old child; with gigantic wings spanning 11-12 feet; short, dark-grey fur; flattened forearms supporting its wings; large, black eyes; and a monkey-like head, with a flattish, man-like face. It was sometimes seen squatting on the forest floor, at which times its wings were closed, pressed up against its flanks; and, of particular interest, its feet appeared to point backwards. When Bartels questioned eyewitnesses as to its lifestyle and feeding preferences, he learnt that it was nocturnal, spending the days concealed in caves located behind or beneath waterfalls, but at night it would skim across rivers in search of large fishes upon which it fed, scooping them from underneath stones on the beds of the rivers. At one time, Bartels had suggested that perhaps the creature was not a bat but some type of bird, possibly a very large owl, but these opinions were greeted with great indignation and passionate denials by his friends, who assured him in no uncertain terms that they were well able to distinguish a bat from a bird! And as some were very experienced, famous hunters, he had little doubt concerning their

235

claims on this score.

Even so, the notion of a child-sized bat with a 12-foot wingspan seemed so outrageous that he still had great difficulty in convincing himself that there might be something more to it than native mythology and imagination - until, that is, the fateful evening arrived when he heard that unforgettable, thrice-emitted cry, because one of the features concerning the giant bat that all of his friends had stressed was that when flying over rivers in search of fishes this winged mystery beast sometimes gives voice to a penetrating, unmistakable cry, one that can be best rendered as 'A-hool! A-hool! A-hool!'!

Indeed, the creature itself is referred to by the natives as the *ahool*, on account of its readily recognisable call - totally unlike that of any other form of animal in Java, as Bartels himself was well aware.

Transformed thereafter from an *ahool* sceptic to a first-hand *ahool* 'earwitness', Bartels set about collecting details of other *ahool* encounters for documentation, and eventually news of his endeavours reached veteran cryptozoologist Ivan T. Sanderson, who became co-author of Bartels's above-cited *Fate* article.

The *ahool* was of especial interest to Sanderson, because he too had met with such a creature - but not in Java. Instead, he had been in the company of fellow naturalist Gerald Russell in the Assumbo Mountains of Cameroon, in western Africa, collecting zoological specimens during the Percy Sladen Expedition of 1932. As Sanderson recorded in his book *Animal Treasure* (1937), he and Russell had been wading down a river one evening in search of tortoises to add to their collection when, without any warning, a jet-black creature with gigantic wings and a flattened, monkey-like face flew directly towards him, its lower jaw hanging down and revealing itself to be unnervingly well-stocked with very large white teeth. Sanderson hastily ducked down into the water as this terrifying apparition skimmed overhead, then he and Russell fired several shots at it as it soared back into view, but the creature apparently escaped unscathed, wheeling swiftly out of range as its huge wings cut through the still air with a loud hissing sound. Within a few moments, their menacing visitor

had been engulfed by the all-encompassing shadows of the night, and did not return.

After comparing notes, Sanderson and Russell discovered that they had both estimated the creature's wingspan to be at least 12 feet (matching that of the *ahool*). When they informed the local hunters back at their camp of their experience, the hunters were petrified with fear - staying only as long as it took them to shriek 'olitiau!', before dashing away *en masse* in the direction furthest from the scene of the two naturalists' encounter! As Dr Bernard Heuvelmans commented in his own coverage of this incident, within his book *Les Derniers Dragons d'Afrique* (1978), 'olitiau' may refer to devils and demons in general rather than specifically to the beast spied by Sanderson and Russell, but as these etymological issues have yet to be fully resolved it currently serves as this unidentified creature's vernacular name.

Several authorities have boldly attempted to equate the *olitiau* with a pterodactyl, in preference to a giant bat. Interestingly, in parts of Zimbabwe and Zambia a creature supposedly exists whose description vividly recalls those long-extinct flying reptilians. It is known to the natives as the *kongamato*, and has been likened by them to a small crocodile with featherless, bat-like wings - a novel but apt description of a pterodactyl!

In the case of the *olitiau*, however, Sanderson remained adamant that it was most definitely a bat of some kind, albeit one of immense dimensions - which is why he was so interested by Bartels's account of the *ahool*, which indicated that undiscovered giant bats were by no means limited to Africa. In fact, it is now known that similar animals have also been reported from such disparate areas of the world as Vietnam, Samoa, and Madagascar - this last-mentioned country's version is known as the *fangalabolo* ('hair-snatcher'), named after its alleged tendency to dive upon unsuspecting humans and tear their hair (a belief reminiscent of the Western superstition that bats can become entangled in a person's hair).

If giant bats do exist, how much bigger are they than known species, and to which type(s) of bat could they be related? The answer to the first of these questions is simple, if startling. The largest living species of bat whose existence is formally recognised by science is the Bismark flying fox *Pteropus neohibernicus*, a fruit bat native to New Guinea and the Bismark Archipelago; it has a total wingspan of 5½-6 feet. Assuming that eyewitness estimates for the wingspan of the *ahool* and the *olitiau* are accurate, then both of these latter creatures (if one day discovered) would double this record. The question of their taxonomic identity is a rather more involved issue.

Known scientifically as chiropterans ('hand-wings' - the greater portion of their wings are membranes of skin extending over their enormously elongated fingers), the bats are traditionally split into two fundamental but quite dissimilar suborders.

The megachiropterans, or mega-bats ('big bats') for short, comprise the fruit bats; often called flying foxes as many have distinctively vulpine (or even lemur-like) faces, these are mostly large, primarily fruit-eating species, and rely predominantly upon well-developed eyes for avoiding obstacles during night flying.

The microchiropterans, or micro-bats ('small bats') for short, comprise all of the other modern-day bats; often small and insectivorous, but also including some vegetarian and fish-eating forms, as well as the notorious blood-sipping vampires of tropical America (certain micro-bats are very large too, almost as big as the biggest fruit bats), these emit ultrasonic squeaks for echo-location purposes when flying at night.

Descriptions of the *ahool* and *olitiau* are similar enough to suggest that they belong to the same suborder - but which one?

In view of their size, it would be reasonable to assume, at least initially, that they must surely be mega-bats, and with the *olitiau* in particular there are certain correlations that seem on first sight to substantiate this.

Paul du Chaillu is best remembered as the (in)famous author of grossly exaggerated, lurid descriptions of the gorilla, as encountered by him during his mid-19th century expeditions to tropical Africa. Less well-known is that he was also the discoverer of this vast continent's largest species of bat - a hideous yet harmless fruit bat with a 3-foot wingspan, and known scientifically as *Hypsignathus monstrosus*. On account of its gro-

Fig. 1 - The Hammer-headed bat - the identity of the mysterious *olitiau*?

tesquely swollen, horse-shaped head and an oddly-formed muzzle that ends abruptly like the blunt end of a hammer, it is referred to in popular parlance as the hammer-headed or horse-headed bat, and is native to central and western Africa, where it can be commonly found along the larger rivers.

This is particularly true during the dry seasons, when the males align themselves in trees bordering the riverbanks, and saturate the night air with an ear-splitting babel of honking mating calls and loud swishing sounds generated by the frenetic flapping of their 18-inch-long wings. A human traveller unsuspectingly intruding upon such a scene as this might well be forgiven for fearing that he had descended into one of the inner circles of Dante's Inferno!

In truth, this hellish gathering is nothing more fiendish than the communal courtship display of the male hammer-heads - each male hoping to attract the attention of one of the smaller, less repulsive females, which select their mates by flying up and down these rows of rowdy suitors, evaluating the potential of each male performer.

On account of its fearsome appearance, large size, and preference for riverside habitats, H. monstrosus has been proposed on more than one occasion as a contender for the identity of the olitiau. Yet even under the dramatic circumstances surrounding their Cameroon visitation, it is highly unlikely that Sanderson and Russell could have mistaken a bat with a 3-foot wingspan for one with a 12-foot spread, especially as they were both very experienced wildlife observers. Moreover, it just so happens that only a few minutes before their winged assailant made its sinister debut, Sanderson had actually shot a specimen of H. monstrosus, so the singularly distinctive physical form of this species was uppermost in his mind; hence, if the mystery beast that appeared just a few minutes later had genuinely been nothing more than a hammer-headed bat, Sanderson would surely have recognised it as such.

Another problem when attempting to reconcile the olitiau with this identity is the olitiau's belligerent attitude - for in stark contrast to this, the hammer-headed bat has a widespread reputation as a harmless fruit-eater, with a commensurately tranquil temperament. Having said that, however, I must point out that this ostensibly mild-mannered monster does have a lesser-known, darker side to its nature too, one that is much more in keeping with its gargoylesque visage. As divulged by American zoologist Dr Hobart Van Deusen (Journal of Zoology, 1968), in startling violation of the fruit bat clan's pledge of frugivory H. monstrosus has been exposed on occasion as a clandestine carnivore - because it has been seen to attack domestic chickens, alighting upon their backs and viciously biting them, and it will carry off dead birds.

Could the olitiau therefore be an oversized, extra-savage relative of the hammer-headed bat? In short, an undiscovered giant member of the mega-bat suborder?

Thought-provoking though this identity may be, when documenting the subject of giant bats in his book Investigating the Unexplained (1972) Ivan Sanderson disclosed that there is also some arresting evidence in support of the converse explanation - namely, that these gigantic forms are in reality enormous micro-bats. This radical notion, which is particularly convincing when applied to the ahool, is substantiated by several independent, significant features drawn from these creatures' morphology and lifestyle.

For example, whereas the flattened man-like or monkey-like face of the ahool and olitiau contrasts markedly with the long-snouted face of most mega-bats, it corresponds well with that of many micro-bats. The presence of both forms of giant mystery bat near to rivers, and the ahool's reputedly piscivorous diet, also endorse a micro-bat identity - many species of micro-bat are active fish-eaters, but there is none among the mega-bats. When the ahool has been spied upon the ground, or perched upon a tree branch, its wings have been closed up at its sides; a micro-bat trait again - mega-bats fold their wings around their bodies.

Perhaps the most curious, but also the most telling (taxonomically speaking), of the statements by the Sundanese natives concerning the ahool is that when observed upon the ground it has been standing erect, with its feet turned backwards. To someone not acquainted with bats, all of this may seem nonsensical in the extreme - after all, whoever heard of bats that can stand upright, and which come equipped with back-to-front feet? Yet, paradoxically, these are the very features that vindicate most emphatically the opinion of Sanderson that this mystery creature not only is a bat (rather than a bird or some other winged animal) but is specifically a giant form of micro-bat.

To begin with: although not widely known, micro-bats are indeed capable of standing virtually erect (even though they mostly run around on all fours when on the ground); mega-bats, however, never attempt this feat. And switching from feats to feet: those backward-pointing appendages of the ahool are worthy of especial note too.

There are a few species of bird that habitually hang downwards from branches in a manner reminiscent of bats. These include Asia's Loriculus hanging parrots (also called bat parrots for this reason); and, during their courtship displays, the males of New Guinea's blue bird of paradise Paradisaea rudolphi and the Emperor of Germany's bird of paradise P. guilelmi. If these birds are observed from the front when hanging upside-down, their feet can be seen to wrap around the front portion of the branch, i.e. their toes (excluding the hind ones) curl *away* from the observer, towards the back of the branch.

With bats, however, the reverse is true - their feet wrap around the rear portion of the branch, with their toes curling *towards* the observer. This is because bats' feet really do point backwards - and so, in the event of a bat standing on the ground, its feet would indeed be projecting backwards, precisely as the *ahool's* Sundanese observers have described.

Combining the *ahool's* rearward-oriented feet with its ability to stand upright when on the ground, its identification as an immense micro-bat is thereby lent credence by note-worthy anatomical correspondences - corre-spondences, moreover, that its native eyewitnesses are unlikely to have appreciated (in terms of their taxonomic implications), and which they would therefore not have incorpo-rated purposefully into their *ahool* accounts if they had merely invented the beast as a hoax with which to fool gullible Westerners.

The possible existence of any type of giant bat with an 11-12 foot wingspan, let alone one that is most probably a micro-bat rather than a mega-bat, is bound to raise many a sardonic eyebrow and inspire many a derisory sniff within the zoological community. The pro-spect, furthermore, that there are other such species, in Africa, Madagascar, and elsewhere too, all successfully evading official discovery and description, may well stimulate even more profound manifestations of incredulity and disdain.

Perhaps, then, these sceptics should pay a visit to western Java and listen for the eerie cry that the wind and good fortune wafted in the direction of Bartels's startled ears; or to western Africa and stand by a silent river to see whether Sanderson's night-winged visitor will swoop out of the evening shadows and into the zoological history books. All of this has happened before - why should it not happen again?

WHEN HOME IS A PILE OF ELEPHANT DUNG

Whereas the previous mystery bats were distinguished by their huge size, the next one is of notably diminutive dimensions - indeed, this is the very characteristic that enables it to indulge in the bizarre day-roosting activity that has incited such scientific curiosity.

It all began in 1955, when John G. Williams, a renowned expert on African avifauna, was taking part in the MacChesney Expedition to Kenya, from Cornell Universi-ty's Laboratory of Ornithology. In June of that year he encountered Terence Adamson, brother of the late George Adamson of *Born Free* fame, and during a conversation concern-ing the wildlife inhabiting the little-explored forests of Mount Kulal, in northern Kenya, Adamson casually mentioned a peculiar little bat that had attracted his particular interest - by virtue of its unique predilection for spending its days snugly concealed inside dry piles of elephant dung!

Bats are well known for selecting unusual hideaways during the daylight hours, requi-sitioning everything from birds' nests to aardvark burrows, but there was no species known to science that habitually secreted itself within the crevices present in deposits of elephant excrement. As a consequence, Adamson had been eager to discover all that he could regarding this extraordinary crea-ture.

He had first encountered one of its kind during a walk through Kenya's Marsabit Forest (of which he was warden). After idly kicking a pile of elephant dung lying on the path along which he was strolling, he saw a small grey creature fly out of it and alight upon a tree nearby. Expecting it to be nothing more notable than some form of large moth, Adamson was very startled to find that it was an exceedingly small bat, with silver brown-ish-grey fur, paler upon its underparts. He was especially surprised by its tiny size - its wingspan was even less than that of the familiar pipistrelles, which are among the smallest of bats. Unfortunately, he was only able to observe it for a few moments before it took to the air again and disappeared, but his interest was sufficiently stirred for him to make a determined effort thereafter to seek out other specimens of this odd little animal.

And as he informed John Williams, during his visit to Mount Kulal he had succeeded in spotting a second one - unceremoniously ejected from its diurnal seclusion when

Adamson had kicked over a pile of pachyderm droppings at the base of the Kulal foothills. Unlike the first specimen, however, this one had flown away without making any attempt to land close by, so Adamson had been unable to make any additional observations.

As Williams noted in what seems to be the only account published until now regarding this coprophilic chiropteran (*Animals*, June 1967), he too became very keen to espy, and possibly even capture, one of these elusive denizens of the dung piles, in the hope of identifying their species. And so, to his travelling companions' great amusement, Williams made a special point from then on of zealously felling as many dry mounds of elephant excrement as he could, on the off-chance that he might conjure forth one of these perplexing little bats.

Despite such valiant efforts, however, the elephant dung bat has still not been captured, and its identity remains unresolved - but as John Williams kindly informed me during some recent correspondence, one species already known to science may provide the answer.

The species in question is a rare micro-bat called *Eptesicus (Rhinopterus) floweri*, first described in 1901 by de Winton, and currently recorded only from Mali and southern Sudan. It is commonly termed the horn-skinned bat, calling to attention the tiny horny excrescences that it bears upon the upper surface of its limbs and tail. This species resembles the elephant dung bat in general size and colour, but an important additional reason why Williams favours its candidature as the latter creature's identity is its remarkable preference for day-roosting within holes in the ground, especially among the roots of acacia trees.

As he pointed out to me, this habitat is really quite similar to the crevices and cracks present within dry heaps of elephant dung, hence it is not difficult to believe that this species would utilise these useful sources of daytime roosting sites if such were available. And as the Mount Kulal region of northern Kenya is not only little-explored but also not too far beyond its known distribution range, this provides further reason for looking favourably upon the horn-skinned bat as a realistic answer to the mystery of the elephant dung bat.

THE BLOOD-DRINKING 'DEATH BIRD' OF ETHIOPIA

In total contrast to the engaging if somewhat offbeat history of the elephant dung bat, the case of the Ethiopian 'death bird' is unremittingly macabre and horrific, more akin to the gothic outpourings of Poe and Le Fanu than to anything from the dispassionate, sober chronicles of zoology. Yet in spite of this, it is only too real; at the present time, moreover, it is also unsolved. I am most grateful to Queensland zoologist Malcolm Smith for bringing this chilling but hitherto unexamined case to my attention, and for kindly supplying me with a copy of the original source of information concerning it.

It was during an archaeological expedition to Ethiopia, shortly before the country was invaded by Italian troops in World War II, that Byron de Prorok first learnt of Devil's Cave, whose grisly secret he subsequently documented in his travelogue *Dead Men Do Tell Tales* (1943). Journeying through the province of Walaga, he resided for a time at the home of its governor, Dajjazmac Mariam, and while there he was approached by one of the servants, a young boy who began to tell him about a secret cave situated roughly an hour's horseback-ride away, near a place called Lekempti. It was known to the local people as Devil's Cave, and was widely held to be an abode of evil and horror - plagued by devil-men who prowled its darkened recesses in the guise of ferocious hyaenas, and by flocks of a greatly-feared form of bat referred to as the death bird.

No-one had ever dared to penetrate this mysterious cavern, but de Prorok decided to defy its forbidding reputation, because he thought it possible that there would be prehistoric rock paintings inside (especially as its notoriety would have served well in warding off potential trespassers, who might have desecrated any artwork preserved within its stygian gloom).

When de Prorok told his young informant of his decision to visit Devil's Cave, the boy was terrified, but after being bribed with a plentiful supply of gifts he agreed very reluctantly to act as de Prorok's guide -

though only on the strict understanding that he would not be held responsible for anything that happened!

The cave was situated high among rocky pinnacles and jungle foliage, but de Prorok succeeded in scrambling up to it, and in removing the several heavy boulders blocking its entrance. Armed with a gun, and leaving his guide trembling with fear outside, he cautiously stepped inside - and was almost bowled over a few minutes later by a panic-stricken pack of hyaenas hurtling down one of the passages to the newly-unsealed entrance. Seeking to defend himself against a possible attack by them, he shot one that approached a little too close for comfort, and the echoes from the blast reverberated far and wide, ultimately reaching the ears of two goatherds who came to the cave mouth to find out what was happening. Here they were met by de Prorok, who had followed the hyaenas at a respectful distance during their shambolic exit, and was greatly shocked by the men's pitiful state - they seemed little more than animated skeletons, upon which were hung a few tattered rags.

When, with the boy as interpreter, they learnt that de Prorok planned to go back inside the cave, they implored him to change his mind, warning him of the death birds. De Prorok, however, was not afraid of bats and made his way once more through the cave's sombre corridors, until he suddenly heard a loud whirring sound overhead. This proved to be a huge cloud of bats, which flew rapidly towards the cave mouth when he fired off a shot in alarm. These, he presumed, must be the dreaded death birds, a line of speculation speedily confirmed when only moments later a rain of bat excrement, dislodged by the shot, began to pelt down upon him from the cave roof, accompanied by an asphyxiating stench that drove him back almost at once to the entrance in search of breathable air.

Outside, he enquired why everyone was so afraid of these bats, to which the two goatherds and the boy all replied that they were blood-suckers - that night after night they came to drink the blood of anyone living near the cave until eventually their unfortunate victims died. This was why the only people living here now were the goatherds (who were forced to do so by the goats'

owners), and was the reason for their emaciated state. The death birds' vampir-esque activities ensured that none of the goatherds lived very long, but they were always replaced by others, thereby providing the goats with constant supervision - and the death birds with a constant supply of their ghoulish nutriment.

To provide him with additional proof of their statements, the two goatherds took de Prorok to their camp nearby; all of the herders there were equally skeletal - and one was close to death. Little more than a pile of bones scarcely held together by a shroud of ashen skin, this living corpse of a man lay huddled in a cot, with blood-stained rags and clothes on either side, and was so weakened by the nightly depredations of the visiting death birds that he was unable to stand, capable only of extending a wraith-like arm. The goatherds told de Prorok that the death birds settled upon their bodies while they were asleep, so softly that they did not even wake; and that they were sizeable beasts, with wingspans of 12-18 inches.

As for physical evidence of the death birds' sanguinivorous nature, the goatherds showed him their arms, which clearly bore a number of small wounds - the puncture marks left behind by these winged leeches once they had gorged themselves upon their hapless hosts?

Nothing more has emerged concerning this gruesome affair, but for zoologists it would have some significant repercussions if de Prorok's account could be shown to be perfectly accurate. Only three species of blood-drinking bat are currently known to science - and all three of these are confined exclusively to *America!*

These are the notorious vampire bats, of which the best-known is the common vampire *Desmodus rotundus*, whose range extends from northern Mexico to central Chile, northern Argentina, Uruguay, and Trinidad; its num-bers have dramatically increased since the introduction of sheep and other livestock to these areas with the coming of the Europeans, serving to expand the diversity and numbers of potential prey victims for it. The other two species are the white-winged vampire *Diae-mus youngi*, recorded from northeastern Mex-ico to eastern Peru, northern Argentina, Brazil, and Trinidad; and the hairy-legged vampire *Diphylla ecaudata*, ranging from southern Texas to eastern Peru and southern Brazil.

(As a thought-provoking digression, there may also be a fourth, giant vampire bat in existence. Within the *Proceedings of the Biological Society of Washington* for 7 December 1988, researchers Drs Gary S. Morgan, Omar J. Linares, and Clayton E. Ray formally described a new species of vampire, 25% larger in size than *Desmodus rotundus*, based upon two incomplete skulls and skeletal remains found in Venezuela's famous Cueva del Guácharo - home of the extraordinary radar-emitting oilbird *Steatornis caripensis*. Dubbed *D. draculae*, this giant vampire bat's remains date from the Pleistocene. However, Brazilian zoologists Drs E. Trajano and M. de Vivo, in a *Mammalia* paper from 1991, noted that there are reports of local inhabitants in Brazil's Ribeira Valley referring to attacks upon cattle and horses by large bats that could suggest the continuing survival here of *D. draculae*, although despite extensive recent searches of caves in this area none has been found ... so far?)

Over the years, a great deal of misinformation has been dissipated concerning this nocturnal, terror-inducing trio of micro-bats - including the persistent fallacy that they actively suck blood *out* of wounds; and the equally tenacious, fanciful misconception that they are enormous beasts with gigantic wings into which they are only too eager to enfold their stricken victims while draining them of their precious scarlet fluid. In contrast, the truth is (as always) far less exotic and extravagant.

Any creature that can subsist entirely upon a diet of blood (sanguinivory) must obviously be highly specialised, and the vampire bats are no exception; Canadian biologist Dr Brock Fenton from Young University in Ontario has lately suggested that they evolved from bats that originally consumed blood-sucking insects attracted to wounds on large animals, but which eventually acquired a taste for the animals' blood themselves. Yet in overall external appearance these nefarious species are disappointingly mundane - with an unimpressive total length of only 2-3½ inches, a very modest wingspan of 5-6 inches, and a covering of unmemorably

brown, short fur. Only when they open their mouth to reveal a distinctive pair of shear-like upper incisors do they display the first intimation of their sinister lifestyle.

These incisors terminate in a central point and have long, scalpel-sharp edges, perfectly adapted for surreptitiously shaving a thin sliver of skin from the body or neck of an unsuspecting (usually sleeping) victim - detected by the vampire's ultrasonic echo-location faculties. The wound that is produced is sufficiently deep to slice through the skin's capillaries, but not deep enough to disturb the victim and thereby waken it (or arouse its attention if already awake) - stealth is the byword of the vampire's lifestyle. Aiding the furtive creation of this finely-engineered wound are the bat's canine teeth, shorter than the incisors but just as sharp.

Once the wound begins to seep blood in a steady flow, the vampire, delicately clinging to the flank or back of its victim with its wings and hook-like thumbs (*not* with its sharp claws - yet another fallacy), avidly laps the escaping fluid with its grooved, muscular tongue. It can also suck it up by folding its tongue over a notch in its lower lip to yield a tube, but it only sucks blood that has already flowed out of the wound. In addition, its saliva contains anticoagulants, preventing the blood from clotting, and thereby providing the bat with an ample supply (but causing its victim to lose more than would have been the case if the wound had been inflicted by some other type of sharp cutting implement).

Indeed, one of these anticoagulants, plasminogen activator (Bat-PA for short), shows promise as a powerful drug in the prevention of the severe physiological damage caused by heart attacks in humans, according to a study of its effects by research fellow Dr Stephen Gardell at Merck Sharp & Dohme Research Laboratories in West Point, Pennsylvania.

The vampire's teeth, tongue, and thumbs are not the only specialised facets of its anatomy - its gut also exhibits some important modifications. Enabling the bat to gorge itself thoroughly before bidding its victim a silent adieu, its stomach has an enormous extra compartment - a tubular, blind-ending diverticulum unattached to the rest of the digestive tract and capable of prodigious distension, rendering it able to hold a voluminous quantity of blood. Sometimes the bat can scarcely fly after feeding, because it is so heavy with freshly ingested blood. Also, its oesophagus is specialised for efficient water absorption, a necessity for any obligate sanguinivore because blood contains an appreciable proportion of water.

What all of this means in relation to the Ethiopian death bird is that any bat thriving solely or even predominantly upon a diet of blood is inevitably a much-modified species, rigorously adapted for such a lifestyle - rather than a mere opportunist species that in certain localities has switched (through some unusual set of circumstances) from its normal diet to a sanguinivorous existence. In other words, if de Prorok's account is a truthful one, then surely the death bird must be a species new to science? After all, there is currently no *known* species of Old World bat that is a confirmed blood-drinker. This, then, is plainly one plausible answer to the death bird mystery - but it is not the only such answer.

I am exceedingly grateful to bat specialist John Edwards Hill, who has recently retired from his position as Principal Scientific Officer at the British Museum (Natural History), for presenting me with a great deal of information that offers a completely different outlook upon this perplexing case. It is well known that the New World vampire bats transmit livestock diseases from one animal victim to another, in a manner paralleling the activities of mosquitoes and other sanguinivorous insect vectors. They also carry rabies to man, though this is a much rarer occurrence than the more lurid reports in the popular press would have us believe. Moreover, bats of many species all around the world are known to contract many different types of bacterial, viral, and protozoan diseases, which can be spread to other organisms via parasites such as body lice and ticks that live upon the bats' skin or fur. Relapsing fever in man, for example, is caused by the bacterium *Borrelia recurrentis*, carried by lice and ticks that have in turn derived it from former rodent or bat hosts.

Accordingly, during communications concerning the death bird, Hill suggested to me that it is possible that humans venturing in or near a cave heavily infested with bats (like Devil's Cave, for instance) would become infected with such diseases - if lice or ticks, dropping from the bats as they flew overhead, bit the unfortunate humans upon which they landed. A parasite-borne infection of this nature would account for the bite-like wounds of the goatherds observed by de Prorok; and, depending upon the precise type of infection, could ultimately give rise to the emaciated condition exhibited by these afflicted persons.

Additionally, native superstition and a deep-rooted fear of bats might be sufficient, when coupled with the distressing effects of a parasite-borne infection, to nurture the belief among such poorly-educated people as these that they were the victims of blood-sucking bats - the notion of vampirism is very ancient and widespread in human cultures worldwide (the Maya of pre-Columbian Mesoamerica even worshipped the vampire bat as a god - Camazotz).

Two other medical explanations for the death bird case were also raised by Hill during our correspondence (though he rated both of these as being less plausible than the likelihood of a parasite-borne disease's involvement), which are as follows.

As Devil's Cave contained large quantities of bat excrement, perhaps these droppings harboured the spores of the soil fungus *Histoplasma capsulatum* (even though this is more usually associated with bird guano); if inhaled, these spores can cause an infection of the lungs known as histoplasmosis, which can prove fatal (but severe cases are not common).

Alternatively, an illness called Weil's disease also offers some notable parallels with the 'death bird syndrome'. Also referred to as epidemic spirochaetal jaundice and as leptospirosis icterohaemorrhagica, Weil's disease is caused by spirochaete bacteria of the genus *Leptospira*, and is usually spread by rodents, but the bacteria have been found in a few species of bat too. Infection generally occurs through infected drinking water, and among the ensuing symptoms of contraction is the appearance of small haemorrhages in the skin, which could be mistaken for bites. Also, the accompanying damage to the kidneys and liver, jaundice, and overall malaise experienced by sufferers could explain the goatherds' haggard, wasted form.

Clearly, then, the case of the dreaded

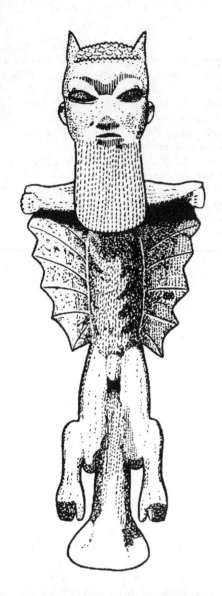

Fig. 2 - Carving of the *sasabonsam* by Osei-Bonsu.
(Line drawing after photo in *West African Review*.)

ciated with Ethiopia in modern times, even this is unlikely to prove an easy task to accomplish.

Until then, the secret of this purportedly deadly, unidentified creature will remain as dark and impenetrable as the grim cave from which its winged minions allegedly issue forth each night to perform their vile abominations upon the latest tragic campful of doomed, defenceless goatherds.

THE 'SASABONSAM' SCULPTURE

One final mystery beast deserves brief mention here if only because it is as likely to have been inspired by encounters with strange bats as by anything else. In an absorbing *West African Review* article for September 1939, J.B. Danquah included a photograph of a carving produced by a member of Ghana's Asantehene people, which depicted a bizarre entity referred to as the *sasabonsam*. According to the carving, the *sasabonsam* has a human face with a broad, lengthy beard, long hair, and two horns or pointed ears; an extremely thin body with readily visible ribs; short stubby forelimbs that, when lifted upwards, reveal a pair of thin membranes resembling a bat's wings; and long, twisted legs terminating in feet with distinct toes. Most authorities dismiss this creature as a myth, but a few have wondered whether it could be some form of giant bat.

Of particular interest to Danquah was the narrative of a youth present in a crowd of people (which included Danquah himself) observing this carving being photographed, because the youth averred that once, at his own Ashanti town, he had seen the body of a *sasabonsam* - killed by a man called Agya Wuo, who had brought its carcase into the town. The youth confirmed that the carving was very like the *sasabonsam* that he had seen, and he added some details based upon the dead specimen.

This had been more than 5½ feet tall; its wings were very thin but when fully stretched out could yield a span of up to 20 feet; its arms (unlike the carving's) were very long, as were its teeth; its skin was spotted black and white; and there had been scaly ridges over its eyes, with hard, stiff hair on its head. The man who had killed it had stated that he had encountered it sleeping in a tree hollow, and that it

death bird and the stricken herders is far from being as straightforward as it seemed on first sight, and may involve any one, or perhaps even more than one, of the above solutions. An aspect of the case that *is* self-evident, however, is the necessity for a specimen of the death bird to be collected and formally studied. Only then might the resolution of this mystifying and macabre cryptozoological riddle be finally achieved - but in view of the perennially uncertain political climate asso-

had emitted a cry like that of a bat but deeper. The body was allegedly taken to the bungalow of L.W. Wood, the region's District Commissioner, who photographed it on 22 February 1928.

Danquah later contacted Wood, who seemed uncertain whether he had indeed photographed such a creature; in addition, he claimed that although he was in Ashanti in February 1918, he was not there in February 1928. It is possible, therefore, that if this account is true, the youth who informed Danquah had become confused regarding the date.

In any event, neither the carving nor the description of the dead specimen bear more than the most passing of resemblances to a bat - but it is equally true that they do not call to mind any other type of animal either! If the fate of the dead specimen (always assuming of course that there really was such a specimen) could be ascertained, its skeleton would solve the currently insoluble riddle of the *sasabonsam's* identity - but until then, this 'bat with a beard' must remain just another one of the varied beings of African mythology that appear to have no known counterpart in the zoological world.

Few creatures are likely to stay hidden from human interference as effectively as those that are nocturnal, winged, and capable of eliciting a profound degree of irrational fear and horror in mankind. Little wonder, therefore, that bats remain some of the most mysterious mammals alive today, with new species appearing - and even supposedly extinct species reappearing - almost every year.

Consequently, the prospect that certain of the more remote, inhospitable reaches of the world could harbour very distinctive bats wholly unknown to science is really not very surprising - on the contrary, it would only be very surprising if this were not the case.

I wish to thank most sincerely John Edwards Hill, Dr Clayton E. Ray, Malcolm Smith, and John G. Williams for their valuable assistance and interest extended to me during my researches for this article.

SELECT BIBLIOGRAPHY

BARTELS, Ernst & SANDERSON, Ivan T. (1966). 'The one true batman.' *Fate*, Vol. 19 (July): 83-92.

DANQUAH, J.B. (1939). 'Living monster or fabulous animal?' *West African Review*, (September): 19-20.

GREENHALL, Arthur M. & SCHMIDT, Uwe (Eds.) (1988). *Natural History of Vampire Bats*. CRC Press (Boca Raton).

HEUVELMANS, Bernard (1958). *On the Track of Unknown Animals*. Rupert Hart-Davis (London).

HEUVELMANS, Bernard (1978). *Les Derniers Dragons d'Afrique*. Plon (Paris).

MELLAND, Frank H. (1923). *In Witch-Bound Africa*. Seeley, Service & Co (London).

MORGAN, Gary S., LINARES, Omar J., & RAY, Clayton E. (1988). 'New species of fossil vampire bats (Mammalia: Chiroptera: Desmodontidae) from Florida and Venezuela.' *Proceedings of the Biological Society of Washington*, Vol. 101 (7 December): 912-928.

PROROK, Byron de (1943). *Dead Men Do Tell Tales*. George Harrap (London).

SANDERSON, Ivan T. (1937). *Animal Treasure*. Macmillan (London).

SANDERSON, Ivan T. (1972). *Investigating the Unexplained. A Compendium of Disquieting Mysteries of the Natural World*. Prentice-Hall (Eaglewood Cliffs).

SHUKER, Karl P.N. (1993). *The Lost Ark. New and Rediscovered Animals of the 20th Century*. HarperCollins (London).

TRAJANO, E. & de VIVO, M. (1991). '*Desmodus draculae* Morgan, Linares, and Ray, 1988, reported for Southeastern Brazil, with paleoecological comments (Phyllostomidae, Desmodontinae).' *Mammalia*, Vol. 55: 456-459.

VAN DEUSEN, Hobart M. (1968). 'Carnivorous habits of *Hypsignathus monstrosus*.' *Journal of Mammalogy*, Vol. 49: 335-336.

VELLUTINI, John L. (1988). 'The pterosaur in modern times.' *Journal of Vampirology*, Vol. 5 (No. 4): 1-6.

VILLA-C, Beatriz & CANELA-R, Maria (1988). 'Man, gods, and legendary vampire bats.' In: GREENHALL, Arthur M. & SCHMIDT, Uwe (Eds.), *Op. cit.* pp. 233-240.

WILLIAMS, John G. (1967). 'An unsolved mystery.' *Animals*, Vol. 10 (June): 73-75.

LAKE CONSTANCE PHENOMENA

Ulrich Magin

There are many approaches open to the Fortean researcher: the study of a particular phenomenon, the analysis of a time-period, the investigation of a geographical area, and so on. German researcher Ulrich Magin concentrates his attention on Lake Constance, on the border of Germany and Switzerland, uncovering a cluster of mystery sounds, lake creatures, UFOs, folklore and the like.

Lake Constance (the Bodensee) is the largest body of water in the German-speaking area of Central Europe. It borders Switzerland, Germany and Austria, occupying an old glacial basin at an elevation of 1,229 ft. With an area of 209 square miles, it is 40 miles long and up to 8 miles wide. Its average depth is 295 ft., although it reaches a maximum depth of 827 ft. Shaped like a giant bird's footprint, it has a shore length of some 125 miles.

The lake's shores have been inhabited since Neolithic times, and a reconstructed Stone Age village is open to visitors at Überlingen. As the lake stores and reflects heat it is the warmest region in Central Europe and one of its islands, the Insel Mainau, has tropical gardens. Charlemagne had an imperial palatinate at the lake, and in the Middle Ages it was a major international crossroads.

A region of this size has naturally experienced its share of Fortean events, and many are connected with the lake. Similarly, it is not surprising that a lake of this size has legends and traditions connected with water.

According to folklore, Lake Constance is connected to Lake Vätter in southern Sweden by underground channels. As Peter Kolosimo remarks, several plants growing around Lake Vätter are otherwise unknown in Sweden, although they are common around Lake Constance.

Lake Vätter is also known for the strange booms heard there, and for the mirages commonly seen on its surface. Local folklore claims that mining work carried out by goblins living in cities at the bottom of the lake are to blame for the booms, while the mirages are reflections of the goblin cities [1]. While an underground channel is clearly impossible, the same phenomena, and more, are regularly reported from Lake Constance.

THE LAKE BOOMS

The most famous and recurring phenomenon is the so-called 'Seeschiessen' (lake booms). These sounds,

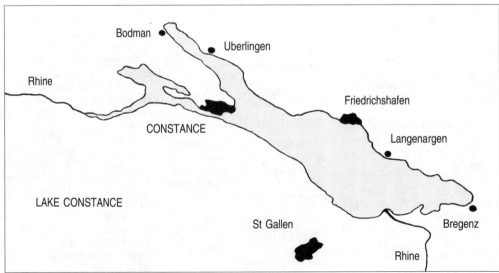

which are similar to the Barisal Guns mentioned by Fort, resemble ultrasonic booms but had been heard well before the invention of aeroplanes. They are common all over Europe, as an article in the German popular science monthly *Kosmos* lists, among others, the English Channel, Belgium, Scottish and Irish lakes and the Black Forest as places where the booms can be heard [2]. A friend of mine has told me that she has heard them often over the Eifel Mountains in Germany. As Forteans are aware, there are many explanations for these booms, the most widely accepted being that they are related to seismic activity or meteorological changes.

A fine witness report comes from the *Neues Tagblatt* of Stuttgart (7 August 1908). A man walking from Friedrichshafen to Manzell reported "a repeated rolling noise like distant thunder, which seemed to come from the Swiss shore. As the sky was completely cloudless I immediately thought it was the lake booms which I have heard for a couple of years now. It is different from detonations of guns in the distance and is most similar, as I have already pointed out, to brief rolling thunder in the distance. In the vicinity of Seemoos I sat down on a shady bench and contemplated the mirror-calm surface of the lake. There was not a ship in sight. At about 10:00am I noticed, about 600 to 800 metres from the shore, a wave about 15-20 m long, which I at first took to be a ridge of lake grass showing above the surface, but looking closer I realised that the wave closed in on the shore in a slow, parallel motion. In front and behind this wave, which consisted of 4 or 5 individual waves close to each other, the lake was as calm as a millpond - therefore, it cannot have been a steamer's wake. Was there any connection to the lake boom heard just half an hour before? It was over the deepest part of the lake, the *tiefe Schweb*, and possibly a landslide had occurred there."

A similar wave phenomenon, the 'Seebär' (sea bear) is known from the western Baltic [2] and is usually seen as the result of an interplay between seismic and meteorological factors. I am reminded of the 'waves without wind' of the Scottish lakes, which could have a similar natural explanation. However, we should note that these mysterious waves also occur on Lake Constance, and might be interpreted as the wakes of lake-monsters.

On 18 September 1908 (a very Fortean year in Germany, with many unusual lights in the sky) the booms were heard at Friedrichshafen. They sounded like subterranean rolling noises. The booms each lasted about two seconds and were separated by four to five minutes. They continued throughout the whole morning until noon and came from the direction of Constance. This proved that they were neither echoes of Swiss artillery fire nor of Alpine avalanches, as the *Frankfurter Zeitung* noted. Witnesses wrote in from all over Germany to report similar booms from the Spessart Forest, the Taunus Mountains and Erzgebirge, all far distant from Lake Constance.

The lake booms have still not been fully explained, despite a call for research as early as 1897 in the *Schwäbischer Merkur*. While it seems that these booms have occurred over every region of Germany, and in many others throughout the world, they take place most often over plains and lakes - Lake Constance being a fine example.

THE 'FIERY FISHERMAN'

The lake also has its ghostlight, the 'fiery fisherman'. I have only seen folkloric reports and thus cannot say with any certainty if the phenomenon is real in any physical sense. The fiery fisherman appears at night and abuses the local fishermen until they throw a rope at him, which soon begins to burn. As long as the rope is burning the fiery fisherman will not feel the pains of hell [3]. This legend is connected to a similar motif, that of the 'water hell', where sinners suffer and sometimes appear as 'fiery men' on the lake surface. The tale is widespread in the Allgäu region, close to Lake Constance.

A similar elemental spirit is the Nebelmännlein ('fog mannikin') which lives at Bodman in Lake Constance. The Löchle ('hole') is a spot in the lake which never freezes in winter, even if the whole of the rest of the lake is covered by an ice sheet. The Nebelmännlein lives there, and it comes out on quiet winter nights to fool the sailors on the lake and cover the grapes with frost [4]. This is clearly a personification of the frosty winter fogs.

THE LANGENARGEN 'FROGMEN'

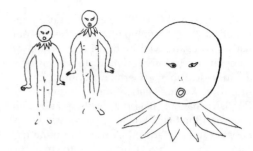

The fiery fisherman is a symbol of all drowned fishermen, yet it could, at the same time, be a rare natural phenomenon. Fiery spirits are no longer fashionable so when, on 22 February 1977, a strange light appeared over Langenargen, on the shores of the lake, it was interpreted as a UFO.

At a distance of 2 km from the shore, six people were sitting in a pub, the Langenargen-Bierkeller. There are indications that they had been heavily indulging in alcohol. At 2:30am they all observed two spindle-like objects with four searchlights, each coming from the lake to hover over the town. The objects came as close as 50 m to the observers, who ran for cover fearing the whistling saucers might crash on them. The objects, now noiseless, carried out several complex manoeuvres before finally disappearing "like a light being switched off". How much of the alleged behaviour of the objects owes to the excite-

Fig. 3 - Sketches of the Langenargen 'frogmen', after Schäfler.

Fig. 2 - Sketch of the Langenargen UFO, after Schäfler.

ment and intoxication of the witnesses is difficult to assess, though a later analysis of the report showed that the objects were definitely a very bright meteor.

One of the group, 27 year old Lothar Schäfler, was on his way to his car after the objects had disappeared when he suddenly perceived two shadowy creatures. At the same time, the object seemed to return, very close to him. He was so badly frightened that he tried to break into a house, smashing a window-pane and injuring himself. He even called the police.

The creatures had a height of 1.3 m and 1.1 m respectively. Their bodies appeared human, but their arms were far longer than a human's, and their fingers appeared cramped. Around their neck they wore a kind of frill with six or seven green pointed ends. Their skin was lighter than a man's, the head was bare and completely round. They possessed neither ears nor nose, and their mouths were circular. Their bodies swung slightly from side to side. As they approached Schäfler he panicked and smashed the window. The German UFO research group MUFON-CES interviewed the witness and called in a hypnotist to recover further details. Although the hypnotist was doing his best to convince the witness that he had lost time and had been abducted by aliens, Schäfler just could not remember being on board the craft [5].

These little green men with fish faces and Kermit-like frills around the neck recall similar creatures observed world-wide in connection with UFOs, but also some monstrous 'gill-men' and 'lizard men' from the USA.

OTHER LAKE CREATURES

St. Gallen, Switzerland, a little to the south of Lake Constance, was founded by the Irish missionary St. Gall in the 7th century after 'a sign from heaven' showed him the spot. St. Gall talked with the demons of the mountains and water, and "undines and nixies ... emerged from the waters to tempt him" [6]. These stories may be Celtic folktales that St. Gall brought with him, but it is interesting to see a human lake spirit crop up again and again in folkloric, religious and ufological contexts.

Besides the nymphs and frogmen, Lake Constance has its own lake monster. A German woodcut of 1590 shows a monstrous serpent which had been discovered in a morass near Lake Constance. Meurger [7]

Fig. 4 - A German woodcut of 1590 depicts a monstrous serpent found on the shore of Lake Constance.

thinks that the broadsheet "transforms an unusual but not unnatural event - the discovery of a large grass-snake - into a monstrous one". The representation of the monster follows the iconography of the time closely - clearly, as with most broadsheets of the period, the religious interpretation of the event was far more important than the accurate detail. Whether the news was really triggered by the discovery of a genuine snake, or whether a German dragon was invented to illustrate a certain moral attitude (as was often the case), is hard to decide after 400 years have passed.

Sadly, a second possible water monster at Lake Constance has turned out to be something of a red herring. Meurger [8] prints a broadsheet engraving that was published in Augsburg (about 80 miles NE of the lake) in 1727 that shows an 'awe inspiring sea-monster' that had been caught at 'Friedrich-shafen' by 400 rustics and their 20 dogs. The monster has a boar's head, a fish body, legs of a horse and duck, and two tails with an eye on each. The broadsheet's monster is a mixture of several monstrous beasts that Olaus Magnus first displayed in his *Carta Marina* of 1539, consisting mainly of an invented monster with a swine's body and fish's tail, all covered with eyes, that Olaus claimed had been seen off Germany in 1532. This drawing was copied and embellished by the Renaissance zoologist Münster, and his engravings were clearly the model for the Augsburg broadsheet. This is fairly typical, as engravers in earlier centuries seldom drew from nature, but worked from

earlier representations. There are several broadsheets from past centuries claiming to show stranded whales, but the picture is always a variation of a broadsheet from 1598 depicting a stranded sperm whale off Holland [9]. The event might have been real, but the picture was drawn from tradition.

However, the Friedrichshafen at Lake Constance was so named only in 1811, and the Augsburg engraving actually refers to Frederikshavn in Denmark. This neatly explains why the depicted monster is so nearly identical to the many-eyed sea-pig shown on Olaus Magnus's map [10].

CONCLUSIONS

It is certainly tempting to interpret all these reports within the framework of Paul Devereux's earthlights hypothesis. Lake Constance is situated at the edge of the Alps and is a very active seismic area. The booms are clearly a seismic/meteorological event. In some cases, slight earth tremors were felt at the same time that the booms were heard. The fiery fisherman could be an anthropomorphised earthlight, and the creature/monster reports various reactions thereto.

However, I favour a social-psychological explanation. As with every lake, Constance has its guardian or god and, as in many traditions, this is represented by the dual symbol of the fireball and the merman/sea-

Fig. 5 - The improbable monster caught at Frederikshavn in Denmark, not at Friedrichschafen on Lake Constance. From an Augsberg broadsheet of 1727.

monster. The lake booms are an unrelated natural phenomenon common over plains and large bodies of water. That earthlights are not the cause of these phenomena is shown by the fact that the Langenargen UFO was only a meteor (which may have triggered a hallucinatory episode in one of the witnesses), that the fiery fisherman and the fog mannikin can be understood symbolically, that the lake monster reports were hoaxes or exaggerations, and that the nymphs of St. Gallen symbolise pagan forces at work. That is, all these Fortean accounts are - consciously or unconsciously - fictions, a rationalisation and personification of natural forces that use traditional imagery adapted to the taste of the times. All the legends of a culturally united area thus give us an alternative, legendary geography and fauna of the area, born of the concerns and daily needs, hopes and fears of those who live there.

It is very interesting to see, once again, how these Fortean motifs mix and merge. The booms probably produce strange waves which look like monster wakes if you need to see them, while the nymphs of antiquity have transformed into space aliens. The fiery fisherman, the glowing elemental of the lake, is split into its two aspects: in the 20th century, the glow is the spaceship and the fisherman is its occupant.

NOTES

1 - Peter Kolosimo, *El Planeta Incógnito* (Plaza y Janés, Barcelona, 1985, p.94). Hoffmann-Krayer, *Handwörterbuch des Deutschen Aberglaubens* (de Gruyter, Berlin, 1987, vol. 1, p.1464). See also my article in the *INFO Journal* 56, 1989, p.26-29, for further examples of this motif-cluster.

2 - 'Rätselhafte Knallgeräusche.' In *Kosmos*, 1909, p19-21. The article lists a large number of 'booms' from all over the world, completing the material that Fort collected.

3 - Hoffmann-Krayer, *op. cit.*, vol. 9, p.135.

4 - Hoffmann-Krayer, *op. cit.*, vol. 6, p.989.

5 - I. Brand/A. Schneider, 'Gleissend-helle Objekte und fremdartige Gestalten in Langenargen.' In *MUFON-CES-Bericht* 4 (MUFON-CES, Feldkirchen-Westerham, 1978, p43-75).

6 - Roslyn Strong, 'Dragon Tale.' In *The Ley Hunter* 100, 1986, p.16-17.

7 - Michel Meurger, *Lake Monster Traditions* (Fortean Tomes, London, 1988, p.151).

8 - Michel Meurger, *op. cit.*, p.230.

9 - Hans Peter Dürr, *Traumzeit* (Syndikat, Frankfurt-am-Main, 1982, p.22-23).

10 - This geographical mix-up is entirely my fault. Meurger merely names the place as 'Friedrichshafen', without further identification. However, it is easy to make the assumption that this is at Lake Constance, and I repeated the error in my recent book, *Trolle, Yetis, Tatzelwürmer* (C.H. Beck, Munich, 1993, p47-48).

PAUL KAMMERER AND THE LAW OF SERIALITY

THE LOST PARADIGM OF COINCIDENCE

John Townley and Robert Schmidt

The Austrian Paul Kammerer (1880-1926) proposed a remarkable theory of coincidence which he called 'seriality'. Long neglected since his death and large replaced in the public mind by the Jungian concept of 'synchronicity', a reassessment of his proposal is long overdue. John Townley and Robert Schmidt, authors of a book-length study of Kammerer and his ideas, (*The Middle Kingdom*, Hindsight Press, forthcoming), guide us through the man's ideas and their various possible applications.

On the afternoon of 23 September 1926, the body of a well-dressed man in a dark suit was found on the slopes of the Schneeberg, a mountain near Vienna, Austria. He was sitting propped up against a rock face, a pistol gripped in his right hand (even though he was left-handed), and had been shot once through the left temple. A suicide note was on the body, and three others had been distributed to friends and relatives - all were typed, not hand-written. Astonishingly, without further investigation it was declared a suicide, and the case was closed.

The event effectively closed the last chapter on the dispute about how evolution proceeded, and closed along with it was the opportunity for science to explain the mysteries of what was later to be labelled 'synchronicity', along with a host of Fortean, occult, and other seemingly unexplainable phenomena. That was because the man on the mountain was world-renowned scientist Dr Paul Kammerer, the last of the Lamarckian biologists, and formulator of the "law of seriality." His primary reputation was for unique and often irreplicable experiments that appeared to prove the inheritance of acquired characteristics in animals, anathema to neo-Darwinian evolutionists, and which earned him bitter enemies among their ranks. The fact that he was also a successful musician and composer and an admired member of Viennese high society also fueled resentment among his academic peers. The summer before his death he had been the subject of a scandal in which someone tampered with one of his experiments, invalidating it and leaving him open to charges of possible fraud. Despite this, he had been given an appointment to head the Soviet Union's most prestigious biological institute, and had been packing up his laboratory to move when his body was found.

But as history quickly buried the biological work of this remarkable scientist (his neo-Darwinian colleagues even expunged his name from scientific biographies), it also banished to obscurity his elaborate work on the phenomenon he called 'seriality,' put forth in his book *Das Gesetz der Serie* (The Law Of Seriality) published in 1919. In this work, Kammerer catalogued and classified hundreds of coincidences (spatial or temporal 'series' of events) he had collected over the years, dividing them into a variety of types, orders and categories in a somewhat Linnaean morphology. Then he proposed a direct, causal way of explaining how they came about. Unfortunately, all of it was done away with a single gunshot.

But Kammerer was not the only scientist mulling over the mysteries of odd coincidences during the years just before and after World War I. So was Carl Gustav Jung, who later published his ideas about the subject using the now-popular buzzword 'synchronicity'. Although clearly influenced in his thinking by Kammerer's work, he went his own route which took the phenomena out of the physical and scientific world and dubbed it 'acausal'. In Jung's view, synchronicity has primarily to do with events meaningful to the observer and which are not connected in any other way except that they happen at the same time. They come, essentially, from some other dimension (specifically, "a realm of *a priori* orderedness") than the ones we know and do not obey the normal rules of causality. The result has been that we now often dismiss unusual events as "just synchronicity," as if that were an explanation, when it isn't one at all - nor did Jung intend it to be.

A further refinement of this 'acausal' causation came later with Rupert Sheldrake's 'morphic resonance', another more 'scientific' attempt to explain the same sort of phenomena. However, Sheldrake's 'morphs', patterns that unite and encourage new synchronistic phenomena, also come from out of thin air - and indeed live there, rather like the shadows on Plato's cave wall.

Kammerer's more concrete ideas never got out of the original German (until our recent translation) and were dealt another blow by science writer Arthur Koestler when he wrote *The Roots Of Coincidence* and a brief biography of Kammerer called *The Case Of The Midwife Toad* in the early 1970s. In both he mentions seriality theory, praises it as important, but then dismisses it as being seductive but acausal - he clearly misunderstood the work. Although it is long and at times difficult, it repeatedly insists on following established causal principles, though the manner in which they apply is more similar to the very latest developments in fractal, chaos, and complexity theories than anything Koestler would have had to draw on to better understand it. Einstein, on the other hand, even reading it at the time of its publication, found the seminal concepts in the work "by no means absurd".

Kammerer's rigorous and analytical approach is immediately evident at the beginning where he classifies and orders 'serial' events before going on to explain their interaction. It is clear he is grappling with a complex problem just from the way he divides up the way series can manifest:

1. A. Simple series (first order).
   B. Series sequence (higher order).
   C. Power series (higher degree).
2. A. Spatial or simultaneous series.
   B. Temporal or succedent series.
3. A. Dependent series.
   B. Collateral series.
4. A. Pure series.

   B. Hybrid or mixture series.
5. A. Single-rowed series.
   B. Multi-rowed series.
      a. Parallel series.
      b. Polytomic series.
         aa. Diverging series.
         bb. Converging series.
   C. Correlation series.
6. A. Segmental or metameric series.
   B. Bilateral or symmetry series.
7. A. Motion series.
   B. Rest series.
8. A. Quantity series.
   B. Quality series.
9. A. Equivalence or identity series.
   B. Similarity or affinity series.
10. A. Homology Series.
    B. Analogy series.
11. A. Row or direct series.
    B. Crossing or inverse series.
12. Opposition or contrast series.
13. Alternating or exchange series.
    A. Alternating series.
    B. Cyclic or circular series.
       a. Cyclical series.
       b. Phasic series.
       c. Periodic series.

Kammerer illustrates his categories with abundant examples of coincidences, many of which seem utterly banal and not worth examination, while others are noticeably bizarre. Where most observers would only notice spectacular coincidences, Kammerer sees an evolution from the barely coincidental to the powerfully unusual, all connected by a hidden structure. After first classifying the types and levels by which coincidental events may be ordered, he then proceeds to propose mechanisms that would explain them scientifically in a direct, causal manner. In the process, he proposes three physical principles upon which the behaviour of complex systems in the everyday world depend, and which take elementary Newtonian laws and apply them not just to physical bodies but to systems of interconnected elements and events.

It is quite obvious to the everyday observer, for instance, that certain types of systems have lives of their own that are more than the sum of their parts and display ongoing qualities even when all of their components have changed. Companies, for instance, or ships - and any kind of bureaucracy. It is as if they have their own kind of inertia and tend to sustain and renew themselves robustly, even in the face of serious assault or damage.

Kammerer calls this quality persistence, the application of physical inertia at the systems level. This inertial quality increases the longer a system stays together, as its environment adapts to it and tends to sustain it from without as well as within. Every part within and surrounding it gains the stamp of the system over time through this process, from the most dense physical parts right up to the lightest, informational parts. When the system finally does break apart, for whatever reason, the pieces travel on along their own paths, carrying with them the stylistic, spatial, and vectoral hallmarks of the experience. Although the visible whole is gone, it lives on in its separate pieces which no longer appear to have anything to do with it, but which continue to evolve and form their own systems. The original has, in fact, not died, but simply passed from the bandwidth where we can recognize it and has become part of the 'background' environment. As in the case of a fractal, self-similar parts of the original whole have been formed but at a size or place where we cannot see it.

Nevertheless, the parts continue to evolve, and themselves break up and reform, until one day some of them run into each other again and surface - often in several different places at the same time, since the same time frame and vectors are involved - and suddenly *an unexplained coincidence arises*, at least so it appears to the outside observer. In fact, of course, everything is proceeding according to nature's laws and what was previously invisible and its origins forgotten has suddenly surfaced to our view. Nothing mysterious here, only complex beyond our ability to see or keep track of.

In developing the concept of persistence and why it should not be overcome and dispersed by entropy, Kammerer enlists two subsidiary concepts, also adaptions of simpler physical laws and also intuitively obvious. He calls them *imitation* and *attraction*.

Imitation is familiar to all. It is a wrap-around term for various types of behaviour we sometimes call mode-locking or entrain-

Fig. 1 - Paul Kammerer

ment - the tendency of larger, stronger, more energetic systems to bring smaller, weaker, less energetic systems under their sway and become more like them. It is the tendency to achieve equilibrium: Newton's Third Law applied to systems. It covers everything from why the moon presents only one face to the earth to why women's menstrual cycles are drawn into sync with that of the dominant female in their environment. In Kammerer's view, neighbouring forms and processes tend to become increasingly alike over time. Physical stuff takes a long time, depending on how malleable it is, but information, having no mass, can adapt almost instantly, transferring form and accompanying function down the line to perpetuate and transform earlier situations which then pop up mysteriously as coincidents as they re-evolve into our view.

Attraction is defined as the tendency for like forms and processes to cluster - everybody knows birds of a feather flock together, right? (so do fish, before raining down from the sky!). Kammerer proposes it as a fundamental principle. In a way, it is the counterbalance to imitation, as where things are already alike, equilibrium is already achieved, at least in part, and change then becomes the only option. Combined with imitation, it suggests a condition of swing-

253

shift reality for systems in general which is very much what leading-edge Belgian chemist and thermodynamicist Ilya Prigogine suggests in his 'swing theory' of open systems, which he proposes to explain the obvious reverse entropy of so much of the observable universe.

What is implied by Kammerer's threefold approach to seriality is virtually a 'Law of Conservation of Information' (our phrase, not Kammerer's) which suggests that at whatever rate its apparent dispersal, *no information is lost*. It only vanishes from our bandwidth of perception, to reappear in altered but often recognizable form down the road. Even where things appear to have come to a complete halt, the very energy and information lost in the race toward equilibrium are stored in adjacent systems and come back in evolved form to rejuvenate the original into new life - which suggests that these adjacent systems are simply part of a functioning larger one that contains them all.

In the case of information at least, as has been previously suggested by information theorists like Claude Shannon, entropy may well be largely in the eye of the beholder, defined by artificial limits imposed by the observer. This kind of approach to the apparent loss of information is also reflected in recent developments of chaos theory where phase-space diagrams and fractal dimensioning reveal order that was previously assumed to be lost.

Kammerer's view, and ours, is that virtually none of it is lost, and it is the type of order and the surroundings in which it is buried that hold the key to where it will burst forth in the future. Whereas chaos, fractal, and information theory tend to be specific and applicational, Kammerer's approach is more universal and embracing, an attempt to tie them all together based on the framework of a paradigm that vanished before it could get a hearing. Its implications allow application of these very much later developments upon a much broader scale than their current proponents have had the imagination (or perhaps audacity) to suggest.

S tarting from the simplest observations and then generalizing from them, Kammerer came up with a world-view we are only now catching up with and upon which many facets of science can draw for further growth. The concept of virtually limitless amounts of form and information imbedded in the environment, in constant motion, and mostly out of our view has wide-ranging implications in a variety of now-troublesome areas.

HISTORY - They say that history repeats itself, and this may be true in an even deeper sense than commonly understood. Human history may in fact be a veritable theatre of seriality. Dramatic events that affect large numbers of people and break down the prevailing causal structure - wars, catastrophes, etc. - free many events so that the natural attraction and affinity of events can allow them to reconfigure serially, thus creating a riot of coincidence.

However, such large scale events also have a great amount of inertia. A great many people experience very similar, intense experiences, not just internally, but the environment itself undergoes a very radical and specific restructuring. When it is over (indeed, as it is happening), these structures branch and effectively go underground, to recombine and surface later in perhaps familiar, perhaps unfamiliar guises, but nevertheless related reincarnations (so to speak). If they should retain their warlike habit, it could mean the onset of hostilities that the best of peacemakers could not avert, being ignorant of the real source.

Thus, seriality could account for much of the history subsequent to these events. It is even possible that seriality is the dominant principle in history, the only way of seeing the overall correlation of causes and events. If so, it would be most important to learn to recognize the various ways in which series become temporarily unrecognizable, only to resurface later.

As for theories of history, instead of singling out a certain type of cause, say, economic, or a cyclical view of the history of nations based on developmental causal models, or seeing history as the unfolding of the Hegelian Idea, we should perhaps only employ these causes as restraining features on the serial process, which may itself the real nerve of the historical process.

ANTHROPOLOGY - There were striking similarities in the implements and technologies of various peoples around the globe in paleolithic and neolithic times, who also shared the habit of building large stone monuments in similar configurations (both sky-oriented and otherwise). These include the stone builders of the Red Clay people around the arctic rim, neolithic northern European peoples, the cultures of Egypt and the Middle East, Southeast Asia and the South Pacific, South America, Africa, and, according to some, legendary Atlantis. These similarities have given rise to much speculation concerning the spread of various peoples around the globe in those ancient times, guided by the general assumption that they must have started in one place and spread out to the rest of the world.

However, according to the serial view, these similarities may have arisen independently through the medium of persistence causality. They may be regarded as simultaneous serial imitations of some common event, well back in the common history of the different peoples when they were all the same stock, in which case little could be inferred about the spread of the peoples from the artifacts. Alternatively, according to the laws of analogical seriality, the common event could even have been some relatively global, inanimate event such as a mountain-raising episode. The imitation of the forces involved in this originating event could manifest as an impulse to erect stone monuments, not necessarily arising as a clear intention in the mind of an individual, but subliminally organizing the efforts of a community.

If this is true, all kinds of 'ancient astronaut' and 'mystic Egyptian' theories

Appendix 1 - KAMMERER'S WORLD VIEW

"I do not want to be a victim of the tragic fate, to finally recant a life consecrated to the clarification of natural occurrences by sinking into the darkness of mysticism; at most I want rather to plunge down into its depths, in order to lift as much of its solid foundation as possible into the light. To free hitherto occult things from mysticism, not to hide things that have already been illuminated behind a mystical veil: that is my goal and task." - P.K.

I magine yourself swimming in the ocean in the midst of a pod of whales: big ones, small ones, moms, dads, and babies. The only evidence you see of them are their dorsal fins above the surface, an occasional rolling back or tail fin, and periodic spouting. From what you see around you, what can you conclude? If you know whales and whale behaviour, you can deduce quite a bit. If you had never seen or heard of whales, you might easily be led to some seriously wrong conclusions. As you see the fins appear above the surface, their location appears to be random - here, there and everywhere, without much pattern. Every now and then two or more will appear and reappear simultaneously in a succession of places. Is it a random occurrence, or is there an underlying causal pattern? Statistically, it would seem to be random, but if you know whales you easily conclude that it is several animals swimming together, perhaps for the purpose of mating, a mother caring for its young, or just companionship, whereas the rest of the fin appearances were random. Even if you didn't know whales, but had the reasonable experience with animals that most of us share, you would probably come to a similar conclusion. By bringing a lifetime of experience to the situation, our human software easily makes the association, but if you were a computer, even a supercomputer, without that background, you would almost certainly conclude on a statistical basis alone that the patterns you saw were random and unconnected.

As a human, the conclusion you made is highly unscientific, however, because it is purely speculative. You don't know exactly why those whales are swimming together, if indeed they are, so you have no right to logically draw the ☛

may be laid to rest, and warring anthropologists and archaeologists may bury the hatchet in the knowledge that at least in part, they all are right.

ANIMAL BEHAVIOUR OR ETHOLOGY - The category of strange, unexplained phenomena has come to be called Forteana after the writer Charles Fort (1874-1932), who along with others like Sir Arthur Conan Doyle, Bernard Heuvelmans, Willy Ley, and Ivan Sanderson collected voluminous lists of strange happenings and coincidences that seemed too bizarre to admit to ordinary explanations. These include frog and fish falls from the sky, multiple sightings of unusual animals, strange meteorological phenomena, and so on.

A number of modern examples have been cited to support Rupert Sheldrake's theories of 'morphic resonance', a kind of updated version of the ideal shadow-forms in Plato's cave manifesting in physical reality on Earth. For instance, little birds called blue tits seemed to learn how to open milk bottles on people's steps all over England simultaneously, even though they were of different sub-species with non-overlapping ranges and thus could not have taught each other to do it. It just occurred to them all at once, which Sheldrake attributes to their sensitivity to some newly-formed etheric morph. Similarly, when rats are taught to perform a maze in Los Angeles, their unconnected counterparts in the U.K. suddenly can do it with ease. According to Kammerer's plan, that's completely logical. When an idea's time has come, it literally and figuratively has - it just surfaces all over the place, following its masked antecedents. Of course, this is why people

☛ conclusion, however correct it may be. Your problem, of course, is you are on the surface and the whales are under the water. Most of the information you need to come to a proper conclusion is simply not within your view. You aren't equipped to see the whole picture. If you were, you would conclude that none of the fin appearances were random as the whales swim together as a whole pod, constantly interacting physically and vocally.

More than that, the whales are also reacting to you splashing about, so some of what you think is random is actually order you are producing yourself without even knowing it. You are haplessly part of the experiment, so to speak. None of it is random - it is all interconnected, but you simply cannot see it.

Despite knowing little about the situation, you still come up with an instinctual analysis of the matter that is at least partially correct, albeit 'unscientific', which is more than a computer can do. Moreover, you don't give it a second thought, any more than seeing three Alaska license plates on the same day. You are used to presuming the rest of the iceberg from its tip, because humans do that sort of thing so well.

Kammerer's world-view is similar: he depicts us as swimming in an infinitely complicated sea of interrelated 'sea-monsters'; complexes of materials and forces which constantly change in shape and scale, only a small part of which we are equipped to 'scientifically' observe or analyze, but which aeons of evolution have prepared us to handle in ways we often do not consciously recognize. It is a universe in which no energy or matter, or *information* is lost, and which does not run down at the end with a whimper but continually reorganizes itself eternally.

Like countless waves crossing in the sea, localized patterns merge, interpenetrate, recombine, resize and then resurface again with subtle changes in a never-ending dance of relatedness and familiarity. Events of the past, long reabsorbed and dispersed, recongeal from their parts in a timely and lawful manner and then go on to transform themselves and once more pass out of our view. We, inseparably in the middle of it all, can only behold it with wonder and join in the dance.

invent the same thing at the same time, independent of each other - it surfaces in the information matrix in multiple places, but flourishes only in the most fecund spot.

GAMBLING - Well, don't look to win the lottery right away, but perhaps you should reconsider the direct use of probability and statistics. Seriality tells us what will tend to happen in an individual context if it is not impeded by outside forces, rather than what will happen for the most part if we average out the effects of a multitude of individual causes. After all, the gambler is right next to the serial process, seeing the individual causes involved, and making a short term prediction about whether an event tends to recur. In this regard seriality may be compared to chaos theory, which can in principle determine what will issue next, employing for that purpose a deterministic law that produces events that appear stochastic and random, hitherto subject only to probabilistic law.

The successful gambler does all this intuitively, by the direct but subconscious perception of the serial process. He knows instinctively when the complex of people and objects at the table momentarily comprise a system isolated from the rest of the environment, so that its serial tendencies will not be impeded by other forces intervening. He senses when the cards represent the 'inertial centre' of this system itself, and then follows the run of cards. He reads not just the cards, but the people, the music, etc., and knows when some apparently unimportant and unrelated event signals the end of the isolation of the system, and the breaking of the streak. Then he folds. If he is very canny, he may even know how to do things to make his luck, how to give a certain twist to the serial process, etc.

This same kind of pattern is commonly intuited by successful professionals in a variety of areas in which science now applies (or attempts to apply) only probability and statistics - the stock market, politics, and advertising demographics, to name just three of the most obvious.

GHOSTS & APPARITIONS - If one of the principal actors in a highly persistent series is entirely removed from the system, the system will tend to replace it with a substitute as best it can.

A similar argument might account for many of the reports of ghosts, particularly the regularly recurring variety. When someone who is at the centre of a highly persistent event complex is suddenly removed, the system may try to restore the presence of that person when the time comes round for an intense peak in the serial process. The system may assemble fog, light reflections, various naturally occurring noises, even plant suggestions in the minds of the observers in an effort to achieve a perfect repetition of the initial event.

MANTIC & ORACULAR DEVICES - One of the most subtle types of seriality is that of correlated series. These result when the individual members of two independent trains of events come together in step with one another and act as if there was a single series with two common unlike features in the repetition. It is a case of two independent series imitating a given, single series, and is a kind of mimicry on the part of nature. This is not to say that these correlations are illusory. They are not. They are merely imitations of imitations.

Most of these correlations would be quite short lived. For example, it may happen that you stub your toe three times on a given day, and each time an ambulance is passing. However, the apparently random sequences produced by mantic devices such as tarot and the I Ching seem to have a strong tendency to correlate with events of a characteristic kind.

SACRED PLACES - In any system there may be certain islands of stability which are left relatively untouched by the continual transformation that forces the remaining bodies to wander all about their 'world'. Here we suppose that there are certain regions that remain virtually unchanged for long periods of time. We might say that these island subsystems have a rather low capacity for spatial adjustment, for mingling their contents with the outside environment. The full range of seriality would have free play within these islands due to the heightened spatial and

Continued on p260 ☞

257

APPENDIX 2 - GETTING LOST IN A SERIES

The varying structures of seriality are simple in their essence, but as individual components in an event begin to move about, switch on or off, or transpose, the resulting picture can get quite dizzying, as Kammerer only begins to suggest in the somewhat blinding diagram A - below - which illustrates his first classification:

1.A. Simple series (first order). A repetition of the same or similar things done twice or more than twice.

B. Series sequence (higher order). A combination of two or more simple series in which one of their

Ausgangsserie	Anhangs- oder Nebenserie		
Serie 1. Ordnung (1. Potenz)	Serie(n) 2. Ordnung (3. Potenz)	Serie(n) 3. Ordnung (6. Potenz)	Serie(n) 4. Ordnung (12. Potenz)

Ausgangsserie:

$$I\begin{pmatrix}a_1\\b_1\\c_1\end{pmatrix}\; II\begin{pmatrix}a_2\\b_2\\c_2\end{pmatrix}\; III\begin{pmatrix}a_3\\b_3\\c_3\end{pmatrix}$$

Serie(n) 2. Ordnung:

$$IV\begin{pmatrix}a_4\\d_1\\e_1\end{pmatrix}\; V\begin{pmatrix}a_5\\d_2\\e_2\end{pmatrix}\; VI\begin{pmatrix}a_6\\d_3\\e_3\end{pmatrix}$$

$$IV\begin{pmatrix}b_4\\f_1\\g_1\end{pmatrix}\; V\begin{pmatrix}b_5\\f_2\\g_2\end{pmatrix}\; VI\begin{pmatrix}b_6\\f_3\\g_3\end{pmatrix}$$

$$IV\begin{pmatrix}c_4\\h_1\\i_1\end{pmatrix}\; V\begin{pmatrix}c_5\\h_2\\i_2\end{pmatrix}\; VI\begin{pmatrix}c_6\\h_3\\i_3\end{pmatrix}$$

Serie(n) 3. Ordnung:

$$VII\begin{pmatrix}d_4\\j_1\\k_1\end{pmatrix}\; VIII\begin{pmatrix}d_5\\j_2\\k_2\end{pmatrix}\; IX\begin{pmatrix}d_6\\j_3\\k_3\end{pmatrix}$$

$$VII\begin{pmatrix}e_4\\l_1\\m_1\end{pmatrix}\; VIII\begin{pmatrix}e_5\\l_2\\m_2\end{pmatrix}\; IX\begin{pmatrix}e_6\\l_3\\m_3\end{pmatrix}$$

$$VII\begin{pmatrix}f_4\\n_1\\o_1\end{pmatrix}\; VIII\begin{pmatrix}f_5\\n_2\\o_2\end{pmatrix}\; IX\begin{pmatrix}f_6\\n_3\\o_3\end{pmatrix}$$

$$VII\begin{pmatrix}g_4\\p_1\\q_1\end{pmatrix}\; VIII\begin{pmatrix}g_5\\p_2\\q_2\end{pmatrix}\; IX\begin{pmatrix}g_6\\p_3\\q_3\end{pmatrix}$$

$$VII\begin{pmatrix}h_4\\r_1\\s_1\end{pmatrix}\; VIII\begin{pmatrix}h_5\\r_2\\s_2\end{pmatrix}\; IX\begin{pmatrix}h_6\\r_3\\s_3\end{pmatrix}$$

$$VII\begin{pmatrix}i_4\\t_1\\u_1\end{pmatrix}\; VIII\begin{pmatrix}i_5\\t_2\\u_2\end{pmatrix}\; IX\begin{pmatrix}i_6\\t_3\\u_3\end{pmatrix}$$

Serie(n) 4. Ordnung:

$$X\begin{pmatrix}j_4\\v_1\\w_1\end{pmatrix}\; XI\begin{pmatrix}j_5\\v_2\\w_2\end{pmatrix}\; XII\begin{pmatrix}j_6\\v_3\\w_3\end{pmatrix}$$

$$X\begin{pmatrix}k_4\\x_1\\y_1\end{pmatrix}\; XI\begin{pmatrix}k_5\\x_2\\y_2\end{pmatrix}\; XII\begin{pmatrix}k_6\\x_3\\y_3\end{pmatrix}$$

$$X\begin{pmatrix}l_4\\z_1\\A_1\end{pmatrix}\; XI\begin{pmatrix}l_5\\z_2\\A_2\end{pmatrix}\; XII\begin{pmatrix}l_6\\z_3\\A_3\end{pmatrix}$$

$$X\begin{pmatrix}m_4\\B_1\\C_1\end{pmatrix}\; XI\begin{pmatrix}m_5\\B_2\\C_2\end{pmatrix}\; XII\begin{pmatrix}m_6\\B_3\\C_3\end{pmatrix}$$

$$X\begin{pmatrix}n_4\\D_1\\E_1\end{pmatrix}\; XI\begin{pmatrix}n_5\\D_2\\E_2\end{pmatrix}\; XII\begin{pmatrix}n_6\\D_3\\E_3\end{pmatrix}$$

$$X\begin{pmatrix}o_4\\F_1\\G_1\end{pmatrix}\; XI\begin{pmatrix}o_5\\F_2\\G_2\end{pmatrix}\; XII\begin{pmatrix}o_6\\F_3\\G_3\end{pmatrix}$$

$$X\begin{pmatrix}p_4\\H_1\\J_1\end{pmatrix}\; XI\begin{pmatrix}p_5\\H_2\\J_2\end{pmatrix}\; XII\begin{pmatrix}p_6\\H_3\\J_3\end{pmatrix}$$

$$X\begin{pmatrix}q_4\\K_1\\L_1\end{pmatrix}\; XI\begin{pmatrix}q_5\\K_2\\L_2\end{pmatrix}\; XII\begin{pmatrix}q_6\\K_3\\L_3\end{pmatrix}$$

$$X\begin{pmatrix}r_4\\M_1\\N_1\end{pmatrix}\; XI\begin{pmatrix}r_5\\M_2\\N_2\end{pmatrix}\; XII\begin{pmatrix}r_6\\M_3\\N_3\end{pmatrix}$$

$$X\begin{pmatrix}s_4\\O_1\\P_1\end{pmatrix}\; XI\begin{pmatrix}s_5\\O_2\\P_2\end{pmatrix}\; XII\begin{pmatrix}s_6\\O_3\\P_3\end{pmatrix}$$

$$X\begin{pmatrix}t_4\\R_1\\S_1\end{pmatrix}\; XI\begin{pmatrix}t_5\\R_2\\S_2\end{pmatrix}\; XII\begin{pmatrix}t_6\\R_3\\S_3\end{pmatrix}$$

Diagram A

features (transverse component) is always taken over into the series that follows and is repeated there.

C. Power series (higher degree). All of the series of the first order that issue from a common series as their origin by means of a changeover of components.

In diagram A - previous page - things start out simple and very soon become horrendously complex. In the first series on the left (Series 1), there is simple repetition of an event with three components a, b, and c. It could be, for example, on day one(I) you run into a strange man(a) wearing a Tyrolean hat(b) and carrying a brass-headed walking stick(c). Nothing of note. On day two(II), it happens again - same guy, same hat, same stick. An interesting coincidence.

On day three(III), there he is again. Is he following you, or what? Day four(IV), you see him again for the fourth time(a4), but he's wearing a bowler(d1) and carrying an umbrella(e1). The coincidence-series is over.

Or is it? Just down the block you spot a different guy(f1) who's wearing a Tyrolean hat(b4) and carrying a briefcase(g1), and around the corner there appears a fellow(h1) wearing a fedora(i1) and carrying a brass-headed walking stick(c4)! Your original experience has split into three.

Two more times(V, VI) you see all three in this new form, and then each of those transforms into two different versions with shared elements - canes, umbrellas, sticks, various hats, and who knows what else. By the fifteenth repetition, what you see may not appear to noticeably resemble your first coincidence, yet it is directly linked.

We began with an arbitrary starting place, however, which made it much simpler than it really is.

Diagram B - below -is a modest effort to show that we reached that starting place as a result of other elements shuffling themselves along until we showed up at that place and time. In fact, one could start at any one of the modules in diagram A and go off in any direction and still find things to be connected. Wherever you are, things are moving in all directions, overlapping and developing both in time (longitudinally, left to right in the diagram) and space (transversely, up and down in the diagram). You, of necessity, are always in the middle of it all, confused by the blinding complexity of it all, yet sensing there is some sort of order here if only you could pull back, God-like, enough to see it.

Zweitvorhergehende Serie (− 2)	Erstvorhergehende Serie (− 1)	„Ausgangsserie" des Schemas S. 57 (+ 1)
$-V\left(\begin{smallmatrix}\mathfrak{F}_1\\\mathfrak{M}_4\\\mathfrak{D}_4\end{smallmatrix}\right) -IV\left(\begin{smallmatrix}\mathfrak{F}_2\\\mathfrak{M}_b\\\mathfrak{C}_b\end{smallmatrix}\right) -III\left(\begin{smallmatrix}\mathfrak{F}_3\\\mathfrak{M}_6\\\mathfrak{D}_6\end{smallmatrix}\right)$ $-V\left(\begin{smallmatrix}v_1\\\mathfrak{P}_4\\\mathfrak{D}_4\end{smallmatrix}\right) -IV\left(\begin{smallmatrix}v_2\\\mathfrak{P}_b\\\mathfrak{C}_b\end{smallmatrix}\right) -III\left(\begin{smallmatrix}v_3\\\mathfrak{P}_6\\\mathfrak{D}_6\end{smallmatrix}\right)$	$-II\left(\begin{smallmatrix}\mathfrak{F}_4\\v_4'\\a_{-7}\end{smallmatrix}\right) -I\left(\begin{smallmatrix}\mathfrak{F}_b\\v_b'\\a_{-1}\end{smallmatrix}\right) 0\left(\begin{smallmatrix}\mathfrak{F}_6\\v_6'\\a_0\end{smallmatrix}\right)$	
$-V\left(\begin{smallmatrix}\xi_1\\\mathfrak{R}_4\\\mathfrak{C}_4\end{smallmatrix}\right) -IV\left(\begin{smallmatrix}\xi_2\\\mathfrak{R}_b\\\mathfrak{C}_b\end{smallmatrix}\right) -III\left(\begin{smallmatrix}\xi_3\\\mathfrak{R}_6\\\mathfrak{C}_6\end{smallmatrix}\right)$ $-V\left(\begin{smallmatrix}\chi_1\\\mathfrak{T}_4\\\mathfrak{U}_4\end{smallmatrix}\right) -IV\left(\begin{smallmatrix}\chi_2\\\mathfrak{T}_b\\\mathfrak{U}_b\end{smallmatrix}\right) -III\left(\begin{smallmatrix}\chi_3\\\mathfrak{T}_6\\\mathfrak{U}_6\end{smallmatrix}\right)$	$-II\left(\begin{smallmatrix}\xi_4\\\chi_4\\b_{-7}\end{smallmatrix}\right) -I\left(\begin{smallmatrix}\xi_b\\\chi_b\\b_{-1}\end{smallmatrix}\right) 0\left(\begin{smallmatrix}\xi_6\\\chi_6\\b_0\end{smallmatrix}\right)$	$I\left(\begin{smallmatrix}a_1\\b_1\\c_1\end{smallmatrix}\right) \quad II\left(\begin{smallmatrix}a_2\\b_2\\c_2\end{smallmatrix}\right) \quad III\left(\begin{smallmatrix}a_3\\b_3\\c_3\end{smallmatrix}\right)$
$-V\left(\begin{smallmatrix}v_1'\\\mathfrak{B}_4\\\mathfrak{W}_4\end{smallmatrix}\right) -IV\left(\begin{smallmatrix}v_2'\\\mathfrak{B}_b\\\mathfrak{W}_b\end{smallmatrix}\right) -III\left(\begin{smallmatrix}v_3'\\\mathfrak{B}_6\\\mathfrak{W}_6\end{smallmatrix}\right)$ $-V\left(\begin{smallmatrix}\check{x}_4\\\mathfrak{D}_4\\\omega_1\end{smallmatrix}\right) -IV\left(\begin{smallmatrix}\check{x}_5\\\mathfrak{D}_b\\\omega_2\end{smallmatrix}\right) -III\left(\begin{smallmatrix}\check{x}_6\\\mathfrak{D}_6\\\omega_3\end{smallmatrix}\right)$	$-II\left(\begin{smallmatrix}v_4\\\omega_4\\c_{-7}\end{smallmatrix}\right) -I\left(\begin{smallmatrix}v_b\\\omega_b\\c_{-1}\end{smallmatrix}\right) 0\left(\begin{smallmatrix}v_6\\\omega_6\\c_0\end{smallmatrix}\right)$	

Diagram B

☞ *Continued from p257*

temporal persistence. Perhaps this is a factor in the 'magical' character of many of the ancient sacred places.

ASTROLOGY - And last, but not least, the old bugaboo that has been hanging around for centuries and engaged some of our greatest scientific minds (Brahe, Kepler, Copernicus, Galileo, Cardano, Paracelsus), and was instrumental in the birth of much of modern astronomy, mathematics, medicine, and psychology. It has fallen on hard times, because laboratory science cannot find **1)**. proof that it works consistently, and **2)**. a physical basis for its operation.

We see different processes at work here, which partly accounts for some of the confusion surrounding it. First of all, there is a strictly causal side to astrology, for which the evidence has steadily been accumulating. The planets apparently regulate solar activity in various ways, producing the variations in the solar wind which have such pronounced consequences on the Earth and its life. Furthermore, a mechanism has been proposed (by astronomer Percy Seymour) by which the planets can have a direct effect on the Earth: they can distort the Earth's magnetosphere by gravitation, thus affecting the geomagnetic field of the Earth itself.

From here on the linkages so far proposed become a bit implausible. We would suggest an application of Kammerer's imitation hypothesis here - namely, that the fluctuating gravitational influence causes fluctuating geomagnetic cycles which tend to mode-lock other large Earthly systems such as land and water tides, weather, geological cycles, etc. These, over the aeons, continue to mode-lock smaller systems, not as a single homogeneous unit, but singly by planet depending upon the nearest associated frequencies or resonances (just as different crystals lock onto different radio wavelengths). Over millions of years, multiple series of integrated systems are set up and continually reinforced. So, it should not be surprising when certain events surface in sync with the return of a given planet to a given position (a transit).

Another process involved in astrological phenomena is just Kammerer's persistence, and it explains the natal horoscope. Seriality takes effect after a system has fully come into independent being. At the moment of birth, a baby becomes an independent system, and effectively removes itself from any further endemic influence of the planets as a subset of its mother's system. It has, so to speak, locked them out, and its internal cycles will continue to persist with the pattern of planetary cycles prevailing at that moment, which will presumably have an influence on its personality. Furthermore, from that time on the planets can be used as indicators of the cresting and superposition of the internal cycles in the person.

These are just a handful of fields where seriality may shed light. Others include epidemiology, evolution, weather, homeopathy, probability, and on and on. By connecting the original ideas of Paul Kammerer with more recent concepts and updating the application of his thought as we are trying to do, a host of mysteries and their logical explanations may come to light. Despite the latest advances in complexity theory and the like, Kammerer's work and our applications of it still outdistance the pack. Perhaps this brilliant, but long-disparaged scientist may yet have his day.

OPTICAL ILLUSIONS
A BRUSH WITH THE ALIENS

Anne C. Silk

Anne Silk is a consultant optician and clinical researcher, and a member of several learned societies. In the following article she proposes that many Fortean phenomena are explicable in terms of ocular anomalies, produced by external energy sources: with particular emphasis on Haidinger's Brush, seen in certain situations where incident energy is polarised, and its relation to 'alien' encounters.

Fortean phenomena and their relationship to little-known areas of orthodox science have long been a personal interest, and 30 years of clinical experience with unusual ocular problems, many impinging on the brain, have led to an in-depth study of some of the more unusual systemic effects of electromagnetic energies on eye and brain. There are frequent reports in Fortean research and 'alien abduction' cases of figures with very unusual black, violet or yellow eyes, shaped like propellor blades or insect eyes. This article is intended to offer some thoughts on the nature of these apparitions, but we must begin by examining the eye and its functions, the ways in which our optical system can be influenced, and the illusory effects which can result.

Rare identical events and rare systemic effects in humans require a combination, often synergistic, of rare causative factors. Science has long studied ionising radiations (X-ray, Gamma, Beta), but the realisation in post-war years that non-ionising radiations (NIR) are emitted not only from the earth but also from man-made systems has enabled theories to be constructed and detailed mapping of the phenomenological effects to be carried out.

We know that the brain is totally transparent to magnetic fields, and that eddy currents are produced as energies traverse differing dielectric surfaces in the brain, much as light 'bends' when entering a substance with a different refractive index (the rod and glass illusion is well-known). As the iris, and thus the pupil of the eye, responds to NIR bands other than the visible spectrum (for example, in the fright mechanism, where a sudden loud noise can trigger pupil dilation) and the pineal gland deep in the brain responds adversely to LAN (light at night) by under-producing melatonin, which is essential for a strong immune system, so the retina and visual cortex will respond in certain circumstances to exogenous as well as endogenous electrical signals beyond the visible. A World Health Organisation report details the amplitude of the magnetic field which produces phosphenes, tiny brilliant flashing lights in the field of view which are readily misinterpreted by the viewer as car lights, figures, horses, etc. (WHO 1987).

Fig. 1 - Electromagnetic Spectrum (not to scale)

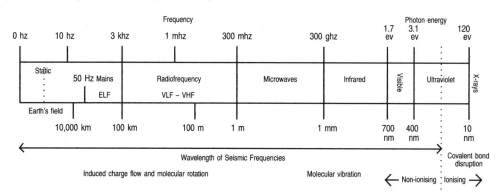

Fig. 2 - The Human Eye

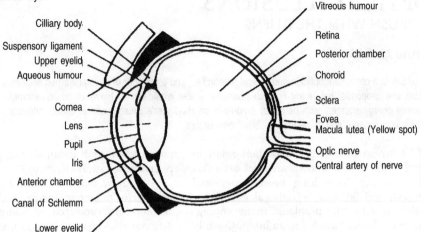

All human eyes are not the same. A few children can see into the ultra violet, while the media (inside) of the eye is still very clear. Many animals and a few adults can perceive the infra-red: these people will see an iron, which has been used but switched off, glowing in a dark room. If the head is irradiated by certain UHF signals, the retina can be so affected and sensitised that the eyes can see in the dark as if by daylight.

From an optical point of view the eye may be said to be at once the most wonderful optical instrument and the worst. The refracting surfaces are not spherical, they are not centred and the various axes are oblique to one another. The media are not homogeneous and they are not completely transparent. In addition, the yellow spot (or *macula lutea*) is polarised (Miller 1978). This means that there is a lack of symmetry in a beam of light. It can be produced by reflection, refraction (bending of light), selective absorption, dichroism (double refraction) and scattering. Light is always a transverse electromagnetic vibration and it is the electric vector which produces polarisation (Bennett 1989).

Light is not only seen by the eyes when the visible part of the spectrum is present but, as is well known, a blow to the head will cause the unlucky recipient to 'see stars'. The aura of epilepsy may produce unusual phenomena caused by energies within the brain spontaneously undergoing a vast surge in amplitude, from both endogenous (within the brain) and exogenous (from outside the brain)

sources (Persinger 1990). Further visual phenomena reported by many writers over the years may bear a direct spatial relationship to place, where seismic activity and electromagnetic 'hot spots' are combined at one point in space.

Many people see *muscae volitantes* ('flying ants') projected on the clouds in the sky, and are well aware that these are simply retinal projections from shadows of ocular debris. Another 'odd' image is the fine web-like structure which is seen apparently overlaying the view ahead when a strong light is shone at the eyes from an angle nearly horizontal to the plane of the face itself. This is a projection of the retinal blood vessels, which cast a shadow on the rods and cones of the eye to which the latter are normally adapted and therefore indifferent; they only become apparent when they are illuminated obliquely, when they will appear to be suspended in space in front of the face like a black lace mesh against a red background. Also, it is not unknown for the movement of the red corpuscles to be seen, projected against a brilliantly illuminated background as small dancing spots that pursue short but regular paths, apparently located in free space ahead of and in front of the subject. A further effect appears at the 400 nm. wavelength (the spectral region absorbed by haemoglobin). Hundreds of minute dancing spots of light may be seen (best against a blue sky): these are projections of the white corpuscles rapidly circulating within the capillaries.

Transduction from light to electrical and chemical energy takes place in photoreceptors and rods and cones lining the retina. The rods and cones contain different photopigments and each is characterised by its absorption spectrum. The ability to capture photons (a photon is a 'bundle' of borrowed energy varying in electron volts) differs as a function of the wavelength of the light striking the rods and cones.

The rod system functions only in night vision, the cones in the day as well. Rods are very sensitive to low light levels but are colour-blind. This inability to distinguish colours is due to the fact that the rods all contain the same photopigment, rhodopsin, which undergoes the same change after the capture of a photon. No matter what the wavelength of the stimulating light the result is the same. In dim light objects will not appear coloured. We shall come to the subject of 'alien eyes' in more detail shortly, but simply from the colour-receptivity of the rods and cones, we can make the following inferences: when 'aliens' have eyes of yellow/gold, the phenomenon is occurring by daylight, when violet/blue in dimmer light and when black, at night or in very low illumination.

Images are processed in the visual cortex at the base of the brain, after being received by the photoreceptors, rods and cones of the retina, and traversing the optic nerve and optical chiasma (from Greek, *chias*, cross) by electrochemical signals. But as with all electrical signals there is two-way traffic. Recent work in Russia indicates that signals not only enter the system via the eye, but also exit via the eye.

In sleep the eyes are seldom still, but dart about beneath the closed lids. In REM (Rapid Eye Movement) sleep it is now thought that certain vital electrochemical processes are in train as people deprived of REM sleep soon begin to suffer adverse effects.

Sudden visual loss can occur if the vessels at the back of and behind the eye are 'pinched'. This will affect transmission along the optic nerve and in the cortex, that part of the brain which processes visual signals. The retina may start to detach from its base and then too minute flashing lights may be seen. (All cases of visual loss, whether transient or permanent, must be seen urgently by a medical practitioner or optician).

The *macula lutea* or yellow spot is the area surrounding the fovea where the inner elements, especially the ganglion cells (which correspond to the foveal cones) are heaped up on all sides of the pit so as to leave an uninterrupted passage of light to this most sensitive area. The *macula lutea* has two curious properties. It is the only part of the eye where there are rods only, and it responds only to polarised energy.

The German mineralogist Wilhelm Karl Von Haidinger was the first scientist to describe the polarisation sense of the eye, in 1844. Since that time many others have investigated the effect which is now considered to be a dichroic effect of the *macula lutea*. As is so often the case in science, workers in one discipline focus in on a phenomenon reported in another. Mineralogists have known for centuries the unusual properties of special crystals which enabled navigators of old to know the exact position of the sun, despite cloud, through the polarising properties of the sunstone.

WHAT IS POLARISATION? Light may be visualised as very long ropes. Being held at the end and randomly bounced along the ground, the ropes will oscillate freely in all directions. But if we place a fence with vertical slats across the path of the ropes, then no matter what we do the 'shake' of the ropes as they reach the fence will *only* be allowed through in an up-and-down direction. The energy in the ropes has effectively been polarised.

The Umov effect means that the darker an object, the stronger is its polarisation. On a dark, rough surface like a curtain, a dark asphalt road or dark earth, light is far more strongly polarised than from white sand, white paper, etc. So the situation changes dramatically at sunset.

POLARISED ENERGY. The TV signal reaches your house from the distant transmitter as a polarised signal. Most signals sent through the air from a transmitter to a receiver are polarised, which means that the energy is only vibrating in one plane. This can be horizontal, vertical, elliptical or circular. That

Fig. 3 - 'Eyes' of a typical 'alien' encounter report can be described as black, yellow, or, more rarely, violet.

is why your TV aerial is angled to one meridian and to one compass point by the installer.

However, there is another signal which is also polarised and that is the piezoelectric energy released over faults, thrusts, etc., when minute movements occur in the earth's crust. The well-known San Andreas fault emits such energy, as does the area beneath Bristol, for example, which is built on faulted quartzite, and the Great Glen Fault in Scotland. There are hundreds of other small faults in the UK alone, and all are mapped and recorded by the British Geological Survey in Keyworth and in Edinburgh.

Light from the sun is also polarised. People who have used polarised sun-spectacles are familiar with the effect: a pool of water with brilliant reflected light is quite opaque until viewed with polarisers, when miraculously the water clears and fish swimming below are clearly seen. Car bodywork reflecting brilliant sunlight becomes 'cooler' in polarised light.

VISUAL ASPECTS OF THE 'GREY' AND 'ALIEN'. The figure most frequently described in 'encounter' cases consists of a disproportionately large cranium and eyes in relation to a reduced body, with vestigial facial features and reduced limbs. It is

predominantly reported as being naked, or with skin-tight body covering, but without sexual organs and having a putty-coloured surface. They eyes are reported as being without ocular structure in terms of cornea, iris, pupil, etc., and having an all-over black liquid appearance (Budden 1994).

There are many very recent examples of 'alien eyes' reported in the UK. Albert Budden, in both his books, *Allergies and Aliens* and *UFOs, the Electromagnetic Indictment*, has carried out meticulous research in the field and has taped conversations with men and women who very clearly describe black insect-like eyes, black lizard-like eyes and 'greys' with black propellor-like eyes which never blink. To these may be added the following cases, tabulated from Jenny Randles *Abductions:*

1946: Iain Johnston (Drumchapel, Glasgow) - 'eyes large and slanted'.
1955: Jennie (Nebraska) - 'eyes like long slits, nobody home in them'.
1957: Cynthia Appleton - 'elongated eyes'.
1978: Elsie Oakensen - 'an hour-glass or egg-timer shape'.
1979: Jean Hingley - 'coal-black eyes, no eyebrows'.
1981: Keith Daniels - saw a pattern across a grey figure 'like 8 on its side'.

Robert Moore, an investigator in East Huntspill, has interviewed a man who 'saw' black wrap-around eyes. The author has spoken to an ex-RAF clerical officer, now living in Wales, who frequently 'sees' black-eyed figures walking through his home; he also sees tiny TV sets in the dark, a clear pointer to the effects arising in the visual cortex rather than the eyes. Shapes resembling TV screens are also, in some cases, precursors of epileptiform attacks.

There is one unusual but well-documented effect which, depending on incident light, whether blue sky, grey sky or night-time darkness, will produce symmetrical elliptical shapes. The shapes are always the same and are known as Haidinger's Brushes (similar to, but not the same as, Haidinger's Fringes). This interesting effect is seen by some individuals (but not all, due to physiological reasons) when circularly, elliptically or linearly polarised light enters the eye at an extremely high degree of polarisation (e.g. > 60%): then a black, yellow or violet shape resembling a figure-of-eight or aeroplane propellor will appear, its orientation depending on the direction of the vibration of the incident light. It will rotate if the plane of polarisation is itself rotating, and it appears in the exact centre of the optical field.

One can practise seeing the effect in linearly polarised light by looking through a polarising filter at a white cloud. It will soon be seen that the centre of the scene is yellow. If the filter is now rotated, the figure-of-eight shape is seen which will rotate as the filter is rotated.

The polarity of the sky at twilight when the sun is very low in the sky is sufficiently strong for this observation. Look straight upwards and move your head slowly to and fro so that your chin points by turns east and west. Most people will then see a small yellow-gold figure pointing like a compass to the sun. If you stay still the figure will fade away as the retina adapts, but if you gently move the head it will stay in view.

When light is faint, as with moonlight, the human eye can hardly distinguish colours so then the nocturnal light seems to us to be black or grey in tone. But polarisation is not confined to light; it can occur with any electromagnetic radiation, such as radar, radio frequency and even X-rays. Both light and energy can also enter the eyes through closed lids, travelling via the retinal - optic nerve - hypothalamic axis to areas deep within the brain. Thus full illumination is not a prerequisite for seeing the Brushes.

There are several current theories as to the mechanism of Haidinger's Brushes: these include macular dichroism, lutein molecular alignment of the lipid bilayer membrane, and bi-refringence of the nerve fibre layer of Henle in the macular. The radial polarisers (the analysers) are located in the photoreceptors and absorb light only when the radial elements are perpendicular to the vibration of the polarised light. In the day, yellow light comes through, but at night, as the rods will only pick up hue rather than colour, grey or black shapes are seen. This fact has been made into a clinical test for macular function, when the Brushes are seen to be revolving in

Fig. 4 - Haidinger's Brush, in the case of linearly polarised light.

rotating blue light seen through a polarising filter.

Lyall Watson, in *Lifetide*, gives two interesting examples of what sound remarkably like Haidinger's Brushes. One is reported by C.G. Jung in 1906, in *Analytical Psychology*. He found a schizophrenic patient standing in front of a window 'wagging his head and looking into the sun'. When Jung asked the patient what he was doing, he said he could see an appendage hanging from the sun. Jung also reported a description of the effect in a Mithraic text. But rather than being, as he thought, a manifestation of the collective unconscious, these reports are more likely to be careful observations of a rare, but natural, phenomenon.

Having described the Haidinger's Brushes effect, let us now return to the 'alien encounter'. Due to the shape and symmetry of the image the brain makes the immediate assumption, within microseconds, that the images are eyes. It then obligingly produces a 'head' to enclose the eyes and then, in many reports, a 'body' of vague colour and form. The brain is so made that recognition and the placing of an image in a rational frame is essential to perception. Two eyes must obviously be in the head and the head must obviously have a body below it. Such a body will probably have clothes on it, and so on (Hopkins 1987, Budden 1994).

There are two constant factors to the 'eyes' of the 'aliens'. They never blink, and they are always the same shape. In the hours of darkness the 'eyes' will be jet black and have no reflex spot. In blue sky perceptions, the 'eyes' will be yellow or golden, and in high UV situations they will appear purple.

There is a further strange effect when the polarised field itself is rotating. The Brushes, or as we interpret them, 'eyes', will start to rotate swiftly much like an aeroplane propeller, and thus may be interpreted as 'wheels' spinning in the heavens. The fact that the image is 'seen' deep in the visual cortex of the brain does not mean that it cannot be projected by the brain to appear as being across a room, or in the sky.

The 'trickster' effects of the eye-brain combination account for many illusory effects. The distances at which the 'aliens' are seen vary from very close, to giant figures many yards away. This misperception of distance is a well-known optical phenomenon. We are all familiar with the observed giant size of the setting sun, or of the moon when it is low in the sky, yet in reality, and when photographed and measured, each disc is exactly the same size as when seen overhead. It is simply the brain's interpretation which is at fault. The brain may be thought of not only as a never-sleeping chemical production factory located within the skull, but as a vast visual and auditory reference library. There are a number of other optical effects relevant to the 'encounter' scenario.

THE FIELD OF STARS. Two identifiable stellate effects are reported (Tyler 1978) which follow rapidly when retinal blood-vessel circulating pressure is blocked (ischaemia). As blood pressure can drop from exogenous environmental causes, so it will affect not only circulation, breathing and the vagus nerve (controlling the heart), but also the eyes and brain. There are two field effects. The first is a random array of yellow coloured points against a dark background which appear to be uniform in size. The second is an array of brilliant violet points which become larger towards the edge of the field of vision. These are frequently reported in 'alien abductions'.

THE FIERY RINGS OF PURKINJE. There are many reports of people waking in a darkened room and seeing two large rings of silvery light in the room, apparently at the foot of the bed. From its compendious store of images, the brain will 'recognise' these as eyes and will then within microseconds produce a 'face'. The phenomenon is called the 'Rapid Convergence Phosphene' or 'Fiery Rings of Purkinje', after the German physicist who described them 1825. When the eye is dark-adapted, rod vision becomes dominant, rather than daytime cone vision; hue discrimination disappears, but luminosity discrimination takes over. In sleep, the eyes are looking up and in, not straight ahead as we might imagine. They are therefore converged. The muscular tension (and hence pressure on the eyeball) between the lateral and medial rectus muscles can be as much as four times greater when they are converged as when not (Tyler 1978).

RED EYED MONSTERS. Phenomenological and ghostly literature has very many reports of what are perceived to be monsters, shapes or animals with one (but not two) large red circular eyes. The odds against all these forms being exactly sideways on to the viewer (and thus with only one of two eyes visible) over the range of centuries and vast geographical distances are colossal. Once again, we can seek an answer in the convergence phenomenon mentioned above. While others will see a dumb-bell shape, a percentage of observers will see only a red disc, due to convergence anomalies. That is to say, where the eyes are closed but the lids are illuminated from an external source (like a night light or the moon full on the face) many will, in certain situations, see 'alien eyes', and others will see Red Eyed Monsters.

MAGNETOPHOSPHENES. A further curious and increasingly reported optical effect is the production of magnetophosphenes. These are tiny, brilliant, flashing lights which appear at the edge of the visual field. A common remark is 'when I turned to look at them, they disappeared'. Between 10 and 50 Hz magnetic fields above 5 mT will produce phosphenes. Ventricular fibrillation (heartbeat irregularities) may occur when current density exceeds 1000 mA/m^2 (H) or 100 mV/cm (E). Depending on the frame of mind and position of the 'viewer' these magnetophosphenes can be interpreted as an oncoming figure (in the middle distance), a distant car with headlights on (far distance) or a nearby white bird, or figure. When the magnetic field is very strong a pattern of scintillating gold or yellow lights is 'seen' apparently across a room, or road. It should be noted that not all present will see such visual effects; only those whose head is in the magnetic field. Dipole orientation effects occur in such systems as DNA, retinal rods and sickle cells at static fields above 1-2 Tesla (WHO 1987).

There are further optical effects which are very specific to place, or rather to electromagnetic fields traversing a point in space. If a radio frequency or microwave signal traverses the eye or brain it can, if enough photons are present, stimulate the retina and visual cortex, right at the back of the brain, into 'seeing' lights. These manifest as tiny white, cream, blue or green 'figures' or 'lights' which flash on the edge of the field of view.

CAUGHT IN THE CORTEX. The visual cortex, deep in the brain, can pick up and transmit signals as if they were real and existed in space. These may be of a regular grid or chessboard pattern, a triangular rayed sunflower effect, or even a shape like a large 'TV screen' (Tyler 1978). The ambient electromagnetic field is critical to these effects, whether as piezoelectricity (from the earth) or manmade (as communications signals). In the experience of the author, few in the eyecare and medical profession seem to be aware of the cause of these apparently strange images. If we stub a toe, we feel pain; if the eye or brain receives an electrical 'kick' a visual image can be created, but these originate, not in space, but deep in the brain.

The interaction of two fields is known as intermodulation and occurs when the earth (DC) and manmade (AC) interact at a point in space. It is especially interesting that Budden, in his ground-breaking book *Allergies and Aliens*, has established with meticulous fieldwork that both fields occur at the houses where his percipients were living at the time of hallucinations and 'alien' illusions.

Every manmade signal from a transmitter has what is known as a reactive nearfield. These are areas which vary according to wavelength and frequency near to a transmitter site. For example, the reactive nearfield of VLF transmitters is about 5 km, more or less depending on ground level, nearby reflective metallic objects, etc. For radio hams, who theoretically are restricted in residential areas to 400 watt peak envelope power (corresponding to 150 watts continuous power), the field strength in nearby houses can be as high as 20 to 30 volt/metre. If the power

quoted above is exceeded, the fields in neighbouring houses will be well above what are considered acceptable levels.

Electromagnetic radiation is emitted from stressed rocks preceding and during earth movements, whether earthquakes, fault slippages or rock fractures (Devereux 1989, Toshio 1985, Derr 1992). The potential mechanisms include tectonic strain, exoelectron emissions, streaming potential, EM excitation of water droplets and the fault zone itself as waveguide. In prehistory our forebears were sensitive to the emitted energies from the earth, via vision (magnetophosphenes), sonic effects and sub-sonic pulses or static build-up (tingling of mucosa and extremities), and carefully marked out these areas for special purposes. But the pressure on housing space in recent centuries has meant that many modern homes are built over these faults and thrusts, which are natural channels for the release of tectonic strain. We should not, therefore, be surprised at observing strange phenomena reported by completely sane people.

However, it is tragic when those reporting hallucinations and strange sensations are so often sent for psychiatric assessment when in many cases all that has happened is that the brain, visual cortex, amygdala, temporal lobes and the highly magnetosensitive pineal gland have received a very high amplitude 'zap' of electromagnetic energy. Peak powers, natural seismic surges and amplified transmitters all combine to trigger effects like the black, unblinking, wrap-around eyes of the 'aliens', as well as many auditory, visual and tactile phenomena.

Although sometimes referred to as 'subtle energies', there is nevertheless considerable hard data which has been published in many scientific disciplines. Cardiologists and neurologists have measured the healing currents emitted from fractures, the heart itself, synapses at nerve junctions, and so on. In geophysics, seismologists have measured emitted energies over faults, thrusts and at subduction plates, which range from Sub-ELF (0 - 3 Hz) through ELF (3 - 300 Hz), ULF (300 Hz - 3KHz) and radio frequency (3 KHz - 300 MHz) to microwaves (3 GHz - 300 GHz). Currents emitted from the cornea-scleral junction are measured in picoTesla and energy from visual evoked potentials has been measured by neurologists.

But eye and brain may possibly be acting like a semiconductor diode, which can both receive light and emit it. Thus an SCD may be both a generator and receptor of light. Krokhalev quotes E. Mendel who in 1904 compared visual hallucinations to "...pictures from a magic lantern. It seems to the patient that he is writing his thoughts on the wall and in the air, and sees them inscribed there." One is reminded of the wall-writing in the home of Mathew Manning and the Bromley 'poltergeist' case written up by Manfred Cassirer. Current Russian research (Krokhalev 1993) indicates that coherent energies from both

eyes and brain will affect film in a camera under hallucinatory situations.

The interaction of eye and brain with exogenous as well as endogenous energy sources, both electric and magnetic, will reveal in scientific terms the rationale for many so-called paranormal phenomena. Everything - atom, cell, crystal, man - is affected in some way, often profoundly, by interaction with other forms of energy. Nothing in this universe exists in isolation, least of all Man. As Sir Eric Laithwaite stated, when President of the Royal Institution, "Nature's problems have all been solved. We have only to be clever enough to unravel the answers".

REFERENCES

S.G.Allen: 'Radiofrequency Field Measurement & Hazard Assessment', *Journal of Radiological Protection*, 1991, 11-1.

A.G. Bennett: *Clinical Visual Optics*, Butterworth, 1989.

A.G. Budden: *Allergies & Aliens*, Discovery Times Press, 1994.

A.G. Budden: *UFOs - The Electromagnetic Indictment*, (in press) Blandford, 1995.

M. Cassirer: *The Persecution of Mr. Tony Elms*, privately published, 1993.

Dr A. Crampin: *A Decade of Shear Wave Splitting*, British Geological Survey, 1992.

J. Cronly-Dillon: *Vision & Visual Dysfunction*, McMillan, 1991.

J.S. Derr: 'Fluid Injection Causes Luminous Phenomena', *Soc. Scientific Exploration*, Princeton, June 1992.

P. Devereux: *Earth Lights Revelation*, Blandford, 1989.

B. Hopkins: *Intruders*, Sphere, 1987.

Prof. G.B. Konnen: *Polarised Light in Nature*, Cambridge UP, 1985.

G. Krokhalev: *Visual Hallucinations Captured on Film*, Aura Z, Moscow, 1993.

M. Manning: *The Link*, Corgi, 1975.

D. Miller: *Duane's Clinical Opthalmology*, Harper & Row, NY, 1978, 1:31.

Y. Miyashita: 'Inferior Temporal Cortex Where Visual Perception Meets Memory', *Annual Review of Neuroscience*, 1993, 16, 245-263.

M.A. Persinger et al: 'Enhancement of Temporal Lobe Related Experiences During Brief Exposure to ELF Fields', *Journal of Bioelectricity*, 1990, 9, 33-54.

J. Randles: *Abductions*, Robert Hale, 1991.

O. Toshio: 'Electromagnetic Radiation from Rocks', *Journal of Geophysical Research*, 1985, 90, 6245.

C.W. Tyler: 'Some New Entoptic Phenomena', *Vision Research*, 1978, 18, 1633-1639.

World Health Organisation: *Magnetic Fields*, Geneva, 1987.

A CHINESE COLLECTION

Steve Moore

The worlds of Chinese historical tradition and traditional cosmology remain relatively unexplored in Fortean circles. Steve Moore, author of *The Trigrams of Han*, examines tales of early Oriental automata, 'occult' battle-strategies, and the cosmological apparatus of the *I Ching* ... mainly with reference to the legend-enshrouded (but historical) figure of Chu-ko Liang.

INTRODUCTION

The five items gathered together here were originally intended to be published as a separate *Fortean Times* Occasional Paper; and, rather than splitting them up, I hope I may be forgiven for exercising my editorial privilege in keeping them as a unit. They derive from my continuing obsession with two interconnected aspects of the Chinese historical tradition: the noted strategist-statesman Chu-ko Liang (181-234 A.D.), and the *I Ching* or 'Book of Changes'.

Chu-ko Liang is one of those fascinating figures who is known to be a fully historical personage, but around whom a number of stories have gathered which seem to range from the apparently semi-historical to the distinctly non-historical. The first essay deals with one of those 'historical/semi-historical' areas: he was said to be responsible for building some sort of wooden automaton with which he transported the supplies for his army, and this piece looks at the evidence and its interpretations. The second piece takes us into that uncomfortable area where historicity blurs into folklore, with a collection of outrageous tales illustrating Chu-ko Liang's near-supernatural genius. Whether there might be any kernel of truth in these stories, I have to let the reader decide; but if we ignore them as fictitious nonsense we risk losing a fully-rounded view of the man and what he has come to represent ... and without that our chances of evaluating the apparently 'historical' material decrease rather than increase. They are, besides, ripping good yarns.

The remaining three pieces are more or less follow-up items to my book on the history of the *I Ching* and its structure, *The Trigrams of Han*, published in 1989. The final chapter of this work was devoted to Chu-ko Liang's use of the *I Ching* to draw up tactical formations on the battlefield. The third essay here, while providing no new insights on the Chinese material, examines some interesting parallels from the Indian tradition of about the same date.

The last pieces (which, from a Fortean viewpoint, might be classified as 'historical revisionism' and 'exploration of other cosmologies') concentrate on two of the arrangements of the eight trigrams of the *I Ching*. The first provides some new evidence for dating one of them, which was unavailable to me when I wrote *The Trigrams of Han*. For this information I am grateful to Peter Eckman MD, of San Francisco; by working together we have been able to clear up at least one minor point about the *I Ching's* history. The second evaluates a curious sequence of the trigrams which has only come to light in comparatively recent archaeological excavation, and demonstrates the dangers of making predictions from unproven hypotheses!

Finally, a word about the transliteration of Chinese words and names. Two choices were available to me here: to use the old-fashioned Wade-Giles system of transliteration, or the more recent New Chinese Phonetics (pinyin). Certain of my friends strongly urged the use of pinyin. Unfortunately, *The Trigrams of Han* was written using Wade-Giles; and as three of the items presented here refer directly to that book, I have thought it more convenient to continue using the same system. My apologies to those who find this decision unspeakable, but I confess myself a pragmatist who prefers maximum convenience. Besides ... I rather like Wade-Giles!

ANCIENT CHINESE AUTOMATA?

THE 'WOODEN OXEN' OF CHU-KO LIANG

Did wooden automata trundle their way, clacking and whirring, across the hills and plains of China 1,800 years ago, carrying army supplies for one of the greatest military geniuses the world has ever known? It sounds like one of those traditional stories which could not possibly have any basis in fact, but there is evidence to show that *something* was, indeed, on the move in the state of Shu all those centuries ago. But were they automata? And if not, what?

Before going any further, a word of warning might be in order. This piece deals with a subject that has fascinated me for years, but which is immensely complicated, highly technical and, finally, results in no positive conclusions at all. It has been 'explained' by experts, but these explanations themselves do not appear to be anything like satisfactory, and need to be examined in their turn. Even so, there comes a time when the available source material appears to have been exhausted, the arguments have been rehearsed, and there's nothing left to do but publish everything that's accumulated. And if, in the end, I can offer little more than negative conclusions, at least the mystery has been laid bare for all to see. Perhaps someone else will

be able to pick up the threads and draw everything together ...

First, then, what exactly is the nature of the beast? According to tradition, Chu-ko Liang (181-234 A.D.), Prime Minister of the state of Shu in China's Three Kingdoms period (220-265 A.D.), built *mu-niu liu-ma* in order to transport supplies for his army; furthermore, the tradition also says that these machines moved under their own power. About the first half of this phrase there is no dispute: *mu-niu* means 'wooden ox' or 'wooden oxen'. *Liu-ma* can be translated as 'flowing horse' or 'gliding horse', neither of which make much sense; the whole phrase is often rendered in English as 'wooden oxen and flying horses'. However, there is a secondary meaning for *liu*, which is 'transport', and thus *liu-ma* could conceivably be translated as 'transport horse' or 'baggage animal'. Allowing this to be the correct interpretation, we could then be dealing not with two different types of 'beast', the ox and the horse, but with one: the 'wooden ox baggage animal'. The evidence for this interpretation will be examined below. However, purely for the sake of brevity, I shall generally refer to the *mu-niu liu-ma* simply as 'wooden oxen'.

Fig. 1 - The manufacture of the wooden oxen. From a modern picture-book of the *Romance of the Three Kingdoms*.

HISTORICAL EVIDENCE AND TRADITIONAL TALES

We have a number of problems to deal with here. Did these wooden oxen actually exist? What was their appearance and function? Did they move under their own power? If they did, how did they move? And if they were not automata, what were they instead? Finally, if answers are proposed to the last question, do they stand up?

First, it should be said that there is no doubt that Chu-ko Liang was a real person. He was as real as, for instance, Alexander the Great, but like Alexander he was also the focus for a great number of later legends. He was engaged in almost continual warfare throughout the latter half of his life, and this provides the motive for our mystery: fighting on or across the borders of his state, he naturally required that considerable amounts of supplies and provisions be delivered to his army. Besides being an astute politician and a remarkable military strategist, Chu-ko Liang also had a considerable reputation as an inventor: a form of multiple-shot siege cross-bow, for example, is attributed to him. While this inventiveness may have given him the means to build automata as well as the motive, the very same quality naturally meant that it was particularly easy for legends and exaggerated tales to gather round him after his death, (some of which

will be examined in the article following this one) and he has become something of a Chinese 'Merlin' figure. So we must proceed with caution.

Let us first turn to the historical evidence. This mostly derives from the *San Kuo Chih*, the official 'History of the Three Kingdoms', hereafter abbreviated to *SKC* [1]. This work falls into two parts. The main body of the text was written by Ch'ên Shou (233-297 A.D.) and was completed in 274 A.D., only 40 years after Chu-ko Liang's death. Ch'ên Shou was a native of Shu, and the *SKC* consists of biographies of all the major figures of the Three Kingdoms period. The second part of the work is a commentary completed in 428 A.D. by P'ei Sung-chih (372-451 A.D.) [2]. Pei's work consists largely of quotations from works either contemporary with, or later than, the Three Kingdoms period.

Ch'ên Shou provides a number of brief references to the oxen, as follows:

231 A.D., 2nd month (21 March-19 April): 'Chu-ko Liang led forth his troops and surrounded Ch'i Shan, transporting supplies with wooden oxen.' [3]

232 A.D.: 'Chu-ko Liang rested his troops and encouraged agriculture; completed making flying horses and wooden oxen at Huang-sha; instructed and trained his troops.' [4]

234 A.D., 2nd month (18 March-15 April): 'Chu-ko Liang led all his hundred thousand troops out from Yeh-ku, transporting his

Fig. 2 - Chu-ko Liang's men immobilise the oxen by turning their tongues. From a modern picture-book of the *Romance of the Three Kingdoms*.

271

supplies by means of flying horses.' [5]

Finally, in a summary of Chu-ko Liang's character, Ch'ên Shou attributes the invention of the device to him alone: 'By nature, (Chu-ko) Liang was good at inventions...wooden oxen and flying horses were entirely his idea.' [6]

So far, then, we have near-contemporary references which indicate the existence of the wooden oxen, obviously in some numbers, and that Chu-ko Liang was responsible for their invention. There seems to be no reason to disbelieve Ch'ên Shou's account. It is hardly embellished, and appears to be a simple, laconic record of events. It seems fairly safe to assume, therefore, that the oxen are not entirely mythical; but we still have no indication as to their nature, nor any evidence that they were thought to move under their own power.

This idea of self-motivation appears fully-formed in later tradition, however, and its main receptacle is the *San Kuo Chih Yen-i* ('The Romance of the Three Kingdoms'), written by Lo Kuan-chung about 1370 A.D. [7]. This classic historical novel is an expansion of the *SKC*, and is said to be 70% fact, 30% fiction and tradition. In summary, the story it tells is this:

Chu-ko Liang proposes to construct wooden oxen and flying horses, at a place called either Shangfang Valley or Hulu Valley (the latter name referring to the bottle-gourd shape of the valley) near Ch'i Shan, on the Wei river.

They require neither food nor water and can keep on the move day and night without resting, and he produces a written plan for their construction [8]. Under his direction, the 'animals' are built by Tu Jui and Hu Chung, and can move over the hills in any direction. With soldiers to guide them, they run constantly from Chien-ko to the battle-front, carrying grain. Chu-ko Liang's opponent, general Ssu-ma Yi of the state of Wei, captures 4 or 5 of the oxen, strips them down, and within two weeks has built a thousand imitations, which also move. All this, however, has been planned by Chu-ko Liang. When Ssu-ma Yi puts his oxen into service, Chu-ko Liang's men capture them by a ruse. As the Wei troops pursue, Chu-ko Liang's men 'give a turn to the tongues of the wooden animals', rendering them incapable of motion. When the Wei counterattack has regained possession of the wooden oxen, they find themselves stuck with a convoy that won't move, and are thus easy prey for a further attack by Chu-ko Liang's troops. Then the victors 'give the tongues a backward turn', after which the oxen move again, and are carried off, together with their supplies.

The whole passage is rather confusing, and there does not appear to be anything in the histories to intimate that the events described actually happened. This suggests that the sequence is to be placed in the material composing the '30% fiction and

Fig. 3 - After their capture, the oxen cannot be moved. From a modern picture-book of the *Romance of the Three Kingdoms*.

Fig. 4 - The manufacture of wooden oxen. A woodcut of 1625.

tradition'. Nonetheless, there is obviously a strong tradition that the wooden oxen moved under their own power; such is the entire point of the passage. In passing, we may also note the importance given to the tongue, here treated as a locking/unlocking mechanism.

Unsatisfactory as this material may appear, it is from the *Romance* that the popular conception of the wooden oxen derives, and our figures 1-3 come from a modern picturebook version of the novel [9]. Figure 4, though rather unclear, is a woodcut from an illustrated edition of the novel, published in 1625 [10]. And this popular conception, taken at face value, remains to this day. Consider this modern piece, with all its quaint English:

Chu-ko Liang later invented a kind of vehicle called *mu-niu liu-ma* to deliver army rations. Such vehicles were installed with a kind of machine which remains unknown to the world. The machines were able to push the vehicle on plains, uphills, downhills or over rugged roads without any labour or fuels. They were as handy as modern jeeps. [11]

THEORIES

Macgowan [12], writing at the turn of the century, handled the problem as follows:

(Chu-ko Liang) set his mind to think, and the result was he designed a number of self-acting

273

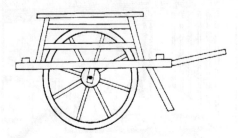

Fig. 5 - The standard form of the Chinese wheelbarrow. A simplified diagram based on photographs and illustrations in Needham (*SCC*)

machines that when wound up would proceed along the roads by themselves, subject only to the guidance and control of those that had the charge of them. The name given to them in the history of 'The Three Kingdoms' is 'the fleet of wooden oxen and horses'. What they were no one at the present day knows, though Chinese writers have discussed them, and men have taken the measurements that have been given in the history and striven to construct similar machines. It would seem that the spring was wound up by the tongue, for as the name implies they were made in the form of oxen and horses.

He also adds a footnote: 'Some have imagined that we have in them the first wheelbarrows that were ever in China.'

Macgowan, who seems to have used both the *SKC* and the *Romance* in constructing his history, here presents the two main theories about the wooden oxen. The first is that the oxen were actually self-motivated by some form of internal mechanism. Macgowan implies that this is a variety of spring-driven wind-up clockwork. Such a proposition would have to be treated with extreme caution. It is true that the gear-wheel was well-known in China before Chu-ko Liang's time, but there is no evidence of the clock-spring, or of the escapement necessary to regulate the mechanism, at anything like such an early date [13]. Furthermore, in none of the available material (including the detailed specification which we shall examine below) is there any mention of an internal mechanism suggesting clockwork.

My point here is not to devalue the genius of Chu-ko Liang (he might, just conceivably,

have invented something like clockwork, but there is no record of it), but that Macgowan is theorising from insufficient evidence. Again, there is nothing in the material to suggest that the 'tongue' is a winding mechanism; if the references in the *Romance* are not entirely fictional, they appear to refer only to a locking mechanism. I suspect that Macgowan may have been romanticising a report that simply baffled him; it is quite possible that Lo Kuan-chung, the author of the *Romance*, was doing the same.

The second theory is that the wooden oxen are to be interpreted as wheelbarrows. As we shall see, this theory is quite old in China, but its main proponent at present is Joseph Needham, who argues his case at some length [14]. With rare exceptions [15], the proposition seems to have been generally accepted, but unfortunately Needham's arguments do not seem to have received the critical examination they deserve. So, in want of anyone better to take on the task, I shall attempt to examine his arguments and material as we proceed. First, though, it is necessary to familiarise ourselves with the Chinese wheelbarrow.

A simplified diagram of the standard form of the Chinese wheelbarrow is shown in figure 5. There are many variants of this, but in the most usual form there is a large single wheel, centrally placed, which takes all the load. There is usually an open-work wheelhousing above the axle, and two side-shafts which extend toward the rear and become the handles by which the barrow is pushed. There are two vertical legs at the rear. The load is carried above the side-shafts, in two sections, one on either side of the wheel-housing. This is obviously different to the western wheelbarrow, which has a small wheel at the front, the large rectangular load-bearing section in the centre, and the legs and shafts at the rear. Needham shows several variants of the Chinese form [16]: none of them has more than two legs, rear-mounted, and the majority have a large wheel.

IN HIS OWN WORDS?

We must now turn our attention to the material that has survived in Chinese. Chu-ko Liang wrote extensively on a variety of subjects, and his

'Collected Works', the *Chu-ko Liang Chi*, ran to more than 100,000 words [17]. Unfortunately, the original *CKLC* is lost. The surviving fragments of his work were collected during the latter part of the Ch'ing dynasty (1644-1911 A.D.) by Chang Shu, and this forms the basis of the modern *CKLC*. [18]

An introductory essay in the modern *CKLC* [19] contains the following brief passage:

> Yen K'o-chun says, in his *Ch'uan San Kuo Wên* [20]: the method of making wooden oxen and flying horses ought to be in *Ch'uan Yun P'ien* [21]. The text appears in the commentary to *Liang Chuan* [22]; also in *Lei Chu* chapter 94, and *Yu Lan* chapter 899. [23]

I have been unable to check the latter two references, but from the way this passage is worded, I suspect that they reproduce the same text as that appearing in P'ei Sung-chih's commentary to the *Liang Chuan*, which we will come to shortly. This text appears in both *CKLC* and *SKC* [24], but the quotation from *CKLC* is preceded by a note from Chang Shu, which reads as follows:

> (Chang) Shu records: Tu Yu says, in his *T'ung Tien* [25], (that according to *Chu-ko) Liang Chi* [26], transport supervisors Liao Li, Tu Jui and Hu Chung, (working) in Ching-ku county, 25 *li* [27] south-west of Po Ma Shan [28], made wooden oxen and flying horses, following (Chu-ko) Liang's ideas. Furthermore, P'ei Sung-chih's commentary on *Shu Chih* [29] quotes the *(Chu-ko) Liang Chi* on the method of transporting by wooden oxen and flying horses, saying:

We now have the supporting evidence of a few names of those involved (two of whom also appear in the *Romance*), which at least adds to the appearance of historical truth; and while the place-names mentioned do not actually confirm those of the *Romance*, neither do they contradict them. Needham [30] adds another name to the list of workmen, P'u Yuan. A fragment of an alleged letter has survived, from P'u Yuan to Chu-ko Liang. It reads:

> I and my workmen now entirely understand your excellent suggestion, and have constructed a

'Wooden Ox' with horizontal timbers joined together and double shafts. (In the time taken by) a man (with a similar burden) to go 6 feet, the 'Wooden Ox' will go 20 feet. A man can carry his whole food supply for a year on it.

There are considerable grounds for suspicion here. Needham does not reproduce the Chinese text, but it is quite obvious that the latter half of this letter reproduces precisely the same wording as will be found in the text from the *CKLC*, allegedly written by Chu-ko Liang himself (see below, Needham's translation in note [35]; also main text at note [48]). We thus have a situation where, if the *CKLC* passage is, in fact, Chu-ko Liang's original specification, P'u Yuan is quoting his own words back at him, which seems pointless. On the other hand, if P'u Yuan's letter is authentic then Chu-ko Liang's specification would appear to be quoting from it, and the specification must therefore have been written after the machine was built. In one or other of these passages, therefore, I strongly suspect the hand of a forger.

Let us move on to the specification for the wooden oxen, given in P'ei Sung-chih's commentary on Chu-ko Liang's biography, and said to come from the original *CKLC*. The text for this is reproduced in figure 6 [31]. Although continuous in the original, the text can be conveniently divided into two parts. Of these, Needham translates only the first, and his version will be given in the footnotes. However, he then continues [32]:

> There follows a long passage in which minute dimensions and measurements are given. It is too tedious to quote, and at first sight so obscure that some have abandoned hope of reconstructing the exact wheelbarrow of Chu-ko Liang's time ... we can only say that a careful scrutiny of the text has led us to the view that the passage is not as garbled as it might seem, and that it points clearly to a wheelbarrow of a type which remained traditional thereafter.

He then proceeds to interpret the passage without translating it. This is unfortunate. By not giving the second part of the text, he risks arousing in the reader's mind a suspicion that it contains information which subverts the original interpretation. As we shall see, there are some grounds for thinking that such a suspicion might, in fact, be well-founded.

I have to say that I agree with Needham insofar as the text is extremely difficult to understand; my translation attempts to reproduce the meaning as literally as possible, without trying to make undue interpretation, or to supply words that suggest what I think the meaning should be [33]. There is also an alternative version of the text given in the Chinese edition of the *Romance* [34], which is somewhat abbreviated and contains a number of variant readings. With the exception of the most inconsequential (e.g., the substitution of exact synonyms), these variants will be dealt with in the footnotes. The text of the first part reads as follows [35]:

The wooden ox: square belly, crooked head [36], one leg, four feet [37]. The head enters the centre of the neck, the tongue is placed in the belly [38]. It carries much in few journeys; it is fit for large tasks, not small ones [39]. Alone [40] it travels several tens of *li*, in a group it travels twenty *li* [41]. The crooked part is the ox's head, the paired parts [42] are the ox's legs [43], the crosswise part is the ox's neck, the revolving parts are the ox's feet [44], the covering part is the ox's back, the square part is the ox's belly, the hanging part is the ox's tongue, the crooked parts are the ox's ribs, the carved part is the ox's teeth, the erect part is the ox's horn [45], the thin part is the ox's halter, the holding parts are the ox's traces and axletree [46]. When the ox's paired shafts face up [47], a man travels six feet, the ox travels twenty feet [48]. Carrying one year's provisions, it travels twenty *li* in a day [49], and the man does not suffer greatly. [50]

This first part of the text, then, gives us a general account of the wooden ox; the second part proceeds to give precise dimensions for its individual components. However, this passage begins 'The dimensions of the *liu-ma* are ...' Now, if *liu-ma* is to be taken as 'flying horse', we find ourselves in the position of having a text that describes the ox in general terms, and then gives the dimensions of a quite separate 'animal', the horse. This would be peculiar, to say the least. A more logical suggestion would surely be to read *liu-ma* as 'baggage animal', and take this to refer to the same thing as the ox. As a result, the second part of the text would then describe the same ox as is mentioned in the first part, and we would then translate *mu-niu liu-ma* as the 'wooden ox baggage animal'; only one object, rather than two variants.

The dimensions in the next part of the text are given in Chinese measurements. These measurements are based on the *ch'ih*, the 'Chinese foot'. In Chu-ko Liang's day, the *ch'ih* was equivalent to 9.094 modern English inches [51]. There are ten *ts'un* (inches) to the *ch'ih*. The *ts'un* is again divided into ten *fên*. Rather than overload the translation with Chinese words, I have translated *ch'ih*, *ts'un* and *fên* as 'foot', 'inch' and 'tenth' respectively, but the reader must bear in mind that we are using a decimal system here, rather than normal English measures.

The second part of the text has peculiar problems of its own, but reads as follows:

The flying horse's dimensions are: the ribs are 3 feet 5 inches long, 3 inches wide, 2 inches and 2 tenths thick, the left and right identical [52]. The front axletree hole *fên-me* [53] is 4 inches behind the head, its diameter is 2 inches. The front leg hole *fên-me* is 2 inches, and 4 inches and 5 tenths behind the front axletree hole, 1 inch wide [54]. The front crossbar hole is 2 inches and 7 tenths behind the front leg hole *fên-me*, the hole is 2 inches long and 1 inch wide. The rear axletree hole is 1 foot and 5 tenths [55] behind the front crossbar *fên-me* [56], all dimensions the same as the front. The rear leg hole *fên-me* is 3 inches and 5 tenths behind the rear axletree hole, all dimensions the same as the front. The rear crossbar hole is 2 inches and 7 tenths behind the rear leg hole *fên-me*, the rear container-fixture [57] is 4 inches and 5 tenths behind the rear crossbar hole *fên-me* [58]. The front crossbar is 1 foot 8 inches long, 2 inches wide, 1 inch and 5 tenths thick. The rear crossbar is of the same sort. There are two rectangular cases of planks, 8 tenths thick, 2 feet 7 inches long, 1 foot 6 inches and 5 tenths high, 1 foot 6 inches wide [59], each one holding 2 *hu* and 3 *tou* of rice [60]. From the upper crossbar hole down to the rib is 7 inches, front and back the same [61]. From the upper crossbar hole to the lower crossbar hole is 1 foot 3 inches; the holes are 1 inch and 5 tenths long, 7 tenths wide, eight holes altogether. Fore and aft are four legs, 2 inches wide, 1 inch and 5 tenths thick. The shape is according to the diagram [62].

澍案：杜佑通典逃云，亮集督運廖立、杜叡、胡忠等，於景谷縣西南二十五里白馬山，推己意作木牛流馬云云。又案裴松之蜀志注引亮集，載木牛流馬法，曰：

木牛者，方腹曲頭，一脚四足，頭入領中，舌著於腹。載多而行少，宜可大用，不可小使；特行者數十里，羣行者二十里也。曲者爲牛頭，雙者爲牛脚，橫者爲牛領，轉者爲牛足，覆者爲牛背，方者爲牛腹，垂者爲牛舌，曲者爲牛肋，刻者爲牛齒，立者爲牛角，細者爲牛鞅，攝者爲牛鞦軸。牛仰雙轅，人行六尺，牛行四步。載一歲糧，日行二十里，而人不大勞。流馬尺寸之數，肋長三尺五寸，廣三寸，厚二寸二分，左右同。前軸孔分墨去頭四寸，徑中二寸。前脚孔分墨二寸，去前軸孔四寸五分，廣一寸。前杠孔去前脚孔分墨二寸七分，孔長二寸，廣一寸。後軸孔去前杠分墨一尺五分，大小與前同。後脚孔分墨去後軸孔三寸五分，大小與前同。後杠孔去後脚孔分墨二寸七分，後載剋去後杠孔分墨四寸五分。前杠長一尺八寸，廣二寸，厚一寸五分。後杠與等板方囊二枚，厚八分，長二尺七寸，高一尺六寸五分，廣一尺六寸，每枚受米二斛三斗。從上杠孔去肋下七寸，前後同。上杠孔去下杠孔分墨一尺三寸，孔長一寸五分，廣七分，八孔同。前後四脚，廣二寸，厚一寸五分。形制如象，軒長四寸，徑面四寸三分。孔徑中三脚杠，長二尺一寸，廣一寸五分，厚一寸四分，同杠耳。

Fig. 6 - The Chinese text of the specification for the wooden oxen.

277

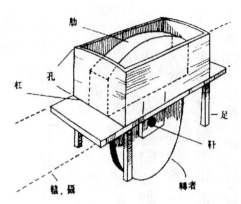

Fig. 7 - Needham's 'Reconstruction of Chu-ko Liang's army service wheelbarrow' according to the specifications in the *Chu-ko Liang Chi.*

The *k'an* [63] is 4 inches long, the face diameter is 4 inches and 3 tenths. In the opening are three leg crossbars [64], 2 feet 1 inch long, 1 inch and 5 tenths wide, 1 inch and 4 tenths thick, all crossbars projecting. [65]

INTERPRETATIONS

As has already been mentioned (see note [14]), Needham interprets the wooden oxen as being wheelbarrows. Now that we have the full specification before us, it is time to examine this interpretation in more detail.

The first thing that has to be said is that this interpretation would be more convincing if the wheelbarrow was unknown before Chu-ko Liang's time. We could then conjecture that Chu-ko Liang was the original inventor and gave his wonderful new machine a poetic name, which thereafter fell into disuse and was replaced by other names such as the *k'uang* or the *jung* mentioned by Needham as early names for the wheelbarrow. However, Needham himself adduces evidence that the wheelbarrow was already known before Chu-ko Liang's time. In my view, this would suggest that if the wooden ox was nothing more than an ordinary wheelbarrow there would be no reason why it should be thought particularly notable, nor why it should have been given a special name. The histories would merely record, if anything at all, that Chu-ko Liang transported his supplies by wheelbarrows. That they do not, suggests

that we are dealing with something different.

It is possible that Needham has been unduly influenced by Chinese writers on this subject. He quotes Kao Ch'êng, of the 11th century A.D., as follows [66]:

> Chu-ko Liang, prime minister of Shu, when he took to the field, caused to be made the 'Wooden Ox' and 'Gliding Horse' for the transportation of the army supplies. In Pa and Shu the ways were difficult, and these (vehicles) were more convenient for getting over the hills. The 'Wooden Ox' was the small barrow (*hsiao ch'ê*) of the present day, and it was so called because it had the shafts projecting in front (so that it was pulled); while the 'Gliding Horse' was the same as that (wheelbarrow) which is pushed by a single person (and so has the shafts projecting behind).

What is being suggested here is that, even allowing for minor differences in design, basically the same wheelbarrow has different names depending on which way it faces, and whether it is pulled or pushed. I do not find this proposition convincing. Furthermore, we have already seen some evidence that might suggest that the 'Gliding Horse' may be read as 'baggage animal'; i.e., it is a term describing the wooden ox itself, not a separate 'animal'. If we are dealing with only one machine, Kao Ch'êng's arguments about the differences fall apart.

Let us now examine Needham's interpretations of the specification translated above. He begins [67]:

> To make the measurements fit, however, it is necessary to adopt certain identifications; for example, the 'ribs' (*lê*) may plausibly be taken to indicate the internal housing which protects the freight from the large revolving wheel. The box of ribs in an animal is, in a sense, a box within a box.

That the 'ribs', of which there appear to be two, each 3 feet 5 inches long, 3 inches wide and 2 inches and 2 tenths thick, can be interpreted as the curved-topped 'internal housing' shown in Needham's diagram (figure 7) is, frankly, something of a strain on my credulity, even allowing the diagram to be more schematic than realistic. As has been repeatedly pointed out in the notes, the presence of this 'large revolving wheel' is somewhat conjectural. This aside, Needham's diagram makes it clear that he is placing this 'internal housing' within a single box which carries the load. Apart from the fact that two boxes are mentioned, we have seen that the rectangular boxes are said to be 2 feet 7 inches long, while the ribs are 3 feet 5 inches long. The ribs therefore cannot possibly fit inside the box, and the idea that they form an internal wheel housing has to be rejected. Needham continues:

> Again, the 'bent part' is the front, the 'cross part' the axle, and the 'double part' the bearings. *Kang* must be taken to mean crossbars, *k'ung* mortises, and *K'an* the small piece of the frame carrying the axle-bearings. The upright sides and ends would be dismountable.

The text, in fact, refers to the 'crosswise parts' as the ox's neck, and the 'double part' or 'paired parts' as the ox's legs. These, of course, are open to interpretation; but even so, this interpretation does seem to be moving rather far from the original context. I have also translated *kang* as 'crossbar', while *k'ung* I have translated as the more general 'hole'; it may perhaps refer to a mortise, but I would not wish to impose so specific a meaning on it when it could equally mean no more than a simple aperture or opening. From his diagram, the small piece of the frame which Needham is taking to be the *k'an* appears to be a flat piece of wood with a hole in it, the axle fitting into the hole. But we have seen that the *k'an* is '4 inches long, the face diameter is 4 inches and 3 tenths'. The 'diameter' must presumably refer to something circular, in Needham's interpretation the hole. But if it is the hole which has a diameter of 4 inches and 3 tenths, then the hole is presumably larger than the piece of wood containing it, which is obviously absurd. The text suggests instead that the *k'an* is drum-shaped. Finally, Needham does not make it clear to what he refers by the 'sides and ends'. I assume he is referring to the boxes; but there is nothing in the text to suggest that these are dismountable.

Let me make myself clear here. I have enormous respect for Needham in general, and I would not wish to deny outright the possibility that the wooden ox is a wheel-barrow. There are certain features ... the horizontal ribs and the double container cases, the shafts which are raised ... which do suggest a Chinese wheelbarrow. But nowhere is there a direct reference to a large central wheel, which would seem to be a remarkable omission if a wheelbarrow is intended; it is, after all, the heart of the whole machine. Besides this, there is the point that he appears to have misinterpreted the nature of the ribs and the *k'an*. Furthermore, there are numerous features, especially in the first part of the text, which Needham does not attempt to explain. Where do the teeth and tongue and traces fit on a wheelbarrow? What of the four legs? This appears to me to show a rather unwarranted selectivity about the evidence: those features which fit with the concept of a wheelbarrow are retained, while those which do not fit are discarded. My overall impression would have to be that Needham has approached the wooden oxen *looking for a wheelbarrow*, rather than starting from the evidence about the ox and attempting to interpret it on its own terms; as a result, he has found exactly what he was looking for. This may or may not be the case, and I would not wish to do him an injustice. But what does seem clear to me is that, whether Needham is right or wrong about the wooden ox being a wheelbarrow, he has not made a convincing argument on the basis of the evidence. Indeed, I would have to say that I am no more convinced by Needham's wheelbarrow than I was by Macgowan's idea of a clockwork automaton.

While rejecting these other interpretations, I also have to admit that, frankly, I don't know what the wooden ox is, on the basis of this specification. Obviously there is no mention of any internal machinery, but neither is there a single large wheel ... and it is certainly very small. The longest dimension is that of the ribs, 3 feet 5 inches long. In English measurements, this is only some 2 feet 8 inches. It appears to have an open-work structure, with horizontal ribs, four crossbars (upper and lower, front and rear) and four legs. We are told that it has four feet, which presumably lie at the end of the four legs, and that the 'revolving parts' are the feet; we also have a front and rear axle. Perhaps, then, we are dealing with a four-wheeled cart, rather than a single-wheeled wheelbarrow. Beyond this, however, it seems unsafe to speculate. But once again we are left with the questions: why would such a cart be considered notable, why given a special name?

CONCLUSIONS

What, then, do we have in the end? We seem to have fairly safe evidence that the wooden oxen actually existed, and were invented and used by Chu-ko Liang. We also have a description and specification which certainly dates back as far as the time of P'ei Sung-chih, in the 5th century A.D. Beyond that, though, nothing seems very certain.

This specification, preserved in the *SKC*, was obviously available to Lo Kuan-chung, the author of the *Romance of the Three Kingdoms*. He reproduces the text in his novel, with minor alterations; and these alterations are so minor that it seems fairly clear that his version derives from the *SKC* text, rather than from a variant source. Perhaps we should put it more broadly, and say that the *SKC* text was available to *whoever* originated the tradition that the wooden oxen were self-motivated, whether that person be Lo Kuan-chung or an earlier predecessor. Now, it is true that there are sections of this text, especially in the first half, which might be read as *suggesting* that the oxen were self-motivated. But suggestions are not evidence, no matter how appealing they might be, and other interpretations would also be possible. Furthermore, there is no description of internal machinery in the specification, and we have discovered no other hard supporting evidence to suggest that the wooden oxen were self-motivated. One possible theory of explanation that we would have to consider, then, is this: that the originator of the tradition has taken the original, highly obscure and confused description, with its mention of horns, teeth, tongues, and so on, its references to the ox moving 20 feet (or 4 paces) while the man moves 6 feet, and, most crucially, the easily misunderstood phrase 'alone it travels several tens of *li*' ... and conjectured from all this that the wooden ox is an automaton, naturalistically shaped like the animal referred to, which moves without the aid of man. If such a theory were correct, we would be left with an excellent story ... but nothing to suggest that it is anything more than fiction.

Which brings us back to the specification. I have maintained that it is not possible to make a convincing interpretation of the wooden ox as either an automaton *or* a wheelbarrow on the basis of the information preserved. Which raises the question, can we trust the specification anyway? All the arguments reviewed so far (Macgowan's, Needham's, and my own) have depended on the notion that the specification is a genuine record of the wooden oxen and was, if not written by Chu-ko Liang himself, at least contemporary with him. And, as we have seen, apart from the references from Ch'ên Shou, this is the prime document from which all other traditions and interpretations appear to descend.

We know that the original *CKLC* was lost. Unfortunately, we have no information as to *when* it was lost. Thus it is by no means clear whether P'ei Sung-chih had the complete work in front of him when he quoted from it in his commentary, or whether he was quoting from a preserved fragment of a work already lost. So, is there any evidence that might indicate what the case actually was?

It has already been pointed out in the footnotes that the text appears to be corrupt in a number of places. Also, we do not seem to have a full set of measurements. For example, there is no mention of the length of the legs. There are also several items mentioned in the first part of the text which have no measurements in the second ... the tongue, the head, the shafts, the halter, and so on. Instead, we have only certain measurements of the 'body' of the ox, and even these are incomplete and confusing. Now, as there does not seem to be any evidence that P'ei Sung-chih was a bad copyist, we would have to assume that the text that he was copying was corrupt and incomplete before it reached him. And as the rest of the surviving parts of the *CKLC* appear to be reasonably literate, we may dispose of the idea that Chu-ko Liang himself wrote a corrupt and incomplete text. All of which suggests to me that P'ei Sung-chih did *not* have the complete *CKLC* before him; only a fragment alleged to come from it. Perhaps, despite the reservations I expressed in note [3] above, he was possibly quoting from the *Wei shih ch'un ch'iu* after all ...

It has also been mentioned (following note [30]) that the correspondence between the letter of P'u Yuan and the first part of the description gives grounds for suspecting that one (or possibly both) of the documents is a forgery. This leaves us with a large question mark over the first section of the specification. Unfortunately, this is the most literate and comprehensible part of the specification; it is the second section which shows most sign of corruption and incompleteness. As such, it is the second section which we would most suspect as having not come directly from the writing-brush of Chu-ko Liang. It would therefore be most unwise to discount the possibility that both parts of the specification translated here are forgeries.

Thus, despite my argument concerning the translation of *liu-ma* (given above following note [50]), which depends on treating the text as one complete item, the fact that we have *separate* grounds for suspecting the authenticity of *each* section of the text would suggest the possibility that the text is, after all, a conflation of two separate items, one treating of 'oxen', the other of 'horses'. There would then be the possibility that, although the oxen and horses are usually treated together, there might after all have been two separate machines: and that we have a description of the oxen, but no specification, while we have a specification for the horses, but no description. But, of course, either part of the text, or even both, could still be forgeries.

Ultimately, then, I would say that while we might accept the original evidence of Ch'ên Shou that Chu-ko Liang did in fact build something called *mu-niu liu-ma*, everything else is unsafe. Mind you, in the final analysis, one is tempted to wonder about even that. Ch'ên Shou, after all, was only one year old when Chu-ko Liang died; he could hardly have seen the oxen with his own eyes, and thus we only have *his report*. Perhaps that report originated in nothing more than Chu-ko Liang's war-time propaganda ... a fairy-tale of 'wooden oxen' to baffle his enemies and bolster his own image. This, of course, is just as much speculation on my part as anything else mentioned here, but I would find it wryly amusing to think that I've spent the last couple of decades, off and on, investigating a huge whopper perpetrated by Chu-ko Liang

himself!

Still, this notion is probably just as unprovable as everything else, so perhaps we should allow Ch'ên Shou's evidence to stand after all. But the specification is probably corrupt and incomplete, and possibly an outright forgery. It is obviously unsafe evidence on which to theorise about some form of automaton. But it is equally unsafe evidence on which to theorise about wheelbarrows. Both must be considered not proven. Indeed, I would go so far as to say that the wheelbarrow notion, despite its *apparent* rationality is quite as much a fantasy as the automaton idea and probably more of a pernicious one: for however fantastic the idea of the automaton may be, it builds up from the data while leaving it basically intact; while the wheelbarrow notion seeks, when not omitting parts of the evidence, to subvert it.

What we are left with, then, is an open field where nothing seems proven or provable, where 'facts' are vaporous and theories nebulous. It is a field ripe for speculation, mystification and fictionalisation. That we, as human beings, are so eager to fill in the gaps with our tales of robot oxen or our rationalisations of wheelbarrows, even to the point where we only add further to the mystery of history, is perhaps a more curious and interesting facet of the entire affair than any kernel of possible 'truth' behind the legend. In the end, though, as with the battle tactics based on the eight trigrams of the *I Ching* [68], Chu-ko Liang seems once again to have taken his secrets with him to the grave. I rather think that it would have amused him to leave us so mystified.

APPENDIX 1

THE AUTOMATA OF MISS HUANG

While final preparations were being made to send this material to press, chance (?) brought to my attention the following item, from G C Stent's century-old introduction to Ch'u-ko Liang, *Brief Sketches from the Life of K'ung-ming* [69]. Stent's series of articles is almost entirely drawn from the *The Romance of the Three Kingdoms*, except for the first item which, after the technicalities discussed above, is so delightful that I reproduce it here in its entirety.

K'UNG-MING ATTACKED BY THE DOG

The first notice we have of K'ung-ming is of a traditionary nature, and, therefore, not to be relied on; it is derived from an old ballad, and is inserted here simply to shew that even in the remote period in which he lived, the ideas, which we in the present times have put into practical form and have brought to such proficiency (viz., the employment of machinery) existed. Foreigners pass this fact over slightingly, or treat it with derision - but in whatever way it may be put, the fact remains the same and cannot be gainsayed: that the *idea* of machinery being employed, as infinitely superior to hand-labour, originated with the Chinese nearly 2000 years before Western nations thought of such a thing, although they failed to carry out their ideas, or after having succeeded in carrying them out, owing to the troublous times in which the inventors lived, or other causes, the art became lost. This is a matter which would doubtless prove an interesting study, and the studying of which might bring to light many curious and startling facts, hitherto undreamt of by foreigners.

In the little ballad above mentioned we are told that K'ung-ming was one day writing a stanza which was to consist of eight lines, and had already composed six of them, but found himself at a loss for the rhyming of the two lines necessary to complete it. He forthwith went out to a neighbour, named Huang, to submit the lines he had already written for his approval, and to request him to write the two lines he was deficient of.

On reaching his friend's house, K'ung-ming entered the door, which he closed after him. Seeing no one in the court-yard, he thought his neighbour had gone out, but on counting his fingers and looking at the palm of his hand, he could tell by his art that Huang was asleep in his library. K'ung-ming thought 'We are old friends, so I will go in without ceremony: it's useless bothering any one to announce me.'

He was proceeding towards the library, when suddenly a large dog he had not before perceived flew out at him and seized hold of the skirt of his robe, which it tore. K'ung-ming hastily retreated two or three steps, crying out lustily for help, at the same time trying to beat the dog off.

Huang was roused from his sleep by the disturbance, and came out to see what was the cause of it, when he perceived that it was his friend K'ung-ming whom the dog was attacking. Huang, on seeing this, cried out 'Don't be alarmed; the dog is only made of willow. Just step aside and stand still; he cannot hurt you!'

'What!' exclaimed K'ung-ming, 'do you mean to tell me that this is a *wooden* dog, or that a wooden dog can bite a person? How is it that it can jump about and fly at one as if it were alive?'

Without replying, Huang went up to the dog, hit it with a stick, and the dog at once lay down without moving.

'This is very extraordinary,' exclaimed K'ung-ming.

'Yes,' replied Huang, 'it *is* somewhat strange, but at the back of the premises I have also a 'willow horse'. This wooden horse every day grinds our corn.'

K'ung-ming said he could hardly credit this, but Huang at once satisfied his doubts by leading him to the mill-room, where he set the horse to work at turning the stones. K'ung-ming was struck with amazement, and exclaimed, 'if Government were only to make use of this invention what a saving it would effect in forage!' He eagerly asked who invented this wonderful horse, and was told by Huang 'that his daughter had carved it out for pastime'.

When K'ung-ming heard this he was amazed and delighted; thinking the girl must be a prodigy. As for the poetry he had come about he made no mention of it whatever, but remarked to Huang, 'the person who is fortunate enough to gain this girl as a bride would, through her means, be able to render great service to the state'. Deeply impressed with what he had seen K'ung-ming returned to his home, but never rested till eventually Huang bestowed his daughter on him. K'ung-ming lived for some time with his young wife in the enjoyment of domestic happiness and a rural life, till he felt himself compelled to leave his quiet home through the exigencies of state and the repeated solicitations of Liu Pei, who personally went three times to entreat K'ung-ming to give him the benefit of his counsel and services.

Thus we find that Chu-ko Liang's *wife* appears to be responsible for the entire notion of wooden automata! Stent mentions that 'we are told that she was coarse and ugly, but that she was possessed of great talent, understanding astronomy, geography and many other sciences, which she taught her husband

- most of the knowledge he possessed being derived from her instructions'. I have been unable to track down the source for these assertions.

APPENDIX 2

THE AUTOMATA OF LU PAN AND OTHERS

Regardless of what the wooden oxen may in fact have been, the concept of automata was far from unknown in Chu-ko Liang's time. Needham [70] provides considerable evidence for Chinese automata of the 'mechanical toy' variety (similar to those produced in Europe over recent centuries) from as early as the 3rd century B.C. As a single example we might mention here the work of one Ma Chun, a near-contemporary of Chu-ko Liang who flourished in the middle of the 3rd century A.D. A mechanical genius who lived in the state of Wei, he improved the silk loom, built a 'south-pointing carriage' (a cart which used a system of gearing to keep a pointer placed on top continuously pointing toward the south, no matter which direction the cart travelled in), irrigation pumps and military siege equipment. More to the point, though, he also built an automated puppet-theatre in which wooden figures of singing girls played music and danced, government officials worked in their offices, acrobats danced on balls and cocks fought [71].

However, fascinating as these 'mechanical toys' may be, they were generally worked by an outside power-source, such as the water-wheel, the power then being transmitted to the machines by ropes, pulleys or gears. The nature of their mechanisms can thus at least be the subject of reasonable conjecture, even if the exact details remain unknown. They are powered from without, and although the individual parts move, the machine as a whole does not move from place to place. They are thus not quite analogous to the wooden oxen, which were traditionally said to be internally powered and capable of full motion. For this type of parallel we must again turn to more traditional and mythological material.

A curious tale of a fully-functional humanoid robot appears in the Taoist classic, the *Lieh Tzu*. This work was written about 300 A.D., but seems to borrow some of its material from as much as 600 years before. The tale that concerns us here is set in the reign of King Mu of Chou, who traditionally reigned from 1001 to 946 B.C. King Mu, travelling in the west of the country, was introduced to a craftsman called Yen Shih. Upon being asked to show the King something he had made, Yen Shih returned with a 'man' who would dance when Yen clasped his hand, sing when he pushed his cheek and do innumerable tricks. So realistic was the figure that King Mu became enraged when it began to wink and beckon to his concubines, and threatened to execute Yen Shih. At this point Yen Shih cut the figure open and revealed it to be an automaton made of leather, wood, glue and laquer. It had a full set of internal organs, all artificial, and when King Mu took out its heart, it could not speak; when the liver was removed, it could not see; when the kidneys were removed, it could not walk. Expressing his wonder, King Mu had the figure loaded onto one of his cars and took it away with him [72].

There is probably little point in seeking any reality in this story, or in the figure of Yen Shih. The *Lieh Tzu* is a book of parables rather than historical anecdotes, and the story is undoubtedly more concerned with the nature of reality than the reality of automata. Besides, Graham points out that the story may well have its origins in India: a similar tale is told in the Buddhist work *Sheng-ching*, which was translated into Chinese in 285 A.D. [73].

Rather more central to our interests are the tales which centre round Lu Pan, who was deified as the god of carpenters. Regrettably, there is considerable confusion about Lu Pan himself, let alone his creations. He has multitudinous names [74], but the general consensus seems to be that he should be identified with the (possibly historical) craftsman Kung-shu P'an; the alternative name Lu Pan apparently deriving from the fact that he was a native of the state of Lu. One possible explanation of this muddle might be this: that a noted craftsman called Kung-shu P'an was later identified with a much more mythical figure, Lu Pan, and that as a result the more mythical traditions connected with the latter figure were then grafted on to the former. Be this as it may, let us first turn our attention to the stories centring on Kung-shu P'an.

The earliest material relating to Kung-shu P'an appears in the *Mo Tzu*, the classic book of the philosophical school founded by Mo Ti, which was written in the 4th century B.C. Here we read that 'Kung-shu P'an constructed a bird from bamboo and wood, and when completed, it flew. For three days it stayed up in the air, and Kung-shu was proud indeed of his skill' [75]. Of course, as with the *Lieh Tzu*, we are once again dealing with a philosophical text, and this story merely serves as a peg on which to hang a riposte from Mo Ti: that however skilful Kung-shu P'an might be, his work has no practical purpose, and is not to be compared with the skill of a carpenter who makes a wooden linch-pin.

Another story concerning Kung-shu P'an comes from the *Lun Hêng*, written by Wang Chung about 83 A.D. Wang Chung was a cynic and a materialist, and quotes the following story in order to criticise its absurdity. Kung-shu P'an is said to have lost his own mother through his skill. He constructed for her a wooden chariot with wooden horses and a wooden driver. When she got into it, it sped away and never returned [76].

Kung-shu P'an is credited with a number of rather more practical inventions besides these, of course, and Needham suggests that there is no real reason to doubt his existence, dating him as flourishing somewhere between 470 and 380 B.C. [77]. This is a rather long period, and elsewhere Needham simply refers to him as living in the 5th century, or flourishing c.470 B.C. However, Chamberlain provides a differing viewpoint [78]. He is aware that the more mythical Lu Pan is given a traditional birth date of 606 B.C., of which more below, and also of the date 'flourishing 470 B.C.'. However, he also points out that Mo Ti (whose dates are uncertain) did not come to prominence until about 420 B.C., and that the episodes with Kung-shu P'an appear to date later than this. Furthermore, Kung-shu P'an appears a number of times in the *Mo Tzu* book, and always in the same structural relationship to Mo Ti: he is Mo Ti's opponent and always ends up being derided. Chamberlain thus suggests that he was a literary counterpoint, invented to illustrate Mo Ti's philosophy. This is a viewpoint which it would perhaps be unwise to discount entirely.

Lu Pan appears to be a more mythical figure, and the stories surrounding him are somewhat more confused. Werner [79] provides three separate biographies, of which the most notable has him being born in Shantung province in 606 (or 506) B.C. He became skilled in metal, stone and wood work, and retired to Mount Li at the age of 40 to become a hermit, learning how to rise into the air and ride on the clouds. The local people, fearing his powers, murdered him. This was followed by a drought, which lasted until a shrine was built to propitiate him. Afterwards he completed his spiritual training in a disembodied state and ascended to heaven, where he built the palace of Hsi Wang Mu, the 'Royal Mother of the West'.

The same stories of the wooden bird and coach are told of Lu Pan as well as Kung-shu P'an, but a third story is told of Lu Pan alone. In this, Lu Pan was said to have been born in Kansu province, and to have built a wooden kite, on which his father flew long distances. When his father flew to Wu-hui, in Kiangsu province, the local people mistook him for a devil and killed him. Angered at this, Lu Pan built a wooden figure of an Immortal (a Taoist 'saint'). When the Immortal pointed its finger toward Wu-hui, a drought afflicted the town. When the inhabitants discovered the cause, they sent presents to appease him. Lu Pan cut off the hand of the figure, after which rain fell in Wu-hui [80]. The parallels between this and the previous stories (the wooden bird, the loss of a parent, and the drought) are obvious, and this story seems to be a summation of all the most important points about Lu Pan. Later folklore also credits Lu Pan with the ability to construct stone dogs to guard houses, and wooden cats that would catch mice [81]. There are numerous other stories about him, but for the most part they do not deal with automata.

Lastly, we might mention two rather more historical figures. Han Chih-ho, a mechanical toy maker of Japanese origin, is said to have come to the attention of the Chinese emperor about 890 A.D. Amongst his other accomplishments, he is said to have built a wooden cat which could catch rats and birds [82]. Perhaps, though, this is just a way of saying that he was as clever as Lu Pan. Chang Hêng (78-139 A.D.), the famous engineer and astronomer, built a wooden bird with wings and pinions, having in its belly a mechanism which enabled it to fly for several *li*. This distance is perhaps exaggerated, but the core of the tale is perhaps not entirely unbelievable. In his own writings, Chang Hêng remarks: 'Linked wheels may be made to turn of themselves, so that even an object of carved wood may be made to fly alone in the air' [83].

What relevance, then, do these stories have to Chu-ko Liang and his wooden oxen? The more historical tales, of 'mechanical toys', and of Chang Hêng's wooden bird, do at least suggest a high level of technology in ancient China, and an interest in the production of automata. Although we have not found any evidence to *prove* that the wooden oxen were automata, this background material at least makes the proposition seem less inherently unlikely. On the other hand, if the oxen were nothing more than some variety of barrow, these tales and myths provide a strong cultural milieu in which stories of their automation could quite naturally develop. We may not be any closer to solving the mystery, but at least now we can see it in a more fully rounded form.

NOTES & REFERENCES

1 - *San Kuo Chih*. 5 vols, in Chinese. Chung Hua Shu Chu, Beijing, 1959. All the material quoted here is from vol 4, *Shu Shu* (The Book of Shu).

2 - Steve Moore, *The Trigrams of Han*, Aquarian Press, Wellingborough, 1989, p151-152.

3 - *SKC*, p896 & 925 (the same information appears in two different chapters). Joseph Needham, *Science and Civilisation in China (SCC)*, Cambridge UP, 1954 onward, vol 4 pt 2, p260. Needham translates the latter ref from *SKC*, which is the least clear of the two, and thus erroneously has Chu-ko Liang coming *from* Ch'i Shan, rather than surrounding it. The first reference makes it quite apparent that Chu-ko Liang is *surrounding* Ch'i Shan, but the affair is further complicated by the fact that in later tradition Ch'i Shan is named in relation to the oxen's place of manufacture (see below, following note [7]). Achilles Fang, *The Chronicle of the Three Kingdoms*, 2 vols, Harvard UP, 1952, 1965, vol 1, p338. Fang's footnote (p354) reads: "The 'wooden oxen' here mentioned apparently were a kind of automaton, a description of which is given in the *Wei shih ch'un ch'iu*, purportedly from Chu-ko Liang's writings..." I have grave doubts about the latter part of this statement,

though it has to be said that Needham, *ibid*, p260, appears to fall into what I believe to be the same error. There is a quotation from the *Wei shih ch'un ch'iu* (by Sun Sheng, c.360 A.D.) given in P'ei Sung-chih's commentary immediately prior to the description of the wooden oxen (*SKC*, p928), but it appears to be quite separate from it, deals with other matters, and makes no mention of the oxen. The description of the oxen then follows, and is clearly stated to come from the *Chu-ko Liang Chi*. In the Chung Hua edition of the *SKC*, the quotations appear in separate paragraphs.

4 - *SKC*, p896. Fang, *Chronicle*, vol 1, p429. The reversal of the usual phrase (flying horses and wooden oxen, rather than wooden oxen and flying horses) is puzzling. This might be seen as evidence that we are dealing with two different types of 'animal', but I shall return to this subject below.

5 - *SKC*, p897 & 925. Fang, *Chronicle*, vol 1, p443. Needham, *SCC*, vol 4 pt 2, p260.

6 - *SKC*, p927. Needham, *SCC*, vol 4 pt 2, p260.

7 - C H Brewitt-Taylor (trans), *The Romance of the Three Kingdoms*, 2 vols. (1925) rpt Charles E Tuttle, Vermont & Tokyo, 1959. Vol 2,

p445-454.

8 - Regrettably, at this point in the translation (p446) we find the following: "Here follows a specification which appears incomprehensible, and is omitted." This sends us back to the Chinese text, of which more below.

9 - *San Kuo Yen-i*, 64 vols. Hsin Ya Ch'i Ts'ai, Hong Kong, 1974, vol 53, pictures 45, 51, 52.

10 - Lu Hsun, *A Brief History of Chinese Fiction*, Foreign Languages Press, Beijing, 1964, p163.

11 - Kam Fung, 'Chariots of Ancient China', *Secrets of Kung-fu*, Tin Lung Publishing, Hong Kong, 1975, Vol 1, no 2, p19.

12 - J Macgowan, *The Imperial History of China*, (1897) rpt Curzon Press, London, 1973, p142.

13 - Needham, *SCC*, vol 4 pt 2. Gearwheels: p85f. History of clocks and clockwork: p435-546.

14 - Needham, *SCC*, vol 4 pt 2, p260-271. In the English language, this 'wheelbarrow' interpretation goes back at least as far as W F Mayers' *The Chinese Reader's Manual*, 1874, reprinted Probsthain, London, 1910, p30, item 88. Mayers says: "The celerity of Chu-ko Liang's movements and his careful provision for the wants of his army gave rise to a story that by means of magic arts he employed in his service 'oxen of wood and mechanical horses', which some writers have sought to identify with the *wheelbarrows* used as a means of transport.''

15 - For example, L Carrington Goodrich, *A Short History of the Chinese People*, Harper, NY, 1943, p78. Goodrich simply rejects the idea that the oxen were wheelbarrows; he offers no alternative explanation.

16 - Needham, *SCC*, vol 4 pt 2, p270.

17 - Moore, *Trigrams*, p150-151.

18 - *Chu-ko Liang Chi* (edited by Chang Shu). Chung Hua Shu Chu, Beijing, 1974. Hereafter, *CKLC*.

19 - *CKLC*, p.xxix. The material quoted here comes from the *San Kuo I Wen Chih* of Yao Chen-tsung, about whom I have no further information, except that he lived in the Ch'ing dynasty (1644-1911 A.D.).

20 - This title translates as 'Collected Writings of the Three Kingdoms Period'. Yen K'o-chun wrote in the 19th century.

21 - *Ch'uan Yun P'ien* is 'punctuated' in the Chinese text with the equivalent of italics, suggesting that the phrase is a book title; it means 'Transport Chronicles'. It may well be a book title, but from the way the passage reads I suspect that this punctuation may be erroneous, and that the correct reading could be simply that the wooden oxen 'deserve a place in the annals of transportation'. The references to the texts then appear in the next sentence. Pre-modern Chinese texts were usually written entirely without punctuation, and the placing of punctuation marks by recent editors thus becomes, on occa-

sion, conjectural.

22 - *Liang Chuan* is the biography of Chu-ko Liang by Ch'ên Shou, that appears in *SKC*. The commentary is that of P'ei Sung-chih. The text mentioned here will be translated below.

23 - *Yu Lan* is presumably an abbreviation for *T'ai P'ing Yu Lan*, an enormous Imperial Encyclopaedia compiled in 983 A.D. On *Lei Chu* I have no further information; it may well be another abbreviation.

24 - *CKLC*, p43-44. *SKC*, p928.

25 - The *T'ung Tien* ('Comprehensive Standards') is an encyclopaedia of material on social and political history, written by Tu Yu, c.812 A.D.

26 - It is far from clear here whether Tu Yu is quoting from the actual and original book, the *CKLC*, or more generally to 'the writings of Chu-ko Liang'. It is uncertain whether the original work survived until his time. He may well have been quoting a fragment, preserved at second-hand.

27 - The *li* is the 'Chinese mile'. It approximates to one third of an English mile.

28 - 'White Horse Mountain'.

29 - *Shu Chih*: the 'Annals of Shu', that part of the *SKC* dealing with the state of Shu. Note here (with reference to note **[3]** above) that Chang Shu makes no mention of P'ei Sung-chih quoting the *Wei shih ch'un ch'iu*; only the *Liang chi*.

30 - Needham, *SCC*, vol 4 pt 2, p263. P'u Yuan's letter is preserved in *Pei T'ang Shu Ch'ao*, chapter 68, compiled by Yu Shih-nan c.630 A.D. The following quotation is translated by Needham.

31 - From *CKLC*. A composite of

the text appearing on pages 43 & 44. Apart from Chang Shu's introduction, the identical text appears in *SKC*, p928.

32 - Needham, *SCC*, vol 4 pt 2, p26l.

33 - Some years ago I had this material professionally translated by an agency which it would, perhaps, be impolite to name. Regrettably, later checking of the translation against the original text showed up a number of outright errors, as well as a number of guesses at the meaning which do not seem justified. I have, therefore, been forced to retranslate the entire passage; and thus I assume full responsibility for any questionable readings.

34 - Lo Kuan-chung, *San Kuo Yen-i*, 2 vols, in Chinese. Chung Hua Shu Chu, Hong Kong, 1985, Vol 2, p830.

35 - Needham, *SCC*, vol 4 pt 2, p260, says that P'ei Sung-chih quotes this passage as being from the *Wei shih ch'un ch'iu*. As already pointed out (see note **[3]**), I am not sure this is the case. Needham, of course, is writing a history of science, and dealing with this material in a section on the wheelbarrow. We shall return to the background of this interpretation below. However, I feel that I have to express a certain caution about his translation, in that it appears to me to have been moulded, in places, by the preconceived interpretation. In brief, he believes the ox to be a wheelbarrow, and translates accordingly. Nonetheless, by providing both his translation and my own, I hope the reader may decide for himself which interpretation to follow. Needham's translation is as follows, and his footnotes are presented alphabetically.

In the 'Collection of Chu-ko Liang's Writings' (*Chu-ko Liang*

Chi) there is an account of the method of making the 'Wooden Ox' and the 'Gliding Horse'. The 'Wooden Ox' had a square belly and a curved head, one foot (*chiao*) [a] and four legs (*tsu*) [b]; its head was compressed into its neck, and its tongue was attached to its belly. It could carry many things, and made thereby the fewer journeys, so it was of the greatest use. It was not suitable for small occasions, but was employed on long journeys; (in one day) it could go several tens of *li* if there was a special need, or about twenty *li* in convoy. The bent part corresponded to the ox's head, the double part [c] corresponded to the ox's limbs (*chiao*), the cross part corresponded to the ox's neck, the revolving part (*chuan chê*) [d] corresponded to the ox's foot (*tsu*), the covered part corresponded to the ox's back, the square part corresponded to the ox's belly, the hanging part corresponded to the ox's tongue, the curved part [e] corresponded to the ox's ribs (*le*), the carved part corresponded to the ox's teeth, the standing part corresponded to the ox's horn, the thin part corresponded to the ox's halter, the handles (*nieh*) corresponded to the traces and whippletree (*ch'iu*) [f] and each half of the axle faced upwards to the double shafts. In the time taken by a man (with a similar burden) to go six feet, the Wooden Ox would go twenty feet. It could carry the food supply (of one man) for a whole year [g], and yet after twenty *li* the porter would not feel tired.

[a] The wheel. [b] Side supports to prevent toppling over. [c] The two bearings of the single axle. [d] The wheel. [e] The housing separating the wheel from the freight. [f] This was a technical term also applied to the swing. In appropriate contexts it could also mean the breeching or crupper straps of harnessed horses. [g] This is quite feasible, assuming a ration of 1 lb a day, which would mean something of the order of 3 cwt. on the vehicle.

I shall examine some of these interpretations as we progress through the text.

36 - The *Romance* here reads 'crooked shinbone' rather than 'crooked head'. At first sight this might appear to be a plausible substitution, but when later references appear to the head being crooked, the substitution is not repeated.

37 - Needham (note [35]) translates 'one foot (*chiao*) and four legs (*tsu*)'. Further on, he translates *chiao* as 'limbs' (i.e. legs) and *tsu* as 'feet'. Obviously this is not consistent, and while this sort of interpretive flexibility might be appropriate to a literary text, it hardly seems permissible when translating a technical specification. Mathews' *Chinese English Dictionary* (American edition, no publisher, 1944) defines *chiao* as the leg or the foot, but *tsu* only as the foot. I have therefore consistently translated *chiao* as 'leg' and *tsu* as 'foot'. Needham interprets 'one leg, four feet' as follows: the 'leg' (*chiao*) refers to the main wheel of the wheelbarrow, and the 'four feet' (*tsu*) to four side-supports. As we shall shortly come to a reference to the 'revolving parts' being the feet (*tsu*), of which there are four, I find this interpretation implausible. Similarly, we shall later come to distinct references to there being four legs (*chiao*), placed fore and aft. There is obvious confusion about the number of legs here, but I can really see no reason why *chiao* should be interpreted as a 'wheel'; unless, of course, one is convinced beforehand that a wheel must be present, in which case whatever material comes to hand must be fitted to the hypothesis. And yet Needham's entire interpretation appears to revolve around this central idea that one main wheel is present. On the other hand, there is some evidence to connect the word *tsu*

with wheels, which comes from Herbert A Giles, *Adversaria Sinica* (1st series), Kelly & Walsh, Shanghai, 1914, p224. Giles there translates a passage from the *History of the Sung Dynasty*, which gives a specification for a 'Measure-Mile-Drum-Chariot' or hodometer. This is a type of cart which, using a system of gearing, causes a drum to be struck when the cart has travelled one *li*. There the main wheels of the carriage are called *tsu-lun* 'foot-wheels': i.e., they are the main supporting wheels, the wheels which actually make contact with the ground. It is, perhaps, notable that this hodometer specification contains minute details of the cogwheels and machinery present in the interior of the cart; no such details appear in the present specification to suggest that the ox is automated. Finally, even allowing for the extreme conciseness of classical Chinese, 'one leg, four feet' does not make a lot of sense. I would therefore have to raise the possibility that the text may be corrupt at this point.

38 - Whatever the 'tongue' may be, its placing in the belly would seem to suggest that it does not in any way correspond literally to a tongue; perhaps some sort of lever is implied.

39 - The words 'it is fit for large tasks, not small ones' are omitted by the *Romance*.

40 - The *Romance* here reads 'by *independent action* it travels several tens of *li*', rather than 'alone'. A similar situation might arise in interpreting the English phrase 'on its own', which could be taken to mean either 'alone' or 'unaided': the *Romance* appears to have decided to clarify the interpretation in favour of the latter possibility, thus reinforcing the idea that the oxen were self-motivated.

41 - Why this should be the case is not apparent. Furthermore, the

Romance reads 'thirty *li*', rather than 'twenty *li*'. It is to be noted here that Needham translates 'in a group' as 'in convoy'. This certainly suggests that the oxen are arranged in a line, and possibly linked together. If the latter were the case, then a convoy of four-wheeled carts seems quite feasible to me; a convoy of one-wheeled wheelbarrows linked together seems impossibly unwieldy.

42 - Needham translates as 'double part', and interprets this as 'the two bearings of the single axle'. Apart from the fact that this provides us with yet another meaning for *chiao*, we shall see that the second part of the text refers to both a front and rear axle. Again, I must seriously query Needham's interpretation. The 'paired parts' would seem to me to refer to the front and back pairs of legs.

43 - The *Romance* here replaces *chiao*, 'leg', with *tsu*, 'foot'.

44 - The *Romance* here replaces *tsu*, 'foot', with *chiao*, 'leg'. Translating the *CKLC* text, Needham here interprets *tsu*, 'foot', as the wheel, where he has previously taken the *chiao* as the wheel.

45 - The references to teeth and horns might suggest that the ox was actually designed to simulate the appearance of a real ox. This is doubtless the reason why later interpretations, such as shown in figures 1-4, portray the machines as ox-shaped automata. However, such decorative touches would seem out of place in a mass-produced military machine. An alternative suggestion might be that these terms are 'coded' references to unidentified parts of the machine. Doubtless it would be possible to make some highly imaginative guesses as to what might lie behind these terms, but they would remain no more than guesses, and would be out of place here. A final possibi-

lity, which we shall return to later, is that the entire text is a forgery, and that the forger has simply overdone the amount of detail, in an attempt to make his 'wooden oxen' more ox-like.

46 - 'Axletree': Mathews' *Dictionary* gives *ch'iu* as 'axletree': i.e., a fixed shaft about which the wheels freely revolve, rather than a rotating axle bearing fixed wheels. Needham translates *ch'iu* here as 'whippletree', which is a pivoted crosswise bar at the front of a vehicle, to the ends of which the traces of the harness are fastened. To translate as 'whippletree' might seem quite plausible in this context, as the word appears in connection with the traces and halter; even so, one would have to wonder where a whippletree fitted on a wheelbarrow with a single centrally-mounted wheel. However, the second part of the text refers to both a front and rear *ch'iu*, and as that is the case I would suspect that 'axletree' is the more likely meaning. Nonetheless, let us consider the possibility that the ox did indeed have a whippletree. This might suggest that the ox was some sort of cart which was drawn by animal power; and this could explain why, if one ox was drawn by an animal it travelled several tens of *li* on its own, while if a convoy was drawn by a single animal, it only travelled twenty *li*. If numerous carts were being drawn in convoy, like the carriages of a train, they would doubtless need some sort of pivoted axles, perhaps somehow cognate to a whippletree, in order to negotiate sharp corners on the road. One is almost tempted to wonder if the entire legend has arisen from such a simple circumstance as this: that Chu-ko Liang was the first to conceive of the idea of using a single animal to draw more than one cart ... and that the wooden 'oxen'-carts 'glided' after the horse; but this, of course, is mere speculation. A less likely possibility is that the ox

itself is being regarded as the traction-animal, and the traces, whippletree, etc., serve to attach it to a cart which it draws. This entire long sentence (from note **[40]** onward) has been translated literally. It might more felicitously read as follows: 'The ox's head is crooked, the legs are in pairs, the neck is placed crosswise, the feet revolve, the back is covered, the belly is square, the tongue hangs down, the ribs are crooked, the teeth are carved, the horns stand erect, the halter is thin and the ox is held by the traces and axletree (or whippletree)'.

47 - Needham's translation of this sentence (note **[35]**) does not seem warranted by the text. If we were dealing with a wheelbarrow, I would have thought that a more logical interpretation would be that 'when the double shafts are lifted from the ground, thus raising the legs and freeing the wheel for motion', then the machine is ready to travel.

48 - 'Twenty feet': this actually reads 'four *pu*'. A *pu* is a measure of five Chinese feet; but the word also means 'a step' or 'a pace'. An alternative reading would thus be 'a man travels six feet, the ox takes four paces'. If the ox actually 'walked', this would suggest a 'stride' of one and a half feet. For an alternative explanation, see Needham's translation (note **[35]**).

49 - The *Romance* omits 'Carrying one year's provisions, it travels twenty *li* in a day'.

50 - Here the *Romance* adds: 'The ox does not need food and drink'.

51 - Rafe de Crespigny, *The Last of the Han*, Australian National University, Canberra, 1969, p406.

52 - There appears to be only one rib per side of the machine, and from the material that follows, they appear to be positioned horizontally, rather than vertically. In the first part of the text they are said to be crooked, or curved. Such 'ribs' would seem to fit with the wheelbarrow interpretation, as the side-shafts of the machine.

53 - The precise meaning of *fên-me* is not apparent. It would seem to be a technical term, and is applied indiscriminately in conjunction with axletree-holes, leg-holes and crossbars. Meanings for the individual words of the pair are to be found in the dictionaries, but the pairing is not. *Fên* is given as: to divide, to share, to separate, to distinguish; a part, a share, function, duty; or a tenth of an inch. *Me* has the meanings: ink, black, dark; silent, lonely; a measure of five feet. It is possible that *me* should be replaced with a similar character, of the same pronunciation and tone, meaning a cord, or to bind. This is written in the same way, but with the addition of radical no 120. Such a substitution of radicals in characters of the same pronunciation would not be unknown in ancient Chinese texts, but this is no more than speculation on my part. My best *guess* as to the meaning would be 'position mark' or 'fixture'...or simply 'position', which would seem to make a fair amount of sense in the contexts in which it appears. It may also perhaps refer to a particular type of joint, such as a mortise and tenon joint; but in the absence of a definite meaning, I have preferred to leave the term untranslated.

54 - The text may be corrupt here, as we have a reference to the front leg hole being two inches, but no indication as to whether this measurement refers to its length, width or position. The *Romance* replaces this sentence with: 'The front leg hole *fên-me* is 4 inches and 5 tenths behind the head, its length 1 inch and 5 tenths, its width 1 inch'. On the surface, at least, this reads more sensibly.

55 - Here the *Romance* reads '1 foot and 5 inches', rather than '1 foot and 5 tenths'.

56 - Here the *Romance* reads 'front crossbar hole *fên-me*'.

57 - I confess slight uncertainty as to the reading 'container-fixture'. Assuming it to be correct, it is curious that only a rear fixture is mentioned, with no corresponding fixture at the front.

58 - The *Romance* replaces the sentences: 'The rear leg hole *fên-me* is 3 inches and 5 tenths behind the rear axletree hole, all dimensions the same as the front. The rear crossbar hole is 2 inches and 7 tenths behind the rear leg hole *fên-me*, the rear container-fixture is 4 inches and 5 tenths behind the rear crossbar hole *fên-me*'. Instead, it reads: 'The rear crossbar hole is 2 inches and 2 tenths behind the rear leg hole *fên- me*. The rear crossbar hole *fên-me* is 4 inches and 5 tenths'. As the last sentence is thereby reduced to meaninglessness, I suspect that the *Romance* reading is corrupt.

59 - Two rectangular cases would fit with the interpretation of the machine being a wheelbarrow, one case mounted on either side of the main wheel. However, we still have no mention of a main central wheel.

60 - The *tou* is taken as roughly the equivalent of an English peck. There are ten *tou* to a *hu*. De Crespigny, *The Last of the Han* (p419) gives the Han dynasty equivalent of the *tou* as 12.1856 cubic inches, but this must surely be in error by a power of ten. If the *tou* is 121.856 modern cubic inches, the capacity of 2 *hu* and 3 *tou* corresponds almost exactly with the measurements of the boxes.

61 - This sentence suggests that the rib is horizontal, rather than vertical.

62 - No such diagram appears to have survived. It will also be noted that no measurement for the length of the legs is provided.

63 - The word *k'an* appears in neither Mathews' nor Giles' dictionaries. The Chinese *K'ang Hsi Tzu Tien* ('K'ang Hsi Dictionary') provides a number of pronunciations and meanings, including 'reins' and 'a bow cover', none of which seem particularly applicable here. Needham's interpretation of the word will be discussed in the main text, below. We may note that the *k'an* is mentioned immediately after the legs, and its description suggests a squat cylinder or drum, 4 inches long and just over 4 inches in diameter. Perhaps the *k'an* is to be interpreted as a very thick 'wheel' ... perhaps the 'revolving parts' that are the ox's 'feet'? Alternatively, it might be a short axle, perhaps for the missing large central wheel?

64 - This phrase appears to be incomprehensible, and the translation is conjectural, to say the least. It is not clear which opening is referred to, nor what the three leg crossbars are. There would seem to be a strong possibility that the text is corrupt here.

65 - The *Romance* omits the phrase 'all crossbars projecting'.

66 - Needham, *SCC*, vol 4 pt 2, p262. The original quotation is from the *Shih Wu Chi Yuan*, chapter 8.

67 - Needham, *SCC*, vol 4 pt 2, p261. Figure 7 appears on the same page.

68 - Moore, *Trigrams*, p144-182. See also *Parallel Arrays*, later in this booklet.

69 - G C Stent: 'Brief Sketches from the Life of K'ung-ming', *China Review* (Hong Kong), Vol. 5 (1876- 77) p311-319. K'ung-ming is the courtesy name of Chu-ko Liang. The series continued in numerous later issues of the *China Review* and Stent also retells the story of Chu- ko Liang and the wooden oxen from *The Romance of the Three Kingdoms* (Vol. 7 (1878-79) p82-84), but this contains no significant new information.

70 - Needham, *SCC*, vol 4 pt 2, p156-165.

71 - Needham, *SCC*, vol 4 pt 2, p39-42. Fang, *Chronicle*, vol 1, p477.

72 - A C Graham, *The Book of Lieh Tzu*, John Murray, London, 1960, p110-111. Needham, *SCC*, vol 2, p53.

73 - Graham, *Lieh Tzu*, p112.

74 - Kenneth J DeWoskin, *Doctors, Diviners, and Magicians of Ancient China: Biographies of Fang-shih*, Columbia UP, NY, 1983, p185. Here we find the following list of names, all referring to the same man: Lu Pan, Kung-shu P'an, Kung-shu Tzu, Pan Shu, Shu Pan, Kung Pan.

75 - *Mo Tzu*, chapter 49. Needham, *SCC*, vol 4 pt 2, p313.

76 - Wang Chung, *Lun Hêng*, chapter 26. Needham, *SCC*, vol 4 pt 2, p574. G Willoughby Meade, *Chinese Ghouls and Goblins*, Constable, London, 1928, p352.

77 - Needham, *SCC*, vol 4 pt 2, p44 & p189.

78 - Jonathan Chamberlain, *Chinese Gods*, Long Island Publishers, Hong Kong, 1983, p150.

79 - E T C Werner, *A Dictionary of Chinese Mythology*, (1932) rpt Julian Press, NY, 1961, p281-282. The following biography also contains material from Chamberlain, *Chinese Gods*, p145-152.

80 - Werner, *Dictionary*, p281.

81 - Jan & Yvonne Walls, *West Lake, A Collection of Folktales*, Joint Publishing Co, Hong Kong, 1980, p30.

82 - Needham, *SCC*, vol 4 pt 2, p163.

83 - Needham, *SCC*, vol 4 pt 2, p574-575.

STRANGE STORIES OF THE SLEEPING DRAGON

C hu-ko Liang, as well as being a man of many talents, was also a man of many names. Apart from his real name, he also bore the 'courtesy name' of K'ung-ming ('Greatly Enlightened'), a polite form of address used in general conversation. After his death, he was given the title Wu-hou ('The Martial Marquis'). But during his life he also bore a nickname, taken in his youth before his talents were fully revealed: this was Wo Lung ... the 'Sleeping Dragon'.

Until his twenty-seventh year, Chu-ko Liang lived as a recluse, and he really only enters upon the historical stage when he became the adviser and strategist of Liu Pei, who later founded the kingdom of Shu in south-west China. After that, the anecdotes of his extraordinary talents come thick and fast. Some of those stories are collected here, but I should perhaps emphasize the word 'stories'. These are not the 'facts' which appear in the histories; nor, indeed, are they the traditions that appear in *The Romance of the Three Kingdoms*. The traditions of the *Romance* are simply too many to cope with in a short piece like this, and I must refer anyone interested to the original [1]. Instead, the stories collected here are even less historical, even more folkloric. It's hardly an exhaustive collection (merely a few tales picked up during some casual reading from English-language sources) but ... take them as you will ... these are the apocryphal stories of the Sleeping Dragon.

I n view of the tradition that Chu-ko Liang's wooden oxen were a kind of automaton, perhaps the most interesting of these stories is that relating to his 'alarm clock'. Unfortunately, the reference [2] is frustratingly brief and lacking in detail. We simply hear that "It is said that he invented a kind of an alarm clock that he used to put under his pillow that would wake him at any particular hour of the morning that he wished to rise." If there's any truth at all in the story, I have no idea what this might have been. There doesn't seem to have been anything that we would understand as 'clockwork' in the 3rd century A.D., and even if it was some sort of water-clock, it would be rather difficult to place 'under the pillow'. We might conjecture that it was something like an hour-glass, where the running of sand (or whatever was used) would eventually build sufficient weight to trip a lever and ring a bell, but there is still the problem of 'under the pillow'. And the main problem here is that the Chinese simply didn't use the soft pillow familiar to us in the 20th century: instead they used a small wooden or porcelain head-rest, which would be rather difficult to place *anything* under. Perhaps Macgowan is just using a romanticizing form of words, but without further information it's difficult to know what to make of this.

In 225 A.D., Chu-ko Liang led an expedition against the Man barbarians of Yunnan province, in an attempt to secure the southern borders of the state of Shu. As his troops were going into an area on the borders of what is now Burma, he took every precaution to protect their health against heatstroke, fever and other tropical diseases. For this purpose he concocted a medicinal powder to be taken in the form of snuff, which would bring about "sneezing to open the seven outlets of the skull" (presumably the mouth, nostrils, ears and eyes). It is apparently still made at the present day, and known as 'Chu-ko's Military Expedition Powder' ... but I don't think I'd care to try it! [3].

More tales of Chu-ko Liang's expeditions to Yunnan. There is a tradition that he built iron-chain suspension bridges over the Mekong river at this time, but this, perhaps, is no more than tradition [4]. He is also said to have set up a column of cast-iron to commemorate his conquests [5]. Later, during the Sui dynasty, an expedition was again sent to conquer the Man barbarians of Yunnan. This was between 594 and 597 A.D., and the expedition was led by Shih Wan-sui. Shih was shown a stone stele set up by Chu-ko Liang to commemorate his conquests, and on the back he found an inscription reading 'Hereafter Wan-sui will conquer Yunnan, but not so gloriously as I did'. Shih Wan-sui thereupon ordered his men to overturn the stele, but underneath they found another inscription reading 'Shih Wan-sui is not to uproot my stele'! Shih had the stele replaced, offered a sacrifice, and left hurriedly [6]. This is probably nothing more than folklore, but it is a splendid example of the omniscience attributed to the Sleeping Dragon.

Perhaps the most outrageous tale of all concerns Chu-ko Liang's tomb. We might start here with a more factual look at what Chu-ko Liang actually requested for his burial. His will has been recorded [7] and the relevant passage reads: 'that he be buried at Ting-chun Shan (Ting-chun mountain) in Han-chung; that his tomb be made in the mountain, sufficient to hold the coffin; that he be shrouded in the garment of the season, without any vessels or other things'. This, it will be noted, is simplicity itself; nothing more than a straightforward interment.

The folktale is rather different. According to this [8], the emperor Hung-Wu (founder of the Ming dynasty, r.1368-1399 A.D.) found himself at Ting-chun mountain, in the neighbourhood of the tomb. He was accompanied by his councillor, Liu Po-wen, and the two men decided to visit it. They were both wearing iron armour, but they managed to force an entrance. They passed through into an ante-chamber which 'contained an inscription to the effect that whosoever visited the tomb should have his hands bound by the defunct'. And indeed, in squeezing through the entrance, both men had had to wedge themselves so that they were virtually incapable of using their arms. They then broke open a second door and found themselves in another room. Within this were several figures made of loadstone, which attracted their armour. As they were dragged forward they hastily cast off their armour, but not before noticing an inscription which Dennys renders in the following doggerel verse:

> I'll strip off the skin
> Of who ventures in
> To open this my grave.

Freeing themselves from this magnetic trap, the two men fled and closed the tomb [9]. The tradition of the visit 'is still recounted by the story-tellers of the neighbourhood'. But not, it seems, by the story-tellers of Pai-ti Ch'éng ('White Emperor City'). This is a city on the Yangtse river, some considerable distance from Han-chung; and yet a modern report tells us that in this place there is a temple to Chu-ko Liang in which are 'enshrined' the bodies of Chu-ko Liang, his son and grandson [10]. Perhaps someone's been shifting the remains; or perhaps these details are insignificant compared with the attractions of the story itself.

Still, death and burial aren't the end, at least not in Chinese folklore. In 639 A.D., a Buddhist monk from the 'Western regions' (Hsi-yu) arrived in Ch'ang-an, the capital of the T'ang dynasty. He is only known by his religious title, Hsi-yu Seng Ch'an-shih (which means little more than 'the Buddhist monk from the Western regions'). He made his way to the house of a certain Mr. Wei, who was giving a party to celebrate the birth of his son. When called upon to forecast the boy's future, the monk announced that the boy was a reincarnation of Chu-ko Liang, and that he had purposely come to Ch'ang-an in order to greet him. The boy later grew up to become an Imperial Secretary (Chung-shu ling) [11].

Finally, we might note that in the Taoist tradition the sacred seals of the Thunder Ritual are said to have been conveyed to Chang Hui-chai (fl. 1264-1300 A.D.) by an 'avatar' of Chu-ko Liang [12]. This is perhaps not surprising, as the Thunder Magic rituals are based on the military tactics of the 'Eight Arrays' attributed to Chu-ko Liang [13]; but who this 'avatar' might have been does not seem to have been recorded.

REFERENCES

1 - C H Brewitt-Taylor (trans), *The Romance of the Three Kingdoms*, (1925), rpt Charles E Tuttle, Vermont & Tokyo, 1959.

2 - J Macgowan, *The Imperial History of China*, (1897) rpt Curzon Press, London, l973, p142.

3 - Leon Comber, *Chinese Magic and Superstitions in Malaya*, Eastern Universities Press, Singapore, 1955, p66-67.

4 - Joseph Needham, *Science and Civilisation in China*, Cambridge UP, 1954 onward, vol 4 pt 3, p205.

5 - Needham, *SCC*, vol 4 pt 3, p201.

6 - Needham, *SCC*, vol 4 pt 3, p201.

7 - Achilles Fang, *The Chronicle of the Three Kingdoms*, (2 vols) Harvard UP, 1952, 1965, vol 1 p459.

8 - Nicholas B Dennys, *The Folklore of China*, (1876) rpt Oriental Press, Amsterdam, 1968, p135.

9 - This tale of the tomb would seem to have an obvious forerunner in the Tzu shih men, the Loadstone Gateway, reputed to have formed the western entrance to the A Fang palace constructed by the First Emperor, Ch'in Shih-huang, in the 3rd century B.C. "Through this gate the 'barbarians' from the west were admitted to the Court, and any weapons that might be concealed upon their persons caused them, through the influence of attraction, to be drawn to the side of the gateway and prevented from advancing. Hence the gate was also called the Ch'ueh hu men, or barbarian-repelling gate." W F Mayers: *The Chinese Reader's Manual*, (1874) rpt Probsthain, London, 1910, drawing on the *Shui ching chu* of Li Tao-yuan, c.500 A.D.

10 - *China Pictorial*, Beijing, September 1989, p12.

11 - E T C Werner, *A Dictionary of Chinese Mythology*, (1932) rpt Julian Press, NY, 1961, p164.

12 - Judith M Boltz, *A Survey of Taoist Literature*, Institute of East Asian Studies, University of California, 1987, p57.

13 - Steve Moore, *The Trigrams of Han*, Aquarian Press, Wellingborough, 1989, p144-182.

PARALLEL ARRAYS

THE MILITARY FORMATIONS OF CHU-KO LIANG AND DRONA

In *The Trigrams of Han* I devoted considerable space to a discussion of the *Pa Chên*, the military formation known as the 'Eight Arrays' [1]. This was a method of arraying troops on the battlefield in a formation based on the eight trigrams of the *I Ching* which, while probably not invented by Chu-ko Liang, was perfected by him and has remained connected with his name ever since. Regrettably, after ten years' research (off and on) I had enough material to write some 40 pages on the subject, but still no answer to the basic question of how the military units functioned on the battlefield. Further research still hasn't produced an answer (perhaps it never will), but it has turned up some interesting parallel material from ancient India.

For details of the *Pa Chên*, as I've been able to put them together so far, I shall have to refer the reader to *The Trigrams of Han*. Briefly, though, the military formation appears to have been based on the 'World of the Senses' (King Wên's) arrangement of the trigrams, as shown in figure 1. There are possible references to it in the 1st century B.C., but it only really seems to have developed to its full form in the 2nd and 3rd centuries A.D. The units of the array were named either from the names of the trigrams or by a series of 'Gates' ('The Gate of Life', 'The Gate of Surprise', and so on). The array appears to have been a hollow formation, and opposing troops were thought to be able to penetrate it by entering at certain of the Gates, and leaving by others ... if they were permitted to. It was possible to 'work evolutions' with the array, moving the troop-units while still retaining the basic formation, although how this was done remains unclear. It was also possible to 'unwind' the formation into a linear array known as the 'Serpent Formation', which was used for surrounding the *Pa Chên* arranged by an opposing general. The *Pa Chên* presents a similar problem to Chu-ko Liang's 'wooden oxen': there appears to be some historical evidence that *something* of this name was actually practiced in the 3rd century A.D., but the major sources of detail derive from folklore, tradition, Taoist magic and barely-understood stone monuments.

The Indian material is hardly of better quality, deriving as it does from the epic poem, the *Mahabharata*. At 100,000 stanzas, this is the longest epic in the world, eight times as long as the *Iliad* and the *Odyssey* put together. It is traditionally said to be the work of Krishna-Dwaipayana Vyasa. While the final version may well have been the work of one author, the epic itself has been compiled from numerous sources: myths, legends, folk literature, heroic narratives and spiritual literature. It appears that there was originally a core of only 24,000 stanzas, but the work reached its present size around the 4th century A.D.; although the process of accretion appears to have been continuous from the 4th century B.C. onwards. Its basic concern is the great war fought between two rival clans, the Kurus and the Pandavas, for the land of Bharata in northern India. It is thought that the epic probably has a kernel of historic truth, as both clans and at least one of the major figures (King Dhritarashtra) are mentioned in the Vedas [2]. This is, perhaps, as far as it is safe to go. Other authors have attempted to read the epic much more historically: as a record of the Aryan invasion of India in the 2nd millenium B.C. [3]. This sort of speculation need hardly concern us here, interesting though it may be.

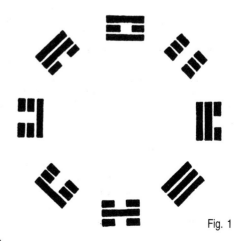

Fig. 1

The written material we have to deal with dates no later than the 4th century A.D., and may have developed in preceding centuries; it is thus (very) roughly contemporaneous with the development of the *Pa Chên* in China.

The *Mahabharata* is composed of eighteen books, and the material in question comes mainly from the sixth, *Bhishma Parva*, the 'Book of Bhishma', and the seventh, *Drona Parva*, the 'Book of Drona'. Many of the arrays are drawn up by Bhishma, who is represented both as a statesman and a general, during his command of the Kuru army; the formation of such arrays appearing to be one of the normal tactical accomplishments of a general. However, the one that is of most interest to us here is the work of Drona. Like Chu-ko Liang, Drona is portrayed as a military genius, although he does not have the same inventive or political acumen. The Kurus were the sons of King Dhritarashtra, the Pandavas the sons of his brother, Pandu. They were raised together as boys and Drona, who as both a Brahmin and an acharya (a 'military preceptor'), was responsible for the military training of both clans. When war eventually broke out between them, Bhishma was the first general of the Kurus, led by King Duryodhana. After Bhishma's death, Drona rather unwillingly agreed to lead the Kurus, but his heart lay with the Pandavas, led by King Yudhishthira; and in particular with his prize pupil, the heroic Arjuna.

As already mentioned, military arrays are drawn up by both Bhishma and Drona; and counter-arrays are also formed by Yudhishthira and the Pandava troops. It is the 'Circular Array', drawn up at the command of Drona, which most concerns us here, but the others seem worthy of mention as well. Yet before examining these, it should perhaps be mentioned that the *Mahabharata* is an epic work, and frequently reaches heights of truly epic hyperbole. Arjuna shoots 'thousands' of arrows without any mention of where he has them to hand; heroes are pierced by sixty or more arrows, feel slightly unwell for a moment, and then continue fighting; hundreds of thousands of troops are slaughtered on the battlefield; and the military arrays are of truly massive proportions. We cannot, then, look for anything like truth in matters of detail. Instead, we must concentrate on the *form* of the arrays.

The arrays are known as *Vyuhas* (which, besides meaning military arrays, can also refer to armies, squadrons, etc.) and fall into various types, representing animals (both real and mythological), geometric shapes and a miscellaneous selection of forms that are often symbolic. Details of the form or purpose of an array are often sketchy and, indeed, once the fighting starts there is usually no further mention of the arrays. All becomes a chaotic swirl of battling heroes in which tactics and formations are quite forgotten.

Lack of space means that we can do little more than list the arrays mentioned in the *Bhishma Parva*. In all cases they consist of mixed troops: chariots, cavalry, elephants and foot-soldiers. They are as follows [4]:

Needle or Needle-mouthed array: this appears to be identical with the Vajra array, the Vajra being explained as either a hard needle for boring gems, or a thunderbolt. It seems to be a pointed wedge, with "bows for its lightning sign".

Krauncharuna (Crane): various rulers and their troops are described as being placed at the beak, eyes, neck, breast, back, joints of the wings, wings and wing-tips.

Garuda: the mythical man-bird of Indian tradition, with the head, wings, talons and beak of an eagle or vulture, and the body and limbs of a man. Again, we hear of positions at the beak, eyes, head, neck, back, tail, and wings. For more details, see below.

Half-moon or semi-circle: this appears to be identical with the Çringataka array, but sounds more like a crescent than a half-moon, as right and left 'horns' are mentioned.

Makara: a mythical aquatic animal, similar to a crocodile or sea-monster. It is often composite, and the parts composing it seem to vary. Here too there are variations: we are told that troops are placed at the head, eyes, beak, neck, back, wings, tail and two feet; or at the eyes, head, neck, middle, front feet and rear feet, and tail.

Hawk or Çyena: beak, eyes, head, neck, wings, back, tail. Emphasis seems to be placed on the beak here.

Mandala: originally 'mandala' simply meant a circle rather than a cosmic diagram. This array is obviously circular, but we also have some significant numerical details. By

294

each elephant is placed 7 chariots; by each chariot 7 horsemen; behind each horseman 7 archers; behind each archer 7 men with shields. The counter-array to the Mandala is the sharp-pointed Vajra.

Sarvatobhadra: a footnote explains that this is a square array with troops facing all sides. It has front, rear, left and right wings.

So much for Bhishma's arrays. The first array instituted by Drona is in the form of a Çakata; which is a type of vehicle, a car or chariot. Virtually no details are given of this. To oppose this, Yudhishthira arrays his army in the form of a Krauncha, a crane [5].

Drona's next array is in the form of a Garuda, mentioned above. Drona himself is positioned in the mouth of the Garuda, while King Duryodhana and his Kuru brothers formed the head. Two famous heroes represented the eyes, while other noted warriors, 'with hundreds of thousands of elephants, steeds, cars, and foot-soldiers, were stationed in its neck'. Other heroes and their followers are mentioned as being positioned in the right and left wings, the bosom, back and tail of the Garuda. We are told that it is a 'super-human array incapable of being vanquished by foes'; that it 'seemed to dance like a tempest-tossed ocean' as it advanced to battle; and that 'warriors, desirous of battle, began to start out from the wings and sides of that array' as battle was joined. Ranked against this, Yudhishthira arranged his Pandava troops in a counter-array in the form of a semi-circle [6].

Chronologically, the next formation mentioned is the Circular Array, but we shall bypass this for the moment and look at Drona's final and most complex array. The main section of the array was part Çakata and part circle. It was 'fully forty-eight miles long and the width of its rear measured twenty miles'. Obviously, we have another case of epic hyperbole here. Behind this was another impenetrable array in the form of a Lotus, and contained in the middle of the leaves of the Lotus there was also a 'Needle' or 'Needle-mouthed array'. One of the purposes of this array was to protect King Jayadratha, who Arjuna had sworn to kill that day. Jayadratha and his troops were placed at the rear, twelve miles behind Drona, to one side of the needle-shaped array. Drona himself was at the front of the array, at the 'entrance' of the Çakata.

Various heroes are mentioned as being positioned at different parts of the array, and the formation is again one of mixed troops [7].

The purpose of this array appears to be mainly defensive and, while the main battle-narrative concentrates on individual combats, it is maintained throughout the day's fighting. Drona generally maintains a position at the 'entrance' or 'gate' of his array, riding out in his chariot to do battle with the Pandava heroes and then returning to his previous post when the particular combat is concluded [8]. The array is penetrated by Arjuna's chariot and Jayadratha is killed; and a couple of other Pandava heroes penetrate the array as well. But these are acts of individual skill and bravery: the array holds against the Pandava army as a whole and is only broken when Drona is absent from his post.

Of the Circular Array (Chakra Vyuha) we have, in fact, very few details. It is, obviously, circular: it has an 'entrance' or 'gate', where Drona is stationed, and King Duryodhana and his troops are in its midst. This reference to a gate has interesting parallels to the 'Gates' of the *Pa Chên*, but there appears to be only one of them. There does not seem to be anything to suggest it is a hollow circle; rather it appears to be filled with the usual thousands of mixed troops. The point is, however, that it is generally impenetrable unless one knows the secret of its formation. Only four people on the Pandava side know how to penetrate it: Krishna and his son, Pradyumna, Arjuna and his son, Abhimanyu. At the time of the array's formation, Krishna and Arjuna have been lured away to another battle, and Pradyumna also appears to be absent. Yudhishthira, finding himself hard-pressed by Drona, asks Abhimanyu to penetrate the array, but Abhimanyu has only been taught how to penetrate the array and not how to come out again. In desperation, Yudhishthira persuades Abhimanyu to undertake the task, promising that he and his troops will follow when the young warrior has opened a passage for them. Abhimanyu manages to penetrate the array, but then King Jayadratha appears, shooting great flights of arrows and closing the passage behind him, preventing the Pandavas from following. After an epic battle, Abhimanyu is eventually surrounded by six chariot-riding heroes, including Drona, and killed [9].

Fig. 2 - A diagram of the Halebid Labyrinth.

Trying to make sense of this array from the material contained in the *Mahabharata* does not seem a very promising task. However, S.C. Brooke [10] draws our attention to a carved stone freeze at the temple of Halebid in Mysore, in southern India. This temple was built by members of the Hoysala dynasty during the 12th and 13th centuries A.D. The frieze, about 9 inches high, shows various scenes from the *Mahabharata* and the *Ramayana*, including a representation of Abhimanyu's death. He is shown still fighting, and close by is a representation of the Circular Array, in the form of a labyrinth. The pattern of this labyrinth is shown in figure 2; on the frieze itself, the pathways are filled with animals and warriors.

To this may be added a depiction from modern sources of a *yantra* ('device') called Chakra Vyuha, which is also in the form of a labyrinth [11]; although here the labyrinth is of a different construction to that shown on the Halebid frieze (see figure 3). This Chakra Vyuha, however, represents a womb and is drawn on a flat surface, much as a western talisman is: after propitiation by a priest, it is used as a focus for concentration by a woman in childbirth. Obviously, no military connection appears here.

Are we then to assume that Drona's Circular Array was, in fact, a labyrinth? Brooke (who seems unaware of the yantra) mingles caution and enthusiasm. On the one hand he says "at present the labyrinth is connected with the Pandavas, but there is no

reason to suppose that this was always the case" and "the labyrinth has been used to symbolise an event described in the sacred epic". For the most part, though, his exposition centres on the explication of the *Mahabharata* story as a tale of human sacrifice, where Abhimanyu is drawn into the labyrinth and killed as a victim in a solar cult; the labyrinth, with its known solar connections, is thus an integral part of this interpretation.

Nigel Pennick (who is aware of the yantra), follows the latter interpretation, although he does not emphasize the solar sacrifice aspect: "In the ancient saga known as the *Mahabharata*, Abhimanyu's death is engineered by means of this labyrinth. There the circular formation known as *Chakra-Vyuha* (the labyrinth) is set up by the agency of Drona, the warrior-magician, who says, 'Today I will slay a mighty charioteer, one of the foremost heroes of the Pandavas. Also, today I will form an array that is impenetrable to the very gods.' Once the labyrinth is made, the victim is lured into it. Although he can enter, it is impenetrable to his comrades, who are powerless to prevent his being slaughtered." [12]

Is this bold assertion, that the Chakra Vyuha described in the *Mahabharata* is a labyrinth, justified? We have seen that Drona's formation has a single 'entrance', but this is also true of the Çakata array mentioned in Drona's final, complex formation; and the Çakata represents a vehicle. The array is said to be 'impenetrable', but this is also said of the Lotus array. And there is no description in the text of any internal structure to the array, labyrinthine or otherwise. This is suprising, when we *do* have details (admittedly vague) of the structure of the other formations. Abhimanyu penetrates the array, intent on breaking it up, after which the entrance is closed behind him; thereafter, the usual chaotic mêlée follows, until he is surrounded by chariots, and slaughtered.

On the other hand, we have the Halebid frieze and the yantra bearing the name Chakra Vyuha, which might seem to be compelling evidence. Yet the Halebid frieze dates to near a thousand years after the epic, and comes from southern rather than northern India; and the yantra quite obviously has no military connotations at all. It seems to me that an alternative proposal could be constructed: that the *Mahabharata's* original Chakra Vyuha was simply a Circular Array of unknown form; that at some later period, prior to the Halebid frieze, this Array was interpreted or symbolised by the labyrinth; that because of this, the labyrinth design gained the name of Chakra Vyuha; and that thus the yantra gained a militaristic name inappropriate to its uses. Perhaps the best that can be said of any interpretation is that it remains 'not proven'.

After this labyrinthine digression, it's time to return to China. There is an interesting parallel to the episode of Abhimanyu's death in the Chinese traditions relating to Chu-ko Liang. The story comes from *The Romance of the Three Kingdoms*, the historical novel written by Lo Kuan-chung about 1370 A.D. [13]. The leading figures in the drama are real enough, but the story itself is probably more traditional than historical. The armies of Shu and Wei are drawn up facing one another, and a contest of military tactics is proposed. Chu-ko Liang arrays the Shu troops in the *Pa Chên* and invites the Wei general, Ssu-ma Yi, to attack it. Ssu-ma Yi deputes the task to three of his captains, each leading thirty cavalry-troops, and tells them how to penetrate the array at the Gate of Life. Unfortunately, Ssu-ma Yi is not as knowledgable as Chu-ko Liang, and the instructions he gives about leaving the array are mistaken. His troops enter the array at the Gate of Life, but are then stopped by a flight of arrows, captured and taken to Chu-ko Liang, who is positioned at the centre of the array. He disarms the troops and returns them to Ssu-ma Yi with a message that he should study further.

This material raises a number of interesting questions, but I fear that any possible answers would have to be speculative. Although it seems a reasonable assumption that the *Pa Chên* had some form of historical reality, even if it is no longer understood, can we say the same about the Indian arrays? There is some independent evidence confirming their existence, at least in theory (though the Circular Array is not mentioned), yet the dating of the material leaves much to be desired [14]. I have not so far found any evidence of them having actually been used on the battlefield; this is merely a lack of positive proof, however. Assuming a reason-

Fig. 3 - The *Chakra-vyuha* as the focus of concentration during childbirth. From Khanna's *Yantra*.

able correlation of dates might be made, we could allow that Vyasa (or whoever wrote the original *Drona Parva*) might be describing something not entirely fictional. As for Vyasa's handling of the material, however, it has to be said that he seems to display little understanding of the function of the arrays he describes, or of military tactics in general. Again, this is hardly conclusive proof of anything. The *Mahabharata* is an epic poem, mainly concerned with story-telling, myth and poetic literature. It remains possible that the author could have been aware of real military practice and used it, or embroidered upon it, without necessarily fully understanding it. Those practices could be as old as the historical core of the *Mahabharata* story, or they could be more or less contemporary with the date of final composition.

Perhaps the safest thing to say is that during the period between the 4th century B.C. and the 4th century A.D. there was a *tradition* (whether historical or literary) of military arrays in India. These arrays were of various forms, including animals and mythological beings, and also the circle. Meanwhile in China, between the 1st century B.C. and the 3rd century A.D., we also have a tradition of military arrays, apparently with a more factual historical basis. The major one of these is the *Pa Chên*, based on the circular arrangement of the trigrams; although later tradition also speaks of an animal-shape, the Serpent Formation. Perhaps this is nothing more than an interesting example of parallel and separate development.

On the other hand, we should not overlook the possibility of influence between India and China. There is some evidence for contact between the two countries as early as the 2nd century B.C. [15], and Buddhism was introduced into China in the 1st century A.D. Whether information about military arrays would have been exchanged must remain no more than a matter of speculation. Obviously the final form of the *Mahabharata* was not written early enough to have an influence on the first formation of the *Pa Chên*; but *possibly* the stories it contains, or the military practices it refers to, could have reached China at a sufficiently early date. And if that material referred to the Circular Array, it is *possible* that the idea of the *Pa Chên* was worked up from this. I have my doubts about this, however. The trigrams on which the *Pa Chên* is based appear to be a purely Chinese invention and the various references to 'evolutions' being worked with it speak of something rather more complex than a simple circle. Alternatively, it is possible that the influence went the other way: we know that the *Pa Chên* was in existence by the early part of the 3rd century A.D., and it is *possible* that stories of some sort of circular array reached India from China before the final composition of the *Mahabharata*. The Chinese context not being fully understood, we would then end up with a simple circular array. But all this is speculation, and hardly seems susceptible of proof.

With regard to the parallels between the stories of Abhimanyu's death and the failure of Ssu-ma Yi's captains, again we can only indulge in cautious speculation. The Chinese story *appears* to be more traditional than historical. If it could be shown to be fully historical, then we would have to concede the *possibility* of the story reaching India before the final recension of the *Mahabharata* was made. On the other hand, the death of Abhimanyu is a major and crucial episode in the *Mahabharata*; while the tale of Ssu-ma Yi's captains is a rather minor episode in *The Romance of the Three Kingdoms*. Similarly, the Indian epic is some 1,000 years older than the Chinese novel. If we are to suppose that one tradition has influenced the other, it would be more logical to assume that the Indian story has influenced the Chinese, rather than the other way round.

It is known that various stories from India's other great epic, the *Ramayana*, reached China during the 1st millenium A.D. The possible influence of these stories on another classical Chinese novel, the *Hsi-yu Chi* ('Monkey', or 'The Journey to the West') is the subject of some dispute [16]. But while the case of the *Ramayana* might be taken as an example of the possibility of literary influence, it has to be said that the *Mahabharata* appears to be much less well-known in China. The similarities between the Abhimanyu and Ssu-ma Yi stories do appear to be quite close. Nonetheless, if we were to accept the possibility that the stories of circular arrays appeared as separate developments in India and China, then surely it would not be straining credibility too far to accept the possibility that similar basic situations would produce similar stories based upon them. Given an impenetrable array formed by a master tactician, an obvious story-telling development would be to have the array penetrated, and for that penetration to ultimately result in failure.

In the end, then, no firm conclusions seem possible. We have parallel traditions, one of which may possibly have influenced the other. Alternatively, the traditions may have originated as quite separate developments, continued to develop separately and, without any cross-influence, have arrived at surprisingly parallel conclusions. And that, perhaps, would be a rather more interesting interpretation than the assumption of one influencing the other.

REFERENCES

1 - Steve Moore, *The Trigrams of Han*, Aquarian Press, Wellingborough, 1989, p144-182. To the references gathered there may now be added Ralph D. Sawyer (trans), *The Seven Military Classics of Ancient China*, Westview Press, Boulder, Colorado, 1993, particularly p326-328, 339.

2 - Krishna Chaitanya, *A New History of Sanskrit Literature*, Asia Publishing House, London, 1962, p200-201.

3 - Ramchandra Jain, *Jaya: The Original Nucleus of Mahabharata*, Agam Kala Prakashan, Delhi, 1979, *passim*.

4 - *The Mahabharata*, translated by Kisari Mohan Ganguli, published by Protap Chandra Roy, Bharata Press, Calcutta; l9 parts, l882-l894. The material quoted here comes from the following volumes: *Bhishma Parva* 1887; *Drona Parva* l888; *Karna Parva* 1889. References will be given according to the following formula: BP 19.4-7 (p61). This refers to the original text of *Bhishma Parva*, section l9, verses (slokas) 4-7; and simultaneously to Roy's translation of the BP volume, p61. The arrays mentioned here are to be found as follows:

Needle/Vajra: BP 19.4-7 (p61); BP 19.35 (p63); BP 82.23 (p295).

Krauncharuna/Crane: BP 50.40-57 (p185-187); BP 75.15-22 (p276); DP 7.24-25 (p17).

Garuda: BP 56.2-9 (p209-210); DP 20.4-16 (p61-62).

Half-moon/semi-circle: BP 56.11 (p210); BP 88.17-21 (p318); DP 20.4 (p61); KP 11.27-32 (p33).

Makara: BP 69.4-6 (p258); BP 75.4-12 (p275); KP 11.14-21 (p32-33).

Hawk/Çyena: BP 69.7-13 (p259).

Mandala: BP 82.10-21 (p294-295).

Sarvatobhadra: BP 100.1-8 (p364).

5 - DP 7.24-25 (p17).

6 - DP 20.24-25 (p61-62).

7 - DP 74.27-28 (p206); DP 87.1-32 (p237-239).

8 - DP 91.2 (p246); DP 96.2-3 (p268); DP 117.34-35 (p345); DP 124.43 (p369); DP 127.56 (p382); DP 128.19 (p384).

9 - DP 34.13-21 (p112-113); DP 35.14-21 (p114- 115); DP 36.15-16 (p117); DP 72.20-21 (p194); DP 73.1-4 (p198- 199).

10 - S.C. Brooke: 'The Labyrinth Pattern in India', *Folklore*, Vol. 63-64, 1952-53, p463-472. A photograph of the frieze is included.

11 - Madhu Khanna, *Yantra*, Thames & Hudson, London, 1979, p157.

12 - Nigel Pennick, *Mazes and Labyrinths*, Robert Hale, London, 1994, p51-52.

13 - Steve Moore, *Trigrams of Han* p161- 162. C H Brewitt-Taylor (trans), *The Romance of the Three Kingdoms*, (1925) rpt Charles E Tuttle, Vermont & Tokyo, 1959, vol 2 p423-424.

14 - This evidence is to be found in the early Hindu law-book, the *Code of Manu (Manu-Sanhita)*, at 7.185: "On his march let him form his troops, either like a staff, or in an even column; like a wain, or in a wedge with the apex foremost; like a boar, or in a rhomb with the van and rear narrow and the centre broad; like a Macara or sea- monster, that is, in a double triangle with apices joined; like a needle, or in a long line; or like the bird of Vishnu, that is, in a rhomboid with the wings far extended." At 7.186: "From whatever side he apprehends danger, to that side let him extend his troops; and let him always conceal himself in the midst of a squadron formed like a lotos-flower." And at 7.189: "Let him at his pleasure order a few men to engage in a close phalanx, or a large number of warriors in loose ranks; and, having formed them in a long line like a needle, or in three divisions like a thunderbolt, let him give orders for battle." M. Kenealy, *Institutes of Hindu Law*, C.W. Hillyear, Watford, 1911, p99. The "bird of Vishnu" mentioned here is the Garuda. It is perhaps worthy of note (particularly with reference to the Makara and Garuda formations) that the arrays are here described in geometric terms, rather than in the poetic and mythological terminology used in the *Mahabharata*; we might speculate that if the arrays were actually used on the battlefield, these geometrical descriptions might give a truer picture of the actual formations. The formations also seem to be used as much for marching as for actually giving battle.

There seems little agreement as to the date of the *Manu-Sanhita*. John Dowson (*A Classical Dictionary of Hindu Mythology*, Routledge & Kegan Paul, London, rpt 1972, p201-2) dates it to the 5th century B.C. W.J. Wilkins (*Hindu Mythology*, (1882) rpt Rupa, Calcutta, 1975, p4) vacillates between about 1000 B.C. and 500 A.D.

15 - Joseph Needham, *Science and Civilisation in China*, Cambridge UP, 1954 onward, vol 1, p206.

16 - Glen Dudbridge, *The Hsi-yu Chi*, Cambridge UP, 1970, p160-164.

SOME NEW EVIDENCE FOR DATING THE TRIGRAMS OF THE I CHING

In collaboration with Peter Eckman

The dating of the *I Ching* and the component parts of its related philosophical system raises some extremely complex questions. I have attempted to deal with these at some length in *The Trigrams of Han* [1]; and I must refer anyone interested in the problem as a whole to those pages, where the arguments are set forth in detail and with references. In brief, though, the conclusion I reached was that while the core-text of the work may well have been written earlier, the book we possess today (including its various philosophical appendices) did not reach its final form until the Han dynasty (202 B.C. - 220 A.D.).

I also concluded that the relative dating of the linear figures used in the *I Ching* should be revised: that (in spite of the Chinese tradition to the contrary) the six-line figures (hexagrams) came into existence before the three-line figures (trigrams), and that the trigrams were derived from the hexagrams, rather than vice-versa. And finally, that the various circular arrangements of the eight trigrams were, perhaps, the latest to appear in this chain of development. It is with the dating of one of these circular arrangements that we have to deal here.

Two of the circular arrangements of the trigrams are well-known: 'The World of Thought' (otherwise known as Fu Hsi's trigrams, or the 'Earlier Heaven' arrangement) and 'The World of the Senses' (King Wên's trigrams, or the 'Later Heaven' arrangement). A third is more obscure and, lacking a name from Chinese tradition, I dubbed it 'The World of the Elements'. With regard to the relative dating of these arrangements, my conclusion was (again, against tradition) that the Elements was the earliest, the Senses second, and Thought the latest. Absolute dating is difficult, but the first two arrangements appear to have been in existence by the beginning of the Han dynasty; the dating of the World of Thought, which concerns us here, is more problematical. This arrangement is shown in Figure 1.

Disregarding the tradition which attributes the arrangement to the mythical Fu Hsi (3rd millennium B.C.), three dates have been posited for the World of Thought. Again, there is insufficient room to rehearse the arguments in detail, and I must refer the reader to my previous work [2], but, in brief, the theories are as follows:

1. That the arrangement was in existence by, or came into being at, the beginning of the Han dynasty (beginning of the 2nd century B.C.). This argument depends mainly on an apparent reference to the arrangement in the *Shuo Kua Chuan* ('Commentary on the Trigrams'). Unfortunately the dating of this document is dubious, and it is by no means certain that the text is definitely referring to the World of Thought arrangement.

2. That the arrangement was in existence by the 3rd century A.D. Apparent references to the arrangement appear in a fragmentary *I Ching* commentary by Yü Fan (164-233) and in the *Ts'an T'ung Ch'i*, allegedly written by Wei Po-yang in 142 A.D. Here six of the trigrams are used in a complex system to describe the phases of the Moon. These six trigrams appear in the same order as the World of Thought, but two (Li and K'an) are omitted. It is not

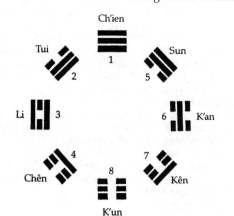

Ch'ien
Tui
Sun
Li
K'an
Chên
Kên
K'un

Fig. 1

Fig. 2 - (a) Ch'ien; (b) Tui, 'Great Yang'; (c) Li, 'Bright Yang'; (d) Chên, 'Little Yang'; (e) Sun, 'Decreasing Yin'; (f) K'an, 'Little Yin'; (g) Kên, 'Great Yin'; (h) K'un.

clear whether this lunar system is derived from the World of Thought, or whether the World of Thought was later derived from the lunar system.

3. That the arrangement only came into being around the beginning of the Northern Sung dynasty (960-1126), shortly before the first printed examples of the sequence appear. This theory would attribute the arrangement to the school of Ch'ên T'uan (c.906-989) and Shao Yung (1011-1077), both of whom are known to have been familiar with the work of Wei Po-yang. The argument largely depends on the fact that the numbering system applied to the trigrams in this arrangement appears to derive from an analytical system worked out by Shao Yung, in which the trigrams and their order are logically derived by division from the yin and yang. The question remains, however: did the arrangement derive from the working out of this logical system, or was the logical system worked out to explain a previously existing arrangement?

At the time of writing *Trigrams* I lacked sufficient evidence to decisively prove or disprove any of these theories, and could only offer a speculative (and largely intuitive) opinion that the second had the greatest likelihood. However, since the book was published I have had the great good fortune to engage in a fruitful correspondence with Peter Eckman, of California; and Peter has brought to my attention some material which allows us to make some progress on the problem [3].

This material is to be found in the corpus of traditional Chinese medical writings: specifically in the *Su Wên* section of the *Huang-ti Nei-ching* ('Yellow Emperor's Classic of Internal Medicine'). There are two main passages of interest here, but the terminology used to describe the trigrams is unfamiliar. From the passages to be quoted below it is apparent that these unfamiliar terms do, in fact, refer to the trigrams; but in order to make the material more comprehensible it may be as well to deal

with the terminology first.

The references to the trigrams are embedded in a complex system including the Five Elements, the calendar, medical theory, and so forth. Six of the trigrams are used to demonstrate the circulation of the 'Six Subtle Energies', but rather than being referred to by their usual names, they are described in terms of their 'yin-ness' and 'yang-ness'. This is probably best understood with reference to Figure 2, which also includes the usual names.

Ch'ien, being entirely composed of unbroken (yang) lines, represents pure yang; K'un, being composed wholly of broken (yin) lines, represents pure yin. The trigrams are here defined as 'yang' or 'yin' according to which type of line occupies the lowest position. Thus Tui, Li and Chên are yang trigrams, Sun, K'an and Kên are yin trigrams. The 'motion' in a trigram is upwards, so Tui, having two yang lines in the lower places, is 'about to become' pure yang, and is thus known as Great Yang; for similar reasons, Kên is known as Great Yin. Li, which normally symbolises the sun, light and brightness, is known as Bright Yang. Chên, with only one yang line, is called Little Yang. The two remaining yin trigrams appear to be named with less logic. Sun is described as Decreasing Yin, as if the presence of a yin line brings about decrease in an otherwise yang trigram, while K'an receives the name Little Yin. The reasons for these names appear to derive from Chinese medical tradition [4] and need not concern us here: the point is that these names are used in our texts, and can be shown to refer to the trigrams. Figure 3 shows the usual circular arrangement with these names in place.

In this circular arrangement, the lower lines of the trigrams are nearest to the centre. Our first passage from the *Su Wên* [5] thus describes the trigrams from a 'viewpoint' of the centre, as follows:

The upper and lower positions are predetermined, and the left and right sides are regulated according to fixed principles. Therefore, on the

301

Fig. 3

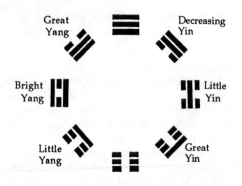

Looking at the circular arrangement, the "upper and lower positions" correspond to Ch'ien and K'un: these represent Heaven (pure yang) and Earth (pure yin) respectively. Their positions, naturally enough, are "predetermined": they play no part in what follows. The "left side" (yang trigrams) and the "right side" (yin trigrams) "are regulated according to fixed principles": this refers to the fact that, moving in a clockwise direction, the 'yang-ness' of the trigrams increases from Chên to Tui, the 'yin-ness' from Sun to Kên. Looked at from the centre, this clockwise direction is a motion toward the right. Thus the Little Yang is followed, to the right, by the Bright Yang, the Great Yang, the Decreasing Yin, the Little Yin, and the Great Yin, before the cycle starts again at Little Yang. Ch'ien and K'un are omitted, having already been dealt with: their "positions are predetermined".

The second passage from the Su Wên [6] again deals with the Six Energies, omitting Ch'ien and K'un. The material of interest here is embedded in a lengthy complex of Elemental, calendrical and medical material, so space permits us only to extract the relevant parts. It will be seen that the arrangement of

trigrams is being regarded as a rotating wheel, with the trigrams moving in a clockwise direction. "When the Great Yang is in control of the heaven ... the Great Yin will be situated beneath the earth". That is, when the circle is rotated so that the Great Yang (Tui) is at the central heaven position (normally occupied by Ch'ien), the Great Yin (Kên) is directly opposite, "beneath the earth", at the earth position normally occupied by K'un. "When the Bright Yang is in control of the heaven ... the Little Yin will be beneath the earth". The positions of the remaining trigrams are given according to the same formula as the 'wheel' is rotated one stage at a time, and we can summarise as follows: Little Yang in heaven, Decreasing Yin beneath earth. Great Yin in heaven, Great Yang beneath earth. Little Yin in heaven, Bright Yang beneath earth. Decreasing Yin in heaven, Little Yang beneath earth.

These two passages, then, appear to describe the World of Thought arrangement in different ways. In the first, the trigrams are described by listing them in a clockwise direction: first the Little Yang, then, to its right, the Bright Yang, and so forth. In the second, they are described as pairs of opposites: the Great Yang is opposite to the Great Yin, and so on. There seems little doubt that, under the variant terminology, the author of the Su Wên is actually describing the trigrams of the World of Thought arrangement. Both these passages would also seem to provide strong evidence in support of the theory I previously proposed [7], that the World of Thought sequence is to be viewed as a *vertical* arrangement, and not a horizontal one aligned to the cardinal points.

If it can be taken that the World of Thought arrangement is described in the Su Wên, the next question would obviously be: when was the Su Wên written? Unfortunately, this is not an easy question to answer.

The Huang-ti Nei-ching is a composite work, and its various parts were composed at differing dates. In general, the book as a whole is dated to the period from the 2nd century B.C. to the 8th century A.D. Lu and Needham [8] dated the Su Wên to the 2nd century B.C.; but more recent work by David Keegan, quoted by Nathan Sivin [9], suggests that it did not reach its final form ... the form

right side of the Little Yang, the Bright Yang is in the reign; on the right side of the Bright Yang, the Great Yang is in the reign; on the right side of the Great Yang, the Decreasing Yin is in the reign; on the right side of the Decreasing Yin, the Little Yin is in the reign; on the right side of the Little Yin, the Great Yin is in the reign; on the right side of the Great Yin, the Little Yang is in the reign.

in which we possess it today ... before the 8th century A.D. However, at least one version of it appears to have existed earlier than this, as the first commentary on it was written by Ch'uan Yüan-ch'i in the 6th century A.D. [10].

This is all fairly vague, but we can draw two conclusions. First, there is nothing to suggest that the *Su Wên*, and its description of the World of Thought, existed before the 2nd century B.C.: so this new evidence cannot be seen as indicating that the World of Thought existed prior to the Han dynasty. There is thus nothing here to suggest a need to revise our previous relative chronology, which places the World of Thought later than the Elements and Senses arrangements.

Second, regardless of the date at which the parts evolved, we know that the *Su Wên* text that we have today was in existence by the 8th century A.D. We can thus say with reasonable certainty that the World of Thought arrangement was in existence by that same date: which means that it would already have been around for some centuries before the time of Ch'ên T'uan and Shao Yung. We are still left with a fairly vague date for the invention of the arrangement (during the thousand years prior to the 8th century A.D.), but at least the third of our possible dates for its composition can be disposed of.

REFERENCES

1 - Steve Moore, *The Trigrams of Han*, Aquarian Press, Wellingborough, 1989.

2 - Moore, *Trigrams*, p90-98.

3 - Peter Eckman MD, *The Book of Changes in Traditional Oriental Medicine*, Traditional Acupuncture Institute, Columbia, Maryland, 1987, p9-10; and personal correspondence. Peter brought to my attention the passages from the *Su Wên*, and pointed out that they refer to the World of Thought; he also provided the medical references listed below. I take responsibility for drawing the inferences about dating.

4 - Eckman, *Book of Changes*, p6.

5 - *Su Wên*, chapter 68. Henry C.Lu (trans), *The Yellow Emperor's Classic of Internal Medicine*, The Academy of Oriental Heritage, Vancouver, 1978, p430-431.

6 - *Su Wên*, chapter 71. Lu, *Yellow Emperor*, p503, 512, 519, 523, 526 & 530.

7 - Moore, *Trigrams*, p105-107.

8 - Lu Gwei-Djen & Joseph Needham, *Celestial Lancets*, Cambridge UP, 1980, p1.

9 - Nathan Sivin, *Traditional Medicine in Contemporary China*, University of Michigan, 1987, p5-6.

10 - Sivin, *Traditional Medicine*, p454.

THE MA-WANG-TUI TRIGRAMS:

PREDICTIONS AND PROBLEMS

As mentioned in the previous piece, some time ago I discussed an arrangement of trigrams which, in the absence of any further information, I dubbed the 'World of the Elements' [1]. This arrangement (hereafter referred to as *E*) seems to have survived outside the mainstream *I Ching* tradition, occurring mainly in magical talismans, and is shown in figure 1.

To summarise briefly, I sought to show that this arrangement was open to interpretation on several levels. It shows the yin and yang symmetrically arranged, the trigrams with the majority of yin lines to the right side, the yang to the left. As the diagram has the trigrams for Heaven at the top and Earth at the bottom, it can be looked at as a vertical arrangement, apparently on a polar alignment. Both the majority of the yang lines and the trigram Li (fire, sun, south) are to the left, making it appropriate to orientate the left side of the diagram toward the south. A similar argument can be made for orientating the right side of the diagram (yin lines, K'an) toward the north.

The diagram also contains a systematic arrangement of the trigrams according to the familial aspects normally attributed to them.

Fig.1

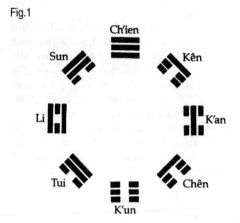

These family aspects are explained as follows. Ch'ien, being all yang, is naturally the Father, and similarly K'un is the Mother. The 'Sons' are those trigrams containing one yang line each, their 'age' depending on the position of the line (lowest 1st, middle 2nd, top 3rd); similarly for the 'Daughters'. Reading round clockwise from Ch'ien we have (1) Father, (2) 3rd Son, (3) 2nd Son, (4) 1st Son, (5) Mother, (6) 3rd Daughter, (7) 2nd Daughter, (8) 1st Daughter. This sequence also appears in the Ma-wang-tui silk manuscript of the I Ching, dating from 168 B.C., where the 64 hexagrams are arranged in eight groups of eight, each group having the same upper trigram. These eight upper trigram groups follow the same sequence as that read clockwise in E [2].

Satisfying as this correlation may be, more recently it has occurred to me that the arrangement of familial trigrams shown in this diagram can also be correlated with a second order of sequencing in the Ma-wang-tui hexagrams. This is the sequence by which the eight hexagrams within each of the eight groups is arranged, following a strict order of the lower trigrams. This sequence is arranged in familial pairs [3], as follows: (1) Ch'ien (Father) & K'un (Mother); (2) Kên (3rd S) & Tui (3rd D); (3) K'an (2nd S) & Li (2nd D); (4) Chên (1st S) & Sun (1st D). If we now look at figure 1 again, we find that pair one is placed on opposite sides of the vertical axis. Moving clockwise from this one place, we find the second pair similarly placed on opposite sides of the circle (Kên & Tui). Similarly, moving one place clockwise again, the third and then

the fourth pair appear in the correct sequence. The arrangement thus corresponds to both sequences of trigrams used in the Ma-wang-tui manuscript. We might also note that a similar double system, of clockwise circling and trigram pairing, appears in the Su Wên description of the World of Thought arrangement, discussed in the previous piece.

I also sought to demonstrate that the Generation Cycle of the Five Elements could be found among the trigrams, by correlating them with the Lo Shu magic square, as in figure 2.

Here, giving the trigrams their standard Elemental designations, we read them in the sequence of the 'magic line' of the magic square of three; but in reverse, beginning at 9 and ending at 1. Thus, following the sequence from Ch'ien (Heaven), we have Metal (9 & 8), which generates Water (7), generating Wood (6 (5 blank) & 4), Fire (3) and Earth (2 & 1) ... the last being K'un, the Earth trigram. Thus we have the Generation Cycle demonstrated, starting from Metal, following a winding course from Heaven to Earth.

On the basis of this evidence, I went on to speculate (in brief), that:

1. As E uses the same sequences of familial relationships as those used to construct the Ma-wang-tui hexagram arrangement, there is likely to be some direct connection between E and the school of interpretation responsible for the Ma-wang-tui manuscript. In effect, I wished to imply that if a circular arrangement of trigrams were to be found associated with the Ma-wang-tui arrangement of the hexa-

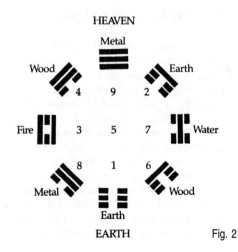

Fig. 2

304

grams, then *E* is what we would expect to find.

2. As the two methods of interpretation (Familial, Elemental) seem to 'coincidentally' fit so well together, in a way that they fail to do in either of the more well-known circular arrangements, then it would be more logical to think that it is in *E* that the trigrams originally received both their Familial and Elemental designations.

3. These designations were then carried with the individual trigrams when they were rearranged into the World of the Senses (King Wên) and World of Thought (Fu Hsi) arrangements, where their sequences became disarranged. And if this progression of events is correct, it is thus likely that *E* precedes both the other arrangements **[4]**.

N ow, some six years after the manuscript for *The Trigrams of Han* was completed, I find that a circular arrangement of the trigrams was, in fact, discovered at Ma-wang-tui, though in a manuscript of Lao Tzu, rather than in direct relationship to the *I Ching* manuscript **[5]**. This arrangement appears in figure 3.

Obviously, the merest glance reveals that this is not *E*, so at least one of my hypotheses will have to be abandoned: the 'received text' of *E* (which is traceable at least as early as the Sung dynasty (960-1279 A.D.) and which, if the somewhat dubious Chinese lineage accompanying it **[6]** is to be believed, may be traced back to K'ung An-kuo (156-74 B.C.) of the Han), does not appear to be the trigram arrangement associated with the Ma-wang-tui hexagram sequence (pre-168 B.C.), as another, obviously different arrangement appears in the same archaeological context. Thus I find myself having to reappraise my thinking on *E* in the light of this new information.

First, though, let us examine the Ma-wang-tui trigram sequence (hereafter denoted as *M*). There are certain similarities to *E*. The left side of the circle contains the majority of yang lines, the right yin, with Li and K'an in the same positions as they occupy in *E*. However, the pairs Tui & Kên, and Chên & Sun, have swapped position relative to *E*. More obviously, the trigrams Ch'ien and K'un have reversed their positions, leaving us with the remarkable situation where K'un (earth) is in

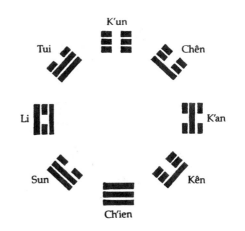

Fig. 3

K'un

Tui

Chên

Li

K'an

Sun

Kên

Ch'ien

the Heaven position and Ch'ien (heaven) is in the Earth position.

Such is the startling unexpectedness of this positioning of Ch'ien and K'un in *M* that one's first reaction on seeing the arrangement might be to dismiss it as an error. However, if the manuscript remains unique (as I gather is the case) it would of course be impossible to prove error, there being no standard to judge it against. On the other hand, the evidence we shall examine below does suggest that the arrangement has been made intentionally, and that Ch'ien and K'un are placed in their unexpected positions as a logical consequence of the system used to construct the arrangement: in short, they are 'correctly' placed. We shall arrive at this conclusion using the same 'tools' as we applied to *E*.

Let us begin with the familial aspects of the trigrams. These are again displayed in an obviously systematic order, and if we apply the Ma-wang-tui hexagram sequences we once again find these extremely productive. Applying the sequence of the upper trigrams, mentioned above, we find the same order, starting from Ch'ien (Father, 3rd, 2nd, 1st Sons, Mother, 3rd, 2nd, 1st Daughters) but this time running anti-clockwise; in *E*, it will be recalled, the same sequence ran clockwise from Ch'ien. If we next apply the paired sequence of lower trigrams, we find that the first pair (Ch'ien & K'un) again occupy the vertical axis, but upside down to *E*. Moving anti-clockwise one place, we find the second pair (Kên & Tui), and so on anti-clockwise

Fig. 4

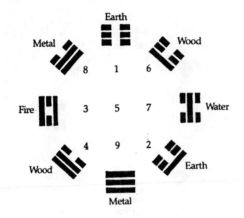

through the remaining pairs. With regard to the familial aspects, then, *M* is perfectly complimentary to *E*: an 'anti-version'.

This complimentarity, however, is far more impressive when we look at the Elemental designations of the trigrams and their relationship to the magic square of three. Yet if we attempt to apply the Lo Shu magic square to *M* in the same way as we did to *E*, we get no meaningful results: the pairs of trigrams with similar Elemental designations are broken up and the order provides no extended correlation to either the Generation or Destruction cycle of the Elements, whether we read the numbers forwards or backwards. However, if we rotate the Lo Shu square about its horizontal axis, so that row 8 1 6 is at the top, rather than 4 9 2, and place this on *M*, the results can be seen in figure 4:

If we now start to read the trigrams in the order of the magic line, from 9 to 1, in the same way that we did with *E*, we find exactly the same result: Ch'ien & Tui (9 & 8, Metal) are followed by K'an (7, Water), Chên & Sun (6 & 4, Wood), Li (3, Fire) and Kên & K'un (2 & 1, Earth). This, of course, is exactly the same sequence of trigrams as appear in *E*, and both show, from a common starting point (9, Ch'ien, Metal), the Generation Cycle of the Elements.

It should perhaps be noted that in manipulating the Lo Shu like this, we have done nothing to damage the integrity of the magic square, the horizontal, vertical and diagonal rows of which continue to add up to 15. The only difference is that the magic line

itself is now a mirror image of what it was in the Lo Shu. And, in fact, this mirror-complimentarity is continued throughout the comparison of the two arrangements. The familial aspects of the trigrams in *M* are presented in an arrangement that is a vertical mirror-image of that in *E* (by both methods of interpretation). The same can be said for the magic square interpretation of the trigram Elements. And, finally, the actual trigrams in *M* are themselves vertical mirror-images of those in *E*. This is not to say, of course, that *M* is simply *E* upside down: that would lead to a wholesale rotation of the figure.

This leaves us, then, with two separate arrangements of trigrams, *E* and *M*, which perform exactly the same functions (systematic arrangement of the familial relationships, demonstration of the Generation Cycle, yin and yang arranged north and south) and are constructed using the same techniques (magic square of three, trigram sequences from the Ma-wang-tui hexagrams), but which are exact mirror images of one another. In terms of function, information content and 'technological complexity', there seems to be no reason why one should be preferred to the other. However, there are two purely aesthetic reasons for preferring *E* to *M*. One is the obvious fact that *E* places Ch'ien and K'un in appropriate Heaven and Earth positions; the other is that the magic square used in *E* corresponds to the standard version of the Lo Shu.

L et us now return, then, to the speculations presented earlier. Having predicted the arrangement (*E*) that 'ought' to go with the Ma-wang-tui *I Ching*, we find instead its mirror-image (*M*). This result is, on reflection, a cause for mingled pleasure: I seem to have been both half-right and half-wrong at the same time. The methodology used to interpret *E* seems to have been vindicated, but the hypothesis based on it appears to have been interfered with by ill-fortune.

If, though, we assume *E* and *M* to be basically variants of the same diagram, then it might still be possible to make an argument, on the same grounds as previously, that the Familial and Elementary designations of the trigrams were first attributed to them using an

E/M original. Again, there is nothing in this new material to actually destroy an argument that these designations were then carried over from *E/M* to the World of the Senses, and so to the World of Thought; but the presence of *M* rather than *E* at Ma-wang-tui would seem to add a further layer of complication to an already speculative theory. Let us, therefore, reconsider the historical circumstances.

We are reasonably certain that the World of the Senses arrangement was in existence by the 3rd century B.C. [7]. If we wish to make a case for *E/M* being the 'original' arrangement of the trigrams, we have to posit that it was in existence before the Senses. This is not inherently impossible, but unfortunately it is not susceptible to proof, either; in this, though, we are no worse off than when we were simply positing that *E* alone was the original arrangement. Regrettably, all we can say is that we know *M* to have been in existence by 168 B.C. This does not preclude the possibility of it having originated prior to the Senses arrangement; but we simply do not know. Similarly, if the manuscript containing *M* is unique, we have no way of determining its history after 168 B.C., except for one thing: if *M* is unique, it has not survived by continuous transmission to the present day.

On the other hand, *E* obviously has survived to the present day even if, as is possibly the case, its meaning and 'compositional key' have been forgotten in the meantime. This arrangement, as we've seen above, can certainly be traced back as far as the Sung dynasty and, with admitted reservations (is the Chinese lineage trustworthy? does it refer to *E* rather than just the Lo Shu? etc.), may possibly be traced back to K'ung An-kuo, around the turn of the 2nd/1st century B.C. All these dates are becoming suggestively close to one another.

If we assume, as would surely seem to be the case, that *E* and *M* are intimately related, two possible models present themselves for their development. The first would be that

they were invented contemporaneously, as a pair. *M* we lose track of early on, while *E* survives, though its history is murky. We might infer that, while both arrangements were equally functional, one was better 'fitted' to survive, while the other became extinct.

The other model of development would be that one or the other of the arrangements had priority, in which case the earlier would obviously be the original, while the later one would be a revision. We might then infer that the revision had been made to some purpose: i.e., to correct some real or apparent defect in the earlier version.

Whichever of these models we prefer, the only real difference between *E* and *M* is aesthetic rather than functional: *E* has better positioning of Ch'ien and K'un and a magic square that matches the Lo Shu. We might thus consider *E* to be 'more correct' than *M*. In the first development-model, this provides a reason for *E* being more 'fit' to survive. In the second model, if *E* is 'more correct', it obviously implies that *M* is 'less correct': i.e., that *M* is the early and original sequence while *E* is the later and revised. And if *E* is 'more correct', this may explain why this arrangement has survived, while *M* died out.

If this second model of development is preferred, one might perhaps posit that the revision from *M* to *E* took place after 168 B.C. It would be tempting to take the Chinese lineage at face value and speculate that K'ung An-kuo might have been responsible, but more caution is perhaps necessary. K'ung was a Confucian scholar of the Old Text school, and so perhaps less likely to be interested in the apparatus of magic squares and Elemental cycles than his New Text contemporaries, who very much specialised in this sort of area. All we can really say is that such a revision would fit very suitably into a Han context; beyond this, as so often with such fragments of ancient thought, it is difficult to say anything definite.

REFERENCES

1 - Steve Moore, *The Trigrams of Han*, Aquarian Press, Wellingborough, 1989, p110-119.

2 - *ibid.*, p112-113.

3 - *ibid.*, p186.

4 - *ibid.*, p117-119.

5 - Zhang Zhenglang: 'Postscriptum pour ''Les 64 Hexagrammes'' du manuscrit en soie', in *Zhouyi Network* No.2, March 1987, p17.

6 - Moore, *Trigrams*, p115-116.

7 - *ibid.*, p62 & 45.

INDEX TO FORTEAN TIMES – 1993

Steve Moore and Bob Rickard

*F*ortean Studies has provided both the opportunity and an ideal way to publish an annual index to *Fortean Times*. It was a monumental slog, but something we have wanted to address for a long time as it will be helpful to scholars and the curious as well as to us in our ongoing productions. Several points must be made ...

We have tried to be as thorough as was practical within the limitations of available time and resources. The aim has been to provide the user with a direct indentification of issue and page numbers (in bold and normal type, respectively). Page numbers prefixed by an apostrophe (eg. '4) refer to the occasional centre-page inserts. The 'Dates' index required a special indicator - an asterisk

suffix (eg. 32*) - to distinguish occurrences dated by the reference material (eg. clippings) only. These dates are necessarily approximations; all other entries refer to actual event dates or dates mentioned.

The 'Topics' index proved incredibly complex and there is no ideal way to organise it. Cross-referencing has been kept to an essential minimum, pointing to major groups and sub-groups. We acknowledge the imperfections of our classifications and stress that they are not intended to infer any system of explanation. Again, our method was to try to anticipate how a user might seek a direct point of entry. Any suggestions for improvement would be welcome.

© Steve Moore & Bob Rickard 1994

TOPICS

Abduction - see: Aliens, Crimes, Hoaxes.

Accidents - see also: Attacks By, Coincidence, Luck.

   Vehicles - Air crash - **67**:12; Child under trailer - **67**:6; Multiple car crashes - **71**:14; Giant hand falls on car - **68**:'6; Tree sinks trawler - **71**:11; Repeated fatal car crash - **71**:9; Pilgrim vehicles collide at Fatima - **72**:18; Pets run over by owner - **67**:12

   Other - Boiler fumes overcome 30 - **72**:18; Hand severed - **72**:14; Boy impaled on railing - **67**:5; Glass eye lost in toilet - **69**:15; Manhole covers, flying - **68**:18; Cold fusion researcher killed - **69**:24; Assoc. with Egyptian mummy - **69**:19; Postman trapped inside post box - **72**:7

Alchemy - Red Mercury - **69**:44-45

Aliens - see also: Entities, Paranormal Exps, UFOs.

   Abduction by - **68**:25, 64; **69**:27-29; **70**:29, 60; **71**:31; **72**:54; of Betty & Barney Hill - **71**:'3; Speculation about - **69**:59; **71**:36-37; **72**:44-45; of Travis Walton - **69**:62; **71**:20, 53; African - **72**:44;

& Birth Trauma hypothesis - **71**:53; & Satanic Child Abuse - **71**:53; & Sexuality - **68**:55; **70**:28; from Aveley, Essex - **71**:'4; from crowded Australian beach - **72**:45; Implants, danger to crematoria - **71**:64; of Linda Napolitano - **67**:53-54; **72**:44; from Pascagoula - **70**:20. See also: *Mental Ph.*

   Encounters with - **69**:27; by Adamski - **71**:20; Documents demanded during - **71**:11; History of - **71**:'1-4; Kelly-Hopkinsville - **71**:'2; 'Martians', Italy - **67**:43; Humanoid, sexual, S. Africa - **71**:'4; Theory of - **67**:65; Villas Boas, alien sex - **71**:20; Fictional - **71**:'1-4; & cattle mutilation - **68**:25; **SETI** - **68**:33. See also: Ancient Astronauts, Religious Ph.

   Forms - **68**:12; **72**:62; **71**:'1-4; silver robots, Alabama - **71**:'4; exotic, Brazil - **71**:'4; Furry, web-footed, USA - **71**:'3; goblin, Kelly - **71**:'2; Lack of genitals - **69**:63; tiny, Malaysia - **71**:'4; Photos of - **71**:'4. See also: Entities.

Altered States of Consciousness - Drunk - **69**:7. LSD - **68**:6; Mushrooms, magic - **71**:35-38.

See also: Mental Ph.

Amnesia - Mental Ph.

Ancient Astronauts - **67**:59; 3000-yr-old 'spaceship' found - **71**:9. See also: Aliens, UFOs.

Animals - Attacks By, Attacks On, Behaviour A, Biology, Cryptozoology, Deaths A, Escapes, Falls (Creatures), Folklore, Giants, Hoaxes, Images, Intelligence, Luck, Out of Place, Palaeontology, Swarms, Talking, Tracks.

Angels - **68**:65; Angels of Mons - **68**:34-37; Moroni, to Joseph Smith - **70**:20. See also: Entities, Paranormal Experiences.

Antiquities

   Ancient sites & structures - Atlantis - **71**:62; Callanish - **71**:52; Great Pyramid - **70**:51; Dinas Bran (castle) - **67**:52; Cerne Abbas Giant - **69**:52; Rennes-le-Chateau - **71**:61-62; Silbury Hill - **70**:62; **72**:52; Callanish - **71**:52; Harold Stones, Trellech - **70**:52; Megaliths, Dressing of - **67**:6; Temples, symbolism - **71**:62; Ultima Thule - **71**:62; West Kennet long barrow - **72**:52

   Artifacts - Ark of Covenant, hunt for - **68**:59; 1940s coke bottles - **71**:7; Rustless iron pillar, New Delhi - **71**:17; Shogun gold, search for - **67**:10; Tunnels - **67**:10

Fakes & Hoaxes - Cave art, Zigoitia - **68**:42; Hominid remains, Indonesia - **70**:42-43; Religious relics - **70**:35-37. *See also: Hoaxes.*

Finds - 13th C. footwear, Wales - **72**:13; Cave art, Sormiou - **68**:42; Cave art destroyed, Tarn-et-Garonne - **68**:42; Chamber in Great Pyramid - **70**:51; Oldest chewing gum, 9,000 yrs old - **71**:7; 3,000-yr-old spaceship - **71**:9; Oldest cloth - **71**:9; Romanov family remains - **67**:45; U-boat in Turkish coalmine - **72**:50; U-boats on sea bed - **72**:50; Twyford Down, 18 skeletons, 7 feet tall - **67**:8

Other - Historical revisionism - **72**:59; Mummified mouse - **68**:7; 2000 yr old seeds grown - **69**:15; Severed Korean noses, Returned for burial - **67**:10; Vegetable Lamb - **68**:63; 'cuplike pram' - **68**:63; Pre-Columbian contacts with America - **67**:58; **68**:61; **70**:62

People - Dr Faustus - **67**:24-27; Kaspar Hauser, death of - **72**:20; Hitlers corpse, fate of - **67**:44-45

Appearances - Caspar Hauser - **68**:60; Materialisations, Sai Baba's, exposed - **69**:64; Mystery footprints - **68**:9; Travelling trolleys - **67**:19. *See also: Embeddings, Teleportation.*

Archaeology - *see: Antiquities.*

Astrology - **67**:61; of chess champions - **71**:54; of Roman emperors - **71**:54; & geographic latitude - **71**:54; John Kent - **70**:52; History of - **71**:60; Indian - **72**:7, 18; Lunar cycles & Stonehenge - **71**:54; of Twins - **69**:53. *See also: Divination.*

Astronomy - **71**:13; Asteroid, Near-miss - **71**:6; Comet Swift-Tuttle - **68**:64; Eclipse, Solar - **68**:6; New solar telescope - **69**:7; Sun, Features on - **69**:7; Uranus, Discovery of - **67**:6; **SETI** - **68**:33. *See also: Cosmology, Meteors, Meteorology, Planets, Scientific Curiosities.*

Atmospheric Optics - *See also: Meteorology.*

Other - Man/mushroom emits coloured lights, Shanghai - **70**:9; Mirages - **68**:64; White cross seen in sky - **68**:36

Parhelia - Parhelia, N. Wales - **72**:64; on Swedish bank-note - **70**:16; 4 suns at Chamdo - **69**:33

Attacks by

Animal mutilators - Cattle mutilation, USA - **68**:23-29; Speculation about - **68**:26-28; Duck shot with crossbow - **69**:6; Horse-ripping - **68**:46-47

Animals - Barracuda leap into boats - **72**:17; Bear rapes & kills cows - **69**:7; Big cat (?) attacks man - **69**:11; Birds, on sheep - **71**:64; Blood-seeking ants besiege town - **70**:6; Brown Recluse spider eats woman - **68**:19; Cat circumcises baby - **71**:9; Cobra kills head of snake-friendly group - **67**:19; Crows, kill lambs - **69**:17; Eagle carries off dog - **71**:6; Eagle, on lamb - **70**:17; Elephants, on cars - **70**:16; Elephants, seeking rum & food - **70**:16; Elephant, on train - **70**:16; Falcon snatches toupee - **67**:19; Giant mice, Turkey - **71**:9; Marmosets eat butterflies in showcase - **70**:18; Monkey plucks out man's eye - **69**:15; Monkeys steal underwear - **68**:13; on Disney-owned TV station, L.A. - **72**:11; Orangutan strips man naked - **68**:13; Pet python - **71**:19; Pig (?) attacks man - **69**:11; Potoroo tears testicles off man - **69**:7; Snake - **67**:65; **68**:'13

Other - Berserkers - **67**:20; Biters - **67**:12; **68**:12; **72**:13; Blood- drinkers - **68**:12, 39-41; **71**:6; Demons - **69**:8; Hairbrusher - **69**:12; Humiliation over telephone - **69**:13; Swedish women 'drugged' - **70**:10; Using food - **72**:16

Attacks on

Animals - Cattle mutilation - **68**:23-29; Duck, with crossbow - **69**:6; Goat blown up in religious ceremony - **69**:12; Horses - **68**:23-29, 46-47; Man drinks blood of goat - **68**:12; Loved white deer killed - **70**:11; Cattle, by sex-crazed bear - **69**:7; Cattle, by UFO (1911 film) - **71**:64; Cattle mutilation, by aliens - **72**:44

Other - Priests - **67**:12; Barbie dolls - **68**:7

Behaviour, Animal - *See also: Attacks, Escapes, Intelligence, Swarms, Talking.*

Long Journeys - Elephant runs 200 miles carrying man - **67**:14; by Dogs - **70**:38-41; Emus flee drought, Australia - **72**:51

Other - Bear uses swimming pool - **72**:14; Beer-drinking goat - **68**:10; Dog brings home human bones - **68**:8; Donkey eats smuggler's hashish - **70**:10; Monkeys steal underwear - **68**:13; Parrot minding chickens - **69**:65; Snake crawls down throat - **70**:16; Beachings, Whales, Tasmania - **67**:49; Bird Battle, Cork - **68**:6; Fainting goats - **71**:63; Falcon snatches toupee - **67**:19; Frog, Swallows gold chain - **67**:6; Panic, Cows, caused by electric shocks - **69**:14; Hibernation, Mistaken for death - **68**:65;

Relationships - Dog jumps cliff after master falls - **67**:18; Dog & Man each with one testicle - **67**:19; Parrot minding chickens - **69**:65

Sexuality - Bull elephant steals female - **70**:32; Bear rapes cows - **69**:7; Potoroos tear testicles off - **69**:7

Behaviour, Human - *See also: Attacks By, Cannibalism, Compulsions, Cults, Crimes, Hoaxes, Impostors, Mental Ph, Panics, Possession, Recluses, Religious Ph, Stupidity, Suicide.*

General - Drunk - **69**:7; Collectors - **68**:60; Forgetfulness, Car drivers leave passengers behind - **72**:12; Frog-killing - **67**:6; Hostage-taking - **69**:4; Incompetence - **68**:13; Blindness, kept secret 70 years - **71**:8; Decadence caused by democracy - **70**:11; Enforced dung-eating - **70**:9; Humiliated by orders over telephone - **69**:13; Jewelry made from excrement - **72**:13; Marketing sweets containing human blood - **71**:10; Protests about speed - **69**:12; Family flees Devil - **71**:17; Woman has palm-prints altered to prolong life - **68**:7; Homosexual protest, tries to wed horse - **68**:7; Not talking, grounds for divorce - **68**:7

Keeping dead bodies - Exhumed from grave daily - **67**:12; Indian guru, believed not dead - **70**:8; Shoppers leave corpse on bus - **70**:10; Bodies discovered in deep freeze - **67**:7. *See also: Deaths.*

Over-reaction - Man shoots lover with crossbow - **67**:20; Boy shot for changing TV channels - **67**:13; Boy stabbed for playing video games - **67**:13; Dog owners assault dog warden - **72**:13; Driver shot for splashing woman - **67**:13; Girl set on fire for cheering team - **67**:13; Hurls glass eye at police - **69**:15; Man shot dead over dog urine - **67**:13; Man suspended for writing 7 wrongly - **71**:14; Mug, assault, abandon man who thinks people good - **71**:14; Psychiatrist shoots 'nut-case' - **68**:19; Undertakers shot arguing over burial - **67**:13; Woman stabbed for hiding milk - **67**:13

Self-mutilation - Removes own tonsils - **68**:18; Bites off own tongue - **67**:12; & Munchausen's syndrome - **70**:23-29; 'Impostor syndrome' - **70**:4

Sexuality - & paranormal - **69**:55; Charged with abuse for enjoying nursing child - **72**:11; In religious context - **70**:27; Fatal intercourse with chicken - **68**:'6; Intercourse with horse - **72**:10; Mass orgasms in cult women - **68**:11; Rapist with 2 penises - **67**:15; Sexual humiliation over phone - **69**:13; Transvestitism - **71**:6; Used schoolgirl panty vending machine - **72**:11; Woman faints at word 'sex' - **71**:7; Stress caused by furry toy penis - **69**:12

Biology, Animal

Interspecies mating - **68**:50-51; Bear with cows - **69**:7; Domestic cats with escaped jungle cats - **72**:46; Wild & domestic cats - **68**:50-51

Other - Butterflies hatch early - **68**:10; Dozen double-yoked eggs - **70**:11; Goat with gold teeth - **69**:8; Sheep with gold teeth - **69**:8; Oldest cow (48) - **70**:11; Rabid raccoons - **67**:19

Teratology - 6-toed cats - **70**:63; Dog with one testicle - **67**:19; Two-headed calf - **67**:14; toad with eyes in mouth - **68**:5; Winged cats - **68**:'14; **70**:63; Sex change, Fish - **69**:8; Albino deer - **70**:11; Bird king - **67**:63; Hermaphrodites, Goat - **68**:10

Biology, Human - *See also: Genetics, Medical Ph, Twins.*

Other - **71**:61; Born circumcised - **67**:64; Brain research -

71:32, 55; Genetics, Patenting - **67**:6; Giants, 7 ft tall skeletons, Twyford Down - **67**:8; Blindness kept secret 70 years - **71**:8; Penile implants go wrong - **68**:13; Strength, Child lifts trailer - **67**:6

Teratology - Hermaphrodite - **70**:18; Man lacks testicle - **69**:63; Man with 2 penises & extra leg - **67**:15; Man with one testicle - **67**:19; Rapist with 2 penises - **67**:15; Siamese Twins - **68**:44-45; Born looking like Ganesh - **69**:9

Cannibalism - **69**:4; Criminal - **69**:7; China, during Cultural Revolution - **69**:48; WW2 Japanese soldiers - **69**:48; Deviant, Zimbabwe - **70**:15; Tribal - **67**:30. *See also: Behaviour H.*

Channelling - **72**:60; Channelled Barbie (doll) - **68**:7. *See also: Entities, Paranormal Exps, Trance Ph.*

Coincidence - *See also: Luck, Good & Bad.*

Accidents - Note for milkman, float crashes with 1000 pts - **71**:14; Air-crash training drill followed by real crash - **67**:12; Driver crashes into same house twice - **72**:7; Family lose 2 children in similar car accidents - **71**:9; Woman twice knocked down by same driver - **72**:7; Simultaneous fall of 2 men - **67**:9

Names & Numbers - **69**:7; **72**:10; **67**:9, 13; Odd product names & foreign words - **70**:6; **72**:63; Actor in Macbeth, arrested by McBeth - **72**:10; Father & son (same name) reunited by hospital rollcall - **70**:8

Other - 7 Family members born 19 April - **71**:19; Ancient footwear found outside cobbler's shop - **72**:13; Angler catches man attempting suicide - **68**:8; Army blow up box of leaflets about bombs - **68**:13; Correspondences between Lincoln & Kennedy assassinations - **72**:32; Cars with identical keys in same park - **71**:19; Dozen double-yoked eggs - **70**:11; Judge dies in trial about emergency procedures - **69**:19; Man & dog each with one testicle - **67**:19; Mice attack Disney-owned TV station - **72**:11; Perfect bridge-hands dealt - **72**:13; Real image appears in fake photo - **70**:7; SPR shares pre-

mises with undertakers - **70**:65; Steals cheque from wife, cashes with husband - **69**:18; Gulf War predicted - **67**:64; Wrong phone number reaches right person - **68**:8; Life imitating art - **67**:64; Lost rings & wallets found - **67**:11

Comets - *See: Astronomy.*

Compulsions - Attacks on Barbie dolls - **68**:7; Unwashed, makes own clothes - **68**:8; Hysteria - **70**:25; Munchausen's syndrome - **70**:23-29; Obscene phone-calling - **69**:13; Priests, attacks on - **67**:12; Rubber eating - **72**:10; Singing, naked man; run down by car - **70**:11; Woman chews same gum for 33 years - **68**:7; Ether drinking - **67**:65; Waves to traffic for 30 years - **69**:12; Doorbell-ringer - **72**:7; Exhumes husband's body each day - **67**:12. *See also: Behaviour H, Panics.*

Conspiracies - Conference on - **68**:30-33; Speculation about - **68**:30-33; Gemstone File - **68**:60-61; Kennedy assassination - **72**:30- 34; Military-industrial complex responsible for cattle- mutilation - **68**:24-25; Red Mercury - **69**:44-45. *See also: Cults.*

Cosmogony - Creationism - **69**:54; Creationism, Orthodox Jews deny dinosaurs - **71**:7

Cosmology - **69**:59; **70**:61; **72**:61

Crimes - *See also: Behaviour H.*

Bizarre - Bridges stolen - **68**:13; Houses stolen - **68**:13; Tranquilliser-laced nipples, robbery - **72**:9; 'Lobster Boy' murdered - **72**:6; Fancy dress - **69**:7; Alfred John, transvestite water goddess, killed 200 - **71**:6; Murdered by wife posing as prostitute - **69**:

Inept - **69**:7; Burglar mistakes human ashes for cocaine - **71**:19; Burglar stuck in chimney - **72**:5; Flees in dark with light-up shoes - **69**:18; Homing pigeons stolen, return - **69**:18; Mugger hands back wrong wallet - **69**:18; Robbers drill out of bank - **69**:18; Robs bank, opens account in same bank - **69**:18; Siphons petrol, swallows it - **69**:18; Steals cheque from wife, cashes with husband - **69**:18

Other - Con trick - **72**:19; Fraud - **67**:9; Cultists steal kneecaps - **68**:9; Imposture -

67:13; Kidnap - 67:12; Murder, Attempted - 67:20; Occult - 67:12; Ritual Murder - 69:7; Serial Killer sues over media portrayal - 72:11. *See also: Hoaxes.*

Using odd objects - Assault with cucumber - 72:16; Assault with ham - 72:16; with strawberry - 72:16; with swede - 72:16; with sausage - 72:16; with eggs - 72:16; Break in with frozen rabbit - 72:16; 'Shotgun' made of cucumbers - 72:16

Crop circles - 69:60-61; 70:59-60, 64; 71:62-3; 72:63; Hoaxers - 69:37-41; Round-up, 1992 - 68:43

Cryptozoology - *See also: Escapes, Giants, Lake & River Monsters, Manimals, Organisms, Out of Place, Sea Monsters, Swarms.*

Mystery Animals - Speculation about - 69:56; Bunyip - 67:'2; Buru - 67:'3; Devil-pig - 67:'3; Dragon - 67:6; Ellengassen - 67:'3; Giant Turtle - 67:'2; Horned anaconda - 70:33; Irkuiem - 67:'2; Kongamoto - 67:'3; Loveland Frogman - 67:6; Minhocao - 67:'2; Mountain Tiger - 67:'2; Nandi Bear - 67:'2; Queensland Tiger - 67:'2; Sucuriju gigante (giant snake) - 67:'2; Tatzelwurm - 67:'2; Thunderbird - 67:64, '3; Tzuchinoko - 67:'2; Waheela - 67:'2; Waitoreke - 67:'3

New & Rediscovered species - 'Living fossils' - 67:'4; 68:54; Bardia elephants - 70:31-33; Bechstein's bat, last seen 1866 - 71:12; Blue-tongue Lizard - 67:17; Dodo - 67:31; Mammoths - 67:'3; 69:47; Moa - 67:'3; 69:42-43; Queensland tiger-cat - 67:31; Tenkin snub- nosed langur, Vietnam - 72:14; Fishes, insects, monkey - 67:28; Hybrids domestic & jungle cats - 72:46; Monkeys, several - 69:10; Poisonous bird - 68:15; Tube worms, 6 ft long - 68:19; Vu Quang ox - 72:14

Other - 70:30-34; Theories of - 68:54; Unknown animals, Various - 67:31

Survival of dinosaur-likes into present - 67:'1-4; Mokele-mbembe - 67:28-31, '2; in Matto Grosso - 67:'2; Mbielu-mbielu-mbielu - 67:'2; Plesiosaur - 67:'3; 'Plesiosaur' identified as rotting shark - 67:'1; Row - 67:'3; Emela-Ntouka - 67:'2; Giant

Turtle - 67:'2

Cults & Movements - *See also: Behaviour H, Conspiracies, Religious Ph.*

Indian - Santan Dal - 70:8

African - Animist water goddess cult - 71:6; Exorcism to prevent haunting - 69:10; Voodoo, Haitian - 67:19

Buddhist, Tibetan - 69:30-33

Christian, Catholicism - 69:5; Believe footprints divine - 68:9; Faxed confessions - 68:7; Cult of BVM - 68:48

Christian, Fundamentalist - 71:17, 25, 30; Divine protection removed from Royal Family - 67:8; Naked family flee devil - 71:17; Poll, population going to hell - 72:10; Ban 'Snow White' - 69:7

Christian, Unorthodox - Branch Davidians, Waco - 68:4; 69:4; Koreshanity (Cyrus Teed) - 68:4; People's Temple, Jonestown massacre - 71:20; White Brothers (Maria Devi Christos) - 72:10; Mormons - 70:11; Millenial cult lets air out of tyres - 67:15

Islam - Islam, Mainstream - 67:9; Fundamentalist - 68:20; Attacks on indecently- dressed women - 67:8; Democracy declared evil - 70:11

Judaism - Faxing notes to Wailing Wall - 68:7; Orthodox, Dinosaurs not kosher - 71:7

Other - Cult round Thai meteorite - 72:9; Goat blown up in religious ceremony - 69:12; Golden Way, The - 68:11; Illuminati, The - 68:33; Philippines cultists steal corpses' kneecaps - 68:9; People Unlimited, Immortality cult - 71:10; New Age Psycho Babble - 71:62; 72:62; Brother Twelve - 67:59; Skeptical, CSICOP - 68:56; Hells Angels - 69:5; Pilgrims & followers in mass deaths - 72:18; Possession cults - 71:31; Religion & Munchausen syndrome - 70:27-29

Satanism - 70:62; Family, The - Charles Manson - 68:24-25; 'Occult, The' - 68:24. *See also: Satanic Child Abuse.*

Spiritualism - 71:13; & Theatre - 70:56

Witchcraft - 68:14; & abductions - 69:59; & Horse-ripping - 68:47

Curses

Cursed objects - Lava from Kilauea - 70:17; Mummy's curse - 69:19; Stones from Ayers Rock, returned - 70:17; 'Crying boy' painting - 69:17

Other - Rain cursed; cross falls on curser - 67:19; Death caused by, After desecration of ancient burial - 67:8; Lifted, by ritual - 69:12

Deaths, Animal

Mass Deaths - Frogs, Slaughtered - 67:6; Bulls, by lightning - 71:47; Pigs, in explosion - 72:10; Lambs, killed by crows - 69:17; Mice, China - 71:7; Birds, Ireland - 71:64; Birds, Mexico - 67:49; Birds, Mexico - 68:6; Birds, Pwllheli, 1904 - 69:65; Birds, Anglesey - 68:6; Fish, in too-pure water - 70:12; Otters in Shetland - 68:13

Other - Last bear in Sarajevo zoo - 67:6; by lightning, Cows - 70:49; Pets run over by owner - 67:12; Cows, Killed by sex-crazed bear - 69:7; Dog jumps over cliff - 67:18; Mouse, Squashed in prayer book - 68:7; Cows killed by electric shocks - 69:14; Saved seals eaten by killer whale - 68:13; White deer killed - 70:11

Deaths, Human - *See also: Accidents, Deaths, Obituaries.*

Bits & Bodies - Severed feet, wearing shoes - 70:18; Dog brings home human bones - 68:8; Noses, Korean, 20,000 - 67:10; Bodies discovered in deep freeze - 67:7; Corpse watches TV 1 month - 70:15; Corpse watches TV 10 months - 70:15; Dead men in cars given parking tickets - 71:14; Found standing, doubled over, head to floor - 69:19. Body keepers - *see: Behaviour H.*

Live burial - 72:56; Comatose drunk buried - 69:18; Survives 45 day entombment - 69:18

Mass deaths - 10 crushed in circumcision ceremony - 72:18; 10 pilgrims in water tower collapse - 72:18; Religious stampedes - 72:18; 134 pilgrims in air crash - 72:18; Bus/coach crashes - 72:18; 30 suffocated in cult butane sniffing - 72:18; 4 die in fire caused by prayer candles - 72:18; 4 mourners in truck accident - 72:18; 50 killed at bathing ceremony - 72:18; 81 mourners in house collapse -

72:18; 87 pilgrims drowned in ferry sinking - **72**:18

Odd, Ironic & Ludicrous - After sex - **72**:19; Anglers drown with flies undone - **70**:10; Anus impaled by broomstick - **68**:19; Blamed on spirits, Thailand - **72**:9; Blown up, mistaking grenade for beer-can - **68**:19; Boulder falls on mobile home - **71**:19; Boy born underwater drowns 5 years later - **67**:46; 4 boys killed by snake in soup - **67**:19; by avalanche - **67**:9; by exploding beer keg - **69**:19; by falling BVM statue - **72**:18; by meteorite - **70**:13; by rockfall, during intercourse with chicken - **68**:'6; by beaver-gnawed tree - **71**:19; Chokes laughing at haircut - **67**:19; Chokes on ring in champagne - **69**:15; Chokes on dentures - **69**:19; Chokes on sunglasses - **69**:19; Crushed by pet python - **71**:19; Crushed in peanut avalanche - **72**:19; Crushed under marshmallow bin - **72**:19; Decapitated by helicopter rotors - **72**:19; Drowns wearing chain & ball - **68**:19; Drowning, In storm - **67**:8-9; Escape car crash. electrocuted - **68**:19; Falling from aircraft - **72**:15; of Faust by devil - **67**:27; Fortune teller shot by client - **68**:13; Heart attack in trial about emergency - **69**:19; Hugged to death - **69**:19; Imitating Romeo & Juliet - **72**:7; Impaled on car statuette - **72**:19; Indian guru, believed not dead by followers - **70**:8; of Lord Carnarvon - **67**:6; by flying manhole cover - **68**:18; Killed falling 1 ft - **67**:9; Killed when suicidal wife falls on him - **67**:19; Killed in snake-handling service - **72**:18; by own booby-trap - **67**:19; Mistakes gun for phone - **71**:19; Jumped on by emu - **71**:19; by falling dog - **71**:19; Murdered by wife in prostitute dress, eaten - **69**:; Of pilgrims & Religious followers - **72**:18; Picks 4-leaf clover, falls over cliff - **67**:19; Priest curses rain, cross falls on him - **67**:19; Puts live fish in mouth, chokes - **67**:19; Singing, naked man run down by car - **70**:11; Survive car crash, run down by rescuer - **68**:19; Suicide on divine command - **68**:19; Swallowed as

ground gives way - **72**:19; Waits 14 years for sex, dies - **68**:19; Wins argument for shade, tree falls on - **72**:19; Woman shot dead by man aiming at dog - **68**:13;

Sudden -After desecration of ancient burial - **67**:8; Allergy to nuts - **69**:19; Fall over cliff - **67**:18; Head of snake-friendly group killed by cobra - **67**:19; Of orienteers - **68**:12

Demons - & sexuality - **70**:28; Attack schoolgirls - **69**:8. *See also: Entities.*

Devil - **68**:9; **71**:17; 'Devil's Hoofprints' case - **70**:65; Face of, in cloud - **68**:'8. *See also: Entities.*

Disappearances - *See also: Appearances, Teleportation.*

People - MIAs - **69**:50-51; Believed dead, actually kidnapped - **67**:12; Col. Percy Fawcett - **67**:31; from Mary Celeste - **72**:20; In odd fog, Romania - **70**:15

Other - Planes, Flight 19 - **72**:20; Ships, Bermuda Triangle - **69**:10

Divination - Astrology - **67**:61; Dowsing - **71**:62; Dreams - **67**:8; Fortune telling - **68**:13; Feng shui - **67**:56; **67**:10; Graphology - **67**:61; Numerology - **67**:13; Palmistry - **68**:7; Psychometry - **72**:39; Witch Smelling - **67**:8. *See also: Prophecy*

Dream - Precognitive - **68**:63; Invention during, Machine - **71**:11; Witchfinding in dream - **67**:8; Coomunication during, with dead - **67**:12; Of former life - **72**:37; Jung's dream of Liverpool - **71**:65. *See also: Mental Ph, Sleep.*

Drugs - *See: Alternate States of Conc, Mental Ph.*

Earth, The - Birthday of - **71**:20; Gravitational field - **67**:7; Magnetic field - **67**:7; Inner core, Oscillating - **67**:7. *See also: Geophysics, Planets.*

Earth Mysteries - **72**:60, 62; Earth Energy - **67**:56; Feng shui - **67**:10, 56; Ley lines - **67**:56; **69**:52; **72**:62; Megaliths, Dressing of - **67**:6; Odd rings - **71**:65; Cerne Abbas Giant - **69**:52; Spirit Paths - **67**:56, 63. *See also: Crop Circles.*

Earthquakes - *See also: Geophysics, Volcanoes.*

Events - Cairo - **67**:49; Colombia - **67**:49; Cumbria - **71**:47;

Greece - **69**:49; India - **72**:51; Indonesia - **68**:49; **72**:65; Japan - **68**:49; **71**:47; Kamchatka - **71**:47; Mariana Islands - **72**:51; Peru - **70**:49

Other - Sensitivity to, by catfish, clams, mice - **70**:19; **71**:7; Seismic Ph, Cause of Taos hum? - **71**:12

Electric People - Human magnets - **68**:11, '15. *See also: Biology H, Feats, Psi Ph.*

Electromagnetic Ph. - Biological effects of - **69**:14; **71**:32, 55; St Elmo's Fire - **68**:6; Street Light Interference - **71**:62; Discharge in ground affects cows - **69**:14. *See also: Forces.*

Embeddings - Needles, by demons - **69**:8; Needles in body - **67**:18; Objects left inside after surgery - **67**:18; Gold nugget in mackerel - **69**:8; Lizard eggs in human stomach - **70**:18; Tree-seedling in ear - **70**:10. *See also: Teleportaion.*

Encounters - *see: Aliens, Entities, Paranormal Exps.*

Entities, Paranormal - Angels of Mons - **68**:34-37; Black Dog - **70**:65; Bowmen of Mons - **68**:34-37; Devil - **68**:9; Ghost, Child - **67**:47; Jesus, in Nairobi - **68**:6; Mephistopheles - **67**:24-27; Fairies - **67**:52; Loveland Frogman - **67**:6; **71**:'3; Owlman - **68**:6; Pan - **72**:64; Thetis Lake monster - **70**:20; Water sprite - **68**:'11; Energy vampire - **68**:12; Flying 'man', Coney Island - **70**:20; Pee paob (living dead), Thailand - **72**:9; Photos of - **68**:'11; **68**:'11; Blamed for deaths - **72**:9; Blamed for factory fire - **72**:9. *See also: Aliens, Angels, Channelling, Demons, Devil, Fairies, Folklore (Characters), Ghosts, Jesus, Phantoms, Poltergeists, Vamipres, Virgin Mary, Werewolves, Zombies; + Names of Fictional Characters (Index)*

Escapes - Eagles, Britain - **70**:17; Pigs - **69**:11. *See also: Out of Place.*

Evolution - Disputes about - **69**:54; Missing links, Unlikelihood of finding them - **70**:53. *See also: Biology, Genetics.*

Explosions - Of Melons - **68**:7; Of toilets - **67**:13; Of TV sets - **67**:13

Fairies - Encounters with - **67**:52; **71**:39-41; Fairylore - **68**:61; **70**:52; Thomas the Rhymer & Fairy Queen - **68**:52. *See also:*

Entities.

Falls - *See also: Flows, Out of Place, Teleportation*.

   Artifacts - Beads, Redcar - **71**:12; Copper bracelet (alleged) - **69**:31

   Creatures - Trout, on Chicago train - **68**:6; Fishes, Australia - **70**:12; Fishes, Florida - **70**:12; Fishes, Havant - **68**:'10; Fishes, Sheerwater - **68**:64; Frogs, Inside hailstones - **69**:6; Periwinkles & crabs, Worcester - **68**:6; Men, from aircraft, etc - **72**:15

   Ice - Hailstones containing frogs - **69**:6; Hailstones with image of BVM - **68**:6; Yellow, smelly, with flash of light - **67**:9; Ice, Southend - **72**:7

   Other - Large stone, Aldeburgh - **69**:6; Sand, SW England - **67**:6; Stones, At tomb of Muslim saint - **67**:9; Stones, Repeating - **67**:9; Tunguska event - **69**:6

Feats - 6 yr old boy drives car 320 miles - **67**:14; Immersion in water, 4 days - **69**:9; Long fasts - **70**:29; Blindness, kept secret 70 years - **71**:8; Passes snake through nasal cavitiy - **71**:5; Rolls water melon 200 miles - **72**:10. *See also: Religious Ph.*

Fires - **71**:14; Caused by prayer candles - **72**:18; Caused by spirits, Thailand - **72**:9; at Hofburg Palace, Vienna - **67**:8; Caused by bird nest in plane - **69**:13; Caused by socks in bathroom - **69**:13; Caused by electrocuted starlings - **69**:14; at Windsor Castle - **67**:8. *See also: SHC.*

Flight - Welsh balloon reaches China in 5 days - **72**:6. *See also: Levitation.*

Flows - *See also: Falls.*

   Of blood - BVM statue weeps bloody tears - **68**:9; from BVM statue, Chile - **69**:20; from BVM statue, Indonesia - **72**:65; 'from abattoir' - **68**:14

   Other Oil from ground, in Ireland - **69**:15; La Mancha Negra, Black sludge on Venezuelan motorways - **67**:16; Raw Sewage, Glastonbury - **71**:64

Folklore - *See also: Hoaxes, Panics, Paranormal Exps, Urban Legends.*

   Characters - Arthurian - **67**:52; Dr Faustus - **67**:24-27; Thomas the Rhymer - **68**:52; Baron Munchausen - **70**:26;

Canonbie Dick - **68**:52; Hekate - **69**:60; Jack O'Kent - **70**:52; King Arthur - **68**:52; King Sil buried at Silbury Hill - **72**:52; Robin Hood - **67**:63; **69**:60; Michael Scot - **68**:52. *See also: Antiquities.*

   Historical - **71**:20; Historical, Cave dwelling musicians - **70**:52; Devil makes Silbury Hill - **72**:52. *See also: Antiquities.*

   Other - Misc. - **67**:6; **68**:6; In Bosnian war - **71**:34; MIAs - **69**:50-51; Angels of Mons - **68**:34-37; Mythic background to cattle mutilation - **68**:26-28; Symbolism of nuclear weapons - **68**:27-28; Red Mercury - **69**:44-45; Superstition - **70**:60; **71**:17

   Traditions - Historical, Fertility rites - **69**:52; Historical, Giant catfish (Namazu) causes earthquakes - **70**:19; Historical, Healing wells - **70**:52; Historical, King under the hill - **72**:24; Polar mythology - **69**:60; Tunnels - **70**:52; 'Shining One' at Callanish on Midsummer Day - **71**:52; Trickster legends - **68**:28; Croglin Grange, Vampire of - **68**:39-41

Forces - *See also: Electromagnetic Ph.*

   Interference with electrical devices - Copiers, computers, typewriters; berserk - **70**:6; Electrocution by phone - **70**:7; Jingle Bells plays on police radios - **67**:14; Penile implant set off by electric car doors - **68**:13; Unwanted radio & TV transmissions - **67**:55

   Runaways - Train - **67**:14; Trekking trolleys - **69**:63; **70**:63

   Other - Manhole covers, flying - **68**:18; Electric discharge in ground affects cows - **69**:14

Fort & Forteanism - **71**:59; **72**:61; History of - **67**:6; Fortean Times, History of - **68**:'2-4; Fort, Charles, Birthday, 6/8/1874 - **69**:6; Investigation methods - **69**:61; UFO conference report, Sheffield - **72**:44-45

Genetics - Cloning - **72**:53; Engineering - **72**:53; Mutations - **70**:53; Patenting - **67**:6. *See also: Biology, Evolution.*

Geophysics - *See also: Earthquakes, Volcanoes.*

   Events - Avalanche - **67**:9; Landslide, Ecuador - **70**:49; Landslide, Japan - **72**:51; Mudslide, Bolivia - **68**:49

   Other - Earth, age of - **69**:64;

Everest lower than thought - **70**:10; Geomagnetic anomalies - **67**:7; Gravity Ph. - **67**:7

Ghosts - *See also: Entities, Phantoms, Poltergeists.*

   Places - **67**:61; **71**:59; **72**:62; In Council Houses, Portsmouth - **68**:17; At West Kennet long barrow - **72**:52; Borley Rectory - **67**:61; Foreign Correspondents Club, Delhi - **69**:9; Hoaxed - **67**:38-42; In video advert - **71**:15; In Bank, Headless - **69**:16; In Factories, Icy mist - **70**:64; in Monastery, spirit sent by Faust - **67**:26; In open air - **68**:53; In Parliament House, Fiji, on video - **72**:19; in restaurant, sounds, multiple witnesses - **67**:47; In TV studio - **71**:15

   Other - Flying Dutchman - **69**:6; Exorcism to prevent - **69**:10

Giants - *See also: Biology.*

   Animal - Anaconda - **67**:31, '2; Snake - **67**:31, 65, '3; **68**:'13; Sturgeon - **67**:10; **69**:63; Turtle - **67**:'2; Crocodiles - **67**:29, 31; Lizards - **67**:31; Mice - **71**:9; Pythons - **67**:29

   Other - Human - **67**:8; Slime mould - **68**:13

Healing - *See also: Medical Ph.*

   Curious - DIY tonsil removal - **68**:18; Holy Water causes infection - **67**:18; tooth removal cures sneezing - **68**:18; X-ray vision finds acupuncture points - **68**:11; Hot milk lures snake from stomach - **70**:16; Serum cripples alcoholics who drink - **69**:17; Cured by phoney 'Holy Water' - **72**:13

   Miraculous - **71**:49; Cured by bleeding statue - **69**:20; by saint's bones - **69**:6; Corpses' kneecaps used in - **68**:9; Faith-healing - **68**:11;

Hoaxes - *See also: Behaviour H, Crimes, Crop Circles.*

   Crimes - Counterfeit money printed on magazine cover - **70**:16; Abduction & rape - **71**:24; Boys set on fire by stranger - **71**:24; Homosexual rape - **71**:24; Kidnap - **71**:24; Teacher raped in school - **71**:24; Emergency call, by woman pretending to be child - **71**:24; Self-victim, Eyelids superglued together - **71**:4

   Other - Alleged lion escape, France - **71**:16; Biggest Chinese sturgeon - **67**:10; Body-warmers for oily birds - **68**:10; Bogus charity drives (bar-codes, ring-pulls) - **70**:12; by police, Radios eavesdroppers conned by UFO story - **72**:14; Crop circles - **69**:37-41; Forged religious relics, Modern, undisguised - **70**:35-37; Ghostwatch TV programme - **67**:38-42; Hampstead seal - **68**:65; Hell found by drilling team, Siberia - **72**:42-43; In Shamanism - **70**:29; Indonesian hominid remains - **70**:42-43; MIA photos - **69**:50-51; Carlos Mirabelli levitation - **71**:43-45; Miracles, Sai Baba's, exposed - **69**:64; Religious, & Munchausen syndrome - **70**:27; Scientific, Letter about false Munchausen syndrome - **70**:26; Shroud of Turin, Faked by Leonardo da Vinci? - **70**:54; UFO crash stories - **72**:55; Vampire of Croglin Grange - **68**:39- 41; War of the Worlds (Welles) - **71**:20

Humour - **67**:7; 'Headlines' - **67**:8; **68**:8; **69**:8; **70**:6; **71**:6; **72**:6

Hybrids - *See: Biology A.*

Hypnosis - Regression in abduction cases - **68**:25; **69**:29; Regression, to former life - **72**:37, 39. *See also: Mental Ph, Trance Ph.*

Hysteria - *See: Behaviour H, Compulsions, Mental Ph, Panics.*

Ice - *See also: Falls, Meteorology (Hail).*

Iconoclasm - Desecration of sacred sites - **67**:9

Illnesses - *See also: Compulsions, Healing, Medical Ph, Panics, Vampires, Zombies.*

   Other - Allergy to nuts causes death - **69**:19; Continuous sneezing - **68**:18; Flesh eaten by spider venom - **68**:19; Deaths of orienteers - **68**:12; Stress caused by furry toy penis - **69**:12; Caused by eating monster flesh - **67**:30; Caused by Holy Water - **67**:18; VD transmitted by inflatable sex-dolls - **71**:11

   Outbreaks - Pneumonic plague; USA - **68**:18; TB - **67**:30; Caused by cutting down trees at saint's tomb - **67**:9; Swedish women 'drugged' by drinks - **70**:10; Rabies, Carried by raccoons - **67**:19; Valley Fever - **67**:63

Images - *See also: Religious Ph, Shroud.*

   Holy - Buddha, on shin bone - **69**:32; BVM on hailstones - **68**:6; Footprints in concrete & asphalt - **68**:9; Jesus Christ, photo of - **68**:'11; Jesus on greasy glasses - **71**:11; Islamic images in clouds - **68**:20; BVM in photograph - **68**:48; Arabic script for 'Allah' - **68**:'5; **68**:19; Sacred Arabic script on seat covers - **71**:10; 'Christ' photo shows Che Guevara - **71**:63; at Baden-Baden, 1872 - **67**:6

   on Creatures - Butterfly wings - **70**:'1-4; Skull on Death's Head hawk moth - **70**:'3; Face on cobra - **69**:9

   on Plants - Letters & numbers in marrow - **68**:19; Arabic script for 'Allah' in aubergines - **68**:'5; Sacred Arabic script in marrow - **68**:19; Fairy Tree, Kensington Gardens - **71**:42

   In Photos etc - Face in carriage window in photo - **69**:65; Jesus Christ in photo - **68**:'11; BVM in photograph - **68**:48; Photos of entities, Jesus, in sky, Italy - **70**:15; Video of ghost, Fiji - **72**:19; Water sprite - **68**:'11; 'Christ' photo shows Che Guevara - **71**:63

   Macro-images - Faces, Cydonia, Mars - **69**:64; **71**:60; Stonehenge on sun - **69**:7; Islamic images seen in clouds - **68**:20; Swastika of larches among other trees - **68**:20; Swastika shaped housing complex - **68**:20

   Simulacra - Butterfly alphabet - **70**:'1-4; Death's Head hawk moth - **70**:'3; Devil face in clouds - **68**:'8; Face in coffee grounds - **71**:8; Face in tuna skull - **72**:7; Face on cobra - **69**:9; Freddy Krueger in smoke - **70**:7; Giant woman - **67**:7; Lion on greasy glass - **71**:11; Of chick & egg in Egg Stone - **70**:9; Sleeping woman, Pairc hills - **71**:52; Tree like sleeping woman - **68**:7; Aural, Talking doll appears to swear - **68**:17

Impostors - Girl pretends deaf-and-dumbness - **68**:14; Mistaken Identity, Man fined for uncommitted crime - **68**:7; Mute boy pretends aircrash survival - **68**:14; Woman pretends to be Army General - **69**:15; Women posing as males - **70**:18; **69**:15; 'Prince Shami', Nigerian Red Mercury trafficker - **69**:44. *See also: Behaviour H, Compulsions, Crimes, Hoaxes.*

Incorruption - of Mao Tse-tung - **67**:15; - in Philippines - **68**:9; Body of Panchen Lama grows new hair - **67**:14; St Bernadette Soubirous - **68**:'7. *See also: Religious Ph.*

Injuries - *See also: Luck, Good (Escapes), Medical Ph.*

   Impaling - Crossbow bolt in head - **67**:20; Crossbow bolt in duck - **69**:6; Nail in brain - **72**:8; Arrow in head - **72**:8; Spike through cheek - **67**:5

   Other - Letterbox amputations - **68**:65; to Hand, Severed, sewn on - **72**:14

   to Head - Railing spike through cheek - **67**:5; by Crossbow bolt - **67**:20; by arrow - **72**:8; Nail in brain - **72**:8

Intelligence - Elephants, exploiting humans - **70**:16; Bicycle-riding bear - **71**:6; Dog brings water to stroke-paralysed man - **67**:18; Dog saves heart-attack man in car - **67**:18. *See also: Behaviour, Animal.*

Jesus - See: Apparitions, Encounters, Entities, Images.

Journeys - *See: Behaviour A, Forces, Swarms.*

Lake & River Monsters - Gill-men - **70**:63; Loch Ness - **70**:34; **71**:20; Loch Ness, Photo, Shiels - **68**:'12; Mekong River, 5-headed dragon - **72**:6; Plesiosaur-like, andes - **67**:'3; Plesiosaur-like, Lake Wenbu - **67**:'3; Thetis Lake monster - **70**:20; Water dragons, Malaysia - **67**:'3. *See also: Cryptozoology, Sea Monsters.*

Law

   Laws - Against vending panties without permit - **72**:11; Man unable to marry horse; too young - **68**:7

   Trials - Dead woman called for jury service - **72**:11; James Randi sues Eldon byrd, defamation trial - **70**:14; **71**:64-65; Judge dies in trial about emergency procedure - **69**:19; Serial killer sues over media portrayal - **72**:11; Uri Geller sues James Randi - **69**:19; 'Lobster Boy' murder trial; freaks give evidence - **72**:6

   Trials of animals - Dog jailed for killing child - **71**:8; Goats jailed for stealing - **71**:8; Rats charged with ruining bread - **71**:8

Levitation - Indian magician, Malaysia - **71**:65; Carlos Mirabelli (medium) - **71**:43- 45; St Joseph of Cupertino - **70**:20, 28-9. *See also: Religious Ph, Saints.*

Light - Flashes from glue - **70**:8; **72**:65; St Elmo's Fire - **68**:6. *See also: Electomagnetic Ph, Meteorology, UFOs.*

Lightning - Kills cows - **70**:49; Kills 111 bulls - **71**:47; Made to order - **68**:8; Warded off by marijuana - **72**:11. *See also: Electromagnetic Ph, Meteorology.*

Luck, Bad - **68**:13; Amnesiac finds he's wanted for crimes - **68**:13; Cancer falsely diagnosed, chain of bad luck after - **71**:14; Escaped car crash, electrocuted - **68**:19; Escaped car crash, run down by rescuer - **68**:19; Cat eats rare bat - **71**:12; Hides jewelry in tin, gives it away - **71**:14; Man killed in 1 ft fall - **67**:9; Picks 4-leaf clover, falls over cliff - **67**:19; Refuses use of phone, own house on fire - **71**:14; Ring given to wrong woman - **69**:15; Saved seals eaten by killer whale - **68**:13. *See also: Accidents, Proneness.*

Luck, Good

Lucky escapes - Child under trailer, Rescued by sister - **67**:6; Railing spike through cheek - **67**:5; Falling angel statue misses - **67**:7; Falls 6 floors, breaks leg - **67**:9; Survives 81 hours in earthquake rubble - **67**:49; Bullet deflected by amulet - **72**:9; Dog brings water to stroke-paralysed man - **67**:18; Dog saves heart-attack man in car - **67**:18; Falls 220 ft, lands on car - **72**:15; Hashish smuggler arrested, donkey eats evidence - **70**:10; Saved from when non-working smoke alarm falls on head - **71**:14; Man carried 200 miles by raging elephant, lives - **67**:14; Of goat from sunken ship - **71**:46; Survives 5th floor suicide attempt - **67**:18; Survives fall when parachute doesn't open - **72**:15; Dumped coke bottles found to be valuable - **71**:7; Talking birds returned - **71**:8. *See also: Accidents, Proneness.*

Shootings - Bullet deflected by spoon held by woman - **70**:19; Shot in head, spits out bullet - **70**:19; Shot in mouth, bullet passes out through back - **70**:19; Bullet deflects off key - **70**:19; Bullet stopped by gold necklace - **70**:19; Bullet stopped

by mobile phone - **71**:14; Bullet stopped by wallet - **70**:19; Bullet deflected by teeth - **70**:19

Magic - **68**:12; **71**:62; **72**:62; Chaos magic - **67**:60; **70**:60; **72**:60; Charms, Corpses' kneecaps used as - **68**:9; Charms/Amulets, Deflect bullet - **72**:9; In Bible - **70**:61; Dr Faustus - **67**:24-27; Aleister Crowley - **67**:60; **71**:20; Michael Scot - **68**:52; Raising Devil - **68**:9; Theory & Practice - **67**:60. *See also: Religious Ph, Shamanism, Witchcraft.*

Manimals - Almas - **67**:32-34; **70**:32, 34; Bigfoot - **67**:33; **71**:59; Loys' Ape - **70**:34; Minnesota Iceman - **67**:33; Wildmen - **67**:32-34; Yeti - **67**:32-34. *See also: Cryptzoology.*

Marine mysteries - Bermuda Triangle - **69**:10; Currents, Traced by floating shoes - **70**:15; Flying Dutchman - **69**:6; 'Mary Celeste' - **72**:20; Trawler sunk by tree, 20 miles at sea - **71**:11; Unidentified Submarine Objects, Sweden - **67**:50-51. *See also: Accidents, Disappearances, Geophysics.*

Mars - **71**:'1-2; Cydonia Face - **69**:64; **71**:60. *See also: Planets.*

Mass Hysteria - *See: Compulsions, Panics, Satanic Child Abuse.*

Medical - **68**:18; Ayurveda - **67**:58-59; Baby circumcised by cat - **71**:9; Dissection - **67**:60; Lizard eggs in stomach, mistaken for drugs - **70**:18; Mass circumcisions - **67**:64; Needles in body - **67**:18; Wrong Operations, vasectomy given instead of circumcision - **68**:13; Penile implant goes wrong - **68**:13; Recovery threatened by infectious Holy Water - **67**:18; Temporal lobe seizures - **71**:32; Tibetan medical paintings - **68**:59-60; Waking up during operation - **67**:65. *See also: Healing, Illness, Injuries, Mental Ph, Obstetric Ph.*

Mental Ph - Amnesia - **68**:13; Multiple Personality - **70**:23-29; **71**:29-30; **72**:65; Munchausen's Syndrome - **71**:30-31; Munchausen's & Shamanism - **70**:27-29; Muchausen's & religious ph. - **70**:27-29; Temporal lobe seizures - **71**:32; Dissociation - **71**:27; Epilepsy - **71**:55; False Memory - **71**:4, 23-32; **72**:54; Forgetfulness - **72**:12, 65; Hysteria - **71**:7; **72**:24; Multiple Personality - **70**:25, 27-8; **72**:24,

26. *See also: Alternate States of Conc, Behaviour H, Dream, Hypnosis, Paranormal Ph, Perception, Possession, Psi Ph, Sleep.*

Mercury - planet - **71**:'1. *See also: Planets.*

Messages - Long-delayed fax - **70**:7; **71**:63; Religious use of faxes - **68**:7

Meteors/Meteorites - Draconid Shower - **67**:49; **68**:64; Perseid Shower - **68**:64

Meteorites - Explodes over Holland - **70**:13; Falls through roof, Japan - **70**:13; Hits house, kills occupants - **70**:13; Hits ship, Japan - **70**:13; Meteorite, wrecks car, New York - **67**:49; **68**:64; **70**:13; Most ancient, found in Chile - **70**:13; Non-random patterns to - **71**:54; Thai meteorite, worshipped - **70**:13; **72**:9

Meteorology - *See also: Atmospheric Optics, Crop Circles, Falls, Lightning, Sounds.*

Clouds - Lenticular - **68**:20; **70**:63; Pictographic - **68**:20; Shield British soldiers at Mons - **68**:35; Shaped like Devil - **68**:'8; Unusual, caused by Mt. Pinatubo - **68**:'8; Miniature rain clouds made to order - **68**:8; Images seen in - **68**:'8, 20

Drought - Australia - **72**:51; Blamed on mini-skirted women - **67**:8; Nigeria - **67**:8; Zimbabwe - **67**:49

Floods - **67**:9; China - **72**:51; Java - **69**:49; Midwest USA - **69**:49; **71**:47; **72**:51; New York - **68**:49; S. Wales - **67**:49; Tuscany - **67**:49; Ukraine & Belarus - **72**:51

Hail - Containing frogs - **69**:6; France - **72**:51; with images of BVM on - **68**:6

Other - **67**:61; Avalanche, Afghanistan - **69**:49; Avalanche, Turkey - **68**:49; Heatwave, Alaska - **71**:47; Heatwave, Australia - **69**:49; Frost affects wine? - **69**:17; Ozone layer, Hole in - **67**:49; St Elmo's Fire - **68**:6

Rains/Storms - **67**:9; Fiji - **69**:49; India - **71**:47; Japan - **72**:51; Localised - **67**:63; 40 days & nights - **67**:49; Ecuador - **70**:49; Bolivia - **68**:49; New York - **68**:49; E. USA - **69**:49; Hampstead - **69**:6; Nigeria - **67**:8

Winds - Scotland - **68**:49; Sandstorm, China - **70**:49; tornado, Oklahoma - **70**:49; Whirl-wind, Wales - **70**:49; Whirlwind, Carries child 2 miles - **68**:14; Winds, Carries 13 children 12 miles - **68**:14

Miracles - Sai Baba's, exposed - **69**:64. *See also: Healing (Miraculous)*

Moon, The - 71:'2. *See also: Planets.*

Mutilation - *see: Aliens, Attacks (By & On), Behaviour H (Self).*

Obituaries - David Bohm **71**:13; Gordon Higginson **71**:13; Ishiro Honda - **71**:13; Brian Inglis - **68**:16; Margaret, Duchess of Argyll - **71**:13; Aime Michel - **71**:13; Jan Oort - **71**:13; Sun Ra - **71**:13. *See also: Deaths.*

Obstetric Phenomenas - 67:7; 3 foetuses removed from 5-month boy - **70**:18; Giving birth in presence of dolphins - **67**:46; Triplets born in 3 different places, over 60 miles - **70**:18; Young Mother, 8 years old - **68**:18; UFOs & Birth Trauma hypothesis - **71**:53. *See also: Biology, Medical Ph, Twins.*

Organisms - Slime moulds, Giant, Chinese - **68**:13

Out of Place - *See also: Cryptozoology, Teleportation.*

Alien Big Cats - Speculation about - **68**:54; **69**:56; **71**:60; Britain - **68**:50-51; Lions, France - **71**:16; Lions, USA - **71**:16

Other - Bechstein's bat, in bathroom - **71**:12; Kangaroos - **69**:56; Wallaby - **70**:63; Walruses in Ireland - **71**:11; Wild boar, Derbyshire - **72**:63; Albatross, Shetlands - **69**:65; Escaped eagles, Britain - **70**:17; Cats, Australia - **69**:11; Cats, Interbred with domestic cats - **72**:46; Piranhas, Rhine - **72**:17; Butterflies - **68**:10; Kangaroo, Isle of Wight; false - **67**:65; Lizard, African, In Swedish forest - **67**:17; Lizard, Asian, Inside car, in USA - **67**:17; Turkish crayfish - **70**:64; Nile crocodile, Frankfurt - **72**:17

Objects - Madagascan Elephant bird egg, Australia - **70**:44; **72**:14; Russian missile in Germany - **70**:11; Trolleys - **67**:19; U-boat in Turkish coal-mine - **72**:50

Over-reactions - *See: Behaviour H.*

Palaeontology - *See also: Antiquities.*

Dating Methods - Radio-metric - **68**:65; **69**:64

Finds, Hominid - Skull, Java - **72**:11; Homo habilis remains - **67**:10; Neanderthals - **71**:62

Finds, Other - Elephant bird egg, Australia - **72**:14; Madagascan Elephant bird egg, in Australia - **70**:44; Mammoths, mini; late survivals - **69**:47; Temnospondyl (fossil amphibian) - **69**:47

Panics - *See also: Behaviour, Compulsions, Hoaxes, Paranormal Exps, Satanic Child Abuse, Urban Legends.*

Mass compulsions - Cult lets air out of tyres - **67**:15; Singing, dancing, crying - **68**:14; Mass fads - **72**:62; Phone-calls to 'dead', Malaysia - **70**:19. *See also: Possession.*

Mass faintings - Jordan - **67**:48; Egyptian schoolgirls - **69**:16; Kosovo - **67**:48; School-children possessed by Devil - **68**:9; Swedish women 'drugged' by drinks - **70**:10; China - **70**:9; Possession epidemics - **71**:29

Scares - Orson Welles' 'War of Worlds' broadcast, Recreated 50 years after in Portugal - **67**:41; Cattle mutilation - **68**:23-29; Child-eating robot zombie scare, China - **70**:9; French child-murder scare - **67**:48; Halifax Slasher - **67**:48; Scapegoat persecuted - **67**:48; End of the World - **70**:64; Organ-kidnapping - **71**:17; Caused by repeated news broadcast - **69**:7; Cannibalism rumour, Zimbabwe - **70**:15; Spy-scare, China - **70**:9; Viewers believe 'Ghostwatch' hoax - **67**:38-42. *See also: Hoaxes, Folklore (Urban Legends)*

Paranormal Experiences - *See also: Aliens, Attacks By (Other), Conspiracies, Crimes (Bizarre), Cults, Curses, Electric People, Entities, Feats, Ghosts, Magic, Mental Ph, Panics, Phantoms, Poltergeists, Possession, Psi Ph, Reincarnation, Religious Ph, Trance Ph.*

General - **68**:16; **72**:59; Afterlife - **69**:61; **70**:62; & sexuality - **69**:55; **70**:28; Assaults by demons - **69**:8; Bedroom Invaders, Vampire, Croglin Grange - **68**:39- 41; Materialisations, Of bench - **68**:53; Message from dead, Solves crime - **67**:8; Icy mist - **70**:64; Out-of-body experiences - **67**:7;

Timeslips Long delayed fax -

70:7; Fax from limbo - **71**:63; Moberly & Jordain case - **68**:53; Phantom restaurant - **69**:34-35

Perception - *See also: Mental Ph.*

Mistaken - Dancing to Walkman, thought electrocuted - **69**:12; Dead men in cars given parking tickets - **71**:14; John Demjanjuk identified as war criminal - **72**:55; Man sheltering from rain thought armed robber - **69**:12; Thought superglue was haemorrhoid cream - **69**:13; Wooden owl mistaken for real bird in trouble - **69**:12; 'Ill' read as '111' - **71**:10

Other - Preposterous Perception, doctrine of - **72**:54

Phantoms - Speculation about - **69**:56; Black Dog - **70**:65; Assailants, Scratching African school-girls - **69**:8; Restaurant - **69**:34-35; Hitchhikers, Exorcism to prevent - **69**:10. *See also: Entities, Ghosts, Poltergeists.*

Planets - Hypothetical extra planets in Solar System, Nemesis - **68**:26. *See also: Astronomy, Earth, Mercury, Moon, Uranus.*

Plants - 2000 yr old seed grown - **69**:15; Algae, Red Tides - **68**:15; Fairy Tree, Kensington Gardens - **71**:42; Melons, Exploding - **68**:7; Olive tree, bears fruit for 1000 yrs - **71**:9; Trees, Appearing, disappearing, moving - **70**:55; Tree sinks trawler, 20 miles at sea - **71**:11; Tree-seedling in human ear - **70**:10; Vegetable Lamb - **68**:63; World's largest flower - **70**:'2

Poltergeists - Enfield case - **67**:41; Flight of objects - **67**:41; **68**:17, '13; Hoaxed - **67**:38-42; **70**:29; in Monastery, sent by Faust - **67**:26; Lights on/off - **69**:9. *See also: Entities, Ghosts, Phantoms.*

Possession - 70:29; by spirits, Thailand, & factory fire - **72**:9; by vampires - **71**:15; Cult of - **71**:31; Devil possesses clothes - **71**:17; Epidemics of - **71**:29; Exorcism, of Devil-possessed schoolgirl - **68**:9. *See also: Entities, Religious Ph, Shamanism, Trance Ph.*

Proneness - to Accidents - **67**:12; Optimist mugged & abandoned - **71**:14; Family lose 2 children in similar car crashes - **71**:9. *See also: Luck.*

Prophecy - Millennial - **68**:60; End of history - **71**:38; End of the World - **70**:64. *See also: Divination, Psi*

Ph.

Psi Ph - *See also: Channelling, Curses, Dream, Feats, Healing, Levitation, Luck, Magic, Possession, Proneness, Stigmata, Teleportation, Trance Ph.*
    General - **68:**16; Clairvoyance - **67:**10; **68:**19; **72:**26; Sees vampires possessing children in video - **71:**15; Crime- solving - **67:**8; Automatic writing, drawing - **71:**49; Dream, Witchfinding - **67:**8; ESP - **72:**62; Magnetising - **68:**11; Rainmaking - **71:**47; Telekinesis - **71:**43; Orgasms by Telepathy - **68:**11; X-ray vision into bodies - **68:**11; Levitation - **67:**6
    Precognition - **72:**37-8; Gulf War predicted - **67:**64; Psychic correctly predicts ear trouble - **69:**17. *See also: Divination, Prophecy.*

Recluses - Cave-dwelling - **67:**9; In hole under caravan - **72:**17; Hides in basement to avoid shame of no holiday - **69:**12. *See also: Behaviour H.*

Reincarnation - Jenny Cockell case - **72:**36- 39; Of Tibetan Lamas - **69:**30-33; Search for new Panchen Lama - **67:**14. *See also: Paranormal Exps, Religious Ph.*

Relics - Karmapa's shinbone, with Buddha image - **69:**32; Spear of Destiny - **70:**36-37; Undisguised forgery - **70:**35-37. *See also: Religious Ph.*

Religious Ph - *See also: Channelling, Cosmogony, Cults, Divination, Entities, Feats, Ghosts, Healing, Images, Incorruption, Jesus, Magic, Miracles, Paranormal Ph, Relics, Saints, Stigmata, Virgin Mary, Witchcraft.*
    General - **67:**6; Glossolalia - **68:**11; Holy Water, Causes infection - **67:**18; Immersion in water, 4 days - **69:**9; Incarnation, Of Ganesh in boy - **69:**9; Saints - **67:**6; & Munchausen syndrome - **70:**27-29; Bilocation - **71:**20; Divine punishment - **67:**8-9; Images, Baden-Baden, 1872 - **67:**6; Karmapa phases in & out of solidity - **69:**30; Stones fall at Muslim saint's tomb - **67:**9

Saints - **67:**6; **68:**6; **69:**6; **70:**20, 28-29; **71:**20; **72:**20; Apparition of St. George at Mons - **68:**34-37; Days - **67:**6. *See also: Levitation, Religious Ph, Stigmata.*

Satanic Child Abuse - **68:**14; **70:**28; **71:**4, 25-32; **72:**47-49, 54; &

Alien Abductions - **71:**53; Litte Rascals Daycare Center case, N. Carolina - **72:**48; in New Zealand - **72:**47-48; in Northolt, London - **72:**49; Orkney case - **72:**49; Wee Care case, New Jersey - **72:**48. *See also: Cults (Satanism), Impostors, Mental Ph. See also: Hoaxes, Panics, Urban Legends.*

Scientific Curiosities - *See also: Astrology, Biology, Cosmology, Electromagnetic Ph, Evolution, Forces, Genetics, Geophysics, Medical Ph, Meteors.*
    General - **72:**62; Battery recharger - **72:**17; Cold fusion - **69:**23-26; Geometrical Solid, conundrum - **72:**63; Location-finder, satellite controlled - **69:**7; Solar Telescope - **69:**7; Fractals - **69:**60; **70:**64; **72:**63; Everlasting lightbulb - **68:**'7; Location finder, by satellite - **70:**65; Red Mercury - **69:**44-45; Wine loses alcohol content - **69:**17; Hawking, deification of - **67:**54; Knapp's Orbital Propulsion system - **70:**60; Symmetry - **71:**62; Virtual Reality, Speculation about - **71:**36-37; Weather control, Miniature rain clouds made to order - **68:**8; Webs used in Bosnian war - **71:**34

Sea Monsters - Discussion - **67:**35-37; Cadborosaurus - **70:**46-48; Gambo - **67:**35-37; Plesiosaur, Identified as shark - **67:**'1. *See also: Cryptozoology, Lake Monsters.*

Sexuality - *See: Aliens, Behaviour, Biology, Crimes, Hoaxes, Medical Ph, Mental Ph, Religious Ph.*

SETI - Search for Extraterrestrial Intelligence - **68:**33. *See also: Aliens, Astronomy.*

Shamanism - **67:**63; & Munchausen syndrome - **70:**27-29. *See also: Behaviour H, Paranormal Ph, Religious Ph.*

SHC - Dr Bentley case - **68:**'9; Fictional case - **68:**63; Geographical distribution of - **72:**65. *See also: Fires.*

Shroud of Turin - **70:**36-37, 54; **71:**65; Faked by Leonardo da Vinci? - **70:**54. *See also: Images, Religious Ph.*

Simulacra - *see: Images.*

Sleep - Long sleeps - **72:**23-29; Case list - **72:**28-29; Sleep paralysis - **71:**32. *See also: Hypnotism, Trance Ph.*

Sounds - Hum, Hueytown - **67:**65;

Hum, Maine - **71:**12; Hum, Taos - **71:**12; In sky - **69:**6; In sky, Conch & cymbals, Tibet - **69:**33; Talking doll seems to swear - **68:**17

Statues - *See: Flows*

Stigmata - Blood Ph. - **71:**48-49; Faked - **70:**27; Non-Catholic, Celtic Christian - **71:**48-49; Of St Francis - **70:**20; Visionary component - **71:**49; Woods, Heather - **71:**48-49. *See also: Religious Ph, Saints.*

Stupidity - **69:**7; Wants ass's milk, buys donkey - **71:**14; Zoo-keepers put marmosets with butterflies - **70:**18; Fatally mistook grenade for beer-can - **68:**19; Killed by own booby-trap - **67:**19; Mistakes gun for phone - **71:**19. *See also: Behaviour H, Crimes.*

Suicide - **72:**7; After watching 'Ghostwatch' - **67:**18-9; **68:**8; **71:**14; **72:**8, 15; Jump from 10th floor - **67:**18; God tells to eat soap & shaving foam - **68:**19. *See also: Deaths, Behaviour H.*

Swarms - Algae, Red Tides - **68:**15; Butterflies, Cabbage Whites - **68:**10; Dragonflies, Yellow Sea - **72:**51; Giant mice, Turkey - **71:**9; Locusts, Hungary - **71:**47; Locusts, Pakistan - **72:**51; Locusts, Somalia - **71:**47; Mice, Los Angeles - **72:**11; Mosquitoes, Poland - **72:**51; Of Blood-seeking ants, Brazil - **70:**6. *See also: Behaviour A.*

Talking Animals - Budgerigars - **71:**8; Cats - **72:**16; Goat - **68:**10; Parrot - **71:**8. *See also: Behaviour A, Intelligence.*

Teleportation - Speculation about - **69:**56; Dr Geraldo case - **68:**6; Mechanised, Speculation about - **71:**56; Of Saints - **70:**20; ; Travelling trolleys - **67:**19; Trees, Appearing, disappearing, moving - **70:**55

Timeslips - *See: Paranormal Exps.*

Tracks - of Almas, in snow, Mongolia - **70:**32; Footprints, in concrete & asphalt, Philippines - **68:**9; Footprints, In snow, New Mexico, like Devil's Hoofprints - **70:**65; of Yeti, in snow, Lhotse - **67:**32. *See also: Cryptozoology.*

Trance Ph. - Sleeping prophets - **72:**25; Seance materialisations - **71:**43-45, 61; Fox sisters - **67:**6; Mediumship - **71:**43-45; **72:**62;

318

& Theatre - **70**:56. *See also: Hypnosis, Sleep Ph.*

Twins - Astrology of - **69**:53; Private language - **67**:12; Siamese - **68**:44-45. *See also: Behaviour H, Obstetrics.*

UFOs - *See also: Aliens.*
   General - **68**:60; **69**:27-29; **70**:62; **71**:13, '1-'4; Disputes in Ufology - **67**:53-54
   Captured/crashed - **70**:60; History of - **72**:55; Roswell incident - **72**:55; Radio hoax - **72**:14
   Sightings/Reports - French wave, 1954 - **71**:'2; Galisteo, 1886, Fish-shaped craft - **67**:6; In 1911 film - **71**:64; Landing, Socorro case - **68**:6; Arnold sighting - **69**:6; Man/mushroom emits lights, Shanghai - **70**:9; & crop circles - **68**:43; on film - **70**:64; **71**:60; Radio eavesdroppers conned by story about - **72**:14; Speculation about - **68**:28, 30-3; **71**:63; & cattle mutilations - **68**:25; conference, Sheffield - **72**:44-45

Uranus - **71**:20; Discovery of - **67**:6. *See also: Planets.*

Urban legends - **70**:60-61; Vampire expected to rise from grave,

Peru - **71**:10; Bogus charity drives - **70**:12; Brezhnev fakes death to marry girl - **68**:19; Candyman - **72**:56; Child- eating robot zombie - **70**:9; Curse on stones from Ayers Rock - **70**:17; Dancing to Walkman mistaken for electrocution - **69**:12; Elephant sitting on car - **70**:64-65; Hell found by drilling team, Siberia - **72**:42-43; Organ kidnappers - **67**:64; **71**:17; Phone-calls to 'dead', Malaysia - **70**:19; Polar bear cub bought as 'puppy' - **69**:8; Snake in stomach - **70**:16; Unwanted radio & TV transmissions - **67**:55; Woman asks for train seat, pregnant 30 mins. - **67**:14; 'Curse of Pele' on lava from Kilauea - **70**:17; McDonald's support IRA - **71**:18; Snuff films - **68**:24. *See also: Folklore, Hoaxes.*

Vampires - *See also: Entities, Paranormal Exps.*
   General - **68**:12, 62; Croglin Grange, Vampire of - **68**:39-41; Energy vampire - **68**:12; Possess children in video - **71**:15; Undead - **71**:34; Undead, Fictional - **72**:56;
   Human illness - **68**:39; **71**:10;

Man attacks goat & woman, drinks blood - **68**:12; 'Bride of Dracula' case, English woman buried in Peru - **71**:10

Vehicles - *see: Accidents, Attacks By, Feats, Folklore (Urban Legends), Forces (Runaways), Luck (Bad) & (Good),*

Virgin Mary - Apparitions of, 'Shining statue', Knock - **70**:20; Black Madonna - **68**:48; Weeping statue of - **68**:9. *See also: Entities, Images, Religious Ph.*

Volcanoes - on sea-bed, S. Pacific - **69**:49; Galeras, Colombia - **68**:49; Philippines - **69**:49; Krakatoa - **70**:20; Mt. Pinatubo, Causes strange clouds - **68**:'8. *See also: Earthquakes, Geophysics.*

Werewolves - **72**:62. *See also: Entities.*

Witchcraft - *See also: Cults, Shamanism.*
   General - **68**:12; **71**:29; Peruvian - **71**:10; Walpurgis revelry - **67**:6
   African - **67**:8, 12; Love-locking rituals - **70**:12; Marijuana wards off lightning - **72**:11; ndoki - **67**:30

Zombies - Theories about condition - **67**:19; **68**:12. *See also: Entities.*

NAMES of PEOPLE mentioned, including Pseudonyms

Acree, Alfred E. - **69**:18
Adamski, George - **71**:'4, 20
Adamson, Robert - **70**:48
Adamson, Shirley - **68**:17
Addy, Liz - **67**:28
Adelmannsfelden, Count Adelmann von - **67**:64
Adinrayanan, S. - **70**:18
Adwait, Kapil - **69**:9
Afifi, Hamid - **69**:18
Afilaka, Michael - **72**:15
Aga Khan - **70**:34
Agathocles - **70**:11
Agnangna, Marcelin - **67**:28-9
Agobard, Archbishop - **68**:25
Aickman, Robert - **67**:56
Akca, Nevzat - **67**:9
Akgun, Onder - **71**:9
Akpinar, Dr Ibrahim - **71**:9
Aldis, Irene - **67**:11
Alekhine - **71**:54
Alexander the Great - **70**:11
Alexander, Andrew - **70**:8
Alexander, Charles - **70**:39
Alexandria, Tsarina - **67**:45
Alexandrov, B. - **68**:19

Ali, Mohammad - **68**:12
Ali, Sohrad - **70**:38
Allan, Mr & Mrs - **68**:53
Allen, Dave - **67**:19
'Alligator Man,' The' - **72**:6
Allitt, Beverley - **70**:23-6, 28-9
Altshauler, John - **68**:29
Anderson, Anna - **67**:45
Anderssen - **71**:54
Andrade, Hernani Guimaraes - **71**:45
Andres, Carlos - **67**:16
Andrews, Colin - **69**:39, 41
Andrich, Jamie - **70**:44; **72**:14
Andronov, Dr - **69**:17
Andropov, Yuri - **68**:19
Andrus, Walt - **67**:54
Antoninus Pius - **71**:54
Anwar, Mohammad - **67**:14
Argyll, Duchess of - **68**:'4
Aristotle - **70**:11
Armstrong, Graham - **67**:17
Arnold, Edwin - **70**:38
Arnold, Jack - **70**:63
Arnold, Kenneth - **69**:6
Arrow, Roy - **69**:11

Ashcroft, John - **69**:18
Asher, Richard - **70**:25-6
Asimov, Isaac - **71**:36
Asjes, Eric - **70**:12
Aspione, Sal - **69**:15
Assilem, Melissa - **71**:28
Atkinson, Prof. Richard - **72**:52
Attila the Hun - **70**:37
Augustus - **71**:54
Avai, Giacomo - **71**:46
Avis, Elaine - **71**:'4
Avis, John - **71**:'4
Azzakov, Dr Dimitri - **72**:42
Bahadur, Jang - **70**:18
Baker, Rachel - **72**:25, 26
Baldwin II - **70**:37
Baldwin, Sue - **70**:6
Bankston, Kenneth - **68**:24
Barbant, Charles - **68**:63
Barger, Ken Charles - **71**:19
'Barker, Col.' - **69**:15
Barnaby, Frank - **69**:45
Barnes, Edward - **69**:7
Baron, Frank - **67**:24
Bartholomew, Peter - **70**:36
Bartlett, Adelaide - **67**:65

Bartlett, Edwin - **67**:65
Bartolomea - **70**:27
Bates, Henry W. - **67**:'4
Baumgarten, Ruth - **67**:39; **67**:42
Baxter, Colin - **68**:46
Bayanov, Dimitri - **67**:33
Beadle, Jeremy - **68**:'4
'Bearded Lady, The' - **72**:6
Bearden, Thomas E. - **68**:25, 28
Beavers, Lawrence - **72**:5
Beavers, Margie - **72**:5
Beckjord, Erik - **69**:41
Beddeleem, Christophe - **67**:48
Begardi, Philipp - **67**:25
Begg, Ean - **68**:48
Bell, Colin - **71**:48
Beloff, Dr John - **69**:55; **71**:45
Bendon, Arthur - **71**:8
Benjamin, Dr Irving - **67**:18
Benning, Michael - **72**:7
Benorthan, Marcus - **72**:13
Benorthan, Phyllis - **72**:13
Bentine, Michael - **72**:64
Bentley, Dr Irving - **68**:'9
Berg, Dr Leo S. - **69**:63
Berlioz - **67**:24
Bernheim, Pierre-Antoine - **69**:48
Bernini - **69**:55; **70**:37
Bernstein, Jeremy - **68**:27
Berry, Dr Paddy - **70**:44
Besterman, Theodore - **71**:43-45
Beyazit II, Sultan - **70**:37
Bezymensky, Lev - **67**:44-5
Bilderburgs, The - **68**:31
Bildt, Carl - **67**:51
Billingsley, John - **68**:7
Birkelund, Palle - **69**:7
Bishop, Christine - **68**:5
Blackmore, Susan - **67**:42
Blades, Ann - **72**:13
Blades, Brian - **72**:13
Blair, Linda - **70**:6
Blake, William - **72**:20
Blashford-Snell, John - **70**:30-34
Bloor, Carol - **69**:13
Bloor, John - **69**:13
Blumenthal, Bob - **69**:44
Bock, Richard - **69**:64
Bogart, Prof Jim - **68**:5
Boggis, Cecilia - **72**:4
Bohm, David - **71**:13
Boito - **67**:24
Bolante, Joy - **68**:9
Bonner, Prof John - **68**:13
Bonnington, Chris - **67**:34
Booth, John Wilkes - **72**:32
Bord, Janet & Colin - **68**:'3
Borg, Bjorn - **67**:51
Botkin, Segei - **67**:45
Botvinnik - **71**:54
Bousfield, Ed - **70**:46-48
Bower, Doug - **69**:38
Boyd, Tommy - **67**:31

Boyenval, Margaret - **72**:28
Boykes, Dr Chaim - **67**:46
Bozan, Haci Ramazan - **67**:9
Bradley, Carmel - **69**:15
Bradley, Johnny - **69**:15
Brahmachari, Thakur Balak - **70**:8
Braun, Eva - **67**:44
Brazel, Mac - **72**:55
Brazier, Mr - **70**:39
Brennan, John - **71**:48
Brezhnev, Leonid - **68**:19
Briggs, John - **70**:64; **72**:63
Brightey, Dennis - **71**:14
Brock, Raymond - **72**:13
Brockman, Tim - **69**:19
Broderick, Fiona - **68**:46
Broderick, Robert - **68**:46
Brodu, Jean-Louis - **71**:16
Broi, Armin da - **70**:39
Brooke, Richard - **67**:39, 42
Brown, Adele - **68**:10
Brown, Catherine - **72**:12
Brown, Ginny - **67**:47
Brown, Harriet - **67**:47
Brown, Henry - **67**:14
Brown, James - **70**:38
Brown, John - **68**:'3
Brown, Judith - **70**:27
Brown, Mariah - **68**:20
Brown, Prof Geoffrey - **68**:49
Brown, Rev Derek - **68**:'10
Brown, Thomas - **72**:12
Bruce, James - **68**:59
Brunvand, Jan Harold - **67**:55
Brutus - **70**:37
Buckett, Katie - **68**:47
Buckland, Frank - **70**:34
Buckmeister, Rudy - **72**:16
Buhler, Rich - **72**:43
Buisson, Denise - **72**:15
Bullard, Eddie - **68**:55
Bulut family - **67**:9
Bumgarner, Roger - **67**:11
Burgess, George - **72**:17
Burke & Hare - **67**:60; **69**:19
Burkholder, JoAnne - **68**:15
Burks, Eddie - **69**:16
Burnham, Owen - **67**:35-6
Burranti, Giacario - **67**:19
Burton, Ian - **69**:19
Bush, Dr Robert T. - **69**:26
Bush, George, president - **69**:51; **72**:54
Bush, Kate - **68**:'4
Busoni - **67**:24
Butler, Harry - **70**:44
Bygraves, Max - **72**:12
Byrd, Eldon - **68**:56; **70**:14; **71**:64-5
Byrne, David - **68**:'4
Byrne, Gay - **71**:64
Byrum, Robin - **71**:26
Caesar, Julius - **70**:37
Cahn, Edward - **71**:'3

Caligula - **70**:37; **71**:54
Callejas, Rafael - **71**:17
Camberton, James - **70**:39
Cameron, Dave - **71**:14
Campbell, Denis - **71**:24
Campbell, Joseph - **70**:29; **71**:32
Campbell, Ken - **71**:65
Campbell, Phyllis - **68**:37
Campbell, Sharon - **68**:65
Campion-Vincent, Veronique - **68**:25
Cantori, Hanibal - **72**:10
Cantori, Laura - **72**:10
Capablanca - **71**:54
Capps, Walter - **69**:50
Capriles, Ruth - **67**:16
Caracalla - **71**:54
Carlini, Benedetta - **70**:27-9
Carlotto, Dr Mark - **69**:64
Carlsson, Stig - **68**:12
Carlyon, Ingrid - **68**:47
Carlyon, Kevin - **68**:47
Carl, Clifford - **70**:47
Carnarvon, Lord - **67**:6
Carr, Capt. Donald - **69**:51
Carroll, Terry - **71**:18
Carvajal, Arturo - **67**:16
Carver, George - **70**:15
Casagrande, Pino - **70**:15
Cassirer, Manfred - **67**:42
Castillo, Julio - **67**:5
Castro, Fidel - **72**:31
'Catwoman' - **69**:41
Cawthorne, Nigel - **69**:50
Cawthorne, Stephen - **71**:19
Cayce, Edgar - **72**:25
Ceausescu - **72**:10
Celebi, Evliya - **71**:9
Celik, Ayfer - **72**:16
Celona, John - **70**:46
Cericola, Tiffany - **71**:19
Cerullo, Morris - **68**:24
Chadwick, Rev. Samuel - **71**:39
Chandler, Evan - **71**:30
Chandler, Jordan - **71**:30
Chapman, Ethel - **71**:48
Chapman, Hilary - **70**:40
Chapman, Philip - **70**:40
Charlemagne - **70**:37
Charles, Craig - **67**:38, 42
Charles, Joseph W. - **69**:12
Charles, Prince of the Belgians - **68**:'4
Chen - **69**:18
Cheops, Pharaoh - **70**:51
Cheramie, Rose - **72**:31
Chernenko, Andrei - **69**:45
Cheshire, William P. - **72**:43
Cheung Xin - **72**:6
Chilton, Samuel - **72**:25, 29
Chirilino, Salvatore - **67**:19
Chodzin - **69**:32
Chorley, Dave - **69**:38
Chorost, Mike - **68**:43
Chorvinsky, Mark - **70**:63

320

Chosroes, King of Persia - **70**:36
Christiansen, Franz - **69**:43
Christos, Maria Devi - **72**:10
Cilingir, Mustafa - **67**:9
Clark, Jerome - **72**:55
Clarke, Arthur C. - **69**:24
Clarke, Stephen - **72**:13
Clarkson, Judy - **70**:11
Claudius I - **71**:54
Claudius II - **71**:54
Cleopatra - **71**:14
Clift, Michael - **70**:54
Clinton, Bill - **68**:32-3
Cloer, Nasine - **72**:17
Clyde, Lord - **72**:49
Coade family - **67**:47
Cochrane, Peter - **71**:56
Cockell, Jenny - **72**:36-39
Cockell, Steve - **72**:36
Cocteau, Jean - **71**:13
Cohen, J. - **71**:55
Coleman, Loren - **71**:64; **72**:4
Collins, Andrew - **72**:44
Columbus, Christopher - **67**:58; **68**:61
Comfort, Corinne Reed - **71**:18
Commodus - **71**:54
Conceicao, Joaquina de - **69**:15
Connally, John - **72**:30
Constantine I - **70**:36-7; **71**:54
Constantine II - **71**:54
Conyers, John - **68**:18
Cook, Keith - **69**:14
Cook, LeAnn - **69**:14
Cook, Melvin - **68**:65
Cook, Rabie - **67**:11
Cook, Wendell - **69**:14
Cooper, William - **68**:31-3; **72**:33
Coppola, Francis Ford - **68**:40
Cordner, Corrine - **68**:18
Cordry, Kelly - **71**:19
Cornell, Anthony D. - **67**:42
Cortez, Fr Roger - **68**:9
Corti, Maria Consolata - **70**:54
Cosgrove, Blanche - **67**:14
Cosquer, Henri - **68**:42
Costa, Alison da - **68**:12
Costa, Cristina - **72**:7
Couch, Michael - **71**:7
Courtin, Jean - **68**:42
Coutts, Angela Burdett - **69**:16
Coutts, Thomas - **69**:16
Coy, Clive - **70**:33
Cozeolino, Peter - **67**:5
Crabbe, Colin - **69**:65
Crabtree, Susan - **67**:11
Crandon, Margery - **70**:28
Crew, Curt - **69**:15
Croesus - **67**:64
Cropper, Paul - **69**:11
Crosby, Susan - **72**:26
Cross, Phil - **70**:7
Crouch, Paul - **72**:43

Crowley, Aleister - **67**:60; **71**:20
Cuanilawa, Pauliasi - **72**:19
Cuellar, Javier Perez de - **67**:53
Cundall, Phil - **70**:7
Cutler, R.B. - **72**:33
Cvetskens, Maria - **72**:28
Czermak, Vera - **67**:19
Dagdelen, Yusuf - **67**:9
Dahinden, Rene - **67**:33
Dalai Lama - **67**:14
Dalby, Keith - **69**:14
Dalhanna, Alla - **69**:19
Daly, Antoinette - **71**:64
Dames, Michael - **72**:52
Daniken, Erich von - **68**:6; **69**:65; **71**:17
Dan, Uri - **67**:46
Darwin, Charles - **67**:'4; **71**:38
Dash, Mike - **68**:'2-'3
Davenport brothers - **70**:56
Davey, Betina - **67**:8
Davey, Stephen - **67**:8
David, King of Israel - **70**:37
Davis, Prof Wade - **67**:19
Dawadi, Shyam Krishna - **70**:7
Dawkins, Dr Richard - **69**:54
Dawson, Elizabeth - **67**:6
Dawson, Lynette - **67**:6
Debaets, Michael - **67**:13
Deck, Catherine - **72**:16
Delashaw, Johnny B. - **72**:8
Delberger, Bo - **70**:10
Delgado, Pat - **69**:41
Della Marna, Ivan - **70**:13
Della Marna, Martin - **70**:13
Demjanjuk, John - **72**:55
Deng Xiaoping - **69**:48
Denham, Carl - **67**:40
Denham, Martin - **67**:40
Denham, Percy - **67**:40
Dent, Alan - **69**:16
Deremier, Jose - **70**:39
Deremier, Lise - **70**:39
Derrida, Jacques - **72**:54
Detaille, Edouard - **68**:35
Deutch, John - **71**:12
Devereux, Paul - **67**:56, 63; **69**:52; **70**:8; **71**:52; **72**:44-45
Devereux, Robert - **69**:16
Dewidar, Ragheb - **69**:16
Dewilde, Marius - **71**:'2
Diana, Princess of Wales - **70**:23, 25
Dickens, Charles - **68**:63; **69**:16
Dimagila, Honora - **67**:15
Dimbleby, David - **68**:16
Dimbleby, Richard - **67**:39
Dingwall, Eric J. - **71**:43, 45
Dinsdale, Tim - **70**:34
Dittemore, Ernest - **72**:17
Doan, Clinton Richard - **69**:19
Domancich, Amadeo - **67**:18
Dominguez, Oscar - **68**:19
Domitian - **71**:54

Donner, Ava - **70**:19
Dorje, Karma Tendzin - **68**:7
Douglas, Elaine - **71**:11
Downs, Prof David - **71**:24
Doyle, Sir Arthur Conan - **67**:31, '4; **71**:39
Drago, Roy - **72**:12
Driesch, Hans - **71**:43-4
Drubtob u-Se - **69**:32
Dryselius, Harald - **70**:16
Dubois, Eugene - **68**:60; **70**:42-43; **72**:11
Dufferin, Lord - **68**:41
Duhamel, Olivier - **67**:48
Dumbacher, John - **68**:15
Dumesney, Warren - **70**:39
Dunbar, Dennis - **69**:42-3
Dunbar, Prof. Robin - **69**:54
Duodo, Nana - **69**:10
Durbin, Ruth - **71**:8
Durham, Bishop of - **68**:53
Dybvik, Arnt Helge - **71**:14
Eades, Rev. Eric - **71**:48
Eames, Craig - **69**:17
Eames, Elaine - **69**:17
Eardley, Paul - **72**:15
Ebbesmeyer, Curtis - **70**:15
Eberhart, George - **69**:56
Ebitass - **67**:29-30
Edalji, George - **68**:23
Edamaruku, Sanal - **69**:9
Eddowes, Michael - **72**:31
Edington, Steve - **72**:51
Edwards, Ivan - **70**:51
Edwards, Rev. Francis - **69**:16
Eggert, Piers - **67**:7
Einstein, Albert - **67**:54; **68**:33
Ekvall, Arthur - **67**:20
Elden, Wilhelmina - **69**:18
Eliade, Mircea - **70**:27
Eliot, T.S. - **70**:28
Elizabeth II, Queen - **67**:8
Ellis, Peter - **72**:47-48
Elverson, Jason - **67**:8
Elwell, Sgt. Ron - **70**:18
Emerson, Hunt - **68**:'2
Enjuabenes, Pierre - **69**:17
Enqvist, Wyn - **67**:51
Epimenides - **72**:24
Erikson, Leif - **67**:58
Ertel, Prof. Suitbert - **69**:53
Esposito, Elaine - **72**:29
Estrada, Gaston - **68**:29
Euwe - **71**:54
Evans, E.P. - **71**:8
Evans, Gary - **70**:8
Evans, Hilary - **67**:39; **72**:44-45
Evans, Norman - **68**:50
Ewing, Mark - **70**:7
Fagny, Marc - **68**:13
Fahd, King of Saudi Arabia - **68**:45
Faldmo, Poppy - **68**:18
Fallar, Florene - **67**:13

Fallar, Joseph, Sr - **67**:13
Fancher, Mollie - **72**:26
Faraday, Michael - **69**:26
Farson, Daniel - **67**:65
Fattah-Sultan, Abdel - **67**:18
Faustus, Dr - **67**:24-27
Faust, Georg - **67**:24
Faust, Johannes - **67**:24
Fawcett, Col Percy - **67**:'2, 31
Ferrie, David - **72**:31
Field, John - **68**:64
Field, Tom - **68**:7
Finnegan, Prof. Timothy F.X. - **72**:54
Finnigan, Judy - **71**:15
'Fire Eater, The' - **72**:6
Fischer, Aimee - **71**:19
Fischer, Bobby - **68**:32-3; **71**:54
Fisher, Capt Edward Rowe - **68**:39-41
Fisher, Dr D. - **72**:63
Fisher, Joseph - **68**:40
Fisher, Thomas - **68**:39
Fitzherbert, Claudia - **71**:28; **72**:48
Fleischmann, Martin - **69**:23-26
Fleming, Dennis - **71**:6
Flood, Chris - **69**:7
Flood, Jackie - **69**:7
Foltz, Debbie - **70**:40
Foltz, Ray - **70**:40
Ford, Carl - **69**:51
Ford, Roly - **70**:11
Forrest, Anne - **70**:7
Fort, Charles - **67**:40; **68**:23, '3-'4; **69**:6; **70**:'3, 36, 38; **71**:56, 61
Foss, Peter - **72**:14
Foster, Jonathan - **70**:25
Foster, Kerry - **69**:19
Fox, Rev Len - **68**:17
Fox sisters (Maggie, Kate, Leah) - **67**:6; **70**:56; **72**:25
Foxley, William - **72**:25
Franklin, Dr Wilbur - **69**:19
Franz Joseph, Emperor of Austria - **70**:37
Frayling, Dr Christopher - **69**:19
Freaney, Paddy - **69**:42-43
Frederick Barbarossa - **70**:37
Freeman-Attwood, Julian - **67**:34; **70**:32, 34
Freemantle, Klint - **72**:15
Freixedo, Salvador - **68**:28
Frenc, Zoltan - **70**:15
Freud, Sigmund - **68**:6; **69**:55; **71**:29, 31-2
Freyd, Pamela - **71**:27
Froderstrom, Dr Harold - **72**:28
Frost, Iris - **71**:8
Fry, Adrian - **69**:14
Futcher, Brian - **67**:8
Fuzeau-Braesch, Dr Suzel - **69**:53
Fyfe, Jack - **67**:18
Gaddafi, Col. - **69**:44
Gaddis, Vincent - **69**:10

Gagliano, Ettore - **67**:12
Gaidar, Premier - **69**:45
Galba - **71**:54
Galloway, Mark - **68**:45
Gantenbrink, Rudolf - **70**:51
Garcia, Jerry - **68**:'4
Garner, Fred - **67**:11
Garner, James - **71**:12
Garrett, Benjamin C. - **71**:34
Garrison, Jim - **72**:31
Gast, Johannes - **67**:26, 27
Gauld, Alan - **67**:42
Gauquelin, Michel - **69**:53
Gefner, Rabbi Zvi - **71**:7
Geller, Uri - **68**:16, '3, 56; **69**:19
George V, King - **69**:6
Geraldo, Dr - **68**:6
Gerstler, Amy - **70**:35
Giancana, Sam - **72**:31
Gibbons, Bill - **67**:28-31, '2; **70**:33
Giegerich, Wolfgang - **68**:28
Gilchrist, Gareth - **72**:10
Gillespie, Debbie - **72**:48
Gilmore, Jim - **72**:17
Gilroy, Rex - **69**:11
Gladstone - **70**:56
Gleason, Jackie - **68**:'4
Glickman, Michael - **71**:63
Godin, David Wayne - **68**:19
Goebbels, Joseph - **67**:44
Goes, Eurico de - **71**:43-4
Goethe - **67**:24
Goff, Suzanne le - **70**:40
Goksu, Izzet - **72**:16
Golding, Prof Jean - **67**:12
Golfo, Mario - **67**:19
Gomes, Gen. Tito Anibal da Paixao - **69**:15
Gomes, Maria Teresinha da Jesus - **69**:15
Goode, R. - **71**:63
Goode, Sgt. Lorne - **72**:7
Goodhew, Geoff - **69**:43
Goodkind, Dr John - **67**:7
Goodwin, Jean - **70**:25, 27
Gopaleen, Myles na - **67**:64
Gorbachev, Mikhail - **71**:17
Gould, Stephen Jay - **69**:24
Gould & Pyle - **72**:24
Gounod - **67**:24
Graham, Eleanor - **71**:12
Graham, Ysenda Maxtone - **70**:54
Grams, K.C. - **71**:12
Graves, Det. L.C. - **72**:34
Gray, Dominic - **70**:65
Gray, Hugh - **71**:20
Gray, William - **71**:7
Greaves, Dr Ian - **67**:18
Green, David - **71**:65
Green, Michael - **69**:40
Green, Tanya - **72**:19
Greene, Sarah - **67**:38-9, 42
Greenshaw, Jeff - **71**:'4

Greer, William - **72**:33
Gregory, Beryl - **71**:10
Grenside, Joanna - **71**:24
Griggs, Jasmin - **68**:17
Griggs, Nicola - **68**:17
Griggs, Sarah - **68**:17
Griggs, Susan - **68**:17
Grosse, Maurice - **67**:39-40, 42
Guattero, Pedro - **72**:10
Guevara, Che - **71**:63
Gul, Saban - **67**:9
Gustafsson, Bengt - **67**:50-1
Gyeltsap - **69**:32
Haaparanta, Toivo - **68**:8
Haddington, Lord John - **67**:42
Hadrian - **71**:54
Hagel, Greta - **67**:13
Hagelund, William - **70**:46, 48
Haggard, H. Rider - **70**:30
Hahn, Benjamin - **67**:46
Haining, Peter - **68**:40
Hall, Tom - **67**:28
Hamouda, Aksam Sayed Ismail - **67**:49
Hancock, Geoff - **70**:39
Hancock, Graham - **69**:65
Hanley, Aideen - **67**:40
Hansson, Lars - **72**:33
Hapsburg family - **67**:8
Harding, Graham - **71**:55
Hardwick, Todd - **67**:17
Hare, Augustus - **68**:39-41
Harms, Mr - **72**:28
Harold, King of England - **67**:47
Harold Godwinson, King - **70**:52
Harper, Charles G. - **68**:40-1
Harrison, Ted - **71**:48
Hascher, Anna - **72**:7
Hashizume, Suzuko - **71**:45
Hassall, Peter - **72**:47
Hassard, John - **69**:45
Hauser, Caspar - **68**:60; **72**:20
Havican, Greg - **71**:16
Hawass, Zahi - **70**:51
Hawking, Stephen - **67**:54
Hawkins, Gerald - **71**:52, 54
Hawthong, Nakorn - **67**:19
Hayakawa, Norio - **68**:31
Haymer, John - **68**:'3
Headrick, Thomas - **71**:52
Hecht, Ben - **67**:6
Hedman, Sten - **70**:16
Heggie, Mark - **68**:12
Heidensohn, Frances - **71**:24
Heineger, Erik - **69**:15
Helmstetter, Georg - **67**:24-5
Hendrix, Jimi - **67**:55
Henry VII - **70**:11
Heporauta, Tuuri - **72**:43
Herbaux, Eloi - **70**:15
Hernandez, Chris - **67**:17
Herod, King of Judea - **70**:37
Herrfurth, O. - **70**:26

Herschel, William - **67**:6; **71**:20
Hester, Monte - **71**:25
Heston, Fr Louis - **70**:40
Heurn, Van - **68**:60
Heuvelmans, Bernard - **67**:31, 33, 36; **68**:54
Hickson, Charles - **70**:20
Hidaka, Sachi - **68**:19
Hidaka, Tomio - **68**:19
Higginson, Gordon - **71**:13
Higton, Rev. Tony - **67**:8
Hilgard, Ernest - **72**:24
Hill, Barney - **67**:53; **71**:'3
Hill, Betty - **67**:53; **71**:'3
Hind, Cynthia - **72**:44
Hitler, Adolf - **67**:44-5; **70**:37; **72**:53
Hiuhu, Charles Wanjohi - **69**:7
Hoaks, Birdie Jo - **70**:18
Hodson, Geoffrey - **71**:41
Hoffa, Jimmy - **72**:31
Hoffer, Eric - **68**:56
Hoffman, Sgt. Karl - **70**:13
Hofmann, Dr Albert - **68**:6
Hofvander, Jenny - **70**:10
Hogshire, Jim - **67**:64
Holbrook, Conley - **72**:29
Holdaway, Dr Richard - **69**:43
Holton, Katie & Eilish - **68**:44-45
Holton, Liam - **68**:44-5
Holton, Mairead - **68**:45
Holton, Mary - **68**:44-5
Home, D.D. - **68**:53
Honda, Ishiro - **71**:13
Honorius - **71**:54
Hoover, J. Edgar - **72**:30
Hopkins, Budd - **67**:53-5; **69**:27-9; **71**:31, 36; **72**:44-45
Hopkins, Matthew - **67**:8
Horapollo - **67**:64
Horne, Rolf - **69**:18
Hort, Ernst - **68**:7
Hort, Suzanne - **68**:7
Hoskins, Bob - **68**:'4
Houdini, Harry - **70**:28
Hough, Peter - **72**:65
Houghton, Tina - **72**:29
Houser, Evelyn - **68**:19
Hovanessian, Mr - **69**:34-35
Howard, Ross - **68**:7
Howard, Thomas - **69**:16
Howe, Linda Moulton - **68**:25; **72**:44- 45
Ho, Gregory - **67**:12
Hu Yaobang - **69**:48
Hufford, David - **71**:32
Hughes, Randy - **70**:41
Hughes-Onslow, James - **71**:42
Hughey, Dr Ken - **69**:42
Hunnicutt, Robert - **71**:'3
Hunt, Jane - **71**:48
Hussein, Sadam - **67**:64; **69**:44-45
Huxley, Aldous - **72**:20
Huxoll, David - **71**:34

Hynek, J. Allen - **67**:53
Ilagan, Jose - **68**:9
Inglis, Brian - **68**:16; **69**:55
Ingraham, James - **70**:15
Ingram, Chad - **71**:25, 32
Ingram, Ericka - **71**:25, 29-30
Ingram, Julie - **71**:25
Ingram, Paul - **71**:25, 27
Ingram, Sandy - **71**:25
Innes, Ivor - **71**:42
Innocent VIII, Pope - **70**:37
Inns, Michael - **69**:39
Irish, Doris - **68**:'7
Irving, David - **67**:45
Irving, Henry - **69**:16
Irving, Washington - **72**:24
Isitor, Godwin - **67**:14
Izzard, Ralph - **67**:'3
Jackson, Bob - **72**:34
Jackson, Frank - **72**:19
Jackson, J. Hughlings - **71**:55
Jackson, Michael - **67**:54; **71**:30
Jackson, Tom - **71**:64
Jacobs, Dr David - **67**:54; **68**:55; **69**:27-29; **71**:36, 53, 64; **72**:54
Jagger, Mick - **67**:54
Jamgon Kongtrul - **69**:32-33
Janecke, James - **70**:19
Jankowski, Dr Bogdan - **67**:34
Jarry, Alfred - **72**:54
Jayalalitha, Mr - **72**:18
Jeffrey, Celia - **70**:8
Jevons, Peter - **71**:55
Joan of Arc - **70**:28, 56; **71**:31
John, Alfred - **71**:6
Johnson, Andrew - **72**:32
Johnson, Dorothy - **67**:19
Johnson, Jackie D. - **71**:19
Johnson, Kimberley - **68**:45
Johnson, Lyndon - **72**:30, 32
Johnson, Page & Sara - **68**:45
Johnson, Rev James - **71**:8
Johnson, Tom - **68**:45
Jones, Bob - **70**:64; **71**:14
Jones, Gareth - **68**:6
Jones, Jim - **71**:20
Jones, Ned - **70**:49
Jones, Stuart - **72**:6
Jordain, Miss - **68**:53
Jorsten, Joachim - **72**:30
Jung, C.G. - **68**:28, 56; **69**:6, 55; **71**:31, 65
Kabanaov, Alexei - **67**:45
Kahraman, Cemal - **67**:9
Kane, Nicole - **68**:18
Kantor, Alan - **71**:19
Kantor, Rochelle - **71**:19
Kaplan, Dr Stephen - **68**:39
Kappinen, Lennert - **67**:17
Karapetian, Lt-Col V.S. - **67**:32-3
Karlsson, Melker - **68**:12
Karmapa, 1st - **69**:31
Karmapa, 16th - **69**:30, 32

Karmapa, 17th - **69**:30-33
Karpov - **71**:54
Kasparov - **71**:54
Katash, Lydia - **67**:7
Keel, John - **67**:64; **69**:64
Keen, Sophia - **69**:19
Kelly, Betsy - **71**:26; **72**:48
Kelly, Robert Fulton - **71**:26; **72**:48
Kennedy, Bobby - **72**:31
Kennedy, Edward - **72**:32
Kennedy, Jackie - **72**:32
Kennedy, Joe - **72**:31
Kennedy, John F. - **72**:30-33
Kennedy, Michael - **72**:8
Kennedy, Robert - **72**:32
Kent, John - **70**:52
Kerry, Sen. John - **69**:50-1
Kerslake, Paula - **70**:41
Keuhne, Horst - **72**:13
Kevran, Louis - **70**:64
Khosa, Simphiwe - **72**:11
Kidger, Alan - **69**:44
Kilgannan, Dorothy - **72**:31
Kimberley, A.W. - **68**:10
Kinchev, Boris - **71**:17
Kingston, Isabelle - **69**:41
Kirby, Robert - **72**:25
Kirk, Robert - **71**:40
Kirkwood, Dr Ralph - **69**:8
Kitamura, Yoichi - **69**:19
Klarer, Elizabeth - **71**:'4
Klass, Philip - **70**:29
Knapp, Michelle - **67**:49; **70**:13
Koenigswald, Gustav von - **70**:43
Kofman, Dr Jeanne - **70**:34
Kofman, Dr Zh. I. - **67**:32-4
Koksal, Mustafa - **67**:9
Kolpashnikov - **67**:33
Komiya, Terumoto - **69**:6
Koresh, David - **68**:4; **69**:4
Korolev, Evgeny - **69**:44
Koubsky, Ann - **71**:19
Kraft, Randy - **72**:11
Kravitz, Herb - **70**:19
Krushchev, Nikita - **72**:31
Kurt, Sukru - **67**:9
Lambert, Pat - **72**:13
Langley, Maj. - **70**:46
Lansdale, Mark - **67**:4
Lasker - **71**:54
Lasky, Harriet - **68**:7
Lauterbach, Antonius - **67**:26
Lautreamont - **67**:6
Lavine, Lynn - **67**:11
Lavine, Marc - **67**:11
Lawley, Sue - **67**:39
Lawson, Alvin - **72**:45
Leakey, Jonathan - **67**:10
Leakey, Louis - **67**:10
Leakey, Mary - **67**:10
Leakey, Richard - **67**:10
Lear, John - **72**:55
Lear, William - **72**:55

Leary, Timothy - 71:35; 72:65
Leavelle, James - 72:34
LeBlond, Paul - 70:46
LeBlond, Philip - 70:47-8
Lee, Christopher - 72:56
Lee, Henry - 68:63
Lee, Paul - 72:49
LeFanu, J.S. - 68:41
Legge, Cyril - 71:11
Leibnitz - 70:20
Lem, Stanislav - 71:36
LePen, Jean-Marie - 70:5
Leslie, David - 69:13
Levin, Bernard - 68:16
Lewis, C.S. - 72:20
Lewis, I.M. - 70:29; 71:31
Lewis, Nicky - 70:18
Lieberman, Robert - 69:62
Lierde, Remy van - 67:'3
Lincoln, Abraham - 72:32
Lincoln, Edward - 72:32
Lincoln, Evelyn - 72:32
Lincoln, Mary - 72:32
Lincoln, Robert - 72:32
Lindgren, Harri - 70:13
Lindsey, Yvonne - 67:13
Lippard, Jim - 69:64
Liu Binyan - 69:48
Liu Deshun - 70:9
'Lobster Boy', The' - 72:6
Locke, John - 69:65
Lockyer - 71:52
Lodge, Geoff - 70:44
Longinus, Gaius Cassius - 70:36
Lopez, Jose - 67:15
Lotti, Rosa - 67:43
Louis, Duke of Savoy - 71:65
Louis IX, King of France - 70:37
Loys, Francois de - 70:34
Lucas, Angela - 67:18
Lucas, George - 71:'2
Lucius Verus - 71:54
Lundy, Maj. Albro - 69:50-51
Lutchner, Gertrude - 72:13
Lutchner, Joe - 72:13
Luther, Martin - 67:26
MacKenzie, Andrew - 68:53
MacKinnon, Dr John - 72:14
Maceachin, John - 72:29
Machen, Arthur - 68:34-37
Mack, Dr John E. - 68:64; 71:36-7
Mackal, Roy - 67:30-1, '2
Madeley, Richard - 71:15
Madonna - 68:55
Magin, Ulrich - 70:63
Magraner, Jordi - 67:33
Magritte, Rene - 67:41
Maheshwari, Dr Usha - 70:18
Maire, T.R. Le - 71:54
Major, Norma - 70:4
Makovnev, Asanassi - 70:40
Malanchthon, Philipp - 67:27
Malik, Rohil - 69:9

Mallasseand, Dr Anne - 67:33
Mallen, William - 69:19
Mallove, Dr Eugene - 69:23, 26
Malory, Sir Thomas - 67:52
Manasseh, King - 68:59
Mangir, Zeynep - 67:9
Manlius, Johannes - 67:27
Mann, Ann - 72:16
Manning, Clark - 72:15
Manning, Lesley - 67:42
Manning, Matthew - 68:16
Manson, Charles - 68:24-5
Mantle, Philip - 72:44
Mao Tse-Tung - 67:15; 69:48
Maples, Dr William - 67:45
Marcus Aurelius - 71:54
Margaret, Duchess of Argyll - 71:13
Maria, Infanta - 70:20
Maringer, Col. Friedrich - 71:14
Marlowe, Christopher - 67:24, 26-7
Marquez, Gabriel Garcia - 67:6
Marrable, Canon - 68:36
Marrable, Miss - 68:36
Marshall, Barry - 67:31
Martin, Bobby - 72:17
Martinez, Debbie - 67:13
Martinez, Jesus - 67:18
Marx, Karl - 71:29
Mary, Queen of Scots - 69:16
Masaru, Matsumoto - 70:13
Masters, Anthony - 68:40
Matt the Tube - 71:5
Matthews, Derek - 70:65
Maude, Prof H. - 67:63
Maunder, John - 72:7
May, Robert - 69:10
Mboo, Joyce - 67:12
Mboo, Namwaka - 67:12
Mboo, Sitali - 67:12
Mbuika, Ndibo - 67:10
McBeth, Heather - 72:10
McCabe, Eamonn - 69:50
McCabe, Sally - 67:47
McCarther, Willia - 68:44
McCarther, Yvonne & Yvette - 68:44
McCrone, Dr Walter - 71:65
McCulloch, Beverley - 69:42
McDonald, Robert C., Jr - 70:8
McDonald, Robert C., Sr - 70:8
McDougal, Dennis - 72:11
McElroy, Tom - 68:7
McGarry, John - 69:8
McGee, Redmond - 69:12
McGirk, Tim - 69:9
McGrath, Dr Ronan - 71:11
McKenna, Terence - 71:35-38
Mckenzie, Alice - 69:43
McKenzie, Rev. Morris - 72:49
McKinnon, Walter - 70:63
McLuhan, Marshall - 71:36
McNall, William - 72:13
McNamara, Dr Ken - 70:44
McPherson, Col. Lachlan - 68:41

Meader, ... 'erence - 69:38, 40
Meadow, Roy - 70:26
Mears, Keith - 68:30
Meech, Laurie - 71:19
Meech, Nanette - 71:19
Méliès, Georges - 68:61; 71:'2
Melling, June - 68:6
Menendez, Erik - 71:28, 30
Menendez, Lyle - 71:28, 30
Menis, Caroline - 69:65
'Merlin' - 69:39
Meyer, Gesine - 72:29
Meyer, Henri - 68:63
Michael, A.C. - 68:36
Michaels, Kelly - 72:48
Michel, Aime - 71:13
Michelangelo - 70:36
Mikhailov, minister - 69:45
Millbank, Charles - 68:19
Miller, Charles - 67:'3; 72:12
Miller, David - 70:48
Miller, Jeff - 71:26
Miller, Kimberley - 72:12
Miller, Marjorie - 72:12
Miller, Wayne - 67:11
Milligan, Spike - 71:42
Millikan, Jack - 70:40
Mills, Dr Randell L. - 69:25
Milton, Richard - 68:65
Minao, Hidenobu - 70:13
Mirabelli, (Carlos) Cesar Augusto - 71:43-5
Mitchell, Terence - 68:25
Mitchell, Warren - 68:'4
Mitchell, Weir - 72:25
Mittermeier, Russell - 69:10
Mizuno, Tomoyuki - 67:10
Mobbs, Sir Nigel - 68:46
Moberly, Miss - 68:53
Mohamad, Mahathir bin - 70:11
Molino, Walter - 67:'2-'3, 43
Monckton, Capt Charles - 67:'3
Mongoumela, Immanuel - 67:29
Monzouros, John - 70:19
Moonlasartsathorn, Phisan - 72:9
Moor, Larry - 67:19
Moore, Steve - 68:'2
Moralee, Alistair - 68:6
Morales, Frank - 72:5
Morey, Leo - 71:'2
Morphy - 71:54
Morris, Chris - 70:44
Morris, Errol - 67:54
Morris, Henry - 68:65
Morris, Jan - 68:8
Morse, Roger - 69:18
Moseley, James - 70:14
Moses - 67:64; 68:26-8
Motha, Dr Gowri - 67:46
Mudford, Kevin 'Mad Dog', - 69:5
Muhammad - 68:20
Mullins, Eustace - 68:31
Munoz, Edgar - 71:10

Murphy, Eddie - **72**:56
Murphy, Sean - **72**:54
Murphy, Willie - **72**:19
Myslinski, Martin - **67**:13
Napolitano, Linda - **67**:53-4; **68**:64; **72**:44-45
Neep, Vic - **69**:65
Nelson, Omaima - **69**:7
Nelson, William - **69**:7
Nero - **71**:54
Neumann, Erich von - **68**:27
New, Colin - **70**:17
Newman, Harry - **72**:6
Newman, Mary - **72**:6
Newton, Isaac - **67**:54
Nguyen, Lam Danny - **71**:19
Nicholas II, Tsar - **67**:45
Nichols, Mary - **71**:26
Niemi, Betty - **69**:19
Nieva, Judiel - **68**:9
Niven, Larry - **71**:56
Nixon, Pres. Richard - **69**:51; **70**:35
Nordqvist, Bengt - **71**:7
Northmoor, Rose - **71**:8
Northumberland, Duke of - **72**:52
Novak, Jean - **71**:19
Novak, Karen - **71**:19
Novak, Lucille - **71**:19
Novak, Ric - **71**:19
Novak, Ted - **71**:19
Novel, George - **72**:33
Noyes, Ralph - **69**:65; **70**:28
Nummedal, Bjarne - **72**:42-3
Nunez, Gonzalo - **69**:20
Nunez, Renato - **69**:20
Nydahl, Hannah - **69**:33
Nydahl, Ole - **69**:33
Obelebouli, Bernadette - **70**:18
O'Brian, Flann - **67**:64
O'Connell, Patrick - **70**:11
O'Donnell, Michael - **67**:14
O'Halligan, Peter - **71**:65
O'Keefe, Lois - **67**:11
Olsson, Carolina - **72**:27-28
O'Neill, Kelly - **70**:44
O'Nolan, Brian - **67**:64
Oort, Jan - **71**:13
Oparin, Vyacheslav - **67**:33
Oppenheimer, Robert - **68**:26-7
Opsasnick, Mark - **70**:63
Orrin, Elizabeth - **72**:25, 29
Orton, Joe - **69**:55
Osbourne, Carol - **72**:16
O'Shea, Mark - **70**:31, 33
Oswald, Lee Harvey - **72**:30-34
Oviedo, Mgr. Carlos - **69**:20
Owen, Alex - **70**:56
Owen, Rev. Keith - **71**:48
Ozawa, Kenji - **68**:8
Ozkan, Kemal - **67**:64
Padzer, Lawrence - **71**:26
Paget, Sir James - **67**:65
Pain, Joyce - **67**:47

Palatinate, Count of the - **67**:26
Pallix, Sylvain - **67**:32-3
Panchen Lama - **67**:14
Pantchenko, Gregory - **67**:33
Papin, Monsieur - **71**:16
Parker, Charles - **70**:20
Parker, Matthew - **69**:6
Parkhurst, Henry - **72**:26
Parkinson, Michael - **67**:4, 38-42
Parks, Bernard - **70**:40
Partridge, Annie - **67**:12
Partridge, Stephen - **67**:12
Patel, Bharti - **70**:19
Patterson, Roger - **68**:54
Patton, General - **71**:63
Paul, Matawa - **67**:28
Pavlova - **71**:40
Paz, Uri - **68**:'3
Pearse, Alfred - **68**:35
Peary, Robert - **68**:6
Peck, Col. Millard - **69**:50
Pegler, Jason - **68**:8
Pekgoz, Behram - **71**:9
Pen, Alelio Bernaldez - **67**:15
Pennick, Nigel - **67**:65
Perini, Don Giacomo - **67**:19
Perkins, Elizabeth - **72**:29
Peron, Pascal - **70**:40
Perot, Ross - **69**:51
Persinger, Michael - **71**:32; **72**:65
Pertinax - **71**:54
Peter the Great - **68**:60
Petrasso, Richard - **69**:26
Petrosian - **71**:54
Petterson, Hans - **68**:65
Pew, Kelly - **70**:44
Pew, Michelle - **70**:44
Pfitzer, Nikolaus - **67**:25
Philip, Prince - **70**:34
Philips, Moira - **70**:41
Philips, Victor - **70**:41
Piaget, Dr Jean - **72**:54
Picknett, Lynn - **70**:54; **71**:65
Pickney, Herbert - **68**:19
Pieri, Bettina - **72**:25, 28
Pierrot, Armand - **67**:48
Pinder, Chris - **69**:11
Pinder, Janet - **69**:11
Pine, Chuck - **68**:25
Pinelli, Armando - **72**:19
Pink, Tim - **69**:11
Piotrowski, Stephen - **68**:10
Playfair, Guy Lyon - **67**:41-2
Pliny - **70**:11
Poe, Edgar Allan - **72**:56
Pomroy, Ron - **68**:17
Pons, Stanley - **69**:23-26
Ponsford, Karen - **68**:14
Porshnev, Boris - **67**:33; **68**:54
Porter, Bob - **72**:34
Porter, Katherine - **72**:24
Porter, Keith - **67**:18
Poselsky, Michail - **67**:45

Potts, Richard - **70**:43
Powell, Jeanette - **72**:46
Presley, Elvis - **67**:55; **68**:55
Prest, Bert - **68**:8
Prest, T.P. - **68**:41
Price, Blaine - **70**:41
Price, Harry - **67**:38, 61
Price, Van - **70**:41
Prince, Clive - **70**:54
Proctor, Floyd - **72**:55
Proctor, Judge J.S. - **72**:55
Proctor, Loretta - **72**:55
Proctor, Norris - **72**:55
Proctor, Timothy - **72**:55
Puienbroeck, Bruno van - **69**:8
Purkinje - **72**:65
Quigley, Carol - **68**:33
Quigley, Dennis - **69**:18
'Rachel,' - **71**:24
Radlich, Gertrude - **71**:19
Radlich, Nathan - **71**:19
Rafferty, Rochelle - **69**:42
Raidi - **67**:14
Rakkorn, Khamla - **72**:9
Ramakrishna - **67**:6
Ramey, Brig. Gen. Roger - **72**:55
Ramey, Lucille - **71**:19
Ramey, Virgil - **71**:19
Ramishvili, Maiko - **68**:11
Ramos, Rafaela - **70**:19
Ramsey, Gloria - **68**:'11
Rand, Ayn - **68**:56
Randi, James - **69**:19, 55; **70**:14
Randles, Jenny - **71**:65; **72**:45, 65
Rao, Nagalakshmi - **72**:7
Rao, Subba - **72**:7
Rardin, Michelle - **69**:7
Rashid, Ahmed - **69**:16
Ratner, Gerald - **72**:13
Rawlins, Dr Dennis - **68**:56
Rea, Dinah - **69**:19
Rees, Dilwyn - **70**:49
Reich, Wilhelm - **72**:44
Rembrandt van Rijn - **67**:26
Rendalen, Age, Jr - **72**:42, 43
Repp, Ed Earl - **71**:'2
Resch, Tina - **68**:'13
Rew, Kelly - **72**:14
Rew, Michelle - **72**:14
Rheinallt, Tristan ap - **68**:10
Rhines & Edgerton - **68**:54
Rich, Dr Patricia - **72**:14
Richard III - **70**:56
Richard, Cliff - **71**:56
Richardson, Bill - **71**:12
Richet, Charles - **68**:53; **70**:28
Rickard, Bob - **68**:'2-'4
Riggs, Doug - **71**:32
Riley, Andrew - **69**:24
Rizzi, Sara - **69**:15
Roberts, Andy - **68**:64
Roberts, Anthony - **72**:8
Roberts, David - **71**:14

Roberts, John - **71**:10
Roberts, Oral - **67**:55
Roberts, Sarah Ellen - **71**:10
Roberts, Vic - **70**:44
Robertson, Col. John - **69**:50-51
Robinson, Roy - **68**:51
Rodriguez, Danny - **71**:17
Rodriguez, Sammy - **71**:17
Rogers, Lois - **68**:45
Rogers, Mike - **69**:62
Romanov, Alexei - **67**:45
Romanov, Anastasia - **67**:45
Romanov, Maria - **67**:45
Romanov, Olga - **67**:45
Romanov, Tatyana - **67**:45
Romero, Claudio - **72**:17
Romero, Derek - **71**:19
Rommel, Kenneth - **68**:24
Rosenblatt, Adam - **68**:11
Rosholm, Rolf - **70**:10
Rothermell, Mark - **67**:31
Rowe, Christine - **70**:39
Rowe, Michael - **70**:39
Rowley, Karl - **69**:65
Rowsell, Joyce - **71**:14
Roy, K.L. - **68**:14
Rubia, Antonio La - **71**:'4
Ruby, Jack - **72**:31, 34
Rugoff, Ralph - **70**:35
Ruiz, Francois - **68**:10
Runcie, Lord - **70**:11
Rutherford, Lord - **69**:24
Rutskoi, Alexander V. - **69**:45
Rutter, Prof Michael - **67**:12
Ruysch, Frederick - **68**:60
Sadykov, Oleg - **69**:45
Saggers, Chris - **72**:15
Sai Baba - **69**:64
Saleh, Hussein & Hassan - **68**:45
Salzman, Catanya - **71**:12
Samuels, Bernard - **72**:13
'Sanchez, Danielle' - **68**:14
Sanders, Ed - **68**:24-5
Sandved, Kjell B. - **70**:'2-3
Sanger, Helen - **68**:7
Santos, Jean Baptista dos - **67**:15
Sartono, Prof. Sastrohamijoyo -
    72:11
Savary, Ruth de - **70**:40
Sawart, Ulf - **67**:17
Scarboro, David - **69**:47
Schlesinger, James - **69**:50-1
Schmidt, Maria - **72**:7
Schmitt, Eric - **69**:4
Schnabel, Jim - **70**:64; **72**:24, 39, 48
Scholten, Joke - **67**:13
Schrenck-Notzing - **70**:28
Schwartz, Henry - **70**:48
Schwarz, Marco - **69**:10
Schwarzschild, Dr Michael - **72**:8
Scot, Michael - **68**:52
Scotford, Roger - **71**:28
Seago, Edward - **71**:39

Seal, Mary - **67**:4; **68**:30-33
Sealy, Peter - **70**:11
Searle, Frank - **68**:54
Selby, de - **72**:54
Sellard, Rick - **70**:40
Sellard, Vicki - **70**:40
Sellard, Virgil - **70**:40
Selva, Serafin Ruiz - **68**:42
Senna, Ayrton - **67**:55
Sepulveda, Dion - **67**:60
Serban, Natasa - **68**:19
Seth, V.N. - **70**:18
Seymour, Ken - **67**:7
Shaffer, Peter - **68**:47
Shakespeare, William - **69**:55
Shakil - **69**:9
'Shami, Prince' - **69**:44
Shamim, Mohammed - **72**:15
Shannon, Fred - **68**:'13
Shapiro, Anne - **72**:29
Shariff, Kwarme - **72**:19
Shariff, Kwasi - **72**:19
Sharma, Kuldip - **69**:9
Sharmapa, The - **69**:32-33
Shaw, Lucy - **70**:65
Sheissenhosen, Prof H.H. - **72**:54
Shelley, Mary - **71**:55
Sher, Andrei - **69**:47
Shiels, Tony 'Doc' - **68**:'12
Shipton, Eric - **68**:54
Shipton, Mother - **69**:55
Shipton, Pat - **72**:11
Shishikura, Dr M - **72**:63
Shuker, Karl - **67**:'2
Sieveking, Lance - **71**:20
Sieveking, Paul - **68**:'2-'4
Sikdar, Chitta - **70**:8
Simcoviak, John - **67**:13
Simmonot, Jean-Paul - **72**:15
Simpson, Doug - **70**:39
Simpson, Gertrude - **69**:10
Simpson, James Kwesi - **69**:10
Singh, Hardial - **68**:19
Singh, Manjit - **67**:12
Sinister, Mr - **69**:37
Sipeung, Saengchaliao - **72**:9
Slack, Paul - **69**:16
Slimp, Valerie - **68**:19
Smith, Carl - **70**:12
Smith, Joseph - **70**:20
Smith, Michelle - **71**:26
Smith, Mike - **67**:38-9, 42
Smylie, Dr Douglas - **67**:7
Smyslov - **71**:54
'Snake, The' - **69**:40
Snowdon, Lord - **70**:39
Sokolowsky, Lilian - **71**:14
Solis, Jesse - **67**:20
Solomon, King of Israel - **70**:37
Somerville - **71**:52
Somsen, Steve - **68**:26
Souza, Godofredo - **72**:29
Spassky - **71**:54

Speer, Sarah - **67**:28
'Spiderman' - **69**:41
Spielberg, Stephen - **72**:53
Spies, Johann - **67**:24, 26-7
Spiro, Herzl - **70**:25
Spittle, Bruce - **69**:43
Spittle, Malcolm - **69**:43
Spitz, Dr Lewis - **68**:44-5
Spohn, Gustav - **72**:43
Sprinkle, Leo - **68**:25, 28
Sreedharam, Mr - **67**:14
St Agnes - **72**:20
St Andrew - **70**:36; **72**:20
St Anne - **70**:20
St Anthony - **70**:36; **72**:20
St Antoninus of Piacenza - **70**:36
St Augustine - **69**:52; **71**:32
St Barnabas - **68**:6
St Bartholomew - **70**:20
St Bernadette Soubirous - **68**:'7
St Cadoc - **70**:20
St Casilda - **67**:6
St Catherine - **72**:20
St Cronaparva - **69**:6
St David - **67**:6
St Dymphna - **68**:6
St Elmo - **68**:6
St Fiacre - **70**:20
St Finbarr - **70**:20
St Francis de Sales - **72**:20
St Francis of Assisi - **70**:20; **71**:48
St Gabriel - **67**:6
St Gemma Galgani - **67**:6
St George - **68**:6, 34-37; **70**:37
St Gerard Majella - **71**:20
St Giles - **70**:20
St Helena - **70**:36
St Hermes - **70**:20
St Hilary - **72**:20
St John - **70**:36
St John the Baptist - **69**:6
St Joseph - **70**:20
St Joseph of Cupertino - **70**:20, 28-9
St Kieran - **71**:52
St Lambert - **70**:20
St Longinus - **70**:36
St Luke - **68**:48
St Martin - **71**:20
St Mary Magdalene - **69**:6
St Maurice - **70**:36
St Michael - **68**:6
St Patrick - **67**:6
St Paul - **72**:20
St Paula the Bearded - **67**:6
St Peter - **68**:48
St Simon Stylites - **72**:20
St Sophia - **68**:6
St Swithin - **69**:6
St Teresa of Avila - **69**:55; **70**:29;
    71:20
St Theodolous the Stylite - **68**:6
St Ursula - **71**:20
St Veronica - **70**:35-6

St Vitus - **69**:6
St Walpurga - **67**:6
Stadelman, Rainer - **70**:51
Stallone, Sylvester - **69**:50
Stein, Dr Gordon - **71**:44-5
Steinacher, Sue - **70**:40
Steinbacher, Dr J. - **67**:63
Steinitz - **71**:54
Stepankov, Valentin - **69**:45
Stevens, Lieut. Larry - **69**:50-51
Stiles, Grady - **72**:6
Stimpson, Tim - **67**:28
Stoker, Bram - **67**:65; **68**:39
Stonor, Charles - **67**:'3
Straiton, Dr Michael - **71**:65
Strecker, Dr Robert - **68**:31
Streiber, Whitley - **72**:54
Stringer, Christopher - **70**:43
Stringfield, Leonard - **72**:55
Stringham, Roger - **69**:26
Strupovets, Viktor - **70**:39
Stuart, John - **71**:'3
Stuart, Lachlan - **68**:54
Stukeley, Dr William - **69**:52
Sulerzhitsky, Lev - **69**:47
Summers, David - **68**:31
Summers, Montague - **68**:40
Sun Ra - **71**:13
Suner, Levent - **69**:8
Surdul, Jurek - **67**:34
Sutton family - **71**:'2
Sutton, Christy - **72**:37
Sutton, Frank - **72**:37
Sutton, Ian - **71**:10
Sutton, Jeffrey - **72**:37
Sutton, Mary - **72**:36-39
Sutton, Phyllis - **72**:37, 38
Sutton, Sonny - **72**:37, 38
Suvorov, Nikolai - **68**:'15
Svensson, Emil - **67**:50
Svensson, Lars Tore - **70**:10
Szilard, Leo - **68**:27
Tadeyev, Ramaz - **69**:45
Tai Situpa - **69**:32-33
Takahashi, Dr Akito - **69**:25
Tal - **71**:54
Talib, Abdul Fadli - **69**:19
Tanabe, Toshiyuki - **69**:48
Tate, Sharon - **68**:25
Tatro, William - **70**:18
Tatum, Mark - **70**:6
Taylor family - **71**:'2
Taylor, Billy Ray - **71**:'3
Taylor, Busty - **69**:40
Taylor, Kevin - **69**:43
Taylor, Prof John - **68**:16
Tchernine, Odette - **70**:34
Teed, Dr Cyrus - **68**:4
Terziski, Vladimir - **68**:31
Thaddeus - **70**:36
Thom, Alexander - **71**:52
Thomas, Christopher - **69**:9
Thomas, Pastor Eugene - **67**:29-30

Thomas, Gareth B. - **72**:46
Thompson, Hunter S. - **68**:63
Thompson, Jim - **70**:47-8
Thompson, J.M. - **68**:53
Thompson, Mary - **67**:11
Thongruen, Lars - **72**:12
Thorne, James H. - **68**:29
Thorpe, Anne - **69**:11
Thouless, Dr Chris - **70**:32-3
Thrasher, Paula - **67**:11
Tiberius - **71**:54
Tinley, Karma Ugyen - **69**:30-33
Tinsley, Chris - **71**:63
Tite, Prof. Michael - **71**:65
Titus - **71**:54
Tokugawa Shoguns - **67**:10
Tomachek, Ernst - **67**:13
Toope, Dr - **72**:52
Torme, Tracy - **69**:62
Tourison, Sedgwick - **69**:50
Toynbee, Arnold - **68**:56
Trajan - **71**:54
Treloar, Dr Norman - **71**:54
Trevor-Roper, Hugh - **67**:45
Trungpa, Chogyam - **71**:55
Truzzi, Dr Marcello - **68**:56
Tudur - **67**:52
Tueux, Marie-Christine - **67**:48
Turner, Carey - **72**:16
Turner, Carol - **70**:30
Turner, Fred - **71**:14
Turner, Gail - **68**:'6
Turner, Josephine - **69**:19
Turner, Ron - **69**:14
Tutankhamun - **69**:19; **70**:51
Tyler, Prof Don - **72**:11
Tzara, Tristan - **67**:6
Umberto, ex-king of Savoy - **71**:65
Umbreit, Helga - **69**:43
Umpat, Marilyn - **68**:9
Umporowicz, Tom - **69**:18
Urban VIII, Pope - **70**:20, 28-9
Urquhart, Ann - **72**:11
Usmanov, Oleg - **71**:17
Ussher, Archbishop James - **71**:20
Utsunomiya, Hiroshi - **69**:15
Valentinian III - **71**:54
Vallance, Jeffrey - **70**:35-37
Vasa, Gustav - **70**:16
Verchomin, Doris - **68**:29
Verne, Jules - **68**:63
Vernon, George - **69**:39
Vetter, Dr Rick - **68**:19
Victor, Jeffrey - **72**:54
Victoria, Queen - **70**:56
Villas Boas, Antonio - **68**:55; **69**:63; **71**:20
Vinci, Leonardo da - **70**:54
Volk, Stephen - **67**:38-42
Volkogonov, Col. Dmitri - **69**:50
Vos, Dr John de - **70**:42-3; **72**:11
Waby, Sam - **69**:42-3
Wadland, Simon - **69**:13

Walker, Alan - **70**:42-3
Wallace - **71**:38
Wallace, David - **69**:19
Walton, Travis - **69**:29, 62; **71**:20, 53
Wang Mang - **69**:48
Wanley, Nathaniel - **72**:25
Ward, Jim - **68**:10
Warhol, Andy - **70**:35
Warren, David - **70**:32
Warren, Deirdre - **68**:5
Washington, George - **70**:37
Waterhouse, Rosie - **71**:28; **72**:48
Watkins, Alan - **70**:38
Watkins, Alfred - **67**:56
Watkins, Debbie - **72**:6
Watson, Simeon - **72**:25
Watts, Alan - **72**:65
Watts, Rev. Dr Fraser - **71**:48
Webb, Alfred - **70**:48
Wei Guoqing - **69**:48
Welles, Orson - **67**:39, 41; **71**:20, 39
Wells, H.G. - **71**:'2
Wesley, Dr John - **68**:45
Westwood, Jennifer - **68**:52
Wetherell, Art - **68**:63
Wheeler, P.W. - **68**:48
Whitehouse, Mary - **69**:55
Whitrow, G.J. - **71**:55
Widner, Dr Rudolph - **67**:7
Wilde, Jane - **67**:54
Wilkinson, Leroy - **69**:12
Will, Ion Alexis - **68**:'2-'3; **71**:13
William of Normandy - **67**:47
Williams, Dorothy - **72**:46
Williams, T. - **71**:8
Willis, Gemma - **68**:17
Willis, John - **68**:17
Willis, Paul - **68**:'3
Wilson - **72**:25
Wilson, Colin - **68**:'4
Wilson, Dawn - **71**:26
Wilson, Edward Arthur - **67**:59
Wilson, Ian - **70**:54
Wilson, Robert Anton - **68**:'4; **71**:16
Wingfield, George - **68**:43; **69**:38-41
Wink, Judy - **71**:16
Wise, Wes - **72**:34
Wolfe, Dudley - **70**:18
Wolfe, Helen - **71**:10
Wolfe, Tom - **72**:56
Woodhull, Victoria - **70**:20
Woods, Heather - **71**:48-49
Worthington, Angela - **69**:17
Worthington, Gemma - **69**:17
Worthington, Sharon - **69**:17
Wright Bros. - **69**:23-4
Wright, John - **67**:26
Wu Gang - **71**:15
Wyant, Chris - **72**:6
Wyley, Graham - **71**:15
Xu Jing - **67**:15
Yamaguchi, Dr Eiichi - **69**:25
Yearick, Archie - **68**:29

Yeltsin, Boris - **69**:45; **71**:17
Yeltsin, Miana - **71**:17
Yikilmaz, Sonmez - **70**:16
Yilmaz, Ayse - **71**:9
Yilmaz, Osman - **71**:9
Yinger, Brian - **71**:14
Yocum, Lorraine - **71**:16

Yoxall, George - **70**:49
Zamora, Lonnie - **68**:6
Zapruder, Abraham - **72**:33
Zawada, Andrzej - **67**:32, 34
Zee, Madame - **67**:60
Zelas, Dr Karen - **72**:47
Zhang Jing - **70**:9

Zheng Yi - **69**:48
Zivojinovic, Milance - **72**:7
Zolotov, Boris - **68**:11
Zuidema, Ellard - **72**:19
Zundel, Ernst - **68**:31

NAMES of CONTRIBUTORS of Articles, Illustrations & Letters

Anonymous
'Cabin Fever' - **70**:64
'Rip-off' - **72**:63
Baker, Gerald
'Unexpected Birth Cycles' - **71**:54
Bayliss, Peter
'Devil's Brother-in-Law, The' - **67**:24-27
Becker, Greg
- **71**:39-41
Beswick, Tim
'Shaman Robin' - **67**:63
Billingsley, John
'Che in the Clouds?' - **71**:63
Blamey, Claire
'Brush with the Black Dog, A' - **70**:65
Bolger, Alan
- **69**:14; **71**:34
Bord, Janet + Colin
'Archive Gems 2: Black Madonna of Montserrat, The' - **68**:48
'Secret Country 7: Dinas Bran' - **67**:52
'Secret Country 8: Eildon Hills' - **68**:52
'Secret Country 9: Cerne Abbas' - **69**:52
'Secret Country 10: Trellech' - **70**:52
'Secret Country 11: Callanish' - **71**:52
'Secret Country 12: Silbury Hill' - **72**:52
Brady, Eric R.
'Lenticular Cloud' - **70**:63
Brookesmith, Peter
'Missing Time' - **72**:44-45
Bruce, Anthony
''Impossible' Solid?, An' - **72**:63
Callaghan, Nigel A.
'Rent-a-Read' - **67**:64
Carr, C.
'Icy Mist' - **70**:64
Carr, Peter
'Frankenstein Vibrations' - **71**:55
Chapman, Brian
'Birds, Sheep and Cremation

Accidents' - **71**:64
'Surgical Rumours and Thunderbirds' - **67**:64
Cheetham, John
'Giant Snakes' - **67**:65
Chrenkoff, Arthur
- **69**:10
'Coincidence or Precognition?' - **67**:64
Clark, Jerome
'Rational Debate' - **71**:63
'Respect for Alien Abductions' - **68**:64
Clark, Tony
'Lunchtime at the Phantom Diner' - **69**:34-35
Coleman, Loren
'Black Lagoon Revisited' - **70**:63
'Really Out-of-Place' - **69**:56
Coleman, Tim
'Interview: Dr David Jacobs' - **69**:27-29
Costello, Peter
'Vegetable Lambs and the Drunkard's Fate' - **68**:63
Dash, Mike
'Bedevilled' - **72**:47-49
'Dragons of Vancouver, The' - **70**:46-48
'In Search of the Yeti' - **67**:32-34
'It Came from Outer Space!' - **71**:'1-4
Dehon, Robert
'Marketing Blunder' - **72**:63
Doble, Adelaide
'Cat's Cradle' - **67**:63
Dorje, Karma Tendzin
'Fractal Challenge' - **72**:63
'Golden Child' - **69**:30-33
Downes, Jonathan
'Art of Jumping to Conclusions, The' - **68**:54
Drapkin, C.M.
'Vampire of Croglin Grange, The' - **68**:39-41
Elliott, R.N.
'Levitation' - **71**:65
Emerson, Hunt
- **67**:1, 21; **68**:1, 21; **69**:1, 11, 21,

26; **70**:1, 16, 21; **71**:7, 21; **72**:21
Evans, Hilary
'Archive Gems 1: Italian Martians, The' - **67**:43
Fisher, Dr David J.
'Fractal Freaks' - **70**:64
Fleming, Glenn B.
'Shooting Down the Myth' - **72**:30-34
Fowler, Christopher
'Albino Lobsters' - **70**:64
Gamon, David
'Bollock!' - **69**:63
Garner, Paul
'Age of the Earth' - **69**:64
Gilmore, Christopher
'Gas or God?' - **67**:65
Glickman, Michael
'Hijacked?' - **70**:64
Godthelp, H.
'Not a Kangaroo' - **67**:65
Gosling, Derek
'Sheerwater Fish Fall' - **68**:64
Goss, Michael
'Down in the Jungle' - **72**:56
Green, Andrew
'Battle Triangle Ghost, The' - **67**:47
Green, Prof. Robert T.
'Sharp Practice' - **67**:64
Greene, Yvonne
'Foetal Memory Metaphors' - **71**:53
Haddington, John, The Earl of
'Face(s) in the Window, The' - **69**:65
Haines, Slim
'Fax not from Limbo' - **71**:63
Hallam, Mary
'It was Crap' - **71**:64
Halstead, Richard
'MIA Photo Mystery, The' - **69**:50-51
Harpur, Merrily
- **67**:16, 18; **68**:9, 12; **69**:12; **70**:10, 12; **71**:12, 14; **72**:12, 16
Harrington, Julia
'Very Local Weather' - **67**:63

Harte, Jeremy
'Reds in the Pond' - **68**:65
Hayes, Anthony
'Music to our Ears' - **69**:64
Hodgkinson, Tom
'Interview: Terence McKenna' -
71:35-38
Holland, Richard
'Bird Death Mystery' - **69**:65
Hollins, Pierre
- **67**:56; **68**:56; **69**:56; **70**:56;
71:56; **72**:56
Howlett, N.M.
'We Stand Corrected' - **70**:65
Impey, Martin
- **70**:19
Inglis, Brian
'Hallucination to Sit On, An' -
68:53
Johnson, D.
'Dream Ticket' - **68**:63
Jones, Nigel
'Solar Phenomenon' - **72**:64
Kennedy, Bruce G.
'Haunted Billabong, The' - **71**:64
Keyworth, David
'Prudes from Space' - **69**:63
Kinney, Jay
- **68**:29
Kirkwood, Jake
'Elusive Pig' - **72**:63
Kollerstrom, Nick
'Radiometric Dating' - **68**:65
Kollins, Martin
'Evolutionary Fast Food' - **70**:53
Langbein, Walter J.
'Von Daniken Got There First' -
69:65
Larson, Gary
- **67**:13; **68**:12; **69**:18; **70**:6; **71**:6;
72:6
Lavery, Eileen
'Quake Miracle' - **72**:65
Lazell, David
'Modern Fairy Tales' - **71**:39-41
Leigh, Dr John
'Letter-box Amputations' - **68**:65
Lies, Christopher
'Of Cats and Shopping Trolleys'
- **70**:63
Lippard, Jim
'Radiometric Dating' - **68**:65
'Sai Baba's Miracles' - **69**:64
Longhorn, David
'Rent-a-Read' - **67**:64
Loveday, Pete
- **69**:38-39; **69**:41
Mays, Nick
'Elephant Sits on Mini - Again' -
70:64
McBeath, Alastair

'Flashes in the Dark' - **72**:65
'Matter of Meteors, A' - **68**:64
McClure, Kevin
'Angels to the Rescue' - **68**:34-37
McLoren, Kirk
'Valley Fever' - **67**:63
McLuskey, Anthony
'Cloning Recipes' - **72**:53
Michell, John
'Crop Thickens, The' - **68**:43
Miles, Ian
'Silent Cities in the Sky' - **68**:64
Milton, Richard
'Age of the Earth' - **69**:64
Mitchell, Alan
'Tricks of the Trees' - **70**:55
Moore, Steve
'Unearthed: Footprints in the
Sands of Time' - **69**:47
'Unearthed: Fresco Fiasco' -
68:42
'Unearthed: Mini Mammoths
Linger Longer' - **69**:47
'Unearthed: Mystery of the
Pharaohs' - **70**:51
'Unearthed: Shooting Tsars' -
67:45
'Unearthed: Something Nazi' -
67:44-45
'Unearthed: Subterranean Sub-
marine' - **72**:50
Noyes, Ralph
'Dead Funny' - **70**:65
'Id, the Ego and the Superna-
tural, The' - **69**:55
Nye, James
'Bibliomania' - **71**:64
O'Neill, Mike
'Importance of Timing' - **69**:53
Owens, Andrew John
'Odd Rings' - **71**:65
Parker, Ainslie
'Grimsby Portents' - **68**:63
Penderton, John
'End was not Nigh, The' - **70**:64
Peters, Ian T.
'Rigor Tortoise' - **68**:65
Petersen, Todd L.
'Fainting Goats' - **71**:63
Picek, Aldo Z.
'Trolley Travel' - **69**:63
Picknett, Lynn
'Answer's in the Negative, The' -
70:54
Playfair, Guy Lyon
'Great Mirabelli, The' - **71**:43-45
Poole, Peter
- **69**:16
Preston, Steven
'Weird' - **68**:63
Radford, Benjamin

'Devil's Hoofprints' - **70**:65
Randi, James
'Randi Replies' - **71**:64
Rickard, Bob
'Archive Gems 3: Bowhead In-
cident, The' - **71**:46
'Fairy Tree in Peril' - **71**:42
'Feeling Cross' - **71**:48-49
'Ghostwatch: Whatever Pos-
sessed Parkinson?' - **67**:38-42
'Hard to Swallow' - **69**:48
'Interview: Bill Gibbons' - **67**:28-31
'Interview: Jenny Cockell' -
72:36-39
'Interview: John Blashford-Snell'
- **70**:30-34
'Other Half, The' - **68**:44-45
'Snap Happy' - **70**:'2-3
'Water Babies' - **67**:46
Rickard, Bob + Olsson, Rolf J.K.
'Big Sleep, The' - **72**:23-29
Ritchie, John D.
'Meeting Pan' - **72**:64
Roberts, Andy
'Curiouser and Curiouser' -
67:53
Roberts, Frank
'Jung's Dream' - **71**:65
Rosen, Sven
'Who's Spying on Sweden?' -
67:50-51
Rubinstein, Prof. Bill
'Localised Combustions' - **72**:65
Sandy, Tony
'Who's in Charge Here?' - **72**:63
Schnabel, Jim
'Crop Correction' - **71**:63
'Memories of Hell' - **71**:24-32
'Munch Bunch, The' - **70**:23-29
'Pick of the Crops' - **69**:37-41
Screeton, Paul
'Dubious Translations' - **67**:55
Sharville, Paul
'Commuting at 186,000 miles per
hour' - **71**:56
Shepard, Leslie
'Bird Rains' - **71**:64
Shipman, Pat
'Boneheads' - **70**:42-43
Shuker, Dr Karl
'Case of the Missing Moa, The' -
69:42-43
'Egg Voyagers' - **70**:44
'Gambo' - **67**:35-37
'Living Fossils' - **67**:'1-4
'Lovecats, The' - **68**:50-51
'Lovecats: The Next Generation'
- **72**:46
Sieveking, Paul
'Deadly Alchemy' - **69**:44-45
'Driller Chiller' - **72**:42-43
'Fear and Loathing in France' -

67:48
  'Horsewatch: Madness in the
    Home Counties' - **68**:46-47
  'Rovers Return' - **70**:38-41
  'Webs of War, The' - **71**:34
Sieveking, Paul + Stillings, Dennis
  'Poor Cow' - **68**:23-29
Sirisena, Ananda
  'Another Face on Mars' - **69**:64
Smith, Peter
  'Childhood Terrors' - **67**:65
Spiromat, Bobby
  'Another Face on Mars' - **69**:64
Stacy, Dennis
  'Alien Bastards!' - **68**:55
  'Hawking Hawking' - **67**:54
  'Roswell the Terrible' - **72**:55
Steiger, Max
  - **67**:10; **71**:19

Sutton, David
  'Spirit versus Energy' - **67**:56
Taylor, Colin
  - **72**:19
Thomas, Lars
  'Bird King' - **67**:63
  'Given the Bird' - **69**:65
Tinsley, Chris
  'Hot Stuff' - **69**:23-26
Treharne, M
  'Herald Angel' - **68**:65
Volk, Stephen
  'Foxing the Public' - **70**:56
Warren, Nick
  'Pimlico Mystery, The' - **67**:65
West, Ruth
  'Obituary: Brian Inglis' - **68**:16
Whittaker, Simon
  'Interview: Mary Seal' - **68**:30-33

Wilson, Ian
  'Shrouded Retort' - **71**:65
Wilson, Robert Anton
  'Atheistic Religions' - **68**:56
  'Munchausen's Syndrome' -
    72:65
  'Preposterous Perception' - **72**:54
Wood, Colin
  'Missing Links' - **69**:54
Wood, Paul
  - **71**:8
Wood, Susan
  'Largest Fish Clarification' -
    69:63
Woodward, Ken
  'Parrot Chicken Minder' - **69**:65
Young, Edward
  'I-Con Man' - **70**:35-37

NAMES of LEGENDARY & FICTIONAL Characters, including Deities & Monsters

Adam - **70**:37; **71**:38
Adonis - **72**:20
Akon - **71**:'4
Aliens - **71**:'1-4
Allah - **68**:20
Almas - **67**:32-34
Angels of Mons - **68**:34-37
Anna Perenna - **70**:20
Antichrist - **71**:17
Aphrodite - **68**:6
Apollo - **71**:52
Archon - **69**:37
Artemis - **71**:20
Arthur, King - **67**:8, 52; **68**:52; **72**:24
Asclepius - **72**:25
Balder - **72**:20
Barbie - **68**:7
Bigfoot - **68**:26, 54
Boulderhead - **72**:47
Bowmen of Mons - **68**:34-37
Bran the Blessed - **67**:52
brilliant being with bat wings - **72**:42
Brunhilda - **72**:24
Buddha, Gautama - **72**:20
BVM - **67**:6, 39; **68**:9, 48; **69**:6, 20;
    70:15, 19-21, 27; **72**:18, 65
Cain - **70**:37
Canonbie Dick - **68**:52
Comrade in White - **68**:37
Consus - **69**:6
Dakinis - **69**:30
Devil, The - **67**:24, 27; **68**:9, 52; **70**:52;
    72:52, 64
Dewi - **67**:6
Diana - **70**:11

Diomedes - **70**:11
Dionysos - **72**:20
Dracula - **67**:64-5; **68**:39-40; **71**:10
Eve - **71**:38
Fairies - **67**:52; **70**:52; **71**:39-42
Fairy Queen - **68**:52
flying man - **70**:20
Frankenstein, Dr - **71**:55
Frogman - **71**:'3
Gaia - **69**:37
Ganesh - **69**:9; **70**:16
Gesar - **72**:24
God - **68**:7, 9, 56; **70**:11; **71**:38, 55;
    72:18, 51
Godzilla - **71**:13
Goodfellow, Robin - **69**:37
Green Man - **68**:6
Greys - **68**:55; **69**:28; **71**:'1
Halifax Slasher - **67**:48
Hamlet - **72**:54
Hekate - **69**:60
Helen of Troy - **67**:24
Helith - **69**:52
Hercules - **69**:52
Hermes - **68**:6
Hood, Robin - **67**:63; **69**:60
humanoids - **71**:'2-'3
Isis - **70**:51
Jack o' Kent - **70**:52
Jack the Ripper - **68**:24
Jahweh - **68**:26-8
Jesus Christ - **68**:6, '11, 53; **70**:15, 20,
    27, 35, 37, 56; **71**:32, 48-9, 63;
    72:20
Jones, Indiana - **70**:30

Kali - **72**:20
Kalouvu (ancestral spirit) - **72**:19
Killer Clowns - **71**:'2
Kirk, Capt. James T. - **71**:56
Krueger, Freddie - **70**:7
Lancelot, Sir - **70**:37
Little Green Men - **71**:'2
Little men - **71**:'3
Little People, The - **67**:52
Loch Ness Monster - **68**:'12
Lucifer - **67**:27
Lugh - **69**:6
Mammy Water - **71**:6
Mars - **67**:6; **69**:44
Martian/s - **67**:43; **71**:'1-'2
Mephistopheles - **67**:24-5, 27
Mercurian - **71**:'1
Mercury - **68**:6; **69**:44
Merlin - **69**:39
Metalunans - **71**:'3
Minnesota Iceman - **67**:33; **68**:54
Mithras - **72**:20
Moon Men - **71**:'2
Moroni, Angel - **70**:20
Mothman - **69**:55
Munchausen, Baron Karl Friedrich
    von - **70**:26
Naakaa - **67**:63
Namazu - **70**:19
Neptune - **69**:44
Old Hag - **71**:32
Old Nick - **69**:37
Osiris - **70**:51; **72**:20
Owl man - **68**:6
Pan - **69**:37; **72**:64

Pater - **67**:6
Pee Paob (living dead) - **72**:9
Pele - **70**:17
Percy - **68**:17
Priapus - **69**:52
Quartermain, Allan - **70**:30
Queen of Heaven, Babylonian - **72**:20
Rer - **70**:51
robot - **71**:'4
robot zombie - **70**:9
Samana - **71**:20
Satan - **72**:10
Screamer, The - **69**:56
Selenites - **71**:'2

Seven Dwarfs - **71**:25
Shadow, The - **72**:54
Shiva - **72**:18
Siegfried - **68**:6
Sil, King - **72**:52
Sleepers of Ephesus, Seven - **72**:24
Sleeping Beauty - **72**:24
Sol Invictus - **72**:20
Spikehead - **72**:47
spirits - **72**:9
Splenditello - **70**:27
Thetis Lake Monster - **70**:20, 63
Thomas of Erceldoune - **68**:52
Trickster - **68**:26-8

Tubal-Cain - **70**:37
Vampire of Croglin Grange - **68**:39-41
Van Helsing, Dr - **67**:38
Varuna - **71**:47; **72**:18
Vegetable Lamb - **68**:63
Venus - **69**:44
Venusians - **71**:'2
Virgin of the Hermits - **68**:6
Vulcan - **69**:44
Wildman - **67**:32-34
Winkle, Rip van - **72**:24
Wotan - **72**:20, 24
Yeti - **67**:32-34

NAMES of ORGANISATIONS,
including Cults, Movements, Societies & Institutions

ABC TV - **67**:44
Adelaide Zoo - **67**:17
Adult Children Accusing Parents - **71**:28
Air Technical Intelligence Center - **72**:55
Albigeois Speleo-Club - **68**:42
Alkor Technologies - **69**:45
American Society of Zoologists - **70**:46
American Tennessee Fainting Goat Assoc. - **71**:63
Astrological Investigation & Research Group - **69**:53
Automobile Association (AA) - **68**:8; **70**:65
Bandung Institute - **72**:11
BBC - **67**:38-42
Beckhampton Group - **69**:41
Bill Bailey Gang - **69**:38-39
Biological Records Centre - **68**:10
Birmingham Accident Hospital - **67**:18
Black Forest Geophysical Observatory - **67**:7
Blackpool Zoo - **69**:7
Branch Davidians - **68**:4
Brazilian Institute for Psycho-biophysical Research - **71**:45
British Expeditionary Force - **68**:34-37
British Horse Society - **68**:47
British Society for the Turin Shroud - **70**:54; **71**:65
British Telecom - **71**:56
Burford Group - **69**:37
C.A. Pound Human Identification Laboratory - **67**:45
Canadian Museum of Nature - **70**:46
Canadian Wildlife Service - **68**:5
Central Middlesex Hospital - **70**:26
Centre for Crop Circle Studies (CCCS) - **67**:42; **68**:43; **69**:37, 40-1

Centre for the Search for Extra-terrestrial Intelligence (CSETI) - **69**:41
Chalk River Nuclear Faculty - **69**:26
Charing Cross Hospital - **67**:18
Chemical & Biological Arms Control Inst. - **71**:34
China Communist Party Central Committee - **67**:14
China Sturgeon Artificial Repro-duction Institute - **67**:10; **69**:63
Christchurch Civic Childcare Centre - **72**:47
Christian Scientists - **68**:56
Church of England - **68**:53
CIA - **69**:29, 40-1; **72**:30-1
Circles Effect Research Group (CERES) - **69**:37
Circles Phenomenon Research Group (CPR) - **69**:41
Clyde Beatty Circus - **68**:44
CNN - **71**:18
Committee for Scientific Investigation for Claims of the Paranormal (CSICOP) - **67**:38; **68**:56; **69**:40, 55; **70**:14
Conservation International - **69**:10
Coutts & Co - **69**:16
Creation Scientists - **68**:56
Darwin College - **67**:42
Dept of Conservation (NZ) - **69**:42-3
Devil's Disciples biker gang - **69**:5
Eclaireurs de France - **68**:42
El Agouza hospital (Cairo) - **69**:16
El Al - **67**:12
English Bridge Union - **72**:13
English Heritage - **67**:8
English Nature Conservation Group - **71**:12
European Southern Observatory -

70:13
Exeter College, Oxford - **69**:16
Expedition Base - **70**:30
Explorer's Club - **70**:30-1
False Memory Syndrome Foundation - **71**:27; **72**:54
Family, - **68**:25
FBI - **72**:31
Federal Communications Commission - **67**:14
Federal Reserve - **68**:31
Field Museum, Chicago - **70**:48
German Archaeological Institute, Cairo - **70**:51
Ghost Story Society - **68**:12
Government Forensic Laboratory - **67**:45
Hammersmith Hospital - **67**:18
Harvard Medical School - **71**:36
Hemdat - **71**:7
Holy Roman Empire - **68**:33
House Intelligence Committee - **71**:12
House Select Committee on Assassinations - **72**:31
HydroCatalysis Power - **69**:25
Hynek Center for UFO Studies (CUFOS) - **69**:4; **71**:63
IBM - **71**:56
International Fortean Organization (INFO) - **68**:'2
Illuminati, - **68**:33
Imperial College - **69**:45
Independent UFO Network - **72**:44
Indian Rationalists Association - **69**:9; **70**:8
Inquisition, - **69**:55
Institut Technique du Vin - **69**:17
Institute for Creation Research - **68**:65
Institute of Psychiatry, London - **67**:12
Institute of Terrestrial Ecology - **68**:10

Institute of Evolutionary Animal
    Morphology - 69:47
International Society of Crypto-
    zoology - 67:28
IRA - 71:18
Jim Rose Circus Sideshow - 71:5
John Birch Society - 72:30
Justice Dept - 72:31
Kagyu, (Buddhist) order - 69:32-33
KCAL (TV station) - 72:11
KGB - 67:44-5; 68:19; 69:50; 72:30-1
Knights Templar - 68:59
Kuwait Airways - 71:10
Latvian Medical Institute - 67:64
League Against Cruel Sports - 70:11
Lincoln Laboratory - 69:26
Little Rascals, day-care centre - 71:26;
    72:48
London School of Economics - 71:24
Los Alamos National Laboratory -
    71:12
LUCE - 70:54
MacArthur Foundation - 70:14
Mafia - 72:30-1
Marine Science & Technology Centre
    - 70:19
Mary Evans Picture Library - 67:43
Masons - 68:33
Massachusetts General Hospital - 72:8
Massachusetts Institute of
    Technology (MIT) - 69:26
McDonald's - 71:18
Medical College of Wisconsin - 70:25
Mental Health Foundation - 67:12
Mercy Hospital, San Diego - 67:20
MI5 - 69:38
MI6 - 69:40-1
Milky Way Falconry - 67:19
Ministry of Defence - 68:31
Monmouth Archaeological Society -
    72:13
Mormonism - 68:28
Mountain Men Anonymous - 72:8
Museum of Archaeology, Istanbul
    - 71:9
NASA - 68:33
National Centre for Scientific Research
    (CNRS) (France) - 69:53
National Geographic Society - 70:42
National Heritage - 71:42
National Islamic Centre, Malaysia -
    68:20
National Museum of Natural History,
    Leiden - 72:11
National Museum of Science, Tokyo
    - 70:13
NATO - 69:44
Natural History Museum - 70:43, 64
Natural Science Museum, Tokyo -
    70:13
Nepal Telecommunications Corp.
    - 70:7

Nippon Telephone & Telegraph
    - 69:25
Noah Technologies Corp - 69:44
NORAID - 71:18
OAS - 72:30
'Occult, The' - 68:24
Octel - 70:64
Operation Congo - 67:28-31
Operation Right to Know - 71:11
Pavlov Institute of Physiology - 70:19
People Unlimited - 71:10
Pesky Critters - 67:17
Plymouth Weather Centre - 67:6
Poor Clares, nuns - 70:37
Procter and Gamble - 71:18
Promecology - 69:45
Public Records Office - 68:30
Quantock Staghounds - 70:11
RAID - 69:4
Religious News Service - 72:43
Reserved Manpower of the Good
    Wisdom... - 67:15
Roper Organization - 68:55; 69:27-8
Royal British Columbia Museum
    - 70:47
Royal College of Art - 69:19
Royal Parks Agency - 71:42
Royal Photographic Society - 70:54
Royal Tyrrell Museum, Alberta - 70:33
RSPB - 68:6
RSPCA - 68:10; 69:12; 70:38
Santan Dal - 70:8
Satanismism - 68:24, 46
Science Photo Library - 70:8
Scientific Exploration Society - 70:30
Scientology - 68:56
Security Ministry (Russia) - 69:45
Seventh Day Adventists - 68:4
Silbury Group - 69:37
SMERSH - 67:44-45
Smithsonian Institution - 70:43, '2
Society for Psychical Research
    (SPR) - 67:39, 42; 68:37; 70:56,
    65; 71:43-4
Spiritualist Association - 67:7
Spiritualists' National Union - 71:13
SRI International - 69:25-6
Stanford Research Institute - 69:24
Teamster's Union - 72:31
Technova - 69:23
Territorial Army - 68:13
Thor Chemicals - 69:44
Tokyo Institute of Technology - 72:63
Tokyo Metropolitan Sewerage
    Bureau - 72:13
Trilateral Commision - 68:31, 33;
    69:40
Trinity Broadcast Network - 72:42-43
Triple Nine Society - 71:54
TVS - 67:47
UN - 68:31, 33
UNICEF - 71:17

United Bureau of Investigation - 69:41
University Hospital, Portland - 72:8
Universities
    Bristol - 67:12, 42
    British Columbia - 70:46
    Cambridge - 71:45
    Canterbury (NZ) - 69:43
    California - 67:7
    California, State Polytechnic -
        69:26
    Chicago - 68:15
    Cincinatti - 67:7
    Edinburgh - 70:8
    Guelph - 68:5
    Heidelberg - 67:24
    Idaho - 72:11
    Johns Hopkins - 70:25
    Liverpool - 71:11
    Louisiana State - 71:34
    Melbourne - 69:48
    Monash - 72:14
    New Mexico - 71:12
    North Carolina State - 68:15
    Open - 68:49
    Osaka - 69:25
    Oslo, Biology Institute - 69:7
    Oxford - 69:10
    Princeton - 71:13
    Strathclyde, Bioscience Dept - 69:8
    Templeton - 69:27
    Tokyo - 67:'1
    University College, London
        - 69:54
    Utah - 69:23-4
    Victoria - 70:46
    Wittenberg - 67:27
    West Indies - 67:14
    Yamaguchi - 69:15
    York, Ontario - 67:7
USAAF - 69:27; 72:55
US Agriculture Dept - 69:14
US Dept of Energy - 69:44
US Military Intelligence - 72:30
US National Oceanic & Atmospheric
    Admin. - 70:15
US Patent Office - 67:6
Vampire Anti-Defamation League -
    68:12
Vampire Research Center - 68:39;
    71:10
Walt Disney - 72:11
Warner Books - 72:11
Wee Care Day Nursery - 72:48
Welsh Office Agricultural
    Development Advisory Service
    (ADAS) - 68:6
Wessex Skeptics, - 69:40
Western Australia Museum - 70:44
White Brothers, (Belye Bratya) - 72:10
World Meteorological Organisation -
    67:49

NAMES of ANIMALS and PLANTS

albatross - **69**:65

algae - dinoflagellates - **68**:15

almas / almasty - **67**:32-34; **70**:32, 34

anaconda - **67**:65; **68**:'13; giant, *Sucuriju gigante* - **67**:31, '2; horned - **70**:33

ant - *Solenopsis* - **70**:6

anteater - **69**:56

archaeocetes - **67**:37

armadillo - **67**:36; **69**:56

aubergine - **68**:'5

baboon - **67**:49; phantom - **69**:56

bacterium - *Pseudomonas aeruginosa* - **67**:18

banana - **69**:49

bandicoot - **69**:11

barley - **68**:43, 52

barracuda - **72**:17

bass - white - **70**:12

bat - Bechstein's - **71**:12

bear - brown - **67**:6; irkuiem - **67**:'2; **68**:54; **69**:7; polar - **69**:8; **71**:6; **72**:14

beaver - **71**:19

bee - **72**:25

beech - weeping - **70**:55

bigfoot - **68**:54; **69**:56; **70**:34; **71**:59

birds - **67**:26, 49; **68**:6; **71**:64

bison - **68**:42

blackberry - **71**:41

blackbird - **69**:65

Black Dog - **70**:65

bluetit - 'king' - **67**:63

boar - wild - **72**:63

bobcat - **71**:16

bream - **70**:12

budgerigar - **71**:8

bunyip - **67**:'2

buru - lungfish? - **67**:'3

butterfly - **70**:18, '1-4; Clouded Yellow - **68**:10; Cabbage White - **68**:10

buzzard - **68**:29

cacomistle - **69**:56

cadborosaurus, sea serpent - **70**:46-48

capybara - **67**:65; **68**:'13

cat - big - **68**:23, 50-51; **71**:60; domestic - **67**:12, 39; **68**:18, 29, 50-1; **69**:56, 64; **70**:63; **71**:9, 12, 16, 45-6; hybrid - **68**:51; **72**:46; winged - **68**:'14

catfish - **70**:19; **72**:6

cattle - **67**:14; **68**:23-29, 31; **69**:52; **71**:40; **72**:44-5

cavy - **69**:56

cetaceans - **67**:37

cheetah - King - **68**:54

chicken - **67**:49; **68**:'6; - **69**:8, 12; **70**:35 - **71**:9, 16

civet - Malay, *Viverra tangalunga* - **69**:56

clover - 4-leafed - **67**:19

coatimundi - **69**:56

cobra - **67**:19; **69**:9

coelacanth - *Latimeria chalumnae* - **67**:'4, 29, 36

cotton plant - **68**:63

cow - **68**:47; **69**:7, 14; **70**:9, 11, 49; double-headed calf - **67**:14; wild Cambodian - **72**:14

crab - **68**:6

crayfish - Turkish, *Astacus leptodactylus salinus* - **70**:64

crocodile - **72**:17; giant (mahamba) - **67**:29; salt-water, giant - **67**:31, 37

crow - **67**:52; **68**:29; **69**:17; **71**:64

cuckoo - **68**:6; **71**:52

cucumber - **72**:16; zombi cucumber - **67**:19

daisy - **71**:41

deer - **68**:29; red - **69**:43; white - **70**:11

devil-pig - **67**:'3

dinosaur - **68**:54; **71**:7; 20th century - **67**:'1-4

diprotodont - **67**:'2

dodo - **67**:31

dog - **67**:13, 26-7, 34, 42, 45, 49; **68**:50; **69**:12, 56, 63-4; **71**:6, 8-8, 19; alsatian - **68**:13; border collie - **68**:47; dachsund - **67**:18; huskie-lab cross - **68**:8; kelpie cross - **67**:18; mongrel - **67**:18; red setter, Irish - **67**:19; Schnauzer - **67**:18; terrier - **67**:12; **72**:13; Jack Russell - **70**:17; trekking - **70**:38-41; white - **67**:52

dolphin - **67**:36, 46

donkey - **70**:10; **71**:14

dove - **68**:6

dragon - **67**:6, '2; **71**:52; **72**:6; water - **67**:'3

dragonfly - **72**:51

duck - pintail - **69**:6

eagle - bald - **70**:17; **71**:6; golden - **70**:17; white-tailed sea - **68**:54; **70**:17

eel - giant - **67**:36

elephant - **67**:14, 30; **70**:16, 64-65; Bardia - **70**:31-3; dwarf - **69**:47; Naumann - **69**:47

elephant bird - *Aepyornis maximus* - **70**:44; **72**:14

ellengassen - sloth? - **67**:'3

emela-ntouka - **67**:'2

emu - **71**:19; **72**:51

falcon - **67**:19; red-footed - **70**:17

fir - Grand - **70**:55

fish - **67**:19; **68**:15, 64, '10; **70**:12

flea - **68**:18

flower - largest, *Rafflesis arnoldi* - **70**:'2

fox - **68**:50

frog - **67**:6; **69**:6; giant - **67**:6; poisonous - **68**:15

frou-frou fish - **67**:19

fungus - **67**:63

gambo - **67**:35-37

garlic - **70**:9

goat - **67**:49; **68**:12; **69**:8, 12; **71**:8, 46; beer-swilling - **68**:10; fainting - **71**:63; hermaphrodite - **68**:10; talking - **68**:10

gorse - **71**:41

guenon - Suntail - **69**:10

guillemot - **68**:10

hamster - **68**:65

hare - **72**:37

herring - **67**:50

hippopotamus - pigmy - **69**:47

horse - **67**:26; **68**:7, 23-4, 29, 36, 42, 46-7, 52, 63; **71**:39; **72**:10, 52

horseshoe crab - *Limulus* - **67**:'4

hyena - *Hyaena brevirostris* - **67**:'2

ichthyosaur - **67**:37

insects - **68**:42

jungle cat - Asian, *Felis chaus* - **68**:50-1; **72**:46

kangaroo - **67**:65; **69**:56

Kellas cat - **68**:54

killer whale - **68**:13; Prude's Bay - **67**:36

king penguin - *Aptenodytes patagonica* - **70**:44

kinkajou - **69**:56

kiwi - **69**:43

kongamoto - flying lizard - **67**:'3

langur - Tenkin snub-nosed - **72**:14

larch - **68**:20; **70**:55

lemur - Golden Bamboo - **69**:10

leopard cat - Asian, *Felis bengalensis* - **68**:51

lion - **71**:11; escaped - **71**:16

lizard - **67**:17, 29, 39; eggs - **70**:18; giant - **67**:31; monitor - **70**:34; pigmy blue-tongue - **67**:17; water monitor, *Varanus niloticus* - **67**:17

llama - **69**:43

locust - swarm - **71**:47

Loch Ness monster - **68**:'12, 54; **70**:34, 46; **71**:20

lynx - **68**:50, 54
mackerel - **69**:8
magnolia - **69**:15
magpie - **68**:29
mammoth - **68**:42; **69**:47
marijuana - **72**:11
marmoset - **70**:18; Maués, *Callithrix mauesi* - **69**:10
marrow - **68**:19
marsupial lion - *Thylacaleo carnifex* - **67**:'2; **69**:11
marsupials - **67**:36
mau - cat - **72**:46
mbielu-mbielu-mbielu - **67**:'2
melon - **68**:7; **72**:10
mermaids, mermen - **70**:63
minhocao - glyptodont - **67**:'2
moa - **69**:42-43; upland, *Megalapteryx didinus* - **67**:'3; **69**:42
mokele-mbembe - **67**:'2, 28-31
monkey - **68**:13; **69**:10
moose - **72**:13
mosasaur - **67**:37
mosquito - **67**:6; **72**:51
moth - Death's Head hawk, *Acherontia atropos* - **70**:'3, 37
mouse - **68**:7; **71**:7; **72**:11; giant - **71**:9
mushrooms - magic - **71**:35-38
Nandi bear - **67**:'2
nautilus - chambered, *Neopilina* - **67**:'4
Newton's mihirung - *Genyornis newtoni* - **70**:44
oak - **70**:49; **71**:42
okapi - *Okapia johnstoni* - **67**:'4
olive tree - **71**:9
onza - **68**:54
orangutan - **68**:13
otter - **68**:13
owl - **69**:12; **70**:37; N. American barn owl, *Tyto alba pratincola (Bonaparte)* - **70**:37
pa fruit - **68**:10
palm tree - **72**:19
panther - black - **68**:50; Oberon - **69**:11; phantom - **69**:56
parrot - **69**:65; **71**:8, 64
peanut - **69**:19; **72**:19
peccary - **69**:56; Chacoan, *Catagonus wagneri* - **67**:'4
penguin - giant - **68**:54
periwinkle - **68**:6
pheasant - **72**:37
pig - **67**:65; **69**:11; **72**:10, 16, 63

pigeon - **69**:18
pine marten - **68**:54
pinnipeds - **67**:36-7
pitohui - hooded, *Pitohui dichrous* - **68**:15
piranha - **72**:17
pla beuk - *Pangasianodon gigas* - **69**:63
plankton - **68**:15
plesiosaur - **67**:'1, '3, 36-7
polecat - **68**:54
poplar - **71**:19
porpoise - Conchito - **67**:36
possum - mountain, *Burramys parvus* - **67**:'4
potoroo - **69**:7
prairie dog - **71**:11
puffin - **68**:10
puma - **68**:50, 54
python - **67**:65; **71**:19; giant - **67**:29
Queensland tiger - **67**:'2
rabbit - **69**:56; **71**:19; **72**:16
raccoon - rabid - **67**:19; **69**:56
rat - **69**:8; **71**:8; rat-king - **67**:55
raven - **67**:52
redwood - **70**:55
rhinoceros - **68**:42
rhododendron - **71**:40
ringtail - **69**:56
robin - **69**:65
rodents - **68**:18
rose - wild - **71**:41
row - **67**:'3
rubber plant - **69**:7
sasquatch - **71**:59
sea lilies - *crinoids* - **67**:'4
sea lion - **70**:46, 48
seal - **68**:13, 65; modified - **67**:36
sea-serpent - **67**:35-37; **70**:46-48
serpent - red - **67**:6; **71**:52
serval cat - **67**:36
shark - **67**:'1; **71**:25; **72**:48; basking - **67**:36; **70**:48; mega-mouth - **67**:35-6
sheep - **67**:52; **68**:23, 52, 63; **69**:17; **70**:17, 49; **71**:40, 64
slime mould - **68**:13
sloth - **67**:'3
snake - **67**:19, 24; **71**:5; **72**:18; black - **70**:16; brown - **67**:17; giant - **67**:'3
snipe - **69**:65
sole - **67**:19
spider - **68**:42; **70**:'3; **71**:34; brown recluse - **68**:19
spruce - Sitka - **70**:55

squirrel - red - **68**:54
starling - **68**:6; **69**:14, 65
sturgeon - **67**:10; Russian, *Huso huso* - **69**:63
swede - **72**:16
sycamore - **71**:11
tamarin - Black-faced lion - **69**:10
tapir - **69**:56
tatzelwurm - **67**:'2
temnospondyl - **69**:47
thallatosuchians - **67**:37
Thetis Lake creature - **70**:20, 63
thrush - **69**:65
thunderbird - **67**:'3, 64
tiger - **71**:34; mountain - **67**:'2
tiger-cat - **67**:31
toad - **68**:5; entombed - **67**:55
tobacco - **69**:49
tomato - **69**:15
tortoise - **68**:65
tree - **68**:7; unidentified seedling - **70**:10; Zelkova - **70**:55
tuatara - rhyncosaur, *Sphenodon punctatus* - **67**:l4
trout - **68**:6; **69**:8
tube worm - **68**:19
tuna - bluefin - **72**:7
turkey - **67**:37; **71**:16; giant - **67**:'2, 36
tzuchinoko - horned snake - **67**:'2
vegetable lamb - **68**:63
Vu Quang ox - *Pseudoryx nghetinhensis* - **72**:14
waheela - **67**:'2
waitoreke - **67**:'3
wallaby - **70**:63
walnut - **69**:19
walrus - **71**:11
weka - bird - **69**:43
whale - **67**:36, 49; Shepherd's Beaked, *Tasmacetus shepherdi* - **67**:36, 37; Japanese Beaked - **67**:36; serpentine, *archaeocete* - **67**:36
wheat - **68**:43
whitebeam, Swedish - **70**:55
wildcat - *Felis silvestris lybica* - **68**:54; **72**:46
wildmen - **67**:32-34
wolf - **68**:23, 54; great white - **67**:'2
worm - **70**:12
worms - intestinal - **70**:9
yak - **67**:'3
yeti - **67**:32-34; **68**:54; **70**:34
yew - **70**:55

ARTICLES, FEATURES and SERIES by TITLE

Age of the Earth
Garner, Paul - **69**:64
Age of the Earth
Milton, Richard - **69**:64
Albino Lobsters
Fowler, Christopher - **70**:64
Alien Bastards!
Stacy, Dennis - **68**:55
Angels to the Rescue
McClure, Kevin - **68**:34-37
Another Face on Mars
Sirisena, Ananda - **69**:64
Another Face on Mars
Spiromat, Bobby - **69**:64
Answer's in the Negative, The
Picknett, Lynn - **70**:54
Archive Gems 1: Italian Martians, The
Evans, Hilary - **67**:43
Archive Gems 2: Black Madonna of
Montserrat, The
Bord, Janet - **68**:48
Archive Gems 3: Bowhead Incident,
The
Rickard, Bob - **71**:46
Art of Jumping to Conclusions, The
Downes, Jonathan - **68**:54
Atheistic Religions
Wilson, Robert Anton - **68**:56
Battle Triangle Ghost, The
Green, Andrew - **67**:47
Bedevilled
Dash, Mike - **72**:47-49
Bibliomania
Nye, James - **71**:64
Big Sleep, The
Rickard, Bob + Olsson, Rolf J.K. -
72:23-29
Bird Death Mystery
Holland, Richard - **69**:65
Bird King
Thomas, Lars - **67**:63
Bird Rains
Shepard, Leslie - **71**:64
Birds, Sheep and Cremation Accidents
Chapman, Brian - **71**:64
Black Lagoon Revisited
Coleman, Loren - **70**:63
Bollock!
Gamon, David - **69**:63
Boneheads
Shipman, Pat - **70**:42-43
Brush with the Black Dog, A
Blamey, Claire - **70**:65
Cabin Fever
Anonymous - **70**:64
Case of the Missing Moa, The
Shuker, Dr Karl - **69**:42-43
Cat's Cradle
Doble, Adelaide - **67**:63

Che in the Clouds?
Billingsley, John - **71**:63
Childhood Terrors
Smith, Peter - **67**:65
Cloning Recipes
McLuskey, Anthony - **72**:53
Coincidence or Precognition?
Chrenkoff, Arthur - **67**:64
Commuting at 186,000 miles per hour
Sharville, Paul - **71**:56
Crop Correction
Schnabel, Jim - **71**:63
Crop Thickens, The
Michell, John - **68**:43
Curiouser and Curiouser
Roberts, Andy - **67**:53
Dead Funny
Noyes, Ralph - **70**:65
Deadly Alchemy
Sieveking, Paul - **69**:44-45
Devil's Brother-in-Law, The
Bayliss, Peter - **67**:24-27
Devil's Hoofprints
Radford, Benjamin - **70**:65
Down in the Jungle
Goss, Michael - **72**:56
Dragons of Vancouver, The
Dash, Mike - **70**:46-48
Dream Ticket
Johnson, D. - **68**:63
Driller Chiller
Sieveking, Paul - **72**:42-43
Dubious Translations
Screeton, Paul - **67**:55
Egg Voyagers
Shuker, Dr Karl - **70**:44
Elephant Sits on Mini - Again
Mays, Nick - **70**:64
Elusive Pig
Kirkwood, Jake - **72**:63
End was not Nigh, The
Penderton, John - **70**:64
Evolutionary Fast Food
Kollins, Martin - **70**:53
Face(s) in the Window, The
Haddington, The Earl of - **69**:65
Fainting Goats
Petersen, Todd L. - **71**:63
Fairy Tree in Peril
Rickard, Bob - **71**:42
Fax not from Limbo
Haines, Slim - **71**:63
Fear and Loathing in France
Sieveking, Paul - **67**:48
Feeling Cross
Rickard, Bob - **71**:48-49
Flashes in the Dark
McBeath, Alastair - **72**:65
Foetal Memory Metaphors

Greene, Yvonne - **71**:53
Foxing the Public
Volk, Stephen - **70**:56
Fractal Challenge
Dorje, K. Tendzin - **72**:63
Fractal Freaks
Fisher, Dr David J. - **70**:64
Frankenstein Vibrations
Carr, Peter - **71**:55
Gambo
Shuker, Dr Karl - **67**:35-37
Gas or God?
Gilmore, Christopher - **67**:65
Ghostwatch: Whatever Possessed
Parkinson?
Rickard, Bob - **67**:38-42
Giant Snakes
Cheetham, John - **67**:65
Given the Bird
Thomas, Lars - **69**:65
Golden Child
Dorje, Karma Tendzin - **69**:30-33
Great Mirabelli, The
Playfair, Guy Lyon - **71**:43-45
Grimsby Portents
Parker, Ainslie - **68**:63
Hallucination to Sit On, An
Inglis, Brian - **68**:53
Hard to Swallow
Rickard, Bob - **69**:48
Haunted Billabong, The
Kennedy, Bruce G. - **71**:64
Hawking Hawking
Stacy, Dennis - **67**:54
Herald Angel
Treharne, M - **68**:65
Hijacked?
Glickman, Michael - **70**:64
Horsewatch: Madness in the Home
Counties
Sieveking, Paul - **68**:46-47
Hot Stuff
Tinsley, Chris - **69**:23-26
I-Con Man
Young, Edward - **70**:35-37
Icy Mist
Carr, C. - **70**:64
Id, the Ego and the Supernatural, The
Noyes, Ralph - **69**:55
Importance of Timing
O'Neill, Mike - **69**:53
Impossible Solid?, An
Bruce, Anthony - **72**:63
In Search of the Yeti
Dash, Mike - **67**:32-34
Interview: Bill Gibbons
Rickard, Bob - **67**:28-31
Interview: Dr David Jacobs
Coleman, Tim - **69**:27-29

Interview: Jenny Cockell
  Rickard, Bob - 72:36-39
Interview: John Blashford-Snell
  Rickard, Bob - 70:30-34
Interview: Mary Seal
  Whittaker, Simon - 68:30-33
Interview: Terence McKenna
  Hodgkinson, Tom - 71:35-38
It Came from Outer Space!
  Dash, Mike - 71:'1-4
It was Crap
  Hallam, Mary - 71:64
Jung's Dream
  Roberts, Frank - 71:65
Largest Fish Clarification
  Wood, Susan - 69:63
Lenticular Cloud
  Brady, Eric R. - 70:63
Letter-box Amputations
  Leigh, Dr John - 68:65
Levitation
  Elliott, R.N. - 71:65
Living Fossils
  Shuker, Dr Karl - 67:'1-4
Localised Combustions
  Rubinstein, Prof. Bill - 72:65
Lovecats, The
  Shuker, Dr Karl - 68:50-51
Lovecats: The Next Generation
  Shuker, Dr Karl - 72:46
Lunchtime at the Phantom Diner
  Clark, Tony - 69:34-35
Marketing Blunder
  Dehon, Robert - 72:63
Matter of Meteors, A
  McBeath, Alastair - 68:64
Meeting Pan
  Ritchie, John D. - 72:64
Memories of Hell
  Schnabel, Jim - 71:24-32
MIA Photo Mystery, The
  Halstead, Richard - 69:50-51
Missing Links
  Wood, Colin - 69:54
Missing Time
  Brookesmith, Peter - 72:44-45
Modern Fairy Tales
  Lazell, David - 71:39-41
Münch Bunch, The
  Schnabel, Jim - 70:23-29
Munchausen's Syndrome
  Wilson, Robert Anton - 72:65
Music to our Ears
  Hayes, Anthony - 69:64
Not a Kangaroo
  Godthelp, H. - 67:65
Obituary: Brian Inglis
  West, Ruth - 68:16
Odd Rings
  Owens, Andrew John - 71:65
Of Cats and Shopping Trolleys
  Lies, Christopher - 70:63

Other Half, The
  Rickard, Bob - 68:44-45
Parrot Chicken Minder
  Woodward, Ken - 69:65
Pick of the Crops
  Schnabel, Jim - 69:37-41
Pimlico Mystery, The
  Warren, Nick - 67:65
Poor Cow
  Sieveking, Paul + Stillings, Dennis - 68:23-29
Preposterous Perception
  Wilson, Robert Anton - 72:54
Prudes from Space
  Keyworth, David - 69:63
Quake Miracle
  Lavery, Eileen - 72:65
Radiometric Dating
  Kollerstrom, Nick - 68:65
Radiometric Dating
  Lippard, Jim - 68:65
Randi Replies
  Randi, James - 71:64
Rational Debate
  Clark, Jerome - 71:63
Really Out-of-Place
  Coleman, Loren - 69:56
Reds in the Pond
  Harte, Jeremy - 68:65
Rent-a-Read
  Callaghan, Nigel A. - 67:64
Rent-a-Read
  Longhorn, David - 67:64
Respect for Alien Abductions
  Clark, Jerome - 68:64
Rigor Tortoise
  Peters, Ian T. - 68:65
Rip-off
  Anonymous - 72:63
Roswell the Terrible
  Stacy, Dennis - 72:55
Rovers Return
  Sieveking, Paul - 70:38-41
Sai Baba's Miracles
  Lippard, Jim - 69:64
Secret Country 7: Dinas Bran
  Bord, Janet + Colin - 67:52
Secret Country 8: Eildon Hills
  Bord, Janet + Colin - 68:52
Secret Country 9: Cerne Abbas
  Bord, Janet + Colin - 69:52
Secret Country 10: Trellech
  Bord, Janet + Colin - 70:52
Secret Country 11: Callanish
  Bord, Janet & Colin - 71:52
Secret Country 12: Silbury Hill
  Bord, Janet + Colin - 72:52
Shaman Robin
  Beswick, Tim - 67:63
Sharp Practice
  Green, Prof. Robert T. - 67:64
Sheerwater Fish Fall

Gosling, Derek - 68:64
Shooting Down the Myth
  Fleming, Glenn B. - 72:30-34
Shrouded Retort
  Wilson, Ian - 71:65
Silent Cities in the Sky
  Miles, Ian - 68:64
Snap Happy
  Rickard, Bob - 70:'2-3
Solar Phenomenon
  Jones, Nigel - 72:64
Spirit versus Energy
  Sutton, David - 67:56
Surgical Rumours and Thunderbirds
  Chapman, Brian - 67:64
Tricks of the Trees
  Mitchell, Alan - 70:55
Trolley Travel
  Picek, Aldo Z. - 69:63
Unearthed: Footprints in the Sands of
  Time
  Moore, Steve - 69:47
Unearthed: Fresco Fiasco
  Moore, Steve - 68:42
Unearthed: Mini Mammoths Linger
  Longer
  Moore, Steve - 69:47
Unearthed: Mystery of the Pharaohs
  Moore, Steve - 70:51
Unearthed: Shooting Tsars
  Moore, Steve - 67:45
Unearthed: Something Nazi
  Moore, Steve - 67:44-45
Unearthed: Subterranean Submarine
  Moore, Steve - 72:50
Unexpected Birth Cycles
  Baker, Gerald - 71:54
Valley Fever
  McLoren, Kirk - 67:63
Vampire of Croglin Grange, The
  Drapkin, C.M. - 68:39-41
Vegetable Lambs and the Drunkard's
  Fate
  Costello, Peter - 68:63
Very Local Weather
  Harrington, Julia - 67:63
Von Daniken Got There First
  Langbein, Walter J. - 69:65
Water Babies
  Rickard, Bob - 67:46
We Stand Corrected
  Howlett, N.M. - 70:65
Webs of War, The
  Sieveking, Paul - 71:34
Weird
  Preston, Steven - 68:63
Who's in Charge Here?
  Sandy, Tony - 72:63
Who's Spying on Sweden?
  Rosen, Sven - 67:50-51

BOOKS REVIEWED by TITLE

Afterlife, The (1993)
Randles, Jenny + Hough, Peter - **69**:61

American Discovery (1992)
Thompson, Gunnar - **67**:58

America's First Crop Circle (1992)
Cyr, Donald (ed) - **69**:60

Arktos (1993)
Godwin, Joscelyn - **69**:60

Atlantis (1992)
Ashe, Geoffrey - **71**:62

Avalonians, The (1993)
Benham, Patrick - **72**:62

Ayurveda (1992)
Svoboda, Robert E. - **67**:58

Beast of Exmoor, The (1993)
Francis, Di - **71**:60

Beast Within, The (1992)
Douglas, Adam - **72**:62

Best of British Men (1993)
(Anon.) - **72**:62

Best of British Women (1993)
(Anon.) - **72**:62

Biological Anomalies: Humans 2 (1993)
Corliss, William R. - **71**:61

Blast Your Way to Megabuck$ ... Sex-power Formula (1993)
Dukes, Ramsey - **70**:60

Brother Twelve (1992)
Oliphant, John - **67**:59

Bye-gones (1992)
Holland, Richard - **67**:61

Caspar Hauser (1992)
Wassermann, Jakob - **68**:60

Character of Physical Law, The (1992)
Feynman, Richard P. - **70**:61

Coldrum Line, The (1993)
Clampitt, F. Russell + Peters, Leslie J. - **72**:62

Columbus Myth, The (1992)
Wilson, Ian - **68**:61

Columbus was Last (1992)
Huyghe, Patrick - **70**:62

Condensed Chaos (1992)
Hine, Phil - **67**:60

Confusion of Prophets, A (1992)
Curry, Patrick - **71**:60

Crop Circles: A Mystery Solved (1993)
Randles, Jenny + Fuller, Paul - **71**:62

Damned Universe of Charles Fort, The (1993)
Kaplan, Louis - **72**:61

Dao De King (1992)
Lao Tzu - **70**:62

Dark Doorway of the Beast (1992)
Hewitson-May, Gareth - **67**:60

Death, Dissection and the Destitute (1989)
Richardson, Ruth - **67**:60

Demons, Doctors and Aliens (1993)
Pontilillo, James - **69**:59

Devil's Notebook, The (1992)
LaVey, Anton Szandor - **70**:62

Dowsing: New Light on an Ancient Art (1993)
Williamson, Tom - **71**:62

Enchantment of the Trossachs, The (1992)
Stott, Louis - **68**:61

Encyclopedia of Ghosts and Spirits, The (1992)
Guiley, Rosemary Ellen - **67**:61

Encyclopedia of Strange & Unexplained ... Phenomena (1993)
Clark, Jerome - **71**:59

Extra Sensory Perception (1992)
MacLellan, Alastair W. - **72**:62

Fandemonium! (1992)
Vermorel, Judy & Fred - **72**:62

Fearful Symmetry: Is God a Geometer? (1993)
Golubitsky, Martin + Stuart, Ian - **71**:62

Finders Keepers (1992)
Purcell, Rosamund Wolff + Gould, Stephen Jay - **68**:60

Fire in the Sky (1993)
(Film) - **69**:62

Forbidden Archeology (1993)
Cremo, Michael A. + Thompson, Richard L. - **72**:59

Fractals (1992)
Briggs, John - **69**:60

Gemstone File, The (1992)
Keith, Jim - **68**:60

Genesis Revisited (1991)
Sitchin, Zecharia - **67**:59

Ghosts and Legends of Yorkshire (1992)
Roberts, Andy - **72**:62

Gmicalzoma (1992)
Vinci, Leo - **72**:62

Goddess Hekate, The (1992)
Ronan, Stephen (ed) - **69**:60

Haunted Nottinghamshire Vol. 2 (1993)
Moakes, Len - **71**:59

Healey and Glanvill's Urban Myths (1992)
Healey, Phil + Glanvill, Rick - **70**:60

Hecate's Fountain (1992)
Grant, Kenneth - **71**:62

Holy Place, The (1993)

Lincoln, Henry - **71**:61

In Search of the Dead (1992)
Iverson, Jeffrey - **70**:62

In Search of the Neanderthals (1993)
Stringer, Chris + Gamble, Clive - **71**:62

Intro. to the Magical Elements of the Bible, An (1991)
Stutley, Margaret - **70**:61

Jung for Beginners (1992)
Hyde, Maggie + McGuinness, Michael - **70**:62

Liber TzBa (1992)
Crowley, Aleister - **67**:60

Little Dutch Boy, The (1993)
Hearn, Ronald - **72**:62

Materialisations (1992)
Boddington, Harry - **71**:61

Matter Myth, The (1992)
Davies, Paul + Gribbin, John - **69**:59

Méliès: Father of Film Fantasy (1993)
(Exhibition) - **68**:61

Messengers of Destiny (?)
(Video) - **71**:60

Millennium Prophecies (1992)
Mann, A.T. - **68**:60

Missing Pieces (1992)
Baker, Robert A. + Nickell, Joe - **69**:61

On Jung (1991)
Stevens, Anthony - **70**:62

Only Planet of Choice, The (1993)
Schlemma, Phyllis V. + Jenkins, Palden - **72**:60

Other Meridians: Another Greenwich (1993)
Gale, Jack - **72**:62

Paranormal Year, The (1993)
Randles, Jenny - **72**:59

Passport to Magonia (1993)
Vallee, Jacques - **70**:62

Plains of San Agustin Controversy, The (1992)
Eberhart, George - **70**:60

Prime Chaos (1993)
Hine, Phil - **72**:60

Robin Hood (1993)
Wilson, Steve - **69**:60

Round in Circles (1993)
Schnabel, Jim - **70**:59

Sasquatch/Bigfoot (1993)
Hunter, Don + Dahinden, Ren͞- **71**:59

Schwa (1993)
Barker, Bill - **72**:62

Science Gap, The (1992) - **70**:61
Rothman, Milton A. -

Sell Yourself to Science (1992)
  Hogshire, Jim - **72**:62
Shamanism and the Mystery Lines (1992)
  Devereux, Paul - **72**:60
Sign and the Seal, The (1992)
  Hancock, Graham - **68**:59
Silbury Treasure, The (1992)
  Dames, Michael - **70**:62
SLI Effect, The (1993)
  Evans, Hilary - **71**:62
Spaceship Conspiracy (?)
  Knap, George - **70**:60
Struggle to Understand, The (1992)
  Corben, Herbert C. - **70**:61
Superstitions (1992)
  Lorie, Peter - **70**:60
Symbolic Landscapes (1992)
  Devereux, Paul - **72**:60
Temple, The (1993)
  Lundquist, John M. - **71**:62

Terrestrial Connection, The (?)
  (Video) - **71**:60
Theory of Almost Everything, A (1993)
  Barry, Robert - **72**:61
Tibetan Medical Paintings (?)
  Parfionovitch, Y. + Dorje, G. + Meyer, F. - **68**:59
UFO Encounters (1992)
  Clark, Jerome - **68**:60
Ultima Thule (1992)
  King, Bernard - **71**:62
Unexplained: 347 Strange Sightings ... (etc) (1993)
  Clark, Jerome - **71**:59
Universe and I, The (1993)
  Ferris, Timothy + Pinn, Ingrid - **70**:62
Unusual Personal Experiences (?)
  Anon. - **70**:60
Vampyres (1992)

Frayling, Christopher - **68**:62
Visions: Complete Astrology System (1992)
  (Computer program) - **67**:61
Warp, The (?)
  (Video) - **71**:60
Weather Watch (1992)
  Moss, Stephen + Simons, Paul - **67**:61
Where Science & Magic Meet (1991)
  Roney-Dougal, Serena - **71**:62
Whole Person Catalogue, The (1992)
  Considine, Mike (ed) - **70**:62
Widow of Borley, The (1992)
  Wood, Robert - **67**:61
Write Stuff, The (1992)
  Beyerstein, Barry L. + Dale F. - **67**:61
Year of the Sorrats, The (1992)
  Richards, John Thomas - **69**:60

BOOKS REVIEWED by AUTHOR

Anon.
  Best of British Men (1993) - **72**:62
  Best of British Women (1993) - **72**:62
  Unusual Personal Experiences (?) - **70**:60
Ashe, Geoffrey
  Atlantis (1992) - **71**:62
Baker, Robert A. + Nickell, Joe
  Missing Pieces (1992) - **69**:61
Barker, Bill
  Schwa (1993) - **72**:62
Barry, Robert
  Theory of Almost Everything, A (1993) - **72**:61
Benham, Patrick
  Avalonians, The (1993) - **72**:62
Beyerstein, Barry L. + Dale F.
  Write Stuff, The (1992) - **67**:61
Boddington, Harry
  Materialisations (1992) - **71**:61
Briggs, John
  Fractals (1992) - **69**:60
Clampitt, F. Russell + Peters, Leslie J.
  Coldrum Line, The (1993) - **72**:62
Clark, Jerome
  Encyclopedia of Strange & Un-explained ... Phenomena (1993) - **71**:59
  UFO Encounters (1992) - **68**:60
  Unexplained: 347 Strange Sight-ings ... (etc) (1993) - **71**:59
(Computer program)
  Visions: Complete Astrology System (1992) - **67**:61

Considine, Mike (ed)
  Whole Person Catalogue, The (1992) - **70**:62
Corben, Herbert C.
  Struggle to Understand, The (1992) - **70**:61
Corliss, William R.
  Biological Anomalies: Humans 2 (1993) - **71**:61
Cremo, Michael A. + Thompson, Richard L.
  Forbidden Archeology (1993) - **72**:59
Crowley, Aleister
  Liber TzBa (1992) - **67**:60
Curry, Patrick
  Confusion of Prophets, A (1992) - **71**:60
Cyr, Donald (ed)
  America's First Crop Circle (1992) - **69**:60
Dames, Michael
  Silbury Treasure, The (1992) - **70**:62
Davies, Paul + Gribbin, John
  Matter Myth, The (1992) - **69**:59
Devereux, Paul
  Shamanism and the Mystery Lines (1992) - **72**:60
  Symbolic Landscapes (1992) - **72**:60
Douglas, Adam
  Beast Within, The (1992) - **72**:62
Dukes, Ramsey
  Blast Your Way to Megabuck$ ...

Sex-power Formula (1993) - **70**:60
Eberhart, George
  Plains of San Agustin Contro-versy, The (1992) - **70**:60
Evans, Hilary
  SLI Effect, The (1993) - **71**:62
(Exhibition)
  M¯ı s:Father of Film Fantasy (1993) - **68**:61
Ferris, Timothy + Pinn, Ingrid
  Universe and I, The (1993) - **70**:62
Feynman, Richard P.
  Character of Physical Law, The (1992) - **70**:61
(Film)
  Fire in the Sky (1993) - **69**:62
Francis, Di
  Beast of Exmoor, The (1993) - **71**:60
Frayling, Christopher
  Vampyres (1992) - **68**:62
Gale, Jack
  Other Meridians: Another Greenwich (1993) - **72**:62
Godwin, Joscelyn
  Arktos (1993) - **69**:60
Golubitsky, Martin + Stuart, Ian
  Fearful Symmetry: Is God a Geometer? (1993) - **71**:62
Grant, Kenneth
  Hecate's Fountain (1992) - **71**:62
Guiley, Rosemary Ellen
  Encyclopedia of Ghosts and

338

Spirits, The (1992) - **67**:61

Hancock, Graham
Sign and the Seal, The (1992) - **68**:59

Healey, Phil + Glanvill, Rick
Healey and Glanvill's Urban Myths (1992) - **70**:60

Hearn, Ronald
Little Dutch Boy, The (1993) - **72**:62

Hewitson-May, Gareth
Dark Doorway of the Beast (1992) - **67**:60

Hine, Phil
Condensed Chaos (1992) - **67**:60
Prime Chaos (1993) - **72**:60

Hogshire, Jim
Sell Yourself to Science (1992) - **72**:62

Holland, Richard
Bye-gones (1992) - **67**:61

Hunter, Don + Dahinden, René
Sasquatch/Bigfoot (1993) - **71**:59

Huyghe, Patrick
Columbus was Last (1992) - **70**:62

Hyde, Maggie + McGuinness, Michael
Jung for Beginners (1992) - **70**:62

Iverson, Jeffrey
In Search of the Dead (1992) - **70**:62

Kaplan, Louis
Damned Universe of Charles Fort, The (1993) - **72**:61

Keith, Jim
Gemstone File, The (1992) - **68**:60

King, Bernard
Ultima Thule (1992) - **71**:62

Knap, George
Spaceship Conspiracy (?) - **70**:60

Lao Tzu
Dao De King (1992) - **70**:62

LaVey, Anton Szandor
Devil's Notebook, The (1992) - **70**:62

Lincoln, Henry
Holy Place, The (1993) - **71**:61

Lorie, Peter
Superstitions (1992) - **70**:60

Lundquist, John M.
Temple, The (1993) - **71**:62

MacLellan, Alastair W.
Extra Sensory Perception (1992) - **72**:62

Mann, A.T.
Millennium Prophecies (1992) - **68**:60

Moakes, Len
Haunted Nottinghamshire Vol. 2 (1993) - **71**:59

Moss, Stephen + Simons, Paul
Weather Watch (1992) - **67**:61

Oliphant, John
Brother Twelve (1992) - **67**:59

Parfionovitch, Y. + Dorje, G. + Meyer, F.
Tibetan Medical Paintings (?) - **68**:59

Pontilillo, James
Demons, Doctors and Aliens (1993) - **69**:59

Purcell, Rosamund Wolff + Gould, Stephen Jay
Finders Keepers (1992) - **68**:60

Randles, Jenny
Paranormal Year, The (1993) - **72**:59

Randles, Jenny + Fuller, Paul
Crop Circles: A Mystery Solved (1993) - **71**:62

Randles, Jenny + Hough, Peter
Afterlife, The (1993) - **69**:61

Richards, John Thomas
Year of the Sorrats, The (1992) - **69**:60

Richardson, Ruth
Death, Dissection and the Destitute (1989) - **67**:60

Roberts, Andy
Ghosts and Legends of Yorkshire (1992) - **72**:62

Ronan, Stephen (ed)
Goddess Hekate, The (1992) - **69**:60

Roney-Dougal, Serena
Where Science & Magic Meet (1991) - **71**:62

Rothman, Milton A.
Science Gap, The (1992) - **70**:61

Schlemma, Phyllis V. + Jenkins, Palden
Only Planet of Choice, The (1993) - **72**:60

Schnabel, Jim
Round in Circles (1993) - **70**:59

Sitchin, Zecharia
Genesis Revisited (1991) - **67**:59

Stevens, Anthony
On Jung (1991) - **70**:62

Stott, Louis
Enchantment of the Trossachs, The (1992) - **68**:59

Stringer, Chris + Gamble, Clive
In Search of the Neanderthals (1993) - **71**:62

Stutley, Margaret
Intro. to the Magical Elements of the Bible, An (1991) - **70**:61

Svoboda, Robert E.
Ayurveda (1992) - **67**:58

Thompson, Gunnar
American Discovery (1992) - **67**:58

Vallee, Jacques
Passport to Magonia (1993) - **70**:62

Vermorel, Judy & Fred
Fandemonium! (1992) - **72**:62

(Video)
Messengers of Destiny (?) - **71**:60
Terrestrial Connection, The (?) - **71**:60
Warp, The (?) - **71**:60

Vinci, Leo
Gmicalzoma (1992) - **72**:62

Wassermann, Jakob
Caspar Hauser (1992) - **68**:60

Williamson, Tom
Dowsing: New Light on an Ancient Art (1993) - **71**:62

Wilson, Ian
Columbus Myth, The (1992) - **68**:61

Wilson, Steve
Robin Hood (1993) - **69**:60

Wood, Robert
Widow of Borley, The (1992) - **67**:61

PLACES

Aalborg, Denmark - **69**:7
Acapulco, Mexico - **68**:29
Ada, OK, USA - **72**:18
Adams Branch, KY, USA - **71**:19
Adams River, BC, Canada - **70**:46
Adelaide, Australia - **67**:17; **69**:12, 49; **70**:18
Agoo, La Union, Philippines - **68**:9
Ainstable, Cumbria, England - **68**:41
Akcadag, Malatya, Turkey - **67**:9
Akpinar, Turkey - **72**:50
Alabama, USA - **72**:10
Alacam, Samsun, Turkey - **71**:9
Alamosa, CO, USA - **68**:23-4
Aland Sea, Sweden - **67**:50
Alaska, USA - **67**:'2; **68**:64; **70**:15, 39
Albany, Jamaica - **68**:10
Alberta, Canada - **68**:24
Albuquerque, NM, USA - **67**:13; **71**:12, 19
Aldeburgh, Suffolk, England - **69**:6
Aldermaston, Berks, England - **67**:45
Aldridge, Staffs, England - **68**:30
Alexandria, Egypt - **68**:6; **69**:16; **70**:40
Alexandroff Glacier, Mongolia - **70**:32
Al-Hoceima, Morocco - **70**:10
Alice Springs, Australia - **70**:17
Alps, The - **67**:'2
Alto Adige, Italy - **67**:19
Alton, Hants, England - **68**:47
Alton Barnes, Wilts, England - **68**:43; **69**:41
Amazon jungle, Peru - **67**:65
Amazon River, Brazil - **67**:'2; **69**:10
Amazonia - **67**:31; **71**:38
America, continent - **67**:58
Amritsar, India - **69**:9
Amsterdam, Holland - **67**:12; **70**:42
Andra Pradesh, India - **71**:47
Anholt Island, Denmark - **72**:50
Angola - **68**:63
Antarctica - **67**:36, 49; **68**:31; **70**:'2
Antioch - **70**:36
Apple Valley, CA, USA - **70**:41
Appleton, Cheshire, England - **72**:14
Arab, AL, USA - **70**:41
Argentina - **67**:'3-'4; **72**:13
Arizona, USA - **67**:63; **68**:18, 29; **70**:39
Arkhangelsk, Russia - **68**:13
Arlington, VA, USA - **69**:56
Armentieres, France - **70**:38
Arnhem, Holland - **67**:13
Arran, Scotland - **71**:40
Aspen, CO, USA - **72**:14
Assam, India - **70**:33

Atlantic Ocean, north - **71**:46
Aurora, TX, USA - **72**:55
Australia - **67**:'2; **69**:6; **70**:15; **71**:10
Austria - **68**:54; **69**:44; **71**:14; **72**:12
Avebury, Wilts, England - **68**:43; **69**:41; **72**:52
Aveley, Essex, England - **71**:'4
Avon, ME, USA - **69**:14
Ayers Rock, Australia - **70**:17
Axum, Ethiopia - **69**:65
Azle, TX, USA - **68**:29
Baci Forest, Romania - **70**:15
Bai River, Congo - **67**:28-9
Baden-Baden, Germany - **67**:6
Bagdogra, Bengal, India - **70**:16
Baghdad, Iraq - **69**:44
Bago City, Philippines - **68**:9
Bahia Blanca, Argentina - **68**:6
Baker City, OR, USA - **72**:12
Bakersfield, USA - **67**:63
Baltimore, USA - **70**:14
Banbury, Oxon, England - **67**:11; **69**:13
Bangalore, India - **67**:14
Bangladesh - **71**:47
Bangkok, Thailand - **72**:9
Bari, Italy - **70**:39
Barking, Essex, England - **68**:12
Barrow, AK, USA - **71**:47
Barrow-in-Furness, Cumbria, England - **71**:47
Basel, Switzerland - **67**:26
Bashkortostan, Russia - **71**:47
Bath, Avon, England - **69**:41
Baton Rouge, LA, USA - **69**:12
Battle, Sussex, England - **67**:47
Beaufort, SC, USA - **71**:14
Beckhampton, Wilts, England - **68**:43; **69**:41
Beersheba, Israel - **70**:10
Beijing, China - **67**:15; **71**:5-6, 15
Belarus - **72**:51
Belfast, N. Ireland - **69**:19; **70**:19
Belfond, Northumberland, England - **70**:17
Belgium - **68**:43
Belize - **67**:31
Belgrade, Serbia - **71**:34
Bennington, VT, USA - **70**:18
Benson, Oxon, England - **70**:63
Benue River, Adamwa, Nigeria - **71**:6
Berga, Sweden - **67**:50
Berkshire, England - **69**:41
Berkeley, CA, USA - **69**:12; **71**:35
Berlin, Germany - **67**:44; **69**:15
Bermuda Triangle - **72**:20
Berryville, AK, USA - **68**:29

Bevealan, Samsun, Turkey - **71**:9
Beverly Hills, CA, USA - **71**:28, 30
Bewbush, Sussex, England - **69**:12
Bhuj-rudramata, India - **69**:49
Bielefeld, Germany - **68**:7
Bihar, India - **72**:18
Birkdale, Merseyside, England - **71**:11
Birmingham, AL, USA - **69**:49; **71**:13
Birmingham, Warks, England - **67**:18-9; **68**:18; **72**:12
Bishops Canning, Wilts, England - **69**:41
Bishops Stortford, Herts, England - **68**:47
Bizen, Okayama, Japan - **67**:10
Bjarkskar, Sweden - **67**:50
Blackburn, Lancs, England - **71**:10
Blackpool, Lancs, England - **68**:'6; **69**:7
Black Sea - **67**:32
Blaine County, OK, USA - **68**:29
Blenheim, New Zealand - **72**:11
Blue Nile - **70**:30
Bnai Brak, Israel - **72**:15
Bodedern, Anglesey, Wales - **68**:6; **69**:65
Bocave River, Philippines - **72**:18
Bodmin, Cornwall, England - **72**:12
Bogota, Colombia - **67**:49
Boha village, Congo - **67**:29-31
Bolivia - **67**:31
Bombay, India - **67**:12; **72**:18, 51
Boonville, MO, USA - **71**:63
Boras, Sweden - **70**:10
Borley Rectory, Essex, England - **67**:56, 59
Borneo - **68**:54
Boston, MA, USA - **70**:28; **71**:36
Botley, Hants, England - **68**:47
Bowden, GA, USA - **67**:11
Boynton Beach, FL, USA - **71**:19
Bradenton, FL, USA - **72**:17
Braga, Portugal - **67**:41
Braintree, Essex, England - **70**:40
Branco, Brazil - **72**:29
Brandon, Suffolk, England - **71**:14
Brands Hatch, Kent, England - **67**:55
Brazil - **68**:54, '13; **69**:63; **71**:20, 43-45, '4
Brazzaville, Congo - **67**:28, 30-1
Bremen, Germany - **72**:29
Bremer Bay, Australia - **70**:44
Brentwood, Essex, England - **68**:19
Bridgnorth, Shrops, England - **68**:51
Brisbane, Australia - **72**:45
Bristol, Avon, England - **67**:65; **68**:13; **69**:39; **72**:12-3

British Columbia, Canada - 67:59; 70:15
Britain - 69:45; 71:10, 54
Brule River, WI, USA - 71:19
Bucharest, Romania - 72:10
Buckinghamshire, England - 68:43, 46
Budapest, Hungary - 69:8
Buinaksk, Dagesan, Russia - 67:32
Bulawayo, Zimbabwe - 69:15
Bulgaria - 69:44
Burford, Oxon, England - 68:47
Burlington, Ontario, Canada - 68:5
Burra, Australia - 67:17
Bursa, Turkey - 71:9
Burton-on-Trent, Staffs, England - 69:17
Busia, Kenya - 71:8
Butte City, ID, USA - 70:41
Buttevant, Ireland - 70:38
Buyukcekmece, Turkey - 67:9
Cabbarus County, NC, USA - 68:29
Cadboro Bay, BC, Canada - 70:48
Cairngorms, Scotland - 68:49
Cairo, Egypt - 67:49; 69:16; 71:17
Calabash, NC, USA - 71:16
Calais, France - 67:48
Calcutta, India - 70:38
Caldwell, KS, USA - 68:25
Cali, Colombia - 67:49
Callanish, Lewis, Outer Hebrides, Scotland - 71:52
Calumet, OK, USA - 68:25
California, USA - 67:36, '3; 68:13, 18; 69:7, 13, 25, 56; 71:20, 54; 72:42-3, 54
Cambridge, Cambs, England - 67:54
Cambridgeshire, England - 69:38
Cambodia - 69:50-51
Cameron Highlands, Malaysia - 71:65
Cameroon - 67:29, 31
Campeche, Yucatan, Mexico - 67:49; 68:6
Canada - 67:49, '2; 70:13; 71:54
Cape Cod, MA, USA - 72:50
Cape St. George, Newfoundland, Canada - 72:7
Caracas, Venezuela - 67:16
Cardiff, Wales - 69:63; 70:38; 71:24
Carisbrooke Castle, Isle of Wight, England - 71:12
Carlisle, Cumbria, England - 72:12
Cartoosa, OK, USA - 70:49
Caspian Sea - 68:63
Castle Gresley, Staffs, England - 69:17
Caucasus mountains - 67:32-3
Cayonu, Turkey - 71:9
Cennina, Italy - 67:43
Cerne Abbas, Dorset, England - 69:52

Cervantes, Australia - 70:44; 72:14
Ceylon - 70:31
Chad - 67:'2
Chaffee County, CO, USA - 68:18
Chamdo, Tibet - 69:33
Chandler, AZ, USA - 70:19
Charles County, VA, USA - 69:18
Charleston, SC, USA - 68:19
Charlieville, Trinidad - 67:14
Chatanooga, TN, USA - 69:49
Chatham Islands, Canada - 70:46
Chedington, Dorset, England - 70:40
Cheesefoot Head, Hants, England - 69:38
Chelmsford, Essex, England - 70:12
Chesham, Bucks, England - 69:7
Chiba, Japan - 68:19
Chicago, IL, USA - 68:6; 69:32, 56; 72:45
Chichester, Sussex, England - 72:29
Chigusa, Japan - 67:'2
China - 67:33; 68:63; 71:47
Chinnor, Bucks, England - 70:17; 72:7
Cholla, S. Korea - 67:10
Chongqing, China - 70:9
Christchurch, New Zealand - 67:'1; 72:47
Chula, MO, USA - 70:40
Cincinnati, OH, USA - 71:7
Clark County, WA, USA - 68:29
Clevedon, Avon, England - 70:18; 72:12
Clifton, England - 68:35, 37
Cluj, Romania - 70:15
Coathill, Cumbria, England - 68:41
Cold River, Canada - 69:26
Cologne, Germany - 71:20
Colombia - 70:34
Colombo, Sri Lanka - 69:49
Colorado, USA - 68:18, 24, 27; 71:11; 72:12
Columbus, OH, USA - 68:'13
Comanche County, OK, USA - 68:29
Commerce City, CO, USA - 71:19
Coney Island, NY, USA - 70:20
Congo - 67:'2; 70:33
Connabarabran, Australia - 71:64
Constantinople - 70:36
Cookham Dean, Berks, England - 71:41
Cooperville, OH, USA - 69:18
Corbridge, Northumberland, England - 69:52
Cordoba, Argentina - 71:8
Corehampton, Hants, England - 68:47
Cornwall, England - 70:40; 71:41
Corona, NM, USA - 70:60
Corrales, NM, USA - 70:65
Cosham, Hants, England - 67:8

Cracow, Poland - 67:24
Craigieburn Range, S. Island, New Zealand - 69:42-3
Crediton, Devon, England - 68:14
Crete, Greece - 72:24
Crimea, Russia - 68:41
Croatia - 71:34
Croglin, Cumbria, England - 68:39-41
Croix, France - 70:15
Crom Castle, Fermanagh, N. Ireland - 70:55
Cuba - 69:49; 72:28
Cumbria, England - 68:52
Cumwhitton, Cumbria, England - 68:41
Cydonia, Mars - 69:64
Cyprus - 69:47
Dadeville, AL, USA - 68:7
Dallas, TX, USA - 71:10; 72:20, 30-34
Damanhour, Egypt - 69:16
Danbury, CT, USA - 69:13
Darlington, ID, USA - 70:41
Dartmoor, Devon, England - 68:51
Dartmouth, Devon, England - 71:14
Dartmouth, Nova scotia, Canada - 68:19
Daruvar, Croatia - 71:34
Darwin, Australia - 70:39
Dawlish, Devon, England - 72:16
Dayton, OH, USA - 68:25; 72:55
Dead Cow River, Atacama Desert, Chile - 70:13
Dead Sea - 70:'2
Dearborn, MI, USA - 71:14
Debrecen, Hungary - 68:12
Decatur, AL, USA - 68:20; 70:41
De Courcy Island, Canada - 70:46
Dedelow, Germany - 68:20
Delaware, USA - 72:12
Delhi, India - 69:9
Denmark - 68:12; 69:33; 70:16
Denver, CO, USA - 68:7; 69:56
Derbyshire, England - 71:49
Detroit, MI, USA - 71:16
Deva, Romania - 68:19
Devizes, Wilts, England - 69:41; 72:52
Devon, England - 67:19; 68:43; 70:40
Dewsbury, Yorks, England - 72:19
Dhaka, Bangladesh - 72:18
Discovery Island, Canada - 70:46, 48
Djambala, Congo - 70:18
Dobbs Ferry, NY, USA - 72:6
Donadea, Kildare, Ireland - 68:44
Donalsonville, GA, USA - 72:19
Doncaster, Yorks, England - 70:65; 71:8; 72:16
Donegal, Ireland - 71:11
Donetsk, Ukraine - 68:19

Dordogne, France - **72**:51
Dorset, England - **69**:38; **70**:7
Dover, Kent, England - **68**:8, 10
Doyran, Samsun, Turkey - **71**:9
Drumtochty, Scotland - **70**:55 Dublin, Ireland - **68**:44; **72**:37
Dubuque, IA, USA - **69**:6
Dulce, NM, USA - **68**:33
Duluth, MN, USA - **68**:7
Dunblane, Perths, Scotland - **69**:11
Dundalk, Louth, Ireland - **69**:15
Dundee, Scotland - **70**:38
Dungeness, Kent, England - **68**:10
Dusseldorf, Germany - **72**:17
East Olympia, WA, USA - **71**:27
Edenton, NC, USA - **71**:25-7
Edinburgh, Scotland - **68**:7, 18, 49; **72**:10, 64
Edmonton, Canada - **68**:29
Effingham, Vancouver, Canada - **70**:48
Egypt - **67**:18; **69**:18-9; **72**:46
Eilat, Israel - **67**:46
Eildon Hills, Roxburghs, Scotland - **68**:52
Ekaterinburg, Russia - **67**:45; **69**:44-5
El-Alamain, Egypt - **69**:19
Elburton, Devon, England - **72**:13
Ellesmere Port, Cheshire, England - **70**:64
Ellos, Orust Island, Sweden - **71**:7
El Toro Air Station, CA, USA - **70**:8
Enfield, Middx, England - **67**:41-2
England, northern - **71**:12; southern - **67**:6
Ennerdale, Cumbria, England - **68**:41
Envira, Brazil - **70**:6
Epena, Congo - **67**:29-30
Ephesus, Turkey - **72**:24
Epping, Essex, England - **68**:47
Erie County, PA, USA - **71**:16
Eskilstuna, Sweden - **70**:10
Estonia - **68**:19; **70**:10
Ethiopia - **69**:44
Europe, Northern - **67**:49
Exeter, Devon, England - **72**:12
Exmoor, Devon, England - **71**:60
Faizabad, India - **70**:18
Falkville, AL, USA - **71**:'4
Farmville, NC, USA - **72**:48
Farnham, Surrey, England - **68**:47
Faroe islands - **68**:49
Fatima, Portugal - **72**:18
Feijo, Brazil - **70**:6
Fez, Morocco - **72**:18
Fiji - **69**:49
Finksburg, USA - **70**:14
Finland - **72**:25
Flores, Indonesia - **68**:49
Florida, USA - **69**:7, 49; **71**:17; **72**:29

Floydada, TX, USA - **71**:17
Foggia, Italy - **72**:19
Folkestone, Kent, England - **68**:8
Fort Lauderdale, FL, USA - **70**:6
Fort Wayne, IN, USA - **72**:18
Fort Worth, TX, USA - **72**:31, 55
Foula, Shetland Islands, Scotland - **71**:64
Fountain's Abbey, Yorks, England - **68**:7
Four Marks, Hants, England - **68**:46-7
France - **67**:33; **68**:10, 35, 54; **69**:23-5; **70**:38
Frankfurt, Germany - **67**:24, 26; **72**:17
Gabon - **67**:29; **69**:10
Galeras volcano, Colombia - **68**:49
Galisteo, NM, USA - **67**:6
Gambia - **67**:35-7
Gansu, China - **70**:49
Garampani, Assam, India - **70**:16
Garfield County, OK, USA - **68**:29
Garo Para, India - **68**:14
Gaston County, NC, USA - **68**:29
Gateshead, Durham, England - **72**:13
Genoa, Italy - **70**:15
Georgia Strait, BC, Canada - **70**:48
Georgia, USA - **68**:49
Georgia, Rep. - **67**:64; **68**:11
Germany - **67**:64; **69**:17, 24, 33, 44-5; **71**:10, 64; **72**:29
Ghana - **70**:'3
Gibsonton, FL, USA - **72**:6
Gijon, Spain - **70**:39
Giza, Egypt - **70**:51
Glacier Island, AK, USA - **67**:36
Glamorgan, Wales - **67**:49
Glasgow, Scotland - **68**:49
Glastonbury, Somerset, England - **71**:64
Glen Truim, Inverness, Scotland - **68**:41
Glenluce, Wigtown, Scotland - **68**:52
Gloucestershire, England - **68**:43; **70**:52
Gockun, Samsun, Turkey - **71**:9
Gouhou reservoir, Qinghai, China - **72**:51
Gourock, Scotland - **67**:36
Granada, Spain - **72**:10
Grange-over-Sands, Cumbria, England - **71**:47
Grant County, OK, USA - **68**:29
Grantham, Lincs, England - **68**:47; **70**:25
Grant's Pass, OR, USA - **72**:8
Graveley, Cambs, England - **69**:13
Grays, Essex, England - **71**:4
Graz, Austria - **72**:16

Great Bridge, W. Mids, England - **68**:51
Great Witley, Worcs, England - **68**:51
Great Yarmouth, Norfolk, England - **70**:65
Greece - **68**:41; **69**:49; **72**:25
Greenford, England - **68**:18
Greenland - **71**:11
Griffin Valley, AK, USA - **68**:29
Grimsby, Humberside, England - **67**:55; **68**:63
Guadalajara, Mexico - **68**:18
Guam, Mariana Islands - **72**:51
Guangxi, China - **69**:48
Guyana - **70**:33
Gwithian Sands, Wales - **70**:49
Hachinoe, Honshu, Japan - **68**:49
Hague, Holland - **67**:13
Hainault, Belgium - **72**:29
Haiti - **67**:19
Halifax, Yorks, England - **67**:48; **71**:14
Halmstad, Sweden - **70**:10
Halwill, Devon, England - **68**:47
Hamburg, Germany - **67**:13; **68**:13
Hampshire, England - **68**:46-7; **69**:38, 41
Hameln, Germany - **69**:13
Hami, China - **68**:14
Hanoi, Vietnam - **69**:50
Harare, Zimbabwe - **70**:15
Harby, Leics, England - **68**:47
Hardin, MO, USA - **72**:51
Haro Strait, BC, Canada - **70**:39
Harpenden, Herts, England - **71**:24
Harrisburg, IL, USA - **69**:56
Harrison City, PA, USA - **67**:13
Hartsdale, NY, USA - **69**:13
Hastings, Sussex, England - **67**:47
Havana, Cuba - **67**:15
Havant, Hants, England - **68**:'10
Havringe, Sweden - **67**:50
Hawaii, USA - **70**:15; **71**:47
Hawkwell, Essex, England - **67**:8
Hayling Island, Hants, England - **68**:50-1
Heathrow Airport, England - **71**:24
Hede, Sweden - **72**:13
Heidelberg, Germany - **67**:24-5
Helmstadt, Germany - **67**:24
Hemel Hempstead, Herts, England - **70**:41
Henry Island, Canada - **70**:48
Hereford, Herefords, England - **70**:55
Herefordshire, England - **70**:52
Hertfordshire, England - **71**:40
High Wycombe, Bucks, England - **68**:47
Himalayas - **67**:32, 34; **70**:18, '3

Hincaster, Cumbria, England - **68**:20

Hindu Kush, Afghanistan - **69**:49

Hokkaido, Japan - **68**:49; **71**:47

Holland - **72**:10, 28

Hollywood, CA, USA - **68**:25

Honduras - **71**:17

Hong Kong - **67**:10; **69**:48; **70**:7;
71:15, 63

Honingham, Norfolk, England -
67:11

Houston, TX, USA - **67**:18

Howick, Northumberland, England -
69:47

Hubei, China - **69**:18

Hueytown, AL, USA - **71**:12

Humberside, England - **68**:46

Hungary - **68**:43; **69**:45; **71**:47

Huntingdon, Hunts, England - **68**:10

Hutton Cranwick, Yorks, England -
69:14

Hyderabad, India - **67**:14; **72**:51

Hydesville, NY, USA - **67**:6; **70**:56

Idaho, USA - **68**:29; **70**:18

India - **68**:51

Indian Ocean - **72**:55

Indiana, USA - **69**:7

Inverary, Argylls, Scotland - **69**:11

Inverkeithing, Fife, Scotland - **68**:10;
70:38

Iowa, USA - **68**:24

Isle of Arran, Scotland - **68**:10

Isle of Wight, England - **67**:55, 65

Ismailia, Egypt - **69**:16

Istanbul, Turkey - **67**:64

Istria, Italy - **70**:13

Israel - **69**:15; **71**:7

Italy - **69**:45; **72**:25

Ituri Forest, Zaire - **67**:'4

Izmir, Turkey - **72**:16

Japan - **69**:23, 47; **70**:19; **71**:10; **72**:50

Java, Indonesia - **69**:49; **70**:42

Jemison, AL, USA - **72**:17

Jerusalem, Israel - **68**:7; **70**:36

Johannesburg, S. Africa - **67**:11;
69:44; **72**:11, 44

Johnstown, Wales - **69**:12

Jonestown, Guyana - **71**:20

Joure, Friesland, Holland - **70**:13

Juniskar, Sweden - **67**:17

Kahta, Adiyaman, Turkey - **67**:9

Kalaotoa Island, Indonesia - **68**:49

Kalimantan - **70**:'2

Kamchatka - **67**:'2; **71**:47

Kansas, USA - **68**:24

Karlskrona, Sweden - **67**:50

Karlstad, Sweden - **70**:10

Karnali River, Nepal - **70**:31

Karnataka, India - **67**:14

Kashmir, India - **72**:18

Kathmandu, Nepal - **69**:33; **70**:31

Kelly-Hopkinsville, KY, USA - **71**:'2

Kendal, Cumbria, England - **68**:20;
71:47

Kent, England - **69**:19

Kentmere, Cumbria, England - **68**:20

Kentucky, USA - **68**:29; **72**:28

Kenya - **67**:8, '2; **71**:8, 17

Kenyon, MN, USA - **69**:14

Kerala, India - **67**:14; **71**:8

Kerguelen, Antarctica - **70**:44

Ketchum, ID, USA - **69**:19

Kham, Tibet - **69**:31

Khilari, India - **72**:51

Kiev, Ukraine - **72**:10

Kilauea volcano, HI, USA - **70**:17

Kilmeston, Hants, England - **68**:47

Kinami, Congo - **67**:29

Kingfisher County, OK, USA - **68**:29

Kings Langley, Herts, England -
70:41

Kiribati - **67**:63

Klang, Selangor, Malaysia - **67**:65;
68:20

Klosterneuburg, Austria - **70**:35

Knock, Mayo, Ireland - **70**:20

Kogoshima, Kyushu, Japan - **72**:51

Kola Peninsula, Lapland - **72**:43

Kosovo, Serbia - **67**:48; **69**:16

Krakatoa, Indonesia - **70**:20

Kuala Lumpur, Selangor, Malaysia -
69:19; **70**:18

Kumbakonam, Tamil Nadu, India -
72:18

Kushiro, Japan - **68**:49

Kuwait - **71**:10

Kuybyshev, Russia - **70**:39

Laos - **69**:50-51

Lacey Green, Bucks, England - **68**:46-
7

La Digue, Seychelles - **68**:7

Lagos, Nigeria - **70**:12; **72**:15

La Jolla, CA, USA - **68**:'11

Lake District, England - **69**:64

Lake Fouloucou, Congo - **67**:28-30

Lake Tele, Congo - **67**:29-31

Lake Tibeke, Congo - **67**:28-9

Lake Vanern, Sweden - **70**:12

Lake Vyrnwy, Powys, Wales - **68**:51

Lake Wenbu, Tibet - **67**:'3

Lamard, Iran - **69**:8

Lamet Islands, Papua New Guinea -
71:7

Lancaster, PA, USA - **67**:14; **69**:25

Landford, Wilts, England - **68**:47

Langley, Vancouver, Canada - **67**:19

Langton Herring, Dorset, England -
68:47

Lascaux, France - **68**:42

Las Brisas, Nambija, Ecuador - **70**:49

Latvia - **67**:64

Leavenworth, USA - **68**:24

Lee County, MS, USA - **68**:29

Lehighton, PA, USA - **71**:16

Leicester, Leics, England - **68**:19

Leicestershire, England - **70**:49

Leipzig, Germany - **71**:14

Lekana, Congo - **70**:18

Leningrad, Russia - **70**:19

Lewes, Sussex, England - **72**:16

Lhasa, Tibet - **69**:30

Lhotse mountain - **67**:32, 34

Libreville, Gabon - **72**:15

Liechstenstein - **69**:45

Likouala River, Congo - **67**:29

Likouala swamps, Congo - **67**:29, 31

Lima, Peru - **70**:49

Lincoln, Lincs, England - **68**:18;
71:48

Lincoln, MA, USA - **69**:26

Lincoln, NB, USA - **67**:11; **70**:40

Lincolnshire, England - **69**:56

Linkoping, Sweden - **67**:51; **70**:10

Lisbon, Portugal - **69**:15

Littledean, Gloucs, England - **69**:11

Liverpool, Merseyside, England -
71:65

Llanelli, Dyfed, Wales - **67**:49

Llanfyllin, Powys, Wales - **68**:51

Llangollen, Clwyd, Wales - **67**:52

Llanystumdwy, Gwynedd, Wales -
68:8

Llipi, Bolivia - **68**:49

Loch Fyne, Argylls, Scotland - **69**:11

Loch Ness, Scotland - **68**:54, '12;
70:34; **71**:20

Loch Rannoch, Scotland - **71**:40

Loire, France - **69**:17

London, England - **67**:7, 18, 24, 26,
46, 64; **68**:44; **70**:19; **71**:28, 39;
Acton - **72**:18; Battersea - **70**:19;
Belsize Park - **68**:16; Clapham -
67:11; Fulham - **69**:19; Golders
Green - **68**:12; **69**:10; Hammersmith - **70**:38; Hampstead -
68:12, 65; **69**:6; **71**:24; Kensington Gardens - **71**:42; Kentish
Town - **68**:12; **70**:64; Lambeth -
68:18; Marchmont Street - **70**:38;
Millwall - **72**:56; Oxford Street -
70:63; Peckham - **72**:18; Rich-
mond Park - **71**:42; Smithfield -
70:20; Southwark - **71**:24; Strand
- **69**:16; Tower Hill - **67**:52;
Tower of London - **72**:25;
Wandsworth - **71**:24; West
London - **69**:15; **71**:24; White-
chapel - **70**:12

Long Beach, CA, USA - **68**:44; **72**:31

Long Newton, Cleveland, England -
67:11

Los Alamos, NM, USA - **68**:27-8;
71:12

Los Angeles, CA, USA - **67**:7; **68**:33, 44; **70**:8, 19, 35; **71**:10, 14, 35; **72**:11, 65

Los Llanos, Sierra Nevada, Spain - **70**:63

Loveland, OH, USA - **67**:6; **71**:'3

Lucena City, Philippines - **68**:9

Ludham, Norfolk, England - **72**:13

Ludlow, Shrops, England - **68**:50-1; **72**:46

Luxheim, Germany - **67**:26

Lyon, France - **68**:14; **72**:16,51

Macclesfield, Cheshire, England - **67**:6

Madagascar - **69**:10; **70**:15, 44; **72**:14

Madiera - **69**:15

Madras, India - **72**:51

Magdeburg, Germany - **67**:44

Maghnia, Algeria - **67**:19

Magonia - **68**:25

Maharashtra, India - **72**:51

Maine, USA - **70**:18; **71**:12

Malaga, Spain - **67**:15

Malahide, Ireland - **72**:36-39

Malawi - **70**:18

Malaysia - **70**:19

Malta - **69**:47

Manchester, Lancs, England - **67**:55; **68**:'14; **69**:12; **72**:16

Manila, Philippines - **67**:15

Manjil, Iran - **69**:34-5

Maplewood, NJ, USA - **72**:48

Marcellus, NY, USA - **72**:25

Margate, S. Africa - **67**:36

Mari, Himachal Pradesh, India - **72**:18

Marlborough, Wilts, England - **69**:19, 41; **72**:52

Marmore River, Matto Grosso, Brazil - **67**:'2

Mars - **71**:'2

Marseilles, France - **72**:19

Martinique - **67**:'4; **69**:10

Maryland, USA - **71**:64

Mashdad, Iran - **72**:18

Mason City, IA, USA - **70**:49

Massachusetts, USA - **72**:8

Maumere, Flores Island, Indonesia - **68**:49; **72**:65

Mauna Loa volcano, HI, USA - **68**:65

Mauritius - **67**:31

Mawnan, Cornwall, England - **68**:6

Mayon volcano, Philippines - **69**:49

Mekong River, Laos - **72**:6

Melbourne, Australia - **69**:5, 49; **70**:39; **71**:14

Melrose, Roxburghs, Scotland - **68**:52

Meon Valley, Hants, England - **68**:46

Mere Brow, Lancs, England - **69**:18

Mersah Matruh, Egypt - **70**:40

Messina, Sicily, Italy - **67**:19

Metz, Belgium - **70**:40

Mexico - **68**:6; **71**:10

Mexico City, Mexico - **72**:13

Mexico, Gulf of - **68**:19

Miami, FL, USA - **67**:17

Michigan, USA - **67**:'2

Middle East - **69**:49

Middlesbrough, Yorks, England - **69**:17

Midlands, England - **68**:'5

Mihonoseki, Japan - **70**:13

Milan, Italy - **67**:12, 19; **72**:12

Minawa Bay, Japan - **70**:13

Minneapolis, MN, USA - **68**:27-8

Minnesota, USA - **68**:25, 54; **72**:12

Mississippi River, USA - **70**:19; **71**:47

Missouri, USA - **68**:29

Missouri River, USA - **71**:47

Mitcham, Surrey, England - **67**:63

Moja, Sweden - **67**:50

Mombasa, Kenya - **71**:11

Mongolia - **67**:33; **70**:34

Monmouth, Gwent, Wales - **72**:13

Mons, Belgium - **68**:34-7, 39; **72**:29

Monsteras, Smaland, Sweden - **72**:27

Montrose, CO, USA - **70**:40

Montserrat, Spain - **68**:48

Moodus, CT, USA - **71**:12

Moon, The - **71**:'2

Moorthwaite, Cumbria, England - **68**:41

Morecambe Bay, Lancs, England - **71**:47

Morley, Norfolk, England - **72**:29

Morretes, Brazil - **69**:10

Morris, AL, USA - **70**:41

Moscow, Russia - **67**:45; **68**:19; **69**:17; **71**:17

Mount Akagi, Japan - **67**:10

Mount Beerway, Australia - **68**:'8

Mount David, NSW, Australia - **69**:11

Mount Everest - **70**:10

Mountfield, Sussex, England - **67**:47

Mount Pinatubo, Philippines - **68**:'8; **69**:49

Mount Rainier, WA, USA - **69**:6

Mount Surprise, Queensland, Australia - **71**:19

Mount Xixabangma, Tibet - **70**:31

Mozyr, Byelorussia, Russia - **70**:39

Mtwara, Tanzania - **71**:8

Muscat, Oman - **69**:49

Musko, Sweden - **67**:50-1

Muwuggwe village, Uganda - **67**:12

Naden Harbor, Queen Charlotte Islands, Canada - **70**:47-8

Na Hang, Tuyen Qang, Vietnam - **72**:14

Nailsea, Avon, England - **71**:8

Nairobi, Kenya - **68**:6; **69**:7, 44

Nakla, Sherpur district, Bangladesh - **70**:38

Nanaimo, BC, Canada - **70**:48

Nannup, W. Australia, Australia - **70**:44

Nantymoel, Glam, Wales - **72**:6

Napier, New Zealand - **72**:15

Naples, Italy - **68**:13

Nasdi, Fiji - **72**:15

Nebraska, USA - **68**:24

Nepal - **70**:7; **71**:47

NV, USA - **68**:18, 31

Nevers, France - **68**:'7

New Delhi, India - **69**:9; **70**:18; **71**:17

Newfield, Durham, England - **69**:11

New Forest, Hants, England - **68**:46

New Hampshire, USA - **71**:14

New Jersey, USA - **70**:18

New Mexico, USA - **68**:18, 24

New Mills, Derbys, England - **72**:63

New Orleans, LA, USA - **72**:29, 31

New South Wales, Australia - **67**:18; **72**:12, 51

Newstead, Roxburghs, Scotland - **68**:52

Newton, NC, USA - **71**:19

Newton Abbot, Devon, England - **68**:47

New York, NY, USA - **67**:14, 38, 49, 63; **68**:49, 64, '8; **69**:49; **70**:11, 18; **71**:35; **72**:19, 29, 47; Bronx - **67**:19; Brooklyn - **72**:26; Manhattan - **69**:44; **72**:44; Palmyra - **70**:20; Queens - **69**:12; Staten Island - **67**:19

New Zealand - **67**:'3-'4; **69**:42-43; **70**:12; **71**:42

Niagara Falls, USA - **69**:56

Niamey, Niger - **67**:8

Nice, France - **70**:5

Nimes, Belgium - **70**:40

Niulu village, Hubei, China - **70**:9

Njurunda, Sweden - **67**:17

Nome, AK, USA - **70**:40

Nordmarka, Ulleval, Norway - **68**:8

Norfolk, England - **68**:47

Norrland, Sweden - **67**:50

Northamptonshire - **69**:38; **72**:36

North Brunswick, NJ, USA - **70**:19; **72**:19

North Carolina, USA - **72**:29, 47

Northern Ireland - **68**:10

North Korea - **69**:44

Northolt, Middx, England - **67**:38; **72**:49

North Sea, England - **72**:19

North Shields, Tyne & Wear, England - **71**:11

Northumberland, England - **68**:52

Norway - **72**:12, 42-3

Nottinghamshire, England - **71**:59

Nottingham, Notts, England - **67**:40; **71**:40

Nova Scotia, Canada - **67**:'2

Nuremberg, Germany - **70**:37

Nyabing, Australia - **70**:39

Oahu, HI, USA - **67**:35-6

Oban, Argyle, Scotland - **72**:29

Oberon, NSW, Australia - **69**:11

Occlestone, Cheshire, England - **70**:49

Oceanside, CA, USA - **72**:5

Ohio, USA - **67**:55; **68**:23

Okfuskee County, OK, USA - **68**:29

Oklahoma, USA - **68**:24

Oklahoma City, OK, USA - **71**:14-5

Oklawaha, FL, USA - **70**:12

Okushiri Island, Japan - **71**:47; **72**:51

Oldland Common, Avon, England - **72**:16

Olduvai Gorge, Serengeti Plain, Tanzania - **67**:10

Olympia, WA, USA - **71**:25, 27

Omaha, NB, USA - **69**:15

Orange County, CA, USA - **70**:41

Oregon, USA - **68**:18; **70**:15

Orense, Spain - **68**:'6

Orkney Islands, Scotland - **71**:32; **72**:49

Orsay, France - **69**:53

Osaka, Japan - **69**:25

Osijek, Croatia - **71**:34

Oskarshamm, Smaland, Sweden - **72**:27

Oslo, Norway - **68**:8; **69**:18; **70**:'2; **71**:14

Osnabruck, Germany - **70**:11

Otslaka, Congo - **70**:18

Overtown farm, Wilts, England - **69**:37

Owslebury, Hants, England - **68**:47

Oxelosund, Sweden - **67**:51

Oxford, Oxon, England - **69**:40

Oxfordshire, England - **67**:7; **69**:38

Ozengeli, Turkey - **68**:49

Pacific Ocean - **68**:19

Pahang, Malaysia - **67**:'3

Pakistan - **67**:33; **72**:51

Palestine - **68**:48

Pamir mountains - **67**:33

Panama - **67**:49; **71**:10

Papua New Guinea - **67**:31, '3; **68**:15; **69**:48; **70**:34

Par, Cornwall, England - **68**:47

Paraiba, Brazil - **67**:13

Paris, France - **67**:48; **68**:14; **72**:15

Park Gate, Hants, England - **68**:47

Pascagoula River, MS, USA - **70**:20

Patagonia, Argentina - **67**:'3

Patmos, Greece - **70**:36

Payas, Hatey, Turkey - **71**:9

Pembroke, Pembs, Wales - **67**:11

Penang, Malaysia - **71**:'4

Penn, W. Mids, England - **68**:51

Pennsylvania, USA - **68**:23, 49, 64, '9

Pensarn, Glam, Wales - **68**:65

Perdelkino Forest, Moscow, Russia - **71**:6

Peterchurch, Herefords, England - **68**:47

Peterlee, Durham, England - **68**:17

Phetchabun Province, Thailand - **70**:13; **72**:9

Philadelphia, PA, USA - **71**:27

Philippines - **68**:13, 28

Phnom Penh, Cambodia - **69**:50

Phrae Province, Thailand - **72**:9

Piano, TX, USA - **68**:29

Pimpinio, Victoria, Australia - **70**:39

Pipawi, New Zealand - **68**:13

Pisa, Italy - **67**:18

Pisco, Peru - **71**:10

Pittsburg, CA, USA - **70**:19

Pittsburgh, PA, USA - **68**:18

Plymouth, Devon, England - **67**:7; **69**:63

Poland - **69**:33, 45; **70**:10;

Portland, OR, USA - **72**:8

Portsea, Hants, England - **68**:17

Portsmouth, Hants, England - **67**:8, 17

Port-Vendres, France - **68**:10

Prague, Czechoslovakia - **67**:19

Prince George, Canada - **68**:8

Princeton, WV, USA - **67**:14

Providence, RI, USA - **72**:33

Providenia, Siberia, Russia - **70**:40

Pulupandan, Negros Occidental, Philippines - **68**:9

Pwllheli, Caernarvon, Wales - **69**:65

Qazvin, Iran - **69**:34

Quantock Hills, Somerset, England - **70**:11

Quarouble, France - **71**:'2

Queensland, Australia - **67**:31; **72**:51

Quezon City, Philippines - **68**:9

Rasht, Iran - **69**:34

Reading, Berks, England - **69**:41

Reddich, Worcs, England - **68**:47

Remirement, France - **68**:6

Rennes-le-Chateau, France - **71**:61

Rhode Island, USA - **69**:10

Rietfontein, Botswana - **69**:8

Rilo, Assam, India - **67**:'3

Ringwood, Hants, England - **69**:7; **70**:11

Rio de Janeiro, Brazil - **71**:17

Rishworth Moors, Yorks, England - **71**:65

River Avon, England - **67**:46

Riyadh, Saudi Arabia - **68**:45

Rochester, MN, USA - **68**:45

Roehampton, England - **70**:12

Roll, AZ, USA - **69**:49

Romania - **69**:44

Rome, Italy - **69**:55; **70**:37; **72**:28; St Peter's Basilica - **70**:36

Roscoff, Brittany, France - **70**:40

Rosendaal, Holland - **67**:13

Rostraver Township, PA, USA - **72**:12

Roswell, NM, USA - **72**:55

Royal Bardia National Park, Nepal - **70**:31

Ruckroft, Cumbria, England - **68**:40

Rumtek, Sikkim - **69**:30; **69**:32-3

Runcorn, Merseyside, England - **72**:45

Russia - **67**:33, 49, 51; **68**:'15; **69**:25, 33; **70**:10

Saanich, BC, Canada - **69**:18

Sacramento, CA, USA - **67**:63; **70**:39

Sagami Bay, Japan - **70**:19

Sahara desert - **71**:37

Salford, Lancs, England - **72**:15

Salihli, Turkey - **67**:9

Salisbury, Wilts, England - **68**:7; **72**:12, 14

Salt Lake City, UT, USA - **68**:18

Salvador, Brazil - **72**:7

Samoa - **68**:19

Samsun, Turkey - **67**:9

San Anselmo, CA, USA - **68**:7

San Bernardino, CA, USA - **68**:19

Sandakan, Borneo - **68**:13

San Diego, CA, USA - **67**:20

Sandusky, IL, USA - **68**:7

San Francisco, CA, USA - **69**:19, 26

Sangiran, Java, Indonesia - **70**:43; **72**:11

San Luis, Batangas, Philippines - **68**:9

San Luis Potosi, Mexico - **72**:18

San Luis San Pedro, Mexico - **68**:29

San Pedro de Uraba, Colombia - **67**:49

Santa Ana, CA, USA - **69**:7

Santa Clara, CA, USA - **67**:13

Santa Fe, CA, USA - **68**:27

Santa Fe, NM, USA - **71**:12

Santee, CA, USA - **70**:40

Santiago, Chile - **69**:20

Sao Paolo, Brazil - **68**:19; **71**:43-5

Sarajevo, Bosnia - **67**:6

Saskatchewan, Canada - **68**:24

Saskatoon, Canada - **68**:29

Sassari, Italy - **69**:15

Sattupali, Andra Pradesh, India - **72**:7

Savannah River, SC, USA - **71**:14

Scarborough, Yorks, England - **68**:10

Scarrowhill, Cumbria, England -

68:40
Scotland - 68:51; 69:65; 72:20
Seaford, Sussex, England - 71:8
Seattle, WA, USA - 69:18
Sedgwick, Cumbria, England - 68:20
Segebro, Scania, Sweden - 71:7
Selah, WA, USA - 70:39
Selbu, Norway - 69:7
Selside, Cumbria, England - 68:20
Senckenberg, Germany - 67:63
Senegal - 67:35-6
Serbia - 67:64; 71:34
Seremban, Malaysia - 69:19
Serengeti - 70:'2
Shaanxi, China - 68:8, 13
Shaba, Zaire - 67:'3
Shaftesbury, Dorset, England - 72:12
Shanghai, China - 67:13; 70:9
Sheerwater, Surrey, England - 68:64
Sheffield, Yorks, England - 70:55;
72:44
Sherbourne, Dorset, England - 67:12
Sherwood Forest, Notts, England -
67:63
Shetland Islands, Scotland - 68:13, 49
Shrewsbury, Shrops, England - 68:51
Siberia, Russia - 67:33, '3; 69:6, 45,
47; 70:34; 72:42-43
Sierra Madre de Guerrero mountains,
Mexico - 68:29
Silbury Hill, Wilts, England - 68:43;
69:40; 72:52
Silverton, OR, USA - 70:39
Sikkim - 70:'3
Singapore - 67:12
Siracuse, Sicily, Italy - 67:'3
Sitgrave-Apache National Forest, AZ,
USA - 69:62
Snowflake, AZ, USA - 71:20
Socorro, NM, USA - 68:6
Solent, The, Isle of Wight, England -
72:14
Solingen, Germany - 70:39
Somalia - 71:47
Somerset, England - 70:63
Songjiang, China - 68:14
Sormiou, France - 68:42
South Africa - 67:'4; 68:10; 69:44;
71:'4
Southampton, Hants, England -
69:38
South Bend, IN, USA - 69:56
South Elgin, IL, USA - 70:40
Southend, Essex, England - 72:7
South Korea - 67:10
South Pacific - 69:49
South Pole - 68:31
Southport, Merseyside, England -
72:13
Spain - 68:19
Speen, Bucks, England - 68:46-7

Springfield, MO, USA - 70:40
Spurn, Humberside, England - 70:17
Sri Lanka - 69:7
Srinagar, India - 72:18
St Valery-sur-Somme, France - 67:47
St Vincent-les-Forts, Alpes de Haute
Provence, France - 71:13
Staines, Middx, England - 70:38
Stanford, USA - 69:24
Stanton, CA, USA - 71:19
Stavely, Cumbria, England - 68:20
Steinfort, Luxembourg - 69:12
Stevenswerth, Holland - 72:28
Stirlingshire, Scotland - 71:40
Stockholm, Sweden - 67:50; 70:16
Stockport, Lancs, England - 72:19
Stockton, Cleveland, England -
68:'7; 70:18
Stoke Bardolf, Notts, England -
68:63
Stonehenge, Wilts, England - 71:54
Strahan, Tasmania, Australia - 67:49
Stranraer, Scotland - 67:31
Stromstad, Sweden - 70:10
Sturt Creek, Australia - 70:12
Stuttgart, Germany - 67:13
St. Albans, Herts, England - 70:11
St. Anne's Bay, Jamaica - 68:10
St. Catherines, Argylls, Scotland -
69:11
St. Charles, MN, USA - 72:28
St. Ives, Cornwall, England - 70:49
St. Leonards, Sussex, England -
68:47
St. Louis, MO, USA - 67:13
St. Petersburg, Russia - 69:45; 72:10
Sudan - 68:45
Suffolk, England - 68:10
Sukhchar, W. Bengal, India - 70:8
Sukla Phanta, India - 70:32
Sulawesi, Indonesia - 68:49
Sumatra, Indonesia - 70:'2
Sumba, Indonesia - 68:49
Sunda Islands, Indonesia - 68:49
Surrey, England - 68:43
Sussex, England - 67:19; 68:43;
69:38, 41
Sutton-in-Ashfield, Notts, England -
72:24
Suva, Fiji - 72:19
Sverdlovsk, Russia - 67:45
Swaziland - 70:12
Sweden - 68:12, 33; 69:12
Swindon, Wilts, England - 72:12
Switzerland - 68:54
Swords, Co. Dublin, Ireland - 71:64
Sydney, Australia - 67:18; 71:24
Sylhet region, Bangladesh - 70:16
Syracuse, NY, USA - 72:11
Szczecin, Poland - 72:51
Taiwan - 69:33

Taiyuan, Shanxi, China - 72:10
Tampico, Mexico - 68:14
Taos, NM, USA - 71:12
Taranaki, New Zealand - 69:14
Tarcoola, Australia - 69:49
Tarn-et-Garonne, France - 68:42
Tarpon Springs, FL, USA - 72:29
Taunton, Somerset, England - 71:12
Teheran, Iran - 69:34-5; 72:18
Telford, Shrops, England - 68:47, 51
Tennessee, USA - 71:63
Tewkesbury, Gloucs, England -
72:12
Texas, USA - 68:24; 70:18
Thailand - 72:18
Thainmee, Surin, Thailand - 72:9
Thannermukkom, India - 67:6
Thenolles, France - 72:28
Thetis Lake, BC, Canada - 70:20, 63
Thorncombe, Surrey, England -
68:39
Three Crosses, Glamorgan, Wales -
68:14
Three Mile Island, USA - 68:27
Tibet - 67:14; 69:30-33
Timor, Indonesia - 68:49
Tinsbury, Somerset, England - 72:29
Tintern Abbey, Gwent, Wales - 70:52
Tipperary, Ireland - 70:11
Tipton, OK, USA - 68:29
Tipton, W. Mids, England - 68:51
Tokyo, Japan - 68:13; 69:6; 72:11, 13
Toprakkele, Turkey - 71:9
Torrance, CA, USA - 70:19
Totnes, Devon, England - 72:12
Toulon, France - 70:40
Treblinka, Poland - 72:55
Tredegar, Gwent, Wales - 67:49
Trellech, Gwent, Wales - 70:52
Trethowel, Cornwall, England -
68:47
Tromelin Islands - 67:31
Trowbridge, Wilts, England - 69:41
Troy, KS, USA - 72:17
Tsurpu, Tibet - 69:30-3
Tucson, AZ, USA - 68:18
Tulsa, OK, USA - 69:56; 70:49
Tunguska, Siberia, Russia - 69:6
Turin, Italy - 70:37, 54
Turkey - 67:9, 64; 69:8; 70:16
Turnditch, Derbys, England - 68:7
Tuscany, Italy - 67:49; 70:27
Twyford Down, Hants, England -
67:8
Tyninghame, England - 69:65
Uelen, Siberia, Russia - 70:40
Uganda - 68:10
Ukraine - 69:51; 72:51
Ulan Bator, Mongolia - 67:34
Umlazi, Zululand, S. Africa - 68:10
Upham, Hants, England - 68:47

346

Urchfont, Wilts, England - **69**:41
Uruguay - **68**:13
USA - **69**:45; **71**:54, '3; east coast - **69**:49; midwest - **71**:'1
Utah, USA - **68**:18; **69**:23
Uthai Thani, Thailand - **67**:19
Uttar Pradesh, India - **67**:14; **70**:33; **72**:18
Valangaiman, India - **69**:9
Valdez, AK, USA - **71**:6
Vancouver, Canada - **70**:46-48
Van Nuys, CA, USA - **70**:64
Venezuela - **67**:49; **70**:34
Vera Cruz, Mexico - **72**:10
Versailles, France - **68**:53
Vibo Marina, Italy - **67**:19
Vienna, Austria - **67**:8; **70**:36; **71**:29; **72**:7
Vientiane, Laos - **72**:6
Vietnam - **69**:50-51
Vincennes, France - **71**:16
Vincenza, Italy - **68**:7
Vineland, NJ, USA - **68**:24
Vinton, LA, USA - **71**:17
Virginia, USA - **70**:14; **72**:25
Vladivostok, Russia - **69**:45
Vogues mountains, Germany - **67**:26
Volga River, Russia - **69**:63
Vologda, Russia - **68**:12
Vu Quang, Vietnam - **72**:14
Waco, TX, USA - **68**:4
Wagga Wagga, Australia - **72**:6
Waimunu, New Zealand - **72**:16
Wales - **67**:6; **68**:13; **69**:41; **71**:41; north - **72**:64; south - **72**:64; west - **71**:40
Wallingford, Berks, England - **70**:63
Warwickshire, England - **71**:41
Warrington, Lancs, England - **71**:18;

72:45
Washford, Somerset, England - **68**:10
Washington, USA - **70**:15, 48
Washington DC, USA - **69**:56; **70**:14; **72**:43
Waynesburg, PA, USA - **68**:19
Weatherford, TX, USA - **68**:29
Wednesbury, West Mids, England - **68**:51
Welshpool, Powys, Wales - **68**:51
Welton, Humberside, England - **68**:46
Wen County, Henan, China - **70**:9
West Bank, Jordan - **67**:48; **69**:16
West Bromwich, West Mids, England - **68**:51
Westbury, Wilts, England - **69**:39
West Drayton, Middx, England - **70**:38
Westfield Common, Surrey, England - **69**:14
West Kennet, Wilts, England - **72**:52
Weston, Staffs, England - **68**:51
Westonbirt, Gloucs, England - **70**:55
West Pokot, Kenya - **69**:44
West Virginia, USA - **67**:19; **68**:64; **70**:18
Wethersfield, CT, USA - **71**:54
Weymouth, Devon, England - **70**:15
Wheeling, WV, USA - **72**:12
Whitby, Yorks, England - **67**:11; **72**:50
White Mountains, NH, USA - **71**:'3
White Plains, NY, USA - **69**:13
Whitehill, Hants, England - **68**:47
Wigan, Lancs, England - **71**:41
Wiltshire, Engalnd - **69**:38-9, 40-1
Winchester, Hants, England - **68**:46;

69:38
Windermere, Cumbria, England - **68**:20
Windsor, Bucks, England - **67**:8
Windsor Safari Park, Berks, England - **70**:17
Winnipeg, Canada - **69**:18
Wisconsin, USA - **69**:14
Wittenberg, Germany - **67**:27
Wolcott, IN, USA - **70**:39
Woodward, OK, USA - **69**:56
Wooster, AK, USA - **68**:29
Worcester, Worcs, England - **68**:6
Wrangel Island, Russia - **69**:47
Wrawby, England - **69**:56
Wrexham, Clwyd, Wales - **72**:7
Wroughton, Wilts, England - **68**:47
Wuhan, China - **67**:10; **69**:63
Wurttemberg, Duchy of, Germany - **67**:27
Wyrley, Staffs, England - **68**:23-4
Xinjiang, China - **70**:49; **71**:7
Yamaguchi, Japan - **69**:15
Yangtse River, China - **67**:10
Yellow Sea, China - **72**:51
Yenice, Samsun, Turkey - **71**:9
Yeoford, Devon, England - **67**:49
Yola, Adamwa, Nigeria - **71**:6
York, Yorks, England - **70**:11
Yorkshire, England - **72**:44
Yuma, AZ, USA - **70**:40
Yunnan, China - **70**:9
Zaire - **67**:29-30; **70**:30
Zambia - **67**:'3; western - **67**:12
Zelenograd, Russia - **68**:11
Zigoitia, Spain - **68**:42
Zimbabwe - **67**:49; **72**:44
Zinder, Niger - **67**:8

DATES

300,000 BC - **67**:58
26,000 BC - **69**:47
18,000 BC - **68**:42
10,000 BC - **69**:47
7000 BC - **71**:7, 9
4004 BC, Oct 22 - **71**:20
3760 BC - **67**:59
3440 BC - **67**:59
1000 BC - **67**:58; **71**:9
500 BC - **67**:58
160 BC - **67**:59
63 BC, Sept 19 - **71**:54
42 BC, Nov 16 - **71**:54
10 BC, Sept 01 - **71**:54
3 BC, Dec 24 - **71**:54
12 - Aug, 31 - **71**:54
28 - **69**:48

37 - Dec, 13 - **71**:54
39 - Dec, 30 - **71**:54
51 - Oct, 24 - **71**:54
53 - Sept, 15 - **71**:54
70 - **68**:7
76 - Jan, 24 - **71**:54
86 - Sept, 19 - **71**:54
121 - March, 26 - **71**:54
126 - Aug, 1 - **71**:54
130 - Dec, 15 - **71**:54
161 - Aug, 31 - **71**:54
188 - April, 4 - **71**:54
214 - May - **71**:54
250 - **72**:24
286 - Feb, 27 - **71**:54
317 - Feb - **71**:54
384 - Sept, 9 - **71**:54

419 - July, 2 - **71**:54
614 - **70**:36
932 - **68**:48
1000 - **69**:47
1066 - Oct, 14 - **67**:47
1098 - **70**:36
1110 - **69**:31
1133 - **70**:20
1224 - **70**:20; **71**:49
1241 - **70**:37
1453 - **71**:65
1466 - **67**:24
1483 - **67**:24
1487 - **67**:25
1487 - March, 1 - **67**:24
1492 - **70**:54; **71**:65
1504 - Aug, 6 - **69**:6

1507 - **67**:25
1532 - **70**:37
1535 - **70**:16
1537 - **67**:26
1539 - **67**:25
1546 - **72**:25
1546 - April, 27 - **72**:25
1548 - **67**:26
1562 - **67**:27
1574 - **71**:9
1587 - **67**:24
1592 - **67**:24
1597 - **67**:10
1599 - **70**:27
1601 - **69**:16
1642 - Aug, 4 - **69**:6
1674 - **67**:25

1680 - 70:55
1692 - 69:16
1694 - 72:25
1696 - 72:25, 29
1697 - Nov, 19 - 72:29
1698 - Feb - 72:29; Aug, 17 - 72:29
1706 - June, 29 - 72:28
1707 - Jan, 11 - 72:28; March, 15 - 72:28
1711 - 72:25
1725 - 67:25
1734 - 72:25
1738 - 72:25, 29; Nov, 15 - 71:20
1740 - 70:55
1746 - 72:29
1751 - 69:52
1752 - 72:25
1753 - 72:25
1757 - Nov, 28 - 72:20
1764 - 69:52
1776 - 72:52
1777 - 72:25
1781 - March, 13 - 67:6
1788 - 72:25, 29
1789 - July, 26 - 72:29
1790 - 72:29
1794 - 72:25
1808 - 71:52; 72:25, 32
1810 - 68:41
1812 - 72:25
1813 - 70:55
1815 - 72:25
1818 - 71:55; Aug, 6 - 71:54
1823 - Sept, 21 - 70:20; 23 - 70:20
1825 - 72:65
1826 - April - 72:25
1827 - 69:63; 72:25
1828 - 68:60
1832 - 67:60; 68:47
1833 - Dec, 14 - 72:20
1836 - May, 17 - 71:54
1837 - June - 71:54
1838 - 72:32
1840 - 68:47
1846 - 72:32
1846 - April, 4 - 67:6
1847 - 68:41; 69:4
1848 - 70:56; 72:26; March, 31 - 67:6
1849 - 72:52
1851 - 69:43
1853 - 72:29
1854 - 70:27, 56
1855 - 70:20, 65
1856 - 71:62; May, 6 - 68:6
1860 - Nov, 6 - 72:32
1862 - Sept - 72:55

1864 - 72:28
1865 - 67:15
1866 - 71:12; 72:26
1868 - 67:10; Dec, 24 - 71:54
1869 - 72:29
1872 - March, 12 - 67:6; Dec, 5 - 72:20
1873 - 68:63; 69:43
1874 - 68:41; 72:28; June - 68:39; Aug, 6 - 69:6
1875 - July, 26 - 69:6; Oct, 12 - 71:20
1876 - Feb, 22 - 72:27
1879 - 68:'7; Aug, 21 - 70:20
1880 - 69:43; Sept, 12 - 70:20
1881 - May, 28 - 68:6; July, 11 - 69:6
1882 - 70:31; June, 16 - 69:6
1883 - 72:28; May, 30 - 72:28; Aug, 28 - 70:20
1884 - 72:29
1885 - 72:28
1886 - 67:65; 72:29; March, 26 - 67:6
1887 - 67:10; 70:42
1888 - 68:61; Oct, 21 - 70:56; Nov, 19 - 71:54
1889 - 70:42; 71:43; 72:65
1891 - 70:42; 71:29
1892 - Oct, 18 - 71:54
1893 - Feb, 28 - 67:6
1895 - Dec, 5 - 72:28
1896 - 69:43; April, 4 - 67:6
1897 - April, 17 - 72:55
1900 - 71:'1
1901 - 67:'4; 68:53; 71:'2; April, 19 - 71:19; May, 20 - 71:54
1902 - 70:43; 72:28, 50; Oct, 19 - 71:24
1903 - 68:23-4; 69:23; May, 28 - 72:28; Nov, 15 - 72:29
1904 - 69:16; 70:55; 72:27; March, 30 - 69:65*
1905 - 68:65; 70:46
1906 - 67:'3; 72:62
1907 - 67:'2; May, 26 - 68:6
1908 - 72:32; April, 3 - 72:27; June, 30 - 69:6
1909 - 68:'7
1911 - 71:42, 64; Aug, 17 - 71:54
1912 - 69:56
1913 - 70:37; June, 9 - 71:10; 13 - 71:10

1914 - 68:34; May, 23 - 71:13; Aug - 68:35; Sept - 70:38; 29 - 68:35; Oct - 68:35
1915 - 68:34, 37; April, 24 - 68:35; 30 - 68:36; July, 30 - 67:37
1916 - 71:41; July, 21 - 68:16
1917 - 70:34
1918 - 71:'2; July, 17 - 67:45; Aug, 13 - 72:50
1919 - 68:'7; May - 70:38; 17 - 71:13
1920 - 68:'11
1921 - 72:29; March, 24 - 71:54; July, 18 - 70:38
1922 - 67:36, 60, '3; 69:47
1923 - 69:50-1; 72:39; Jan - 69:56; April, 6 - 67:6; Aug, 15 - 70:39
1924 - 71:59; Feb, 15 - 70:39
1925 - 67:'2; 70:28
1927 - 67:59; 71:43, 47; 72:37
1928 - 69:43; - 71:43; March, 6 - 67:6
1929 - 69:15; June, 17 - 71:54
1930 - 67:36; 68:20; 70:44; 71:45; July - 71:43
1931 - 68:35; 71:56; April, 24 - 70:38*; July, 4 - 70:38*; Aug - 71:41
1932 - 67:11; 72:36, 39; Oct - 72:37
1933 - 67:'2; 68:'12; 70:46; Jan, 30 - 67:44; June - 71:41; Nov, 12 - 71:20
1934 - 71:43-4; Aug, 22 - 71:44
1935 - April, 14 - 68:6; Dec - 71:43
1936 - 70:30; 71:39; March - 71:40; April - 71:40; May - 71:41; Nov, 19 - 71:54
1937 - 67:36; 70:47-8; 72:14; Jan, 30 - 71:54; June, 7 - 68:6
1938 - 67:37, 39, 41, 48; 70:18, 37; 71:46; Dec - 67:'4; 22 - 67:36
1939 - 67:33; 71:'1-'2; 72:32
1940 - 69:43; - 72:44
1941 - 67:32; - 68:'7; Aug, 6 - 72:29
1942 - 67:36; 70:40
1943 - March, 9 - 71:54;

April, 16 - 68:6
1944 - Oct - 72:50
1945 - 68:26; 69:48; April, 30 - 67:44; May, 4 - 67:44; 5 - 72:50; July - 70:60; Dec, 5 - 72:20
1946 - 67:44; 72:32
1947 - 70:48; 71:'1; 72:44; June, 24 - 69:6; July - 72:55
1948 - 67:'3; 71:'1
1949 - 67:11; May, 14 - 68:44
1950 - 67:'3; 68:31; 70:42; April - 72:27; Nov - 69:56
1951 - 70:25-6; 71:45; April, 19 - 71:19; May, 23 - 71:54
1952 - 68:42; 72:55; Nov, 20 - 71:20
1953 - 67:63; 71:'2
1954 - 67:'3; 68:53; 70:55, 63; 71:13, '2; Nov, 1 - 67:43
1955 - 68:54; 71:'3, 59; Aug - 71:'2
1956 - 69:34; June - 67:'2
1957 - 67:39; 68:55, 60; 69:63; 71:'3; Oct, 15 - 71:20
1958 - 67:36; 70:14, 64; 71:'3
1959 - 67:17, '3; 69:30; 70:48; 72:31
1960 - 67:30; 68:56; 70:8, 48, '2; Nov, 8 - 72:32
1961 - 71:'3
1962 - 70:44, 55; 72:31
1963 - 68:60; 69:43; 70:36, '2; 71:'3; 72:29; April, 13 - 71:54; Aug - 69:56; Nov, 22 - 72:20, 30; 24 - 72:34
1964 - 72:64; April, 19 - 71:19; 24 - 68:6
1966 - 67:'4; 68:23, '9; 69:38; 72:7
1967 - 70:64; 71:59; Sept - 68:23
1968 - 70:17, 30, 46, 48, 60; 71:34; 72:52; Jan, 1 - 69:65; May, 31 - 68:6; Dec - 72:16
1969 - 68:25; 70:30
1970 - 67:44; 68:24-5; 70:55; 71:'4; 72:43, 55; Aug - 69:56
1971 - 68:24; 69:51; 70:30
1972 - 68:24; 70:63; 71:'3; Jan, 18 - 70:7; March, 3

348

- **67**:6; Aug, 19 - **70**:20; Nov, 16 - **68**:9

1973, - **68**:24-5; **70**:39, 47, 55; **71**:43-4, '4; **72**:31; Oct - **70**:39; 11 - **70**:20; 16 - **68**:25; Nov - **68**:'2

1974 - **68**:25; **69**:56; **70**:30; **71**:'4; Dec - **68**:25

1975 - **68**:63; **69**:15, 19, 27, 38; Aug, 14 - **69**:6; Sept - **70**:65; Nov, 5 - **69**:62; **71**:20

1976 - **67**:15, 35-6; **68**:24, '2; **69**:19, 64; **70**:17, 40; **70**:40; **71**:65; April, 17 - **68**:6; June - **68**:'3; Dec - **70**:39

1977 - **67**:41; **69**:44, 65; **70**:8, 26, 40-1; **71**:'4; April, 25 - **67**:'1; May - **68**:'12; June - **70**:39; July - **70**:40; Dec, 5 - **70**:40

1978 - **68**:8, 29; **70**:30, 39, 60; Nov, 18 - **71**:20

1979 - **69**:48; **70**:34, 39, 41; **72**:29, 31, 45; April - **70**:39; May - **70**:39

1980 - **68**:20, 24-5; **69**:39; **70**:40, 59; **71**:26, 30; **72**:37

1981 - **67**:50, 56; **69**:32, 56

1982 - **67**:64; **70**:32, 34, 40; **72**:6; Oct - **72**:7; Nov - **69**:15; **71**:54

1983 - **67**:36, 50; **68**:47; **69**:16, 48; **70**:41, 55; **71**:65; **72**:7, 29, 54, 65; Jan - **68**:47; March - **67**:48; April - **67**:48; June, 11 - **67**:35

1984 - **67**:18; **68**:'13; **69**:44; **70**:13, 30, 47-8; **71**:54; **72**:43; Feb - **68**:48; Dec - **67**:31

1985 - **67**:12, 28; **68**:29; **69**:8, 10; **70**:65; **72**:37; Sept - **70**:24

1986 - **67**:'2; **68**:29, 45, 64; **70**:14, 56; **71**:54; **72**:51; May, 30 - **68**:14; Dec - **72**:47

1987 - **67**:51, '2; **71**:52, 63; **72**:37; Jan, 3 - **70**:41; April - **68**:45; Sept, 27 - **69**:30; Oct - **70**:55; Dec - **67**:50

1988 - **67**:34, 41, 64; **68**:14, 51; **69**:17, 41, 50; **70**:14; **71**:9, 65; **72**:37, 47; June, 11 - **68**:6;

July, 26 - **68**:50; Aug - **68**:44; Sept - **70**:54; Dec - **69**:13

1989 - **67**:18; **69**:23-4, 26; **70**:39, 42; **71**:14, 18, 26, 65; **72**:29, 37; Jan - **67**:14; Feb - **67**:18; **69**:12; 3 - **68**:50; **72**:46; May - **72**:51; July, 10 - **67**:5*; July, 23 - **68**:26; Aug - **72**:42; Nov - **67**:53; 6 - **67**:14; **72**:7; 30 - **72**:44; Dec - **67**:29, 47

1990 - **67**:30; **68**:29, 42, 51, '5-'6, '8, '10; **69**:38-9; **70**:30; **71**:45; **72**:9-10, 36-7; Jan, 7 - **72**:42; 17 - **68**:29; March - **67**:48; **69**:16; April, 8 - **68**:29; 13 - **70**:40; May, 5 - **72**:24*; 25 - **69**:50; 27 - **70**:15; June - **71**:43; 21 - **68**:'15*; 26 - **68**:29; July, 1 - **70**:40; Aug - **67**:47; 20 - **68**:29; Sept - **68**:29; **70**:40; Oct, 2 - **68**:29; 3 - **68**:47; Nov - **72**:49; 4 - **68**:29

1991 - **67**:29, 31, 33, 50, 53, 64; **68**:11, 25, 29, 51; **69**:9-10, 40-1, 45; **70**:19, 25, 31, 59; **71**:7, 15, 34; **72**:29, 36

Jan - **70**:44

Feb - **67**:53; **68**:29; **72**:49; 2 - **68**:29

March, 1 - **67**:11*; 16 - **68**:47; 22 - **67**:14*

April - **68**:29; **69**:13; 18 - **67**:33*

May - **68**:9; **71**:12; **72**:47; 15 - **67**:11*

June - **67**:10; **68**:'8; 12 - **68**:45; 13 - **68**:46

July - **67**:45; **69**:50; **70**:40; 1 - **68**:29; 5 - **70**:16*; 8 - **69**:18; 11 - **71**:60; 19 - **70**:16*; 23 - **67**:14*; 27 - **68**:12; 31 - **69**:50

Aug - **67**:11; **68**:17, 51; **72**:43; 1 - **68**:18; 2 - **69**:51; 7 - **69**:18*; 9 - **72**:16; 15 - **71**:8*

Sept - **68**:29; **71**:28; **72**:43; 21 - **69**:51; 29 - **71**:9*

Oct - **67**:18; **68**:42; **69**:25; **70**:43; 7 - **67**:9*; 12 - **68**:13*; 19 - **68**:29

Nov - **68**:29; **69**:44; **72**:18, 47; 8 - **71**:34; 15 - **70**:63; 27 - **69**:12

Dec - **67**:18; 11 - **69**:12*; 14 - **70**:16*; 20 - **67**:7*; 29 - **69**:14*

1992 - **67**:'2, 8, 44, 50, 65; **68**:7, 14, 20, 27, 37, 43, 51, 56; **69**:9, 17, 19, 40-1, 50; **70**:12, 15-6, 31-2; **71**:'4; **72**:14, 36

Jan - **67**:11; **68**:29, 42, 51; **69**:24; **72**:18; 9 - **68**:30; 10 - **70**:18*; 11 - **68**:8; **71**:8*; 13 - **68**:13*; 18 - **67**:9*; 19 - **67**:9*; 25 - **68**:29; 27 - **69**:19; 31 - **69**:19

Feb - **67**:46; **69**:11; **70**:16; **72**:18; 1 - **69**:19; 3 - **68**:25; 5 - **68**:18; 8 - **67**:9*; 10 - **67**:11*; 12 - **72**:15*; 19 - **67**:50; 21 - **70**:17; 27 - **71**:60

March - **69**:32; **70**:17, 19, 43; **71**:27; **72**:13, 18, 47; 5 - **69**:14*; 8 - **69**:17; 19 - **68**:19*; 20 - **70**:9; 27 - **67**:65*

April - **67**:34; **70**:9; **72**:19; 1 - **68**:12*, 44; 19 - **69**:8*; 21 - **67**:12; 26 - **69**:33

May - **67**:7, 13-4, 19, 45, 50; **68**:10, 51; **69**:11; **70**:13, 46; **71**:49; **72**:18; 4 - **67**:19*; 7 - **67**:13; 12 - **72**:12*; 14 - **71**:14*; 19 - **69**:43; 22 - **69**:13*

June - **67**:45; **68**:51; **69**:41; **70**:15; **71**:34; 8 - **67**:20; 10 - **72**:16*; 12 - **69**:13*; **70**:18; 16 - **68**:12, 29; 17 - **67**:64*; 20 - **68**:18; 22 - **68**:19; 24 - **69**:18*; 29 - **67**:17; **69**:14

July - **67**:18, 45, 50; **68**:10, 12, 29; 1 - **67**:17; 7 - **67**:17*; 10 - **67**:9; 11 - **68**:43; **69**:15*; 12 - **68**:47; 14 - **69**:11; 15 - **72**:29*; 16 - **68**:10; 17 - **67**:8; 19 - **67**:13; 20 - **67**:13*; 22 - **68**:14*; 25 - **68**:19*; 26 - **68**:20; 27 - **67**:13*; 28 - **68**:8*, 13*

Aug - **67**:16, 46, 50;

68:10, 13-4, 16, 18, 20; **69**:7, 40-1, 45; **72**:34; 2 - **67**:13*; **69**:12*; 3 - **67**:19*; **70**:18*; 5 - **67**:12*; 6 - **67**:9; 13 - **68**:46; 15 - **67**:13; 18 - **68**:8; 19 - **68**:18; **69**:18; **70**:13; 21 - **68**:19*;; 21 - **69**:12*; 25 - **72**:16*; 26 - **67**:19*; **68**:18; 27 - **72**:12; 29 - **68**:29, 45; 31 - **68**:13*

Sept - **67**:33, 45-6, 53, '2; **68**:10, 19; **69**:9; **70**:65; **72**:18, 64; 1 - **70**:38*; 2 - **68**:18; 3 - **72**:16*, 47; 4 - **67**:6*; **68**:5, 13*; 10 - **67**:34*; **68**:7*; 11 - **71**:14; 12 - **67**:12; 13 - **67**:50; 14 - **68**:46; 16 - **67**:50; **68**:10*; 17 - **67**:45*; 18 - **67**:6, 18*; 19 - **69**:13*; 20 - **71**:14*; 21 - **67**:50; **69**:19; 23 - **67**:51; **71**:14*; 25 - **67**:13*, 48; 26 - **67**:51; **71**:14*; 27 - **69**:30; 28 - **68**:7*

Oct - **67**:14, 17, 19, 47-8; **68**:6, 15, 46; **69**:10, 12; **70**:6; **71**:13; **72**:13, 29; 1 - **67**:13*; 2 - **68**:8; 4 - **67**:13*; **68**:13; 5 - **69**:13; 6 - **67**:19*; **68**:14; 7 - **67**:49; 9 - **67**:49; **68**:64; **70**:13; 12 - **67**:14*, 49; **68**:19; 13 - **67**:49; 15 - **69**:15*; 16 - **68**:13, 19*; **70**:15*; 18 - **67**:49; 21 - **67**:63; **72**:6*; 22 - **70**:55*; 24 - **67**:49; **68**:8*; 26 - **69**:7*; 27 - **67**:7*; 28 - **67**:19*; 30 - **67**:6, 10; 31 - **67**:4, 42

Nov - **67**:6, 11, 15, 19, 50; **68**:12, 46; **69**:11, 45, 51; **70**:12, 18; **71**:13-4, 16; 5 - **67**:40, 49; 6 - **67**:18; 8 - **69**:9; **71**:14*; 12 - **72**:7*; 14 - **69**:20; 18 - **69**:12; 20 - **67**:8, 19*; 18*; 19* - **68**:19*; 22 - **67**:19*; 23 - **67**:8*; **72**:7; 27 - **67**:8; **68**:19*; 28 - **67**:19*; 29 - **68**:7*; 30 - **67**:49

Dec - **68**:13, 51; **69**:7, 11; **70**:46; 1 - **69**:12*; 7 - **68**:6*; 8 - **68**:49; 10 - **70**:13; 11 -

68:49; 12 - 68:49;
72:65; 15 - 70:12;
71:24; 17 - 69:20; 18 -
67:14*; 20 - 70:19; 21 -
72:12*; 22 - 67:15*; 23
- 68:9; 69:10; 25 -
68:17; 27 - 69:7*; 28 -
67:15; 71:13; 30 -
72:11*

1993 - 68:51; 69:6; 70:17,
19, 32; 71:7, 17; 72:59

Jan - 69:45; 70:6;
71:13; 72:18; 2 - 68:44,
46-7; 4 - 72:5, 12*; 5 -
69:14; 6 - 68:47; 10 -
68:9; 11 - 68:49;
70:10*; 12 - 68:18; 13 -
68:9; 69:13; 14 - 68:49;
15 - 68:64; 68:7*; 16 -
68:49; 69:7; 17 - 68:46-
7; 18 - 68:49; 20 - 68:7;
69:42; 21 - 68:13*, 46-
7; 70:13*; 22 - 68:9, 19,
46-7; 23 - 68:47; 25 -
69:42; 26 - 69:42; 27 -
68:9, 47; 28 - 68:47;
69:43; 71:17; 29 - 68:7;
30 - 68:47

Feb - 67:31; 69:18;
72:18; 1 - 68:47; 2 -
68:47; 69:49; 3 - 68:47;
69:49; 4 - 70:9*;
72:16*; 5 - 69:49; 7 -
68:7*; 9 - 68:18*; 10 -
70:7; 69:12*; 11 - 68:9,
16; 71:14*; 12 - 68:47;
71:12*; 14 - 72:15*; 15
- 68:47; 70:11; 16 -
69:49; 18 - 69:15*;
70:18; 71:8*; 18 -
69:18*; 19 - 68:47; 20 -
67:6; 68:10*; 21 - 67:6;
68:7*, 47; 70:16;
71:14*; 23 - 68:47;

71:19; 25 - 67:6; 68:45;
69:49; 70:11- 2; 26 -
68:47; 69:7*, 15*; 27 -
71:8*; 28 - 67:6; 71:13

March - 69:7*, 65;
70:9-10, 44; 71:19, 24;
72:18, 48; 1 - 67:6;
68:47; 70:12*, 19*; 2 -
68:47; 70:9; 3 - 70:11*;
4 - 69:19*; 72:8*; 5 -
68:47; 70:6; 13 -
69:18*; 71:12*; 14 -
69:15*, 17*; 70:5; 17 -
67:6; 18 - 69:49; 19 -
70:19*; 20 - 67:6;
69:49; 72:16; 23 -
70:11, 15; 72:14*; 24 -
67:6; 69:49; 26 - 69:7*,
15*, 17*, 49; 71:18; 28
- 69:19*; 72:16*; 29 -
69:8*; 72:14*; 31 -
70:19

April - 69:15;
70:10, 51; 71:12, 24; 1 -
69:16; 72:15; 3 - 70:8*;
4 - 70:15*; 5 - 70:10*,
18; 72:19*; 6 - 71:9*; 8
- 69:18*; 72:9*; 9 -
67:6; 71:7; 11 - 67:6; 14
- 71:6; 16 - 70:10*; 17 -
70:15*; 72:12*; 18 -
70:49; 71:48; 19 - 69:4;
19 - 71:19; 71:15; 20 -
68:6; 21 - 68:18*;
71:17; 23 - 68:6; 71:24;
24 - 72:19; 25 - 70:49;
28 - 70:11*; 29 - 69:15;
29 - 71:16; 30 - 68:6;
71:8*

May - 70:18-9;
71:7; 72:11, 13- 4, 18; 1
- 68:6; 70:64; 72:8; 3 -
71:16; 5 - 70:8, 49; 8 -
68:6; 9 - 70:49; 10 -

72:9; 11 - 70:49; 12 -
71:16; 13 - 69:4; 71:19;
15 - 68:6; 70:49; 18 -
70:11*; 20 - 71:6, 11*;
21 - 68:6; 72:7; 22 -
70:11; 25 - 70:8, 19;
72:11*; 26 - 70:18;
71:11*; 28 - 68:6; 30 -
71:13; 31 - 71:16

June - 70:11; 71:12;
72:9, 49- 50; 1 - 70:8;
72:10*; 2 - 68:6; 71:16;
4 - 70:14; 71:8*; 6 -
71:8*; 8 - 71:10, 47, 64;
11 - 70:4*; 71:47; 13 -
70:13; 72:9; 14 - 71:14;
15 - 69:6; 70:18, 49; 17
- 72:9; 18 - 71:12*;
72:19*; 20 - 71:6*; 21 -
69:6; 71:6*; 72:12; 23 -
71:47; 72:6; 26 - 71:47;
27 - 72:11*; 28 - 72:6;
30 - 70:8

July - 71:12, 19, 47;
72:50; 1 - 71:47; 3 -
72:18; 5 - 71:11; 7 -
69:6; 71:11*; 8 - 72:15,
17*; 9 - 72:17; 10 -
72:17; 11 - 71:47; 12 -
71:47, 51; 72:7; 14 -
71:47; 15 - 69:6; 71:19;
72:19*; 16 - 71:19, 47;
72:13, 15; 19 - 71:47;
72:14; 20 - 71:19, 47;
21 - 72:19*; 22 - 69:6;
72:6*, 9; 25 - 72:10*;
26 - 71:13; 29 - 70:13*;
30 - 72:51; 31 - 72:15

Aug - 72:13; 1 -
69:6; 3 - 71:14*; 72:14;
5 - 71:16; 72:9; 6 -
71:16; 7 - 72:51; 8 -
72:51; 9 - 72:51; 11 -
71:17; 72:19*; 12 -

72:51; 13 - 71:7*;
72:51; 14 - 72:44; 15 -
72:44, 51; 16 - 72:11,
2*; 17 - 72:10*; 18 -
72:13*; 19 - 71:17; 20 -
71:5*; 72:51; 21 -
72:10*; 23 - 72:10*, 50;
24 - 70:20; 72:7*; 26 -
71:24*; 72:16*; 27 -
72:51; 28 - 72:14; 29 -
72:12

Sept - 72:9, 50; 1 -
70:20; 2 - 72:19; 4 -
72:50; 8 - 70:20; 72:17;
13 - 72:12; 16 - 70:20;
72:7; 17 - 70:20; 18 -
70:20; 21 - 72:51; 22 -
72:11*, 63*; 25 - 70:20;
29 - 72:51

Oct 4 - 70:20; 16 -
71:20; 21 - 71:20; 25 -
72:6; 30 - 71:20; 31 -
71:20

Nov 1 - 71:20; 11 -
71:20; 13 - 71:20; 24 -
72:10; 25 - 72:20; 30 -
72:20

Dec - 68:51; 4 -
70:12; 8 - 72:20; 21 -
72:20; 21 - 71:19*; 25 -
72:20

1994 - Jan, 1 - 72:20; 5 -
72:20; 9 - 67:4; 14 -
72:20; 17 - 72:20; 20 -
72:20; 25 - 72:20; Feb,
1 - 72:20; Feb, 6 -
72:20; Feb, 19 - 72:20;
April - 67:31

2000 - 68:60; 69:47

2006 - 71:52

2012 - 71:38

2126 - 68:64

2500 - 72:52